I0822983

KILLING THE DEAD

Killing the Dead

VAMPIRE EPIDEMICS FROM MESOPOTAMIA TO THE NEW WORLD

JOHN BLAIR

PRINCETON UNIVERSITY PRESS
PRINCETON & OXFORD

Published by Princeton University Press
41 William Street, Princeton, New Jersey 08540
99 Banbury Road, Oxford OX2 6JX

press.princeton.edu

GPSR Authorized Representative: Easy Access System Europe - Mustamäe tee 50, 10621 Tallinn, Estonia, gpsr.requests@easproject.com

Library of Congress Control Number: 2024952167

ISBN 9780691224794
ISBN (e-book) 9780691226965

British Library Cataloging-in-Publication Data is available

Editorial: Ben Tate, Josh Drake
Production Editorial: Elizabeth Byrd
Jacket: Chris Ferrante
Production: Danielle Amatucci
Publicity: Alyssa Sanford (US), Carmen Jimenez (UK)

Printed in the United States of America

10 9 8 7 6 5 4 3 2 1

For

IDA

a strong woman

CONTENTS

PREFACE AND ACKNOWLEDGEMENTS

I AM A HISTORIAN and archaeologist of medieval culture, and it may surprise some colleagues that I decided to write this book. The subject has always curiously intrigued me, and perhaps I needed to get it out of my system. (One of my earliest clear memories is illicitly reading Tolkien under the bedclothes with a torch, paralyzed in terror by the barrow-wights whom he modelled on one group of the Scandinavian undead.) More seriously, I have always realized that to understand people in the past, we must explore what made sense to them and not just what makes sense to us. Scholars who shy away from topics that seem distasteful or irrational are re-framing past world-views in the image of their own. For many protagonists in this book, predatory corpses were threats more daunting and imminent than high prices or poor harvests.

However, intensive work on a subject so remote from my 'official' teaching and research has had to wait for the luxury of retirement. The Queen's College, Oxford, is very generous to its Emeritus Fellows, and I consider it an immense privilege to remain fully part of that hospitable and stimulating community, so wonderfully free from the managerial culture that breeds the vampires of our own day. Colleagues at Queen's have contributed more to this book than they know or I can remember. Near at hand, the Bodleian Library and the Art, Archaeology and Ancient World Library have provided deeply appreciated resources for archaeological data, early printed books, and modern scholarship.

I am equally fortunate that my publisher, Princeton University Press, has shown its usual energy and enthusiasm for producing a high-quality book. Among the first-rate team with whom I have been so fortunate to deal, I would especially like to thank Ben Tate, who has encouraged the project so warmly from the start (and suggested the title), and Dimitri

Karatnikov, who worked his magic on some previously inadequate illustrations.

The originators and copyright owners of many images have generously allowed them to be reproduced, and I am most grateful to all of them. They are acknowledged individually in the "Illustration Sources and Credits" chapter.

Many friends and colleagues have answered queries, clarified puzzles, and contributed snippets of information. My grateful thanks go to Robert Bartlett, Sarah Clegg, David d'Avray, Elizabeth Edwards, Leszek Gardeła, Jenny Guest, Ronald Hutton, Philip Jones, Carolyne Larrington, Tom Licence, Christopher Metcalf, Howard Morphy, Graeme Murdock, Alexander Murray, Alexandra Nachescu, Elizabeth O'Brien, Chris O'Callaghan, Richard Parkinson, Roger Pearson, the late Siegbert Prawer, Frances Reynolds, Levi Roach, Ritchie Robertson, Kemal Stachowski, Veronica Strang, John Thornton, Nina Anna Trzaska, Carl Watkins, Shamara Wettimuny, Andrew Wilson, and Martin Worthington, with apologies to any others whom I have accidentally omitted. The two anonymous referees contributed valuable insights, and I think gratefully of the large number of other scholars whom I have never met but whose works—listed in the bibliography—have taught me so much. Morten Kringelbach invited me to speak at the Centre for Eudaimonia and Human Flourishing, which gave me some very helpful reactions from the perspective of neuroscience. I must also thank my ancestor James Blair for helping to demystify the European living dead (see p. 430).

This project has taken me far outside my academic comfort-zone, and I owe a big debt to the specialists in other fields who patiently read and corrected draft chapters: Michael E. Bell (the United States), Kanerva Blair-Heikkinen (Finland), Robert Evans (the Habsburg lands), Anna Kjellström (taphonomic processes), Diarmaid MacCulloch (Reformation Europe), Meleisa Ono-George (Africa and the Caribbean), Claudia Rapp (Byzantium) and Selena Wisnom (Mesopotamia). Naturally, they are not responsible for any remaining errors.

Kanerva Blair-Heikkinen, Christopher Whittick, and Selena Wisnom read the whole book in draft. Their incisive and searching comments have enriched it, as have Selena's distinctive insights into so many byways of the supernatural in the ancient world and beyond. While I was pursuing this weird topic, the three of them saved me from ever feeling like a lone eccentric.

My greatest debt is to my family: they have not just tolerated a research topic that many people would find repellent but have warmly shared it. Kanerva's enthusiasm for the thought-worlds of traditional societies (not least in her own Finnish background), and for the world's languages, has been a constant stimulus and source of strength. She has shared the funny side of vampire beliefs, and has helped me not to take them too seriously. Katri, Olavi, Kirsti, and Seppo have been positive and supportive as always. Edward and Ida progressed from childhood to young adulthood during a time when my thoughts and conversations were excessively dominated by the living dead and mutilated corpses. All of them endured these temporary obsessions with extraordinary good-humour; they need to endure them no further. Ida's strong and distinctive view on the world, never daunted by convention, would have marked her out as a powerful 'wise-woman' in some of the societies discussed in these pages. This book is therefore for her.

Introduction

> The reader may or may not find persuasive any of the various theoretical attempts to illuminate the vampire of tradition. But at the very least, the reader may come to understand that the vampire is much more than simply a scary creature of the human imagination. . . . It is truly a matter of life and death!
>
> —ALAN DUNDES

IN MARCH 1732, English men and women sat down to their morning papers and read of lurid events in Serbia. Suspicious villagers had dug up several corpses, and had found them undecayed and bloated with blood. Recognizing the marks of vampirism, they had mutilated them in various ways and had then burned them (p. 376).

In fact, such episodes were not rare in the Carpathians and Balkans. What made this case different was that the Habsburg military authorities had investigated it, and had produced a report. That brought the Serbian vampires to the attention of the Austrian and German press, and thus to newspapers in Paris and London.

Released on the world, the story had an impact that would transform sensational popular literature over the next two centuries. Those first readers must have been most struck by its sheer exotic weirdness: a bizarre transaction across the boundary between life and death, in a wild zone of Europe about which they knew nothing. Surely it could never have happened in civilized England?

To see how wrong they were, let us go back six centuries, to a churchyard near Burton-upon-Trent in Staffordshire around the year 1090 (p. 253). The villagers stand nervously beside the graves of two recently buried men who have been seen wandering around with their coffins on their backs, banging on doors, and summoning the inhabitants to sickness and death. The graves are opened, and as the coffin-lids are wrenched off, expectations of an unholy continuing life seem to be horribly confirmed: the corpses have resisted the natural processes of decay, and the cloths over their faces are stained with blood. The dead stand condemned, and the living proceed at once to execution. The heads of the corpses are cut off and placed between their legs, their hearts are torn from their chests, and the graves are backfilled. The hearts are carried across the running water of the Trent and burned on a hilltop. As the smoke rises, the vampires' victims recover but a black crow flies up from the flames.

If that leaves any room for doubt, we can go back another four centuries: to Ely, in the fenland of eastern England, around the year 680 (pp. 207–211). Near the richly furnished grave of a girl, a young woman has been buried with a bag of amulets and other magical objects. But something is wrong: people see her walking around, or perhaps they blame sickness or bad luck on evil power emanating from her grave. Her corpse is dug up, and, although in reality starting to decompose, it looks uncannily intact: drastic measures are needed. Someone wrenches her torso towards one side of the grave, twists it over, pulls off the head, throws the jawbone to the end of the grave, and places the cranium level with her chest.

As these two stories illustrate, there was once a time when people in England believed in restless and dangerous corpses. So why did the stories that trickled in from the Balkans in the 1730s find no local resonance? This amnesia illustrates how belief in the unquiet dead is capable of fading away as well as emerging. Nor is England unique in that. Although this belief-system has indeed been very widespread across the globe, it cannot be found everywhere. It was much stronger at some times, and in some places, than others, and it could take some very different forms. There have been patterns of ebb and flow, which, on occasion, could reach epidemic proportions.

Since corpses do not in reality climb out of their graves and walk around, or become bloated with the blood of living victims, the question remains why people sometimes think that they do. Here is a puzzle worth exploring.

Many books have been written about vampires in sensational literature.[1] There are many others about vampires in actual human belief, but in one way or another they leave something missing. The various popular and encyclopaedic works[2] are essential reading for anyone who tries to get to grips with the subject on a global scale, and I could scarcely have managed without them, but they can lack coherence and critical analysis. Occasional anthropologists have engaged with living cultures of vampire belief, but work of that kind is all too rare. Archaeology refreshes the subject by contributing 'deviant' burials, of which growing numbers are excavated as the years pass, but analysis lags behind data-collection. So perhaps there is room for a book like this, which tries to make some coherent sense—on both general and local scales—of this strange belief and why people held it.

There are significant omissions. I say little about vampire fiction from the eighteenth and nineteenth centuries, and nothing about that from after 1900. (For earlier periods, the line between folklore and fiction is harder to draw: people told stories about things they believed in, and often believed the stories they heard.) More surprisingly, to some readers, the events of the 1730s, and vampire folklore from the more easterly parts of Europe since 1800, only get summary treatment. These rich, abundant, and compelling stories have been discussed many times in print, to the exclusion of much else. To emphasise them here would have been distorting as well as unnecessary: earlier (otherwise excellent) authors have generalised unjustifiably to the whole belief-system from this very specific context, and I want to avoid that trap.

Starting from problems of perception and definition, I trace how the 'European vampire' is just one species within a large family of predatory supernatural entities, including the female flying demons of South-east

Asia and the lustful *yoginīs* of India. After visiting the shamanic circumpolar zone, the Assyrian Middle East, and China, the book concentrates on Europe. Inevitably, that reflects my own historical and linguistic range: whole books could be written about the dangerous dead in Asia, for instance. But I hope that future scholars of other regions will find my approaches useful, not least because I did my best to establish consistent definitions. This book (like the occasional vampire) feeds on itself: general problems and approaches must be clarified first, and readers eager for the specific case-studies are asked to be patient.

The issue of gender, barely considered in previous works, is thrown into sharp relief by the two examples just mentioned: revived corpses were almost entirely female in seventh-century England, largely male in the eleventh to twelfth centuries. If belief in the undead reflects underlying fears or resentments, there must be social and cultural explanations for why those emotions were sometimes focused on men and sometimes on women. A recurrent strand identifies these supernatural yet physical beings as female, starting with the predatory flying monsters that emerge from a deep layer in the human imagination, continuing through the *lamiae* of the Graeco-Roman world, and culminating in the wise-women and witches of medieval and post-medieval Europe. When it comes to legacies in imaginative fiction, Sheridan Le Fanu's Carmilla embodies a more genuine tradition than Bram Stoker's Count Dracula, though we will also meet plenty of troublesome corpses that are male.

Vampires were not killed by science or modernity. In Europe east of the Elbe, dramatic manifestations of the belief continued through the nineteenth and early twentieth centuries; in a region of southern Romania, they continue still. The human tragedies of colonialism and slavery generated some distinctive if contained episodes in Australia and West Africa, and to the African diaspora in the Caribbean we owe that distinctive oddity, the Haitian *zombi*: undead but not dead. Strangest of all, perhaps, is New England between the 1780s and 1890s, where European folklore and popular medicine fused with the psychological trauma of tuberculosis deaths to create a distinctively modern kind of vampire.

While historians, literary scholars, anthropologists, and psychologists have all suggested theoretical models, this book is concrete and (literally) down-to-earth. I am certainly not averse to using theoretical approaches when they seem helpful and appropriate, but I prefer to start from hard evidence. My approach is pragmatic, and not beholden to any particular school or fashion. It is often functionalist, while also laying much emphasis on the power of inherited culture: as one scholar puts it, 'as anthropological interpretations, function and culture are hardly incompatible'.[3]

I have tried to be broad in scope, in the hope that light may be thrown in dark places by breaking down the boundaries of regional intellectual traditions as well as disciplinary ones. For example, English historians and archaeologists—tacitly reluctant to acknowledge forms of 'irrationality' in past world-views—have been remarkably resistant to the plain message of the evidence. That stands in sharp contrast to regions like Serbia or Poland, where the reality of beliefs in the dangerous dead is taken completely for granted because they are within recent experience. Cross-cultural analogies can be over-worked, but it is perverse to ignore them when they make coherent sense of what is otherwise baffling.

Although this book is not about fictional vampires, they cast a long, dark shadow over it. The subject's lurid overtones have attracted a diverse range of commentary and discussion: sometimes scholarly and effective, sometimes the opposite. Folklore and literature have it in common that they both tell stories, but the stories (at least in origin) are qualitatively different. Some recent books treat ethnographic field reports and *Dracula* as though they were sources of like kind. This habit of mind is hard to take seriously, but it is deep-rooted and goes back centuries. The labyrinth of borrowings and muddles, repeated from source to source and sometimes infecting supposedly objective reports, is hard to negotiate and full of snares. It is too much to hope that I have avoided them all, but I have done my best.

The theme is a difficult one for modern and rational people to discuss, and there will still be those who view it as bizarre, unhealthy, or repulsive. But nothing that was important to people in the past is off-limits for historians. Our own society keeps the physicality of death at a distance, but for many past societies it was a normal and familiar part of life: belief in animated corpses is only repellant from a sanitized modern perspective. Nor is it necessarily pathological or harmful: indeed, I want to argue that it has positive outcomes. The 'vampire epidemics' discussed in this book occurred at traumatic junctures, of the kind that have often turned communities against marginalized groups within them. By mirroring the distinctive anxieties of the societies that generated them, they provided a therapeutic, largely innocuous outlet for impulses of fear, hatred, and paranoia. Killing the dead is better than killing the living.

A Note on European Geography and Place-Names

A substantial part of this book deals with the eastern half of Continental Europe. That presents a practical problem: many places that had German names at the time of the events discussed (and in the sources that discuss them) now have Polish, Czech, Hungarian, Romanian, Slovakian, or Ukranian names, and lie within the boundaries of post-1918 nation-states. It also presents the moral problem of avoiding vocabulary that seems to ascribe peripheral, colonial, or dependent status to places or ethnic groups within that zone. On the first count, I have initially given names in dual form (thus 'Lemberg / Lviv', 'Groß-Mochbern / Muchobór); thereafter I give them in the German form when early modern texts are being cited, but in the modern form when the reference is to archaeological rather than documentary data. On the second count, it is not always possible to avoid using terms like 'central Europe' or 'eastern Europe' (though with lower-case initials), but readers must understand these as descriptions of physical location and nothing more.

PART I

Approaches

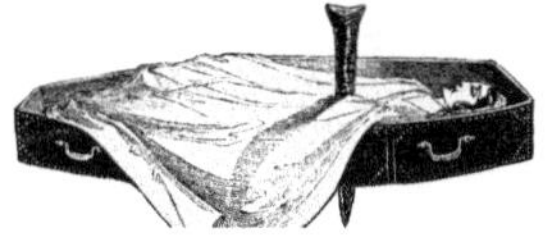

THIS BOOK is not about ghosts. It is about corpses: corpses that get up from under the earth and walk around, or lie in their graves in a state of unholy incorruption, absorbing the health or life-blood of the living. How were these strange constructs of the imagination conceived and visualised, and in which parts of the world were they thought to live?

To tackle those questions, we need to understand the varied approaches to the problem that have been taken by a range of specialists: psychologists, anthropologists, folklorists, scholars of literature and print culture, and archaeologists. Starting with definitions, the chapters in Part I aim to lay down those foundations.

1

Who Were the Dangerous Dead?

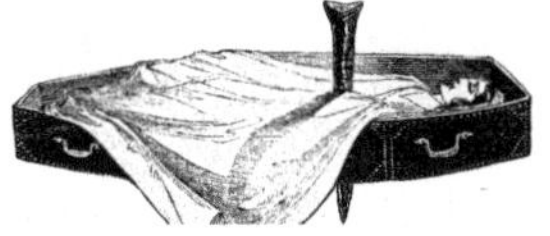

Nothing that relates to this subject has astonished me more than the accounts of the vampires of Hungary, Moravia and Poland; of the Broucolacks of Greece; and of the bodies of excommunicated persons which are said never to rot. I thought myself obliged to give it all the attention I was capable of.

—DOM AUGUSTIN CALMET, 1746

IS A WALKING CORPSE really 'just' a corpse? Readers of this book may often be tempted to ask that question, and definitions can prove slippery. That said, these pages make abundantly clear that many people have believed literally in walking corpses, others in ghosts, others again in ambiguous entities; and that those distinctions are socially and culturally conditioned. To ask for them always to be clear and consistent is asking too much of normal human cognition. For those who hold them, beliefs in physically animated corpses are no less real and vivid because they have fuzzy boundaries, and in broad terms they show some recurrent patterns.

Defining the Dangerous Dead

> By her side stood a tall, thin man, clad in black. His face was turned from us, but the instant we saw [him] we all recognized the Count. . . . With his left hand he held both Mrs. Harker's hands, keeping them away with her arms in full tension; his right hand gripped her by the back of the neck, forcing her face down on his bosom. Her white nightdress was smeared with blood, and a thin stream trickled down the man's bare breast which was shown by his torn-open dress. . . . His eyes flamed red with devilish passion . . . ; and the white sharp teeth, behind the full lips of the blood-dripping mouth, champed together like those of a wild beast.[1]

This is the most famous description of vampire activity, and the most misleading. In real folk-belief, predatory vampires are rarely aristocratic, rarely centuries old, and only in some specific contexts do they suck blood; nor are their physical attacks on the living described in such detail. Bram Stoker's research for his novel led him to material that was not entirely typical, and that he then transformed for dramatic effect. For instance, his use of an early eighteenth-century story, 'that those who have been tormented or killed by the *Vampyres* become *Vampyres* when they are dead', developed into a universal orthodoxy, but in fact this mechanism for creating vampires is only rarely mentioned.[2] To understand what people actually believed, we must forget Count Dracula and go back to basics.

All dead bodies are at least *slightly* daunting and troubling: that is a human universal. Most cultures have viewed the interval between death and final disposal as an anxious time, requiring alertness and elaborately formalized rituals to ensure a peaceful transition to the world of the dead. Usually, all goes well: the soul or life-force departs or diffuses, and the individual rests in peace. Trouble happens in the minority of cases where that process is frustrated or impeded. In a high proportion of cases, the undead are not created by the addition of something new but by a failure to complete.

In societies envisaging a universal life-force and multiple souls, it might be just one of those entities that hangs around. By contrast, the

FIGURE 1: The vampire who never was: Count Dracula, as pictured by E. A. Holloway in 1913. The anti-hero of Bram Stoker's misleading masterpiece reigns supreme in modern perceptions. In fact, he is very unlike the dangerous corpses in which people have actually believed.

Christian and Islamic belief in a single indivisible soul, which departs at the point of death, is not easily compatible with the belief in animated corpses. That puts pressure on theologians and clerics to rebrand the phenomenon as diabolical possession, which—fortuitously—is not so different from animistic cultures where unsettled corpses can be vulnerable to occupation by randomly straying spirits. The instinctive reflex is always essentially the same: *this corpse, from which all energy should have departed, is playing host to some force or entity that is dangerous, evil, or simply stuck.* Whether that entity is envisaged as the dead individual, as some element of the dead individual, or as something entirely different, is much more variable.

Why is this thought to happen? The single most widespread reason—and maybe the oldest—is uncompleted ritual. Rites of passage are badly performed, the body is not watched properly during the wake, or some unpropitious accident occurs. Alternatively, a life tragically cut short means that the soul's natural passage hits a dead end. The drowned, the murdered, women who die in childbirth, and girls who die before marriage, are stuck in that moment. They cannot return to human life, but nor can they move on, so that their needy, envious personalities lurk poisonously in their physical bodies. But even a properly completed sequence may not be foolproof: sometimes—as in early modern Germany or later New England—blameless and correctly buried corpses mysteriously mutate in the grave to send out lethal emanations.

In none of those cases do the individuals' personal qualities explain their fate (though the people cut short untimely are assumed to be resentful). Slightly different is the idea of the undead state as a posthumous continuation of malevolence in life, or even sometimes as a punishment. In medieval Europe or nineteenth-century Russia, for instance, typical subjects were dishonest, faithless people, often magicians or witches. This more moralistic framework probably resulted from specific social and religious circumstances, but it highlights individuals who, being marginal or subversive in life, were feared as uncontrollable forces after death.

The restless dead have taken a range of forms. Some appear as in life, some monstrously transformed, some as shape-shifters into animal

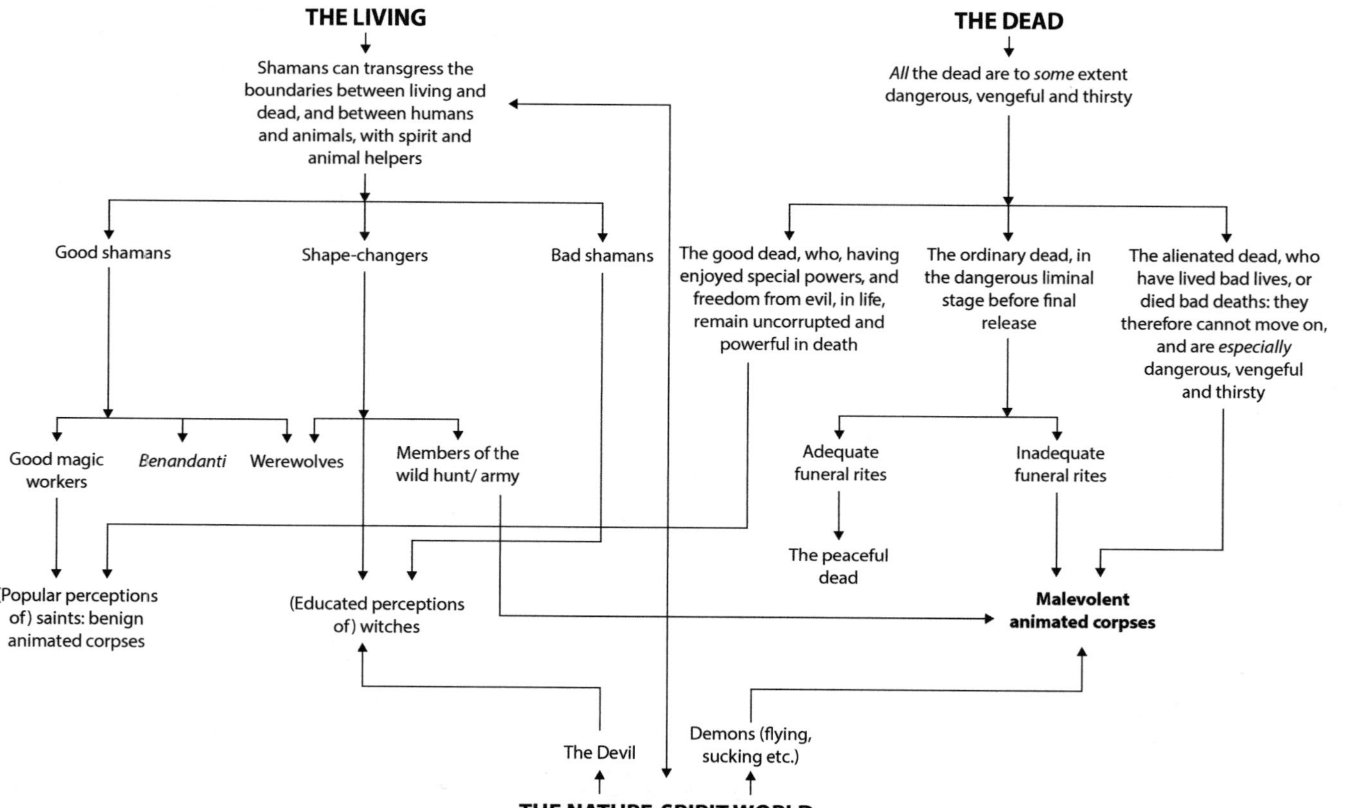

FIGURE 2: An attempt to frame the various supernatural concepts underlying world-wide beliefs in malevolent corpses.

guise. The really slippery conceptual issue is the relationship between the corpse and the walking, talking entity. Sometimes it is explicit that they are identical (for instance, because the grave is empty), but dead people 'seen' walking are usually ambiguous: you can touch, hit, or even wound them, but then they can shape-change, or pass through solid walls and their own grave-earth. As Martha McGill puts it, 'the returning dead persistently displayed a kind of "spiritual corporeality"'.[3] It is a constant, however, that the physical integrity of the buried corpse is a necessary condition for its spiritual part to materialize and harm the living: disabling the corpse will end the activities.[4]

Naming the Dangerous Dead

Let us not get tied into knots over terminology. Above all, let us avoid the kind of self-confirming argument that makes a fluid or even anachronistic conception or definition into an inflexible standard: 'Vampires drink blood; the predatory dead in *X* do not drink blood; therefore *X* does not have vampires'. Such logical fallacies open long and winding paths to a dead end.

Modern discourse cannot completely discard the word 'vampire', but the baggage that it has picked up during nearly three centuries of fictional and popular usage compromises it severely. First used in English in the 1730s,[5] it quickly emerged as the pre-eminent term for the beings explored in this book, and since the nineteenth century (especially in fiction) it has meant a bloodsucker. It is because of this essentially literary construct that historical discussions have hugely over-emphasized bloodsucking.

In this book I try to avoid tendentious terminology, but I have not restricted myself to words that are current in the periods being discussed (which would be impossible), and I have felt free to ring the changes. In general, I only use 'vampire' in post-1700 contexts, and when discussing the works of modern writers. My more usual expressions are 'dangerous corpses', 'dangerous dead', 'restless dead', 'undead' (a helpful term coined by Bram Stoker), 'revenant', or—when appropriate—'walking dead'. Distinguishing genuine oral terms from niche literary vocabulary is not always straightforward, especially in post-medieval Europe with its echo-chambers of pseudo-scholarly discourse on the subject.

That said, the words that people used in their own day to describe dangerous corpses are interesting and informative. So is their absence. If the last paragraph seemed vague, that is because a stable, dedicated vocabulary for dangerous and restless corpses did not exist in Europe north of the Carpathians before 1700. The reason, apparently, is that conceptually they were *still just people*: a grandfather who died last year remains a grandfather, not something different, even though he insists on walking around. (Nickname-like terms in folklore from the Aegean Islands and Pomerania—'wide-mouth', 'fatty', 'glutton', 'after-eater', 'sitter-up', and so on—are in an informal register and perhaps not very old.[6])

As we move southwards and eastwards—into the Carpathians and Balkans—we do encounter some consistently used terms. Even those, however, are borrowings from vocabulary that had once described beings of different kinds. That fact speaks of a different conceptual world (closer to that of South-east Asia), in which the restless dead merged ambiguously into a diverse supernatural family. We will often encounter these terms, so some discussion of the more important ones is useful here.

Slavonic *upiór* and its cognates are the sources of the term that entered Western European languages as *wampyr* and then *vampire*. Its origins remain debatable, but we can trust a sophisticated recent analysis that reviews twenty-three alternative etymologies.[7] The authors opt for a reconstructed Proto-Turkic noun **ōpyr*, 'that which sucks, that which swallows', which then followed a range of different semantic paths with meanings in the broad range of 'evil spirit' (Figure 3). There is nothing to suggest that these beings were conceived as animated corpses, but that was the destination to which this tortuous semantic path would eventually lead.

Romanian *strigoi*, Albanian *shtriga*, Istrian *strigon*, and so on descend from the classical Roman *strix*: a bird-like demon—one among the huge tribe of airborne demonic females—that enters houses at night to attack babies (p. 125). Elements of that identity survived, but in Istria by the 1680s the *strigon* was a predatory corpse, as the *strigoi* has been more

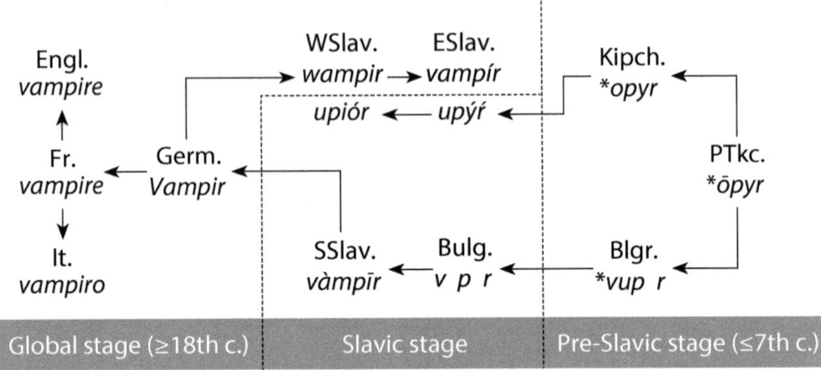

FIGURE 3: The complex ancestry of the word 'vampire'. This diagram illustrates Kamil Stachowski's hypothesis of an origin in Proto-Turkic **ōpyr*, transmitted via Bulgarian and South Slavic to produce German *vampir*. That form was adopted in more recent centuries into French, English, and Italian, as well as cycling back into West and East Slavic.

recently in Romania (pp. 343, 409).[8] The other standard Romanian term, *moroi*, is a borrowing from a widespread Germanic term for a night-pressing demon (as in 'night-mare'), and indeed was used as recently as 2004 in the specific sense of a night-pressing corpse (pp. 302, 438).

Greek *vrykólakas* is a loan from *vukodlak* and its many cognates, a widespread term across the Slavic and Baltic zones. The original form of the Slavonic word is again mysterious, but the likeliest option among several seems to be a compound meaning 'wolf-hair'.[9] The overwhelmingly most common meaning is straightforwardly 'werewolf', though *kodlak* in Croatia and Serbia, and *vurkollák* in Albania, morph into something closer to 'vampire'.[10] In Greece, *vrykólakas* usually means a malevolent walking corpse (p. 308).

In all four cases it is by association, not semantically, that these words denote animated corpses. Originally referring to demonic or shape-shifting entities with malignant supernatural powers, they only later embodied the idea of those powers residing in the physical bodies of dead humans. The implication seems to be that the animated corpse was a later arrival in the company of demonic beings. (A modern analogy would be our word 'computer'—something that makes computations—

which tells us that adding-machines were invented before email and the internet.) To put it another way: belief in demonic forces is always there in the background, but belief in the dangerous dead comes and goes.

Locating the Dangerous Dead

Corpse-killing is neither universal nor consistent, but it does crop up at one time or another over a large proportion of the world. At this point, the reader may be expecting me to map the practice on a global scale and throughout human history. But there are two big stumbling-blocks to any such attempt. The first is simply a lack of evidence. Some societies (such as Mesopotamia or China) have written sources going back millennia; others (such as Australia or Siberia) have no written sources at all before modern colonial contacts. For large areas of the globe, the evidence is folkloric, anecdotal, and very recent.

That means that our global map will lack time-depth, which is the second stumbling-block: it will show recent outcomes, but only hint at the deep processes lying behind them. As will be argued in this book, dangerous-dead beliefs can appear and disappear in response to socio-economic, religious, and cultural change. For instance, it seems likely that in AD 900, the English believed in the walking dead whereas the indigenous Australians did not; in AD 1900, the opposite was true. One or two thousand years ago, the map would have looked different.

But maybe it would not have looked *completely* different. Plotting relatively recent beliefs in the unquiet dead, and in related supernatural entities, does in fact show us some interesting things (Map 1).[11] Manifestations group within vast but distinct areas of the globe, mostly in what might be termed the 'vampire belt' running from Scandinavia and the North Sea through central and eastern Europe, western Russia, the Near East, India, and China to Indonesia. Two observations, to be picked up later, are worth making here. One is that these regions had 'shamanic' cultures in the hinterlands, mostly in the direction of the North Pole. The other is that one important cluster of manifestations, in West Africa, lies entirely outside the corridor.

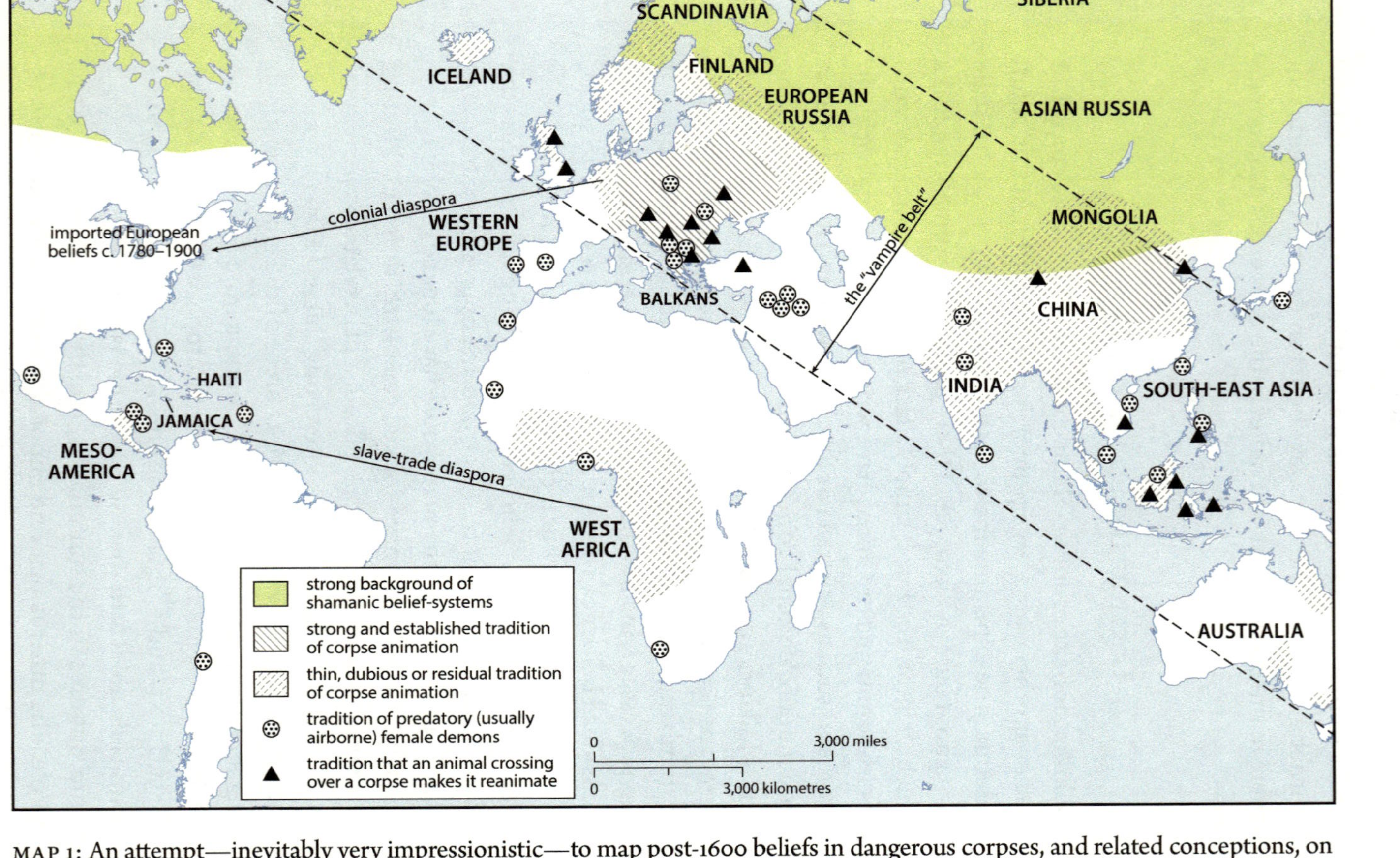

MAP 1: An attempt—inevitably very impressionistic—to map post-1600 beliefs in dangerous corpses, and related conceptions, on a world-wide scale. Since the data are relatively recent, it gives little sense of change over time. It does, however, highlight the clusters in Europe and Asia, and their relationship to the huge zones of deep-rooted shamanic belief that lay north-eastward. The suggested 'vampire belt' is an artificial construct, but a useful one to think with.

Map 1 also plots two distinctive belief-complexes that are distinct from the dangerous dead but have an immediate bearing on them. One is the belief that a cat jumping over a corpse will make it reanimate (p. 58). To anticipate, let us note that this strange idea—like belief in animated corpses itself—is widespread but not universal, with dominant clusters in the Balkan zone of Europe and in South-east Asia.[12] The second complex concerns demonic flying entities that were bird-like, female, and especially prone to attack mothers and young children. This was particularly intense in two zones: one on the western Pacific edge through Japan southwards to Indonesia, the other around Mesoamerica and the Caribbean. The motif seems to reflect a very early stage in the emergence of the belief-system and a deep layer in the human psyche (p. 122), even though it assumed specific regional identities.

Starting from these recent patterns, we can take some cautious steps—the deeper into the dark the further back we go—towards understanding where they came from. Burial archaeology potentially tells us something about the deep past of dangerous-dead beliefs. In the Upper Palaeolithic (50,000–12,000 years ago), it was individuals with striking physical anomalies, rather than social and political elites, who were buried in elaborate and distinctive ways:

> The very practice of burying bodies intact, and clothed, appears to have been exceptional in the Upper Palaeolithic. Most corpses were treated in completely different ways: de-fleshed, broken up, curated. . . . The corpse in its complete and articulated form—and the clothed corpse even more so—was clearly something unusual and, one would presume, inherently strange. . . . In many such cases, an effort was made to contain the bodies of the Upper Palaeolithic dead by covering them with heavy objects: mammoth scapulae, wooden planks, stones or tight bindings. Perhaps saturating them with clothing, weapons and ornaments was an extension of these concerns, celebrating but also containing something potentially dangerous.[13]

In the context of similar cases in this book, it is a plausible if not conclusive inference that these people were considered physically dangerous to the extent that restraint was needed to prevent their return.

Nonetheless, prehistoric 'deviant' burials are too rare and sporadic to give us a very coherent picture. Occasional prone, mutilated, or stone-laden corpses occur through the Neolithic and all later periods across the then-inhabited world. But even if we could confidently distinguish measures to restrain the dead from executions and shaming rituals (Chapter 7), there is in practice no way of knowing whether they represent the direct forerunners of later beliefs or entirely independent episodes.

With the emergence of written sources from ancient Mesopotamia onwards, some things start to come into focus. In China and India, we can see the 'flying female demon' complex morphing into charismatic and lustful entities that shape-changed between hyena/ fox and human forms, and started to be conceived as actual dead women. After about AD 100, developed 'vampire' stories building on this theme started to appear in both China and the Eastern Roman Empire, presumably diffused through long-distance economic and cultural exchanges.

How these traditions fused with others from the steppe region and from north-western Europe is elusive, but the combination that eventually emerged is distinctive (Figure 48). The diffusion of religious and spiritual ideas across the later Roman Empire may have tended to encourage homogenization. In Europe, corpses come in two versions—walking and grave-bound—which may have split from a single early prototype (p. 238). Walking corpses spread disease and fear, and sometimes shape-shift; bloodsucking is occasionally present, perhaps as an exotic introduction from the Black Sea zone. Grave-bound corpses do (by a mysterious process) absorb human blood, becoming red and bloated, and characteristically chew their shrouds.

Vampires and Witches

In his transformative survey of witch beliefs, Ronald Hutton observes that 'alternative explanations for misfortune that rule out or marginalize witchcraft are found across the world', and that the minority of global cultures *not* believing in witchcraft ascribe their misfortunes to other supernatural entities.[14] Those entities have included nature-spirits and unruly life-forces which—so the present book will argue—were the ultimate underpinning for beliefs in dangerous corpses.

And yet, in one crucial respect, a dangerous corpse differs from a nature-spirit and resembles a witch: as a physical entity, it can be tracked, examined, condemned, punished, or destroyed.[15] The procedures for identifying and neutralising witches and vampires were sometimes quite similar, and we will visit places where witches, wise-women and controlling matriarchs became even more dangerous after death. As reservoirs of unholy, lethal power, the restless dead had much in common with witches.

However, the geographical incidence of the two forms of persecution was more often complementary than overlapping, as the great witch-hunts of early modern Europe illustrate. There are exceptions, notably the apparent succession from witch-killing to corpse-killing in seventeenth-century Moravia (p. 351). But the regions of Europe where the witch-craze was at its most intense—Belgium, the borderlands of France and Germany, Switzerland, Austria, and Hungary—are broadly those where we will *not* meet many of the restless dead in this book. This tends to suggest that persecution of witches and persecution of corpses were *alternative* responses to similar stresses and anxieties, though both operated in societies where blaming nature-spirits was no longer enough.

Pursuing that point is made harder by the fact that whereas we have decades of systematic and thoughtful research into the social, cultural, and psychological contexts of witch persecution, approaches to corpse persecution have so far been rudimentary. But one does not need to scratch the surface far to find parallels. For instance, a group of essays on the Scottish witch-hunt make the points that belief in witchcraft is widespread but not a human universal; that it can have social and psychological benefits; that it can be a reaction against controlling mothers; that it can be either endemic or epidemic; that gender patterns are variable; and that romantic or fictional publications on witchcraft can encourage actual belief.[16] In the present book, all these points are repeatedly made about corpse-killing. Likewise, Hutton observes that 'witch-hunting, all over the world, has tended since records began to burgeon dramatically at particular times and die away or fall to a low level at others', which applies equally to hunting the dangerous dead.[17]

Accordingly, it should perhaps not surprise us that the factors that provoked epidemics of witch-killing and of corpse-killing remain equally hard to pin down, because they are equally complex and variable. Writing this book, I have often felt the frustrations expressed by Andreas Holzem in a recent study of central European witch persecution: 'All these clusters of conditions are ambiguous and contradictory in themselves—they always invite counterexamples. The manifestations of witch trials can evidently be understood only as the consequences of a complex amalgam of factors for which particular conditions of realization existed in certain parts of Germany. It was the disastrous interplay of a multitude of conditions that killed so many people in these regions, while others were left unscathed.'[18] In some regions little touched by witch-hunts, this 'interplay of a multitude of conditions' led to the alternative outcome of attacking corpses. That was less disastrous: the witches were alive, but the corpses were dead.

For us, there is another big difference: witch-hunting was often orchestrated from above through bureaucratic and legal mechanisms, whereas (notwithstanding occasional exceptions) that was only rarely true of corpse-hunting. An important consequence is that the copious documentation left by the persecution of witches is almost completely lacking for corpses. Even in well-documented societies, we may be grossly under-estimating the number of attacks on the dead.

This broad-brush survey raises more questions than it answers, and fleshing out the details is the task of the present book. In a few specific cases, it is possible to infer that some forms have displaced others. Migrations in the deep human past must have spread the ubiquitous 'demonic flying female'. Where this motif is muted or absent, that may be because it was superseded by versions in which the undead human body remains active in an essentially unmodified form (and can therefore be of either gender, for instance). But then why are the undead sometimes conceived as conscious individuals, sometimes as corpses powered by *zombi*-like brute forces? Most fundamentally, why do such beliefs exist at all and why do they come and go? The next chapters try to tackle these difficult questions.

2

Fearing Dead Friends, Killing Dead Enemies

ARE ANIMATED CORPSES A HUMAN CONSTANT?

'No, he's no more! He's no more, and in the place where he was there is something alien and hostile, some dreadful, terrifying, and repulsive mystery . . .'

—MARYA BOLKONSKAYA, ON THE DEATH OF HER FATHER (LEO TOLSTOY, *WAR AND PEACE*)

STRONG EMOTIONAL FEELINGS towards dead bodies—of fear, grief, alienation, reverence, or denial—are in the makeup of *homo sapiens*, inherited from hominin predecessors.[1] But here we are exploring something more specific and more culturally variable: the corpse that is not just an inert residue, but interacts with the living because of an indwelling agency or life force. That idea brings its own perplexities. Is the personality—or part of it—still there? If so, is it the one that we knew, or has it been hideously changed? Or has the corpse been occupied by some alien, demonic being?

The Psychological Approach: Innate Anxieties?

For the detached observer, a more clinical question follows: are such fears hard-wired in the human psyche to the extent of generating a universal illusion that corpses can exert agency of their own accord? Unsurprisingly, Sigmund Freud thought so:

> The assumption . . . that immediately after death the beloved member of a family becomes a demon, from whom the survivors have nothing but hostility to expect, so that they must protect themselves by every means from his evil desires, is so peculiar that our first impulse is not to believe it. Yet almost all competent authors agree as to this interpretation of primitive races. . . . [According to Rudolf Kleinpaul] this relation culminates in the conviction that the dead, thirsting for blood, draw the living after them. . . . Later moderation has restricted the malevolence of the dead to those categories where a peculiar right to feel rancour had to be admitted, such as the murdered who pursue their murderer as evil spirits, and those who, like brides, have died with their longings unsatisfied. Kleinpaul believes that originally, however, the dead were all vampires, who bore ill-will to the living, and strove to harm them and deprive them of life. It was the corpse that first furnished the conception of an evil spirit.[2]

Given Freud's huge influence across the past century, it is amazing to discover that these confident views are based on a popular book of folk-psychology by a journalist and general humanities writer, Rudolf Kleinpaul.[3] His account of vampires owes more to psychological interpretations of literature than to history or ethnography, and barely ranges outside Europe. Certainly it is nowhere near an adequate basis for assessing whether belief in walking corpses is a human universal.

In 1931, Freud's follower Ernest Jones pursued the problem in an account that—although more solidly based—still takes the Freudian framework for granted.[4] Thus the dead are feared because of an unconscious sexual guiltiness which 'owes its origin to infantile incestuous wishes'; 'morbid dread always signifies suppressed sexual wishes'; and 'in the Vampire superstition proper the simple idea of the vital fluid being withdrawn through an exhausting love embrace is complicated by more perverse forms of sexuality, as well as by the admixture of sadism and hate'.[5] He lays great emphasis on sleep paralysis of the night-mare kind, especially its sexual forms. We will see that the night-mare is a significant factor, and that corpses can sometimes be amorous. But many of the dangerous dead have nothing to do with sex.

Equally predictably, Carl Jung and his followers saw humanity's abiding fascination with the vampire type as reflecting its archetypal character. To quote a recent summary: 'From this point of view, a vampire lives within each of us. We project this inner reality on both male and female persons, members of other "tribes" and ethnic groups. We all have a dim awareness that this demonic yet tragic figure is real. However, we usually fail to grasp that this outer image is an expression of an inner reality—a reality that is elusive, threatening to self and others, and that can be effectively engaged only through a combination of empathy and heroic effort.'[6]

The basic problem with all of this is the sheer variety of different cultural forms, open to such a range of different interpretations, that these early psychologists squeezed into their respective procrustean beds. Jung gave more weight than Freud to cultural variety, but his model still ignores those large areas of the world where nothing remotely resembling the European vampire belief has ever been recorded. Rather than manifesting in all populations, or even in a consistent subsection of them, fears of the restless dead can remain low-key through millennia, and across large tracts of the globe, until awoken by complex conjunctions of forces that tend to be locally specific. Likewise, only certain revenants have been 'demonic yet tragic'.

These approaches will not be invoked much in this book, but they still leave us with questions to ponder. In 1998 the folklorist Alan Dundes re-worked the Freudian model in a culturally specific version, acknowledging that 'the vampire is *not* universal by any means'. His starting-point is that vampires are suckers of blood and other fluids because they are, above all, thirsty. That becomes comprehensible in the 'structural framework, apparently common to Indo-European and Semitic worldview in antiquity, [which] involves a set of bisecting humoral binary oppositions: hot and cold, and wet and dry', and in which *all* the dead are thirsty.[7] Again we hit the problem of over-definition—there are many members of the undead tribe who do not suck anything—but the suggestion that these beliefs are specific to certain (albeit very big and ancient) cultural groups is worth remembering.

Of course, there has been more recent and more technical research—mainly on psychology's frontier with anthropology—into the cognitive roots of supernatural beliefs. Remarkably little of it bears specifically on the dangerous dead: there is more on monsters, and on the special case of non-quite-dead *zombis*.[8] One scientific paper of 2015, by Vladimír Bahna, does try to explain vampirism through methodologies associated with the evolutionary psychologist Pascal Boyer. Bahna sees the vampire as one of those supernatural constructs that—in Boyer's view—are particularly well-adapted to cultural transmission. They contrast with disembodied ghosts in being corpses, thus triggering an instinctive emotion of disgust; equally, their physicality means that they can be attacked and destroyed. Since they display little or no conscious agency, they are more like instinctive predators: 'the actions of a vampire are not influenced by personal relations, knowledge or positive or negative preferences'. Accordingly, these beliefs 'represent a cognitively attractive combination of a hazard and relevant actions to eliminate it'.[9]

There are big problems with this rather mechanistic analysis. We will see that there is a spectrum between ghosts and unquiet corpses; that the walking dead do sometimes display aims and emotions; and that they regularly attack specific people (notably relatives) for specific reasons. Still, we can take some helpful pointers from Bahna's analysis. Vampires are indeed made all the more compelling by their lurid physicality. Most crucially, they can be detected, maimed, or destroyed, whereas the real sorrows and evils for which they stand proxy are all too immune from neutralization. If people who have been magically, socially, or sexually unbridled and dominant in life come back to trouble us, we can quell them once and for all by eliminating their corpses.

The basic limitation of approaches like Bahna's is that they aim to adduce general psychological phenomena, whereas beliefs in the unquiet dead are altogether more varied. For instance, not all humans have been disgusted by corpses, and those who see interaction with them as natural (Indigenous Australians, for instance) tend not to expect them to come back. That is not to decry the psychological approach—far from it—but to insist that research methods should acknowledge the cultural embeddedness of supernatural beliefs.

Recent work on the psychology of ritual is helpful here because it is more context-specific. Many vampires are obsessive-compulsives: chewing their shrouds, counting grain scattered in their graves (pp. 237, 94). But then, so are their killers, whose tasks must often be performed with ritual precision. To exhume and mutilate a decaying corpse is indeed a ritual, and a powerfully distressing one. Like other effort-intensive rituals, it drives its practitioners onwards because they have already invested so much in it: the more corpses we kill, the harder it becomes to see corpse-killing as a pointless activity. This 'effort justification' dynamic helps to explain why an initial outbreak can generate an epidemic lasting for years or decades.[10]

Night-mares

Some of the episodes described in this book involve the sleep-paralysis experience, in which one wakes up, unable to move, with an unwelcome supernatural visitor pressing on one's chest.[11] This phenomenon is sometimes called the 'Old Hag'—with reason, since the perceived attackers are so often female—though here I shall call it the 'night-mare' (not 'nightmare') in the original sense of that term. Much about it remains puzzling, but we know that it is common world-wide, that it is vividly real to its percipients, and that it can be studied as a problem in neuropsychology. In his fascinating exploration, David J. Hufford demonstrates that many of its details are cross-cultural to the extent of apparently being universal.[12]

To that extent, the night-mare is significantly different from beliefs in witches or in the restless dead. But it concerns us here because the perceived attackers have often been identified, in a range of permutations, as living witches or as recently dead people. The connection is well known from witchcraft trials, as with the Salem accuser of 1692 who testified that 'he did awake in the Night by Moonlight, and did see the likeness of this Woman grievously oppressing him; in which miserable condition she held him, unable to help himself, till near Day'.[13] A modern Philippine version replicates the motif of a malignant female—assimilated to the local form of a flying demon—who is again a real, identifiable woman; this time, however, she is already dead (p. 128).

The night-mare had a similar role in some European vampire epidemics.[14] A Buckinghamshire story from the 1190s tells how a dead man terrified his widow by returning and night-pressing on her (p. 255). Likewise, after rumours spread in 1591 that a shoemaker of Striegau/Strzegom (now Poland) who received Christian burial had in fact committed suicide (p. 336), he was seen around the town as he looked in life and 'terrified sleepers in a more horrid form'. As the problem escalated, he attacked beds, 'clung to the sides of those lying there, and redoubled ghastly attempts to suffocate', so that by morning the victims were covered in livid bruises and the marks of his fingers. When exhumed, the corpse was duly found intact and bloated with blood.[15]

Even in New England, as late as 1799, the 'vampire' Sarah Tillinghast first manifested as a night-mare. Her younger sister fell ill and died soon after her, having complained that 'Sarah came every night and sat upon some portion of the body, causing great pain and misery. So it went on. One after another sickened and died until six were dead, and the seventh, a son, was taken ill. The mother also now complained of these nightly visits of Sarah. These same characteristics were present in every case after the first one'.[16]

These episodes, so widely separated, have important messages for this book. One is the intense physicality with which night-mare victims perceive their attackers: as research has repeatedly shown, they seem every bit as *real* as if their objective existence were proved scientifically. When those beings take the form of recently dead neighbours or relatives, the sufferers will form an understandable conviction that those people have come and sat on them as actual corpses. That is certainly not to explain how *all* beliefs in the dangerous dead started, but it provides one reason why those beliefs have been held so strongly.

FIGURE 4: A Lilith-type demon as night-mare. This re-working of Henry Fuseli's *Nightmare* by the engraver Tony Johannot (1845) conveys both the form and the horror of female flying demons in Middle Eastern and Graeco-Roman imaginations.

It therefore becomes relevant to ask where night-mare experiences come from, and whether they have any causal links to dangerous-dead experiences. Shelley R. Adler's study of a South-east Asian refugee community in the United States, the Laotian Hmong, helps us here. In the 1980s, these people suffered a strange epidemic: 'seemingly healthy people died in the night, on their backs, with looks of terror on their faces'.[17] The Hmong are traditionally shamanistic and animistic, believing in multiple human souls and multiple nature-spirits, and already before migration they feared the night-mare spirit (*dab tsog*).[18] In America, they met a host of social traumas and cultural challenges: community and family dispersal, an alien host society, a new religion, and long hours of hard work for bad pay. As children started to grow up with Western values, inter-generational stress heightened the sense of alienation. Above all, mass conversions to Christianity without proper instruction generated a rich mix of guilt, resentment, anxiety, and disorientation. As one informant put it: 'There are also many, many individuals who are converted without knowing what's going on. They just did it because their friend did it. They just did it because their sponsors are Christian. So they did it without knowing. When they converted, they continued to feel terrible. They go home and they talk to relatives and friends, and they keep saying, "Well, this is what happened to me. I already did it, but I didn't want to do it. Please continue on the old tradition", and so forth'.[19]

The sudden nocturnal deaths, so prominent among the refugees, were less familiar in the Vietnamese homelands, but the Hmong themselves associated them with *dab tsog*. The exclusion of traditional safeguards thus exacerbated the problem: 'In the old tradition, if [a night-mare episode] happens, then they need a shaman to come and give them the metal [ring] for the neck or ankle, but the Christians—now I am Christian—I just pray and pray'.[20]

Adler's study added a scientific dimension that acknowledges how acute psychological disturbance can have adverse physical effects: it looks as though cultural fear of *dab tsog*, combined with conditions of high stress (including fatigue and sleep loss), have indeed had fatal consequences for certain vulnerable individuals, to the point of explaining the sudden deaths among Hmong immigrants.[21]

Let us beware of reductionist and single-cause explanations. Most night-mare experiences are not fatal; most night-mare assailants are not identified as dead people; most narratives of the restless dead do not report night-mare elements. Still, there are promising avenues here. If at least *some* restless-dead experiences start with the night-mare, cultures with a vivid sense of predatory nature-spirits like the *dab tsog* might be more prone to them: South-east Asia illustrates this effect vividly.[22] More generally, we see how insecurity, anxiety, and a demoralizing lifestyle can intensify fears of malignant supernatural forces. If that seems obvious, Adler's research highlights a specific trauma that we will meet again: the destruction of traditional support systems, both spiritual and social, because of religious change driven from above.

Physiology, 'Human Universals', and Culture

In contrast to the psychological approach is the materialistic one, based on forensic pathology, which Paul Barber developed in his excellent and entertaining book *Vampires, Burial, and Death*.[23] His central argument is that natural physiological processes of bloating, swelling, reddening, contortion, and the oozing of blood have created a widespread illusion that some kind of life persists in recently dead corpses. To the extent that Barber's theory—like Freud's—seeks to universalize, it faces the same problem that only certain societies have been prone to draw this wrong conclusion from the observed physical changes.

Unlike Freud, though, Barber acknowledges the powerful role of oral transmission in conditioning responses: 'One event gives rise to multiple folkloric forms, which, when reformatted by the observer—made coherent by being provided with motives, then told as a process—take on forms that we may not even recognize as the original event. . . . It is thus, evidently, that the European vampire came into being. Dead bodies do bloat and bleed at the mouth—as our informants tell us—but these functions are seen not as evidence of decomposition but as a consequence of their having sucked blood from the living'.[24]

A framework within which specific and generalizing explanations can potentially find common ground, or at least a meeting-place, is offered by the conception of 'human universals': 'those features of culture, society, language, behavior and mind that, so far as the record has been examined, are found among all peoples known to ethnography and history'.[25] If that sounds too sweeping, scholars subdivide it further, into 'near' universals (as against 'absolute' ones), 'conditional universals' (which always happen when particular conditions are met), and 'statistical universals' (which 'may be far from absolutely universal' but occur 'in unrelated societies at a rate that seems well above chance').[26]

Those options allow flexibility: maybe enough to give restless-dead beliefs some 'universal' status, even though they are not found worldwide. They meet the standard for 'statistical universals'. Since they regularly appear under specific combinations of social, religious, cultural, and epidemiological stresses, they might also be called 'conditional' ones. The model allows that 'observable variation in behavior or culture is entirely compatible with a panhuman design of the mind', which seems to admit the range of cultural agency proposed in this book.[27] All this provides a context for how underlying pressures can generate remarkably similar belief-systems.

Without trying to judge further between the evolutionary psychologists and the cultural anthropologists, we can accept some basic facts: that there is a human propensity to suspect that some of the dead are not really dead; that certain physical and psychological effects can often strengthen that suspicion; but that the suspicion must still be triggered by attitudes, perceptions, and fears that are not automatic, but spring from social, economic, political, religious, and cultural variables.

Dangerous corpses only make sense in the contexts of the societies that feared them, and of belief-systems that may surprise some modern readers: systems like those in which individuals have two or three souls; in which death is not an event but a journey or process; in which shamans can travel between different worlds; and in which relationships, affections and hatreds continue to play out across the frontier between life and death. We will now examine some of those contexts.

3

The Dangerous Dead in Society

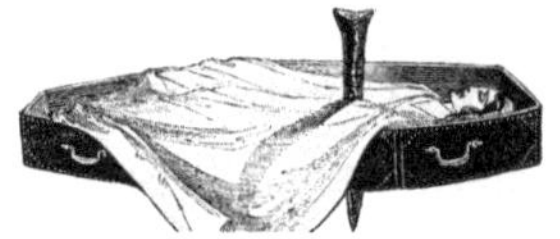

> Upon examining closely the narrations of the death of these pretended martyrs to vampirism, I discover all the symptoms of an epidemical fanaticism, and am convinced that their death is occasioned by nothing but the impressions of their own fear.
>
> —DOM AUGUSTIN CALMET, 1746

HOW CAN WHOLE societies come to believe that the dead walk among them? Understanding that requires moving beyond theoretical approaches, and engaging with tangible human communities and their world-views. We will first visit two very different societies in which the veil between life and death has been thin. The dead have been close: sometimes to be revered, sometimes to be feared, but regularly to be interacted with, if not unambiguously in a bodily form. Both case-studies manifest an endemic layer of anxiety, capable of intensifying under stress into something more concentrated and physical.

The Sora of the Indian East Coast

The Sora are an indigenous, long-stable society.[1] They are slash-and-burn farmers, with linguistic and cultural affinities looking outwards to

South-East Asia. Their strong sense of sociability, mutual sharing, and interdependence crosses the life/ death boundary. The engagement of the living with the dead is continuous and immensely complex, to the point of influencing large areas of social and ethical practice. Cremation happens swiftly, but is followed by extended negotiations to help the dead along the road from the short-term 'Experience' stage—when they may be resentful, conflicted, or dangerous—to the stable and serene 'Ancestor' stage.

That is hardest for those who have died badly: they can seek to pull the living after them, setting up chains of unquiet deaths.[2] In such cases, 'inquests' are held: public meetings to settle differences across the divide, in which conversations with the angry dead—mediated by female shamans—can become very direct and informal. Here for instance are snatches from a dialogue between a little girl who had died recently and her aunt (representing the girl's mother):

> DEAD GIRL [arriving from the Underworld, faintly]: Mother, where are my nose-rings?
>
> LIVING AUNT: They must have burned up in the pyre, darling, we looked but couldn't find them . . .
>
> DEAD GIRL [petulantly]: Why aren't you showing me my nose-rings?
>
> LIVING AUNT: They were so tiny. . . . Oh my love, my darling, don't cause your own illness in others. Can you say that your mother and father didn't sacrifice for you? . . .
>
> DEAD GIRL [addressing herself to her silent mother, and crying]: Mother, you were horrid to me, you scolded me, you called me Scar-Girl, you called me Leper-Girl, you said, 'You're a big girl now, why should I feed you when you sit around doing nothing?'
>
> . . .
>
> LIVING AUNT: So don't you pass it [her illness] on, don't you give it to your mother and little sisters!
>
> DEAD GIRL: If I grab them I grab them, if I touch them I touch them, if I pass it on I pass it on: that's how it goes. . . .[3]

In this culture of universal cremation, corpses cannot straightforwardly get up and walk. Even so, the deceased's 'ghost' (*kulman*) is tangible enough to be coated with ash from the pyre, to have hair that the living can touch, to rummage around the kitchen looking for food, and to need restraining from returning home.[4] In the following story (which reads rather like an origin-myth for the cremation rite), a dead woman who has *not* been cremated seems physical enough to her family:

> A family lived in isolation in the jungle. One day the mother died and since he did not understand what death was, the father just abandoned her corpse. But every day when he left his children and went out to find food, her *kulman* returned and swept the house and cooked. . . . [The children told him, so he] stayed behind one day to see for himself. His wife did indeed come and start to work. He was overwhelmed with joy and rushed up to her and threw his arms around her. But as soon as he clasped her, she turned to ashes in his embrace. Only then did he understand that he had to cremate her and plant a stone for her.[5]

As elsewhere, the ambiguity in such narratives may reflect ambiguity in perception: do the dead *really* walk? It may well be that the Sora, if pressed, would say that they do not do so in a literally corporeal sense. But if such a society were to suffer socio-cultural trauma and externally-driven religious change, leading for instance to the abandonment of cremation, might this aspect of their cognitive world assume a more lurid physicality?

Eastern Finland

Nilsiä, a small town in eastern Finland, belongs to a traditional society of mixed subsistence farming, little touched by modernity before the 1960s. In June 1998 a retired farming couple, Helmi and Uuno Heikkinen, were drinking coffee at home. A friend called Pikilän Helmi had dropped in, and was telling them about the death of her husband Jussi a couple of years earlier. While he was still unburied, Pikilän Helmi and her sister Elsa were preparing for the funeral. That night, Elsa slept beside her sister in what had been Jussi's place. During the night, Jussi came with his walking-stick, shouted 'Get out of my bed', and drove Elsa away with blows on the leg. In the morning, her leg was red and swollen. Some time afterwards, Jussi visited his widow a second time. 'Would you like to come with me?' he asked, in a friendly, enquiring fashion, adding, 'but you still have some time left'. Later he came a third time, saying, 'Now it's time to go: you haven't much time left'.

The meeting with the Heikkinens was soon after that. In fact, Pikilän Helmi had come because she thought it would be her last chance to meet them, and she did indeed die shortly afterwards. Also present on that occasion was Elvi Kuosmanen, who recalled Sanni Hyttinen, a former resident of the same building whose husband had died in the Winter War of 1939–40. Recently, when Sanni had just moved to an old people's home, her husband had come and told her that it would soon be time for her to go: 'It's good that you now live in such nice quarters, but you won't have much time to enjoy them'.

Helmi Heikkinen told this story to members of her family in July 2006,[6] but her daughter-in-law and grandchildren agree that on previous occasions, they heard her narrate a simpler version: that Pikilän Helmi's dead husband would regularly return to sleep with her, and that she essentially took that for granted. They suggest that Helmi Heikkinen unconsciously remoulded the story in her mind into a more structured version (perhaps influenced by fairy-tales with the three-visit motif), and also filtered out the implied sexual aspect.

For us, this story has two lessons. One is about how oral transmission works: genuine memories are reported and handed down, but in the process they can be re-shaped into recognized narrative forms, with elements emphasized or suppressed to suit current sensibilities. The other—counter-intuitively for modern readers—is its *normality*. It just describes ordinary life, as perceived in pre-industrial societies across the globe through countless millennia: there is nothing sinister about Jussi's return.

Going back another generation, we meet something darker and more eerie. Helmi's mother-in-law, Anna Lovisa Heikkinen (1878–1961), was a hard woman in a tough environment. Her keen-sightedness seemed almost outside the human range, and her granddaughter remembers once seeing horns on her head. As she lay dying, she asked mysteriously to be buried with her hair. Soon after her funeral, footsteps were heard in the attic, where a search revealed a bag of hair and nail clippings. This was buried in a bog, and the footsteps ceased. Years later, her great-granddaughter saw her bible lying in a cupboard on the house porch and sensed that nobody liked to touch it.[7]

These stories from a traditional Finnish family preserve traces of a perceptual world that once covered large areas of Europe. The boundary between the living and the dead is thin and permeable, and it becomes perilously frail when daunting individuals, having crossed it, show signs of coming back. Jussi and Anna Lovisa are not returning corpses, but they are physical enough to attack someone with a stick or tramp across a timber floor. Jussi's story illustrates the particular dangers of the interval between death and burial. Anna Lovisa represents the strong, potentially dangerous matriarch whom we will meet later. But there is a distinct difference between these two dead people: one behaves in a normal, predictable fashion, whereas the other is sinister and provokes countermeasures. What would another stage along this spectrum look like?

Anthropological Perspectives

By now, we should have some grasp of the kinds of mindset that could—given the right stimuli—generate fears of the walking dead. What then were the stimuli? To pursue this further we need specific and close-grained analyses, but sadly those are few and far between. The heroic pioneers of anthropology, while intensely interested in comparative religious systems and concepts of the soul, gave little thought to the specific problem of corpses with an in-dwelling life. Sir James Frazer's *The Belief in Immortality and the Worship of the Dead* and *The Fear of the Dead in Primitive Religion* make six volumes between them, in which beliefs across the globe are rehearsed in mind-numbing abundance.[8] Even so, the dangerous physical dead barely feature there, outside a rather breathless catalogue of corpse-killing practices that is useful as a source for examples, but in no way analytical.[9]

More recently, those anthropologists who have shown interest in the problem have tended to follow the universalizing lead of the psychologists. There has been valuable work on the dangerous dead in animistic and multi-spirit cultures, notably Katherine Swancutt's fine-grained analysis of 'vampiric imps' in the complex family structures of Buryat Mongols.[10] By comparison, the few surviving pockets of European corpse-killing have (sadly and surprisingly) seen little attention. A few case-studies do nonetheless exist, and two especially deserve our attention here.

Carl-Ulrik Schierup is a sociologist interested in ethnicity, migration, and multiculturalism: his study of vampire beliefs among Wallachians in Denmark and Sweden starts from research on those expatriate communities. Back home, in north-eastern Serbia, the beliefs are endemic, but why do they 'not only survive, but are even invoked more often in immigrant communities, than in the pre-migratory rural situation'?[11] Schierup's answer lies in heightened tensions between expatriates and their home families, whose distinctive structure, dominated by the elderly, continues to exert a hold on them. He begins with one Milorad, who is working late in his suburban Danish house in 1983. He hears a knock, and lifts his tired eyes: 'His deceased mother is hovering outside the window in her white burial attire, muttering in a distant voice: "Why have you left me . . . ?"' To his friends, it is only too predictable: 'They knew before I did that she might come. . . . I had gone against my mother, and married Zlatka, who was a simple girl and not good enough for me according to Mamma. Then later, when I moved from my mother's house to bring peace to the family, my mother condemned me. . . . People knew that my mother was strong and that her judgement was a hard burden to bear. They knew that she might return.'[12]

Schierup locates such anxieties in the 'Timok family type', which comprises up to five generations in the same household (now often alternate, as couples temporarily migrate, leaving children with grandparents). It is made practicable by an early age of marriage and a low birth-rate. The senior generation, which dominates property-rights and household decision-making, seeks to maintain control by arranging marriages—often doomed ones—for malleable teenagers. Predictably, many young couples defy the system and make their own choices. Such marriages tend to be more successful, but they can cause bitter and

FIGURE 5: A new bride bows to her mother-in-law, whose welcome does not look warm: Russian Karelia, 1894. It is easy to imagine how such a woman, domineering and oppressive in life, could have been conceived as a vampire after her death. Note the large key hanging at her waist, a sign that she rules the household.

long-lasting conflict between the generations. 'Thus the ultimate moral sanction of the older generation, lies in the fact that they might reappear [after death] and revenge themselves'.[13] After about 1970, a new factor was temporary migration to Scandinavia. Migrants regularly returned to their home villages and families, with which they still identified and where life-cycle events happened, but the potential for conflict grew as younger generations became more educated and cosmopolitan. The elders responded by falling back on traditional ideology and magical sanctions: 'Thus, the strategic importance of 'vampires' tends to increase as integration in Scandinavian society grows'.[14]

There are anthropological insights of a different but complementary kind in Juliet du Boulay's unique and brilliant paper 'The Greek Vampire', based on her fieldwork in the village of Ambéli (in Euboea on the

Aegean coast of Greece) in 1971–3.[15] In contrast to Schierup's sociological and functional approach, du Boulay explores symbolic meaning. Sadly, her work stands so completely on its own that generalization from it is risky, but it adds such richness in context and significance that it needs close attention here.

The ritual life of Ambéli was dominated by a pervasive cyclic symbolism, represented by the traditional ring-dance, in which all movement was in a spiralling anti-clockwise ('auspicious' or 'right-handed') direction. In rituals of both marriage and death, blood is a central motif, and that blood must circulate auspiciously, out of the kindred rather than turning back upon it. In the case of marriage, men stay in their own kindreds whereas women move outside them: 'the movement of women between the kindreds is equated with the movement of blood, and expresses the principle that this movement should be unidirectional and should not be reversed'.[16]

When death comes, the Angel of Judgement 'with his drawn sword cuts the victim's throat, and drenches with blood not only the dead person but also the house and everyone in it': thus the individual is transformed from a this-world being of flesh and blood to an insubstantial soul.[17] But that process can go horribly wrong if a procedural accident—usually a cat or some other creature or object passing across the corpse—occurs between death and burial. This breaks the outwards-flowing spiral movement of the blood, turning it back on itself, and may also block a vertical axis passing through the corpse between the upper and nether worlds.[18] The corpse is then reanimated as a predatory and lethal vampire.

There is thus a parallelism—though not a direct causal link—between the good and bad directions of blood circulation in marriage and in death:

> Blood going to 'strange' blood [by marriage well outside the kindred] pours in a life-giving spiral through the community; while blood going to blood that 'resembles itself'—that is to say, stays where it is—halts and doubles back. Similarly, the life in which the outpouring of the blood in death has not been frustrated moves on without

> check into the new and auspicious categories of the other world; while a life by which this outpouring is, by some inauspicious action, checked and turned back on itself, returns to devour the succeeding generations, and imperils the destiny of its own soul.[19]

The parallel elucidates a dramatic moment in du Boulay's research when she overheard two women deploring a marriage between second cousins: 'In this context the comment then uttered takes on a startling significance, for, said as an aside and half under the breath, it took the form of a well-known proverb: "The vampire hunts its own kindred" (*vrykólakas tó sói kynigáei*). The image of the vampire returning from the grave to hunt its own kin sprang intuitively to mind in the context of the blood which in second cousin marriage returns to destroy its originators'.[20]

Du Boulay's work gives rich texture and meaning to motifs found in many (but not all) dead-killing cultures. One of those, of course, is blood: vampires are rarely caught sucking it, but they sometimes accumulate it in their bodies and graves. Another is social ritual, shockingly transgressed if the dead cannot die. A third is the motif-complex of blocking, frustration, and diversion onto the wrong path, many versions of which appear in this book. Whenever we meet these, we should remember her insights.

Whether she explains why the people of Ambéli came to believe in vampires in the first place is perhaps not so clear. Other Greek regions may be different (as she fully acknowledges), and places further afield may be different again. We will see that beliefs in dangerous corpses were deep-rooted in the Balkans, but may only have developed in Greece during the later Middle Ages (p. 285). Rather than the Greek vampire being created as a sinister counterpoint to the auspicious spiral, it seems more likely to have been assimilated into that symbolic system from a different source.

What sustained it? The Schierup and du Boulay models have one social institution in common: rigid and heavily-determined marriage patterns based on extended kindreds. But whereas du Boulay dissects attitudes at a moment in time, Schierup emphasizes stresses building up because of social change, migration, and inter-generational strife.

Conflicts between norms imposed by family elders and the inclinations of young couples must have occurred in Ambéli, too, where mothers-in-law were proverbially cross-grained[21] and old women could mutter under their breaths about vampires. In the expatriate Wallachian communities, the vampires were the grandmothers themselves.

If this recalls the Freudian idea of 'relative-as-demon', it must be stressed that it is just one scenario among several. It introduces some important themes that we will meet again: distinctive kinship structures; dominant and sinister matriarchs (Figure 5); disempowered but rebellious teenagers; heightened stresses within migrant communities. But there will be other cases where few or none of these factors apply.

There is a distinction between societies like those explored in these two studies, where 'the vampire hunts its own kindred', and the many others where it attacks neighbours rather than family and is a general public nuisance. Intra-family tension is one layer, but socio-economic change, trauma, and disease have added others. In a global context, the Ambéli cameo is one point on a fluctuating trajectory.

Epidemics?

Even if fear of the dangerous dead is a human propensity, the cultural factors activating its more intense forms have been absent from large regions of the world. In other regions, the fear has existed at a mild level through long timespans; in others again, it has risen to intense levels during short or occasionally lengthy phases. It seems appropriate to adopt clinical terminology: chronic versus acute, endemic versus epidemic.

Some well-documented outbreaks of vampire-killing erupted quite suddenly: in Saxony and then Silesia from the 1540s, in Moravia from around 1650, and in New England from the 1780s (pp. 323, 325, 350, 390). They then ran for up to a century, with gradually diminishing intensity. That helps to make sense of an older case: eleventh- to twelfth-century England, where the start of the outbreak remains hazy, but its geographical retreat and then near-disappearance after 1200 was quick and obvious (p. 313).

Elsewhere, and further back in time, the evidence is rarely adequate to calibrate the rise and fall of epidemics: we tend to find specific clutches of stories, or of excavated burials, that suggest intense phases of corpse-killing without giving much idea of their length. With at least some of these, their very isolation might suggest short, acute episodes. On the other hand, there are large areas—northern Europe through the first millennium AD, for instance—where sporadic episodes are most convincingly ascribed to low-level but long-lasting fears, perhaps punctuated by brief local peaks.

The clear epidemic cases arose against backgrounds of acute trauma: foreign invasion combined with socio-economic and religious change in medieval England; bubonic plague, the Reformation and re-Catholicization in central Europe; violence and disease at the interface of Turkish and Habsburg imperial domination in Serbia; and the devastating scourge of tuberculosis in New England. Epidemic disease may be the most powerful driver, but any grossly disorientating and destabilizing change could potentially arouse concerted attacks on the dead—so long as a basic cultural propensity was already there in the background. In other cases we will need to explore different factors, such as the anthropologists' models of family structure, and religious tensions between Catholic, Orthodox, and Muslim traditions.

In the end, the dead are most likely to be blamed when external forces bring grievous burdens of sorrow and fear. These can be social, cultural, and religious changes, up-ending the customs and belief-systems that underpin stable life. They can be the grief and outrage of the colonized or the insecurities of colonizers. They can be destructive wars. They can be religious transformations. Above all, they can be epidemic diseases.

Faced with such catastrophes, inaction is intolerable: one must do *something*. Tragically, vengeful hatred has often been directed irrationally against neighbours, for instance those identified as ethnic, religious, or sexual deviants. But suppose the culprits are recognised among the dead? That may be irrational too, but it will spare the living.

Few reflective comments have come through to us from societies that actually practised killing the dead. But we can listen to a relative of the last New England 'vampire' (exhumed in 1892), recalling the tuberculosis that devastated his family and neighbours, and their way of coping with it: 'Do I believe in vampire? No. No, I don't believe in that. I'm not sure they did, but they had to come for an answer. And it turned out that maybe that was the answer. And some of them old people probably died with that in their mind, that they did the right thing.'[22]

4

Rest in Peace (and Don't Come Back)

HOVERING ON THE THRESHOLD OF DEATH'S DOOR

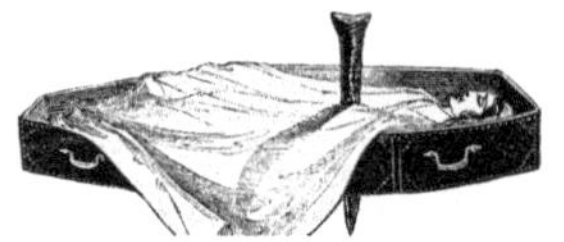

No exorciser harm thee!
  Nor no witchcraft charm thee!
Ghost unlaid forbear thee!
  Nothing ill come near thee!
Quiet consummation have;
  And renowned be thy grave!

—WILLIAM SHAKESPEARE, *CYMBELINE*, ACT 4, SCENE 2

IN CONTRAST to the (historically abnormal) attitudes of the modern Western world, most past societies have viewed death as a process, not an event. It is a multi-stage journey, in which the cessation of breath, the laying-out, the liminal stage at the wake, the burial, and the ensuing physical decay are steps along a road that must be followed precisely. Nor does it necessarily end there: disposal of the corpse has often been two-staged, only finished when the defleshed bones are exhumed and laid to their final rest. In his classic study of rites of passage, Arnold van Gennep tells us that he initially expected funerals to emphasize separation rites; in fact those turned out to be few and simple, whereas long and complex rites of transition have dominated the process in most cultures.[1]

This is not the place to review the huge anthropological literature on death rituals.[2] Performances that ensure the soul's safe passage do concern us, however, because such dire consequences have been ascribed to their absence. When there have been specific grounds for concern, further pre-emptive measures have been remarkably consistent in societies where the physical return of the dead is feared. The dead who take a wrong turning may encounter a blockage or even be forced to turn back. In the worst case they may never leave the living world at all but hang around frustrated, unable to move on.

Rites of Passage

Preparation of the body for burial follows a range of cultural norms, and details (inclusion of grave-goods, for instance) can only be properly understood in the context of their specific cultures. But alongside basic respect and decency, certain aims recur, if sometimes felt instinctively rather than concretely stated: to encourage egress of the soul(s); to prevent ingress of unwanted external forces; and to prepare the individual—still poised ambiguously between life and death—for the next stage. The grave-clothes must be loose and free of knots so as to liberate the soul on its journey—or, by contrast, must include multiple knots so that any unquiet corpse will take years to untie them.[3] Among Votians and Karelians, facial orifices were covered to cut off sense-contact, and the mouth was bound shut to prevent the soul from re-entering (Figure 6): an explicitly rationalized version of the practice of jaw-binding.[4] The Finno-Ugric Mordvins laid a sickle across the belly of the corpse:[5] a standard rite there, but modified as an anti-vampire measure in northern Poland (p. 348). In rural Greece, the washing and re-clothing of the corpse transform it from a polluted to a holy entity.[6] Like any traveller setting out, the dead person must be properly prepared and see a clear road ahead.

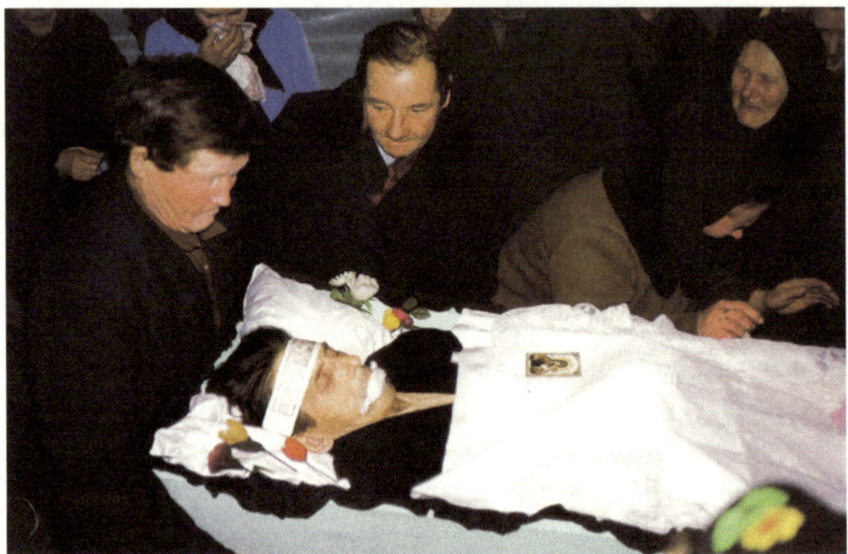

FIGURE 6: Blocking the corpse's mouth: this modern version of the ritual, photographed by the folklorist Lauri Honko at a Karelian funeral in 1977, perpetuates the old conception of preventing the return of the spirit.

The liminal phase between laying-out and burial, while the corpse still lies at home, is a time of great danger. It must not be rushed: however virtuous the deceased, failure of this process can have disastrous consequences. With the Skolt Sámi, for instance, 'if the dead man was buried before three days had elapsed, he would turn into a man-eating ghost, *rōmâs*, with teeth of iron'.[7] During these long hours the wake can take many forms—sometimes mournful and solemn, sometimes drunken and raucous—but guarding the body is conducted with iron discipline to avoid mishaps (Figure 7).

In du Boulay's Greek village, a crucial function of the wake was to perpetuate the auspicious anti-clockwise cycle in the movement of mourners around the corpse.[8] Special care was taken to avoid the most disastrous of all accidents: a being or object, usually a cat, crossing the body. In this culture, it had particularly grim consequences:

> In Ambéli only one type of action is believed to create a vampire, and this is often initially framed in terms of the prohibition against cats. . . .

FIGURE 7: The wake of Koksi Leisa on Kihnu island, Estonia, 2008. The photographer Anne Helene Gjelstad was admitted to this intimate scene in the dead woman's kitchen, where women from the village gathered to pray, mourn, and sing. Guarding the corpse with such earnest attention, they smoothed Koksi's passage to the next world.

> [This, however, is] a short-hand expression of a danger which is much more general, and which is represented by any action which crosses over the body. . . . And it is this action—whether it is performed by stepping across the body, or by handing anything across it to someone on the other side, or by leaning over the body to place something on the ground opposite—which creates the conditions for a demonic possession so absolute that, whatever the virtue of the person during life, the soul loses for ever its own nature, and becomes immediately an urgent and terrible danger to those it leaves behind.[9]

This stark conception—unchristian in both the theological and the moral senses—was in fact mitigated by a flexible idea of the soul(s) (p. 101). Still, it illustrates a particularly intense fear of *transition interrupted*: the door stands open for the safe passage of the soul, but with one false move it shuts forever.

FIGURE 8: A stage in a traditional Philippine funeral: the corpse is taken out through a window rather than the door so that it will find it harder to get back inside.

The wake safely completed, the corpse is removed from the house. Since it might try to find its way back through the door, it can be hoisted out through a window or a hole in the roof (Figure 8).[10] The Sámi employ other measures to confuse the dead, including turning the hut door upside-down and piling firewood against it.[11] Then the corpse is buried and left to complete its journey towards physical dissolution.

If that journey is impeded, the implications can be horrifying. We will encounter many corpses that were exhumed, found incorrupt, and killed over again. Such dire cases make the fullest sense in the context of belief-systems in which total decay is the visible and necessary sign of safe passage. In parts of rural Greece, exhumations—usually five years after burial—are momentous and public occasions. The priest recites Psalm 51: 'Wash me, and I shall be whiter than snow. / Let me hear joy and gladness; let the bones that you have crushed rejoice. / Hide your face from my sins, and blot out all my iniquities'. If the bones are found clean and white, it is a sign that the dead person has indeed attained 'joy and gladness', iniquities blotted out. But if any flesh remains, bystanders can mutter: '[The bones] didn't come out well'; 'He didn't have a good soul'; 'The earth didn't forgive him'.[12] It is unusual for such sentiments to be so overt, but they give concrete expression to a latent fear that pervades this book.

Such motifs, in different varieties and permutations, recur very widely. That does not mean that they have always had the same aims and resonances: measures that are reassuring or merely routine when the dead are not a threat take on a different order of urgency when they are. Something moving across the body, which caused existential disaster in Greece, might be merely indecorous elsewhere. In post-medieval Britain, for instance, a very similar repertoire of wake rituals was observed, but not invested with such high-stakes concerns: they had 'a Janus-like ability to be understood either as a friendly gesture of protection towards the body and soul, or as an expression of dread, revealing a desire to prevent haunting'.[13]

Consider three accounts of how a corpse should be equipped for burial. The first concerns the great Northumbrian saint Cuthbert (died 687), as described by a near-contemporary monk of Lindisfarne: 'His whole body was washed, his head was wrapped in a head-cloth, and a consecrated wafer was placed on his holy breast. He was robed in his priestly vestments, wearing his shoes in readiness to meet Christ, and protected with a waxed shroud'.[14]

Thirteen centuries later, in the broadly European context of a marginalized Roma community, a child was buried in Romania: 'Luciano was wearing a clean brown sweater and a pair of brand-new jeans. His pockets were stuffed: blue wads of lei notes in one, and a comb, a small mirror, and a sewing kit in the other—provisions for the road. On his feet he had factory-fresh plastic slippers, dark brown and molded to look like tie-up shoes. . . . He had one hand over his heart. . . . Deep in the coffin beside his head rested a plywood model boat'.[15]

Also in the twentieth century, but working among the African-descended communities of Haiti, an anthropologist described traditional funerals:

> The corpse is next dressed. . . . No buttons or pins are used on new clothes, which are sewn into place, and if the body is dressed in

> clothing he wore while alive, the pockets are torn so that nothing can be carried away in them. Shoes were at one time put into the coffin—or sandals in the country—beside the dead, rather than on his feet, so that he would not be tempted to walk, but today in Mirebalais and the surrounding country the dead are buried barefoot or in stocking feet, since, as it was explained, 'otherwise they make too much noise as they go about'. . . . In the coffin are placed a rosary, a scapulary, soap, a comb, a handkerchief . . . ; but no strong drink is included because, were the spirit of the dead person to become drunk, this would be dangerous; and no money, for if so much as a single sou were given to the dead, he would return and take the rest of the family wealth. . . . Pins are carefully excluded, because if the dead were given sharp objects, he would return to prick the family.[16]

The items provided are broadly comparable—smart clothes, useful accessories, shoes—but they are understood in different ways. The Lindisfarne passage is the oldest, but it comes from a religious milieu and refers to an unambiguously holy corpse. Beneath the Christian veneer, though, it betrays a more traditional conception of a dead man walking to a physical destination wearing physical shoes. In the Roma case, the physicality of the journey is more explicit but still essentially innocuous: the dead boy simply needs equipping, and there is no sense that he might misuse his shoes or money. By contrast, the Haitian preparations are about restraining rather than facilitating, and sinister expectations drive them: the dead man must be *prevented* from walking around malevolently (or at any rate noisily), *prevented* from getting drunk and disorderly, *prevented* from coming back to steal money, *prevented* from pricking his relatives with pins.

These embedded motifs of ritual behaviour can be articulated to a wide spectrum of understandings—from saintly purity to uncanny malevolence—about what the dead can do to the living. But they presuppose at least a modicum of intuitive anxiety, even when that is low-level and unarticulated. When corpse-killing epidemics erupt, it is usually from this kind of background.

Lives Cut Short: The Unfulfilled, the Quarrelsome, and the Unforgiving

Time and again we will encounter the troublesome corpses of those whose lives were cut off suddenly, violently, or unnaturally early. Most such cases fall into three categories: people who have not fulfilled their potential; people who have died with their natural life-course unfinished; or people who have left the world without resolving enmity or wrongdoing between themselves and others.

Infants are the extreme case, especially victims of infanticide. Their capacity to be feared (a fear surely reinforced with guilt) is illustrated by the 'Nordic dead-child motif'.[17] Norway and south-western Finland have strong and deep-rooted traditions of supernatural beings representing murdered infants, especially those who have been exposed or dumped in bogs. They relate to the broader southern Scandinavian tradition of the *myrting*, a dead person who has been murdered or hidden in a marsh.[18] These unfortunates have either had no place in society or have been violently ejected from it: their pain and resentment keep them bound to the world of the living. In medieval Poland, infants buried in normal cemeteries (who have presumably died naturally) are sometimes bound or stoned, suggesting that their return may also have been feared.[19] In a Greek version, unbaptized or aborted babies take revenge by causing disruption in the maternal home; if exhumed a year after burial they are found incorrupt, with their hands in their mouths and smiling, and are suppressed by pouring boiling vinegar on them.[20] This fear of dead infants is not universal: for instance, 'dead-child beings' are absent from the more easterly parts of Finland that had little contact with the west.[21]

The most important class of the unfulfilled, though, are those who die in late childhood or early adulthood, especially females. We meet many of them in this book, their frustrated adolescent angst and reproductive urges noxiously pent-up in their corpses. And then there are the nasty-minded: the unsociable, sullen, faithless, grudge-bearing, unforgiving or domineering, and those (aptly known today as 'mood-hoovers') who suck the energy and joy out of others.[22] They cannot pass cleanly and peacefully from the society of their fellows because they were never reconciled to it, and no loving friends are there to smooth the way. Of similar kind are the resentful matriarchs, enraged that death has ended their control over their offspring. Still worse is the case of those who have died violently—fighting, in drunken fits, murdered, drowned, struck by lightning—since the speed and violence of their deaths leaves no chance of reconciliation. Broken promises, unresolved quarrels, and stagnant resentments tie them to the world's pains and sorrows, and a poisonous life-force clings to their physical bodies.

The dead cannot be pursued for unsettled scores—unless they choose to return. In a lightly fictionalized autobiography describing an Estonian farm around 1880, the farmer's relationship with his wife is soured by memories of her first husband, who has hanged himself and been buried in unconsecrated ground:

> Andres was silent. Then his face turned scornful and angry. 'How long, then, will Juss stand between us?', he asked.
>
> 'I don't know', Mari answered simply.
>
> 'When he was alive, he ran from me even with a knife in his hand, but in death he's bolder. I would strangle him with my bare hands if I could, just to get free from him', said Andres. . . . 'You have your Juss and there's nothing I can do about it. I've managed to overcome every obstacle . . . , but I can't overcome Juss.'
>
> 'Juss is dead, so how could you?', said Mari.
>
> 'That's so', said Andres. 'When he was alive, I could beat him with one hand tied behind my back, but now that he's dead, two hands aren't enough.'
>
> 'No one can beat the dead', Mari said firmly.[23]

Juss's absent presence is hovering in the air like a thundercloud of resentment, fear, and guilt. And the dead have an unfair advantage: you cannot fight back at them. Or can you? If they return physically, they lay themselves open to physical punishment. One good reason for believing in restless corpses is that they are exposed to human violence and vengeance.

Not, however, in this Estonian story: what Juss the suicide does *not* do is to return as a revenant or ghost. So far as we know, he lies quiet. That is an exception worth exploring.

Why Do European Suicides Rarely Return as Corpses?

Classically, unquiet corpses were people who lived and died badly. There is one highly revealing exception: only rarely—at least in Europe west of the Vistula—have they included those who died by their own hands.[24] This seems strange: suicides have regularly been considered no less undesirable than the undead, and treated in similar ways. In many cultures they were outcasts, shamed in this world and damned in the next, condemned to ignominious modes of burial. Suicide was wrong, Aristotle declared, because it injured the city-state: hence, 'the Athenians cut off the feet of a suicide's corpse before they bury it'.[25] If such a burial were excavated, it could well be interpreted—apparently wrongly—as a disabled walking corpse.

In later medieval and early modern Europe, supernatural phenomena in the wake of suicides more often take the form of storms and flooding. Almost uniquely, a case of 1591 at Striegau / Strzegom (now Poland) does link suicide to revenancy: a shoemaker is buried honourably despite his suicide but walks and attacks people, so the corpse is exhumed, found intact, and eventually burned (p. 336). Compare and contrast a Zürich suicide in 1417: he is likewise buried honourably, but people protest that this wrongful burial has caused bad weather and ruined the harvest, so the corpse is removed from consecrated ground. There are similar stories from Venice in 1342, Basel in 1439, and Metz in 1484.[26] Apart from the Striegau case, the substitution of the foul-weather motif suggests unease with the idea the suicides might return physically (or simply unawareness of it, given that the real point of these stories is divine displeasure at suicides being buried in unconsecrated ground). This seems to be a facet of the more general pattern, noted by Alexander Murray, that medieval suicides rarely manifested as ghosts.[27]

Why did these particularly noxious corpses lie quiet? There only seems to be one plausible answer, and it tells us something profound about the corpses that *did* cause trouble. Suicides may have been wicked, desperate, and eternally damned, but *death did not cut them short or leave them resentfully unfulfilled.*[28] Instead, by defiantly completing their lives on their own terms, they blew away any unruly life-forces that might otherwise have infested their earthly remains. What makes corpses troublesome is that uncompleted lives cling to them. To employ an abused phrase correctly, suicides are the exception proving that rule.

We have now explored some recurrent fears and anxieties, and the nightmarish images that they generate in the human brain. The reader may be thinking that this process has often happened independently and spontaneously, and in deep history, that could well be right. But human beings also tell stories and transmit social memories. Once written history begins, we start to pick up themes that can be followed through the centuries, and that circulated in Europe with increasing intensity as manuscript culture expanded from the eleventh century and print culture from the sixteenth. Circulation brings its own problems, as literate narratives become increasingly self-referential, and opaque in their interactions with oral culture. But to understand the making of 'vampire' beliefs and folklore in the Western world (and sometimes much further afield), the challenge of trying to separate belief from literary artifice has to be faced.

5

Understanding Stories (1)

THE SPOKEN AND WRITTEN WORD

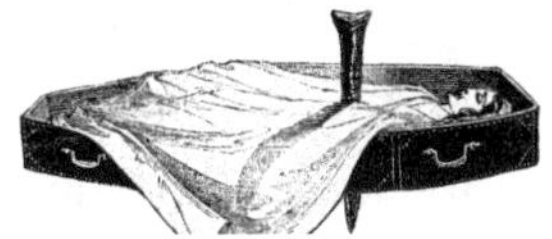

Man, sub-creator, the refracted light
Through whom is splintered from a single White
To many hues, and endlessly combined
In living shapes that move from mind to mind.

—J.R.R. TOLKIEN, *MYTHOPOEIA*

IT IS THROUGH STORIES that people communicate their traditions, hopes, and anxieties, and the rich fruits of their imaginations. Stories from across the globe have been collected and analyzed by textual scholars, folklorists, and oral historians in huge abundance, and some of them concern the dangerous dead. But their very survival means that the popular has been mediated through the scholarly, and the oral has become written. Can we get a grip on this slippery mass of material and understand how it fits together?

The Problem of Narrative Motifs

Folklorists break narratives down into their distinct components ('motifs'), which can be classified and indexed. The supreme achievement of this approach is Stith Thompson's *Motif-index of Folk-Literature* (1932–6, revised 1955–8), where we can find a world-wide range of occurrences for every motif. Supernatural engagements with the dead are listed under fifty-two headings, occupying 114 pages, that describe the return of dead people (not necessarily in bodily form) for almost any likely or unlikely purpose.[1]

The trouble with motif-spotting is knowing what to make of it all. We may be intrigued to find that dead people who return to demand stolen rings have been reported in Lithuania, England, and North Carolina (motif E236.1.1), but to explain it, some hard questions must be asked. We can readily guess that the motif reached North Carolina from England, but does the Lithuanian parallel reflect early English trade in the Baltic? Or a common Indo-European inheritance from before the Baltic language-group separated? Or independent invention? Without more fixed points, we are left guessing.

That brings us back to the problem of 'human universals', which, in the anthropologist Donald Brown's view, can include myths and legends.[2] Could it be that some stories about the restless dead flow naturally from basic human cognition? One motif that has been claimed as a sort of 'universal' should interest us here, since it concerns the reanimation of corpses. This is the idea that if an animal (especially a cat) jumps across a corpse, the corpse reanimates. Gregory Forth and Svitlana Kukharenko argue from its very wide incidence that it is one of Brown's 'statistical universals', occurring with non-random frequency in unrelated societies: thus 'the representation might not be a direct expression of pan-human cognition but might instead be a function of other features that are similarly widespread and occur simultaneously in all societies that manifest the aversion.'[3] And indeed they identify a broader range of perceptions—that animals or people crossing or transitioning over other beings are considered transformative—as a cognitive matrix within which this particular variant looks less singular:

> Reanimation of the corpse . . . is so widespread as to be considered something that, regardless of cultural influence, human thought naturally appends to the image of animate beings traversing a corpse. The reason is not difficult to discern. If traversal by animate beings can radically transform living as well as deceased beings (as shown with reference, for example, to sleeping humans and reclining dogs), then in the case of a corpse—an inert object that cannot obviously suffer the sort of partial or progressive consequences applicable to living beings—the consequence can hardly be anything other than reanimation.[4]

This is ingenious and could be partly right, but it sits uneasily with some other factors. This belief-system is *not* universal; indeed, it maps persuasively onto those regions where other dangerous-dead beliefs are recorded and is entirely contained within the 'vampire corridor' (Map 1).[5] So, are the dangerous-dead beliefs in those regions simply a product of the jumping-cat beliefs? Given everything else known about them, that would be a bizarre conclusion: the converse seems much more likely. But in any case, why must we assume that they emerged 'regardless of cultural influence'? Human movements across the globe have been vast in scale and complexity, as ancient DNA is now showing us. It is surely not so unlikely that story-motifs emerged at a very early date, and crossed equally vast extents of time and space. Equally, the fine-tuning of their meanings and intensity must be specific to cultures, as du Boulay's different interpretation of the cat motif illustrates (p. 41).

Can the deep origins and development of human mythology ever be recovered? Michael Witzel has tried to do just that, in a book of vast scope.[6] He argues that by correlating motifs and narratives from across the globe, two broad myth traditions can be distinguished: 'Laurasian', comprising Europe, most of Asia, North Africa, North America, South America (patchily), and Polynesia; and 'Gondwanan', comprising Australia, sub-Saharan Africa, and Melanesia. The 'Laurasian' system, which produced the mythic cycles familiar from later European and Asian cultures, had, in Witzel's view, taken shape before people crossed the Bering Strait some 20,000 years ago. So ambitious a scheme can never be proved, and Witzel has come in for some severe criticism,[7] but one should admire his intellectual courage in formulating a hypothesis that future work can support or undermine. For present purposes, we will note that the global incidence of dangerous-dead beliefs maps closely onto the 'Laurasian' zone—notably in emphasizing the northern hemisphere—except that it also includes Australia and West Africa: those exceptions will therefore need special attention.[8]

Anyone who studies mythology, epic, or folklore will know the headache-inducing puzzle of similar (sometimes elaborately similar) stories that turn up at entirely different places and times. That comes back to the debate between anthropologists and psychologists: cultural transmission, or universal human cognition? The direction in which one tends to be drawn—inferring elaborate intertextual relationships, or alternatively assuming independent invention—depends to an extent on temperament: hence the division of scholars into 'lumpers' and 'splitters'.[9]

The interrogation of an amiable Latvian werewolf in 1691 (p. 290) is the subject of a fascinating debate, published verbatim in 2020, between a 'lumper', Carlo Ginzburg, and a 'splitter', Bruce Lincoln.[10] The argument weaves between Ginzburg's model of a deep cultural tradition—surfacing in fragments—of people assuming supernatural powers to battle evil forces, and Lincoln's conviction that class oppression in different times and places generated independent if similar responses. Personally I feel much closer to Ginzburg's position, and suspect cultural links between many of the dangerous-dead beliefs explored in this book. Equally, I acknowledge that similar pressures, exacerbating the basic human uneasiness about corpses, can potentially create belief-systems that look remarkably like each other.

As Ginzburg says, the way forward is to see 'at which level the convergence becomes sufficiently unlikely to constitute a proof of historical connection'.[11] Sometimes, the consistency and complexity of parallels make the 'splitter' position untenable. Thus one 'lumper', Bruno Currie, shows how the Akkadian poem *Etana* is echoed in a Greek fragment, in an Aesop fable, and in versions in India, Egypt, and the Baltic. 'It seems next to impossible here to assume polygenesis', writes Currie. 'Extraordinary as the conclusion seems, these folktales and *Etana* must be genetically related. Thus *Etana* becomes an intriguing test-case of the 'historic-geographic' method in folklore studies'.[12]

Stories Written Down

With the appearance of writing—at very different stages across the globe—we gain the huge advantage of time-depth: stories collected from oral culture can be cross-checked against texts dating back hundreds and sometimes thousands of years. But here we face the problem that writers are, by definition, educated: members of an elite whose ideas have often been very different from those of 'ordinary' people. For most times and places in the past, the world-views and traditions of human societies ('popular culture') are only known to us—beyond what archaeology has to offer—through the writings of scholars and religious specialists ('elite culture'). That can cause genuine problems, but in this book I reject any idea that the 'elite' and 'popular' worlds were insulated from each other and recognize a continuous feedback-loop between them.[13]

Let us explore that enigma through three examples, starting with the most dramatic and explicit story of the walking dead to survive from the ancient world (below, p. 136). Preserved in a compilation of about AD 120, but set in Thrace, it tells of a dead girl called Philinnion who makes amorous nightly visits to a young man. A nurse spies them through a door-crack, and tells Philinnion's parents. When they burst in and greet her joyfully, she rebukes them for violating rules set by the other-worldly powers and falls (genuinely) dead. While the first half of this story fits an established Eurasian template, the second half is unique in ancient sources. But astonishingly, it is widely reported—with gender roles reversed—in the recent oral folklore of Ireland:

> A servant girl, sent by the mother to peep through the key-hole of the bedroom, looked and saw Máire with a baby in her arms and a man sitting at her bedside. She ran to tell her mistress, who declared that the man was her [dead] son. The woman told the servant to tell Máire that it was necessary to store some things in her room; then the farmer's wife was secretly bundled up and carried into the room. That

> night she saw her son come and sit down beside the bed. Losing patience the mother threw off the clothes on top of her and caught hold of her son. 'May God help us now, mother!', he exclaimed, saying that if she had only waited two hours more, she would have had him forever. Now he must spend seven years in hell because of her.[14]

Independent invention seems unbelievable; hardly less so the idea that the story travelled across two millennia from the Graeco-Roman world to Ireland. Did early medieval visitors from the Mediterranean take it to Ireland? Or did some later Irish story-teller read an early printing of the Philinnion story? And why the gender-reversal? This insoluble puzzle warns us against dogmatism in interpreting links between written and oral material.

Usually, the narrative sequence is more formulaic than this: burial, unholy revival, depredation, exhumation, destruction. But it can include distinctive elements. The unusual motif of the corpse that walks back home to do jobs makes a good illustration. An early fifteenth-century collection tells of a Breton baker whose wife and children, after his death, continued getting up at night to knead their dough:

> Suddenly the dead man appeared among them, rolled his sleeves up to the elbows, and started kneading with them, urging them on in a loud voice to continue skilfully and energetically with the job that they had started. But they ran here and there in a state of terror. . . . After that he often appeared—and not just at night—and went around the houses throwing stones at people. He did not go by the open road but where there was the most mud, so that he was muddy up to his knees and thighs. The inhabitants . . . did not know whether it was a dead man or some evil spirit who did these things. They went to his grave, dug him up, and found the corpse muddy up to the knees and thighs, just as they had seen him going around. Also, they saw that he had thickened arms from kneading with the others. Seeing this, they back-filled the grave, but he soon appeared as before and became a really bad nuisance to people. In the end they decided to pull him out of the grave and break his thighs. This was done, and he was not seen again.[15]

Far away, among the Greek islands, a French visitor reported in the 1650s:

> The great familiarity that one of these *vrykolakes* showed to his living wife caused much amazement on Santorini. He was called Alexander, a shoemaker by trade, and dwelt while alive at Pyrgos castle. After his death, he appeared to his wife as he had been in life. He came to work in her house, mended her children's shoes, drew water from the cistern, and was often seen in the dells cutting wood to maintain his family. After he had been doing this for some time, the horrified people dug up his corpse and burned it, and with the smoke of the fire the demon's powers evaporated.[16]

We can only guess whether these exceptionally handy revenants were independent creations, or fragments from a lost tradition. Perhaps the widespread folklore about supernatural beings (deities, fairies, demons, dwarfs) who do practical tasks for humans was assimilated into walking-dead beliefs.[17]

For a third illustration, we can focus on a small but significant detail: human flesh polluted by faithlessness, and therefore doomed to unclean survival. This idea surfaces in a fourteenth-century account of a Yorkshire revenant, condemned to wandering because of her fraudulent property dealings: 'it is said that downy cobwebs hung in strands from her right hand, and that it had turned black, and that when she was asked why this was, she replied that she had often held up this hand to swear false oaths'.[18] Compare this scene from 1970s Greece, when the time came for the bones of a popular twenty-year-old girl to be moved to the ossuary:

> Many women . . . were surprised and puzzled by the poor condition of Eleni's remains. Why after five years had Eleni's hair and clothes not decomposed? Why were the bones not clean and white? Some women . . . believed that a person whose body did not fully decompose and whose bones were black and unclean had committed sins that had not been forgiven. They all knew, though, that Eleni's reputation had been beyond reproach. Her parents were highly respected

> as well. Someone asked about her grandparents. An older woman nodded knowingly and said that Eleni's grandfather had been a rural policeman and had often been called on to testify in court during disputes over land ownership and property damage. He may have testified falsely on occasion or accepted a bribe. After all, the proverb says, 'The sins of the parents torment their children'.[19]

Elini's case belongs to the Greek world, where physical incorruption was held to reflect moral pollution (p. 50). But medieval Yorkshire was not like that, and the story shows that the idea had a wider and deeper currency than its familiar eastern Mediterranean context.

Scholarly Narratives of the Demonic in the Christian West

Much of this book deals with the Christian societies of medieval and early modern Europe. The abundant works of clerics and theologians engaged with what people really believed, but in trying to make sense of those beliefs they gave them a coherence and moral value (in this case a negative one) that could potentially be recycled back into folk-culture. In particular, the Christian binary conception of Good versus Evil encouraged the demonization of supernatural entities that, while powerful and daunting, need not in origin have been perceived as purely noxious. After 1100, the consolidation of an increasingly complex theological framework brought learned conceptions more and more heavily to bear on popular consciousness.

Western Europe between 1100 and 1250 produced a rich crop of stories about dead people leaving their graves, which have been studied intensively by historians and literary scholars. I admire—and have profited from—the insights of so much careful scholarship on high medieval theology, spirituality, and historical culture. But there are problems. While this research often draws on contemporary literary theory, it makes little use of anthropology and almost none of archaeology. That is a symptom of a fundamental limitation: the topic is treated exclusively in terms of learned discourse, so that the real men and women in the villages and fields who fled from the dangerous dead, and opened graves to destroy them, have become stage-props with no imaginations or agency of their own. For instance, we read in a recent discussion of scholastic thought:

> The abandonment of active revenants in favor of passively animated corpses was gradual, taking place roughly between 1130 and 1230. During this transitional century, revenants are described frequently, but they presented a problem for learned reporters, . . . because of their corporeality, the fact that they had or are bodies. It became more difficult for the learned clergy, many of whom were also natural philosophers, to imagine that a soul would ever come to reside in a dead body. . . . This difficulty was created by the many twelfth-century thinkers who promoted a new definition of a human being as a balanced unity of body and soul.[20]

Setting aside whether there really was such a transition from 'active' to 'passive' (which is dubious), this formulation takes no account of underlying popular beliefs. What 'really' happened may have indeed been very different from the written reports, and may in time have been modified by learned rationalizations. But no amount of scholastic thought would have made the medieval laity believe in animated corpses unless they had a socio-cultural predisposition to do so. The essential characteristics of high medieval European revenants owe nothing to the schools of Paris or Oxford, for we will meet them in entirely different global contexts. That is not to belittle the scholastic contribution to a dynamically evolving Western world-view, but rather to insist that the feedback-loop is essential to any adequate interpretation.

In the end, we must accept that the 'living shapes that move from mind to mind' will never be slotted into a coherent family tree: their complexity is too great and the record too incomplete. But just as a few pieces of a torn-up map can make some sense when the fragments are laid out in the right relationship to each other, but not when they are arbitrarily joined, so we can make the most of our scraps of evidence by acknowledging the gaps between them. They do show patterns, which in some parts of the world can be linked to broad chronologies that reveal change over time. Few dead-killing motifs may have been completely new by the historical period, but they continued to be restructured and reinterpreted in distinctive ways. To borrow a metaphor from biology, they had to be adaptive to prosper: we can learn something about the societies that sustained them by observing which were emphasized and which dropped out.

6

Understanding Stories (2)

VAMPIRES IN PRINT

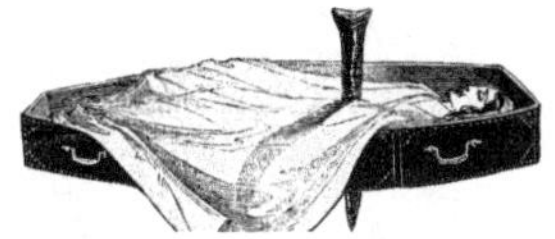

[They] took up his Body, 40 Days after he had been dead, and found it fresh and free from Corruption; that he bled at the Nose, Mouth and Ears, pure and florid Blood; that his Shroud and Winding Sheet were all over Bloody; and that his Finger and Toe Nails were fallen off, and new ones grown in their room. By these Circumstances they were perswaded he was a *Vampyre,* and, according to Custom, drove a Stake thro' his Heart; at which he gave a horrid Groan. They burnt his Body to Ashes, and threw them into his Grave.

—THE *GENTLEMAN'S MAGAZINE* REPORTS THE ARNAUT PAVLE CASE, MARCH 1732

WITH THE INVENTION OF PRINTING, the circulation of European stories about restless corpses moved up several gears. As later chapters will show, occasional early references were followed by a clutch of theological and philosophical discussions during c. 1580–1610, and then—from the 1670s—a steadily growing volume of printed academic and historical debate and commentary, reaching a climax in 1732.

FIGURE 9: The father of vampire studies: Dom Augustin Calmet, in a posthumous engraving commissioned by his community at Senones. Below it they placed Voltaire's verse in his honour, presumably not registering its potentially satirical undertones: see p. 381.

Another landmark came in 1746 when the Benedictine scholar Dom Augustin Calmet published his survey of supernatural beings, which was quickly re-issued in several editions, including an English one of 1759 (Figure 9). This book's section on vampires was the most influential academic work on the subject ever published. Its straightforwardly evidence-based approach was a breath of fresh air after a long series of increasingly derivative works (p. 380). It achieved its remarkable popularity because it entered the market at the right point: saturated with so much fragmented and repetitive discussion of 'vampires' (still a relatively new word), the reading public wanted a textbook.

Calmet inspired a huge progeny of followers and popularisers, bringing the stories to a much wider readership; a good example of the genre is the *Histoire des vampires et des spectres malfaisans* of 1820, a pocketbook that re-packages Calmet for the mass market.[1] In print, the topic assumed an oddly self-referential character, as educated writers crafted an image of 'popular' vampire beliefs, for other educated writers to attack in turn as ignorant superstition (Figure 10).

Whether directly or through these later channels, Calmet's book remains the ultimate source of much modern vampire literature in Europe and America, both fictional and supposedly historical, and was transformative in bringing the topic to a wider reading public. There and elsewhere, stories were now frozen on the printed page, where later generations could read them. But they were stories still: not necessarily more reliable, and by no means stable in transmission.

Confusions of the Feedback Loop: Drinking Vampire Blood

The complexity of interactions between learned discourse and popular practice is illustrated by one particularly bizarre and repellant (not to say dangerous) strand in the belief-system. This is the practice of ingesting blood or organs from a supposed vampire corpse, or ashes derived from burning them, as a remedy for vampire-induced illness. Although not wholly dissimilar from the idea that victims will recover as they watch the smoke rise from burning vampire organs—already known in

Reafon and virtue are alike ferene ;
Undaunted midft the roaring thunder's fmile,
Nor know one tremor in the midnight fcene,
Whofe fhades imprefs grim horror on the vile.*

But fee, far glittering through the dufky night,
Yon blaze, whofe ruddy ftreaks illume the fky,
Shed on the devious path its wanton light,
And dart its beams upon the indignant eye !†

Behold Religion from the fpot retire,
Her mild cheek mantled with a crimfon glow :
While Superftition guards the lighted fire,
Waves high the torch, and triumphs in her woe.

And there the infatuated father ftands—
Forgot each gentle feeling of his foul—
Virtue no more his harden'd breaft commands,
Nor pity melts, nor can e'en love control.

To

* " ———quorum———
Horror ubique animos, fimul ipfa filentia terrent."—VIRG.

† Alluding to the following paragraph from the Albany Gazette of the 26th of April laft :—" Two children of Mr. Jofiah Grant Huit, of Ballftown, being lately attacked with fymptoms of a confumption, he was advifed, in order to their cure, to dig up and burn the body of a daughter, who died of the fame diforder, about twenty months ago.—Strange to relate ! the unfeeling, infatuated father, tore the remains of his child from her coffin, placed them on a pile, and reduced them to afhes !"

C

FIGURE 10: The paradox of folk-belief in print culture. In this poem of 1790, Thaddeus Mason Harris attacks the 'vain superstition' of New England vampire exhumations from the heights of Enlightenment rationality, ponderously loaded with classical quotations. But the practice, apparently introduced less than a decade earlier, may itself have been stimulated by popular print and ideas derived from Paracelsian medicine.

To the lone ſpot by Superſtition led,
(Fondly unkind,* and indiſcreetly brave)
Where reſt in ſacred ſleep the ſilent dead,
To rob his lovely daughter's peaceful grave.†

Ere her chill'd brow had loſt its pallid hue,
Ere faded on her cheek the dying ſmile—
Torn from the ſhroud, her form expos'd to view,
Rudely he plac'd upon the kindled pile,

Thus

* The deſign was to reſtore to health two remaining children :—Apparently pardonable; but at the ſame time irrational and cruel. For *no end is attained but by the proper means*; and what connexion is there, can there be, between the means here uſed and the intended effect ?

"*Nam febrem vario depelli carmine poſſe*
Vana Superſtitio credunt tremulæque parentes."

'A vain ſuperſtition, and credulous parents, would believe that the fever may be cured by a charm.' [Serenus Sammonicus, a Roman phyſician and poet, who lived in the reign of the Emperor Severus and Caracalla his ſon, makes the foregoing obſervation in his poem on the art of healing and remedies.] A ridiculous ſuperſtition only could have ſuggeſted ſuch a belief. Reaſon and reflection could never admit it.

† "De mortuis nil niſi bonum," was a Roman law of the twelve tables. Reſpect for the dead is common to every period of civilization; and is inſeparable from every humane breaſt. It is eſtabliſhed upon principles univerſally felt and acknowledged. Its violator would be ſeverely puniſhed in moſt nations—deteſted in all.

FIGURE 10. (*continued*)

eleventh-century England (p. 239)—its shocking physicality sets it apart. Did people in pre-modern Europe really do this?

A complicating factor is the medicinal use of human blood and body-parts, in accordance with the theories of the physician, philosopher, and alchemist 'Paracelsus' (Theophrastus von Hohenheim, c. 1493–1541).[2] A brilliant experimenter, Paracelsus believed that substances healed through occult 'influences' or 'spirits', the most powerful being those derived from what they were meant to cure: the human body. The fact that medicine now rejects these hypotheses should not make us view them patronizingly: in the early modern period, ingesting or anointing with substances from Egyptian mummies or the blood of executed criminals seemed as rational as doing the same with any other substance.

These Paracelsian ideas entered popular practice: at a beheading in Vienna in 1668/9, a man ran forward and caught the spouting blood to cure his epilepsy.[3] It is especially interesting that in New England, where vampire-killing would start a century later, the Puritan poet Edward Taylor (c. 1642–1729) had both a library containing Paracelsian books and a 'dispensatory' from which he provided human- and animal-based medicines.[4]

The tangled story of consuming blood from vampire corpses starts in a different and very unexpected place. In 1687, a major ethnographical account of parts of West Africa by the Capuchin missionary Giovanni Antonio Cavazzi was published in Bologna. In it, Cavazzi describes magical and medical practices among the Mbundu of Angola, including a method of obtaining vital curative fluid from undecayed corpses:

> When they are in a fresh and intact state when unearthed, their heads are cut from their bodies, from which it is said that blood flows out (which may happen through some illusion or deceit). It is collected and made into poultices for the sick, or mixed into their food, which infallibly guarantees health. Thereafter the dead person, having lost his strength, will no longer be able to harass them.[5]

From Angola to Paris: in May 1693, a story appeared in the society magazine *Mercure Galant*. The author was the courtier and polymath Pierre des Noyers (1607–93), who spent several years in Poland in the entourage of Queen Louise-Marie.[6] Much earlier, in 1639, he had written to a friend about the being known as *upior* (Ruthenian) or *striga* (Polish): born with teeth; eating its shroud and then its hands and arms in the coffin; causing successive deaths of family members; and extinguished by decapitation and release of pent-up blood.[7] This story is rather highly-coloured (eating the hands and arms is unusual), but it does probably originate in genuine oral accounts of the shroud-chewer belief.

Very different is des Noyers's account from 1693.[8] Now the *striges* and *upierz* have become corpse-hijacking demons: 'It is said that the demon takes this blood from the body of a living person, or from certain animals, and carries it into a dead body; for it is alleged that the demon goes out from this corpse during a certain period, between noon and midnight, after which it returns and stores there the blood that it has gathered'. The blood comes out of the mouth, nose, and ears of the corpse, the corpse swims in blood, and it starts to eat its shroud. The demon especially troubles former associates and relatives of the dead 'host', appearing to them in the guise of parents or friends, and does not leave until all the family members have died in succession. The remedy is to exhume the corpse, which is found soft, flexible, bloated, and red:

> When they are found in that state, having the likeness of those who had appeared in dreams, their heads are cut off and their hearts are opened, and a quantity of blood flows out. It is collected and kneaded into flour, which is made into bread, which is a certain remedy to guarantee against such a terrible affliction. After the heads [of the dead people] have been cut off, those whom the Spirit torments at night are no longer troubled by it, and are well thereafter.[9]

This narrative has problems. The idea of the demon using the corpse as a safe-deposit for its hoard of blood seems to be unique; so, probably, is the time-slot between noon and midnight.[10] These read like clerical rationalizations, perhaps fed to des Noyers by some Polish priest and overlaid on his earlier, more authentic observations. But more fundamentally, it seems obvious that des Noyers's account of Poland shamelessly re-works Cavazzi's account of Angola, published eight years previously. It might not be quite so simple. An earlier common source, still unidentified, remains possible. The descriptions of mixing blood into food and poultices look remarkably close to Paracelsian ideas, extended from ordinary corpses to undead ones: was even Cavazzi's account distorted by his own medical learning? But in any case des Noyers's account is a piece of unprincipled plagiarism, worthless as evidence for Polish folk-belief.

Even so, it has bounced down through the echo-chambers of vampire literature ever since. The following year, a lawyer called Marigner built on the narrative—which he took at face value—with long philosophical musings on the nature of vampires.[11] Inevitably, in 1746, it was republished in Calmet's book, which made it permanently available to vampire-aware readers. While otherwise faithful to des Noyers, Calmet's version irons out the motif of demonic corpse-possession by calling this predator a vampire 'or a demon in its form'.[12] This process of moulding to a more familiar template culminates in a recent version that presents the story as straightforward ethnographic reporting, omitting the demonic motif completely.[13]

So far, this has just been a morality tale of plagiarism and uncritical copying. But in 1713, at Dąbrówka (now western Ukraine), some villagers were tried in the Uniate episcopal court for exhuming a woman's corpse and mutilating it in inventive ways. They admitted to the exhumation (because the dead woman had been walking around and attacking people), and to drinking the corpse's blood mixed with vodka. They denied cutting out the heart, mixing the blood into flour, and baking cakes with it, but the judges were sceptical and made them swear an oath.[14]

This will sound very familiar to readers of early modern witch trials, where suspects were regularly bullied into admitting bizarre fantasies formulated by the persecutors. In this case, it seems clear that at least the idea of the blood-cakes was *suggested by the judges*; the same could be true of the blood-drinking, even though the accused were induced to confess that. It is distinctly possible, not to say likely, that an ordinary corpse-killing was embellished with luridly fictitious detail by judges who knew des Noyers's report from twenty years earlier.

Apparently in the 1740s, a steward of the Łubieńskis was buried in their family crypt (at Łowicz?), but found to be active and lifelike in his coffin. He was therefore beheaded, and the dowager Countess Łubieński ordered 'everyone in the household to drink some of the blood so as to be tormented no further' (a phrase which distinctly echoes des Noyers).[15] It was later believed that around the same time, members of the aristocratic Wollschläger family in West Prussia had died in quick succession; the corpse of the first was found to be red-faced and supple, and when a member of the family cut off his head a great spout of blood gushed out, which the vampire-killer caught in a cup and drank.[16]

The next stages may have had something to do with the discovery and development of inoculation, which in Poland inspired eccentric folk-remedies as well as scientific interest.[17] In 1770–1, the educated were making horrified comments about peasants drinking the blood of corpses in times of plague.[18] In the same year a landowner at Bilobozhnytsya (now western Ukraine), whose serfs wanted to leave because of the plague, led them instead to the cemetery 'with the help of a nobleman he knew', and ordered them to exhume some corpses, behead them, and drink the blood (which they presumably did because they had no choice).[19]

A striking and unusual feature of all these episodes is their top-down character: ecclesiastical judges started from a preconception that peasants made cakes out of vampire blood; aristocrats believed that drinking it was an effective remedy, and therefore imposed it on their dependents. There are no good grounds for viewing it as a genuine vernacular belief before 1800.

Nonetheless, there is persuasive evidence that in nineteenth-century Poland and Prussia, people really did occasionally drink blood from corpses thought to be vampires.[20] A less unhealthy alternative, the drinking of fluid mixed with burnt vampire organs, was practiced in nineteenth-century New England (p. 398). In Romania this was first attested in the 1890s, and it quickly became common there;[21] the latest reported case was in 2004 (p. 439).

Once again there were multiple channels, and we have little means of choosing between them: did the New England practice, for instance, derive from Edward Taylor's Paracelsianism or from German quack-doctors' reading of Calmet? What we should *not* imagine, though, is that the drinking of blood from undead corpses was some ancient European folk-practice: its adoption into popular usage was imposed downwards and only became habituated later. Maybe those unfortunate serfs at Bilobozhnytsya would never have been forced to do it if Fra Cavazzi had not published his book on Angola.

It's Printed, so It Must Be Right

We should not, then, underestimate the power of learned discourse in print to modify or even reinforce popular beliefs. And books could end up in unexpected places and be interpreted in unpredictable ways. In the 1650s the Jesuit François Richard visited the Aegean island of Santorini, where he observed burnings of *vrykólakas* corpses. He treated the belief seriously, but when an Orthodox abbot boasted about the superiority of his religion—no Turks or Catholics were punished after death like that—he replied quick-wittedly that, on the contrary, demonic possession pointed to damnation rather than salvation for the Greeks. Richard would have been surprised to know that, sixty years later, his book would be shown to a sceptical French visitor as evidence for the reality of the *vrykólakas*: 'He was a Catholic, they said, so you've got to believe him'.[22] One might even wonder whether, as time passed, Richard's account could have gained canonical status as a handbook for performing such vampire-burnings on Santorini?

There is a real possibility that people in eastern Europe—guided by their Francophone priests and medical practitioners—adopted not just blood-drinking but a range of other practices detailed by Calmet and related works. Once books describing folk-beliefs were widely available, they could in turn influence or even generate such beliefs. It may be that continuing vampire ideas in eastern Europe were encouraged and fortified by the flood of publications and intense public interest since the 1730s, telling people how they 'ought' to understand and deal with their vampires. For historians, that has a sobering implication: vampire folklore collected in nineteenth-century Europe could have been influenced by any number of motifs potentially supplied by a reading or re-telling of Calmet.

The interchanges between oral and written narrative, and between written and printed, have never been just in one direction. That comes as no surprise to readers of Carlo Ginzburg's classic *The Cheese and the*

Worms, which explored the intellectual makeup of an independent-minded Friulian miller. This Menocchio sparred with the Inquisition in the 1580s over his highly unusual views on the Creation. Ginzburg showed that Menocchio's ideas drew on wide if eccentric reading that included the Bible, the *Golden Legend,* Mandeville's *Travels,* Boccaccio's *Decameron,* and perhaps even the Koran. Equally, they drew on traditions deep-rooted in his own locality. He was not alone: two decades earlier, a Lucchese rustic had expressed equally heterodox ideas, some of them resembling Mennochio's, in a prophetic poem.

Their similarities, Ginzburg writes, go beyond the reading that they had in common: 'The crucial element is a common store of traditions, myths and aspirations handed down orally over generations. In both cases, it was contact with written culture through their schooling that permitted this deeply rooted deposit of oral culture to emerge.'[23] With traditions about the dangerous dead—only a minority of which are attested before the invention of printing—this kind of symbiosis is an ever-present possibility.

The Chinese Calmets: Yuan Mei and Ji Yun

It was not just in Europe that eighteenth-century scholars took an interest in the dangerous dead. In China, where these beliefs also had a very ancient history (Chapter 11), the huge majority of narratives derive from two collections of wonder-stories issued during 1788–9.[24] Yuan Mei (1716–97) was a poet, artist, and bon viveur, whose scandalous lifestyle and religious scepticism shocked many. His collection *Zi buyu* (*Censored by Confucius*) was a vast compendium of the conventionally inappropriate, including many stories about the malevolent dead whose corpses are exhumed, found intact—though usually covered with white hair—and burned. (Characteristically, he gives us what may be the world's only story of two walking corpses having sex with each other.[25]) Ji Yun (1724–1805), a civil servant and philosopher, was exiled during 1768–71 to Ürümqi in the far north-west of China, an unstable borderland through which many people passed. He found it a rich source of folklore, which he combined with his own experiences, and those of his friends and relatives, in the five volumes of *Yuewei Caotang Biji* (*The Shadow Book*) during 1789–1800. Less sceptical than Yuan Mei but not uncritical, he tried to make spiritual and philosophical sense of brutal animated corpses and seductive dead women.

In 1907, the Dutch Sinologist J.J.M. de Groot noted that Chinese stories of animated corpses seeking human flesh and blood start with Yuan Mei, and astutely asked: 'Is this coincident with the vampire-panic . . . [in central Europe] in the last years of the seventeenth century, . . . occupying the minds of scholars and theologians of Europe in the first quarter of the next?'[26] That question still stands. Was there actually a Chinese vampire epidemic that was contemporary with the European one? Or did European preoccupations stimulate literary interest?

No direct influence of Calmet is visible in the two Chinese collections, which derive from (and perhaps intensify) indigenous beliefs. Nonetheless, they resemble him in their systematic approach to the material and in their reflective and scholarly detachment. Late eighteenth-century China had economic, diplomatic, and religious contacts with western Europe, including Jesuits at the imperial court:[27] it is not impossible that educated Chinese met people who had read Calmet. Be that as it may, Yuan Mei and Ji Yun certainly had a Calmet-like effect on later writing: much of the content of popular modern works on Chinese vampires can be traced back to them.

As an Irish playwright memorably put it, 'a strange man is a marvel, with his mighty talk; but . . . there's a great gap between a gallous story and a dirty deed.'[28] Hearing or reading spine-chilling tales is one thing; opening a grave to hack and pull at the putrid, stinking corpse is quite another. People liked to talk or write about killing the dead, but how often did they actually do it? Luckily, we have another source to demonstrate in abundance that they really did: the mutilated corpses themselves.

7

Understanding Corpses

THE EVIDENCE OF BURIAL ARCHAEOLOGY

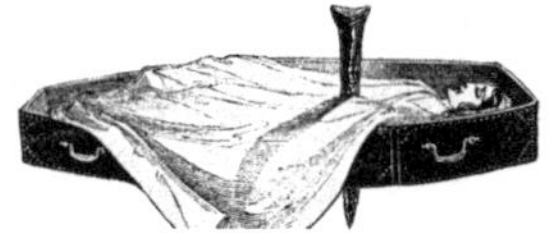

'How long will a man lie i' the earth ere he rot?'

—WILLIAM SHAKESPEARE, *HAMLET*, ACT 5, SCENE 1

MUCH OF THIS BOOK is about corpses thought to have resisted natural decay. That abnormal condition was occasionally benign—indicating a saint—but more often malign—indicating a vampire. With high-risk individuals, pre-emptive measures could be taken before burial to prevent the second of these outcomes. But usually, the unnatural state of the corpse only became apparent if disturbances drove people to reopen the grave.[1]

How should apparent incorruption be explained in reality? What traces of pre-emptive and preventive countermeasures have been left for archaeologists to find? And can corpse-killing be convincingly inferred from archaeological evidence alone? In the first instance I approach those problems more as a historian than as an archaeologist: not starting from the burials, but using narrative evidence to infer what kinds of traces the burials would display. Since we do have written sources describing this aspect of human cognition and behaviour from many parts of the world, going back into the deep past, it seems perverse to exclude it from informing our interpretations. Thus informed, it should be possible to establish a consistent archaeological methodology for assessing the likelihood of posthumous killing when written evidence is lacking.

Archaeothanatology

The term 'deviant burial', widely current in Anglophone literature, is vague as well as tendentious. Warfare, judicial execution, murder, sacrifice, and a desire to shame can all result in abnormal modes of burial. And although excavated burials have the great advantage that they are independent of textual bias, and represent events that really happened, they convey motivation implicitly rather than explicitly. Only through rigorous observation, comparison, and disciplined inference can we distinguish natural and accidental causes from deliberate attacks on corpses and—within the second category—distinguish measures intended merely to shame or insult the dead from ones explicitly designed to keep them in their graves.

Recent decades have seen a creative rapprochement between archaeologists, physical anthropologists, and biological scientists, which has produced more rigorous and sensitive methodologies for understanding post-depositional changes in corpses. The literature is huge; suffice it to say here that publications since the 2000s have identified many potential reasons for bodies being disturbed, in most cases acknowledging deliberate corpse-killing among them.[2] However, a sense started to develop that corpse-killing had been invoked too indiscriminately. Scientists pointed out that the biochemical effects of decomposition inside coffin voids, and intruders such as burrowing animals, can disrupt the bones to an extent that looks misleadingly like violent human intervention.[3]

So far, so good. But if literary-critical approaches can become rigid and oppressive, so can archaeological theory: there are signs of new dogmas entrenching themselves. The new discipline of 'archaeothanatology' seeks to establish a theoretical and methodological framework for recording and interpreting excavated human remains. This sets some welcome and valuable standards, but for present purposes it is remarkably unhelpful. The discipline seems to entertain no possibility of dead-killing activities, which do not receive a single serious reference in the 768 pages of its recent *Handbook*.[4] To assert that chopping-marks on the lower limbs of several early medieval burials in northern France were accidental products of grave-robbing, or that the cranium and lower jaw in another burial were removed and separated 'to create a space to stand or crouch', are surely lapses in common-sense.[5] Historians of ritual need to respect the relevant science, but scientists should also recognize that actions driven by belief and fear did actually take place and left material outcomes. It is no denigration of the archaeothanatologists' achievements to say that in this respect they have a blind spot.

This chapter, which argues that a range of processes (some archaeologically visible, others not) did indeed aim to kill the dead, revisits ground covered by Paul Barber's *Vampires, Burial, and Death*. It would be superfluous to repeat his detailed medical and folkloric evidence, though I often refer to it. I do, however, widen the chronological and cultural scope: Barber worked largely from European sources of the eighteenth century onwards, which gave a skewed sample. And to accept (as one must) his exposition of how biological processes make corpses seem alive does not remove the problem of selectivity: the processes are universal, but only a small minority of corpses have ever been interpreted in that way. Vampirism is in the eye of the beholder.

Incorruption: Saints and Vampires

Corpses can really be—or at least seem—incorrupt. Barber describes in detail (probably too much detail for some readers) the stages through which typical buried corpses are likely to pass, and the reasons why atypical ones can appear unexpectedly intact.[6] A new experimental study, within the framework of archaeothanatology, monitored the decomposition over time of two coffined and buried corpses.[7] It is, however, hard to generalize from this experiment to individual past cases: soil conditions, humidity, the condition of the corpse, and the nature of its container and wrappings, will all have influenced the outcome.

Normal biochemical processes produce swelling and bloating in the early stages of decay; rarer ones can make occasional corpses seem incorrupt and lifelike.[8] Although these effects are different, they have both been regularly identified as signs of supernatural continuing life. To observers whose fears are aroused, the bloated corpse is unambiguously sinister, since it is assumed to be swollen with other people's blood. But the lifelike corpse is ambiguous: is it very holy, or very unholy indeed?

Those who have linked incorruption to self-denying sanctity may not have been entirely wrong. It seems from the self-mummifying Buddhist monks of the Himalayas and Japan that extreme asceticism can trigger physical changes, capable of arresting decay.[9] Was there something of that with the famously incorrupt St Cuthbert of Lindisfarne, who died in 687 on a diet of raw onions? When his coffin was opened more than four centuries later he looked like a living man, his joints flexible: not like 'ordinary' incorrupt saints whose bodies are wrinkled and stiff, an admirer tells us gleefully.[10]

But what about those more wrinkled saints: how incorrupt does incorruption need to be? When outcomes are wanted or expected, there is room for negotiation. In 1544, a Russian ecclesiastical commission sent to investigate the locally-promoted St Iakov Borovitskii found that 'the flesh had dried to the bones, and the right hand was missing three fingers. However, the commission pointed to the intact head, face, fingernails, and toenails, and declared the body to be substantially incorrupt'.[11]

As Juliet du Boulay explains for modern Orthodox Greece:

> It may seem strange from a purely conceptual point of view that lack of corruption is one sign of a saint, when . . . it is also a sign of a vampire and, in less extreme cases, indicates at the exhumation the presence of 'sins'. But the villagers, living by experience rather than by theory, do not find it difficult to distinguish the uncorrupt and holy from its mirror image, the uncorrupt and demonic dead. . . . And the underlying rationale is similarly secure, for while most of humanity dies still full of sins—fat, gross, opaque, as it were, to the spiritual world, needing still the long process of purgation and forgiveness before their soul is truly free—the flesh of the saint in whom the spirit has already taken up its

> abode, having already achieved purgation, has no need of this process. The vampire's flesh betokens the presence of such evil that it cannot decompose; the saint's flesh betokens such a presence of holiness that decomposition is no longer necessary.[12]

Still, such distinctions are guided by experience, and people could have remembered different experiences. If Cuthbert's followers had not known him as a man of God, might his lifelike corpse have raised concerns? And did everyone necessarily take the same view of him? The prospect of real ambiguity is illustrated by the Russian case of St Artemii Verkol'skii:

> In 1577, a deacon found the uncorrupted body of a boy who had been struck by lightning and been buried in the woods. He brought it back to the village church in Verkola, claiming it belonged to a saint. The local peasants at first insisted upon leaving the body outside the church on the porch—the place where excommunicants and repenting sinners had to stand during services. The placement marked the body's uncertain status: whether it was a miracle-working saint or an evil-doing vampire was yet to be determined.[13]

Usually, we know of such cases from the reports of literate ecclesiastics invested in the saintly interpretation rather than the vampiric one. Voices now silent might have made comments of a different kind.

Reaching Stasis: Defleshing, Cremation, and Mummification

Sinister abnormalities imply a norm with which they contrasted: the ordinary dead, decaying gently in their graves. But that norm was not universal: where it did not apply, did people fear the dangerous dead? Three alternative and very different processes—defleshing, cremation, and mummification—are arguably linked by a common aim to achieve a condition of inert stasis.[14]

As we saw, funerary rites have often been multi-stage journeys, culminating in those deposits of unfleshed bones that archaeologists find in many different contexts. Whereas close engagement and manipulation of progressively decaying human flesh (especially that of near relatives) seems unspeakably revolting to modern Western societies, some people—native Australians, for instance—have seen it as a natural, healthy, and cathartic way of saying farewell to the dead and speeding them on their way.[15] In a sense, the modern Greek exhumation ritual is a more sanitized means to the same ends: once the clean bones have been washed and placed in the ossuary, 'no one worries that these once hallowed remains are left to the mercy of any chance event. . . . The physical remains have moved into a phase unrelated to sin or salvation, the soul gone elsewhere'.[16] This is *completion*: the absolute antithesis of the stagnant dead-end that spawns vampires.

Cremation also seems a straightforward separation rite, but perhaps it was not always quite so decisive. Extended rituals of defleshing or decay leave dry bones, bereft of life-force and danger; by contrast, the suddenness of cremation may give no time for the spirit and life-forces to depart, leaving the burnt residues as a locus of energy. In a spectacular Viking-age case, five spears were stabbed down into the ashes of a woman who had already been cremated with ten knives (p. 228). Certainly to *omit* cremation, among people who normally practised it, might well arouse fears that an individual had failed to move on in the normal way. A recurrent flash-point for heightened concern is likely to have been when a polytheistic cremating society converted to Christianity or Islam, and therefore switched to inhumation: we will meet cases of that in early medieval Europe.

What of the other extreme: a society where corpses are *normally* incorrupt because of active efforts to preserve them? The obvious case is Pharaonic Egypt, where the mummified dead occupied a continuing place in society.[17] They had to be placated with proper funeral rites and continuing offerings, and were capable of being malevolent and vengeful, or inflicting disease. But it was as one of their multiple incorporeal souls that the dead manifested themselves: mummies stayed in their tombs, and (ironically, given modern film fantasies) there is no trace in the abundant literature that they ever pursued the living.

Perhaps the intensive process of embalming and bandaging sanitized the corpse in a psychological as well as a physical sense, making it inert

FIGURE 11: Eleventh-century burial at the Baltic trading port of Wolin (now Poland). This man lay prone, with his head detached and twisted sideways, and his ankles tied. Reconstruction by Mirosław Kuźma.

and unthreatening like dry bones or ashes. What these cases have in common is *the completion of process*. As Barber puts it, 'though cremation and embalming seem to imply radically different philosophies (since the one process destroys the body while the other preserves it), in a sense they actually do the same thing: both render the body inert, preventing its transformation into a monster'.[18]

A long procession of mutilated corpses weaves its way through this book. Despite great regional variation, certain forms of mutilation appear repeatedly in the written and burial records. We therefore need to understand what they are, and in particular to assess how far their archaeological appearance is unambiguous, and how far open to other interpretations.

Countermeasures (1): Disorderly and 'Live' Burial

When skeletons are found lying in disorderly postures, premature or even deliberately live burial is often—probably too often—invoked as explanations. People have, on occasion, been buried alive, both accidentally and deliberately. The accidental form might in theory produce twisting and distortion capable of being misunderstood as irregular burial, though it is questionable whether this has ever actually been demonstrated. Since distortion on its own is never a reliable indicator of dead-killing, this need not concern us.

Deliberate live burial is theoretically impossible to rule out since we can never be *sure* that *any* coffined, shrouded or bound corpse was not alive when it went into the ground. This issue becomes acute in the occasional case of face-down burials with wildly spread limbs, illustrated by a famous case from sixth-century Yorkshire. We will return to that problem (p. 189), but it bears emphasizing here that a corpse past the *rigor mortis* stage, when thrown roughly down on its front and weighted with stones, is extremely hard to distinguish from a living and struggling person in the same circumstances: those who regard these burials as 'self-evidently' alive may not be standing on very solid ground.

Countermeasures (2): Prone Burial

Burial in the prone (i.e., face-down) position has been practiced widely throughout human history but not uniformly, appearing mainly in Europe, North Africa, Mesoamerica, and South-east Asia.[19] One study suggests that it normally indicates deviant or excluded members of society, especially in contexts of disruption, migration and contact between different groups.[20] Perhaps it was not inevitably shaming. Famously, the body of the Frankish king Pepin the Short (died 768) was found prone when exhumed in 1137, most likely a gesture of humility.[21] That sentiment may have existed more widely during the early and high Middle Ages in Scandinavia and German-speaking central Europe, where male prone burials are often otherwise regular, and in favoured locations.[22]

In the narrative and folkloric data, however, laying corpses face-down (or turning them over at a later stage) is one of the most widely recognized forms of corpse-killing. The rationale given in recent folklore, that if such a corpse tries to dig out it will dig downwards (pp. 413, 416), may or may not be ancient.[23] But there is also an intuitive sense—perhaps

FIGURE 12: The shameful burial of a criminal: detail from 'The Deposition from the Cross' by Geertgen tot Sint Jans (c. 1460/5–1490), part of a triptych from the chapel of St John in Haarlem (Netherlands). One of the thieves crucified with Jesus is buried prone, with his waist bound, and is thumped in the back with the butt-end of a spear. Is that simply to shame him, or to pre-empt his posthumous activities?

because it inverts the normal order, or because a face-down posture is ignominious or submissive—that to bury someone like this is a shaming act (Figure 12).[24]

Prone burials are among the most common potential cases of corpse-killing, and a recent study favours that interpretation for excavated

Slavic burials from the eleventh century onwards.[25] Here they will be considered potentially indicative, but only when the prone position accompanies other diagnostic features of treatment or location.

Countermeasures (3): Loading with Stones

Large stones placed on top of a corpse are common finds, especially in prehistoric periods when social contexts were undocumented. Intuitively, throwing stones on top of a human being (living or dead) carries some kind of intention to keep them down. But this too can be merely shaming: as the priest says of the self-drowned Ophelia, 'for charitable prayers / Shards, flints and pebbles should be thrown on her'.[26] There are late folkloric reports of throwing stones on the heads of suspected vampires.[27] Again, this cannot be taken as unequivocal evidence of corpse-killing but is a suggestive factor in combination, especially when the stones are very massive. We will encounter some persuasive cases in medieval northern Europe (Figure 54).

Countermeasures (4): Decapitation and Jaw Removal

Other things being equal, the favoured explanation for a corpse buried without its head will usually be execution. But beheading is often accompanied by other abnormalities, and context helps. Cemeteries specifically for the executed tend to be easily recognized, whereas the occasional decapitate in a normal cemetery is odder, and might have a different explanation. Where decapitates are a large minority of regular burials in regular cemeteries (as notably in late Roman Britain; see p. 179), the case that these are posthumous measures against the restless dead seems stronger.

The narrative and folklore evidence for posthumous beheading is so abundant that it must always (outside clear execution cemeteries) be considered a realistic possibility, and a likely one when combined with other indicative traits.[28] The practice of detaching the head with a spade as the corpse lies in the grave is widely documented in medieval and early modern Europe. Unlike execution by beheading, this need not necessarily (depending on the stage of decomposition and condition of the bone) have left marks of chopping on the neck vertebrae.[29] In the recent experiment, the joint between the cranium and the spinal column disarticulated after about three months, after which the head could easily have been pulled off.[30]

An important related question is the detachment of the lower jaw from the cranium, which we will regularly encounter (Figures 30, 35–37, 39–40, and 46–47). In the experiment, the relevant joints became disarticulated only one to two months after burial.[31] There is then a natural tendency for the jawbone to shift slightly, though clearly not to a different part of the grave.

Countermeasures (5): Bending and Binding Limbs

As the archaeothanatologists have shown, limbs and other bones can be disordered—sometimes dramatically so—by natural processes. But when they are found bent into sometimes unnatural positions that would only stay in place when tied (in contrast to normal wrapping in a shroud), there is a clear intention to restrain.

This would be consistent with binding a prisoner before execution, with a purposeful attempt to prevent a corpse from moving, or even with deliberate live burial. In contexts where execution and live burial seem implausible on other grounds, restraint of the potentially active dead is therefore the favoured option. A late Anglo-Saxon sketch of a damned corpse shows shackles on his ankles (Figure 53), and the ethnographic data include contexts where limbs were *routinely* bound to pre-empt unquietness.[32]

Countermeasures (6): Removing or Maiming Feet or Limbs

This looks quite persuasive, though as a caution we should remember Aristotle's statement that the Athenians cut off the feet of suicides (p. 55).[33] In ancient Greece, the practice of removing the feet and other extremities of dead enemies was designed to shame them, but also to disable their capacity for vengeance (p. 163). The symbolism of the act does surely embody a perception that the corpse might (literally) walk, and it seems more purposefully targeted than prone burial or stoning. It is the symbolic opposite of giving a dead person shoes for walking to the next world and implies that this corpse will not be going anywhere, in either direction.

Cuts made by chopping and hacking at the lower limbs might be interpreted as battle injuries, but that is unlikely when they occur on female burials, as in one early medieval Frankish cemetery (p. 184). They are interesting as the kind of thing that might be done when the grave of a suspect corpse was opened, rather than during the funeral rites. It parallels the late medieval Breton story where a troublesome revenant's neighbours 'decided to pull him out of the grave and break his thighs' (p. 62).

Countermeasures (7): Piercing and Impaling with Stakes and Nails

Driving a wooden stake through the body is the classic folkloric recipe against vampires,[34] and is mentioned in the early eleventh-century Rhineland (p. 235). By its nature it will rarely show up archaeologically, but there are occasional examples (Figure 54).

There is a better chance of detecting iron nails driven into the corpse or its clothing (Figure 13), though some excavation reports just note frustratingly that the grave contained 'some nails'. We will see that this was a common rite in the late Roman Mediterranean. In a clear case from Anglo-Saxon Surrey, nails were driven into or next to the joints of selected corpses (Figure 45). How that might have happened is vividly explained in a description from 1930s Jamaica:

> When it came time to place the body in the coffin there was a great deal of talk back and forth. Some few said that he had been a fairly good man and that they were sure that once buried, he would not return. All the trouble of keeping the ghost or duppy [revenant] in the grave was unnecessary. But the majority were for taking no

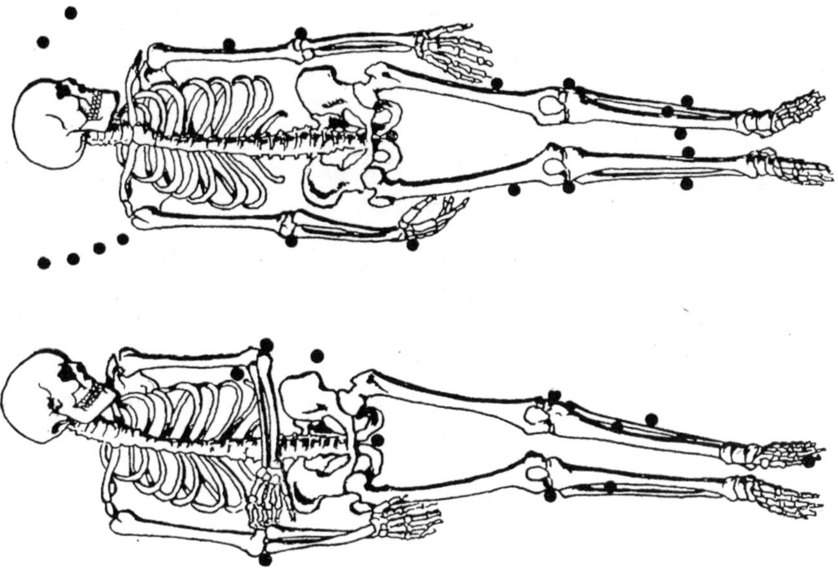

FIGURE 13: Medieval nailed burials in the Jewish cemetery of Deza (Soria), Aragón, Spain.

> chances. . . . They took four short nails and drove one in each cuff of the shirt as close to the hand as possible to keep the hands firmly in place. The heel of each sock was nailed down in the same way. Now the duppy was 'nailed hand and foot'. The brother of the corpse was summoned and he spoke to the dead and said, 'We nail you down hand and foot. You must stay there till judgement. If we want you we come wake you.'[35]

Similarly, an account of the Morlachs (a predominantly Romance population group in Dalmatia) from 1774 relates: 'When a man dies who is suspected of becoming a vampire (*Vampiro o Vukodlak*) . . . their practice is to cut his hams, and puncture him completely with pins, alleging that after these two operations he will be unable to walk around. It sometimes happens that before he dies, a Morlach, foreseeing that he will have a great thirst for children's blood, asks his heirs to promise to treat him as a vampire before putting his body in the tomb.'[36]

FIGURE 14: A large pair of shears has been laid across the body of this infant, aged about 16 months, buried in a churchyard at Visby (Gotland) in the twelfth century.

Countermeasures (8): Pinning Down with Edged Weapons or Tools

Unlike stakes, spears or knives stabbed into burials will survive for archaeologists. While this action could have different aims (as has been suggested for cases from Iron Age Yorkshire; see p. 179), maiming the dead or pinning them down seems on the face of it the most obvious. The Anglo-Saxon case where a spear was driven through the corpse's heart (Figure 32), or the medieval Finnish one where the coffin-lid was pinned down by multiple edged weapons (p. 228), will convince most people.

Uncertainty comes with the many cases of knives found in ill-defined locations on the corpse: were they grave-goods to help the dead in the next world, or countermeasures to prevent them from returning to this one? The placing of sharp objects to keep the corpse down is widely recorded in the folklore and ethnographic evidence.[37] Sickles have been used as grave-goods, with a range of symbolism that does not necessarily indicate fear of the dead.[38] However, a group of seventeenth-century female burials in northern Poland with sickles hooked around their throats are unambiguous cases of corpse-killing (Figure 61), which was still remembered by a West Prussian informant in 1933 (Map 10).

Countermeasures (9): Blocking, Binding, or Separation of the Jaws

The functions of the human mouth are to eat, drink, suck, chew, and speak. Performed by the dead, these actions are threatening and can be forestalled by binding the jaw or by forcing it open (Figure 6). When a stone is found in a corpse's mouth, or gaping jaws imply a 'gag' made of cloth or some other organic substance, that is the most reasonable explanation (Figures 45 and 59). In recent Kashubian tradition (West Prussia), 'a brick is put under the chin so that he may break his teeth on it'.[39] When the aim is to prevent the soul from re-entering (p. 47), the thinking is different but the goal is similar.[40]

One might imagine circumstances in which the purpose was simply to shame or take revenge on the deceased (with a cursing or scolding individual, for instance), but the abundant documented concerns about oral activity by the dangerous dead make that idea look forced. Setting bloodsucking aside, the widespread European belief in noxious shroud-chewing corpses provides reason enough. One of the very earliest relevant texts, from Mesopotamia in the seventh century BC, refers to 'a dead person blocked with cloths, uprising, complaining' (p. 160).

Countermeasures (10): Extraction or Piercing of the Heart

Puncturing or cutting out the heart is one of the most frequently described counter-measures, and turns up regularly in this book.[41] European written sources from the twelfth century onwards mention the procedure, which became standard after the Middle Ages. It also has the distinction of having survived to modern times: the hearts of Mercy Brown (New England) and Petre Toma (Romania) were cut out to halt their vampiric activities in 1892 and 2004 respectively (pp. 45, 439).

This mutilation should be visible archaeologically, because of the necessary disturbance to the upper left side of the ribcage. In older and less professional excavations, however, it may often have been missed or not reported: excavators do not expect it, and natural snapping of ribs under earth pressure is normal. There are occasional convincing cases from Britain, and one from early medieval Ireland where the *inside* of the ribcage shows cuts from a knife inserted under it in the appropriate place (pp. 182, 214).

Countermeasures (11): Use of Fire or Heat in the Grave

The burning of a corpse already laid in its grave is generally rare, and a minority practice when it does occur. Given that it is both unpleasant and technically difficult, it seems best understood as an afterthought, when it has become apparent after the funeral that the corpse needs further suppression. Plausible cases have been recognized in Neo-Assyrian Mesopotamia and in Anglo-Saxon England (pp. 161, 186). Two others, from the twelfth or thirteenth century, were in eastern Swedish cemeteries: at Rissne, where someone opened the grave, disturbed the remains, broke the coffin-lid and set it on fire; and at Gnista, where a fire lit on top of a conventionally buried corpse contained timbers, animal remains and pieces of rope.[42]

This last case recalls a modern Romanian story: 'At night Dimitriu and his son took candles and went to dig up the grave. They were seized with horror at what they saw. There she was, sitting like a Turk, with long hair falling over her face, with all her skin red, and with finger nails frightfully long. They got together brushwood, shavings, and bits of old crosses, they poured wine on her, they put in straw, and set fire to the whole. Then they shovelled the earth back and went home.'[43]

Countermeasures (12): Scattering Grain

The scattering of grain or seeds in the coffin or grave-earth of a suspect corpse is mentioned widely. Where rationalized in recorded folk-belief (as in Haiti; see p. 427), the usual explanation is that the dead person will feel obliged to count them and will never finish. The use of mustard and poppy seeds against vampires is widely mentioned in Slavic folklore. In one eleventh- to twelfth-century Polish cemetery, black mustard seeds mainly occurred in female burials,[44] though that might point to magical practitioners rather than restless corpses. By its nature, such evidence very rarely survives archaeologically, though there are examples from English graves of the sixth and tenth centuries.[45]

Countermeasures (13): Exhumation Followed by Burning or Dispersal

This, by definition, will leave nothing on the original burial site except an empty grave, for which there could be many other reasons. Modern retrieval of debris from the process could only happen by the merest chance, though there is one persuasive case from medieval Yorkshire (p. 259).

Countermeasures (14): Deliberate Mutilation after Burial

The opening of graves to remove objects is of particular interest to the archaeothanatology school, which has developed new and discriminating ways for analyzing a range of behaviours that used to be labelled 'robbing'. It has been shown that these acts were not always straightforwardly for gain, and could be ritualized.[46]

Our concern here is different: the opening of graves with the intent to mutilate the corpses. Such episodes must be interpreted as—in some sense—aggressive attacks on the dead individuals, but again distinctions are necessary. For instance, the violent and apparently public mutilation—more than a century later—of corpses in ninth-century Norwegian ship-burials may well have been to stop the dead from walking, but if so, the belief cannot have depended on physical incorruption (p. 229).

A more interesting scenario is when the corpse is attacked long enough after the initial burial for decomposition to set in, but soon enough for the illusion of incorruption to remain viable. For obvious reasons this would be an extremely unpleasant process, not to be undertaken lightly. Sharp tools would not be necessary, however, because the joints could simply be pulled apart.

How soon after burial this might happen is of considerable relevance. In the recent experiment described above, the jawbone would have been detachable after one to two months and the cranium after three. Although there must have been huge variation, this is helpfully compatible with the kind of time-frame within which concerns about a potentially restless corpse might arise and spread.

It will be important to distinguish repetitive procedures from random ones. Systematic, stereotyped actions look purposeful rather than merely malicious, especially if they regularly take the form of disabling the joints necessary for walking, talking, or chewing.

Almost always, there will be a balance of probabilities rather than unequivocal certainty. The strongest cases will be those showing repetitive combinations of maiming actions, especially when performed on corpses in a semi-decayed state, and where accretive data form patterns. Overall, the archaeological evidence abundantly supports the textual evidence: corpse-killing was a frequent and widespread reality.

Having now surveyed a range of evidence and approaches, we will continue to take a wide-angle view as we tease out and interpret some strands of belief that emerge from the deep human past. When these broad cultural traditions have been defined, developments in specific regions and on a historical timescale will start to come into focus.

PART II

Dynamics

A COMPLETE FAMILY TREE of the dangerous dead is not achievable, but we must start somewhere. Any idea of a teleological evolution from 'simple' to 'complex' would be mechanistic and inadequate. However, beliefs that were continuously reconstructed and reinterpreted can be understood in at least a relative sequence, showing some recurrent developmental linkages.

This was a dynamic process. If some motifs reflect socio-cultural change over the last two millennia or so, others seem more embedded and organic. Motifs that look like preserved fossils in some cultures have been alive and meaningful—at least into the era of ethnographers and anthropologists—in others. Beliefs do not emerge from nowhere, and where we find them making cultural sense, we are probably getting closer to their original form and meaning.

The chapters in Part II have a world-wide range, seeking to define some of the major visualisations of the dangerous dead, and chart how they spread, combined, and adapted. They construct a new framework to support a closer-grained view of developments in western Eurasia.

8

The Circumpolar World and Northern Asia

CORPSES AND LIFE-FORCES

> The *bong* [walking corpse] looked and the girl was washing her head in the water. This way and that he hovered. The *bong* put his head in the other basin imitating them, but there was oil in his basin. Speechless and silent he copied them. The girl now finished washing her hair and took the iron box and put it in the water to wash it. The *bong* took the birch-bark bag and put it in his bowl. The girl put the box on her head. The *bong* took the bag and put it on his head. Now his oily head burst into flames.
>
> —FROM A DAUR MONGOL JOKE ABOUT THE STUPIDITY OF WALKING CORPSES

WHEN CORPSES COME BACK to life, what animates them? Often, in this book, that question lurks in the background unresolved. Has the beloved (or feared) grandmother, who died last month, returned to her family as the person she used to be? Or has some new occupant moved in: an external spiritual or demonic force? Or could it be just *part* of grandmother—her life-force (or her anger) without her rational intelligence?

Whenever the dead are thought to return, these underlying uncertainties about their nature, and about how corpse, life-force, and personality interact, are there to some degree.

The conception of corpses being occupied by a fluid range of spiritual entities is prominent and consistent in the circumpolar region, and across the vast tract of the globe comprising Siberia, Mongolia, and Manchuria. It coexists there with the complexes of belief and ritual traditionally labelled 'shamanic', and with a sense of permeable boundaries between the human, spirit, and animal worlds. These thought-patterns were not unique to the region (some of them also occur in Africa, for instance), but they are accessible through some helpful anthropology. If we want to understand the dangerous dead in a pan-spiritual thought-world, this is a good place to start.

Life-Forces and Multiple Souls

Most people in modern Western cultures conceive themselves and others as distinct and individual entities. They might envisage immortal souls if they come from Christian or Muslim backgrounds, or biological organisms if they come from materialistic ones, but in either case human beings are conceived as indivisible centres of consciousness. In the past, across large areas of the world, people have seen things differently: a universal life-force generates multiple souls, which animate individuals in pairs, threes, or even more, and in some cases can move between humans and animals.

In ancient Egypt, for instance, each person had a *ba*, a *ka*, and an *akh*: the *ba* could occasionally leave the body during life; the *akh* (the most personal, and only possessed by the virtuous) could travel from the tomb while the other souls stayed; and the *ka* (represented by the dead person's *ka*-statue in the offering chamber) seems to have been closest to a basic life-force.[1] Anthropologists have often identified such conceptions in west and central Africa: thus the Dahomey believe in three souls embodying respectively the biological life-force, the personality and voice, and the intellect and conscience.[2] We will meet the Chinese *po* and *hun* later.

Siberian, Mongolian, and Manchurian peoples had an all-embracing idea of life-force and soul permeating all people and animals. Humans have a 'true soul' (consciousness and self-cognition), a 'soul which precedes' (higher-order physiological functions and reproductive power), and an 'external soul' that returns to the spirit-world but may be reincarnated in people or animals. Occasionally, this third soul can be wayward, hanging around the corpse or wandering at large until it finds a new host.[3] With the Sámi, the 'free-soul' escapes at death, but the 'life-soul(s)' have to stay around the corpse, restrained by the shroud if necessary.[4]

In European societies, this way of thinking is rarely explicit but not necessarily absent. Juliet du Boulay's Greek case-study gives subtle insights into how it can survive at an inchoate level. Reflecting on two simultaneous but incompatible beliefs—that the Angel takes every person's soul at the moment of death, and that an accident at the wake turns a virtuous person into an irredeemable vampire—she observes:

> This contradiction presents a difficulty, not only because the same word *psychí*, denoting the soul, is used in both contexts, but also because villagers do not differentiate in any conscious sense between the two uses of the word. Nevertheless, there are hints . . . which may suggest that at a relatively inexplicit level the soul is understood in what are virtually two distinct senses. . . . [T]here exists in rural Greek thought, running alongside those beliefs which relate to the destiny of the soul separated from the body and taken by the Angel, a parallel belief that the rupture between the body and the person who inhabited it is not made absolute on death, but is only finally completed when the flesh, as villagers say, 'has dissolved' (*échei liósei*) from the bones—a process indicating also the dissolution of sins. . . . According to this latter series of ideas, then, possession by the devil of the *body*, of the flesh and blood, would necessarily involve in some way the possession of a psychic element of the person also—of that psychic element whose dissolution is equivalent to the dissolution of sins; and this is said to occur despite the fact that another psychic element has already left the body with the Angel. . . . [The villagers] are untroubled by the contradiction between the two uses, and the nascent distinction thus suggested would account for the fact that they are much less concerned about the fate of the vampire's soul than they are about the reanimation of the corpse, and for the

> corresponding fact that they are much less fearful of actually becoming a vampire than they are of making or meeting with one.[5]

This contradiction—teased out so painstakingly by a deeply sensitive anthropologist—has far-reaching implications: was it latent in other societies with vampire beliefs? In many stories in this book, survivors seem oddly unconcerned about the spiritual fate of the dead friends or relatives whose corpses they hack or burn: did they have a 'relatively inexplicit' understanding like that of the Ambéli villagers?

In the modern industrialized world, someone claiming multiple personalities would be diagnosed with 'dissociative identity disorder'. But is it necessarily a disorder? The anthropologist and clinician Rebecca J. Lester writes movingly about a traumatised young woman, manifesting twelve distinct personalities, who was helped by treating her as 'a community of selves within one individual', in need of balancing rather than curing: 'Given my anthropological training, I approached Ella's DID symptoms differently than many clinicians might. Ella looked to me like a community—a dysfunctional one at that moment but a community, nonetheless. My concern was less with the number of selves she had than with how those selves worked together—or not—in her daily life. Was it possible to bring those selves into a harmonious coexistence?'[6]

That 'harmonious coexistence' is precisely what spiritual practitioners in many cultures have tried to achieve. But for them, it could occasionally go wrong in a different way. One or more of an individual's life-forces might linger unnaturally after death. Or, unruly and free-floating spirits might somehow miss their true path and enter a dead body. When that happened, the result was a dangerous animated corpse. But in circumpolar cultures, it was just one in a range of physical and spiritual entities in the animate world that could morph and combine.

Shamans, Spirits, and Were-Animals

'Shamanism' is a contested concept.[7] Shamans were practitioners within a particular kind of spiritual, cosmological, and economic culture-zone, but did not control or define it. Indeed, the essence of such a belief-complex is that it was not a 'system' but decentralized, variable, and fluid.

FIGURE 15: A female shaman in Bronze Age Siberia: reconstruction from grave-goods.

One can find broader or narrower definitions, but it clarifies if we think in the first instance of the circumpolar zone, with its challenging ecology and dependence on animal protein for human survival. From there, recognizably similar phenomena extend into adjoining parts of Asia (Siberia, Asian Russia, and Mongolia), northern Scandinavia, and North America. An interesting point to emerge from global mapping is that all the major Eurasian zones of dangerous-dead beliefs border north-eastwards on shamanic societies (Map 1).

For present purposes, the crucial aspect is interaction between the seen and unseen worlds: between humans, animals (especially wolves), animal-spirits, and the dead.[8] Animals were hunted for survival, but on the spirit plane they could also be powerful guides and protectors. After a long, dangerous process of transformative initiation, the shaman moved between the worlds of people, spirits, or ghosts in a state of ecstatic trance induced by drum-beating. As one observer puts it,

> the Subarctic shaman . . . becomes spirit. 'Shaman-as-Wolf' and 'Wolf-as-Shaman' are interchangeable concepts. The interchangeability of

> shaman, spirit, and animal-familiar means that many aspects of ordinary reality in the Subarctic are felt to be imbued with spiritual power or force and are therefore potentially dangerous and need to be regarded with caution. The animal that one hunts may prove to be a shaman's animal-familiar, just as the lone hunter who shuns camp life and duties can be a *Windigo* [a life-sapping spirit], or the woman who refuses to marry and does not participate socially a *Windigokwé* [the female version] in disguise.[9]

Here the dangerous dead are no great abnormality, because they are just one among several categories of daunting spiritual forces. They do not usually manifest as physical corpses, but the divide of death is a thin barrier, readily crossed and re-crossed: if the dead can prey on the living, the living can also prey on the dead. In Northern Kamchatka (northeast Russia on the Bering Sea), unpopular women are suspected of 'vampirically' touching corpses at wakes to draw out their residual life-force, keeping themselves fit and young. One woman who came home too late for her father's funeral 'saw the vampire sitting in the room, with an infuriatingly satisfied look on her face. Marina knew what she had done, and in anger she walked up to the woman, touched her on the shoulder, and said, "I take back my father's energy which you stole." Marina then left the house and went home. The brazen insult was dangerous, but she did not suffer from any retaliation, and later, in private, witnesses confided to Marina that she had done the right thing.'[10]

Among the Buryat Mongols, complex intra-family negotiations are played out between the living and the dead with the mediation of shamans. Hostile dead relatives take the form of 'vampiric imps' (*chötgör*), who are small, ambiguously corporeal, but sometimes capable of being trapped (Figure 16). In family feuds, they can waste the resources and drain the energy of rival branches until a shaman expunges them from the genealogy.[11]

Shamans themselves—daunting in death as in life—occasionally became animated corpses of a more familiar kind. With the Haida of West-Coast Canada and North America, special rites speeded up their transition to the underworld; their remains were deposited in remote

FIGURE 16: A Buryat Mongol vampiric imp (*chötgör*), drawn by the shaman Yaruu for the anthropologist Katherine Swancutt.

places, since encountering their graves would bring sickness and death.[12] A nineteenth-century Skolt Sámi shaman, Grigori Riisä, was pre-emptively taken to a peat-bog for burial but refused to go quietly:

> One of the reindeer pulling the dead man's corpse was suddenly frightened and when the man looked round, he saw the dead man sitting on his coffin. The man asked the dead man what he was doing up at night and told him to go and rest. . . . They finally reached a place known to the driver where there grew two pine trees. There the man stopped the reindeer and climbed one of the trees. The shaman followed him and began to gnaw at the trunk of the tree. He could not climb the tree as his hands had been bound together by the blessing he had been given. The man then broke off a branch of the tree and threw it down. The shaman ceased to gnaw for a while but then continued again. The man threw another two branches at Grigori but finally the pine began to sway. The man climbed across to the other pine tree, which stood close by. . . . [This continued until at last] the shaman noticed that dawn had come. The shaman then returned to his coffin. The man could then

> continue the journey to the burial place without being worried any more. On arrival he first made a fire and burned the dead man's heels. The coffin he placed in the grave upside down so that the shaman would not be able to get out. After this the shaman was heard to wail his complaints for seven years until he had sunk so far into the ground that he could no longer be heard.[13]

What kind of being was this undead Grigori? Evidently his life-force soul remained, but not his moral consciousness. He was sentient to the extent of chasing prey, reacting to daybreak, and bewailing his fate, but otherwise displayed mere animal savagery. Reduced from the personality that he must have been in life, he resembled the brute-force 'lumpen' corpses explored later in this book.

Although an exception in the 'shamanic' north, Grigori illustrates how spirit-based beliefs could occasionally produce gross corporeal expressions. Why? A useful analogy may be the sudden intensification of were-animal beliefs among the Daur Mongols after 1900, when the 'crisis of modernity', with its sudden influx of alarming foreign ideas, challenged traditional modes of dealing with the spirit-world.[14] It is not hard to guess that stress and trauma also generated the lurid image of the monstrous Grigori.

The *Bong* and the *Ibagan*: A Case-Study in Shifting Categories

For a book like this, which tries to understand thought-processes from long ago, clear categories of supernatural beings are hard to establish. That is scarcely surprising, since rigid definitions have not troubled most believers. To sketch out a broad landscape of beliefs in combination and flux can be more productive, and first-hand ethnographic studies illuminate the past. A case in point is the Russian anthropologist Sergei Shirokogoroff's fieldwork in the 1910s among the Tungusic peoples in Siberia, Mongolia, and Manchuria.

Shirokogoroff identified a corpse-based being normally called *bon(g)* by Tungus speakers and *ibagan* by Manchus, but essentially similar across the groups studied in this vast area. It is created when the first two souls have departed and the life-force becomes inactive, but before the corpse starts to decay. At that point, some spirit—often a soul that has not found the world of the dead—can enter the corpse and reanimate it. It 'would not possess the characters proper to the living person, because the second soul would be absent, but even physiological functions to some extent might be restored.' Often 'a spirit introduces itself into the buried corpse which begins to move and which again may have physiological needs'. Those who have seen *bong*s say that they 'are very short in stature, less than a metre tall, and they live on the meat of the badger'; they also have long hair, a small lower jaw, and a third eye. Most of them are female. Stories tell of *bong*s being seen returning to their coffins. The Manchu *ibagan* is covered with hair, and jumps instead of walking. When the Manchus catch an *ibagan* they kill it with an axe and burn the body, together with the bodies of any people that it has killed.[15]

Corpse-burning is used pre-emptively in one other case:

> About the middle of the last [nineteenth] century, the corpse of girls of less than twenty years old were burnt together with the coffins. The reason was that [because the girls would have married outside the clan] there was nobody, after their death, to take care of soul and body. . . . However, since the soul is the soul, so it may produce great harm to the people, and the corpse may be used by other spirits in which way the girl's corpse may become *ibagan*, the safest way is to destroy the body.[16]

Fifty years later another anthropologist, Caroline Humphrey, investigated the *bong* among the Daur Mongols. The conceptions described by Shirokogoroff survived, but with a tinge of ridicule. 'They were feared, but also thought rather pitiful and funny', and comic stories were told about their stupidity. One woman told her 'that the life force (*ami*—breath) should come out of the body via the arm-pits, but if for some reason it did not, because the body had been incorrectly buried, then the ghost would hang around. "Oh, there are many *bong* around here", she said.'[17]

The inconsistencies in these accounts are striking. Shirokogoroff was told that the occupying spirit came from outside, Humphrey that it was its own life-force (or ghost?) hanging around. The jokes about the *bong*'s stupidity imply that it has cognitive faculties, but at a low level. And how could physical human corpses be pictured as small, grotesque, hairy, three-eyed badger-eaters, which sound more like cousins to the Buryat 'vampiric imps'? There is a conceptual elision here between corpses occupied by external spiritual forces, corpses occupied by their own life-force spirits but residually conscious, and quasi-demonic 'little people'. The hairiness of the *ibagan* suggests animal transformations. All this is important and valuable, because we will meet such category-confusion again: the Tungusic case proves that believing communities really can entertain them simultaneously.

Descendants of the Were-Animal

In the light of these beliefs, it is interesting to remember the semantic evolution of Slavonic *vukodlak* from 'wolf-hair' to 'werewolf' to 'vampire'. An occasional but persistent theme of the walking dead in medieval and post-medieval Europe is that they shape-shift, often into dogs or wolves; post-medieval Chinese stories regularly say that errant corpses traced to their graves are found covered with long white hair.[18] One was 'covered all over with white hairs, as if it wore a robe of silvery rat-skins inside-out. Its face too was overgrown with such hairs; its eyes were deep and black, and had green eye-balls emitting glaring rays.'[19] In modern Taiwan, this motif of were-animal ancestry fuses with some other relevant ones:

> It is partly the capacity of the corpse to turn into a dangerous and powerful monster, or *iau-kuai*, that is feared at the coffining. While the corpse is in an indeterminate state between a living man and a buried ancestor it is relatively less predictable and controllable. . . . [In one case when the sun and moon were allowed to shine on the coffin], the corpse was able to turn into a *iau-kuai* with long white hair, huge fangs, and a long tongue. The dead man's soul was able to leave the corpse and cause sickness and other troubles for the people of the area.[20]

Here the monstrous corpse does not *itself* leave the grave and walk; its transformation allows the soul to do so. This conceptual shift will interest us when we consider the 'grave-bound' vampires of medieval and later Europe.

The jumping *ibagan* allows us to tease out another thread. A subspecies of the possessed corpse in China was a hopping variety, widely attested in folklore.[21] This idea seems to have been conflated with a ritual in which corpses were 'walked' home for burial, prodded by the 'walker' to hop forward. This eerie effect of a corpse apparently walking on its own was described by an eye-witness in the 1950s: 'One dark and overcast afternoon I was strolling along the village road when a bulky, black object suddenly passed me, sending a chill down my spine. The thing was covered with a huge inky-colored robe. . . . The footsteps were heavy and made a repetitive, thudding noise, like someone knocking the ground with a block of wood. Just then, my friend Piggy scurried up to me and whispered in my ear: That's a corpse'.[22] Perhaps this ritual recalls a time when corpses were really thought to walk home (as in Africa more recently, p. 422), and perhaps the jerky movements of the corpse-walker under the big robe were assimilated to the idea of a 'hopping corpse'. In any case, the resemblance to the Manchu *ibagan* implies deeper roots and animal origins.

The *bong* raises two further issues: gender and intelligence. Since dangerous young females are prominent in the rest of this book, it is very interesting that *bong*s were mainly female and that girls under twenty were cremated as a high-risk group. In contexts explored later, these categories were separated out by gender: wily, shape-shifting females, against males blundering around as strong, stupid corpses.

Turkic Suckers

Finally, a different kind of supernatural being must be introduced. Since the evidence for it is entirely philological, it is a shadowy presence, and not demonstrably part of the story of the restless dead before the 1660s. But it gave us the word 'vampire', and hovers in the background of eventual European beliefs in 'vampires' that suck blood.

This is the sucking and/or swallowing entity implied by the reconstructed proto-Turkic noun **ōpyr* (p. 15). It was perpetuated in the later folklore of Turkic peoples as a monstrous being, able to 'shapeshift into different creatures, especially wolves, dogs, cats and other animals, or a ball of fire' and 'is said to devour everything that it encounters', but its root meaning is unequivocally 'sucker'.[23]

Demons might potentially suck substances other than blood: milk from the animals on whom pastoralists' livelihood depends, for instance, or milk from mothers' breasts.[24] In the folklore of diverse Turkic cultures, however, the *obur* was one of a range of voracious, sometimes night-pressing demons and monsters whose common feature was that they drank blood.[25] The sense 'sucker' is an important piece of evidence, especially since the first recorded application of the term to walking corpses is associated with bloodsucking (p. 292).

This chapter has visited a northern and Asian world where animated corpses were one element in a continuum of psychic perceptions. Spiritual entities and life-forces, ranging from the universal to the personal, could take up residence in living people, living animals, corpses, or ambiguously physical entities. Boundaries between were-animals, walking corpses, and 'little people' were permeable. One thing, however, these corpses were *not*: rational and fully conscious personalities of former living humans, continuing within their physical bodies.

Where this belief-complex existed in other regions, it has been infiltrated and overlain by different ideas: for instance, women transformed after death into quasi-demonic but still physical forms, or dangerous individuals who just will not die properly. These fusions explain why neat classification of the dangerous dead is impossible: even when they are more personal and individual, traces of multiple souls, life-forces, and shape-shifting regularly intrude.

9

India and China

LUMPEN CORPSES AND LUSTFUL HYENA-WOMEN

'A ghost is made from the vital *qi* that's left behind after a body dies. With time, such *qi* will naturally disperse. However, by feeding on the vital *qi* of the living, ghosts can delay their disappearance from our world. Female ghosts generally seduce human beings to draw out their *qi*. Male ghosts generally kill people to draw out their *qi*. This is the difference between draining blood from an animal over time or hacking it into meat straight away.'

—SHI LIANGSHENG, TAOIST MASTER, C. 1700

THE EARLY TEXTS from India and China show some broad similarities in their supernatural beliefs. With the spread of Buddhism, some of those parallels became direct and explicit. They included two prototypes for the dangerous dead: corpses occupied by violent or brutal life-forces, and lustful female beings who shape-change between human and animal forms. Both probably crystallized out of beliefs like the Mongol and Siberian ones described in the last chapter.

Gender Templates in India: *Vetāla, Dākinī,* and *Yoginī*

As Tantric practices developed in India from the seventh century AD onwards, some supernatural entities came into sharper focus. The two that concern us here could hardly be more different, but they probably grew from similar origins, and they emerged in parallel to the 'vampire' in both Asia and Europe.

Vetālas were monstrous, violent spirits or genies, prone to hanging around cremation-grounds and occupying corpses. They were not necessarily unintelligent (the *vetāla* in a famous story-cycle is brilliantly quick-witted[1]), but they represented brute-force masculinity. Fearsome though they were, Tantric sorcerers and *yoginīs* could master them, riding them across the sky like hot-air balloons as the furious *vetāla* belched fire through the mouth of the corpse.[2]

Female demons, by contrast, took the form of beautiful women, lustful, predatory, and shape-shifting (Figure 17). By the seventh century they had crystallized as *dākinīs* and *yoginīs,* who moved around in swarms, conferring enlightenment on adept practitioners but eating the incompetent and ordinary.[3] *Yoginīs* always had a strongly erotic aspect, which from the tenth century was emphasized in picturing their encounters with humans: they devoured special men ('Virile Heroes') in a sexual rather than a gastronomic sense.[4] In a memorable story from the Rājataranginī (a chronicle of Kashmir) under AD 1148/9, the narrator

> saw on the burial ground *yoginīs* enveloped in a halo of light. . . . Intoxicated by drink, they had felt the desire for sportive enjoyment of a lover, and not finding a Virile Hero, had carried off that skeleton [of Sandhimati]. One by one, each of them placed [upon the skeleton] one of her own limbs, and then quickly bringing a male organ from somewhere, they made his body complete. Next, the witches, magically drawing back the spirit of Sandhimati—which was still roaming about without having entered into another body—put it into that [body]. Resembling a person just risen from sleep, he was covered by them with heavenly ointments, and he, the leader of their circle, was carnally enjoyed by them to their fullest desire.[5]

FIGURE 17: A *yoginī*: ninth-century sandstone carving from central India. The traces of sharp, projecting teeth are a warning that her voluptuous appearance may give a false sense of security.

In all of this, *yoginīs* controlled and manipulated male bodies. They rode *vetāla*-powered corpses; they reconstructed the bodies of dead heroes for sex; and they demanded the body fluids of their partners. Human interactions with them were sacrificial as well as transformative. As David Gordon White memorably puts it, 'few would argue that offering one's body up to hordes of predatory female were-creatures is not a most unusual path to salvation. Among all the possible ways to transcend the human condition and realize unity or identity with God, this surely ranks among the strangest'.[6]

Their mythology took a path that did not identify them with dead women, but for present purposes, the *yoginī* are enlightening offshoots from the main stem. As passionate, erotic devourers of men and suckers-out of their life-forces, they were not-so-distant cousins to some of the walking dead.

Gender Templates in China: *Jiangshi* and *Huli Jing*

In old age, the Chinese philosopher Ji Yun looked back on his childhood in the 1720s and his father's friend, Dr Hu Gongshan. Dr Hu had been a brave man and a tough fighter, but two adventures had made him horribly afraid of the dark. The first happened when he was walking through a wood as a young man, and a *jiangshi* attacked him. He climbed a tree to escape; it made stiff, automaton-like attempts to get up, but as dawn broke it gradually lost animation and clamped itself tightly onto the tree. When he examined it by the light of day he saw that it might once have been a man, but it was covered with 'a snowy something resembling fur or mould, and possessing blood-coloured eyes, talon-like hands, and pointed teeth so long that they jutted past the lips, the deep wrongness of the creature—which managed to be both aesthetic and moral—disturbed Dr Hu to his core'.

Dr Hu's second encounter happened in a guest-house in a remote place in the mountains. He was woken at night by movements under his sheets. As he watched, the thing turned into something the size of a human head, and then a body. Then a woman's head poked out, and 'it stretched its way onto his pillow as its owner's naked body turned to him, feverishly warm. Despite the woman-thing's beauty and the silky heat of her flesh, Dr Hu felt no lust. But he was so paralyzed with fear that he did not fight her either when her impossibly long arms wound around him and crushed him close. Nor did he fight when she forced her stinking mouth against his in a kiss so pungent with decay and blood that he gagged and passed out.'[7]

Ji Yun wrote on the borders between folklore and fiction, and this neat story-pair—a vehicle for defining and distinguishing the two modes of predatory undead—must be a literary construct. But as a scholar's exposition of the beliefs embedded in his culture, it tells us what we need to know.

As a violently animated corpse, the identity of the *jiangshi* seems stable and straightforward.[8] To quote Ji Yun again:

> They are corpses that have been dead long enough to be buried in their coffins, but then have become reanimated by an outside agent (a spell, lightning, a pregnant cat walking across their grave). However, the deceased are not what they were. While in the grave, their emotions have soured, their thoughts gone feral, and their rank bodies have fermented and stiffened into more monstrous possibilities.

> If freed from the soil, these fiends will spread terror in the night—killing, infecting, feeding, and leaving the dry husks of their victims in their wake. As depraved as they are, there is a complexity to these creatures. Sometimes, a lingering attraction to family and friends remains—albeit in a perverted form.[9]

In some versions it is the *po* or earthy life-force soul that animates the corpse when the more ethereal and personal *hun* has departed. That turns amiable people into monsters, who can attack and kill their own former relatives. They can manifest as 'running corpses', which leap up from their biers before burial and rush after their victims. In a particularly terrifying story of c. 1700 by Pu Songling, a recently dead and coffined woman attacks four travellers at an inn, killing three and chasing the fourth; the fugitive hides behind a tree, to which she clamps herself and becomes immobile (Figure 18).[10] More usually, the *jiangshi* are male, and they show little sign of consciousness beyond basic blood-lust. Dr Hu's first assailant so closely recalls the undead Sámi shaman Grigori Riisä (p. 105) that a common motif-sequence seems likely.

By contrast, the 'woman-thing' that so horribly disturbed Dr Hu's sleep was a version of the fox-spirit or *huli jing*.[11] This is a much more complex being. She shape-shifts between the forms of a fox and a beautiful woman; she seeks out handsome young men to devour them sexually and suck out their vitality; but at times she melts into a softer and more human love for her victim. She is conscious, individual, and crafty, outwitting the young men (and sometimes even her fellow-vixens[12]) with her stratagems.

Prototypes and Chronology

There are obvious similarities between the wily, foxy females of India and China, the *yoginī* and the *huli jing*. Those between the *vetāla* and the *jiangshi* are less clear, and indeed when Buddhism came to China it was thought necessary to translate *vetāla* with a new word, *qishigui* (ghost that could raise a corpse).[13] What they have in common, though, is a

FIGURE 18: A tree-hugging vampire in China. This running corpse has chased her victim to a Buddhist monastery. He dodges behind a willow-tree, but she tries to grab him. When he falls to the ground, she clamps herself to the tree.

corpse hijacked by an entity different from its former occupant: in one case an external demon, in the other the non-rational part of its own life-force. This last idea goes back a long way in China: in a story from the fourth century BC, a learned man observes that in cases of violent death, the *po* and *hun* which everyone has at birth can hang around and become licentious demons.[14]

It is in India, on the other hand, that we first recognize the wily animal-woman. Stories from the Vedic period (c. 1500–500 BC) mention the creature called in Sanskrit *śālāvṛkī*, literally 'house(?)-wolf'.[15] Stephanie W. Jamison argues that the *śālāvṛkī* is the striped hyena, a formidable species of predator in which the female dominates. In Vedic myth, the warrior-god Indra takes the form of a female *śālāvṛkī* to circle the earth three times (probably a reference to the striped hyena's 'circular tour' while feeding), and feeds her cubs with *yatis* (itinerant male ascetics resembling later yogis). Semantic evidence makes it fairly clear that the shape-shifting and ravenous *yoginīs* were humanized adaptations from this prototype, demonstrating their ultimate origins in were-animals. The *yati* tradition, as David Gordon White shows, 'may have been the scriptural precedent for . . . the tantric yogi's self-sacrifice to the predatory shape-changing *ḍākinīs* and *yoginīs*'.[16]

What then of the Chinese fox-spirits? Charms against them date from 168 BC, but it looks as though their assimilation to lustful supernatural females happened under Indian influence, perhaps especially with the tentative percolation of Buddhism during the first to second centuries AD.[17] By the fifth century, Chinese Buddhist monks were being warned against 'fox-phantoms, some of them taking the form of brides, richly apparelled, who will stroke and caress the mediator's body and speak of things contrary to Law'; seventh- and eighth-century texts explicitly equate fox-spirits (including flying ones) with jackals and *ḍākinīs*.[18]

These equivalences were eventually reinforced by Tantric Buddhism, but must have pre-dated it. The chronology, however, is tight. A Chinese story in which a fox-spirit hijacks a woman's corpse to have sex with a traveller dates from c. 180; more remarkably, an apparent derivative set in the eastern Roman empire had been recorded in Greek by c. 130 (pp. 132, 136). We will see that in Europe and the Near East, the first century

AD was a transformative period for dangerous-dead beliefs. Was it so in China too?

The Siberian and Mongolian anthropology of the last chapter helps us to position the entities discussed in this one. When we remember that the *bong* is produced by one of several souls hanging around the corpse (or a stray soul entering it), and that it moves around with a life-force but not much cognition, we can infer prototypes for the *jiangshi* and possibly for the brighter *vetāla*. When we remember that it is usually female, and takes curious, shape-shifting forms, we can perhaps also glimpse where the *yoginī* and *huli jing* come from, notwithstanding their higher intelligence. When circumpolar shamans transition between human and animal forms, they are not stupid or lacking in resourcefulness.

Yoginī and *huli jing* were spirits, not dead women, even though they assumed forms solid enough to engage in sexual activity. A further stage remained, to be completed in one of two ways. The first was a collapsing of the categories discussed above, so that female animal-spirits hijacked corpses: here the corpses walk and talk, but not with their own personalities. The second was a cognitive merging—perhaps encouraged by the night-mare effect—in which predatory female spirits were identified as specific dead women: here the dead personality does occupy her own corpse. In both cases, the physical incorruption of the body is a necessary condition, whether it is seen to move around or to lie in the grave as a reservoir of sinister power.

These mechanisms will help to explain the more developed story-type to be discussed in Chapter 11, but they also have a more general relevance. Female demons and dangerous dead women are almost inextricably connected in many world cultures, displaying similar motivations and posing similar threats. Fundamental cognitive bridges, probably reinforced by the ubiquity of the night-mare experience, link the demons and the women across time and space. At this point, we widen our gaze to Mesoamerica, South-east Asia, and the Middle East.

10

Flying Demons and Dangerous Women

> [Your] forms will be like the forms of the dead. [You make yourselves visible in the shape of] father and mother, grandfather and grandmother, a lad and a lass, a pregnant woman and a child-bearing woman. . . . [in the shape of] winged animals of the earth and birds of the sky.
>
> —ARAMAIC INCANTATION AGAINST LILITHS

IN AZTEC MEXICO, dramatic statues glared at travellers from roadside shrines. They showed corpse-like demons with skull heads, big eyes, and claw-like hands outstretched (Figure 19). These were *cihuateteo*: women who had died in childbirth and who preyed on young children in their anguished resentment.[1]

Compare that with this modern account of the *churel* among leather-tanners in northern India:

> She is the ghost of a woman who has died while unclean, or while pregnant, or in child-birth; or . . . during the Dewali festival. She is described as having pendent breasts, large, projecting teeth, thick lips,

FIGURE 19: A resentful dead mother, now preying on living children: Aztec *cihuateotl,* fifteenth century AD.

> unkempt hair, and a black tongue, and as of dreadful appearance. Her feet, like those of most evil spirits, are turned around. . . . She is especially malignant towards her own family. To lay the ghost of a woman who has died as described above . . . the body is sometimes buried face downwards, and some fill the grave with thorns and heavy stones to keep down the ghost. Again, small round-headed nails are driven through the nails of the forefingers and the two thumbs, and the great-toes are welded together with iron rings.[2]

Or again, a British visitor to Malaysia observed in 1881:

> If a woman dies in child-birth, either before delivery, or after the birth of a child and before the forty days of uncleanness have expired, she is popularly supposed to become a *langsuyar,* a flying demon. . . . To prevent this, the following precautions are sometimes taken in Pêrak: a quantity of glass beads are put in the mouth of the corpse, a hen's egg is put under each arm-pit and needles are placed in the palms of the hands. It is believed that if this is done the dead woman cannot become a *langsuyar,* as she cannot open her mouth to shriek (*ugilai*), or wave her arms as wings, or open and shut her hands to assist her flight.[3]

With a characteristic fluidity of definition, these three examples drew on a heritage of beliefs about overlapping supernatural entities: the female demon who preys on the vulnerable; the living woman who crosses boundaries between the seen and unseen worlds, between the living and the dead, and between human and animal life; and the resentful dead woman or child, cut off in their prime and deprived of motherhood and life, who return to avenge themselves on the living. In the Malaysian case, the dangerous entity is also identified as bird-like.

To us, especially if our training is academic and analytical, the distinctions seem clear-cut; we might even become irritated with the fuzziness of ethnographic writers—or their informants—for leaving them fluid. That would be the wrong approach: the ambiguity of these boundaries is so recurrent across time and place as to suggest that it is rooted in human cognition. Of course, it is culturally modulated too: societies believing in demons have not necessarily had powerful female practitioners, and have not necessarily believed in restless corpses. This malleable belief-complex, expressed within a range of permutations, is central to the themes of this book.

Airborne Female Demons: Asia, Mesoamerica, and the Caribbean

The wing-flapping *langsuyar* of the Malaysian case illustrates one of the most basic types of all: not universal, but so widespread that it was surely in the minds of some of the earliest *homo sapiens* outside Africa. To conceive flying creatures as supernatural comes easily; since some flying creatures are dangerous, it is equally natural to conceive those as evil entities. The various species of vampire bats were established long before human evolution, and could have become a model for airborne demons once humans reached Central and South America. Equally, the fugitive, evanescent fluttering of birds, bats, or butterflies readily suggests the idea of human souls liberated after death.

Recovering some 'original' belief-system is impossible, but perhaps the Taino (who migrated from northern South America to the Bahamas and Antilles some 2,500 years ago) can point us towards an early one.

They conceived the dead as living happily by day in a hidden land, but coming out at night in various animal and human forms to eat guava fruit and seduce the living. In fact, it is tropical bats that hide in caves by day and emerge to eat guava by night. In Taino art, skull-like images referring to death fuse dramatically with images of bats and of those other night-flyers, the owls.[4]

Birds and bats fly; demons fly; the souls of the dead fly; at times they can all be dangerous or vicious. To those basic ideas must be added two others: that the vicious entities are female (or young); and that they are malevolent because they resent deprivation of sex, children, or life. We cannot possibly say where those concepts started, but we can say that they have existed widely in pre-modern human cultures around the globe. They also appear in the West African view that corpses of women who die pregnant or in childbirth are especially dangerous and polluting (p. 423).

This line of thought takes us back to the Indian *yoginīs*. There are strong cultural and philological linkages from earthbound foxes and jackals to fox-bats or flying foxes, and thence to bats, owls, and other noxious winged creatures. Indian fox-bats are huge flying mammals, noisy and dirty, appropriate to a conception of *yoginīs* as 'filthy birds of the night'.[5] To quote David Gordon White once again: 'Imagine you are a tantric yogi, hallucinating from sleep deprivation, as well perhaps from drugs and the consumption of blood and raw flesh. It is the dark of the moon and the dead of night. Suddenly loud animal cries appear from all around, from the air above as well as the earth below. The night is teeming with screeching *yoginīs* (which, when they are flying foxes, resemble birds when aloft and foxes when on the ground), so many "skin jackals" on the hunt for prey.'[6]

Modern South-east Asia provides a close variant on this theme. A rich body of folklore rings the changes on a range of characteristics: the entities are demons, or women who have died virgins or in childbirth, or living female 'witches'; they divide their bodies at the waist, so that the upper half can fly off leaving the lower half inert; the upper half flies with its entrails dangling, or takes the form of an owl or bat; and because of its resentful anger it preys on animals and people, especially babies. The Philippines and Malaysia have a remarkably varied vocabulary for beings in these forms (*aswang, langsuyar,* and *mannananggal* are merely the most common terms),[7] reflecting an intensity of beliefs approaching epidemic proportions. In Cambodia, Thailand, Vietnam, Japan, and Sri Lanka, the same motif-complex occurs in milder versions.[8]

Half-way around the world, the supernatural predators of Mesoamerica look like variants on the same theme.[9] Witches transform into owls;[10] the *tlaciques* divides at the waist like its South-east Asian counterparts, and there are monstrous female forms like the *cihuateteo.* Re-branded as a regenerative Aztec goddess, Coatlicue has the skull-like head, flaccid breasts, and raised claws of the vengeful-woman type, 're-claiming the bodies of the children to whom she had given the breath of life'.[11] Other variants occur in India, including the *churel* already mentioned.[12] In the Caribbean and West Africa, the *asema, jumbie, soucayant,* and *loogaroo* belong to the same family, modified by colonial intervention (the last term is *loup-garou,* French 'werewolf').[13]

Historical origins, and geographical ebbs and flows, are lost. But it cannot be a coincidence that supernatural predators around so much of the world's equatorial zone took this distinctive form in recent centuries. Once, this age-old belief-complex extended further north, where its trace-elements—scattered and submerged, but unmistakable—can be recognized by homing in on Europe and the Middle East.

Airborne Female Demons: Mesopotamia and Europe

In Poland and the Balkans, folklore preserves some of the basic motifs—resentful female revenants, or demons and unbaptized infants taking the form of vampiric birds or moths—in a range of combinations.[14] Except that division of the body into a flying upper and an inert lower half seems not to occur, these entities bear a strong resemblance to the South-East Asian ones. And in the Middle East and eastern Mediterranean, with their ancient literate cultures, a time-depth behind the late ethnographic evidence becomes visible at last. The demonic entities of cuneiform tablets and Graeco-Roman authors are well-known, but now we can see them afresh, in a wider field of vision where they look altogether less exceptional.

Documented in Mesopotamia from the second millennium BC are two female beings: the goddess Lamaštu and the demon Lilītu.[15] Lamaštu's father, the sky-god Anu, expelled her from heaven when she requested human babies for dinner. Thus demonized, she became a feared predator against infants, tricking mothers and midwives into letting her suckle them. Amulets portray her with an animal head, a woman's body with sagging breasts, and a bird's talons for feet—very similar, in fact, to the Indian *churel* and Aztec Coatlicue (Figure 21). The pattern for Lilītu—or rather for the plurality of *lilītus*—is a desolate girl who, having died an unfulfilled virgin, visits the living at night in a wind-borne guise to find sex and children.

These entities—abundantly documented in the charms and rituals against them—are formally different, but their traits overlap in their envious attacks on infants and parents. In the light of the folkloric material just surveyed, it seems pretty clear that they are personalized outgrowths from the same motif-complex, who must have diverged in prehistory just as they would converge again later. Lamaštu, and the male Pazuzu who is re-deployed as her adversary, are the only evil Mesopotamian demons regularly depicted. Whereas Lamaštu's iconography appears on both cheap and expensive amulets, cheap amulets against the amorphous Lilītu are especially abundant.[16]

An older Mesopotamian stratum is implied by a rare but consistent depiction of sexual activity, in which a squatting woman—seemingly suspended in the air—mounts a recumbent man (Figure 20).[17] There is one very early version, on a pot of c. 5000 BC, and then a small group of cylinder-seals from around 2000 BC. Both figures are headless in the earliest image, and the man probably so in one of the later ones. On two of the seals, a second man attacks the woman with a dagger. Interpretation is disputed, but where the participants lack heads their energetic sexual activity can scarcely be on a human plane. With her squatting posture, this woman is surely the night-mare in her sexualized form, whether or not we call her a *lilītu*.

Gallû, a male Mesopotamian demon, underwent a sex change when he was swept up, along with Lamaštu, into archaic Greek culture. That may have happened in the seventh century BC,[18] when we encounter

FIGURE 20: A Mesopotamian night-riding demon: three depictions.

'Gello' in Sappho's sinister and ironic reference to her as 'child-loving' (p. 157). The origins of 'Lamia' and 'Gello' are thus clear, but they tended to merge over time, and their later Greek counterpart, the *aōrē*, was not necessarily their direct descendant. As Sarah Iles Johnston writes, 'In analyzing the Greek *aōrē*, we should consider the possibility that some of her individual features may have been borrowed from elsewhere in the Mediterranean basin, but we must keep in mind, as we do so, that the recognition of such borrowings only becomes useful when we take the further step of explaining how or why they upheld or toppled *existing* Greek taxonomies and beliefs.'[19] That analysis chimes with the present approach: by insisting on a broad background, and by noting that demonic beings had to be 'adaptive' in the evolutionary sense.

A fourth entity, the *strix*, appears in Roman sources from c. 200 BC. Etymologically a screech-owl, she is identified as either a bird or a (living) old woman, who enters houses at night—probably in immaterial spirit form—to attack babies.[20] She shares with the Philippine *aswang*-type the unusual habit of extracting her victims' intestines, and may represent a tradition different from the Greek models.[21] As that again illustrates, only fragmentary genealogies are possible for demonic females in the ancient world. It happens that we know about Lamaštu, Lilītu, Gello, and the *strix*, but they are just four out of what may have been countless variants who have left no written trace.

More confidently, we can trace how their traditions were channelled into the post-Roman societies of the eastern Mediterranean and the Middle East.[22] The *lamia* as female demon retained a rather vaguely-defined afterlife into late antiquity and the Middle Ages, and semantic derivatives of the *strix* were among the main vampiric beings of eastern Europe (p. 15). The Iberian *bruja*—a night-presser and child-killer who could enter rooms through the tiniest cracks—is an obvious relative, even if the nature of the relationship is unclear.[23] Gello's descendants, the *gelloudes* of Byzantine and Ottoman Greece, remained powerful presences. However, they were not corpses but demons, or the living women whom demons possessed. Continuous through the Middle Ages and beyond, this tradition is summarized by a Byzantine writer in the 840s. He describes how, a century earlier, some women were hauled before a judge in Constantinople,

> accused of murdering suckling infants after having penetrated through the house fissures or closed doors and clandestinely killing the new born children. . . . It is indeed a myth related by the Greeks that a certain woman, Gello by name, after meeting an early death, is in the habit of visiting babies and new-born children in the guise of ghosts and plotting against their life. Deceived by the same evil spirit of the myth, those who give credit to such things attempt in some way to confer this abominable power upon women as though it were true and ascribe the cause of untimely death to these [women] who are transformed into spirits.[24]

In Greece this intense fear of *gelloudes* survived through the Ottoman conquest and long after.[25] In eleventh-century Europe, Burchard of Worms picked up this strand, condemning women who think they can go through closed doors, kill people, 'and cook and eat their flesh and in place of their hearts put straw or wood . . . and when they are eaten make them alive again'.[26]

Lilītu/Lilith, and her generic progeny the *liliths*, may have had the biggest long-term impact on ideas of the returning dead. There is rich evidence for their various incarnations in the Jewish world: in Talmudic literature and in the fascinating lay-produced texts inscribed on incantation bowls from late-antique Mesopotamia.[27] Still rather ambiguously perceived as unfulfilled dead women, but also demonic, they attacked children and 'married' themselves to men, who then needed letters of divorce.

Demons and Matriarchs

The physicality of the dangerous dead can be ambiguous. That applies especially to flying demonic beings with their elusive identities. Although the Taino dead were likened to bats or owls, they were tangible enough when in human form for the living to feel their bellies to check whether (being dead) they lacked navels.[28] The Malaysian and Philippine entities were conceived as actual dead women in some cases, but not in all.

A crucial link between airborne demons and sinister appearances of known humans—living or dead—must surely lie in the sleep-paralysis and night-mare complex. How did those monstrous beings, squatting on our chests as we lie powerless, first get there? Maybe through the air, passing through walls, doors, or cracks: that is the behaviour of a *lilith* or *strix*. But they are horribly, palpably solid, pressing down and threatening to smother, strangle, or extract sexual energy: whatever can do that must surely be a physical body. The cylinder-seal pictures suggest this link. It becomes explicit in Aramaic texts on sixth- and seventh-century incantation-bowls, like the one heading this chapter, which accuses *liliths* of appearing as various dead individuals: parents, grandparents, children, pregnant women, birds, and winged beasts. Another, written around a sketch of a bound and wildly struggling female (Figure 21), condemns the evil *lilith* who 'appears in a dream of the night and appears in a vision of the day. . . . As a nightmare-demon she falls [upon her victims], she kills boys and girls, [male] babies and [female] babies'.[29]

That re-visits a familiar ambiguity: corpses animated by their own personalities, or by external spiritual forces? Fuzziness for us may mean

FIGURE 21: Female demons through the ages. *Left*: The Assyrian demonic goddess Lamaštu, with her animal head and raptor talons, holding a comb and spindle, as shown on a late Bronze Age amulet. *Right*: A wild Lilith on an Aramaic incantation bowl, sixth century AD.

fuzziness in the past, but the potential to recognize a known individual—if people feared her enough—must always have been there.

The same applies to a different female prototype: rather than lacking children, she angrily dominates her extended family. In a modern Philippine story, the attacker in one sleep-paralysis episode takes the local form of an *aswang*, divided at the waist. But rather than an anonymous demon, or even an unfulfilled mother, she is a specific sinister matriarch, terrifyingly real to the victim:

> At about one o'clock, Aguas felt that somebody was staring at him. He opened his eyes and looked around. At the window he saw an old woman, the lower part of her body missing, staring at him, her greying hair standing up and with her lips open in a devilish grin. Her eyes were bloodshot and big. He was so frightened that he tried to scream but nothing came out of his mouth. He tried to wake his companion up but he could not move. He tried to close his eyes but couldn't. After a couple of minutes, the *aswang* flew away. . . . At breakfast he was about to tell the owner of the house what happened but he was astonished at the portrait he saw . . . of the landlord's [dead] mother,

> [who] looked exactly like the *aswang* he had seen. The landlord . . . told him it was his mother and not to worry about her because she wouldn't disturb them any longer.[30]

In this variant, a mature woman, presumably overbearing in life, continues to exert her oppressive power after death. It recalls the template of the controlling matriarchs—lethal when thwarted—in the Wallachian example (p. 39). An odd Christianised version is one incarnation of the popular ascetic saint Paraskevi ('Saint Friday'), a fierce enforcer of the Friday fast in Orthodox rural Greece: 'Seen always as an old woman dressed in black, sometimes with two teeth "one above and one below", she appears in dreams and strikes fear into the hearts of the disobedient. Thus housewives who, for whatever reason, have kept on working on a Friday evening, or may have forgotten to light the icon lamp, tend to have dreams of waking up with a suffocating sensation, or of having had some visitation by a black-clothed woman whose very presence is a reproof.'[31]

The themes of this chapter are almost uncontrollably elusive: the kaleidoscope gyrated for millennia, and its movements usually escape us. One motif, however, always turns up: the demonic or dead female who is predatory, deadly, and sexually needy. She lurks there in the background, ready to shape fears of the restless dead when other pressures aggravate them. But her identity is moulded by context: resentful virgins and would-be mothers are emphasized in some cultures, overbearing matriarchs or numinous magic-workers in others. Or, as the next chapter shows, imaginative re-workings of the theme can cast her as a tragic anti-heroine.

11

The 'Carmilla Template' in China and the Eastern Roman Empire

> Machates pretended that nothing was wrong, since he wished to investigate the whole incredible matter, to find out if the girl he was consorting with, who took care to come to him at the same hour, was actually dead. As she ate and drank with him, he simply could not believe what the others had told him.
>
> —STORY OF PHILINNION

THE STORY of an unsuspecting young man visited amorously by a deadly (but not wholly unloving) dead woman appears in both China and the eastern Roman Empire during the early centuries AD. However it was diffused, its origins apparently lie in Asian conceptions rather than European ones, and the extent to which it influenced actual European beliefs remains unclear. Centuries later, though, it was to have a major impact on Romantic vampire fiction.

FIGURE 22: Carmilla on the prowl: wood engraving by C. M. Jenkin after a drawing by D. H. Friston, from the first publication of Le Fanu's story.

Dead Women Who Love the Living and Destroy Them

We saw how Indian *yoginīs* and Chinese *huli jing* shape-shifted between carnivorous mammal (hyena and fox respectively) and female human. Perhaps they were demonic in origin, but the conceptual sleight-of-hand that assimilated airborne demons to dead women was at work here too. Most of the beings discussed in this chapter are dead humans, but they betray traces of their hyena, fox, and demon ancestors. They are predatory yet transformational; they bring love and death; their lovers are their victims; and they are female.

In 1876, the Irish novelist Sheridan Le Fanu published his novella *Carmilla*. Its anti-heroine—the second best-known fictional vampire—has been thoroughly eclipsed in popular fame by the first. Yet whereas Count Dracula bears little resemblance to any monster in whom real people have believed, the undead Carmilla recreates a genuine tradition at the point when it crystallized into a template.

Befriended by the unsuspecting Laura, Carmilla pursues a relationship that is both romantic and lethal, picking up the emotional charge of the ancient stories in her agonized, predatory love:

> 'Think me not cruel because I obey the irresistible law of my strength and weakness; if your dear heart is wounded, my wild heart bleeds with yours. In the rapture of my enormous humiliation I live in your warm life, and you shall die—die, sweetly die—into mine. I cannot help it; as I draw near to you, you, in your turn, will draw near to others, and learn the rapture of that cruelty, which yet is love; so, for a while, seek to know no more of me and mine, but trust me with all your loving spirit.'[1]

If Le Fanu is melodramatically Victorian (and departs from the models by making Carmilla lesbian), he gives a first-person voice to beings who are normally portrayed from the outside as threatening monsters, yet who are conscious personalities capable of love and pain as well as desire. Acknowledging Le Fanu's feat of imaginative recreation and his sensitivity to the psychological undertones, I shall call this the 'Carmilla template'.

Predatory Dead Females in China

In China, around the first or second century AD, the fox-woman shapeshifter becomes the protagonist in a recurrent narrative. A traveller stops for the night at a wayside inn, has sex with the lonely female innkeeper, but wakes to find that he is lying on a tomb.[2] Elaborations develop during the late second to fourth centuries. A story of c. AD 180 tells of the haunted Ximen Inn in Ruyang County, where lodgers come to bad ends. One day an official called Zheng Qi approaches it, and a good-looking woman asks him for a ride. After some hesitation, he agrees; they enter the inn and (despite a servant's warning) go upstairs. Zheng Qi sleeps with the woman, but gets up very early and leaves before daybreak. When the servant comes to clean the room, he finds a dead woman. She is traced to a family several miles away, from which a female corpse has mysteriously vanished. Zheng Qi sickens and dies, but another visitor to the inn catches and kills the spirit, who turns out to be an old fox.[3]

In this version the corpse is just a vehicle, hijacked by a fox-spirit who happens to find it at the right time. But the *Anecdotes about Spirits and Immortals* of the court scholar Gan Bao, compiled around AD 350, includes a story that introduces the mature template, with the dead woman acting in her own personality.

> Zhong You, of Yingchuan Prefecture . . . , was absent from court meetings for months. Meanwhile, he kept behaving strangely and entertained odd ideas. When someone asked him the reason, he said, 'A woman often comes to me, and she is extraordinarily beautiful.' The man talking with him said, 'She must be a ghost. You should kill her.' When the woman came again, she stopped outside Zhong You's door instead of going straight to him. Zhong You asked, 'Why do you not come in?' The woman answered, 'You intend to kill me.' Zhong You said, 'I have no such intention.' He invited her again and again, until she came in. In spite of his reluctance and regret, Zhong You struck at her with a knife, which cut her thigh. She ran out of the house at once, and, as she ran, she kept wiping the blood with a piece of new silk wadding. The next day, Zhong You sent men to search for her by following the drops of blood. In this way, they came to a big grave. In the coffin was the corpse of a beautiful woman, like that of a living person. She was clothed in a white silk blouse and a red embroidered waistcoat. There was a cut on her left thigh, and silk wadding had been torn out of the waistcoat for wiping the blood away.[4]

Another variant is recorded in the tenth century. A beautiful woman appears to the prefect of the Xinfan district. He is charmed by her and keeps her with him for some months, but one morning she makes a sad farewell, saying that she must go because her husband is coming. She leaves him a silver wine cup to remember her by, and he gives her ten pieces of silk. Soon afterwards the military commander, whose wife has died and been coffined, visits the prefect. Seeing the silver cup, he is astonished: 'This is from my wife's coffin—I can't understand how it gets here'. The prefect tells him the whole story. The angry commander goes to his wife's coffin and opens it, sees her lying with the pieces of silk in her arms, and burns her.[5]

For the tradition's progression through later centuries, we turn inevitably to the huge 1780s compilations by Yuan Mei and Ji Yun, where the developed 'Carmilla template' turns up among the more numerous and prototypical stories of amorous fox-spirits.[6] Two of Yuan Mei's stories, veering between pathos and bawdy comedy, illustrate both its resilience and its flexibility.

The first concerns an intelligent, good-looking young man called Zhang in Zhili (now Hebei Province). As he studies in his parents' house, a beautiful woman appears at the window. He calls to her, and shortly afterwards she walks into his chamber. She says, 'I live to the west of your house', and they become lovers. This goes on for a year, and Zhang becomes more and more emaciated. The father becomes suspicious and decides to investigate. He goes to the chamber, hears a woman's voice, and breaks in; only Zhang is there, but under the pillow is a gold hairpin. Zhang's father beats him, and brings in a Daoist exorcist. That night the woman comes again, but in tears: 'Our secret is out so I must say goodbye', she says. She promises to meet him in Huazhou twenty years on, and disappears. Twenty years later, he is taken to Huazhou to meet a new bride, whom he recognizes as his old lover. She tells him that she is just twenty, and he thinks: 'That fox fairy must have been deeply in love with me. She's been reincarnated as my new wife.'[7]

In the second of Yuan Mei's stories, the protagonist is a young servant of the Yongzhou magistrate. One evening he notices a bright light glowing under the eaves, which proves to be a firefly. That night, as he lies in bed, he finds the firefly crawling on his penis. It turns into a woman, who stimulates him to have sex. The same thing happens the next night, and she tells him: 'My father used to be a magistrate here, so this magistry was my old home. Unfortunately, when I was only eighteen I fell in love. But the romance turned sour and I pined away and died. Pear blossoms were my favourite flower, so I asked my mother to bury me beneath the pear tree just outside. When I saw you, so young and virile, I couldn't resist.' Realising that he has been sleeping with a corpse, the boy throws a pillow at her and runs out screaming. His relatives advise him to rub himself with cinnabar (and to put his trousers on). The next day they investigate the base of the pear tree, find a coffin containing the preserved body of a beautiful young woman, and burn it.[8]

The stories concentrate in east-central China (the old heartland of the Han dynasty), and could reflect a nucleus of deep-rooted beliefs in the active dead comparable to the Scandinavian and Balkan ones. The later versions demonstrate the continued adaptation (and vitality) of the inherited motif-sequence. In all cases, the narrative is stereotyped in its first half (young man visited sexually by female fox-spirit or dead woman), but then becomes free to diversify, working towards a range of possible outcomes. The same applies to the Roman-era stories to which we now turn.

Corinth: Apollonios and the Lamia

In Europe, the 'Carmilla template' is represented by two well-known stories from the eastern Roman Empire. One is an adventure of the philosopher Apollonios of Tyana, supposedly set in the first century AD but recorded in the 220s.[9] A handsome young man called Menippos is walking along a road near Corinth when a 'spectre' (*phasma*) approaches him in the form of a rich and beautiful woman, who invites him to her house with promises of song, wine, and love. Menippos is enthralled, and begins a regular sexual relationship with her. Despite Apollonios's warnings ('it is a snake that warms you, because your woman is not marriageable') he resolves to marry her, and invites Apollonios to the party. Eying up her finery, he observes: 'This excellent bride is one of the *empousai,* though most people think they are the same as *lamiai* and *mormolukeia*. These female beings fall in love, and they crave for sex, but most of all for human flesh, and they use sex to ensnare the men upon whom they wish to feed.' She insults him and tries to throw him out, but all the gold, silver, wine, and servants vanish into thin air. 'The *phasma* pretended to weep, begging him not to interrogate it or force it to confess its true nature. But Apollonios insisted relentlessly until it confessed that it was an *empousa,* fattening Menippos with pleasures in order to feed on his body, since it was its custom to devour beautiful young bodies because their blood was fresh.'

Phasma normally means a ghost, but this one was physical enough to pursue a sexual relationship. Defining her as one of the *empousai, lamiai,* and '*mormo*-wolves'—not clearly distinct from each other—looks back to the depiction of these same three dangerous females by Aristophanes:[10] Greek categories have been imposed on the story-line. Yet here, as in some of the Chinese stories, we can pick up hints of human feeling: not simply vengeful and envious, the *lamia* knows love and pain while still enslaved to the destructive urges of her nature.

Thrace: Machates and Philinnion

The other Graeco-Roman narrative is of higher literary quality and takes a different turn. Referring to a distant and essentially fictional past, it existed by the early second century (and so, in purely textual terms, is the earliest known evidence for the mature template). The moving story of Philinnion is not a myth or folk-legend but a work of fiction—indeed, the first novella with a tragic undead heroine.[11]

A young man called Machates comes to the Greek city of Amphipolis (western Thrace), and stays in the guestroom of a couple whose newly-married daughter, Philinnion, has died six months earlier. One evening, an amorous girl visits and sleeps with him. They exchange love-tokens—a gold ring from her, an iron ring and gilded wine-cup from him—and she leaves before dawn.

On the second night she returns, and through a crack in the door a nurse spies the pair. She tells the parents how the girl resembles their dead daughter, and in the morning they confront Machates: 'The youth was anxious and confused at first, but hesitantly revealed that the girl's name was Philinnion. He told how her visits began, how great her desire for him was, and that she said she came to him without her parents' knowledge. Wishing to make the matter credible he opened his coffer and took out the items the girl had left behind—the golden ring he had obtained from her and the breast-band she had left the night before.'

The parents recognize the items, and on the third night they burst in and greet their daughter. But she responds sadly: 'Mother and father, how unfairly you have grudged my being with the guest for three days in my father's house, since I have caused no one any pain. For this reason, on account of your meddling, you shall grieve all over again, and I shall return to the place appointed to me. For it was not without divine will that I came here.' Thereupon she falls dead. The civic authorities take over: they open Philinnion's tomb, and find her corpse missing from its bier. Accordingly, they burn her body outside the city limits, and 'perform an apotropaic sacrifice to Hermes Chthonios and the Eumenides'. Machates sinks into depression and kills himself.

This story embodies two layers of inherited narrative. One is the template of the Chinese stories, where the animated corpse seems reassuringly human to her lover, and where the dire fate of the victim is expressed in Machates's eventual suicide.[12] The other is a universal folktale sequence in which infernal powers agree to release a dead person but insist rigidly on their terms of the bargain: the intrusions of the nurse and parents violate those terms, and necessitate sacrifice as a rite of closure.[13] But Philinnion herself seems different again. An emotional human being, she presents her own point of view in her own voice. She is desolate in a first life unfulfilled (she had died at the point of marriage), needy for stable love, and ready to enter the commitment implied by the exchange of tokens. And, as she says, she has 'caused no one any pain'.

Or has she? Do we suspect that she could be a *lamia* after all, secretly draining Machates's life-blood? There is a powerful tension here in the ambiguity between devoted lover and deadly parasite. It helps to explain the modern impact of these stories, inspiring as they did the classic female vampires of Romantic and later literature: Goethe's Bride of Corinth, Coleridge's Geraldine, Keats's Lamia, Le Fanu's Carmilla, Stoker's Lucy. Thus the vampiric *femme fatale* was born.

Diffusions: The Direction of Travel

These stories present a difficult problem of origins and transmission. Going purely on the surviving texts, the mature motif-sequence is recorded earlier in the Roman world than in China. Nonetheless, there are persuasive grounds for inferring a Chinese origin.

Female predatory shape-shifters are deeply embedded in Asian folklore, and the various motifs from which the 'Carmilla' sequence was constructed are documented in China by the third to fourth centuries AD. Gan Bao collected several other stories of men becoming the lovers of women who turn out to be dead or divine; of dead people found alive in their coffins long after burial; and of items removed from coffins or found inside them, implying physical movements between the coffin and the world of the living.[14] (It is striking that a precious wine-cup appears in both the Xinfan story and the Philinnion one.) Only the Zhong You story continues with the sequence in which the amorous woman is traced and unmasked as a physical corpse, but it draws on the same pool as the others. In Roman collections, by contrast, the first halves of the Apollonios and Philinnion stories stand ready-formed and without context, with no hint that their constituent elements had any European background.

A lost first-century Chinese prototype thus seems the most economical hypothesis. This suggestion is less outlandish than it might initially seem, given the overland and maritime commercial routes traditionally called the 'Silk Roads'. That is a contested concept: certainly the Mediterranean's contacts with China are more elusive than those with India, and most of them may have happened indirectly via Indian sea-ports.[15] All that matters here, however, is the existence of *some* economic and cultural interchange between Han China and imperial Rome around AD 100, and for that the evidence is solid. The Begram Hoard (Kushan Empire, now Afghanistan) included lacquered woodwork of Han origin, alongside Indian-style ivory carvings and glassware and bronzes from Roman Egypt and Syria.[16] Conversely, the Han-era tombs at Hepu (Guangxi, west of Hong Kong) contained a pot from the Parthian Empire and glass bowls and beads from the Mediterranean.[17] Where such objects could travel, so could a story.

If the 'Carmilla template' did indeed make its tortuous journey from China to Thrace, it could have picked up stray influences along the way: perhaps from the Mesopotamian and Levantine flying demons and their Greek descendants, as in the *lamia* story. Indeed, it was to be reworked in a medieval Jewish version where Lilith becomes a celestial *agent provocateur*:

> She adorns herself with many ornaments like a despicable harlot, and takes up her position at the crossroads to seduce the sons of man. When a fool approaches her, she grabs him, kisses him, and pours him wine of dregs of viper's gall. . . . That fool goes astray after her and drinks from the cup of wine and commits with her fornications and strays after her. What does she thereupon do? She leaves him asleep on the couch, flies up to heaven, denounces him, takes her leave, and descends. That fool awakens and deems he can make sport with her as before, but she removes her ornaments and turns into a menacing figure.[18]

In the Roman world, prostitutes often doubled as sorceresses.[19] The link between supernatural power and sexual enticement would have been intuitively familiar in the early centuries AD.

Just Male Fantasies?

Readers may well be thinking that there is a large dose of male fantasy and anxiety in all this. One scholar observes that 'in traditional Chinese fiction, where even the vernacular stories were written virtually all by males, the female more often than not appears only as a creature of fantasy—both affectionate and threatening, both desired and feared. The biases of culture and gender could not be more apparent.'[20] Is the 'Carmilla template' simply a genre of fiction, in which men fantasized about 'amorous female ghosts who could ignore social etiquette and offer their unabashed love to a man for no particular reason'?[21]

The fact that these entities were deadly as well as erotic undermines that view, since it embeds them in the ancient belief-complex that produced the *dākinī*, *yoginīs*, and *huli jing* discussed in Chapter 9. So do some modern derivatives, like the belief in Gujarat that a 'ghostly *Dakan* lives with a man as his wife, brings him dainties, and turns the refuse of food into flesh and bones. The man gradually becomes emaciated and ultimately dies. It is believed that generally a *Dakan* kills a man within six months.'[22] That hardly sounds like an enticing male fantasy, though it does embody anxiety and perhaps misogyny.

FIGURE 23: Taiwanese spirit brides, photographed by the anthropologist David K. Jordan in 1966–68. Living men required to marry dead girls in the form of these dolls are sometimes less than enthusiastic.

Taiwanese 'spirit marriages' preserve another variant. Girls who have died young appear in dreams or divinations, and ask to be married to bridegrooms of their choice. To avert vengeance, the men—not always delighted—go through marriage ceremonies with dolls made of paper and cloth (Figure 23). As one of them observed: 'If you are going to marry a spirit, how do you know it is the right spirit? If it is the wrong one, then later on things become even more troublesome, so the reason for inviting the host god of my village [Yang Fuu Tayshy] on the wedding day was to make sure it was the right spirit; and the divination instrument of Yang Fuu Tayshy led the bride's taxi. Since the wedding with the spirit, the family has been very peaceful, and nothing unfortunate has happened.'[23]

In one sense, these are stories of female agency and empowerment. Are we picking up male anxieties about autonomous and empowered women, rather than about uninhibited and available ones? And might those reflect social realities? Taoism embodied a tradition of female religious specialists, analogous to the female shamans of Mongolia or West Africa introduced in the next chapter.[24] During the third to sixth centuries AD, China saw a significant loosening of gender restrictions. The moralist Ge Hong complained that women were free to go out as they wished, socialize at celebrations and religious events, visit friends and relatives, sing and drink, go home late, and stay out overnight.[25] Earlier, in the Hellenistic world, there had been a slow but steady increase in the legal and familial autonomy of (at least upper-class) women, some of whom were highly educated and significant patrons, and had growing influence in the public domain. And again, male philosophers had railed at this destabilizing trend.[26] Perhaps, if the 'Carmilla template' percolated westwards in the late- to post-Hellenistic era, it took root in fertile ground.

———

This template—at least unmodified—dropped out of mainstream narratives in post-Roman Europe. Instead, the offending female corpses were often those of magic-workers and eventually witches. If anxiety was a driving force, it shifted away from the sexual to focus on the magical, even though the subjects were still mainly female.

It would be absurd to deny that the sources discussed in this and the previous two chapters speak overwhelmingly with male voices, and sometimes with misogynistic ones. That does not negate the fact that they speak to female power, which is the theme that we will now pursue. Some women could escape gender constraints—even in very patriarchal societies—by carving out roles for themselves as ritual practitioners. Autonomous and charismatic, they were correspondingly (in male perception) daunting. The dangerous dead of the medieval West were mirrors reflecting real and powerful women.

12

Wonder-Working Women

THE POWER AND THE DANGER

They were loud, yes, loud when they rode over the [burial-]mound; they were fierce when they rode across the land. Shield yourself now, you can survive the strife. *Out, little spear, if there is one here within.* It stood under/ behind . . . a shield, where those mighty women marshalled their powers, and ?they sent shrieking spears.

—THE OLD ENGLISH CHARM 'WIÐ FÆRSTICE'

IN A 1931 PHOTOGRAPH, the Daur Mongol shaman Huangge stands resplendent in her outfit with jangling metal ornaments, holding her drum and beater. But the best shamans keep up with the times: in the background stands the thoroughly modern car in which she travels to tend the sick (Figure 24). There could be no better icon of the female ritual specialist in her prime: revered, independent, and preserving tradition adaptively through social change.

In Europe, women like Huangge had long since been eclipsed and rebranded ignominiously as 'witches', but they once existed there too. Feared for their daunting powers (and perhaps targets of male anxieties

FIGURE 24: The shaman Huangge sets out from her tent. She will travel—in the car parked behind—to tend to the sick in Hailar city, northeastern Inner Mongolia. Photograph by Ethel John Lindgren, 1931.

and resentments), they were prominent among the dead who would not stay down.

Powerful Women: Shamans, Ritual Specialists—and Night-Mares

In the spiritual systems of many cultures, women have been important as shamans, diviners, and prophetesses.[1] The status of being 'possessed' is ambiguous, and easy to misrepresent as passive: the woman is entered and occupied by unearthly powers for which she is just a mouthpiece.[2] Yet prophecy has often been ritualized, most famously at the Greek oracle sites of Delphi, Didyma and Claros, where the prophetesses were awe-inspiring figures whose enigmatic words carried huge weight.[3] A range of historical junctures—often at points of social upheaval—have briefly opened up a dynamic role to female charismatics, but patriarchy has usually reasserted itself in the end.[4] In ancient Mesopotamia, female deities—and the women who served them—both declined between the third and first millennia BC: consecrated wise-women (*qadištus* and *nadītus*) were reduced to the marginalized status of 'witches', despite retaining an important role in childbirth rituals.[5] We will meet that pattern again.

During the first millennium AD, many—perhaps a majority—of northern European seers, augurs, and magical practitioners were female. That is indicated by comments of Caesar, Tacitus, and other Roman writers, by Roman inscriptions, and by later Old Norse sources.[6] A rich vocabulary in Old English and related languages described female supernatural entities, at some stage assimilated to living women (p. 187). That again suggests frontier-crossing, by practitioners moving between the seen and unseen worlds. Its legacy is the tradition of wise, capable, and prescient women that runs through later Old English literature.[7] Likewise, burials from sixth- and seventh-century Francia and England show that certain females—including infants—wore special ritual costumes and equipment (Figure 25).

It need not follow that early medieval wise-women were religious leaders in an institutional sense. Perhaps more likely, they enjoyed a distinctive status based on their numinous power (ascribed early in life or even from birth), set apart from whatever male hierarchies existed.[8] Arguably, that is implied by its Christian-era outcome: the seventh-century boom in rich nunneries in northern Francia and England, ruled and occupied with remarkable autonomy by female members of royal and princely dynasties (p. 195). These nuns could not be bishops or priests, but they could be almost as free and wealthy. But only ladies in the elite Christian nexus could re-invent themselves like that. Their humbler counterparts were increasingly marginalized: as 'cunning-folk',

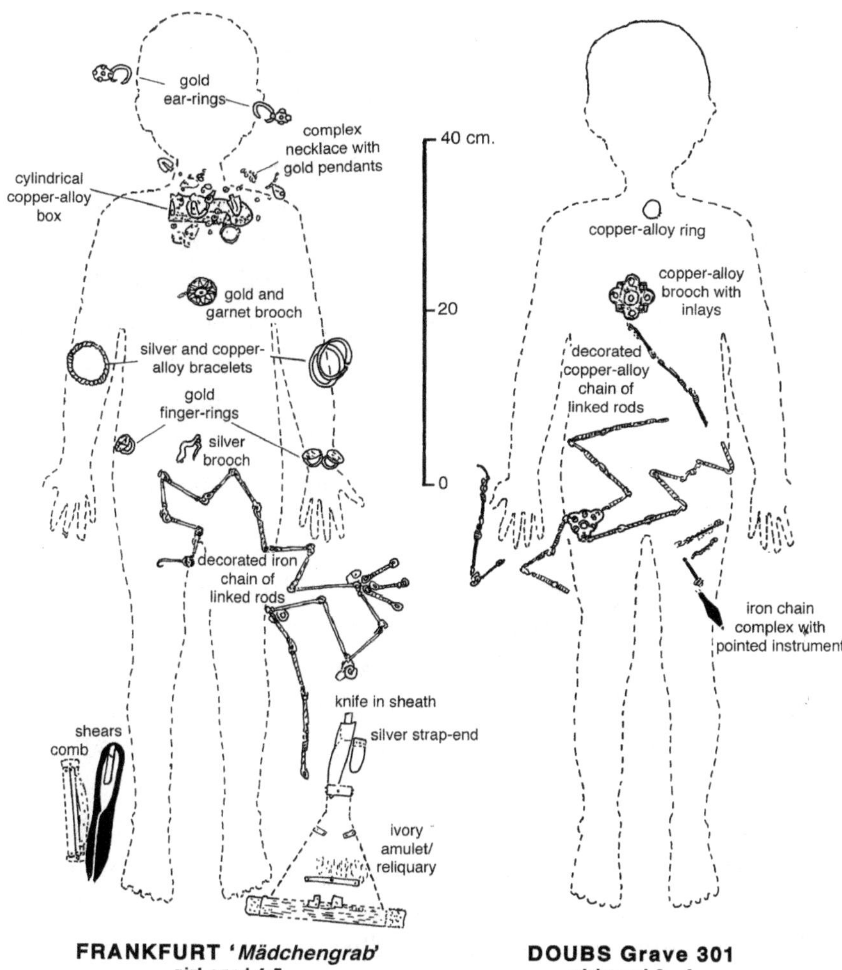

FIGURE 25: Seventh-century Frankish burials of young girls loaded with jangling chains and other ritual equipment. They illustrate that in this society, as in some others, numinous power could be ascribed to exceptional females from an early stage in life.

as organisers of death-rituals, and—because of their medical skills—as midwives.

The charismatic wise-women of the ancient world and early medieval Europe can only be glimpsed in a broken and distorted mirror, and they are beyond the range of anthropology. But modern analogies may offer some pointers. The first takes us back to the Sora of the eastern Indian coast, where shamans of the top rank—'funeral shamans', who communicate with the dead—are always female. An anthropologist writes:

> Women start to become shamans at a very early age, usually around seven or eight years old. In the dreams of the future shaman, *rauda sonums* [personalities of dead shamans] come and escort her down to the Underworld. The path is terrifying, as little girls have told me, but the *sonums* are kind and reassuring. At first these dreams come only occasionally, but later they are repeated every night and come to lose their fearsome quality. Around puberty the girl marries [in the Underworld] a *sonum* who is the son in the Underworld of a living shaman known to her. . . . It is this marriage and consecration which will give her the ability to enter trance.

These women sometimes also have 'this-world' marriages, which tend to be abnormal or unstable: 'if she is in the more intense funeral tradition her husband usually finds it unbearable to share her with a dream-husband of elevated status'. It is a profession not easily combined with family life, so funeral shamans tend to stand outside normal social structures.[9]

The second analogy comes from the Edo people in Benin (Nigeria), where the deity Olokun is conceived as a great chief who commands pathways between the unborn, the living, and the dead. Women in general worship him, but some are specially selected to be his devotees: because they have distinctive physical features from birth, or because they have suffered dissociative misfortunes, illnesses, or altered states of consciousness. After initiation, these women start practising as mediators with Olokun, and the more successful ones build a reputation (Figure 26):

> With this recognition comes economic success, and priestesses begin to acquire considerable amounts of money, which they commonly invest in real estate. . . . When a new ontological status as ritual specialist also includes economic success, this combination can be translated into two major (and ultimately related) achievements: individual

FIGURE 26: The priestess Eduzemegie Eweka in a state of possession, Benin City, West Africa. She diagnoses social and medical problems and relays the demands of the god Olokun to his devotees. Photographed by the anthropologist Paula Girschik.

autonomy and high social status. . . . In the traditional Edo family structure, women are subordinate to men . . . But when Olokun priestesses begin to earn significant sums of money they tend to move out of their husbands' compounds and set up their own residence. . . . The movement away from her husband's domination is expressed in the idiom of divine demands; that is, the priestess claims that Olokun has

> demanded that she live apart from her husband. . . . With economic success and personal autonomy, the priestess moves beyond the level of commoner and propels herself into the elite. . . . Within her circle of devotees, the priestess functions like a Benin chief.[10]

Three characteristics of these special Sora and Edo women seem likely to have applied equally to their earlier counterparts in Europe: status as mediators with the unseen world who are born, not made (though their skills must be trained and indeed 'marketed'); economic success and high social status; and emancipation from what is otherwise a norm of male dominance. For the first, we need only consider those sixth- to seventh-century graves in the Rhineland and England where girls as young as four were buried with the full panoply of amulets, relic-boxes, and clanking metal chains worn by adult wise-women (Figures 25, 34, and 39–40). As for the second and third aspects, the trajectory through professionalized skills to wealth and autonomy parallels the high status of wise-women in Germanic areas up to the sixth century, followed after conversion by investment in plutocratic nunneries (like the Benin 'real estate'?) in the seventh.

That women of this kind might be thought dangerous after death is clear in England at least, where female corpses—one of them well-equipped with amulets—were chosen for posthumous killing (Chapter 17). But there is also a linguistic clue: the fact that in early medieval Germanic languages, night-mare entities were gendered female. The root word—Old High German and Old Norse *mara,* Old English *mære*—is invariably a feminine noun, describing a female supernatural being that pressed down on its victims at night, occasionally as a sexual predator.[11] Yet this differs from modern clinical experience, where night-mare victims tend to identify their attackers as of the opposite gender.[12] Cultural conditioning—reflecting the charisma of certain special women—was evidently at work here. Given the known cases of night-mare attackers recognized as dead individuals, it is a fair inference that the *mara/ mære* was in many cases experienced as a specific (perhaps powerful or threatening) dead woman. For victims, the belief that such women were walking around in the flesh was scarcely unreasonable.

'Electric Girls' and Adolescent Power

As a demographic group, females between the ages of about twelve and twenty-two keep turning up in this book. An obvious reason is that they include two prime categories of the dangerously resentful dead: girls who die before marriage, and mothers who lose their babies or die in childbirth. But did that, on its own, make these individuals so powerful and threatening that they were feared after death? Probing deeper can uncover another dynamic: the psychological, physiological, and physical phenomena associated with adolescent and young-adult women.

We can start with the work of the neurologist Suzanne O'Sullivan, who has studied outbreaks of mysterious psychosomatic ('functional') illnesses across the globe. Common to these episodes is that the subjects have suffered some kind of fear, hopelessness, or traumatic constraint, to which they react subconsciously in extreme ways: 'mass psychogenic illness tends to happen in contained communities under strain'.[13] O'Sullivan's cases are very largely concerned with young women, and while rightly scathing about patronizing and patriarchal concepts of female 'hysteria', she does observe that at least two-thirds of people with functional neurological disorders are women:[14] 'Truthfully, nobody really knows why young women are more likely to be affected by these disorders. There are many factors, but I am convinced that their voiceless position in society is one of them. . . . There may also be something in young women's physiology that makes them more vulnerable to functional disorders . . . The frequent bodily changes that come with cyclical hormones might create more abundant white noise, which young women have to learn how to decipher.'[15]

Equally, O'Sullivan sees the outbreaks as social phenomena arising from group interaction: 'In a sense, they were mass hysteria events that evolved into functional disorders, but not necessarily *psychogenic* functional disorders. These are sociogenic phenomena. The explanation for each event lies in the society in which the outbreak occurred, not inside the girls' heads.'[16] This perspective converges with my own for corpse-killing epidemics: human constants are there, but special kinds of social and cultural stress are necessary to activate them.

It also adds a dimension to early modern witchcraft. Most accused witches, of course, were women, but what matters here is that in cases of possession through the agency of a witch, just over 80 percent of *victims* in England were female, as were 86 percent of those in New England (p. 394).[17] 'Victimhood' could empower powerless girls, giving them second-sight, visionary capacities, and a voice. Some witch-possessed children and young adults—especially unloved or repressed ones—relished the attention, concern, and freedom from social restraints, like two Lancashire children in the 1590s who delighted in 'filthie and unsavoury speeches'. As one historian puts it, 'the possessed were appropriating language and behaviour in ways that were intensely personal and liberating'.[18]

The link between adolescent girls and poltergeists is a variant of the same dynamic. To take a classic case in 1960, the pubescent, eleven-year-old Virginia Campbell was sent from Ireland to stay with her brother's family at Sauchie (Clackmannanshire, Scotland) in stressful domestic conditions. The parish minister reported hearing loud knockings and watching a chest move around. The knockings intensified when Virginia's niece joined her in bed (which she resented), but stopped when she went into trances or fell asleep.[19] At Bouvigny (Orne, France) in 1846, the celebrated 'electric girl' Angélique Cottin—aged fourteen, of low intelligence, and about to make her first communion—caused furniture to fly around, and a basketful of dry beans jumped up and danced when she raised her hand (Figure 27).[20]

Much remains unclear about such happenings. Researchers with no taste for the paranormal, noting that agents in poltergeist cases are often in a poor medical condition, invoke psychological tensions, epilepsy, or 'recurrent paroxysmal events in the central nervous system'.[21] Known cases span seventeen countries in three continents; 79 percent of agents reported during 1612–1899 were females (with an average age of fourteen), whereas the genders were equally balanced during 1900–74.[22] That change surely moved in step with female emancipation: it reinforces the idea that in some way these poltergeist episodes—like O'Sullivan's functional disorders and the witch possessions—reflect subconscious rebellion or self-assertion by the disempowered. To observers, they looked like magic.

FIGURE 27: The 'electric girl': Angélique Cottin of Bouvigny (Orne), 1846. As she stretches out her hands, a basketful of beans jump up and dance around.

The Monstrous Regiment: How Many Restless Corpses Were Female?

We can now restore a lost dimension to past narratives of the dangerous female dead. Since the effects described in the last section have been so widespread for at least four centuries, it is hard to see why they should have been any less so in the remoter past: when we ask why women in their teens could have been perceived as powerful, sinister magic-workers, we need look no further. If the implication is that they lost their powers when they grew older, evidence from Anglo-Saxon grave-goods may support that (p. 187). But what if they died first—suffering the fate of the unfulfilled virgin or the bitter *gello*—when still at the height of their powers? Imprisoned in such unquiet corpses, their undiffused supernatural energies would be daunting.

How many of the dangerous dead have, in fact, been women is surprisingly hard to define. In seventh-century England, nearly *all* corpses chosen for countermeasures were apparently female, whereas by the eleventh century they were nearly all male (Chapters 17 and 21). Again, the abundant cases from early modern central Europe show a clear though not overwhelming preponderance towards females,[23] but with considerable local variation. For instance, dangerous corpses were largely male in Moravia/Silesia during 1590–1660, and on the south Habsburg borderland during 1700–30, but two-thirds female in Moravia/ Silesia during 1660–1760.[24]

In patriarchal societies, it will often be men whose public functions and activities catch the spotlight when they become troublesome after death; conversely, the tendency to identify women as witches may create the opposite bias. In the rare epidemics for which we have detailed evidence, the *initiating* cases often seem to have been female even when many subsequent ones were male, as with Miliza at Medvedia (Serbia) in 1731, or Dorothea Pihsin and Anna Tonnerin at Cavnic (Transylvania) in 1752.[25] The long-term decline in female supernatural power may help to explain the shift over time from an exclusive to a moderate female bias in Europe.

If it was not always women who became vampires, women still had a crucial role in defining them. Just as midwives—bringing children into this world—remained the antithesis of envious Gello, it was also an abiding female role to conduct mortals out of this world. By orchestrating that anxious passage across the threshold of death, women had an opportunity and a responsibility to prevent return traffic. An eleventh-century writer in the Rhineland condemned such women for staking dead mothers and infants (p. 235), but their numinous power was too important socially to be suppressed. Reflecting on Balkan society during c. 1700–1900, an anthropologist has written:

> The task of women, generally speaking, was to prepare dead persons for the coffin by washing and clothing them. In so doing, they were always expected to examine the entire body of the deceased in order to look out for signs that might announce his or her fateful transformation into a vampire. . . . Mourning the dead was one of the duties of the women of the village. They burst out into spontaneous and emotional laments, . . . [which] served as a means of direct and final communication with the dead and with the world he or she was now entering. . . . *Mediation with the dead*—this was the main function of women, and as such, they had their place not only in burial rites, but also in popular vampire belief.[26]

PART III

From the Ancient Middle East to the Early Medieval North

THESE CHAPTERS BEGIN *a historical tour, starting around 1200 BC and culminating with the spectacular eruptions of corpse-killing in eighteenth-century Europe and nineteenth-century North America. What that tour will* **not** *be is a continuous or comprehensive survey, which is impossible: it is a patchwork, full of holes that sometimes extend over centuries and are bigger than the patches of firm data. Rather, it tries to trace the episodic surfacing of phenomena that conform too closely to those already described, and to each other, for likely coincidence, and to identify cultural links that might explain how they were transmitted.*

13

Mesopotamia, Greece, and Rome before Christ

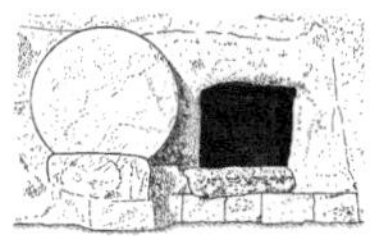

'Fonder of children than Gello' is a saying applied [by Sappho] to women who die prematurely, or to those who are fond of children but ruin them by their upbringing. For Gello was a maiden, and because she died prematurely, the people of Lesbos say that her ghost haunts little children, and they also blame her for the deaths of those who die prematurely.

—ZENOBIOS, COMMENTING ON A LOST POEM BY SAPPHO

THE TOUR STARTS with the ancient societies of the Fertile Crescent: Sumerian, Babylonian, and Assyrian. Because clay tablets inscribed in cuneiform writing survive to be excavated, we have an exceptionally early body of literature that casts an intense (if narrow) beam of light on several aspects of these cultures, including ritual and belief.[1] Among those are the earliest known references to the restless dead.

Mesopotamia: The Neo-Assyrian Restless Dead?

This was a world in which people had a close, constantly renewed relationship with the world of spirits and demons. Everyday lives were regulated by rituals of extraordinary complexity, defined and interpreted by learned professionals. The literature includes incantations, invocations, and omens in huge abundance, engaging with an array of supernatural beings. These unseen but intensely felt presences included the dead. Irving Finkel writes: 'Ghosts were taken entirely for granted as part of human life within the surrounding world. On top of that, Mesopotamian ghosts were, I think, to a considerable extent tolerated and even treated with sympathy, for many ghosts were literally familiar, and ghostly encounters did not necessarily add up to much. The grievance and resentment that characterised the worst kind of ghost, however, could easily develop into outright malice and the need for vengeance with unpleasant consequences for the victim.'[2]

The texts' concern with protection from malevolent forces may overemphasise the unhappiness and hostility of the dead. It has been argued that in the second millennium BC, the *kipsum* ritual, with offerings made at the grave on a monthly or semi-monthly cycle after burial, was a means of keeping deceased relatives close within the family circle, buttressing a sense of community between the living and the dead.[3] That would make this society look like more recent ones in which the dead retained a capacity for positive or negative interaction, much as living people do: good ritual practice is like good social practice, keeping the community in harmony. In any case, the boundary between the seen and unseen worlds was thin, and those on the other side of it were powerful and constant presences.

That does not mean that they necessarily moved among the living in physical form. Normally, the returning dead appear as insubstantial ghosts (*eṭemmū*), and before the late second millennium BC there is no unambiguous suggestion that they were anything else. A possible exception is a group of dream omens from the Old Babylonian period (c. 1900–1600 BC), predicting legal consequences when a dreamer's dead father, 'after he has been buried, lives and is killed [again] and for a second time they anoint and bury [him]', or alternatively 'comes up from the grave, is stuck until his middle, but passes through [eventually]'.[4] These describe dreams rather than waking life, and may envisage the miraculous or surreal, but at least they show that a dead man leaving his grave was an available cognitive motif.

With the collapse of the great Late Bronze Age states and the subsequent rise of the Neo-Assyrian Empire, hints at the beliefs explored in this book start to become clearer. By the reign of Ashurbanipal (669–631 BC), whose library preserved so much of what we now know, Assyria had become the biggest empire the world had ever seen. It rose from ruins left by political chaos, and it was not built peacefully. Warfare was bloody, plunder and retribution horrific, and defeated peoples could suffer mass deportation.[5] That was nothing new—the whole ancient world was violent—but it could have created a trauma of instability and anxiety that, like other traumas described in this book, found an outlet in concrete visualizations of the noxious dead.

The first straw in the wind is an adaptation of the old Sumerian poem *The Descent of Inana*, which describes how that goddess passed the seven gates of the Underworld to visit her sister, the Queen of the Dead. An Akkadian version, which apparently existed by about 1200 BC (because it seems to be quoted in the *Gilgameš Epic*), is heavily shortened but adds one new passage: Inana/ Ištar threatens that if she is shut out, she will smash the gate and 'bring up the dead to consume the living, and the dead will outnumber the living'.[6] Aggressive dead people bursting from the Underworld sound more physical than *eṭemmū*: this adaptation hints that a conception of walking corpses was starting to emerge well before the time of Ashurbanipal.

With that possibility in the background, the documented history of the restless dead starts in the city of Nimrud and the tomb of Queen Yabâ, whose husband died in 727 BC. Placed in a wall-niche was an alabaster tablet inscribed with a formidable curse against any violator of the tomb, ending with the hope that powers of the Underworld will 'impose eternal not-sleeping on his corpse and ghost' (Figure 28).[7] Lack of context restricts our understanding, but it seems a fair assumption that a not-sleeping corpse is a restless one.

Luckily, this text is not completely isolated. The encyclopaedic omen series known as 'Šumma Alu' ('If a City'), built up over several centuries but standardized on a series of tablets around the mid-seventh century BC, catalogues omens taken from events in people's everyday lives. Many refer to spirits or ghosts, but one group (Tablet XXI, 1–18) lists

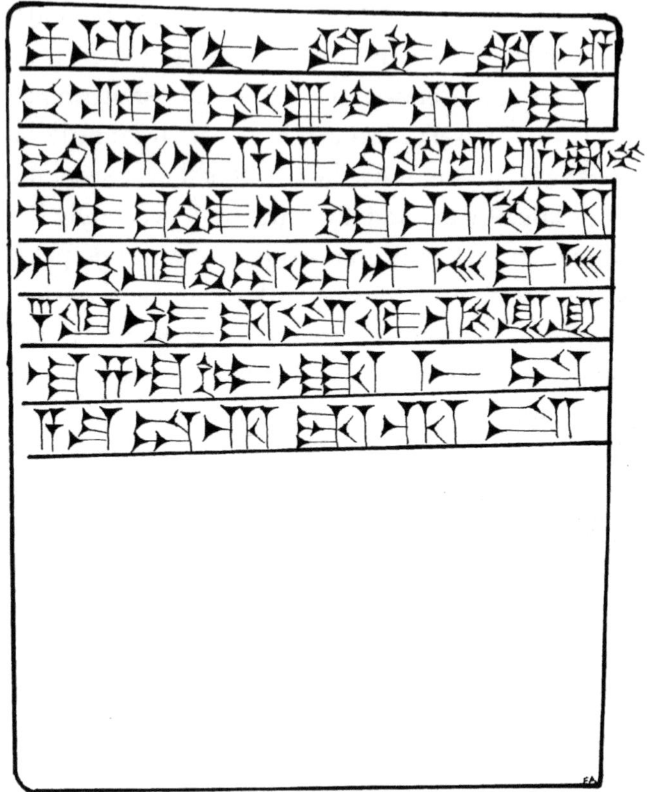

FIGURE 28: The world's oldest written reference to the concept of a restless corpse? Inscription in the tomb of Queen Yâba at Nimrud (now Iraq), eighth century BC.

the various things that will happen if one sees a 'dead person' or 'corpse'.[8] The text is fragmentary, but includes appearances of 'a dead person wearing a garment', 'a dead person wearing a dirty garment', and—especially intriguingly—'a dead person blocked [i.e., constrained and/or gagged?] with cloths, uprising, complaining'. Even more explicitly, one clause describes the outcome 'if a corpse in the grave comes back to life with people nearby'.

As with Yabâ's inscription, it is hard to know how to understand these isolated references, but there is no obvious objection to taking them at face value: they describe appearances of 'dead people', in contrast to the demons and spirits mentioned in other clauses.[9] The word translated as 'garment' in the first two cases is specific to clothing. In the third, however, the word for 'cloths' (*lubāru*) is a general one that can mean any piece of cloth or rag, and 'blocked' (*ku-ru-uk*)—applied elsewhere to waterways and, in one case, to a gag in a magic figurine's mouth—indicates obstruction.[10] This dead person was either bound to prevent movement, or gagged to prevent biting or talking—or perhaps both. 'Uprising' and 'complaining', is he/she angrily struggling to escape this imprisonment? To invoke the later shroud-chewing revenants is tempting; even if that goes a step too far, the text does suggest a burial-rite in which the corpse was bound or gagged with a view to preventing such activities.

Many centuries would pass before the next known literary appearance of revenants. Nonetheless, it does seem that the Neo-Assyrians believed in the walking dead, even if we cannot know whether this was an isolated phase or the start of a long tradition. Tablets show that some of these texts were still being copied in the last centuries BC in southern Iraq.

The cuneiform texts only concern the elite and literate, but the everyday milieu of the omens implies that these beliefs extended beyond palace walls. Just possibly, some very strange burials excavated in the urban sites at Dūr-Katlimmu and Ziyaret Tepe, spanning the ninth to sixth centuries BC, offer another clue.[11] These are on-site cremations, performed (surely with horrible effects) in built-up zones including house courtyards. If that makes them extraordinary, they are still more so given the entrenched Assyrian aversion to cremation as a mainstream practice. Burning was applied to images of supernatural enemies, as in one exorcism ritual: 'As these figurines dissolve, melt, and drip ever away. / So may my warlock and witch dissolve, melt and drip ever away'.[12] Enkidu, asked by Gilgameš whether he saw 'the man who burned to death' in the Underworld, replies: 'I did not see him. His ghost is not there, / His smoke went up to the skies'.[13] While there remains ambiguity about whether funerary cremation had the same annihilating effect, its connotations were highly negative.[14]

There must have been something special about these people; the burning of their remains suggests that it was something negative.[15] Yet they had full sets of grave-goods and food offerings, which imply a future in the next world. A possible solution is that they were first buried normally, but then burnt—still lying in their graves—because they were perceived to be causing trouble. Were these the 'dead people' of the omens, who would have walked among the living without such countermeasures? It may—subject to future work—prove significant that the one group of these cremations for which anatomical data are available shows a strong bias towards women and children.[16] The gender and age bias would then point to anxieties about women, and the untimely dead, that are not made explicit in the texts, but would be consistent both with fear of Lilītu and with the general psychological pattern.

Ancient Greece

In broad terms, there is no question that Mesopotamian cultures influenced archaic Greek ones.[17] Those influences may have been especially strong in the seventh century BC (as it happens, the time when 'If a City' reached its final form), and included the re-moulding of Lamaštu and Lilītu into their Graeco-Roman identities. There was scope, then, for Neo-Assyrian ideas about the restless dead to influence Greek belief.

Did that happen? Sarah Iles Johnston concludes that before c. 700 BC, the returning dead are conspicuous by their absence in any shape or form. By the fifth century, that had changed: 'Greek beliefs evolved from a system in which the dead were relatively weak and unlikely to affect the world of the living, except under very special circumstances and then of their own volition, into a system in which the dead were an active force in the world of the living and could be called into action when the living chose.' It seems very likely that the opening-up of Greece to cultural influences from Mesopotamia and Egypt explains that change.[18] This is one illustration of a recurrent process whereby Middle Eastern religious and magical ideas moved westwards through the Aegean and Mediterranean, eventually to reach the western provinces of the Roman Empire. The 'Carmilla template' illustrates that such influences could come from as far as China.

In Classical and Hellenistic Greece, insistence on correct performance of funeral rituals suggest the obsessive anxiety, seen in so many other cultures, that the dead should have a peaceful passage and nothing to resent.[19] That was not achievable for those who died unfulfilled, unsatisfied, or unavenged: the *ataphoi* (lacking proper burials), the *aōroi* (dying prematurely or untimely), and the *biaiothanatoi* (dying by violence).[20] These were daunting, potentially dangerous entities, who had to be negotiated with and appeased, and they were now visualized in a more concrete way as individuals with their own aims and resentments.[21] Curse tablets placed in graves suggest that the agency of the dead was important for making the curse effective, and the graves of *aōroi*, who had died prematurely, were especially targeted.[22] That said, these Greek dead rarely seem very physical—their complex interactions with the living are essentially mental and psychological—and to that extent they resemble the dead of ancient Egypt.[23]

This was not, then, a society in which corpses walked regularly, but it does look like one where corpses *might* occasionally walk when activated by special stresses and anxieties. Are there any signs of that? One possibility is the practice of *maschalismos* ('armpitting'), which involved the cutting off of the feet, hands, nose, and other extremities of a dead enemy and hanging them under the armpits. This was a shaming ritual, but its purpose does also seem to have been to disable and disempower the potentially vengeful subject.[24] Whether the anticipated attack would have been physical or ghostly, the pre-emptive measure was physical enough.

More important for the future were what Johnston calls the 'childless mothers and blighted virgins': the demonic Lilītu/Gello types assimilated to actual human women who died untimely. This motif, with its Assyrian ancestry, is prominent in Classical and later Greek sources. Sappho's cryptic comment on Gello's lethal 'fondness' for children indicates its presence by c. 600 BC; two centuries later, Aristophanes and other writers presented Empousa, Lamia, and Mormo as unhappy souls who revenged themselves upon the living.[25] Johnston makes the important psychological point that these entities had a scapegoat role, enabling displacement of anger and resentment from neighbours and relatives. Ascribing envy-driven malevolence to the living is socially disruptive; far better to ascribe it to the dead. The *aōrē* performed this function all the better because 'she began as a real, living woman, fully normal except insofar as she was childless'.[26]

Early Rome

During its aggressive expansion in the second and first centuries BC, Rome clashed violently with the Hellenistic world but also embraced much of its culture. Whether or not Greek ideas about the restless dead were already common to the eastern Mediterranean region, they were absorbed as Rome moved towards great-power status.

Unsurprisingly for a ceremony-conscious society, we find plenty of references to appropriate closure rituals or the lack of them. Vergil famously described the unburied dead crowding longingly on the bank of the Styx, unable to cross to the Underworld; Horace pictured a stranded, threatening corpse that demands burial.[27] The Eleusinian Mysteries adopted the figure of the *empousa* as a restless spirit.[28] From a relatively early date, heads of Roman families appeased the household's *lemures*—its untimely dead, including infants buried on the premises—with the nocturnal rituals of the Lemuria.[29]

All this suggests inherited perceptions of which dead people might prove restless, and of how to keep them quiet. But as in archaic Greece, so in Republican Rome, there is a resounding lack of evidence for walking corpses of any kind. That would soon change.

So far as the fragments go, the ancient Near East and the Mediterranean were not regions where concerns about walking corpses reached epidemic levels over long stretches of time. There are persuasive though isolated clues from twelfth- to seventh-century Assyria, and then some suggestive background noise—but nothing more solid than that—in the Mediterranean during the later centuries BC.

Perhaps we should expect no more: most of our sources are not of a kind to record popular beliefs. If this belief-complex did indeed show itself in the form of spasmodic, epidemic-like eruptions, with longer intervening phases of low-level anxiety and passive folkloric transmission, most of what happened will almost certainly have escaped us.

There is therefore nothing implausible about linking the Neo-Assyrian references to texts from centuries later. If there was a long quiescent phase, hints started to appear during the first century AD that the dead were on the move again, in the Eastern Roman Empire and perhaps also in Asia. Meanwhile, people were becoming aware of a new, charismatic religion with a crucified leader who got up and walked out from his tomb.

14

The Later Roman World and Christianity

> For I handed on to you . . . : that Christ died for our sins . . . , and that he was buried, and that he was raised on the third day . . . , and that he appeared to Cephas [Peter], then to the twelve. Then he appeared to more than five hundred brothers and sisters at one time . . .
>
> —I CORINTHIANS 15:3–16

CHINA AND THE HELLENISTIC world both have good written sources for the later centuries BC, but the dangerous dead rarely figure in them. Does it reflect some more general sea-change that the 'Carmilla template' appeared, around AD 100, in both these widely separated zones? At just this time, stories were being told around the eastern Mediterranean about the restless dead as physical earthly bodies, able to rise from their graves and walk around as they had done in life. Among them, spread by Christians, were stories about the most memorable resurrected body of all.

This was a period when new religious and philosophical ideas were circulating at extraordinary speed and range, often percolating from the Near East into the Eastern and then Western Empires. It was also an age of intensely vivid and powerful mental images, when literary narratives, including saints' lives, portrayed the monstrous, the diabolical, and the ghostly.[1] In the Western Empire, the move during the second and third centuries from cremation to inhumation—itself a Near Eastern influence—was surely another powerful factor. No longer converted by the pyre into a radically different substance, the corpse in its grave was a more ambiguous entity, its inertness not quite so obvious.

Was there, in fact, a pan-Eurasian epidemic of anxieties about the dangerous dead? The sources are inadequate to support such a conclusion, but it is not impossible. Perhaps religious change, provoking destabilization and a spiritual identity crisis, did cause the dead to be visualized in more lurid and concrete forms. If so, the evidence is tantalizingly indirect, and it does not help that most of what survives is literary rather than folkloric, and is sometimes satirical. A good case can be made for a submerged body of folk-belief, but it has to be read between the lines of the sophisticated writers who parodied it.

Empty Tombs

Returning to Philinnion, we should pause on the episode (absent from all the Chinese parallels) that finally proves her undead state: 'When we opened the chamber into which all deceased members of the family were placed, we saw bodies lying on biers, or bones in the case of those who had died long ago, but on the bier onto which Philinnion had been placed we found only the iron ring that belonged to the guest and the gilded wine cup, objects that she had obtained from Machates on the first day.'[2] Here the stark revelation that a corpse is not in the tomb, and must therefore be walking outside it, makes its first appearance in a secular story of the undead. But there is, of course, one very obvious parallel:

> They found the stone rolled away from the tomb, but when they went in, they did not find the body. While they were perplexed about this, suddenly two men in dazzling clothes stood beside them. . . . The men said to them, 'Why do you look for the living among the dead? He is not here, but has risen!' . . . Returning from

> the tomb, they told all this to the eleven and to all the rest. . . . Peter got up and ran to the tomb; stooping and looking in, he saw the linen cloths by themselves.[3]

Jews and Greeks who heard the Resurrection story would have recalled heroic or meritorious individuals being carried up to heaven by God or the gods: assumption or apotheosis, not resuscitation.[4] That is also the explanation that first occurs when, in a novel by Chariton of Aphrodisias, a grieving husband visits his newly-dead wife's tomb and finds it empty: 'When [Chaereas] arrived, he found the stones moved away and the entrance [of the tomb] open, and seeing this, he was dumfounded. A report of the mystery came quickly to the residents of Syracuse, who all ran together to the tomb: . . . amazingly, the dead girl [Callirhoe] was not lying there!'[5]

The resemblance of this to the gospel narratives is striking. Callirhoe, however, is not a walking corpse (she has simply revived and been abducted by tomb-robbers), whereas Jesus and Phillinion get up and leave their tombs after genuinely dying. They also—like revenants of later centuries—combine an unambiguous physicality with a capacity to pass through barriers. That parallel would have horrified the first Christians (some of whom found the bodily Resurrection problematic in itself), but it is plausible that the genre starts with Jesus. Philinnion's story existed by c. AD 120 and Callirhoe's by c. AD 200, so it is entirely possible that both authors heard a version of the gospel narrative, and combined it with material of a drastically different kind to enliven their fictions.

Animated Corpses in Later Antiquity

As this illustrates, walking-dead beliefs in the eastern Mediterranean could have been affected by contacts with the increasingly prominent followers of the risen Christ. Christians knew that Elisha had revived a dead child, that Jesus had raised Lazarus and Jairus's daughter, and that Paul—more recently—had revived a young man killed by falling from a window.[6] Tertullian (c. AD 155–220), the first great Latin theologian, could cite these scriptural marvels and contrast them with the vaporous phantoms raised by pagan magic: because they were tangible, physical bodies, they were both genuine and holy.[7] In fact, though, the Eastern Mediterranean around this time had stories of equally physical pagan corpses, that revived briefly in order to prophesy, give messages or perform some task.[8]

Whether pagan or Christian, these episodes are set apart by their *public* character: corpses are either revived by charismatic holy men or revive themselves in the presence of observers. As spectacles, they resemble the marvellous and monstrous prodigies beloved by writers of the time. That makes them rather different from corpses that get up and leave their tombs through some mysterious and hidden process, as Philinnion and her Chinese analogues (or indeed Jesus) had done. They still matter here, because they show that the idea of animated corpses was not just dismissed as ludicrous; indeed, the scriptural cases made that reaction impossible for later Christian clergy, however sophisticated. To that extent, they portray a world in which Philinnion could seem a reality.

Other stray fragments are suggestive, if not quite conclusive. We might make something of one of Apuleius's picaresque short stories (c. AD 150–180) where a witch summons up a dead woman 'yellow like boxwood and foully emaciated', her 'unkempt hair partially grey and caked in the ashes that had been scattered over it'. She has the capacity to pull someone into a room and kill him, but her status as a physical corpse remains ambiguous.[9] The same could be said of a dead woman in a tongue-in-cheek story by the Syrian satirist Lucian (c. AD 125–180+): returning to complain that one of her golden sandals was left off her pyre, she sits down on a couch next to her grieving husband, who embraces her.[10]

A late Roman legal exercise—of the comical kind that sets up an impossible lawsuit for forensic debate—is much more explicit, though again it poses the challenge of inferring real beliefs from satire. A wife sues her husband for imprisoning their dead son in his tomb because he comes out and visits her: 'She was not confronted in the night by a face covered in dismal cinders or a head sprinkled with ash, but her son came to her in his former shape, a young man of beautiful mien. Nor was he content just to be seen and watched, but, if you put any faith in the needs of the poor woman who was the only one to see him, he embraced her, kissed her, and lived the whole night.' But the husband employs a magician, who binds the son: 'he has not just been shut in with words (for perhaps he could have got past those), but bonds of iron and tight knots have escorted him back to death.' When the spell is laid, 'for the first time the son becomes a corpse and shade'. He is constrained with chains and bars, 'and now his poor mother thinks about those iron points that have gone down into his body and his limbs'.[11]

This text is fascinating: in its explicit physicality; in recalling Philinnion (the son appears as in life and displays human affections); and in describing countermeasures—incantations, ligatures, stabbing with iron—that were applied to unquiet corpses in other times and places. The context is crazy, but these details accord so closely with known practices that they must surely draw on a contemporary reservoir of stories or folk-belief.

The poets and novelists of the eighteenth- and nineteenth-century Romantic era who wrote about vampires did not believe in them; Graeco-Roman authors and their sophisticated readers may have been similarly sceptical. Yet the new appearance of such stories in the first to third centuries cannot have happened in a vacuum, any more than it did in eighteenth-century Europe: these texts surely did respond to genuine beliefs and anxieties that the corpses of some dead people walked from their graves. In a feed-back loop between literate and oral culture, the emergence of genres that drew on—or even parodied—such fears may in turn have modified them, cycling more coherent narratives back into popular belief.

Nailing Down the Dead: Corpse-Killing in the Late Roman Empire

In the legal exercise, the mother laments the sharp iron points (*mucrones*) stabbed into her son's corpse.[12] Archaeology shows precisely that ritual, used extensively across much of the Roman Empire after AD 300 (Map 2). While caution is needed (nails as grave items do not necessarily imply corpse-killing), the hammering of nails into a corpse's head or limbs is scarcely ambiguous.

Skulls pierced by one or more nails—their contexts often unclear—have been found on late Roman sites in the Rhine and Moselle valleys

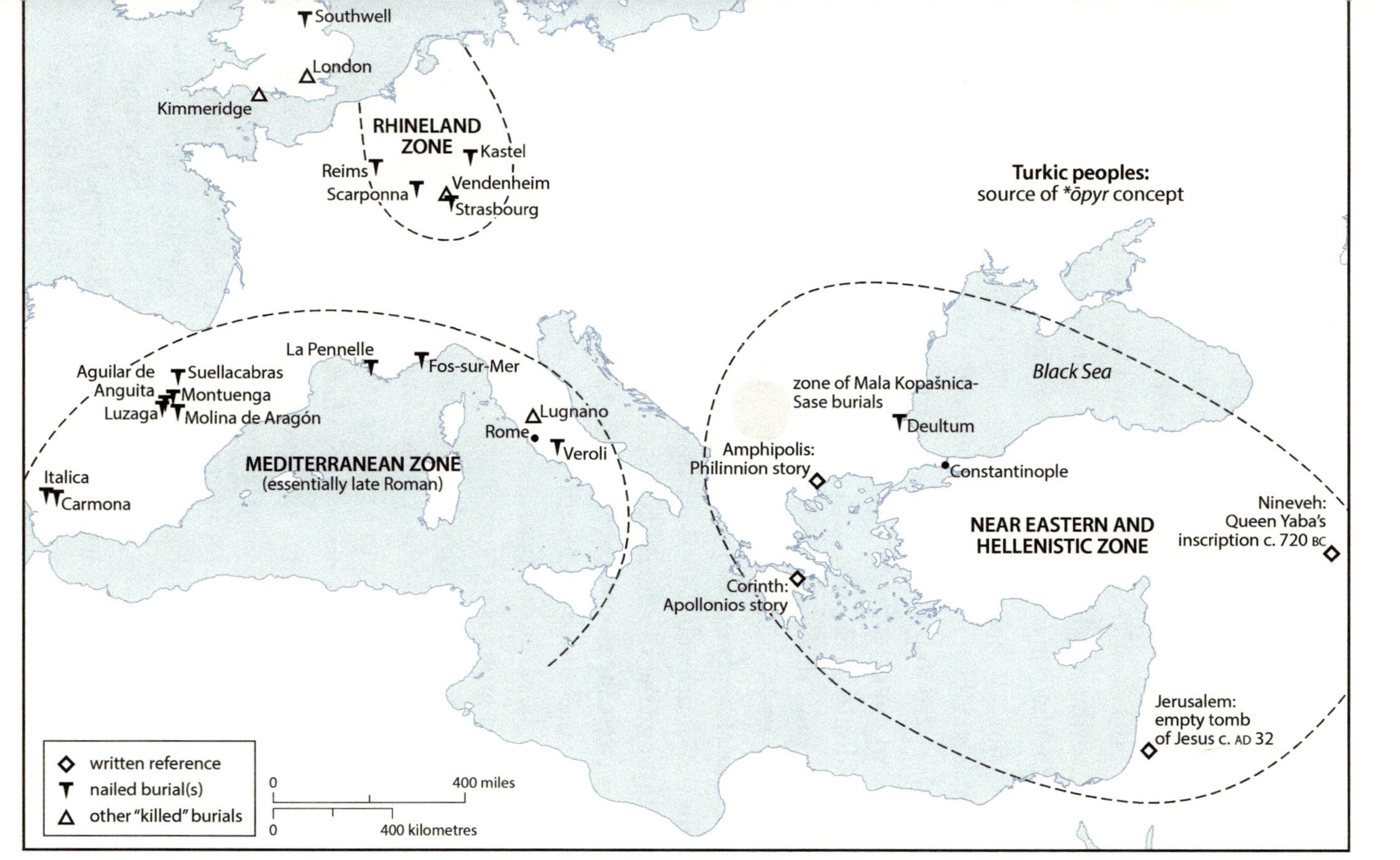

MAP 2: Dangerous-corpse beliefs in Europe and the Near East up to c. AD 500. Three distinct zones are suggested: (1) the Hellenistic world, perhaps influenced by both Mesopotamia and the Caucasus; (2) the late Roman Mediterranean world, where the beliefs would soon largely die out; and (3) the Rhineland, representing the southern fringe of the North Sea and Scandinavian belief-zone that lies outside this map.

and on the Italian coast.[13] Others are known from old finds at Sassari and Caligari on Sardinia.[14] Perhaps more useful are the cases where in-situ skeletons are found with nails driven not just into the skulls, but through limbs or feet. Examples from Gaul are at Rheims in the north and Fos and La Pennelle on the Gallic Mediterranean coast.[15] These can be dated between the late fourth and sixth centuries, at the interface between Roman and Visigothic control. In a third-century cemetery at Bologna (northern Italy), one burial had a single nail in the top of the skull; another had three nails in the skull and four in the right shoulder, arm, and hand.[16] In Iberia, a concentrated group of five cemeteries with nailed burials in the north-east (Aragón), with two outliers in the south-west, were dated to the immediately post-Roman to early Visigothic period.[17] An important implication of these cases is that post-Roman invaders adopted a Roman nailing practice, which—remarkably—would revive in Aragón centuries later (p. 282).

Late- or post-Roman Britain provides just one example of the same genre: a burial overlying second-century demolition features in the villa complex at Southwell (Nottinghamshire) had rivet-like iron studs driven through the shoulders, ankles, and heart.[18] This raises practical questions (were the rivets closed in position by a smith?), and the burial is otherwise undated, but a fourth- to sixth-century range seems plausible in the light of the other cases.

One further group is important for its location and for what it may foreshadow. Debelt (Roman Deultum), on the Black Sea coast of Bulgaria, has produced six very thoroughly 'killed' burials. The skull of one adult male had been pierced twice by a pointed tool. Five more adult males lay nearby: in each case, a large nail had been hammered into the back of the skull; nails had been driven into the right and left temples and the shoulders; the palms had been nailed to the pelvic bone; other nails pieced the leg-bones; and the feet were set apart with a small stone between them.[19]

These burials should probably be placed in the later Roman period, perhaps the fourth century. Although currently isolated, they might have a background context in the 'Mala Kopašnica-Sase' type burials of the nearby Roman province of Moesia Superior (Serbia). In this rite, the ashes of a cremated body were placed in a pit already burned with a

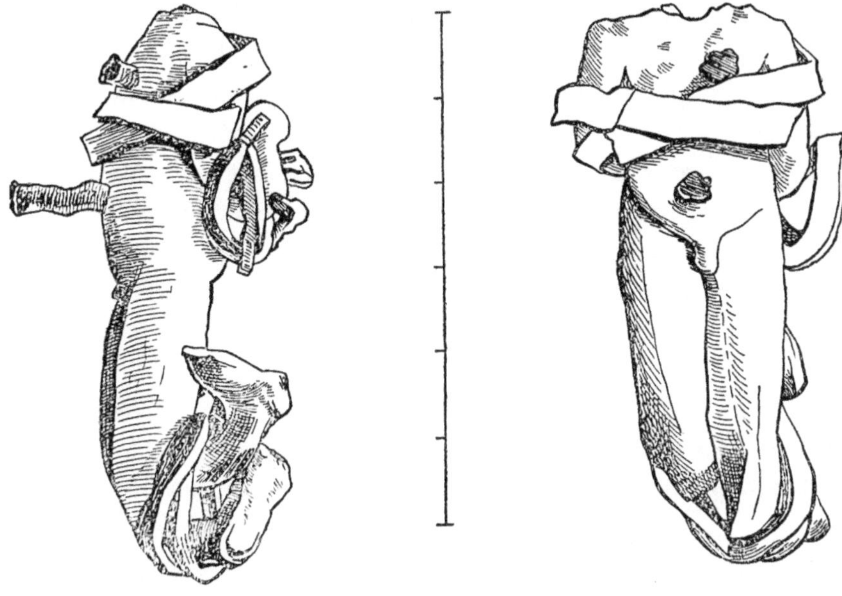

FIGURE 29: 'Killed' lead figurine from Attica, probably third century BC. The mutilation of this figure—beheading, binding, bending-back of the legs, staking through the belly, piercing of the heart—prefigures the 'killing' of so many actual human corpses in later centuries. The scale is in centimetres.

separate fire; they were often mixed with nails, not easily interpreted as structural.[20] While hard to decode, some purification or closure ritual was evidently involved.

Where did the idea of nailing come from? Although most known cases are in the Western Empire, an eastern origin seems likely. In the Greek world, images were 'killed' by transfixion as far back as the third century BC (Figure 29),[21] and the placing of nails in Greek and Graeco-Roman cremations was probably apotropaic.[22] As Christianity triumphed, and other eastern belief-systems spread into regions of the Western Empire that had quite recently abandoned cremation, it would be unsurprising if Hellenistic modes of pinning down the restless dead came in their wake. Only Thrace separates Deultum from Amphipolis, the scene of Machates's fictional adventure with Philinnion.

A different but equally suggestive rite occurs in a fifth-century infant cemetery at Lugnano, north of Rome. Its context must have been traumatic: a malaria epidemic at a point when the Roman Empire was fragmenting. The infant burials were associated with offerings to the Underworld powers, including puppies lacking either crania or lower jaws, and—more exceptionally—one ten-year-old child was buried with a large stone in the mouth.[23] A local panic about vengeful returning children can probably be inferred (p. 53). More generally, the fourth- to sixth-century evidence does (rather predictably) suggest an epidemic of dangerous-dead fears in the collapsing Roman world.

The Special Christian Dead

By that time, a powerful new theology was confronting traditional beliefs throughout the Empire. Christianity taught that Jesus would return on the last day to judge the living and dead, reuniting souls with their miraculously reconstituted bodies. Until then, corpses would lie quiet. As St Augustine argued, this scheme left little room for corporeal dead people who hung around familiar scenes, and little option for clergy to ascribe restless corpses—when layfolk reported them—to anything other than demonic possession.[24]

Or did it? In the 590s, Pope Gregory the Great related two stories about dead sinners, both set in Roman public baths. Their punishment was to serve as bath attendants, in one case standing in hot water. Although it is not stated explicitly, they sound physical enough: they could pull off bathers' shoes, hold their clothes, and feel discomfort.[25] That one of the greatest pastors of the Western church could tell such stories illustrates how easily folk-belief could permeate hardline doctrine.

Equally, scripture had described the reanimation of good and holy people. Might those who had suffered and died for the resurrected Christ in the days of persecution be glorified too in their own bodies? As the cults of saints multiplied and rose to prominence, their graves in churches and cemeteries across the (now officially Christian) Empire acquired the numinous force of the pagan temples they supplanted. The wonder-working servants of God were both powerful and present in the body, and those physical bodies could be out of the ordinary. In the 390s, Bishop Ambrose of Milan took a revolutionary step:

> [He] exhumed the body of the holy martyr Nazarius, which had been buried in a garden outside the city [of Milan], and had it moved to the basilica of the Apostles, by the Roman Gate. In the grave in which the martyr's body was lying we saw the martyr's blood as fresh as if it had been shed that day. . . . His head, moreover, which had been cut off by the impious men, was so complete and uncorrupted, with its hair and beard, that it had the appearance of being washed and laid in the grave at the very hour it was taken out. And why wonder, seeing that Our Lord promised in the Gospel that 'not a hair of their heads shall perish'? We were surrounded also by a strong scent that surpassed all perfumes in sweetness.[26]

For Ambrose and his clergy, Nazarius's lack of physical corruption manifested his spotless freedom from any spiritual taint. But . . . an undecayed corpse lying in fresh blood? That image will become familiar to readers of this book in drastically different contexts.

Some contemporaries surely had the same thought, as well as detecting a disturbing whiff of magic. The discovery of miraculously incorrupt saints was widely and enthusiastically pursued, but it exposed fissures in Christian devotional culture. The papacy disapproved of moving martyrs' remains, and did not generate stories of miraculous corpses.[27] This question must always have been slightly double-edged (p. 82). In emotional and charismatic circles, however, the impact could be powerful, and the practice spread to different cultural zones within the Christian world.

The nailed burials suggest beliefs endemic across the southern Empire from Gibraltar to the Black Sea (Map 2). However, it seems that they only survived or re-emerged in specific parts of this zone: the Alps, a pocket of Aragón, and above all the Balkan peninsula. Some of these nodes eventually connected with traditions percolating from the non-Roman north and east, though in that case, the process was drawn out over many centuries.

One crucible for this cultural interchange is suggested by the nailed burials at Deultum in eastern Bulgaria, where a mixed Thracian, Slavic, and Turkic population would become enthusiastic practitioners of corpse-killing some centuries later (p. 284). Another is the northern European world—Scandinavia, eastern England, the Rhineland—to which we now turn.

15

The British Isles and Northern Francia, 200–600

SOCIAL TRAUMA, WISE-WOMEN, AND MORTUARY THEATRE

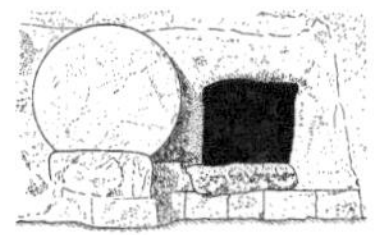

> Nobody knows where *helrunan* roam
> around on their business.
>
> —*BEOWULF*, LINES 162–163

BETWEEN THE LATE Iron Age and early Middle Ages, corpse-killing in Britain and northern Gaul may have been widely endemic but only rarely epidemic. That inference must be based on excavated burials, since written sources before 1000 are either absent or irrelevant. We can never be *certain* what the burials mean, but a combination of the general principles described in Chapter 7 with later narrative sources leads to conclusions that are at least persuasive.

One useful fact is that corpses targeted in distinctive ways show a female preponderance. Were these women guilty of crime in life, or of causing trouble after death? Later narratives contain no support for the first option but plenty for the second. The cases where female bodies

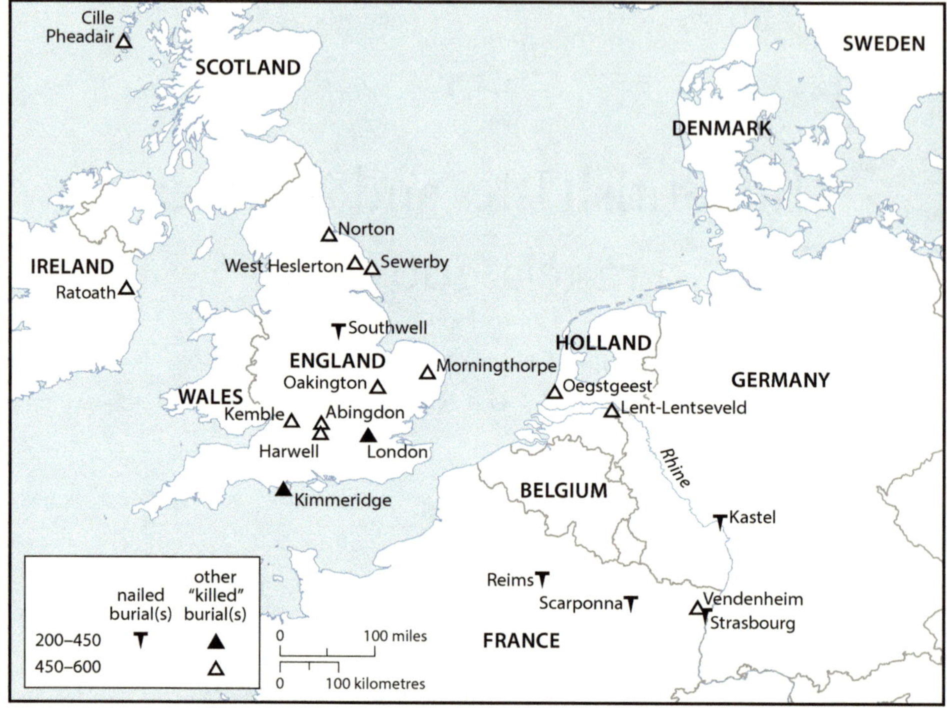

MAP 3: Known corpse-killings in north-west Europe, c. AD 200–600.

were attacked *after* the initial burial, once decay had set in, point in the same direction. The conclusion must be that women were thought to pose a posthumous danger, men much less so.

Late Prehistory

During the later centuries BC, a gradual shift from cremation to inhumation in parts of central to northern Europe could potentially have raised fears about unquiet corpses. The late Iron Age societies of Gaul and Britain had strongly-developed traditions of human sacrifice and the ritual display of severed human heads,[1] but for present purposes those traditions hinder more than they help: they make it extremely difficult to isolate any potential minority of cases involving mutilation of corpses for other reasons.

However, hints start to emerge in eastern Britain and Ireland. In East Yorkshire, multiple spears were sometimes driven down into the graves of high-status warriors. 'Was this a mark of honour or a gesture of fear?' asks a recent discussion.[2] We cannot answer, but the second is at least possible. Perhaps less ambiguous is the burial of a mid to late Iron Age woman at Bodicote (Oxfordshire), above a carefully placed dog skeleton and horse skull: in a pattern that will become familiar, her head was detached at some point after the initial burial.[3] At Barnetby-le-Wold (Lincolnshire), closer in time to the Roman invasion, a woman was buried in the fill of an enclosure ditch: prone, headless, her right foot detached, her wrists and ankles tied, and her head in a separate pit nearby.[4] Other cases are reported from late Iron Age Ireland, notably an adult male at Carroweighter (Co. Roscommon) who was buried prone in a ditch, his right foot amputated and placed between his legs.[5]

Roman Britain

As army units carried religious, magical, and mystical practices from the eastern to the western provinces, some of the late Asian, Hellenistic, and Mediterranean beliefs explored in the last two chapters could have fused with indigenous ones. As elsewhere in the Empire, the combination of these influences with Christianisation, and with the abandonment of cremation, may well have heightened anxieties.

Decapitated and prone (face-down) burials in Roman Britain have attracted much interest and comment.[6] Both rites were used widely—in rural and urban contexts, and for both sexes—across midland Britain. Decapitation (usually performed by chopping, the head being placed between the legs) was a distinctive British peculiarity, and increased markedly during the third and fourth centuries. Prone burials tended to occur in more marginal locations, and to involve people of poorer health and lower nutritional standards. Otherwise there are no clear patterns, and in both cases the evidence falls short of demonstrating an aim to keep the dead down.

That said, the decapitated and prone groups each comprise fewer than 4 percent of known Romano-British inhumations, which seems a viable proportion of people thought likely to cause trouble after death.

Perhaps, when more burials are dated, specific corpse-killing epidemics will emerge. Meanwhile, more eloquent post-mortem mutilations are occasionally found. Among fourth-century burials are a skull pulled off when semi-decomposed, a prone burial with a pot replacing a cut-off foot, and a young man buried prone with half a pair of shears by his left hand and a pot upside-down on his buttocks.[7] These are certainly distinctive, and could reflect heightened anxieties as cracks started to appear in traditional Roman culture.

The new religious influences in third- to fourth-century Britain (perhaps Christianity above all) may have changed perceptions of female spiritual power,[8] and the gender bias is persistently visible from this point onwards (Figure 30). At Kimmeridge (Dorset) a female in a stone cist, buried after c. AD 290, had her cranium and lower jaw removed and placed separately by her lower legs; a second burial on top of the cist, also female, had the jawbone by her knees.[9] The cranium of a woman buried c. AD 270–400 in the eastern cemetery of Roman London was also lifted out (perhaps through a gap in overlying rubble, where it was replaced by an iron key) and laid on the pelvis; this must have happened when the corpse was semi-decomposed, since the jawbone remained in situ.[10] This purposeful attack on a woman's organs of thought, biting, and speech was to reappear centuries later, in an Anglo-Saxon context and then a Scandinavian one (pp. 202, 224).

The Atlantic Zone

As the Western Empire collapsed, social and political trauma must have caused familiar and reassuring landmarks to dissolve. From the presences—and absences—of corpse mutilation, hazy geographical patterns start to emerge. The Brittonic-speaking world (Wales, Cornwall, and Brittany) presents a striking absence: there is almost no evidence, either archaeological or folkloric, for dangerous-dead beliefs.[11] That seems strange, until we remember that Iron Age mutilated burials concentrate near the Humber Estuary, and Roman ones in the south-east midlands.[12] Did British revenants essentially inhabit the eastern seaboard, facing the North Sea and Scandinavia?

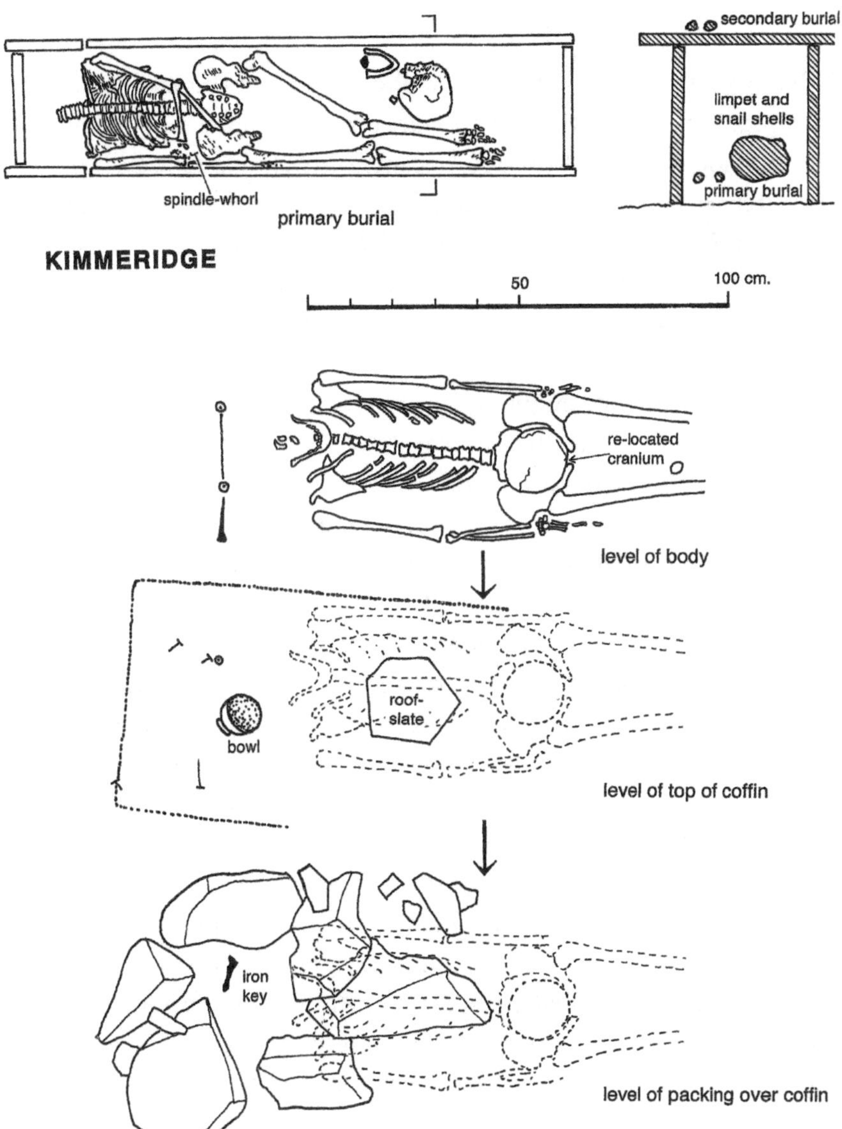

FIGURE 30: Two 'killed' female burials from Roman Britain. *Above*: At Kimmeridge (Dorset), an elderly woman was carefully buried in a stone cist, but her cranium and lower jaw were removed and placed separately by her legs; on top of the cist was placed another corpse, again with the lower jaw near the knees. *Below*: In the eastern cemetery of *Londinium*, this grave of a fourth-century woman was re-opened when the body was semi-decomposed, the cranium lifted off (leaving the lower jaw behind) and placed on the pelvis; heavy stone packing was laid on top, possibly with a gap through which the cranium was extracted.

Even so, they may have had Gaelic cousins in the Irish Sea zone. Decapitations—of both genders—are common in Ireland.[13] Crouched burial, standard in the Iron Age, became restricted to specific individuals, potentially including revenants.[14] A fifth- to sixth-century crouched female at Ratoath, Co. Meath, lacking her head, hands and feet, looks a promising case.[15] Irish prone burials are mainly though not exclusively juveniles and women, suggesting a narrowing-down of the practice to high-risk categories.[16]

This Irish evidence might offer a context for an isolated but dramatic case on the extreme north-western edge of Britain (Figure 31). At Cille Pheadair in the Hebrides, in the fifth or sixth century, a woman of around forty was buried in a stone cist facing the open Atlantic.[17] She lay on her back, her left arm by her side with the fist clenched, her right arm flexed with the hand on her upper chest. A rounded pebble apparently rested on the genital area. After decay had begun to set in, the cist was re-opened. The torso was twisted over onto its left side, and held in place by a slab extracted from the cist lining and wedged behind her back. Her right hand and lower arm were bent downwards from the chest to the pelvic area, leaving finger-bones behind. The skull was apparently not attacked, though a parting of the jaws could reflect an organic object wedged between the teeth. More dramatically, the sternum was removed and the rib-cage folded open on the upper left side, a configuration strongly suggesting deliberate removal of the heart.

What followed is equally enigmatic. After this mutilation, the cover-slabs were replaced, and the grave was left for an interval. Then, an impressive Pictish-style square cairn with a stone kerb and raised shingle surface was built over the grave.

Who was this woman: feared enough to be savagely mutilated in her grave, but then revered enough to be commemorated by an exceptional and typically high-status monument, looking out to the Atlantic and perhaps a landmark for sailors?

The arthritic wear on her bones suggests a life of heavy labour, but the real surprise comes from the isotope signatures of her tooth-enamel, which 'point to early-life origins in eastern Scotland, Ireland or England'. Square Pictish cairns are more common in eastern Scotland, so perhaps

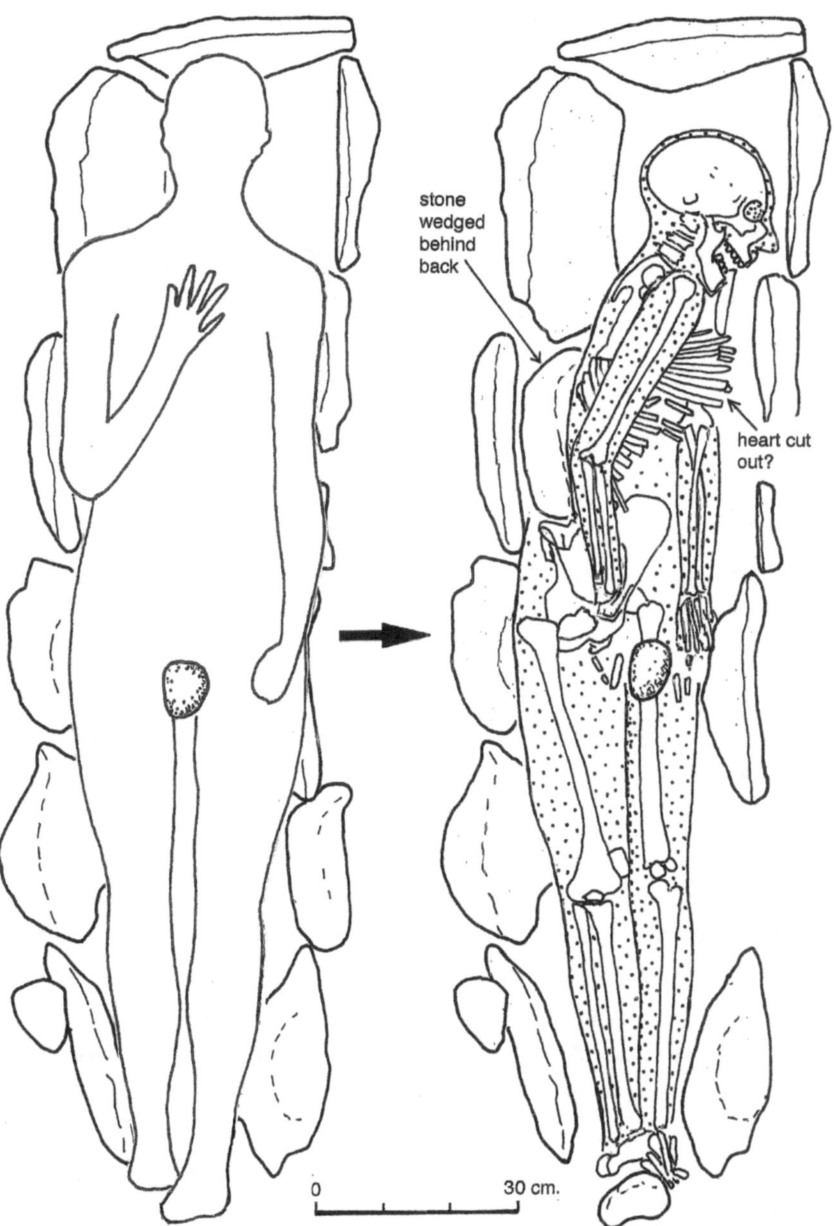

FIGURE 31: Cille Pheadair (Hebredes): the 'killed' burial of a fifth- to sixth-century woman in a stone cist, with inferred outline of soft tissue, and hypothetical outline reconstruction of the posture of the corpse as initially buried.

she came from there, but an Irish origin might also make sense. Was she an itinerant but charismatic wise-woman, both feared and revered after her death?

The Frankish Zone

After Rome, northern Europe assumed a new form. The present France, Low Countries, western Germany, and Austria, under Frankish ('Merovingian') rulers, contained peoples of multiple ethnic origins, including 'Celtic', Gallo-Roman, 'Germanic', and Frisian. Did the dead walk among them?

That question is clouded rather than clarified by an abundance of ambiguous evidence. Grave-opening was extremely common across the entire Merovingian zone, rising to a peak in the seventh century. In many cases, the purpose was to remove objects. Some of that was straightforward robbery, but recent work—associated especially with the 'archaeothanatology' school—has built a more nuanced and complex picture, emphasizing social, cultural, and ritual factors.[18] What matters here is that these interventions often involved disturbance to the head/skull, which could be relocated within the grave or removed entirely.[19]

The challenge—to distinguish corpse-killing from other plausible reasons for these interventions—is not made easier by the archaeothanatologists' current tendency to avoid the subject. More work is needed, but there are suggestive if isolated cases (Map 3). Some Bavarian examples have been reported of head-disturbance 'before fleshly decomposition was complete', involving 'reversal, repositioning or turning crania upside down'.[20] The Rhineland offers one very strange episode: in the cemetery of Vendenheim (Alsace), 16 percent of burials display multiple slashes and chop-marks across their lower legs. These attacks occurred through the fifth to seventh centuries, affected both sexes, and were made when the bones were relatively new and probably still fleshed.[21] This behaviour is hard to explain, unless as a countermeasure to the corpses (literally) walking.

The best parallels might eventually turn out to be in the Netherlands, though poor bone preservation is an obstacle there. From Lent-Lentseveld comes a burial (of c. 450–550?) where the cranium had—

once again—been lifted off and placed on the pelvis, leaving the lower jaw behind.[22] In a rather odd cemetery at Oegstgeest, also containing several prone males of whom one was partly burned, a young woman had damage to the ribcage consistent with heart removal.[23] If the Low Countries eventually produces more cases like this, they may reveal affinities with practices just across the North Sea.

Corpse-Killing among the Pre-Christian English

Descendants of fifth-century colonists from southern Scandinavia and north-west Germany, the early English interbred with an indigenous population who—though preserving little of Roman culture—had known centuries of Roman rule and retained Roman Christianity. But they formed their own identity in reaction and contrast: a polytheistic, non-urban warrior people whose social organization was based on extended kin-groups.

The little that we know about English pre-Christian religion suggests that it was decentralized, with undeveloped cult sites dispersed in the natural landscape, and with a strong emphasis on the supernatural animals encoded in the highly stylized art forms.[24] The English were only formally converted to Christianity from the 590s, but their contacts with Britons, Irish, and Franks started well before that. External influences on their ritual practice, including ones that were ultimately Roman-derived, are therefore not implausible.

There are no descriptions of religious specialists, and burial archaeology is our only source. Fifth- and sixth-century burials were characteristically accompanied by grave-goods. Usually these signalled status in family, life-cycle, and gender, but some people (notably women) apparently stood outside the normal social nexus. And already, it seems, there were occasional restless individuals who had to be kept down.[25]

Decapitations and prone burials, both male and female, are not infrequent at this date; occasionally a prone female lay in the grave-earth above the primary burial, which might suggest sacrifice or punishment rather than corpse-killing.[26] A male at Kemble (Gloucestershire), whose feet were cut off at the ankles and placed near the knees, is less ambiguous; so

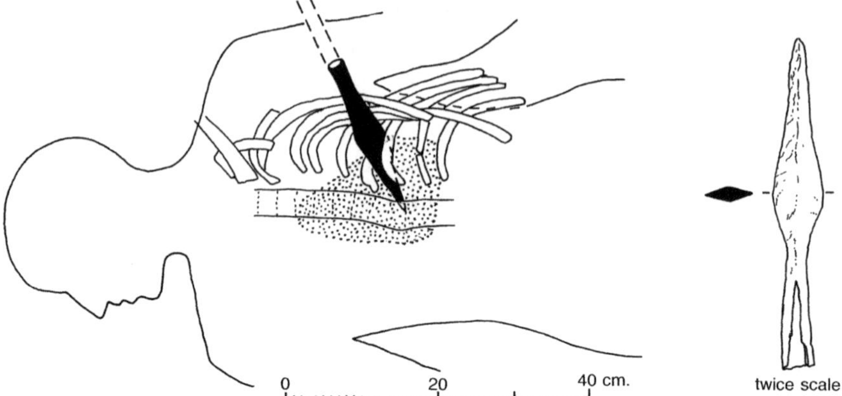

FIGURE 32: Harwell (Berkshire): the corpse of this sixth-century man was speared through the heart in the grave.

are three young adult females at Abingdon (Berkshire) who lay not only prone, but with legs and arms doubled up, body-parts missing, and in one case an overlying stone-pile.[27] In a dramatically clear case, a young adult male on the edge of a sixth-century cemetery at Harwell (Berkshire) was pierced directly through the heart with an iron spearhead (Figure 32).[28] Occasionally a fire was lit in the grave, either above or below the corpse: with analogies from ancient Assyria and modern Romania (pp. 161, 94), grave-opening to kill a revenant is a plausible interpretation.[29] Finally, one extraordinary group of female burials requires closer attention.

Female Ritual Specialists

In England, as in parts of Francia (especially the Rhineland), amuletic grave-goods identify certain sixth-century girls and young women as ritually special (Figure 25). Evidence is then lacking for several decades, since most English burials during c. 580–640 are unfurnished. It seems likely, though, that these empowered women could be recognized by their distinctive equipment through the whole period from c. 450 to c. 680 (and perhaps, for all we know, beyond that).

Anyone could wear amulets, but the 'special' women carried them in distinctively elaborate ways: complex assemblages hanging on cords and chains, usually at the left hip. In the sixth century a young woman was buried at Bidford-on-Avon (Gloucestershire) with accessories including an amulet-bag, a scalpel-like knife, and a neck-bag or bib decorated with twelve miniature bucket-shaped pendants: her appearance would have been highly distinctive, and her functions surely included magic and healing.[30]

A particularly distinctive item was the so-called girdle-hanger, a symbolic key-like object of copper-alloy, usually worn in pairs, found in many female graves in the eastern (Anglian) zone of England during c. 450–550. Analysis by Kathrin Felder (Meents) has enriched our understanding of 'special' women, their functions, and their place in society.[31] She finds a correlation of girdle-hangers with other amuletic objects, but not with the finest dress fittings or jewellery. These women were therefore not the richest in society, but had a distinct and parallel function because of their magical and medical powers.

Felder argues that 'wearers of girdle-hangers in early Anglo-Saxon communities formed part of a deeper-rooted European tradition of female authority in the domains of spiritual knowledge and healing magic', and that they may have had a role in aiding conception and safe birth.[32] These were specialists but not rare specialists (perhaps one in each extended family?), and they were seemingly integrated into the communities who buried them. A final point—unsurprising to readers of this book—is that girdle-hangers often accompanied adolescent girls, and that two-thirds of the adult women carrying them whose ages are known died between seventeen and twenty-five.[33]

Old English words for female magical practitioners and supernatural beings are helpful here. Inevitably we only know them from later (strongly negative) references, but *hægtesse, helrune, heahrune,* and *burgrune* all plausibly refer to powerful women skilled in mysteries, with a certain ambiguity about whether they were this-worldly or other-worldly:[34] maybe they were adept at crossing that frontier. This is a far richer vocabulary than anything ascribed to male practitioners, but after the eighth century it disappears, supplanted by the negative and reductionist *wicce* 'witch'. That speaks volumes about the decline of female power.

One Foot out of the Grave: Mortuary Theatre in Eastern England

These women were sometimes buried in odd ways.[35] At Empringham (Rutland), four out of the five mid-sixth-century women with girdle-hangers lay in a flexed posture (otherwise rare in that cemetery), while at Morningthorpe (Norfolk) the skull of another was displaced to the side of her grave.[36] At Oakington (Cambridgeshire) around 550, a young woman with girdle-hangers was buried—uniquely—with a cow, surrounded by four of the five prone burials (all female) found in this cemetery.[37] Heightening the sense of theatre, one of these prone females clutched a brooch and beads in her right hand, while her left hand rested on the arm of a child who had been placed to face towards her.[38]

The cemetery at West Heslerton (North Yorkshire) produced three graves with girdle-hangers.[39] The body in grave 152 (early sixth century) was again flexed. The other two were very strange indeed. Grave 139 (c. 530–70), a female probably in her twenties, lay supine but with her legs drawn up in front of her so that the knees were just below the ground-surface. Grave 113 (c. 550–80), a girl in her teens with girdle-hangers and an elaborate collection of amulets, lay semi-prone so that her skull faced downwards, with her legs flexed 'with the feet almost projecting from the grave'.

Other burials in this cemetery had equally bizarre postures.[40] In grave 16 (an unsexed adult with two knives), 'the lower legs were jammed up against the northern edge of the grave with the feet almost at the surface'. In grave 114 (c. 550–80), a young adult female lay prone, with her left foot missing, and her legs—bound together at the knees—splayed up the sides of the grave. Grave 132 (c. 550–80) contained an adolescent girl with an unusually complex amulet assemblage and brassica seeds in a cup; she lay prone, her legs tightly folded back, and the left upper arm was 'flexed and raised at the elbow to nearly the top of the grave as excavated'. Completing this collection of oddities, the women in graves 89 and 166 lay prone, in grotesquely contorted attitudes, as though their central bodies had collapsed into voids.

These illustrate a larger category that one might be tempted to call 'wild' burials: face-down, with the limbs splayed and flailing. The most famous case is the supposed 'live burial' of c. 550–80 at Sewerby (East Yorkshire). This woman overlies a conventional female burial, and was placed half-way up the grave fill, with a rock on her back and her feet kicking up towards the surface.[41] Given that this is one of several early Anglo-Saxon graves where an aberrant corpse overlies a normally arranged one, human sacrifice is not implausible; even so, the many parallels must now throw serious doubt on the idea that the woman was thrown into the grave alive. At Norton (Co. Durham), the occupant of grave 99 lay in a very similar posture; both she and the prone male in grave 91 had their feet—yet again—raised to the surface of the grave (Figure 33).[42]

Of the eleven burials just discussed, one was male, one uncertain, and the rest female: the bias towards women must be deliberate. Further, four of the eleven had collections of amuletic objects. Rather than 'disorderly', this group should be read as carefully staged funerary tableaux. The strangely broken appearance of some of them—notably West Heslerton 89 and 166—might be explained by lost timber structures (hurdles or chests?) over which the prone corpses were draped. Most bizarrely of all, one or more limbs were nearly always positioned so as to reach upwards to the surface of the grave. That might occasionally have happened by chance, but not regularly; the raised arm in West Heslerton 132 would have required careful placement. Was there some idea that the living needed to be in close contact with the powerful dead, either to absorb energy or to check that they rested quietly?

These abnormal sixth-century female graves differ from their seventh-century successors in that they do not show disturbance or mutilation *after* burial. Maybe people held these women in awe while they lived, and knew that they had to be treated appropriately in death. We need not infer that they were thought evil, or that the treatment was shaming, but they were reservoirs of supernatural energy. Some of that energy remained in their corpses and had to be controlled. The details are irrecoverable, but it is a reasonable conjecture that these distinctive and theatrical funeral rites were designed both to appease

FIGURE 33: Norton (co. Durham), burials 99 and 91. This sixth-century woman (*above*) and man (*below*) were laid so that their feet projected upwards to the surface of the grave.

them and to discourage them from returning. After that, they were not disturbed again.

The grouping of these burials in the years c. 550–75 is notable. Was there some specific cause? During the 540s, the populations, economies, and societies of Europe reeled under the blows of volcanic-induced climate change followed by bubonic plague.[43] Existential anxieties and spiritual traumas might have intensified fear of the numinous dead. Why that should manifest in east-coast England remains unexplained, though the regional congruence with abnormal burials of the later Iron Age might not be irrelevant.

This chapter has suggested that traditions of corpse-killing came into clearer focus, and concentrated more strongly on female subjects, during the fourth century. The techniques, especially the separation of the cranium and jawbone from the corpse and from each other, were to reappear in future centuries. However, eastern England—perhaps reacting to the plague of the 540s—controlled its dangerous female corpses with a different kind of ritual, involving theatrical prone postures rather than mutilation. Plague would return in 664, but to a very different England: more hierarchical, more cosmopolitan, and more polarized in its religious beliefs. Attitudes to dangerous dead women changed accordingly.

16

The Christian English, 600–700 (1)

SAINTLY WOMEN AND HOLY INCORRUPT BODIES

'I saw the body of God's holy virgin raised from the tomb and laid on a bed like one asleep. . . . All the linen cloths in which her body was wrapped appeared as whole and fresh as on the very day when they had been put around her chaste limbs.'

—CYNEFRITH DESCRIBES THE DISCOVERY OF ST ÆTHELTHRYTH'S BODY, INTACT AFTER SIXTEEN YEARS, IN 695

FROM ABOUT 640, a new wave of female corpse-killing becomes visible in England. It looks different from the other: rather than being buried in eccentric postures and then left alone, selected women were buried normally, but then savagely attacked when half-decomposed. Women were still the target, but something had changed.

In contrast to the undocumented fifth and sixth centuries, we do have narratives by seventh-century Christian authors. They did not care to discuss the dangerous dead, but at least they tell us about the cultural context. The complex changes that followed conversion brought trauma as well as widening horizons: these strange attacks on corpses surely reflect a need to identify dead scapegoats. I propose that they represent the dark side of a spectacular expression of autonomous female agency: the foundation of rich, female-led monastic houses in northern Francia and England. They belonged to a brilliant high culture celebrated in Latin texts, whereas the corpse-killing was a response to undocumented popular fears. But they were linked: to understand the mutilated bodies, we must first try to understand the nuns.

Towards Christianity

The English courts were converted to Christianity between the 590s and the 660s. By then, aspects of the indigenous religion were already starting to look more centralized: monumentally built shrines, perhaps something like a coherent priesthood.[1] For its own part, Christianity would prove remarkably adaptable to the landscapes and textures of traditional belief: re-branding holy places in the countryside, tolerating (up to a point) a range of medico-magical rituals, and assimilating 'tamed' versions of animal imagery into religious art.[2]

When it comes to burial practice, it is hard to distinguish specifically Christian influences from the larger package of changes. From around 570, 'normal' burials ceased to have any grave-goods that are visible to us; a small minority of elite males during c. 590–630 were furnished with spectacular treasures, including gold-and-garnet jewellery of astonishing richness and quality; and then finally—during c. 640–80—special groups of females received carefully-constructed modes of furnished burial.[3]

There is no evidence that the Church forbade grave-goods, and these changes do not map onto the conversions in any tidy way. They must, however, reflect some decisive conceptual shifts in relations between the living and the dead. There was an additional source of unease in those Anglian-settled areas of eastern England that switched from the cremation rite to inhumation in the years around 600. As always, that must have raised anxieties: had the dead relative or friend *really* moved on?

That question encapsulates the broader tension between death as a journey and the grave as a permanent residence. The famous and superlative burial of c. 625 in the royal cemetery at Sutton Hoo, Suffolk, illustrates the ambiguity. The great king's ship was set up for his voyage to another world, probably recalling earlier traditions in which the death-ships of sea-kings were literally launched out to sea and an unknown destination. But amidships stood the timber house in which he lay with his regalia, weapons, and feasting equipment, and above his ship was raised a great mound, widely visible from sea and land. Had he sailed away? Or was he still there under his barrow, a source of other-worldly power like the saints of the new religion in their shrines?

Change and Anxiety: Landmarks Melt Away

Before the 650s, the efforts by Italian, Frankish, and Irish missionaries to convert the English to Christianity had not penetrated far outside the circles of kings and their courts. Now, however, they began to impinge on society at large, to the point where long-held beliefs were marginalized or even outlawed.[4] To replace them, ideas and practices flowed in from the wider and more complex Continental world that still maintained the legacy of Roman civilization. The great historian Bede wrote of King Eorcenberht of Kent (640–64): 'He was the first English king who ordered idols to be rejected and destroyed through his whole kingdom, and the Lenten fast to be observed, by royal authority. And so that his commands might not be lightly neglected, he prescribed suitably heavy punishments for offenders. His daughter Eorcengota—a child worthy of her father—was a maiden of outstanding virtues, serving the Lord in a monastery founded in the Frankish region by a very noble abbess called Fara in the place called Brie'.[5]

Christianisation was the vehicle for a creative fusion between post-Roman Mediterranean culture and the cultures of the British Isles. From the 650s, this new order started establishing itself in the countryside. If the growing pressure to abandon old beliefs had some creative outcomes, it must also have been destabilising. The Tyneside farmers who abused some monks at about this time because they 'have abolished people's old devotions, and nobody knows how the new ones should be observed', may have had a point.[6]

These were decades of drastic change in other ways: the shift from gold to silver as the main precious metal, the spread of coinage, the rise of large coastal emporia for international trade, and reorganization of rural settlement patterns.[7] On top of all that came the epidemic—probably bubonic plague—which struck Britain in 664–6 and 684–7, with milder episodes between.[8] A disaster on that scale must have seriously undermined the population's morale and psychological wellbeing. This has become a familiar story for us: the shocked and bereaved, needing someone to blame, can turn to blaming the dead.

Nunneries, the Holy Sisterhood—and the Dark Side

Eorcengota was a nun in Francia, but from the 650s, English nunneries on the Frankish pattern were founded during an extraordinary burst of enthusiasm and lavish patronage.[9] This was the golden age of English female monasticism. Royal and noble women, often highly cosmopolitan and educated, ruled rich monasteries—and exercised political power from them—with a freedom unequalled until modern times. It was a very specific movement, starting in northern Francia, spreading through the English kingdoms, but rapidly dying away everywhere after 750. Why did so many women become abbesses and nuns, and why were abbesses so powerful?

An important background factor is surely that they represented continuity from the numinous women of the immediately pre-Christian era. Faced with the new religion, with its sophisticated structures and powerful backers, English wise-women must have seen the road forking ahead of them. If they remained true to their calling, or lacked patrons, they could probably have continued as traditional practitioners without much interference. But as decades and then centuries passed, they would have been increasingly marginalized; eventually, they would be stigmatized as 'witches'.

Alternatively, with the right inclinations and relatives in high places, they could re-brand their supernatural power as Christian and themselves as abbesses or nuns. But perhaps neighbours and subjects clung to a traditional world-view in which they remained wonder-working *hægtesse*—and perhaps they relished that role more than the texts choose to tell us. Strictly speaking, interpreting dreams and predicting the future were forbidden, but nuns still did it. When one of them dreamed that a stream of purple thread came out of her mouth, 'an aged nun who was known to possess the spirit of prophecy, because other things that she had foretold had always been fulfilled', assured her that it presaged the holiness of her future teaching.[10] Beyond the Christian overtones, was that very different from what a *hægtesse* might have done?

There is just one Christian text—the 'Life of St Leoba'—in which fear of the restless dead seems to break the surface. This biography recalls an episode set in the nunnery of Wimborne (Dorset), probably in about the 720s. The prioress—a strict, bad-tempered disciplinarian—died without being reconciled with her sisters. A mound was heaped over her grave, and the young nuns jumped on it and cursed their dead tormentor. The abbess protested, but on visiting the grave she was horrified to see that the mound had sunk, and now lay about six inches below the surface. 'She understood from the subsidence of the ground how the dead woman had been punished, and judged the severity of God's sentence upon her from the sinking of the grave'. So she called the sisters together and urged them to forgive the dead prioress, and to pray for remission of her sins and the repose of her soul. After a three-day fast the abbess prayed, and the grave 'suddenly began to fill in and the ground rose, so that the moment she got up from her knees the grave became level with the surface of the ground': thus she knew that the prioress was absolved.[11]

The circumlocutions are hard to read behind: precisely *how* had she been punished? The almost unique motif of the sinking grave has a relevant parallel, if a much later one: in nineteenth-century Serbian folklore, it was believed that 'if the grave has sunk in . . . [it] suggests that the deceased has transformed himself into a vampire'.[12] That the earth sank because the prioress's unquiet corpse had come out from beneath it is therefore a plausible inference. The prioress looks a good candidate for that fate: grumpy and unsociable, cut off with grievances left unassuaged. At least the story embodies some conception that the unquietness of the soul could be visited on the grave.

The Two Wives of King Ecgfrith

The careers of two Northumbrian queens illustrate both the surface Christian narrative and the possible hidden depths. The first is Æthelthryth, daughter of the East Anglian king Anna, who married an east midlands nobleman and then King Ecgfrith of Northumbria.[13] She was strong-willed and self-confident, preserving her virginity through both marriages. In 673 she left Ecgfrith, founded a great nunnery on her own lands at Ely (Figure 38), and became its first abbess. A respected and self-denying ruler, she was thought by some to have a 'spirit of prophecy', predicting both the plague that would kill her in 679 and the number in the community who would also die.

What propelled Æthelthryth to illustrious sanctity was her successor's decision, in 695, to move her bones into the church from the grave where she had been laid sixteen years earlier. Bede, who knew eyewitnesses, describes the dramatic scene: the tent raised over the grave, the sounds of shovelling, and then the astonished cry 'Glory be to the name of the Lord'. The body was 'as incorrupt as if she had died or been buried on that very day'. The wound from a large tumour below her jaw, cut out just before her death, had healed leaving only a slight scar. She was carried triumphantly into the church and laid in a re-used Roman sarcophagus, where miracles followed. Here was one kind of incorrupt corpse.

Our second example is Iurminburh, King Ecgfrith's wife after his debacle with Æthelthryth.[14] If she looks such a contrast to her saintly predecessor, that is partly because she crossed swords with the combative St Wilfrid. We know about her from Wilfrid's admirer and biographer, Stephen of Ripon: a less sophisticated and more polemical writer than Bede, and (helpfully for us) less reticent about popular culture. In Stephen's eyes, Iurmenburh was a 'sorceress' (*venifica*) like the biblical queen Jezebel, turning her husband against Wilfrid with her poisoned arrows of eloquence. But after Ecgfrith's death—as Stephen tells us in a comical volte-face—the chastened Iurmenburh was transformed 'from a she-wolf into a lamb of God, a perfect abbess and excellent mother of her community'.

We learn about Ecgfrith's queens from two very different writers, but they had more in common than appears on the surface. Both were embedded in the plutocratic world of Anglo-Saxon elites, and well-versed in its politics and opulent culture. (Even the ascetic Æthelthryth confessed to a teenage liking for fine necklaces, presumably of the gold-and-garnet type.) Both were ascribed powers of a vaguely supernatural kind, even though one is labelled a holy prophetess and the other a poisonous sorceress. Stephen calls Iurmenburh a Jezebel—hinting at false prophecy, foreign gods, and sacrifices in pagan shrines—yet she too ended her career as abbess of a royal nunnery.

Objects of Power: Christian or Traditional?

One of Iurmenburh's misdeeds occurred around 680, when the king had imprisoned Wilfrid on her urging. She 'took away the reliquary of the man of God which was full of holy relics, and . . . hung it next to her both when she stayed in her chamber and when she travelled in her carriage'. That was a bad move: she was suddenly possessed by a demon. Seeing her agonized contortions, the wise abbess Æbbe told the king: 'Send back to him [Wilfrid] the holy relics which the queen robbed from his neck, and carried about from town to town like the Ark of God, to her own destruction'.

This reliquary must have been a container or capsule, probably of precious metal and small enough to hang around his neck: it sounds very like the relic-capsules found in some seventh-century female graves (Figure 34). For Wilfrid, the relics inside it were both sacred and protective. Iurmenburh would have conceived similar functions, but did it cross the fine line from relic to amulet or magic charm? For Æbbe, it seems to have possessed something like autonomous agency, inflicting demonic agonies on its abductor.

In this period of intense cultural interchange, portable objects invested with numinous power were bridges between the thought-worlds of literate Christianity and traditional English belief. Were they Christian relics or traditional amulets? We must ask the same question about these powerful women: Christian (and miracle-workers), or traditional (and diabolical)?

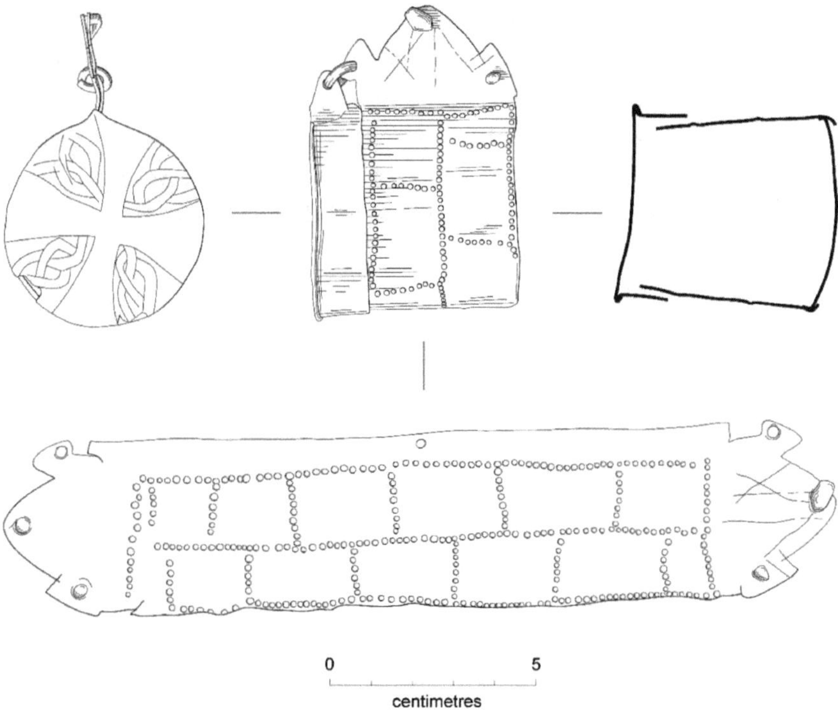

FIGURE 34: An object of power, but was it Christian power? This copper-alloy capsule from a seventh-century female grave at North Leigh (Oxfordshire) must have contained some powerful amulet or relic. It is interesting that the lid marked with a prominent cross seems to be a replacement: maybe Christianising an item that had previously held different associations? For a similar capsule in context, see Figures 39–40. Analytical drawing by Vicki Herring.

Iurmenburh, with her stolen reliquary, stands for a generation of strong women whose power was daunting and ambiguous. Educated religious writers saw a gulf between the women who dedicated themselves to God and those who (as their critics would have put it) dedicated themselves to the devil. For most of the laity, the difference would have been less stark and a traditional layer of similarities more apparent.

All these special female bodies were imbued with numinous power, but of what kind? Traditions would have remembered the wise-women who, a century earlier, were buried face-down to keep their dangerous life-energies in check. The new Christian world had a binary framework, in which the dangerous could more readily be labelled evil. Here let us remember Orthodox Russia, where incorrupt corpses could be either saints or vampires (p. 83). Did all contemporaries necessarily share Bede's starry-eyed view of Æthelthryth's incorrupt body?

17

The Christian English, 600–700 (2)

SINISTER WOMEN AND DANGEROUS INCORRUPT BODIES

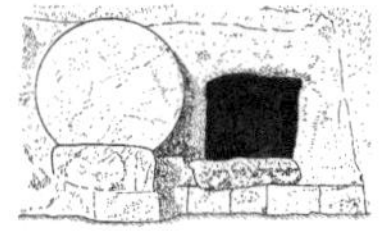

I saw her, the grave sheet was round her,
  Months had passed since they laid her in clay;
Yet the damps of the tomb could not wound her,
  The worms had not seized on their prey.

—VERSES ON A MASSACHUSETTS VAMPIRE,
PUBLISHED 1822

WHILE THE RICH abbesses were living and dying in their monasteries, other women were still being buried with traditional-style amulet groups. There were, however, some new items: elaborate complexes of iron chainwork, and cylindrical metal boxes that may copy Christian reliquaries but contain items that look magical (Figure 34).[1]

Although we know nothing about these women's activities, they must have been ritual specialists not unlike their sixth-century predecessors. We cannot prove, but can easily guess, that the new Christian establishment disapproved of them. But it seems that one underlying conception—other-worldly forces operating through female agency—empowered both the nuns and the wise-women. This background may help to explain why the corpses 'killed' in England during these decades were almost entirely female.

Sinister Women, and How to Keep Them Down

In contrast to the burial tableaux of the earlier phase, we now find corpses that were initially laid out in the normal way, but then mutilated when they were semi-decayed but still articulated—in other words, within a range of weeks or months. The treatment entailed two or more out of three standardized measures: twisting of the torso into a prone or semi-prone position; detachment and repositioning of the cranium, leaving the lower jaw either in place or scattered in the grave; and removal of the heart. The first two are obvious; clear recognition of the third is much harder in normal excavation conditions.

All this makes a big claim, and one that some English excavators, drawn to 'rational' explanations, find it hard to accept. The contorted attitude in which one of these women ended up is ascribed in the excavation report to 'delayed burial, grave robbing, disturbance by plough or a combination of these factors.'[2] Positively bizarre is the interpretation of another, whose head is rotated through 180 degrees, as a live burial: 'in her struggles to get out she dragged her right arm under her body to lever herself up.'[3]

My argument is that these burials reflect a culture of killing the dead, so it is important—and only fair to the sceptics—to make the case thoroughly. Casual damage can be ruled out by showing that the procedures were systematic rather than random. So let us now look at how four corpses were treated. The drawings (Figures 35–38 and 40) allow consistent comparison by showing the burials as excavated (with normal body outlines added) alongside outline reconstructions—inevitably schematic and at times conjectural—of their potential postures when first buried.

Wolverton (Buckinghamshire): Burial 2088 in this broadly seventh-century cemetery was a female in her twenties or early thirties (Figure 35).[4] She only had one surviving grave-good (a spindle-whorl made

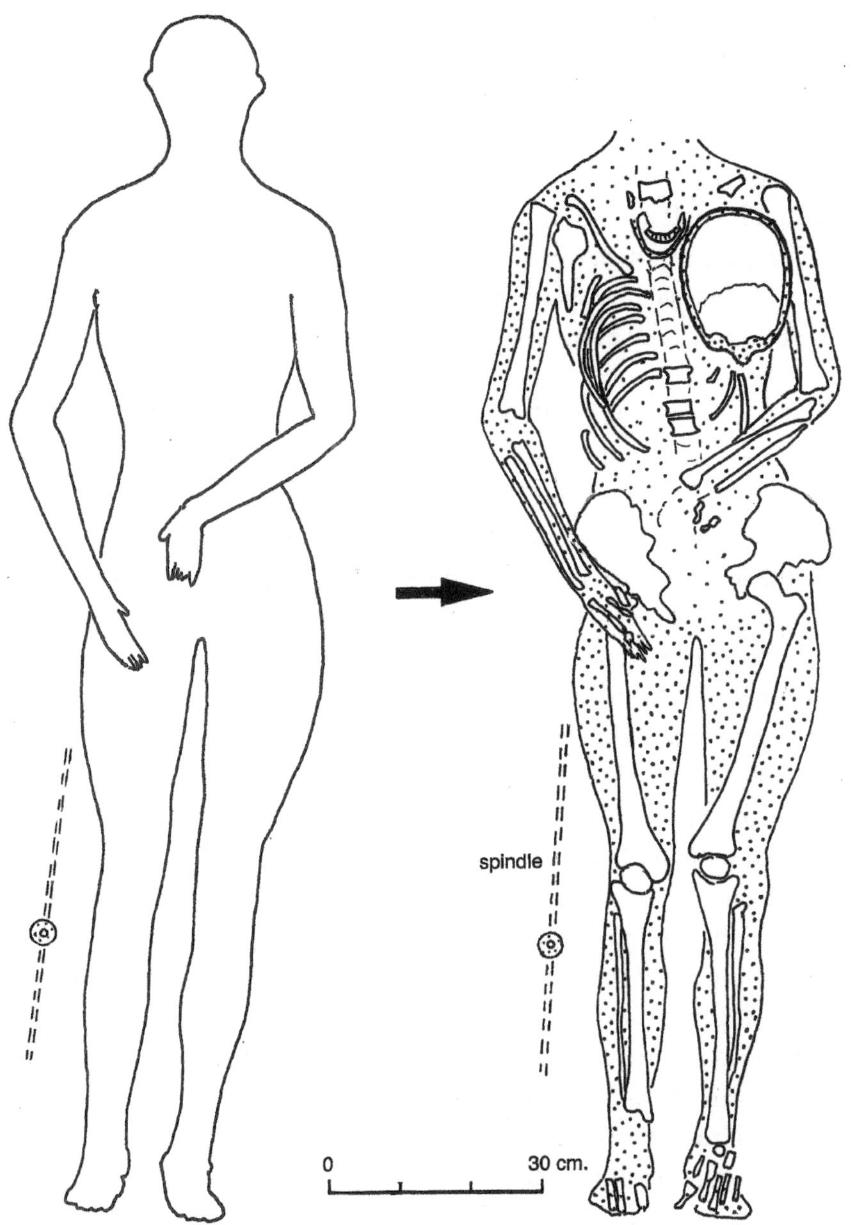

FIGURE 35: Wolverton (Buckinghamshire), burial 2008, with inferred outline of soft tissue, and hypothetical outline reconstruction of the posture of the corpse as initially buried.

from a Roman pot, perhaps representing a spindle laid parallel with her right leg), and was in a group of regularly aligned and largely unfurnished graves. These features tend to locate her in the later part of the calibrated radiocarbon range obtained from her skeleton, AD 580–660. She was laid on her back, with her legs straight, her right hand on her hip and her left hand in the pelvic area.

The grave was then re-opened. The torso may not have been disturbed much, if at all: slight displacements of the left femur and pelvic bone could result from natural processes. More dramatically, the head was detached from the spinal column and re-positioned in two parts: the cranium on the left side of the chest directly over the heart, and the jawbone centrally on the upper chest. In the absence of cut-marks, it seems that the head was simply pulled off, presumably at a stage when the muscles of the neck and cheeks were relatively decayed. The published plan and photograph suggest that the rib-cage was quite disturbed, especially on the left side.

Lechlade (Gloucestershire): Burial 74 in this large and important cemetery was a girl aged about nine (Figure 36).[5] No radiocarbon date is available, and the cemetery spans the sixth to seventh centuries, but as one of a group of unfurnished graves in a rather peripheral area she can probably be placed in the post-600 range. From the position in which her corpse finally rested, it can be inferred that she was initially laid on her back with her hands near her hips or pelvic area.

The disturbance was more violent than at Wolverton. The whole body was twisted around into a prone position, fragmenting the left foot and leaving the right leg crossed behind the left. The cranium was removed (again probably by tugging, since no cut-marks are reported), and placed upside-down above the left buttock; the jawbone was rotated, but in its natural location, so it may not have been completely detached from the neck. The rib-cage, seen from behind in the plan and photograph, was apparently splayed open.

Dover Buckland (Kent): Burial 67 was a woman in her twenties, buried c. 650–80 in a small cluster of graves focused on a Bronze Age barrow (Figure 37).[6] She wore a fine necklace including one gold pendant, three silver-gilt pendants, and beads of amethyst, shell, glass, and bronze. She also had a copper-alloy wire bracelet, and a lump of iron

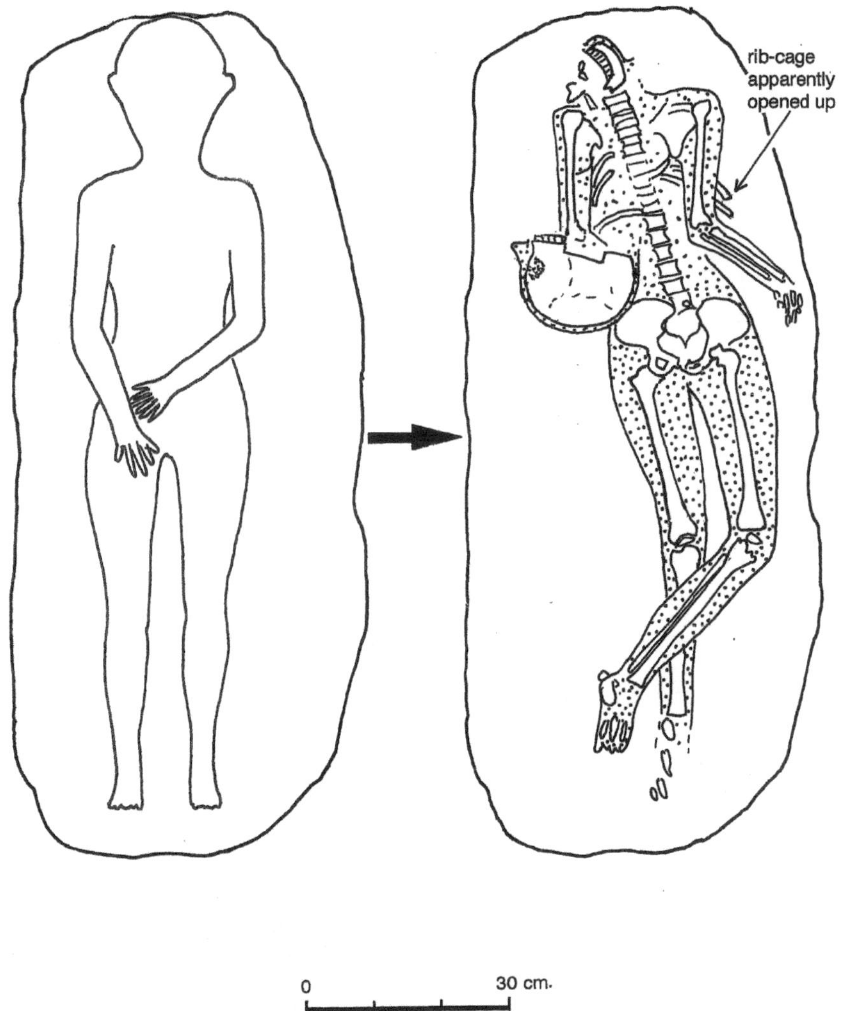

FIGURE 36: Lechlade (Gloucestershire), burial 74, with inferred outline of soft tissue, and hypothetical outline reconstruction of the posture of the corpse as initially buried.

pyrites (probably amuletic) placed by her left foot. The disruption of the skeleton leaves aspects of the original posture unclear, but it seems that her left leg was straight and her right leg sharply flexed,[7] her left arm by her side or on her chest, and her right arm flexed with the hand towards the head.

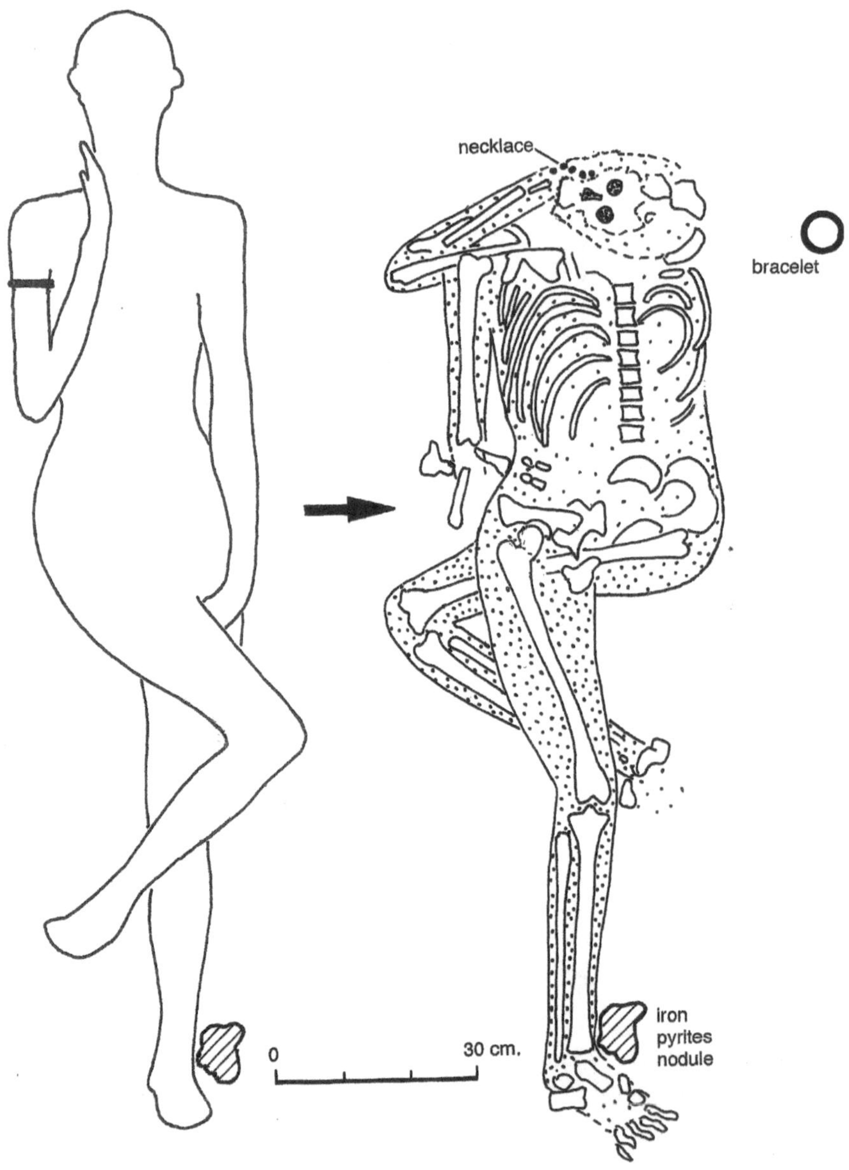

FIGURE 37: Dover Buckland (Kent), burial 67, with inferred outline of soft tissue, and hypothetical outline reconstruction of the posture of the corpse as initially buried.

When the body was semi-decomposed but still at least partly articulated, the torso was twisted over to lie prone. The right femur was pushed unnaturally tight against the underside of the pelvis, and the right arm apparently detached from the shoulder. The cranium was removed, and repositioned sideways and facing upwards. The jawbone and lower left arm were apparently missing. The bracelet was dislodged to the side of the grave, most likely from the detached upper-right arm.

Ely (Cambridgeshire): This fourth example, unlike the first three, has an enlightening historical context (Figure 38).[8] Westfield Farm is only a mile from the core buildings of the great royal nunnery at Ely, where we have already encountered the incorrupt body of St Æthelthryth. A girl aged ten to twelve was buried there—apparently under a barrow—with rich grave-goods including silver, gold, and gold-and-garnet pendants and rare glass cups. Around her barrow, fifteen further burials were placed, spanning ages from teenage to mature adult. Six of these were female, the rest certainly or probably male.[9] The females (with one crucial exception) lay against the northern perimeter of the barrow, the males further out.

All the graves fall in the date range c. 660–700, and the site must have lain on the nunnery's land, so the rich girl was presumably a relative or associate of Æthelthryth and her family. This looks like a case where a close female relative was accorded different funeral rites: the abbess in her church among her nuns, the secular princess in her demonstrative barrow-burial surrounded by her own attendants. It recalls Minster-in-Thanet (Kent), where the princess Eormengyth was buried—at much the same time—a mile east of the nunnery ruled by her sister Mildthryth.[10]

Burial 2—which lay slightly further away than the other females—is extraordinary (Figures 39 and 40).[11] A girl in her mid-teens was apparently laid on her back in a straight position, with her right arm by her side and her left arm flexed so that the hand touched her shoulder or face. At her knees—and perhaps originally hanging on her left knee, the usual position for such items—was a cloth or leather bag containing a cylindrical metal relic-box, a Romano-British brooch, two hobnails (probably also Roman), five amethyst beads, iron and copper-alloy rings and iron nail fragments. This odd collection was clearly amuletic

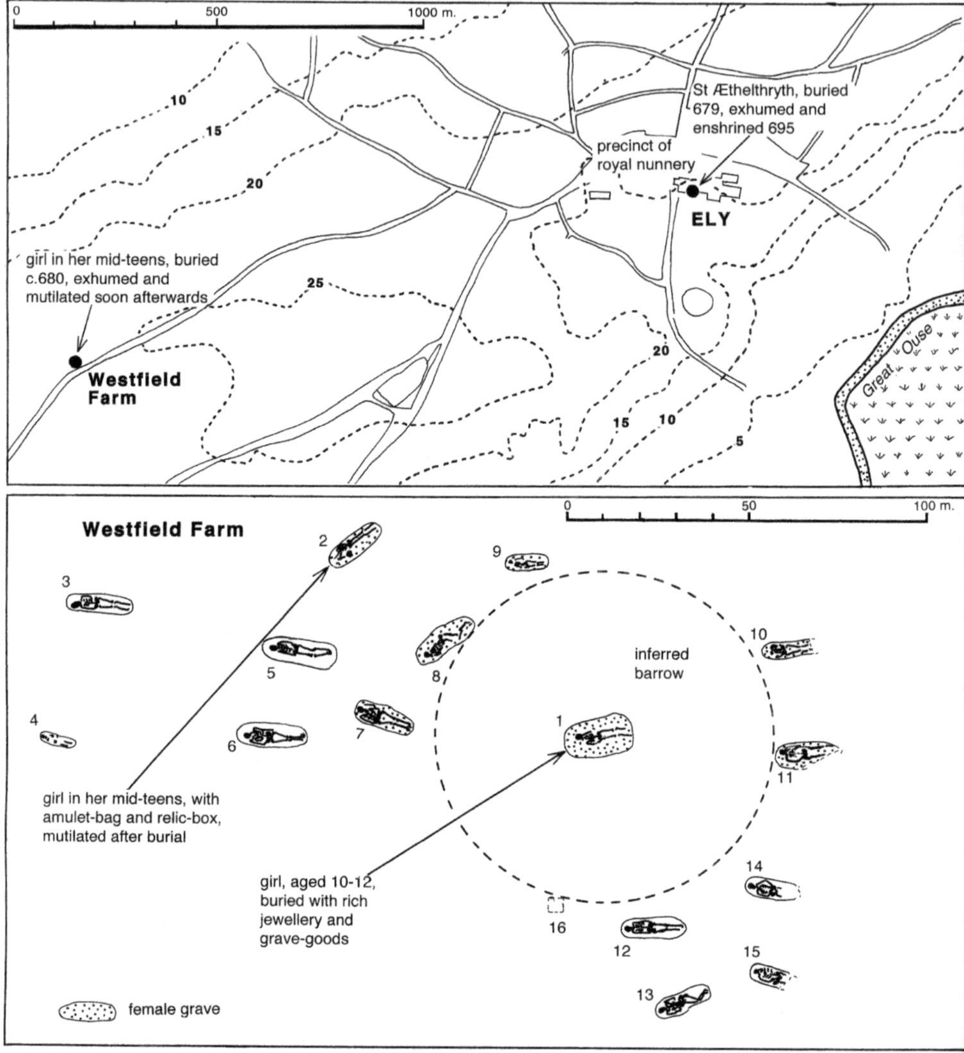

FIGURE 38: Seventh-century Ely (Cambridgeshire): the burial-sites of two incorrupt female corpses that were treated very differently.

or magical, and is fairly typical of the amulet-bags buried with female ritual specialists.[12]

When the girl's body was decaying but still partly articulated, it suffered a violent attack. Someone apparently grasped the upper torso and twisted it in a clockwise direction, hauling the corpse to the side of the

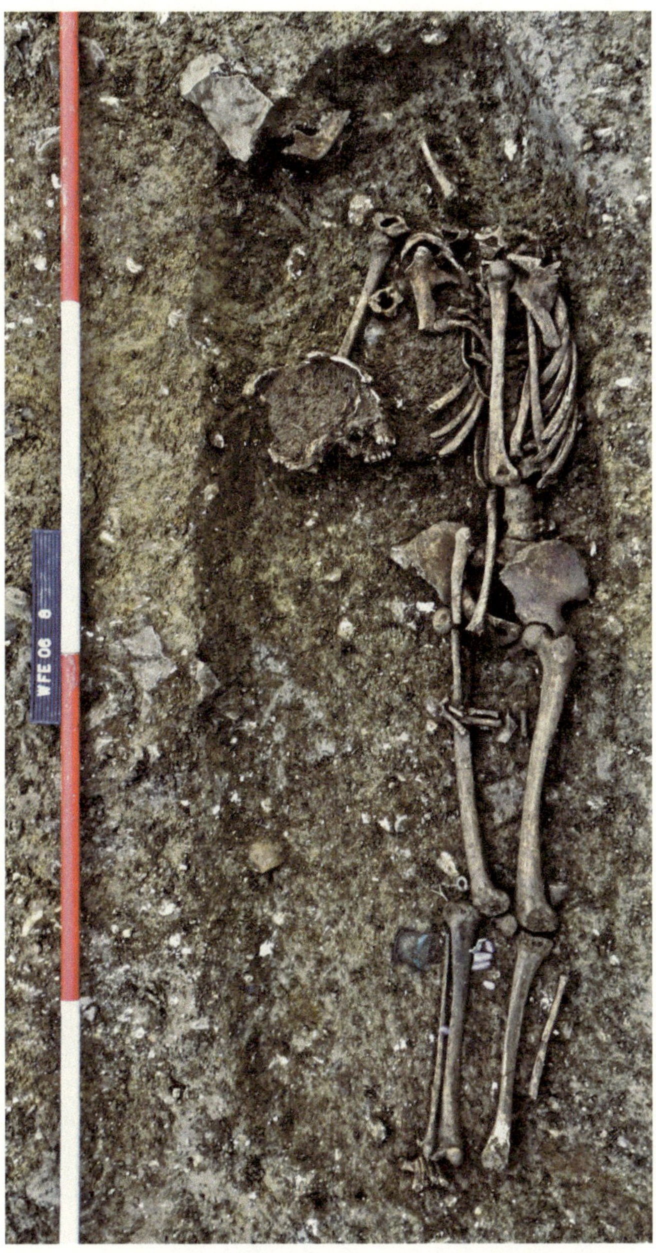

FIGURE 39: Westfield Farm, Ely, burial 2. This late seventh-century woman, with her amulet-bag at her knees, has been violently turned over, and her head and lower jaw pulled off and separated, when the corpse was still semi-articulated. The metal relic-capsule by her leg (green) resembles the one in Figure 34.

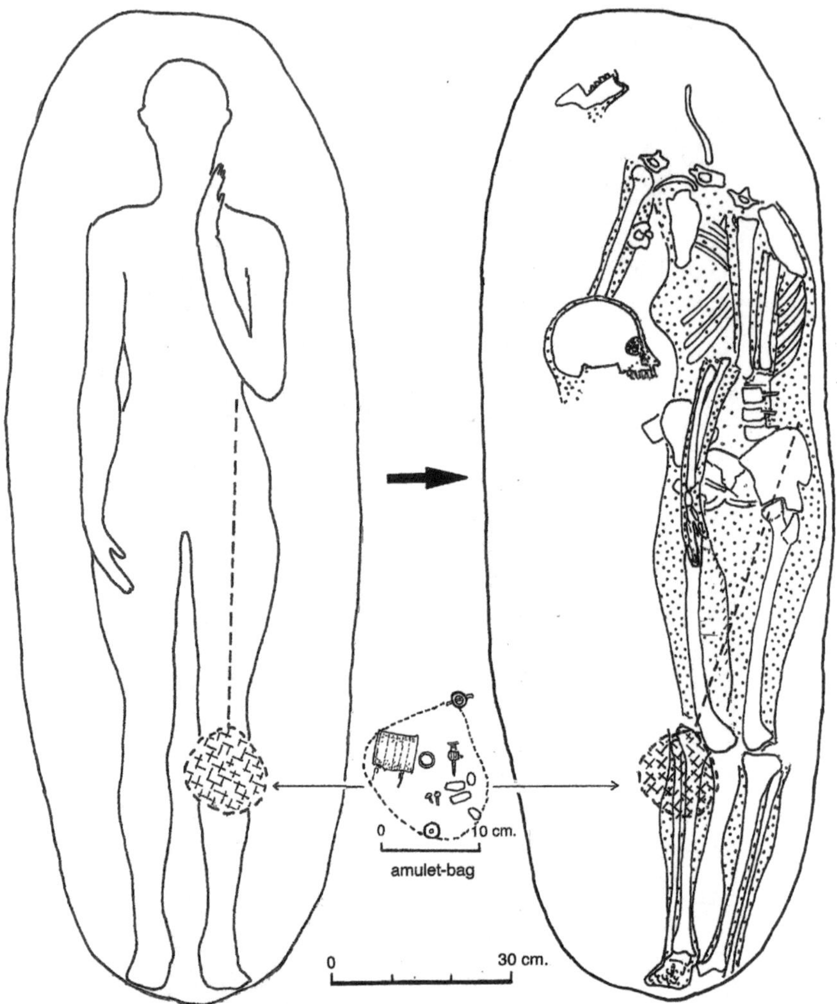

FIGURE 40: Westfield Farm, Ely, burial 2, with inferred outline of soft tissue, and hypothetical outline reconstruction of the posture of the corpse as initially buried.

grave. This broke it at the knees (so that the upper legs and trunk lay on the right side while the lower legs remained supine); separated the right arm at the elbow; jammed the left hand against the shoulder-blade; and rolled the amulet-bag onto the right knee. Again the head was wrenched off with no sign of cut-marks, displacing the collarbones, and the cranium was laid on its side facing the chest; the jawbone was dispersed towards the head end of the grave. The rib-cage was significantly disrupted, though it is unclear whether that was deliberate or an effect of the rough treatment.

These well-reported cases are far from alone. Up to ten further instances of separately displaced crania and jawbones (and in one case the jawbone only) are known from excavated cemeteries in southern England. Details are limited in some cases, but so far as the evidence goes they are—with only two exceptions—female, and most, perhaps all, are from the seventh century.[13] Others will surely turn up. At present, this looks like a distinctively southern English practice and suggests at the least a sharply heightened concern during a period of some decades.

Æthelthryth's Other Contemporaries: An Unholy Sisterhood?

From the cases just described, clear patterns emerge. There is a strong emphasis on separating the cranium and lower jaw from the body and from each other; on rotating the body from a supine to a sideways or prone position; and (plausibly though not demonstrably) on removing the heart. All these are actions of *disablement*: to destroy the organs of vitality and thought, to impede forward and upward movement, and to prevent biting and eating (and talking and cursing?). Most crucially, they were performed *at a stage when decomposition had started but was far from complete.*

Why go through the revolting business of uncovering and mutilating a half-rotten corpse? Arguments based on the impossibility of alternatives are dangerous, but here there really is only one viable explanation, amply supported by the analogies from other times and places reviewed in this book. These individuals were buried normally, but fears then emerged that they were causing trouble, either because they were seen walking around, or because they were thought to be spreading illness and misfortune from their graves. In due course they were exhumed, judged to be 'incorrupt', and dealt with accordingly. It is unlikely that the appearance of these corpses was exactly pristine, but incorruption is a flexible concept.

The subjects were almost entirely female, and the treatment of the Lechlade girl implies that dangerous power could be innate from an early age. The same may be true of the teenager at Westfield Farm, where the focal burial of a still younger girl with gold jewellery speaks of the female-centred world at Æthelthryth's Ely. Did the early deaths of these girls enhance rather than diminish their numinous power in their graves?

How did these women fit into their own communities? Lechlade was a fairly conventional cemetery with some rich graves and few abnormalities, so the girl in burial 74 looks marginal. The woman in Dover grave 67 was among the richer though not the richest in this cemetery, and apart from the presumably amuletic pyrites nodule there is nothing distinctive about her grave-goods: in being thus singled out, she was alone in her community and generation. At Wolverton, on the other hand, burial 2088 was not the only case of preventive measures: out of some eighty burials, six were laid prone (including a female with an amulet-bag and an adolescent with a spearhead placed on the upper body), which might suggest that this decapitation was an extreme expression of endemic concerns.[14]

The cemetery at Westfield Farm evidently served a smaller and more distinctive group, perhaps the household or dependents of the girl whose barrow dominated it. If the gendered arrangement of the graves suggests a female inner circle and a male outer circle (a microcosm of Æthelthryth's nunnery?), the teenage girl in grave 2 was rather peripheral. On the other hand her amulet-bag, and the distinctive copper-alloy relic-box that it contained, mark her out as someone special. Although hers is the only known relic-box grave that displays such drastic mutilation, it is hard to believe that her possession of amulets had no connection with the treatment of her corpse.

What also gives this burial special interest is that it was so close in time and place to Æthelthryth's. The mutilation of Westfield burial 2 happened close to the time of Æthelthryth's death in 679. Just up the road, Æthelthryth's own incorrupt corpse was exhumed and translated some fifteen years later: observers of the first dramatic event could well have witnessed the second. Did any spectators in 695 harbour subver-

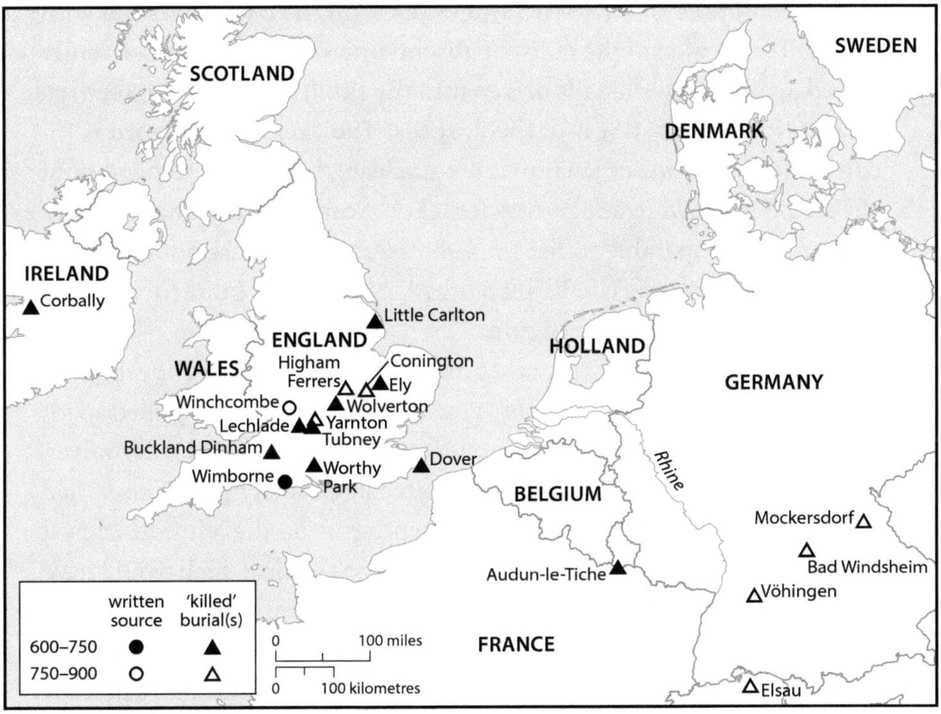

MAP 4: Known corpse-killings in north-west Europe, c. AD 600–900.

sive thoughts: another dangerous corpse with sinister in-dwelling life, so why treat it differently?

Wider Contexts: Francia and Ireland

How did the seventh-century English learn this mode of killing corpses? The conspicuous absence of cases from Wales and Cornwall argues against western British influence. The separation of the cranium from the lower jaw is a technique already noted in fourth-century southern Britain and the fifth-century Low Countries (pp. 180, 185). A good place to look might be north-eastern France and the Rhineland (Map 4), since it is there—together with eastern England—that female amulet-complexes are most prominent in graves. One seventh-century cemetery, at Audun-le-Tiche (Moselle), produced a remarkable number of mutilated burials: several with stones piled on the corpse, several with the skull re-located in the grave or absent, one with the corpse violently pulled apart, two with nails driven into the skull, and one (two teenage boys) with arrows shot into the corpses. The excavation record is incomplete (locations of jawbones are unclear), but about 70 percent of affected burials were apparently female.[15] Some of these methods are potentially comparable to the English cases, if others are not (the nails look like a continuing late Roman practice). We must hope for a better-excavated cemetery in the region.

Some contemporary Irish cases might also be relevant. They differ in showing an emphasis on juveniles, who are found with joints pulled apart, hands and feet chopped off, or large stones in their mouths.[16] However, a woman buried over the fill of a ring-ditch at Corbally (Co. Clare) 'had sharp-force trauma to the sixth and seventh ribs on the left side, caused by an upward single action with a double-edged blade, which would have pierced her heart'; her left arm was bent so that her hand rested on the wound.[17] This recalls the Cille Pheadair case (p. 182), but is closer in time to the English mutilations. There were abundant Christian and scholarly contacts between the seventh-century Irish and English: might those have been conduits for less orthodox practices?

Much more work is needed before the relevance of such parallels becomes clear. But in this cosmopolitan world, it seems unlikely that English anxieties about dangerous dead women were purely insular.

In England through the fifth to eighth centuries, corpse anxieties may have been endemic. But two peaks can be recognised: the later sixth century in the eastern zone, and then the years c. 640–80 in southern England. The different treatment of the two groups of women implies different ideas about who they were and what they did.

If it is right to infer that the women of c. 550–80 were perceived as powerful rather than evil, ideas had changed by the 660s. Now the leaders of society were Christian, and were busily transferring social and financial capital to the exciting new female world of the nunneries. Traditional beliefs and practices survived for a long time to come, but their practitioners may have been increasingly isolated. Ironically, the destabilizing effect of new ideas—introduced through the monastic high culture—could have contributed to a superstitious persecution of the dead that must have horrified scholars such as Bede.

The radiocarbon evidence suggests that the second corpse-killing epidemic had started by the 640s, which points to the combined stresses of social and religious change as the likely cause. Two decades later, a real medical epidemic—the bubonic plague of 664—could well have intensified it. The shocking violence with which some female corpses were attacked would then speak of panic in the face of this inexplicable new terror, and a search for culprits to blame with concentrated hatred. It is not too fanciful to imagine how some people thought: *That enigmatic girl, radiating uncanny energy, who died last month: is she taking revenge for her life cut off, sending out poisoned darts to the neighbours who are now dying horribly?*

The sixth- and seventh-century cases surely represent a continuum, but with changing practices reflecting different contexts and anxieties. It would be unsurprising if new ideas and influences after 640 brought new ways of neutralizing the dead, which were then luridly intensified by the plague.

Equally, it may be that as the force of the plague gradually lessened, and the dominance of the monastic culture faded, corpse-killing declined correspondingly. Over the next three centuries, episodes were occasional rather than regular, until the millennium produced a new set of anxieties.

Around the later eighth century, the author of 'Beowulf' deplored—from a Christian perspective—the evil progeny of Cain that troubled the world: 'ogres, elves, hell-corpses (*orcneas*) and giants'.[18] If these *orcneas* were the traditional walking dead, they are thoroughly demonized in this context. The poet describes the monster Grendel in terms not only presaging the savage dead of later Iceland (p. 249), but also suggesting the terrors of the night-mare experience.[19] Perhaps by that point the undead had become less familiar, and more likely to be conceived as semi-legendary horrors.

18

Francia, England, and Scandinavia, 700–1000

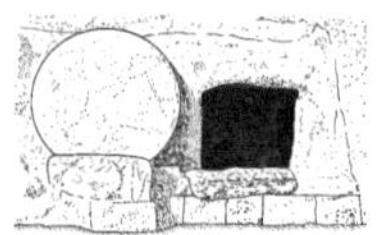

Then Odin rode by the eastern doors,
where he knew the seeress's grave to be;
he began to speak a corpse-reviving spell for the wise woman,
until reluctantly she rose, spoke these corpse-words:

'Which man is that, unknown to me,
who is making me travel this difficult road?
I was snowed upon, I was rained upon,
Dew fell on me, dead I've been for a long time.'

—'BALDR'S DREAMS'

ENGLAND PROVIDES the clearest evidence for corpse-killing during the seventh century, but this may have been part of a wider pattern, less visible elsewhere. It seems possible that across the whole north European zone, revenant beliefs were endemic at a lower level: people just accepted that the dead had to be lived with. A brooch of c. 700 from Strand, Norway, bears the inscription 'brooch is corpse-protection': the oldest explicit textual reference from northern Europe, assuming that it protected *against* corpses rather than protecting a corpse.[1] Less ambiguously, a ninth-century runic amulet found at Ulvsunda (Sweden) enjoins: 'do not be over-lively outside [your grave], revenant! May the evil-doer get woe. . . .'[2]

Carolingian Francia

As the Frankish culture-zone expanded eastwards during the eighth and ninth centuries, previously undocumented beliefs came within the range of written sources. A sermon of c. 800 from Lorsch Abbey (on the Rhine) exhorts the baptized not to consult *strigae* or to believe in 'fictional wolves'.[3] This might be an early hint at beliefs in night-battles between (evil) demons and (good) werewolves (p. 290), but it does not define the *strigae*. More expressively, Charlemagne's legal code for recently-conquered Saxony prescribes death for two kinds of offender: one who believes 'according to pagan custom that some man or woman is a *striga* and eats men, and because of this burns him/her, or gives his/her flesh to be eaten, or eats it'; and one who 'causes the body of a man to be consumed by flames, and reduces his bones to ashes, according to the pagan rite'.[4]

This is frustratingly obscure. We can infer that *strigae* were humans, believed to double as demonic entities who devoured people. It is unclear whether they were burned alive, or (if their corpses proved troublesome) after death; the reference to eating their flesh has no independent support of any kind. The second clause is usually taken to describe ordinary cremation, but in context it might conceivably refer to the exceptional burning of the dangerously animated dead.

Whether these texts point to beliefs in undead corpses, or simply to the kind of magical context that often generated those beliefs, remains unclear. Nor—if the normal remedy was burning—will archaeology help. Occasional burials point to mutilation in the grave. The ninth-century settlement of Vöhingen (on the Rhine near Stuttgart) contained a prone male burial with the legs trussed tightly to the body.[5] At Bad Windsheim (Bavaria), a ninth- to tenth-century male, initially buried supine, was twisted over to a prone posture when semi-decomposed, leaving one leg in situ.[6] Further south, the late Roman practice of nailing the skulls of corpses was still occasionally used in Bologna.[7]

Most intriguing is a cemetery at Mockersdorf in Bavaria—close to the present Czech border—from the decades around 800. This contained six abnormal burials (out of forty): two prone, one piled with stones, two with the crania displaced from the jawbones, and one with the right forearm thrust through the cranium and jawbone.[8] This was a frontier zone, where eastwards Frankish expansion faced Slavic peoples. The grave-goods are not distinctive to either group, and would be compatible with a mixed population. Until comparable cemeteries are found, this seems most likely to reflect a local epidemic of corpse-killing, prompted by ethnic confrontations on a violent frontier.

The most memorable of Carolingian unquiet corpses was found at Elsau in Zürich canton, near the sources of the Rhine. In the ninth century, a severely disabled middle-aged woman was buried in what seems to have been the north porch or annexe of a small church (Figure 41). Her ankles were bound, and there may have been an attempt to cut off her right foot. But that was not enough: within one to six years, the grave was re-opened and the skull pulled off and rolled sideways. The grave was then re-filled with boulders, on which were placed a sea-eagle's foot (over her head) and a fox's foot (over her feet). Finally, a mortar floor was laid in the room, hiding all traces of the grave.[9]

The motivation and rituals cannot be fully decoded, but they must have been dramatic and unusual. The woman was initially buried in an honorific Christian space, so she cannot have been marginal in life. But perhaps events after her funeral cast a more sinister and threatening light on her, so that drastic measures were needed to keep her down, and then to conceal the presence of her grave. The animal talismans are unique survivals, but they recall later European magic and witchcraft. Were spirit-animals expected to bind her body in their respective realms: a creature of the air for her head, a creature of the earth for her feet? This looks like a respected but daunting wise-woman, on the older northern European pattern, in a world of complex frontier-crossing magic.

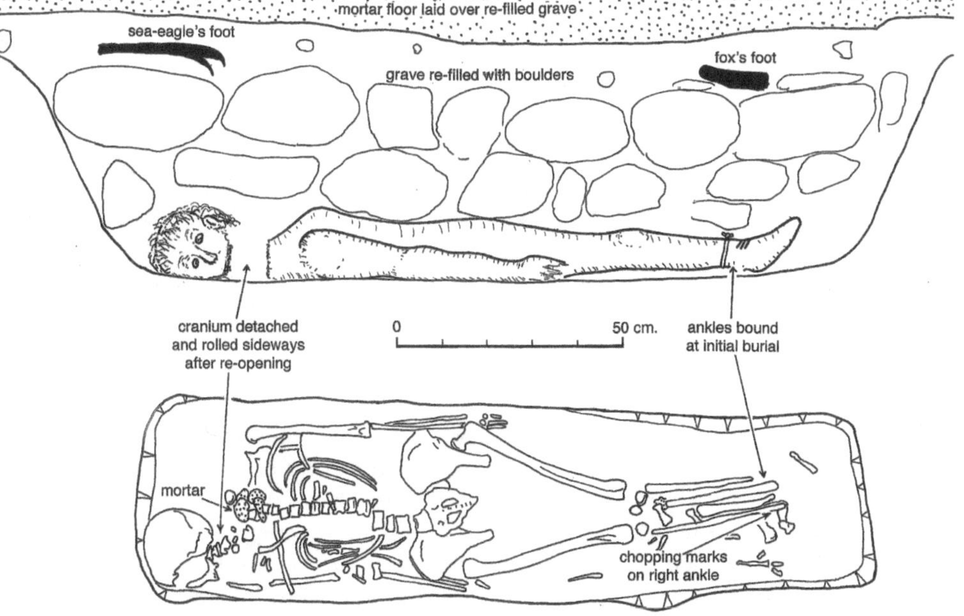

FIGURE 41: Elsau (Switzerland), the grave of a powerful Carolingian woman: plan as excavated, and interpretative reconstructed section. In addition to more familiar expedients, two detached limbs from creatures of air and earth were laid on top to keep her down.

Lying Undead in a Ditch: England, 700–1000

By 1000, the wise-women and abbesses of the seventh century were just memories. Violent, unstable northern Europe in the tenth and eleventh centuries was a man's world, and its dangerous dead were largely male. That said, female subjects only gradually disappeared from England, and at one point the counter-measures took an even more violent turn. Rather than mutilated in their own graves, young women were dismembered, trussed, and buried in the boundary ditches of settlements.

Helpfully, three examples of this are dated by radiocarbon. At Yarnton (Oxfordshire), a girl of thirteen to nineteen (AD 780–895) was dumped in the ditch of an enclosed rural settlement, face-down with her legs tightly trussed backwards (Figures 42 and 43). Below and around her lay the lower jaw and ribs from a child of about six, and the crania of four

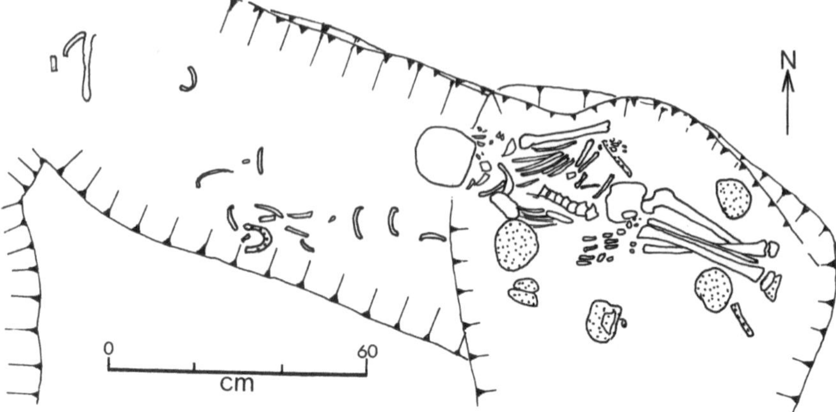

FIGURE 42: Yarnton (Oxfordshire): debris from a ninth-century rampage of corpse-killing? In a settlement boundary ditch, the crania of four children (shown with stippled shading) were placed. Above them, a teenage girl was dumped face-down with her legs tied back. Scattered nearby in the ditch-fill were a lower jaw and rib fragments, again from sub-adults. The targeting of the heads, jaws, and rib-cages (to remove the hearts?) suggests intense fear that a group of dead children would return.

children.[10] At Conington (Huntingdonshire) and Higham Ferrers (Northamptonshire), young adult women (AD 680–880 and 770–890 respectively) were buried prone in the boundary ditches of royal resource-processing complexes (Figure 44).[11] The Higham Ferrers woman, lacking her head, arms, and shoulder-blades, was already semi-decayed when she went into the ditch as a tight bundle; two adult male jawbones, of similar and slightly earlier dates, were in the backfill nearby.[12]

These cases look very similar, including their overlapping date ranges. The disarticulated remains associated with two of them, comprising crania and jawbones, suggest that their deposition followed the mutilation of other corpses (children at Yarnton, adult males at Higham Ferrers). Although the radiocarbon ranges are too broad for certainty, it is intriguing to speculate whether they might all be close in date, and reflect a specific epidemic in the early to mid-ninth century. It might be relevant that Irish burials in ditch terminals (with a preponderance towards juveniles) also seem to concentrate in this period.[13]

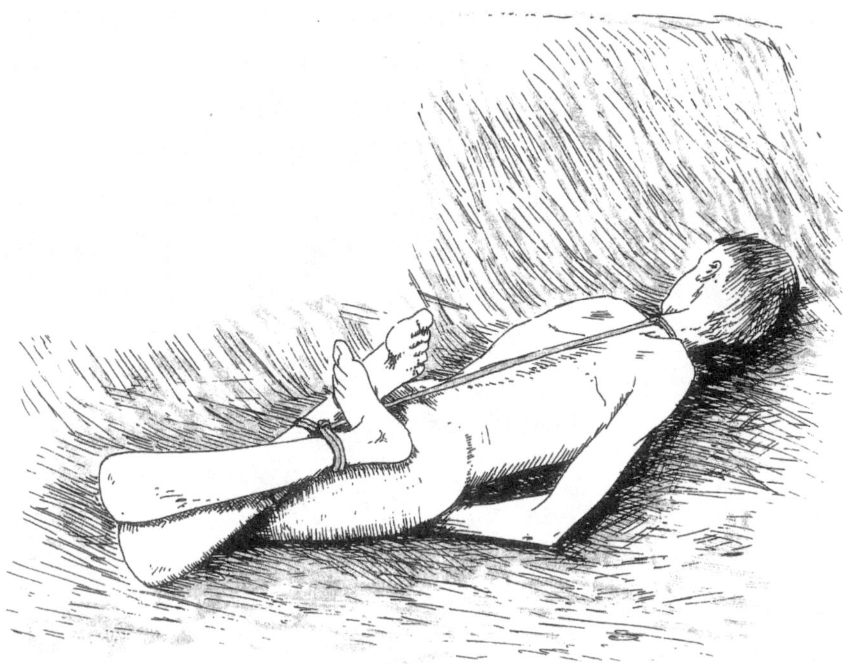

FIGURE 43: Artist's impression of the girl buried in the ditch at Yarnton.

Why were these young women selected for this particularly shameful treatment? Perhaps by now they were less like seers and healers and more like witches. Something of this may be glimpsed in the mysterious Old English poem known as 'The Wife's Lament'—probably composed in Mercia during c. 750–850—where an unquiet dead woman is imprisoned in an earthen dugout under an oak-tree, in a sinister, joyless landscape.[14]

The last word on the mighty host of female walking dead comes from the 'Life' of St Kenelm of Winchcombe, written during c. 1040–80. This narrative—from an Anglo-Saxon world becoming Anglo-Norman—presents Kenelm's sister, the royal abbess Cwoenthryth, as a fratricidal Jezebel, who recites Psalm 109 backwards 'by some kind of witchcraft' until her eyes drop out onto the psalter. 'The wretched woman died shortly afterwards, and they say that she could not be kept buried in the church, nor in the cemetery, nor in the open field, but that a brilliantly shining child [the martyred Kenelm] appeared to someone, and ordered

FIGURE 44: Conington (Huntingdonshire): an eighth- or ninth-century woman buried prone in one of the terminals of the boundary ditch around a high-status settlement.

her to be thrown into some remote deep place.'[15] After this succession of failed interments, she would presumably have looked not unlike the excavated Higham Ferrers woman.

Cwoenthryth really existed—she was abbess of Minster-in-Thanet in the 820s—but no genuine source mentions her scandalous end. Rather, this fiction of an anti-heroine looks back on the lost culture of female monastic dominance through the lens of eleventh-century misogyny. It was probably remembered that powerful abbesses had once been daunting in death, but the undead Cwoenthryth is re-cast as a deviant who must be banished to the margins.

Among the more ordinary dead, countermeasures are hard to recognize in this period. One exception is the relatively subtle practice found in a cemetery at Godalming (Surrey), in use during c. 850–1120.[16] At least 4 percent of burials, mostly male, have nails driven into the joints of the neck, elbows, hips, or knees (Figure 45). This is clearly a corpse-

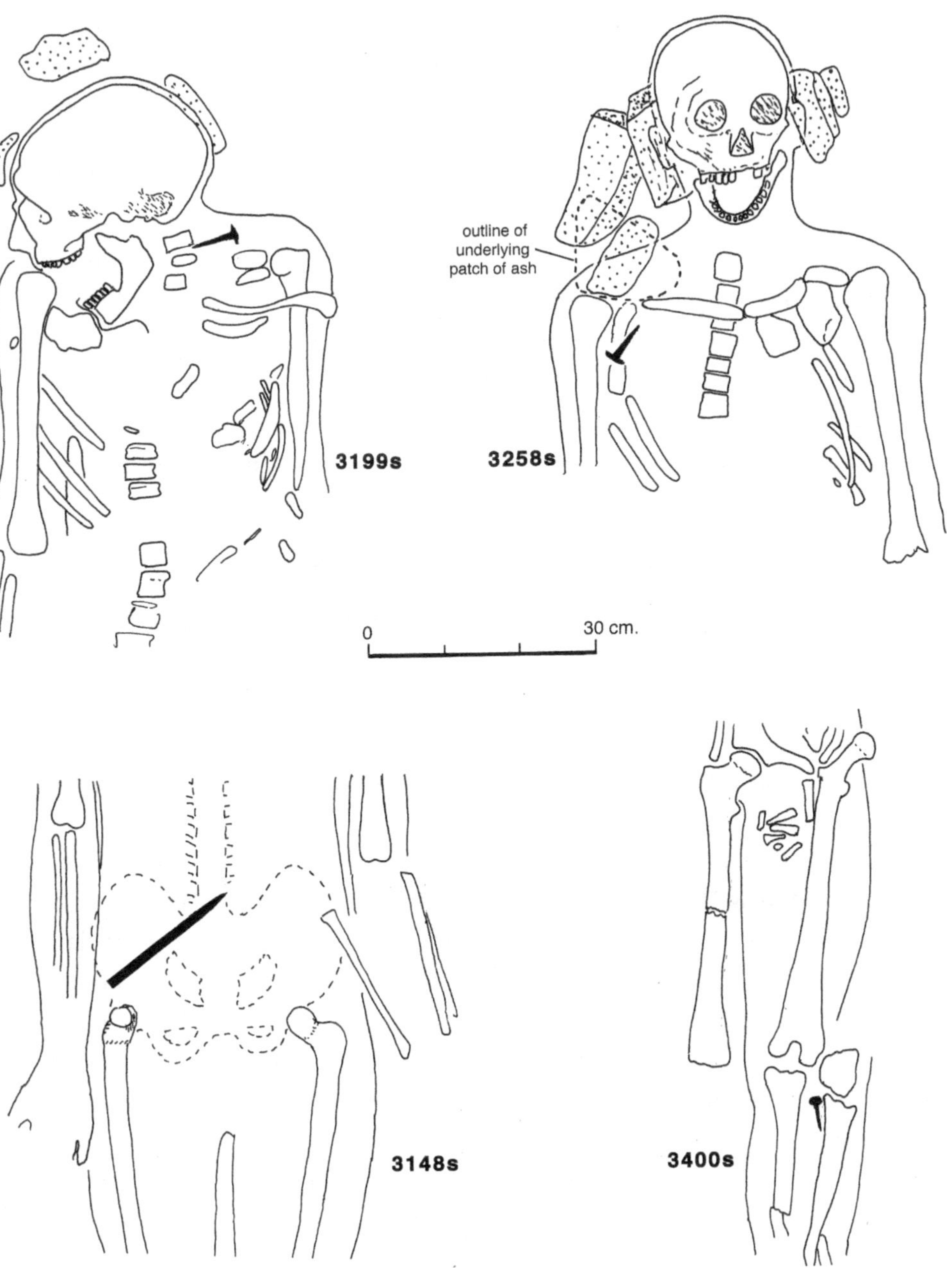

FIGURE 45: Nailing down the late Anglo-Saxon dead. Selected burials from the cemetery at Godalming (Surrey), illustrating the piercing of shoulders, necks, and knees with iron nails and the presumably similar use of a large iron spike.

restraining practice (as in Jamaica, p. 90), though of the low-level kind that could have been performed privately at the laying-out or wake. These burials, which span the life of the cemetery, imply a belief persisting over many generations: about one corpse in twenty was threatening to the point of needing tactful restraint.

Two sites in south-west Britain imply a slightly different tradition. At Glastonbury (Somerset), 14 percent of burials in an apparently monastic cemetery lay prone; a small coastal cemetery near St David's (Dyfed) contained one headless, folded-up corpse, and another that lay prone with rocks on its back.[17] Both cemeteries were active around the ninth century, both were accessible from the Bristol Channel and Irish Sea, and both had religious associations: Irish influence seems likely.

Scandinavian Sisters

In one of the medieval Icelandic poems that draw on the pagan past, Odin visits the underworld to have some alarming dreams interpreted. He resurrects a seeress (*vǫlva*) buried in the eastern doorway, who reluctantly answers his questions (p. 216). The source is late, but it catches an echo of a female-dominated ritual world that survived longer in Scandinavia than in England.

A category of powerful, daunting, and respected wise-women, equipped with wrought-iron ritual staffs, remained prominent up to Christianisation.[18] They and their equipment are found (especially at Birka in Sweden) in graves of c. 900–50, which recall with an odd precision the female graves of conversion-period England. These wonder-working women were sometimes buried amid bizarre funerary tableaux, including being seated in chairs or accompanied by sacrificed animals.[19]

Posthumous mutilation is rare, but occasional women did require extreme measures. Grave Bj.959 at Birka contained a well-dressed woman with brooches, beads, shears, tweezers, an iron ring, a knife, and a bone needle-case.[20] Her skull was cradled in her right arm; the jawbone was completely absent, but a pig's jawbone lay across her throat (Figure 46). Some crucial details of this burial are unrecorded, but we have more data

FIGURE 46: Birka (Sweden), burial Bj 959. This tenth-century woman's head was detached and relocated; the lower jaw was removed entirely, and a pig's jawbone laid across her throat in substitution. Reconstruction by Mirosław Kuźma.

for grave T at Bogøvei, Langeland (Denmark), a woman accompanied by a knife, beads, and a shell (Figure 47).[21] Leszek Gardeła's interpretation of the sequence here deserves quoting:

> Sometime after the coffin was lowered into the grave-pit and the funeral ceremonies had passed, someone decided to open the grave. It is

FIGURE 47: Bogøvej (Denmark), burial T. This tenth-century woman's head and lower jaw were detached and re-located separately from each other. Reconstruction by Mirosław Kuźma.

difficult to determine when that happened, but we may suspect a moment when the body was in an advanced state of decomposition. The grave was opened and the head/skull was ripped from the spine (no signs of cutting were identified on the bones . . .). During that process the jaw was damaged and it broke in half. . . . Then, the person(s) re-

> sponsible for the whole act threw or placed the woman's head/skull on her left leg, right below the knee. In the process of moving the head, the jaw fell off from the head/skull along with the cervical vertebrae (the vertebrae and the jawbone were found to the west from the skull and between the thighs . . .). Afterwards, the grave was back-filled again.[22]

Readers will note the convergence of this reconstruction with my own independent reconstruction of the seventh-century English burials (p. 202). Indeed, Gardeła draws the same conclusion: 'Perhaps the people who opened [the grave] cut the woman's head off because she haunted the local society? Maybe she was seen as responsible for some misfortunes that fell upon the members of the nearby farms?'[23] The capacity to eat, bite, or curse has again been disabled by separating the two jaws (at Birka, even by replacing the woman's lower jaw with a pig's).

These Scandinavian parallels to English practices three centuries earlier—both the demonstrative signalling of numinous female power, and the very specific procedure for neutralizing dead women who have turned troublesome—are intriguing. Direct influence is not impossible, but there is a large time-gap to be bridged (as indeed between the late Romano-British burials of this kind and the seventh-century ones). It seems more likely that we are seeing discrete traces of a northern European continuum. Pulling a dead woman's head apart would not have been done lightly, but maybe there was always an understanding that it worked in extreme cases.

Stoning and Stabbing

Mutilation of buried corpses was not confined to females, nor to the dangerous dead. Across Scandinavia, many Viking-age cases of beheaded and stoned corpses—both male and female—have been found.[24] These are more ambiguous than the Birka and Bogøvei examples, and the well-attested ritual sacrifice of slaves creates a further problem: it probably explains the several double male burials in which one of the pair is decapitated. The cases where stones are piled over corpses, or laid on their heads or feet, are perhaps more promising.

So is a different kind of ritual where weapons are stabbed down vertically into the burial deposit, seen for instance at Kaupang in Norway.[25] Even this could be ambiguous: in Iron Age Yorkshire, weapon-stabbing has been tentatively explained as a vigorous gesture of respect by the dead warrior's comrades (p. 179). That scarcely explains a tenth-century episode beside a lake at Dalstorp in southern Sweden, when five spears were stabbed down into the ashes of a woman who had already been cremated with ten knives: her neighbours in life were extremely determined to keep her quiet in death.[26]

It seems a fair inference that female subjects remained important in Scandinavian corpse-killing until at least the later tenth century, but that male subjects were also present, and possibly gained prominence over time. That may apply especially to the high-status dead who occupied chambers within barrows, and who became the subjects of an important folklore motif.

The Scandinavian Mound-Dwellers

Around 1200, the historian Saxo Grammaticus re-worked a story from the legendary Danish past. The princes Asvith and Asmund have made a vow of friendship: when one dies, the other will be buried with him. Asvith dies first, so Asmund is enclosed alive in the barrow, but robbers break in and rescue him. Horribly disfigured, Asmund relates in verse the horrors of the tomb:

> Beyond all this I have struggled against a phantom's energy, wrestled with grievous strain and immense peril. Asvith returned from the other world with ghostly violence; his gashing nails attacked me, renewing fierce battle after his death.
>
> . . . .
>
> By some piece of hellish daring
> Asvith's spirit was launched from the shades

with ferocious teeth to devour the steed
and lift the dog to its monstrous jaws.
But horse nor dog sated its hunger;
swiftly it turned its lightning talons
to slash my cheek and take off my ear.
. . . .
I was quick to scythe off its head with my sword
and thrust a stake through its wicked body.[27]

There were multiple versions of this template across early medieval Scandinavia. Mostly they only survive in the late and unreliable medium of Icelandic sagas, but they are so numerous and consistent that they must reflect an embedded belief. The protagonists are male. Some are horrific, like Asvith; others are dangerous and daunting rather than evil, sometimes reciting their own death-songs in skaldic verse.[28]

Attacks on corpses in barrows really happened, as shown by events at the two great Norwegian ship-burials at Oseberg (two women buried in 834) and Gokstad (a man buried c. 900).[29] Between about 950 and 980—in other words during early Christianisation—intruders tunnelled into the chambers on both ships. They smashed furnishings, dragged out the (now skeletal) corpses, and mutilated them with extraordinary violence; in particular, the skulls were smashed into small fragments. The scale of the operations shows that these were not secret robberies, but public attacks on the dead. While political motives are possible, the saga narratives encourage the view that these potentates were viewed as noxious and dangerous forces inside their barrows, requiring neutralization.

When we penetrate below the atmosphere of high drama, these mound-dwellers are actually not so different from grave-bound corpses further south. Horrific though they are, they do not stray from their tombs. To his former loving friend, Asvith is an evil monster to be beheaded and staked: the ambiguity (is it the 'real' Asvith or a diabolical re-animation?) recalls the conceptual sleights-of-hand when modern Greeks neutralise their dead relatives (p. 101). A ravenous consumer of horses, dogs and people, Asvith can be read as a dramatised version of the shroud-chewers, lying in their graves bloated with blood; he is dispatched by identical means. The point is underlined by another of Saxo's stories—set in a fictionalized context—which might as easily have come from twelfth-century England or early modern central Europe: 'His wickedness even appeared after his decease; anyone nearing his tomb was quickly exterminated, and his corpse emitted such foul plagues. . . . The citizens, overwhelmed by this evil, disinterred the body, decapitated it and impaled it through the breast with a sharp stake.'[30]

Revenant beliefs were endemic across the northern zone, but they fluctuated over time, notably in shifting from female to male subjects. In sixth-century England, there had been some correlation between female amuletic equipment and abnormal burial. Late seventh-century England and early tenth-century Scandinavia were each, in turn, at the point of being transformed by Christian culture. In both contexts there were female ritual specialists; some female corpses were perceived as dangerous; but these two categories only partly overlapped. Except at Ely, the most drastically mutilated corpses were not those with explicit ritual equipment. The common factor may therefore be a more generalized conception: *numinous power resides in women.*

As Christian theology took hold, the sinister diverged from the powerful. That took time: the ninth-century woman at Elsau looks as dramatic as any other. 'Witches', though socially marginalized, were still powerful, hence the long-continuing female strand in central European beliefs. But in Scandinavia and England it was increasingly the male leadership of local society—warriors, farmers, officials, priests—that produced grumpy and dishonest individuals whose malevolence persisted beyond the grave.

Within the continuum of this period, there may have been occasional local peaks. Perhaps the Mockersdorf cemetery represented one, and the girls dumped in ditches in ninth-century England represented another. The fights with Scandinavian mound-dwellers could represent a third peak, although those narratives (setting aside the intrusions at Oseberg and Gokstad) are only documented much later. But as magnate domination and colonial violence traumatised Europe, and the dreaded millennium approached, there was a change of gear: the dangerous dead intensified their activity and extended their range.

PART IV

Europe in the High Middle Ages

SOURCES FOR THE DANGEROUS DEAD are scarce in medieval Europe, but the impression of heightened activity after 1000 is too widespread to discount. As well as probable epidemics in Iceland and England, evidence starts to emerge around the edges of the Viking culture-zone, including Finland and the southern Baltic coast. Were these local eruptions all facets of a Europe-wide epidemic? The millennial year 1000 initiated quite enough angst: fears of the end of the world were unrealized, but rapid economic and urban growth, combined with political disruption and the consolidation of harsh aristocratic power, overthrew many familiar landmarks.

Many people think of vampires as inherently Slavic. A different scenario is proposed here: that distinct zones of belief, in northern Europe on the one hand and the Black Sea region on the other, reflected a common background but took different paths over many centuries. Their influences diffused, but eventually coalesced again after 1600. Over time, local developments responded to changing social and psychological needs, causing the belief-system to fade in some regions and intensify in others.

19

Motifs Taking Shape

THE MAKING OF THE 'EUROPEAN VAMPIRE'

They found them intact, but the linen cloths over their faces were very horribly bloody. They cut off the men's heads and placed them in the graves between their thighs, tore out their hearts from their corpses, and covered the bodies with earth again.

—DEALING WITH THE STAPENHILL REVENANTS, C. 1090 (*MIRACLES OF SAINT MODWENNA*)

IN THE 1010S, a Rhineland bishop wrote down a long list of superstitious errors, including two that concern us here. Adopting the voice of a probing confessor, Burchard of Worms asked:

> Have you done what certain women, inspired by the devil, are in the habit of doing? When some infant dies unbaptized, they take the little one's corpse, and put it in some secret place, and transfix its tiny body with a stake, saying that if they do not do this, the little child would rise up and would be able to injure many. . . . [And] when some woman needs to give birth but cannot, and dies in that misery

during her fruitless labour, they transfix both mother and infant with a stake driven into the earth in the same grave.[1]

This is the first central European reference to measures against the restless dead; some English stories run it close. Over the next two centuries, chroniclers would document these beliefs in Latin, and saga-writers would start to weave them into Old Norse narratives. For the first time, the European revenant was a topic for literate description and learned speculation, and the dialogue between 'elite' and 'popular' becomes visible to us.

How far did academic theology absorb lay beliefs, and how far did it modify them? When clerics picked up interpretations from penitentials and chronicles, did their preaching and pastoral care influence the illiterate laity? Both English chroniclers and Icelandic saga-writers used the motif of the violent, lumpen male corpse, but were they drawing it independently from oral tradition, or from motifs that spread in the milieux of literate discourse and creative writing? We must always keep these questions in mind, even when we cannot answer them. Here as always, there was a feedback-loop rather than an impermeable cultural barrier.

The European Melting-Pot

Burchard of Worms's perceptions that the restless dead were women and children, and that it was a female task to restrain them, would later be diluted but not effaced: suspect corpses in some parts of early modern central Europe still showed a strong female bias. By contrast, the English undead were now male. There is an impression that European beliefs were both intensifying and undergoing new modifications. But as a package, they also emerge as distinctly different from those in other parts of the world.

The phenomenon is not Europe-wide: a line drawn from London to Athens would leave only occasional post-Roman cases to its south-west, in Brittany, Italy, Iberia, and the Mediterranean. North-east of that line, there is a remarkable homogeneity (with some local variations) about the belief-systems delineated in medieval England and Scandinavia, in early modern Germany, in Poland, in the Balkans, and in the Aegean. The main difference is that the south-east European beliefs include bloodsucking, and adopt the terminology of demonic beings. But a case can be made that the scattered eruptions of similar motif-sets reflect a thick, embedded stratum, that was sometimes submerged, and sometimes exposed, but eventually resisted erosion in some regions more than others.

The formation of this stratum may go back ultimately to common roots, and may owe something to religious interchange in the late Roman Empire: even if Nordic and Balkan cultures of belief were separated for centuries, they had basic ingredients in common. Evidently the complex had an inherent psychological power, which preserved it as a layer of smouldering embers liable to flare up when combinations of religious, social, or medical disruption reached critical levels of stress.

Defining the Prototypes: Walkers, Bloaters, Shroud-Chewers, and Bloodsuckers

Undead corpses of the European zone come in a range of variants. The vital power (and occasionally the personality) of the living person is retained after death within the corpse, which sometimes walks around, sometimes remains confined to its grave, but in either case is animated by a life-force that is understood as abnormal, noxious, and unholy. If it walks, it can shape-change into animal forms—a capacity which, like passing through doors and walls, raises questions about its literal physicality when out of the grave. Such a corpse does not visibly suck blood, though sometimes it can mysteriously absorb the blood of others while dormant. It will often become bloated and swollen, and acquire a livid appearance.

One seemingly trivial but distinctive feature provides a trace-element for cultural links. This is the corpse's behaviour towards its own shroud or face-cloth, which it is liable to tear, chew, or swallow. Of course, Paul Barber would point out that both bloating and tearing can be outcomes of natural decomposition. Still, the motif is so regularly emphasized (and so conspicuously lacking in some other cultures) that it must reflect transmission rather than independent observation. These undead seem to be obsessive-compulsives: neurotically biting and tearing at the constraining shrouds in their malevolent frustration, their outrageous lusts pent up by restrictions on their movement.[2]

At some point, a basic difference emerges between those who are seen walking, and those who never leave their graves but lie there exuding evil power. It is unclear when that occurred, and there will have been different trajectories in different regions. No coherent time-line should be expected, and the sources do not suggest one. It just happens that there are particularly useful narratives from twelfth-century England, so we will start there.

What seems to be the archetypal European revenant occurs in a story preserved in an English chronicle of the 1190s, and almost certainly set at Annan in south-western Scotland (p. 254). It tells how a corpse left its grave each night and wandered through the town, spreading sickness and death. Two brothers accordingly opened the grave 'and soon exposed the corpse, which was distended to a huge corpulence, with a swollen, livid face. It was observed that the shroud, which had been wound around it, was completely shredded up (*sudarium . . . concissum penitus*). Too angry to be frightened, the young men struck a blow at the lifeless corpse, whereupon such a flow of blood gushed out that they understood it to be a sucker of many people's blood (*sanguisuga . . . multorum*). Dragging it out of the town, they quickly built a pyre'.[3] A link between the breaking of the shroud and the swelling and animation of the corpse becomes explicit in later Baltic, Finnish, and Sámi folk-tales, where the corpse arises when the shroud or coffin bursts.[4] Widespread in later Europe was the idea that re-animation could be prevented by placing a barrier between the corpse's mouth and its wrappings.

The other important point about the Annan revenant is that he is called a bloodsucker. However dubiously the motif entered later vampire literature, this story is from the twelfth century: it is unique, but unambiguous. Bloodsucking—not emphasized in Roman-era material—suggests that there was some obscure and distant link here with the **ōpyr* tradition (p. 292). Even so, ambiguity remains. This revenant is not seen biting his victims Dracula-style: he wanders around spreading poisonous vapours, and his corpse is swollen with blood, but how did the blood get there? The 'after-eating' corpses of later central Europe will present the same enigma.

The Mobile Dead: Walkers

The Annan revenant walked *and* accumulated blood in its grave, but other English stories present walkers in apparent distinction from grave-bound corpses. The richest medieval narrative of all (in a monastic chronicle written around the 1130s) discusses two labourers who had died at Stapenhill, near Burton-upon-Trent in Staffordshire, in about 1090.[5] This account is so exceptionally circumstantial that it bears detailed comparison with later folklore:

- They made false accusations against their lord.
- They died of sudden seizures and were buried.
- That evening, they appeared carrying their coffins on their backs.
- They also appeared as animals.
- They behaved threateningly and spread disease, so that many people died.
- Their graves were opened and the bodies were found intact, with the cloths over their faces 'very horribly bloody' (*deformissime cruentatis*).
- Their heads were cut off and placed between their thighs, their hearts were cut out, and the graves backfilled.
- The hearts were burned on a hilltop, crackled with a loud noise, and a crow flew up from the flames.
- Both the disease and the apparitions stopped; the surviving victims recovered when they saw smoke rising from the fire.

Amazingly, every one of these details can be matched from folklore ranging across northern and eastern Europe (p. 257). Here, surely, the precise and sustained parallels go beyond any plausible coincidence, and make a 'splitter' position untenable: eleventh-century England and post-medieval Romania were heirs to the same deep stratum of tradition.

A recurrent feature of European walking corpses is the animalistic wildness of their behaviour. They shape-shift, they roam around with barking dogs, they drive animals mad or even dance among them, and they especially attack shepherds and their sheep. There is clearly a fusion here with other motifs of supernatural disorder, notably the wild hunt of the damned (p. 291): hunters and their hounds, all 'black and loathsome', were seen and heard around Peterborough in 1127.[6] A revenant in 1190s Buckinghamshire, and a later one near Prague, indulged in wild antics among the farm animals (pp. 255, 345). The emphasis on shepherds suggests a background in which rampant corpses, like other kinds of monsters, had lurked on the wild margins of society, though it may also reflect the role of transhumant pastoralists in disseminating these types of supernatural fear (p. 367).

Conversely, the bloating and chewing motifs are toned down in the Stapenhill narrative: the corpses are just said to be intact, and only the face-cloths suggest bloodsucking. This evolution of the prototype points forward to the 'active' type of revenant that would be familiar across much of Europe in the following centuries. Although Scandinavia and Iceland lack shroud-chewers, the monstrous, black, bloated revenants of those regions cannot be very distant relatives.

The Grave-Bound Dead: Bloaters and Shroud-Chewers

Meanwhile, the bloated shroud-chewer also evolved into a different and more passive kind that was never seen to leave its grave at all. This variant is illustrated in a judgement of the Ottoman jurist Ebussuud Efendi (1490–1574), probably referring to the Turkish-ruled Balkans:

> QUESTION: Some deceased people, after being buried, tear their shrouds in the grave, their organs fill with blood, and their bodies turn reddish. What is the reason for this occurrence?
>
> RESPONSE: If it happened, it is [because of] the graceful will of the just Lord. Then it shows, 'the wicked spirits possess dead bodies of people who were partnered with them during their lifetime in terms of deeds and morals.' It is not beyond the power of the Almighty.
>
> QUESTION: When the aforementioned occurrence is seen, what should be done to the related corpse?
>
> RESPONSE: You need to cover up the grave if it is Muslim [since] the revenant is harmless.

QUESTION: Are people allowed to take out [the corpses] from their graves and burn them according to the sharia?
RESPONSE: No, they are not.[7]

An interesting aspect of this dialogue is that the Muslim jurist, from a different religion and culture, acknowledged the reality of the phenomenon (rationalized here as diabolic possession) but thought it essentially harmless: a wicked life leaves the corpse vulnerable to demons, but nobody else suffers. In Greece, Orthodox clergy were similarly relaxed about the bloated but inert *tympaniaios* (p. 308). That was not the view of their Catholic and Lutheran neighbours to the west, in northern Germany and Poland, who had to confront the bloated, immobile, but still deadly shroud-chewer. As we will see, that terror would even have a distant and bizarre future among the inhabitants of nineteenth-century Pennsylvania.

The 'Southern Slavic' Problem

There is an elephant in the room: doesn't everyone know that vampires are Slavic? The concentration of undead beliefs in the Balkans since 1800—highlighted by travel writing and fiction—encouraged a presumption that the southern Slavic zone was the 'original' epicentre. An early proponent, the German scholar Ernst Havekost, acknowledged the lack of firm evidence, but still saw the 'rich treasury of folk belief and poetry', combined with the interlinking of undead beliefs with others across the Romanian, Bulgarian, Czech, Polish, Russian, and Greek areas, as betokening a deep-embedded belief.[8] Thus, in Havekost's view, it was Viking entrepreneurs who channelled these stories from the southern Slavs via Novgorod and Finland to northern Europe.[9]

But the intensity of a phenomenon at a late date does not prove that it existed from an early one. The one zone of the post-Roman Balkans where we can be certain of corpse-killing practices persisting through the early Middle Ages is Bulgaria (p. 283), where the population was ethnically very mixed. Most other Slavic populations practiced cremation, which tends in itself to militate against such beliefs. In the light of the evidence to be discussed, diffusion through the Balkans from an origin on the Black Sea coast of Bulgaria seems the most plausible scenario.

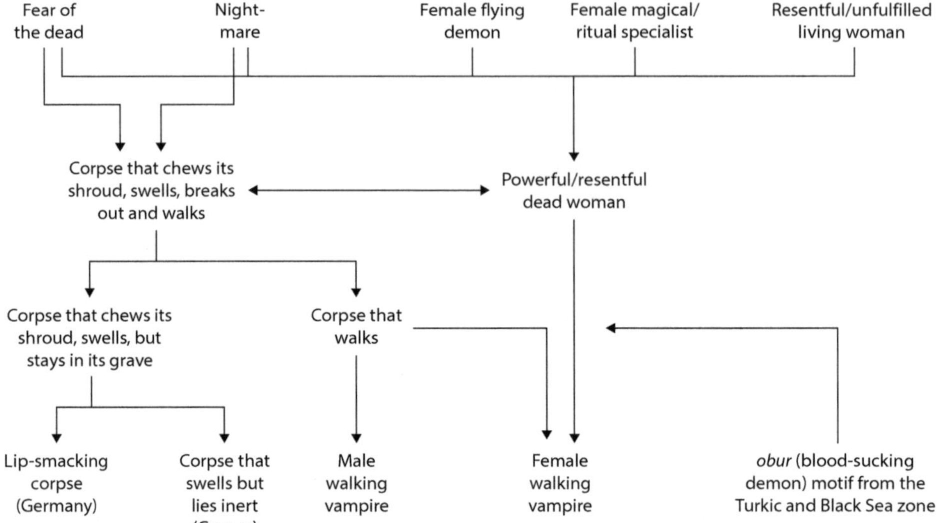

FIGURE 48: An attempt to frame the various supernatural concepts underlying European beliefs in malevolent corpses.

Anchoring belief-systems so rigidly to specific ethnic/linguistic groups is tricky at the best of times. In this case, the abundant evidence now available for corpse-killing in regions of northern and western Europe from the sixth century onwards fatally undermines the idea that the beliefs had anything exclusively Slavic about them.

When the various threads are pulled together, a tentative 'family tree' of restless-dead motifs in the European zone can be suggested (Figure 48). Needless to say, this is an abstraction to think with, not a definitive or comprehensive solution. Gaps between sources are vast, and reality must have been both more complex and more fluid. Still, this visualization of motifs that travelled side-by-side, cross-pollinating as they went, is probably somewhere near the truth. It does help to explain why the region looks different from the rest of the world, and why the 'European vampire' seems distinctive.

20

An Icelandic Epidemic?

> As soon as the fires were burning, [the dead] Thórodd and his companions came in, all dripping wet. They sat down by the fire and began wringing the water from their clothing. After they had sat down, [the dead] Thórir Viðlegg and his six companions came in; they were all covered with earth. They shook it out of their clothing and spattered the earth over Thórodd and his men. The people of the household rushed from the room.
>
> —EYRBYGGJA SAGA

THE SAGAS OF ICELANDERS, written in Old Norse, contain some of the most celebrated and highly-coloured stories of the walking dead.[1] To readers of this book, these beings will seem less bizarre and unfamiliar than they do to other readers. Equally, the peculiarities of Icelandic society moulded some distinctive types of revenant, and distinctive conceptions of how to deal with them.

These sagas, written after 1200, cannot be relied on for factual information. They are not historical narratives but imaginative and sophisticated constructs, drawing both on the Icelandic past and on European literary models. Still, they embody rich traditions about the Icelanders, their ways of life, their social customs, and their beliefs.[2]

The motif-sequences about the walking dead were certainly based in oral culture: they occur so vividly, and so often, that they must have been prominent in the story-telling tradition. Might that in turn mean that these beings were real and threatening presences for Icelanders during c. 930–1030, the period in which the stories are set?

Traumas of Icelandic Society: Colonization, Feud, and Conversion

Settled by Norsemen during the decades around 900, Iceland developed a distinctive social and political order reflecting both its colonial character and its harsh climate.[3] A 'republic' of slave-owning warrior-farmers, it was governed through a system of public courts. The strong emphasis on collective decision-making reflected a society where standing depended on generosity and good-neighbourliness: 'the ungenerous, the authoritarian, or the inept simply lost support and thus status'.[4] In this unforgiving ecological niche, all areas of life depended upon co-operation: violating it was a deed of the monstrous.

The Icelanders accepted Christianity—after some debate—in the year 1000. This was traumatic for many, and an added psychological stress on a society that already operated near the margins of social and economic viability. It also heightened fears that the rejected supernatural forces would prove resentful and vengeful. Such a phase of transition, uncertainty, and emotional trauma can breed monsters.[5]

The secondary and fictionalized nature of the saga material rules out any firm chronology. Still, the exceptional prominence of dangerous-dead motifs, in stories set in and around the conversion era, may reflect a reality: that there was indeed an epidemic of such beliefs in eleventh-century Iceland, where fears already endemic in Scandinavia were intensified for a few generations.[6] The parallel material in Chapters 19, 21, and 22 strengthens this possibility. Archaeology is of limited help here (perhaps because suspect corpses were normally burned), but the piling of stones on suspect corpses is sometimes mentioned in sagas, and three

Icelandic male burials from the period are indeed weighted down with extremely large stones.[7]

Neighbours from Hell

The Icelandic beliefs were outgrowths from the Scandinavian ones, and the debt is clear. There are several barrow-guardians, including the monstrous Raknarr in 'Bárðar Saga' and Kár in 'Grettis Saga', where the motif-sequence of the Asvith case is repeated: a living man struggles with the revenant, whose head is eventually cut off and laid against his buttocks.[8] A very different member of the same tribe is Gunnar, the wise, chivalrous hero of 'Njal's Saga', who sits upright in his barrow in a state of 'high good humour': 'It seemed to them that the mound was open, and that Gunnar had turned around to face the moon. There seemed to be four lights burning inside the burial chamber, so that there were no shadows. They could see that Gunnar was cheerful and looked exultant. He chanted a verse so loudly that they could hear it at a distance.'[9]

Gunnar is exceptional: in general, the Icelandic revenants (*aptrgangur*) are even more noxious than their Scandinavian prototypes.[10] They are mostly men: outsiders, boorishly antisocial in life, thuggishly brutal after death. They violate the most basic norms of status, property, and reciprocity. Unlike the barrow-dwellers, they roam around spreading mayhem. They are outside the law and break it with impunity, since they have no kinsmen who will owe compensation for their misdeeds.[11]

Three examples will illustrate this type, and all are outsiders: Víga-Hrapp, from a Scottish/Hebridean background; and Thórólf and Glám, Scandinavians newly settled in Iceland.[12] 'Laxdæla Saga' tells of Víga-Hrapp, a big, aggressive man who has fled to Iceland to avoid compensating for his crimes, and whose neighbours dislike him. On his deathbed, he asks to be buried standing up under his threshold 'so that I can keep an even better watch over my house'.[13] But 'difficult as he had been to deal with during his life, he was now very much worse after death': his corpse kills his servants and ravages neighbouring farms. It is moved to a distant spot, but Hrapp appears as a seal and causes a boatload of men to drown. Eventually, Hrapp's corpse wrestles with a farmhand and is speared in a fight. When the grave is opened the next day, his body is found undecayed and accompanied by the spearhead. Hrapp is therefore burned on a pyre, and his ashes carried out to sea.[14]

Thórólf Lame-Foot of 'Eyrbyggja Saga' is an equally antisocial farmer, who steals, bribes, and kills.[15] Dying a bad death, he is taken out through a hole in the wall, hauled away on a sled, and buried under a large cairn. But

> people became aware that Thórólf was not resting quietly in his grave; they could never go out in peace after sunset. As well as this, the oxen which had hauled Thórólf's sled were ridden to their deaths by trolls, and all the livestock which wandered near his grave went mad and bellowed themselves to death. The shepherd at Hvammur often came running home because Thórólf had chased him. . . . [Later] the shepherd was found lying dead not far from Thórólf's cairn; his body was black and blue all over, and every bone in his body had been broken.[16]

Matters go from bad to worse: livestock die, Thórólf takes to climbing on the roof (a favourite revenant activity),[17] and then to coming indoors. After the farmstead is abandoned, Thórólf begins haunting the whole valley and many people die. Eventually, the distraught locals break open his tomb and find the body undecayed but hideous. They haul him onto a ridge, but the oxen go mad and break loose. Thórólf is now so heavy that they can barely drag him to the new grave, which they strongly fortify.[18] Some years later, the troubles resume. So once again, 'they broke into the cairn and found Thórólf lying there. His body was uncorrupted and hideous to look at. He was as black as death and as large as an ox. . . . [With great difficulty] they rolled him down to the foreshore and built a great pyre there; they set fire to it and bundled Thórólf onto it and burnt everything to ashes.' Even that is not enough: a cow licks the site of the pyre and a calf is born, which grows into a monstrous and eventually lethal bull.[19]

In 'Grettis Saga', Glám from Sweden is 'a well-built man and very strange-looking, with wide blue eyes and wolf-grey hair'. Employed as a shepherd capable of outfacing a revenant, he dies in the encounter and is found 'dead, blue as hell, and bloated to the size of a bull'. Buried on the spot in a shallow grave, Glám soon comes back to cause trouble: he roams around, drives people mad, climbs on the roof, and kills men and livestock. Finally, the warrior Grettir sleeps in the hall and confronts him. There is a mighty struggle; Grettir overpowers Glám, cuts off his head, and places it (yet again) against his buttocks, after which Glám's body is burned. But Grettir is left under a curse, haunted by the memory of Glám's eyes.[20]

Dangerous Women Again: Thórgunna the Naked Cook

So far, this has seemed a very male world, but residues of female power survived in the Icelandic belief-system. In 'Laxdæla Saga', an evil-looking woman appears in a dream and complains that someone is annoying her by praying at night over her grave in the church. The next day, they dig up the grave and find 'blue and evil-looking' bones, a brooch, and a large wise-woman's staff.[21] This is a funerary assemblage like those in the Swedish female graves (p. 224), presented here as a relic from the bad pre-Christian days.

'Eyrbyggja Saga', with its extraordinary sub-plot of the restless dead, gives us a formidable female protagonist: Thórgunna from the Hebrides. This uncanny woman is rich in fine clothes and textiles, but 'neither easy-tempered nor talkative'. As she rakes hay at the Fróðá farmstead it rains blood, which never dries where her rake had touched.[22] Thórgunna looks like another relic from the old world of female practitioners, an impression strengthened by her dying wishes: 'I want my bed and all its furnishings to be burned to ashes, for they will bring no good to anyone. I am not saying this because I begrudge anyone enjoying all this finery if I thought it would do them any good; the reason I am so insistent', she said, 'is that I would not like it if people suffer the afflictions I know will follow if they do not respect my wishes.'[23]

Her wishes are ignored, and a terrifying sequence of events unfolds. Her burial party are caught in a storm, stop at an inhospitable farmhouse, and go to bed hungry, but Thórgunna herself—naked—occupies the kitchen and cooks dinner for them. After the funeral they return home to Fróðá, and a 'doom-moon' keeps appearing against a panelled wall. Then a shepherd dies and is buried, but he starts to hang around the farm and kills a visitor, after which the two of them are often seen together. Thórodd, the householder of Fróðá, goes out fishing with his men, and that night a seal's head keeps rising through the floor of the hall and glares at Thórgunna's bedclothes.[24]

Preservation of the bedding has unleashed a storm of uncanny force. Thórgunna's role is enigmatic: her cookery shames the surly hosts, but why is she naked? Probably to make the point (explicit in an ancient Greek version of the same motif[25]) that she lacks her rich textiles in the afterlife. The failure of the bedding to follow Thórgunna out of this world is the controlling dynamic, allowing wild forces to break their normal bounds.

Corpses in Court

It gets worse. The next morning, the fishermen are all drowned at sea. On the evening of their own funeral feast they walk into the hall, dripping wet, and are made welcome.[26] But as the drenched revenants return night after night, their presence becomes tiresome, especially when the dead shepherd and his own party turn up and pick a fight with the others. Then uncanny portents appear again, the food stores are spoiled, and people start to die. These include the aptly-named Thorgríma 'Witch-Face', who has previously been paid to kill a man in a blizzard and who now joins the other active dead.[27]

That is the last straw: a priest and his helpers are brought in. First, Thórgunna's bed-furnishings are burned. Then a court is convened, and the corpses are formally charged with 'trespassing in the house without permission and depriving people of life and health'. Accepting their guilty verdicts in a series of short, rueful statements ('We won't get much peace here so let's get going'), the dead acknowledge that they have had their fun and must now leave. Prayers are said, holy water is sprinkled, and normality returns.[28]

This story seems comical, and contemporaries probably did not take it very seriously. But the conventions that it parodies were deadly serious. In a society so famously regulated by collective debate and decision-making, the formality of the process—restitution, arraignment, judgement—is crucial. So is the corpses' acceptance of the verdicts passed on them. In achieving this consensus, the Fróðá people can at last close the breach in the barrier between life and death that their neglect of Thórgunna's wishes had broken open.[29]

———

The sagas recycle two basic motif-sequences—the 'rampaging revenant' and the 'ferocious barrow-dweller'—in lightly disguised variants to suit different story-lines. In 'Grettis Saga' the two are fused, with the fight inside a barrow transposed to a hall. But we happen to know that this version was itself much older: Glám's last fight replicates the struggle between Beowulf and Grendel in the English epic *Beowulf*.[30] In adopting such episodes into their narratives—set thereafter in unchanging parchment and ink—the saga-writers drew on a long story-telling tradition.

In so doing, they mapped out the world of the undead in a way consistent with northern European patterns of the tenth to twelfth centuries. There are occasional survivals from the female-dominated past (the wise-woman under the church floor, Thórgunna, Thorgríma). More prominently, there are faithless lumpen males (Víga-Hrapp, Thórólf, Glám). Their bodies—diabolically blue and monstrously distended[31]—have obvious affinities with English, central European, and Greek types.

Yet some different visualisations have also found their way into the sagas. Their treatment of the undead is not constrained by the moralizing, binary world-view of most other Christian-era texts: despite their late date, they acknowledge a lost world where the dead could coexist with the living. Gunnar—not evil in any sense—lives happily in his earthen home, singing about his past exploits. The gate-crashers at Fróðá resemble the lumpen type, but at a higher cognitive level: they are rowdy guests who have outstayed their welcome. They enjoy partying around the hearth, but then make little speeches accepting their banishment. Even the monstrous Glám curses his nemesis in a coherent speech.[32]

It is enlightening now to turn to England, both for the similarities and for the contrasts. Like the dominant Icelandic type—though more exclusively—the undead are noxious, unsavoury males. But in a society moving away from feud and collective decision-making towards royal government and legalism, their moral personalities are rather different: less like boorish neighbours and more like furtive criminals. Iceland and England between 1000 and 1200 had some deep cultural roots in common. There were several English scholars in late twelfth-century Iceland, so direct transfer of motifs at a literate level is quite possible.[33] They were, however, different societies, and their undead differed accordingly. To compare and contrast them highlights how closely the dangerous dead mirrored varying realities.

21

The English Walking Dead, 1000–1200 (1)

STORIES AND CORPSES

That corpses of the dead—moved by I don't know what spirit—leave their graves and wander around, terrifying and harming the living, and return to the same graves which open up for them, would be hard to credit if there were not numerous modern cases and abundant reports. . . . For me, it would be just too laborious and burdensome to write down all episodes of this kind that I have heard to have happened in our own times.

—WILLIAM OF NEWBURGH, 1190S

AS THE UNDEAD of the sagas stalked Iceland, England was experiencing its own distinctive epidemic. For several reasons, eleventh- and twelfth-century England could well have been traumatized and insecure. There were Viking raids, and then successive conquests in 1016 and 1066: crises that transformed but did not impair the unusual strength of English central government. Economic and urban growth brought wealth to many, but also unsettled the social order.[1] The organized Church tightened its grip on spiritual culture; new conceptions of the afterlife, salvation, and penance were exhilarating but also disturbing. If the English phenomena were part of something broader, local circumstances still gave them a distinctive colouring.

Too Boring to Write About: Stories of the Walking Dead

Twelfth-century England provides ten stories that describe dead people walking in physical form: four by the Augustinian canon and chronicler William of Newburgh, three by the courtier and satirist Walter Map, one by the great Benedictine historian William of Malmesbury, and the remaining two in monastic chronicles (Map 5).[2] This is the richest body of historically-specific written evidence known from medieval Europe: it allows unique insights into how these perceived threats were conceptualized, addressed and explained.

Context is important. After a very long gap, this era saw a sudden, rich flowering of historical writing in England, some of which took a lively new interest in the marvellous and bizarre. It is quite possible that beliefs now brought onto the radar were in fact long-standing, and indeed three of the episodes described happened before 1100. (That chroniclers and historians largely *stopped* writing about the walking dead after 1200, by contrast, seems unambiguous.) We should, however, take seriously William of Newburgh's perception that these phenomena were new in 'our own days'. He is surprised to find nothing about them in 'books from old times' that, he says, discuss everyday matters and would not suppress such horrors. Nowadays, by contrast, there are so many walking corpses that to describe them all would just be tedious.[3]

Heeding William's warning, I take a light touch here: the stories are more rewarding when analyzed as a group than when repeated individually. In the following summary list, the items are referred to by number in the subsequent discussion:[4]

1. c. 1000, Bury St Edmunds (told by Herman the Archdeacon, 1090s): a wicked judge walks from his grave; he is sewn into a calf-skin and sunk in a lake.[5]

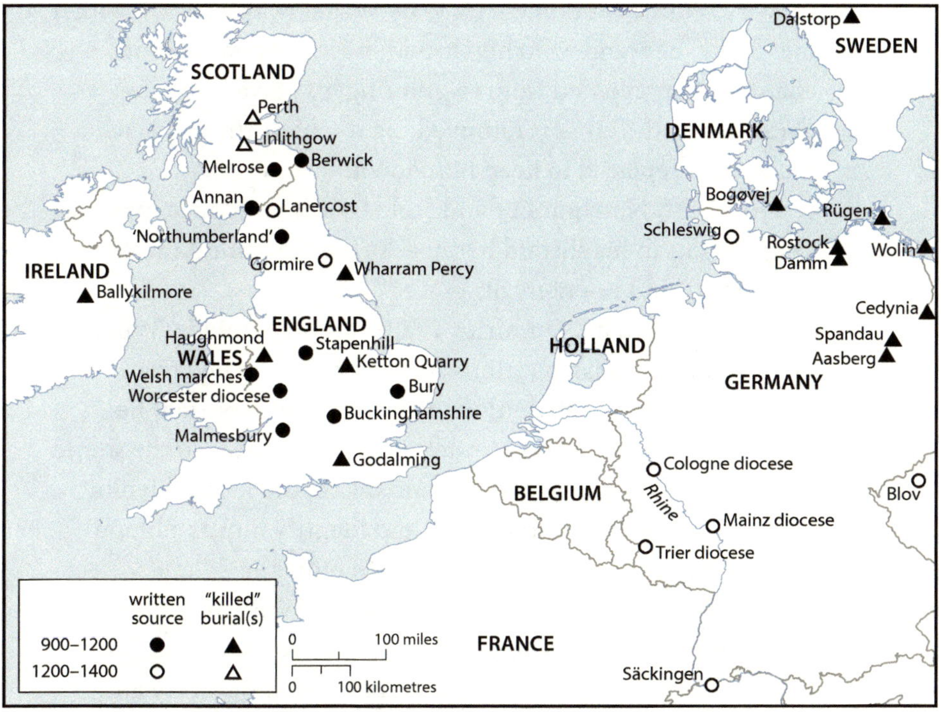

MAP 5: Known corpse-killings in north-west Europe, c. AD 900–1400.

2. 1019–23 or 1052–3, Malmesbury (told by William of Malmesbury, c. 1125): the dissolute Abbot Brihtwold walks from his grave; he is sunk in a bog.[6]
3. c. 1090, Stapenhill near Burton-upon-Trent (told by Geoffrey of Burton, c. 1120–40): two faithless villagers die badly; they walk from their graves to the village, carrying their coffins and sometimes shape-changing; they cause illness and death; they are exhumed and found intact, with the cloths over their faces soaked in blood; they are beheaded, their hearts cut out, and the hearts burned.[7]
4. 1148–63, Welsh marches (told by Walter Map, c. 1190): a Welsh malefactor dies badly; he walks from his grave to the village and summons people, causing illness and death; his corpse is beheaded and holy water sprinkled; he walks again; a knight chases him to his grave and splits his head with a sword.[8]

5. 1164–79, Worcester diocese (told by Walter Map, c. 1190): a man dies badly; he wanders in his shroud; he is trapped in an orchard; he is prevented from re-entering his grave by a cross placed on it; the cross is removed; he re-enters the grave, where the cross is replaced to keep him down.[9]
6. c. 1170s–80s?, Northumberland (told by Walter Map, c. 1190): a knight walks in his shroud because he died excommunicate; he is absolved, and re-enters his grave.[10]
7. c. 1170s–80s, Annan, Dumfries and Galloway? (told by William of Newburgh, 1190s): a jealous steward, who had fled from Yorkshire to evade retribution, dies badly and is buried; he walks from his grave and wanders around the town to the sound of howling dogs, causing illness and death; the locals dig him up, find him swollen and bloody, and identify him as a bloodsucker; they cut out his heart and burn him.[11]
8. c. 1190s, Melrose, Roxburghshire (told by William of Newburgh, 1190s): a dissolute chaplain known as the 'hounds'-priest' walks from his grave, wanders in the monastery and outside, and makes groaning noises; when a man wounds him with an axe, he returns to his grave; the locals dig him up and burn him.[12]
9. c. 1190s, Berwick-upon-Tweed (told by William of Newburgh, 1190s): a wicked man walks from his grave and wanders to the sound of howling dogs, spreading illness and death; the locals dig him up and burn him.[13]
10. c. 1190s, Buckinghamshire (told by William of Newburgh, 1190s): a man walks from his grave, returns to his wife at night, then dances around among the animals; the first reaction is to burn him, but the bishop gives an absolution instead.[14]

Dissecting the Narratives

The protagonists, without exception, are bad men. Three are defined respectively as excommunicated, in need of absolution, and just sinful (6, 10, 9). Two are unworthy ecclesiastics: an incompetent, drunken abbot, and a household chaplain addicted to hunting known as the 'hounds'-priest' (2, 8). There are two villagers who make false accusations against their lord and die suddenly while feasting; a crooked and disagreeable steward; and an unjust judge (3, 7, 1). That leaves two men who are just said to have died 'faithlessly' (4, 5). In fact, *faithlessness* is the feature defining them all: they have broken their obligations to God, to their lords, or to their callings in life.

In at least five cases, the basic if tacit assumption of the locals seems to be that the walking corpse is simply the man himself—bad in death as in life—who has somehow failed to die properly and has thereby entered a monstrous state (3, 5, 6, 7, 10). The sinister failure to move on is betrayed by the incorruption of the corpse (3, 10), or—still worse—by its bloody, bloated state (7, 8). Blood-drenched cloths covering faces (3), and the shredded-up shroud of a manifest 'blood-sucker' (7), are reminiscent of the later Continental shroud-chewers. Unlike them, however, these corpses are walkers, not grave-bound.

Some of them merely frighten people by wandering around in their shrouds (1, 2, 6, 5). The 'hounds'-priest' causes a nuisance by obstructing visitors to Melrose Abbey, and makes groaning noises outside the chamber of the noble lady who had employed him (8). The Buckinghamshire revenant is notable for the range and inventiveness of his depredations, including the only explicit night-mare case (10):

> He was buried, and on the following night he entered his sleeping wife's bedroom, and not only frightened her but almost suffocated her with his unbearable overlying weight. The night after, he afflicted the astonished woman in the same way. Terrified by the danger, she faced the third night's battle sleepless with the protection of a group of guards. He came, but was driven back by the shouts of the guards, and left unable to do harm.
>
> Thus repulsed by his wife, he annoyed his own brothers in the same village . . . [who took similar precautions.] Then he took to dancing around wildly among the animals in and near the houses, as their restlessness and abnormal behaviour showed. This was an equal nuisance to friends and neighbours, who also had to keep watch at night. . . .
>
> After a period of these nocturnal leapings, he then started wandering around by day, frightening everyone though visible only to some. For if

he met a group of many people together, he was only visible to one or two of them, even though the others could sense his presence.[15]

Then there is a clutch of four narratives that share motifs: the revenants walk around to the noise of barking dogs, or in one case (3) carry coffins on their backs and shape-change into animals; they summon fellow villagers by name (3, 4), or spread foul air (7, 9); the victims sicken, and in many cases die; in consequence, the villages are almost deserted; but there is (partial) recovery once the revenants are neutralized. This looks as though it was originally a single story-sequence, preserved here in a range of orally-transmitted variants.

How to deal with such monsters? There are pragmatic and secular remedies: cut off the head with a spade, or (when that fails) split it with a sword (4); cut off the head, put it between the thighs, cut out the heart and burn it (3). A different approach was to dump the offending corpse in a standing pool or bog (1, 2). We have already noted this practice in relation to Queen Cwoenthryth at Winchcombe, and will encounter it later in Yorkshire (pp. 222, 314). One more case can be suggested: in 1040, King Harthacnut had the corpse of his predecessor Harold I exhumed, beheaded, and thrown in a fen or river, which sounds like a pre-emptive strike against his potentially undead and resentful half-brother.[16] The latest stories, in William of Newburgh's collection, describe total burning of the corpse, usually performed by a posse of tough young men; in one case the heart has to be cut out and torn to pieces before the corpse will burn (7).

Some ecclesiastics preferred gentler methods. Bishop Gilbert of Hereford recommended holy water (though only after detaching the head with a spade), while Bishop Roger of Worcester trapped a revenant in its grave by laying a cross on top (4, 5). These bishops were trying to protect the living rather than to save the dead, but in two other cases the remedy was absolution (6, 10).

The implication—that troublesome corpses can contain human souls capable of being saved—forces us to confront the hardest question of all: what was the nature of these entities conceived to be? That is where the ecclesiastical veneer really obstructs our view, since all these writers internalized a Christian scheme of salvation and damnation that did not necessarily run along the grain of inherited popular belief. They must have known this themselves, and indeed the unresolved differences in the narratives betray divergent viewpoints.

Genuinely-Held Beliefs: Motif Parallels and the Message of Archaeology

The educated ecclesiastics who wrote these stories were steeped in Christian theology. Even so, they grew up in families, with parents, siblings, and lay neighbours: they may have been trained to despise popular culture, but they knew a lot about it. For Gilbert Foliot, the aristocratic Anglo-Norman bishop of Hereford (1148–63), beheading a troublesome corpse was all in a day's work (4). By contrast, the saintly Hugh, bishop of Lincoln (1186–1200), who came from south-eastern France, was astonished by the whole idea, although his English advisors knew that 'these things often happen in England' (10). The astute folk of Berwick-on-Tweed predicted only too surely that the foul air spread by a walking corpse would cause sickness and death, because so many had done it before (9). William of Malmesbury laughed at the credulity of the English who believed in walking corpses, but the implication is that many did.[17]

These are not clerical fictions: an embedded and widespread nexus of folk-belief shows through, even if aspects have been massaged to suit theological understandings.[18] That becomes clear from the many and detailed parallels between motifs in these stories and material collected elsewhere by ethnographers and folklorists, especially in eastern Europe. In the story from Stapenhill (3), a point-by-point analysis matches almost every detail with motifs from Romania, Serbia, Slovenia, Greece, Norway, and the Baltic.[19] The story of the miscreant in (7) has enough in common with Víga-Hrapp's to suggest that William of Newburgh and the 'Laxdaela Saga' drew on the same motif-sequence. Other parallels can be found throughout this book.

Burial archaeology helps less than might be expected. Far fewer tenth- to twelfth-century cemeteries have been extensively excavated than earlier ones; in any case, corpses burned or dumped in lakes would normally leave no trace. One dramatic exception is the grave of a young

FIGURE 49: Haughmond Abbey (Shropshire), burial 4245: covering up a twelfth-century embarrassment? This man was buried honourably, outside the west door of the canons' church. But then his body was twisted over into a prone position when still semi-articulated, and the head pulled off.

man, probably from c. 1120–30, at the Augustinian priory of Haughmond (Shropshire), placed immediately outside the west door of the church (Figure 49).[20] He lay prone, in a twisted attitude, with his cranium detached and his right leg separated at the knee. In the light of the seventh-century cases discussed earlier, this looks like a conventionally-buried corpse that was later uncovered, twisted over and partly dismembered in a state of semi-decomposition. Haughmond is in the Welsh marches: Walter Map's story (4) comes to mind.

An extraordinary discovery in the deserted medieval village of Wharram Percy (Yorkshire) may tell us more about popular practice. A fourteenth-century pit-group contained a mixed-up assemblage of damaged, broken, and sometimes burned human bones from a minimum of ten individuals, including two adult females, two adult males, two teenagers, and two children. These people were probably of local origin, and radiocarbon results show that all but two of them (who were later) died between 950 and 1200. There was evidence of burning on 12 percent of the bones; this had happened while the flesh was still present, and there are indications that the corpses were decapitated before burning. Thirteen percent of the bones showed marks of cutting and chopping, concentrated around the shoulders, the lower jaw, the base of the skull, and especially the upper left rib-cage (Figure 50). There was also some breakage of leg-bones.[21]

Discounting cannibalism (improbable in a Yorkshire village over several generations!), revenant corpses seem the only viable explanation. The remains are precisely what would be left after the procedures described by William of Newburgh: disablement, hacking apart, stabbing or removal of the heart, and partial burning on an amateur pyre. Then they presumably accumulated on some dump, from which they were later removed for burial.

This is evidence—of the most dramatic and compelling kind—that the corpse-killings described in the texts really did happen. There is no reason to think Wharram Percy atypical in its zeal. To envisage a total of (say) fifteen individuals would give, on average, around one revenant per decade burnt in this village. That hardly sounds like an epidemic level—but then Wharram Percy was a small place.

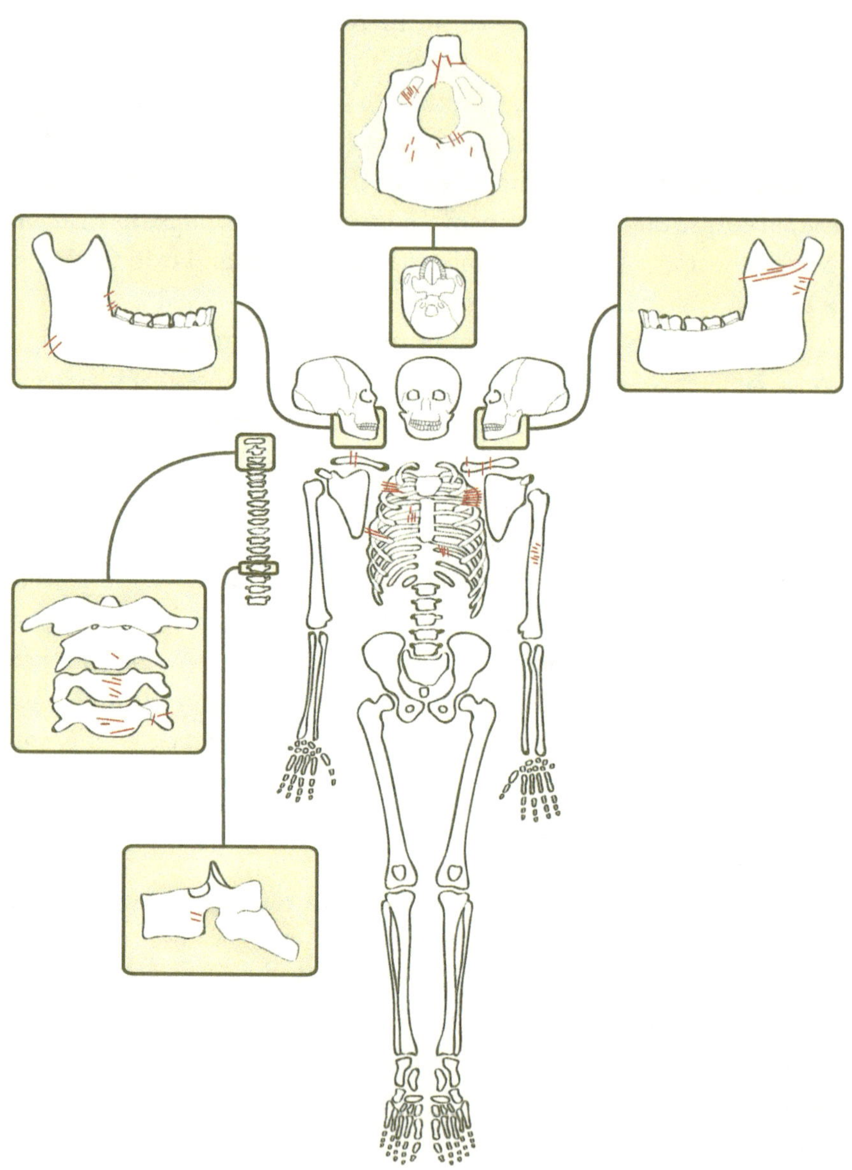

FIGURE 50: Wharram Percy (Yorkshire): a dump of defeated revenants? Composite diagram showing the incidence of cut-marks on the tenth- to twelfth-century disarticulated bones in a pit. The pattern suggests an emphasis on separating the skull from the lower jaw, and on attacking the rib-cage; it looks especially significant that cuts concentrate on the upper-left ribs, near the heart.

FIGURE 51: Ballykilmore (Ireland): a middle-aged female, eleventh to twelfth century. The cranium has been removed and replaced by a head-shaped stone, and another stone has crushed the upper ribcage. (The legs of an underlying burial are also visible.)

Finally, two isolated female burials must in some way be part of the same story. In a graveyard at Ketton Quarry (Rutland), a girl of about eleven, with a calibrated radiocarbon date of AD 973–1150, was buried with her head placed between her feet.[22] At Ballykilmore (Westmeath), in central Ireland (Figure 51), a middle-aged woman, with a calibrated radiocarbon date of AD 1024–1176, was buried semi-prone, also in a normal graveyard. Her cranium had been replaced by a rounded stone of equivalent size (leaving the jawbone in place), and a large stone lay on her broken and disordered upper ribs.[23] Like the Cille Pheadair woman six centuries earlier (Figure 31), she is an enigmatic outlier in the long tradition of dangerous dead females.

The evidence for corpse-killing in eleventh- and twelfth-century England is compelling, and mostly tells the same story. There is, however, one possibly crucial discrepancy: whereas the narratives deal exclusively with adult males, the Wharram Percy corpses cover the whole demographic range, and the Ketton and Ballykilmore burials are both female. Do the written sources distort the picture by selecting for a particular type of dead malefactor? There are reasons why that might be so.

22

The English Walking Dead, 1000–1200 (2)

BREAKING GOD'S LAW AND THE KING'S

A man of evil deeds, fearing either the law or his enemies, fled from Yorkshire to the lord of [Annan] castle. . . . [He died without the sacrament.] He received Christian burial, although unworthy, but it did him no good: each night his corpse, driven by Satan, left his grave and wandered through the streets and around the houses . . .

—WILLIAM OF NEWBURGH, 1190S

THESE ENGLISH REVENANTS sprang from two layers in the cultural imagination. One was organic and Europe-wide: it explains the folk-motif parallels. The other—contemporary and dynamic—was moulded by developing ideologies, guided from above, about authority, legitimacy, purity, and life after death. Assertions of social or moral inclusion highlighted the excluded: both Church and state targeted out-groups, including criminals, oath-breakers, heretics, and even lepers, with an intensifying rhetoric that labelled them unclean.[1] An important reason for the rise of the walking dead—noxious by nature—may be that they became dark mirrors for the noxious living.

Shifting Conceptual Landscapes: Demonic Possession, Purgatory, and Lay Spirituality

The idea of a human soul animating its earthly body after death was never easy for twelfth-century literati to swallow. Almost inevitably, there were alternative explanations that invoked forms of demonic possession (doubtless made easier by the belief, apparent in some pre-Conquest texts, that demons could enter wicked corpses at the point of death[2]). In one of our stories, Bishop Gilbert muses whether 'the Lord has given power to the evil angel of that lost one to move around in that dead body' (4): an odd phrase that echoes descriptions of demons as 'bad angels', but also recalls older conceptions of 'animal souls' remaining with corpses (p. 108). William of Newburgh expresses puzzlement at whatever kind of 'spirit' moves them (p. 251). William of Malmesbury mocks the credulous (clerical?) English for thinking that 'the corpse of a wicked man after death is possessed by a demon and walks'.[3] In the Berwick story, the revenant is called a 'soulless apparition' that moves around 'by the operation of Satan' (9).

Most complex is the Bury hagiographers' treatment of the unjust judge (1). Herman says that he troubled people 'doubtless to bemoan his own unrest, though it is permissible to acknowledge that it was not him but a demon in his likeness'. Goscelin of Saint-Bertin develops this by hoping 'that he was handed over to Satan for the present for this purpose: that his spirit might be saved on judgement day'. This odd idea relies on St Paul, when he instructs the Corinthians how to deal with a sexual sinner: 'you are to hand this man over to Satan for the destruction of his flesh, so that his spirit may be saved on the day of the Lord.'[4]

Paul's words remain enigmatic, but medieval thinkers could read a comforting message that even when Satan controlled a corpse and moved around in it, the soul might ultimately be saved. This is a version of the widespread rationalization that demons, not human souls, make corpses walk.[5] Ælfric used it around 1000 when he wrote that 'witches still go to crossroads and heathen burials with their delusive magic, and call to the devil, and he comes to them in the likeness of the man who is buried there as though he rise from death'.[6] But here, as in the revenant stories, only the corpses of the reprobate are vulnerable to this diabolical hijacking: a walking corpse means a soul in torment.

The stories show divergence—and real disagreement—on whether such souls had any hope of salvation. Bishop Gilbert calls the undead Welsh malefactor 'that lost one' (4). The view expressed by one of Bishop Hugh's advisors in the Buckinghamshire case, that the 'body of this most wretched man ought to be burnt', suggests a perception of a former human being in a tragically and irrevocably corrupted state (10). Hugh's own approach, and that of the priest towards the excommunicated knight (6), are by contrast more purgatorial: these sinners are suffering justly for their misdeeds, but God's mercy can rescue them. In the second case, the corpse is clearly equated with the dead knight himself rather than some demonic squatter.

The slipperiness of these concepts is underlined by a further story from William of Malmesbury that, while not exactly describing an undead corpse, belongs to the same thought-world.[7] A witch at Berkeley (Gloucestershire) is on her deathbed, fearing damnation. She tells her children that they cannot change the sentence already passed on her soul, but begs them to 'lighten the burden of her torments' by saying masses for her and protecting her body. She asks to be sewn into a stag-skin and placed in a stone coffin, its lid fastened with iron and lead and then bound with three huge iron chains. This is done, but on each of the first two nights, demons burst in and break one of the chains. On the third night, the biggest demon summons the dead woman by name, breaks the third chain, and carries her off as she screams frantically for help. The implication must be that her sentient personality still resides in her corpse, and that when the demon takes her, he is seizing her body and soul. But how was protecting her body meant to shield her from punishments already ordained? If this is a genuine English folk-story, its theology is incoherent.

The references to penance and absolution in stories 1, 6, and 10 only make sense in the context of developing ideas about purgatory, where souls destined for salvation suffered purifying torment. Purgatory certainly had a place in late Anglo-Saxon theology, but conceptions of it became more defined and complex in the twelfth century: views on the spectrum from damned monster to salvation-seeking soul depended on the up-to-dateness or otherwise of the participants' and reporters' theological training.[8] Lay attitudes will have developed in symbiosis with scholarly ones, if tending more towards the traditional and down-to-earth. In negotiating interpretations within communities, or between communities and clergy, there was scope for considerable flexibility in how far the soul was blamed for the corpse's misdeeds. Whether the dead offender was a beloved relative or a detested enemy may have made a difference.

Yet it would be wrong to exaggerate the humane and merciful strand in twelfth-century thinking about undead corpses. For their ordinary lay victims, they were monsters to be exterminated; most clergy before 1150 would have agreed. The ghastly thought—*if I misbehave, I might become like that*—was too powerful to be disarmed by ideas of demonic possession or purgatory. Possibly too (though this is never stated explicitly), it was a tool in the hands of late Anglo-Saxon and Anglo-Norman rulers and reforming churchmen, aspiring to build an integrated Christian society under the law of God and the king. Revenants presented a powerful warning to offenders, and embodied what might happen to them in this world and the next.

Faithlessness, Damnation, and Unclean Burial in the Ideologies of Church and State

The revenants of the English stories share with the Icelandic ones their maleness and their brutality.[9] But they are more socially integrated, and correspondingly more sinister. Rather than obvious loners, they are people of usually good standing and sometimes high status. Rather than openly rejecting Christian burial like some of the Icelanders, they creep at night from their churchyard graves. Rather than openly pursuing grievances, they prey furtively on neighbouring villagers. Rather than lurking on the wild margins, they are a poison at the heart of communities.

In fact, the English revenants of this period look closer to later Romanian and Greek vampires than to Icelandic walking corpses: less like wild monsters, more like human criminals. Law-breaking in contemporary England was pursued ruthlessly through a fearsomely rigorous penal system, and condemned by ecclesiastical rhetoric that increasingly identified crimes against public order as crimes against God. While a stream of law-codes prescribed savage penalties for the wicked in life, a new contrast also emerged for the dead: between 'clean' or 'Christian' burial in a consecrated churchyard with due rites, and 'foul' or 'heathen' burial that was the very opposite. Archaeologists have found many cemeteries on marginal sites—often at parish boundaries or meeting-places—where the executed (and perhaps others) were thrown shamefully into pits, beheaded, face-down, or with hands and feet tied.[10]

In all this, there is an intriguing similarity between the treatment of living criminals and the treatment of walking corpses. When revenant corpses in the stories are mutilated in their graves, or deposited in pools or bogs, their fate recalls the prone, beheaded, and disorderly corpses found in execution cemeteries. Crucially, in the stories with this motif—Queen Cwoenthryth, the Bury judge, Abbot Brihtwold, Harold I (perhaps by implication), and a later Yorkshire case (p. 314)—the watery grave is a *prison*: the corpse would not previously stay quiet, so has to be placed where it cannot escape. Beheading and heart-removal had similar aims. Here containment, disablement, and punishment coincided.

All this went beyond mere shaming: its implications were more fundamental and sinister, since the fate of corpses really mattered. Late Anglo-Saxon writers had a very material conception of the soul, and the idea that even the faithful dead had some kind of continuing consciousness in the grave was never far below the surface.[11] The tenth-century rite for consecrating churchyards presented them as serene resting-places where the virtuous dead were shielded from evil forces.[12] By contrast, the manner in which the wicked were buried was an outward and visible sign of their damnation.[13]

Bogs had a long conceptual history as liminal sites of enduring punishment: preserving flesh from decay, they held dead miscreants in a state of painful stasis from which they could neither move on to the next world nor return to plague this one. Old 'pagan' earthworks on boundaries could do the same. Sarah Semple cites an image of damnation in

FIGURE 52: Prisons for the unholy dead in early eleventh-century England? The Harley Psalter contains these two strange scenes of mutilated corpses inside mounds. One group seem to be engaged in animated speech, despite their chopped-off feet. It has been plausibly argued that these images depict the 'hell on earth' suffered by criminals and social outcasts, condemned to a living death in burial-places from which they could neither move on to the next world nor return to this one.

FIGURE 53: This eleventh-century English drawing illustrates a story told three centuries earlier by Bede. A delinquent monk—already known to be damned—is buried with his legs bound and perhaps with something gagging his mouth.

the eleventh-century Harley Psalter, showing four individuals with chopped-off feet inside a mound (Figure 52): it shows, she suggests, 'a living-dead existence, trapped within the earth . . . This Anglo-Saxon vision of hell and damnation combines Christian tenets and popular beliefs'.[14] Likewise, an eleventh-century manuscript of a story told by Bede, about a damned monk who was 'buried in the remotest places of the monastery', is illustrated with a sketch showing ropes or shackles around his legs and possibly a gag in his mouth (Figure 53).[15]

Laws from the 920s onwards variously forbid hallowed burial to perjurors, the unchaste, 'notoriously untrustworthy' men, and thieves.[16] One threatens a sexual offender that he will 'forfeit clean burial and God's mercy'; the twelfth-century translation of another renders 'unclean burial' as 'buried amongst the damned'.[17] A Church-influenced code of 1020–1 warns the lazy man who fails to learn even the Lord's Prayer and Creed that 'after his death he cannot rest in a hallowed grave among Christians'. An eleventh-century homily says that those who die flagrantly corrupted by sexual lust should 'not even be carried to the heathen pit but dragged without a coffin'.[18] It is likely, then, that not all the prone or decapitated burials found on 'heathen burial' sites were execution victims. Could some of them have been the walking dead, re-located in this fashion after conventional Christian burial had failed to keep them quiet? As we saw, Ælfric envisaged witches trying to resurrect corpses in 'heathen' burial-places.

No formal trials of corpses are recorded in England, but the exhumations, proofs of guilt, and 'executions' in the narratives have the air of judicial processes, performed by village communities and authorized in at least two cases by diocesan bishops (3, 4). The hearts of the Stapenhill revenants were carried across the Trent to be burnt at a typical site for executing felons: a hilltop beacon at a junction of parish boundaries. And the revenants of the Anglo-Norman narratives—degenerate ecclesiastics, lying tenants, a dishonest steward, an unjust judge, all of them faithless—look very like the miscreants condemned in the law-codes. Both groups, the living and the prospectively undead, were members of a Christian community who perversely flouted its normal bonds and pledges. Every society has its criminals, and many societies have had their restless dead, but the late Anglo-Saxon and Anglo-Norman establishments coloured both with a distinctive kind of moral reprobation.

Just possibly, this helps to explain the narratives' exclusive concentration on male subjects: public misuse of power, neglect of professional ethics, and violent criminality were pre-eminently masculine offences. The chroniclers and their informants, who mostly belonged to an elite establishment, may have seized on narratives illustrating a particular, ideologically charged dimension of the walking dead. The Wharram Percy finds, on the other hand, do not suggest any gender bias.

That reminds us that medieval writers did not select their material to help modern historians. Their aims—theological, moralistic, or political—were entirely different, and the stories that survive were written to serve those aims.[19] The parallels and the archaeology show that people really believed in these beings, but the image we can construct of them may be distorted and incomplete.

Persecuting Mentalities?

According to the historian R. I. Moore, twelfth-century Europe saw 'the formation of a persecuting society'.[20] As an educated clerical caste rose to prominence, it buttressed its moral and theological hold by defining 'out-groups' as wicked, dangerous, or polluted: heretics, Jews, lepers, and sexual deviants. Such imagined threats to righteous Christian society had to be neutralized by exclusion, execution, or fire. Prejudices that started at an elite intellectual level were imposed downwards until people internalized them, perceiving enemies where there were none. Thus, in Moore's argument, began the history of European persecution with all its ghastly later outcomes.

Does corpse-killing fit that model? There is significant common ground. Since the dead are not in reality a danger to anyone, the epidemic recalls the deranged hysteria against Jews. In its psychological impact, neutralizing dangerous corpses was not wholly remote from the liturgy separating lepers from society, in which the afflicted person stood in an open grave and was made symbolically dead while living.[21]

William of Newburgh's revenants, who walk around spreading noxious contagion, are indicative here. In general this is a rather unusual activity for the undead, but it is precisely how twelfth-century heretics (not to mention lepers) were conceived in the paranoid minds of their persecutors. William uses essentially the same metaphor in describing the one English heresy episode, at Oxford in 1163: the heretics' hut was burnt and they were driven out to die, so that the disease would not appear in England again.[22] Concerns about heretics and concerns about walking corpses were felt in the same ecclesiastical circles: Bishops Gilbert of Hereford and Roger of Worcester, who took action in two of our cases (4 and 5), corresponded with each other about what to do with the Oxford heretics.[23]

Burning whole corpses diverged from normal English judicial penalties (at least for males), but resembled the new Continental penalty for heresy. This started at Orléans in 1022, gathering pace in a series of burnings in the Rhineland from the 1150s, and then a dramatic case at Reims in the late 1170s.[24] Against that background, it is intriguing to note that burning only starts to figure in the English narratives with those reported by William of Newburgh, from the 1170s onwards. It is in fact pretty clear that English corpse-burning tracked Continental heretic-burning. The English (exceptionally in contemporary Europe) did not burn heretics at this date: is there some sense in which they burned revenants instead?

The English dead-killing epidemic did not start in this context: it was well under way a century earlier, and obviously it was not imposed to consolidate elite power. Perhaps, though, the rise of persecution moulded and intensified the belief-system—already linked to criminality—so that people associated walking corpses with other undesirables needing isolation or elimination. Is it even possible that paranoiac fears directed against them, rather than against heretics, help to explain the curious absence of heresy trials in twelfth-century England? If corpses became scapegoats for the ills of society, they could not feel pain or sorrow like the other scapegoats. Persecution of the undead was a relatively innocuous—perhaps even therapeutic—aspect of a persecuting society.

The noxious and agonized undead cast a long shadow over living offenders. The law and the Church wanted to impose honesty, oath-keeping, and religious purity: what ghastlier warning could there be than the crooked perjurers who did not move on after death? If caught in evil-doing, those who violated society's revered bonds and obligations risked excommunication, execution, and unclean burial. Even if not caught—even if rich and secure—undeath would find them out. Nobody wanted to end up like Abbot Brihtwold of Malmesbury: revealed as an unquiet corpse, ejected from his Christian grave, and thrown into a bog—'from which', says William of Malmesbury, 'from time to time rises a foul smell that breathes a noisome miasma over the locals'.[25]

23

Central and Southern Europe, 1000–1400

[Henry Nodus] was sadistic, viewing rape, adultery, incest, perjury and such things as virtues. After he died in the Maifeld district, he appeared to many in the sheepskin that he often wore in life, especially frequenting his daughter's house. Neither the sign of the cross nor the sword could drive him away. People often hit him with swords, but they could not wound him: he just made a sound like a soft mattress being hit.

—CAESARIUS OF HEISTERBACH, 1220S

THE LAST EIGHT chapters explored Scandinavia, England, and northern Francia. But a similar belief-complex, percolating southwards from the Baltic and perhaps eastwards from the Rhine, becomes visible in central Europe after 1000. Meanwhile, in the Balkans, an independent version of the European prototype was emerging, perhaps from a nucleus of inherited late Roman belief on the west shore of the Black Sea. How these two zones of corpse-killing intensified, expanded towards each other, and eventually met will be the theme of Part V.

Careless labelling hampers attempts to understand the European revenant. 'Vampires' are said to be 'Slavic' or 'Balkan', 'Romanian', or 'Polish'.

Such thinking assumes an unproven relationship between ethnicity and belief, and is framed by national boundaries that did not yet exist. This chapter tries instead to follow the evidence, examining references and archaeological findings geographically. As beliefs once held widely in the Roman world faded in some regions, intensified in others, and were supplemented by new traditions from outside the Empire, patterns started to crystallise.

The Central European Undead: Viking Origins

The main—and radical—argument of this section is that Scandinavian colonisation and trade created a diaspora of Viking-style revenants. A restricted area of south-west Finland, under strong Scandinavian influence in the late eleventh to early twelfth centuries, is a good starting-point for exploring the dynamic. Dating from that phase is a group of elaborately-constructed burials with spearheads, knives, and even swords stabbed down into the grave and around its edges, sometimes with several weapons at a time.[1] Some of them also have piled-on stones, and there are occasional prone burials.[2] The stabbing rite is unusual, but it cannot be a coincidence that within Finland these practices are only known in the Scandinavian-influenced region.

The Baltic was a Viking-dominated sea, and similar effects were spreading southwards. Slavic populations practised cremation up to around 1000: except in abnormal cases, it is unlikely that they needed measures to keep corpses down, nor feared the sinister incorruption of buried corpses. Corpse-killing, therefore, must have been either a new autonomous development or an introduction from outside. Viewed without preconceptions, the burial archaeology carries a clear message: the dangerous dead of Slavic central Europe came primarily from Scandinavia, and penetrated southwards up the rivers that flow into the Baltic (Map 6).

Among burials from c. 1000–1250 within 150 kilometres of the Baltic coast, especially between the Elbe and Oder, a minority of graves show aberrant practices like those already discussed in Scandinavia, notably prone burial, decapitation, and the piling of stones on limbs or the whole body.[3] These phenomena are also widely found in Poland and the Czech

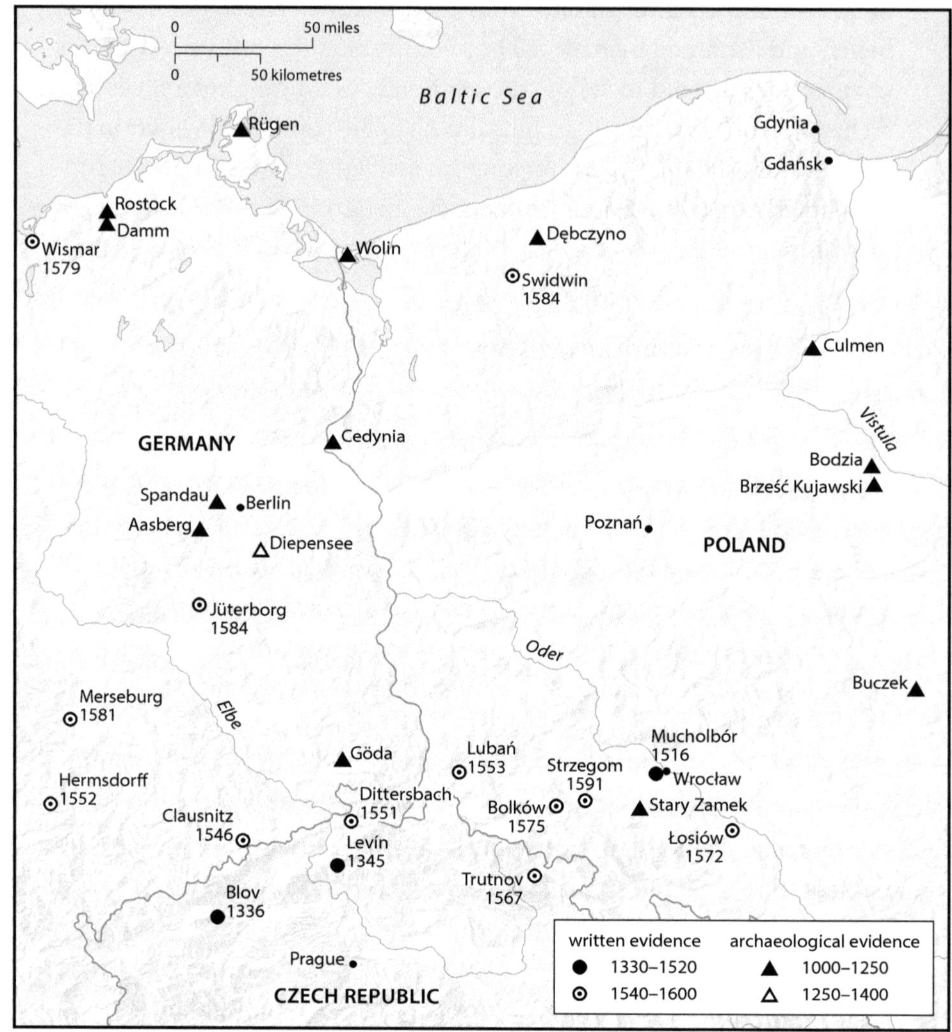

MAP 6: Known corpse-killings in north-central Europe, c. AD 1000–1600.

Republic.[4] They can be ambiguous (it is often suggested that these people were criminals or slaves), but occasional cases are more expressive. In the coastal zone, burials at Damm (Rostock) and Rostock-Gehlsdorf had combinations of iron nails with stones in the mouth and under the chin.[5] An adult male at Ralswiek, Rügen, was initially buried with nails and subsequently heaped with stones when the grave was re-opened; another at

Wolin was buried prone, with his ankles tied and his head detached and twisted sideways (Figure 11).[6] Three graves at Debczyno in West Pomerania were grossly attacked: in two cases to remove and re-locate the head and feet, in the third by a large pit in which bones were extracted, burned in situ, and loaded with massive stones.[7] Cases at Spandau (Berlin) and Aasberg (Brandenburg) illustrate combinations of coins between the teeth, post-burial disturbance and probable staking.[8] A curious cemetery at Cedynia (western Poland) contained multiple decapitations and stonings, and a female with nails through her hands and feet.[9]

Some distinctive cases, mostly from the eleventh century, have been found further up-river (Figure 54). Several graves at Göda (east of Dresden) had knives, needles, and other iron objects in the mouth and heart area, combined with post-mortem neck dislocations.[10] On the Oder, a female at Stary Zamek (near Wrocław) was buried prone, with her lower limbs raised upwards, and a line of stakes (pegging down a beam?) through her left buttock, lower spine, and the crook of her right arm.[11] On the Vistula, signs of anti-revenant treatment occurred on up to two per cent of burials in the large cemetery at Culmen, including decapitations in the grave with a sharp instrument.[12] Male burials at Brześć Kujawski and Buczek had wooden stakes, still partly preserved, apparently driven through their hearts.[13] At Bodzia, near the first of these, a woman in her early twenties, accompanied by items including coins up to c. 1020 and a spindle with a rare and precious stone whorl, had a huge piece of quern-stone laid on her face and upper chest: a unique arrangement that looks more purposeful than ordinary graves with stones, and might suggest a traditional kind of daunting wise-woman.[14]

Practices continuing later in the region are illustrated by excavated burials dated c. 1250–1400. At Diepensee (near Berlin) one male was buried on the edge of the churchyard, abnormally aligned, with one leg chopped off and a charred board laid over the upper body; three others had mouth-stones.[15] A female at Klein Hoym (near Magdeburg) lay prone, her cranium detached and inverted after decomposition had set in.[16] Two fourteenth-century corpses in the Benedictine cloister of Harsefeld (near Hamburg) were 'killed' following the initial burials: in one case by dropping a boulder down a shaft dug over the head of the coffin, in the

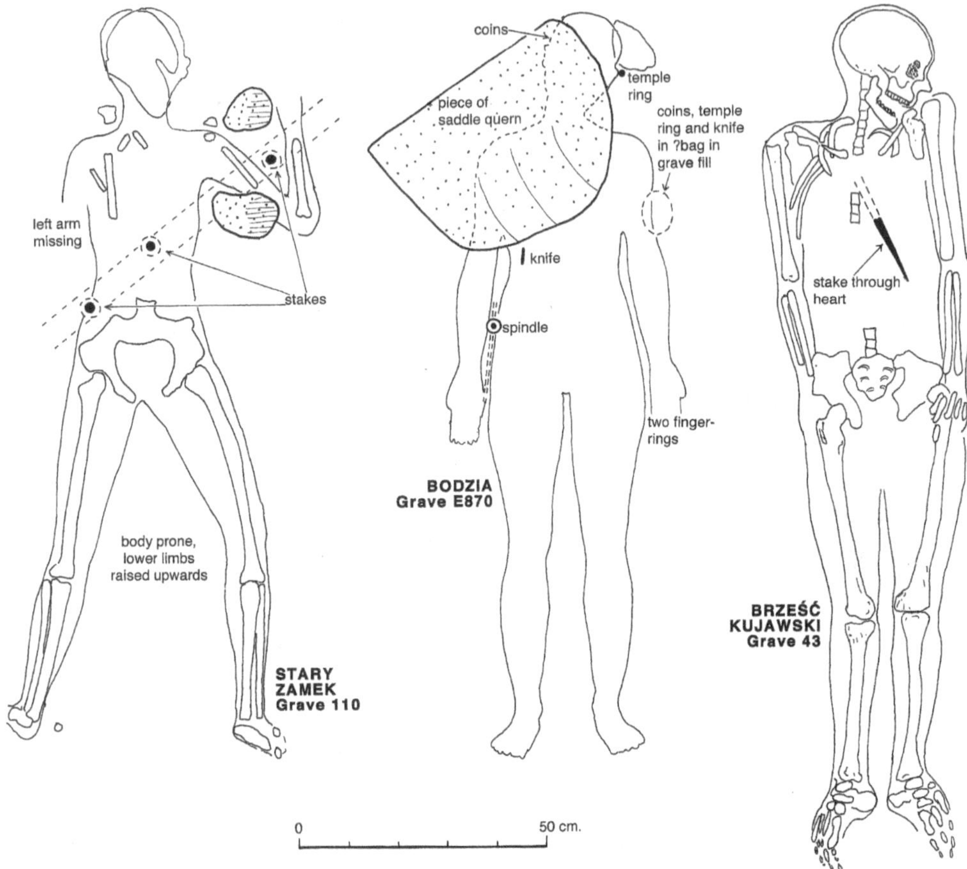

FIGURE 54: Three eleventh-century 'killed' corpses in north-central Europe.

other by opening the grave, turning the coffin upside-down, and then sealing the backfilled grave with a carefully laid brick pavement.[17]

Here is a context for the undead King Abel of Denmark, a suspected fratricide, who died in 1252. He was initially buried in Schleswig cathedral, but caused such disruption that his body was sunk in a marsh with a stake through the coffin. This story—and Abel's reappearances as a demonic huntsman—had become local folklore by the sixteenth century, illustrating the resilience of this belief-complex in the borderlands of Scandinavia with Germany.[18] Further south, in east Saxony, Bohemia, and Moravia, the early excavated examples at Göda and Stary

Zamek are closely juxtaposed with documented cases at Blov (1336), Levín (1345), Muchobór (1516), and a localized epidemic of corpse-killing from the 1540s onwards (pp. 334, 324). This region, like others in Mecklenburg and Pomerania, was still a nucleus of anxiety about restless corpses as late as the 1930s (p. 411).

All this creates a strong case that corpse-killing emerged in what are now northern Germany, north-western Poland, and the Czech Republic from about 1000, and became endemic in the more restricted zones where epidemics would later erupt. How and why did it start? The resemblance to Scandinavian practices described earlier is very clear. The trading-place of Wolin was much frequented by Viking merchants, and there were abundant opportunities for Scandinavian influences to penetrate deep inland. The Elbe, Oder, and Vistula were perpetual highways; for instance, Norwegian-made whetstones were extensively used in Wolin and further up the Oder.[19] The whole area covered by Map 6, and extending northwards into Scandinavia, produces abundant finds of ninth- and tenth-century Islamic coins: evidence of a complex trade in enslaved Slavic people implicating both Viking merchants and the violently competing Slavic polities.[20]

From the 960s, the success of the Piast dynasty in building a strong Polish state involved a turn towards Christianity under Frankish and Bohemian influence, but archaeology shows that people on the Vistula near Bodzia retained links with the Scandinavian world and its culture up to 1100.[21] Further west, between the Elbe and Oder, the more fragmented Slavic groups were also orientated commercially towards the Baltic, and interacted regularly with both Scandinavians and Franks. Colonizing pressure from the eastern Frankish empire was always intense, but successfully resisted between the 980s and 1140s.[22]

Several of the usual stresses that generate fears of the dead are visible here: the trauma of violent ethnic and political competition; population movements; enslavement with the consequent disruption of families; socio-cultural change; and the outlawing of traditional belief-systems. As inhumation became established—perhaps with attendant anxieties—the dangerous-dead beliefs already rooted in Scandinavia could easily have been introduced alongside other influences on burial practice:

aristocratic chamber-graves of Viking/Rus' type, for instance, occur widely across the region, including at Cedynia and Bodzia.[23] Intriguingly, all this was contemporaneous with the inferred epidemics in England and Iceland.

Rhenish Revenants

In about 1223, the Cistercian preacher and writer Caesarius of Heisterbach finished a long sequence of stories, set in his native Rhineland, about the dying and the dead. Between the lines of his monastic and didactic priorities, a belief that the dead could return in physical form emerges in several stories. Three of them, set respectively in the dioceses of Cologne, Trier, and Mainz, seem unambiguous (Map 5).

In the first, two feuding villagers are buried in the same grave, but then one of them has to be moved because they start fighting 'like wild horses'. In the second, a wicked knight called Henry Nodus appears to many people after death, impervious to the sword-blows that bounce off him. In the third story, a priest's concubine on her deathbed begs to be buried in a new, well-studded pair of shoes, saying, 'I'll really need them'. She dies and is buried, but before dawn, a travelling knight encounters her, wearing just her shirt and the same shoes. She rushes up, shouting 'Help! Help!', as a hellish huntsman and dogs approach. The knight makes a circle around himself and the woman with his sword, and twists some of her hair around his left arm. But she screams 'Flee without me, he's coming' and rushes off, leaving her torn hair. The demon catches her, throws her across his horse, and vanishes. The next day they open the woman's tomb, and find that the hair wrapped around the knight's arm has been torn from her head.[24]

The second story recalls one from Lanercost Priory that shows a similar interest in the revenant's physicality; the third assimilates motifs resembling William of Malmesbury's 'Witch of Berkeley' narrative to the 'wild hunt of the damned' template (pp. 317, 264, 291).[25] The material has clearly been processed through monastic contacts and teaching, but a folkloric substrate specific to the Rhineland seems likely: for Caesarius, this kind of thing is not too bizarre. The point is emphasized by another of his stories, in which enemies chase a man past a churchyard where he regularly prays for souls: the grateful corpses rise from their graves to defend him with swords and scythes.[26]

Didactic stories from elsewhere in Germany and France avoid such motifs,[27] and the Paris theologian William of Auvergne is emphatic that the dead do *not* return in bodily form.[28] Caesarius's material confirms that the beliefs implied by early medieval burials, and then condemned by Burchard of Worms, were still alive in the thirteenth century. But this was their last appearance: the Rhineland would soon become a backwater in the current of revenant fears.

The High Rhine and the Alps

Far from home, between the Black Forest and the Alps, the Irish missionary Fridolin asked two rich brothers to endow his new nunnery at Säckingen. Urso readily gave his share of their common property, but died soon afterwards, whereupon his brother Landolf took legal action to reclaim the land. But the saint had a trick up his sleeve: going to Urso's tomb, he broke it open and summoned him. Hand in hand, Fridolin and the obliging corpse walked six miles to the local court, where the dead Urso quickly got the better of his startled brother (Figure 55). The land safely secured, Fridolin walked the corpse home and returned it to eternal rest.[29]

Obviously this is fantasy, a fourteenth-century addition to the imaginative biography of a saint from the misty past. But it interests us here because it made local sense: devotees around Säckingen did not baulk in disbelief at the idea of a corpse walking around. This suggests that (less virtuous) active corpses were still part of their belief-system, as they had been at the time of the spectacular Elsau burial (Figure 41). Later medieval evidence is otherwise thin, but a corpse in the cemetery of the Holy Spirit hospital at Konstanz was laid prone, with the legs tied together crosswise.[30] And there is one documented episode that probably took place somewhere near the source of the Rhine. Published in 1486 in the notorious *Hammer of Witches*, it also makes the first of those rare links between active corpses and European witchcraft:

FIGURE 55: The walking corpse as friend and ally, as conceived by a Swiss glazier in 1547. The Irish saint Fridolin walks hand-in-hand with the dead benefactor of his monastery, who brandishes the title-deed.

> One of us inquisitors found that a certain town had been almost depopulated through the dying of the inhabitants, and the rumour was widespread that a certain buried woman was swallowing bit by bit the shroud in which she had been buried, and that the plague could not stop unless she ate the shroud entirely and swallowed it into her stomach. After there was consultation about it, the chief judge and the mayor dug up the tomb and discovered that almost half the shroud had gone down into her stomach through he mouth and throat. Agitated at the sight of this, the mayor drew his sword, and after cutting off her head, he threw it out of the grave. With this, the plague suddenly stopped.[31]

Some decades later, when this motif-sequence re-emerged in Saxony, it would be understood rather differently (p. 324). In the meantime, the Reformation and the witch craze had re-contoured the borderlands between human society and magic, and between the living and the dead.

Facing the Mediterranean: A Roman Inheritance?

Our southwards journey now takes us across the Alps, into Mediterranean regions where subjects and successors of the late Roman Empire had killed corpses by hammering nails into them. Despite the long evidence gap, it seems possible that this practice had not died out.[32] Suggestive, if frustratingly isolated, is a tenth-century burial transfixed with a wooden stake at Molzbichl, in the hills on the Austrian/Italian border north of the Friuli.[33] And in the twelfth- to thirteenth-century monastic cemetery at Novalesa, on the Alpine edge west of Turin, fourteen burials (representing 2.2 percent of identified individuals) had their skulls pierced with uniform square holes made by iron spikes.[34]

More perplexingly isolated is a group of spectacularly nail-killed burials in Aragón (north-eastern Spain): the only substantial episode known from south-western Europe after the fifth century. What makes these stranger still is that all or most of them occur in twelfth- or thirteenth-century Jewish communities. Out of four or more cemeteries, only

Deza is published in any detail, and there an amazing two-thirds of all the excavated burials were pierced by nails (Figure 13). Both sexes and all ages are represented. A regular pattern of nails between the bones of the arms and legs evidently fastened the corpses down to boards or coffin-bases. Other nails were disabling: in the head, the vertebrae, the heart, and (with a few females) the genital area.[35]

This must be in some sense a continuation or revival of the corpse-nailing found in precisely the same upland region of north-east Spain during the fourth to sixth centuries (p. 172), perhaps now made visible—after a long gap in evidence—by a specific epidemic eruption. Given the scrupulous reverence accorded to human remains in Hebraic tradition, the Jewish context is perplexing. But inscribed objects found with the corpses leave no room for doubt, and the practice seems to have left an echo in the otherwise unintelligible Aragónese curse 'May you be nailed like a Jew (*Clavado te veas como Judío*)'.[36]

Whatever made these communities adopt such an ancient but culturally alien tradition, there is no problem in envisaging a trauma-induced epidemic of fear. The later twelfth century brought great anxieties for Jews in Iberia, caught between the hardline Islamic regime of the Almohad Caliphate and the Christian conquest from the north. If the burials are of that date, these communities were in precisely the zone of the advancing Christian frontier. There was ample scope here to alleviate fears and miseries by transferring blame to the dead.

The Balkans and Greece

At last, we reach the zone of south-eastern Europe where 'vampires' lurk in popular imagination. The whole Balkan peninsula south of the Danube had belonged to the eastern Roman (Byzantine) Empire, but what are now Bulgaria, Serbia, Bosnia, and Croatia were lost to Slavic and Turkic Bulgar invasions during the late sixth and seventh centuries. Bulgaria and Serbia both established formidable military states, though Serbia was intermittently under Byzantine or Bulgarian control. Most of Greece remained part of the Byzantine Empire until the Ottoman conquest of 1453 (though alongside Crusader rule in some areas), and in practice the whole peninsula was heavily permeated by Byzantine cultural and religious influence.

Despite popular perceptions, it may have been relatively late that dangerous-dead fears intensified north of the Danube, in Romania and Transylvania. Bulgaria, however, has produced more than a hundred potentially 'killed' skeletons. They start with occasional seventh- to early eighth-century cases, become more frequent through the ninth to tenth centuries, and apparently tail off after the thirteenth. If corpse-killing was so prevalent there over such a long timespan, Bulgaria may be a key to much that is otherwise mysterious. Luckily, this material has been ably collected and discussed by Petar Parvanov, whose work makes my analysis possible.[37]

Most of the Bulgarian cases show combinations of mutilation, abnormal body position, and stones laid on the corpse. Missing or misplaced bones of the feet or lower legs, and tied wrists or ankles, are especially common. The head is detached in about a quarter of cases—sometimes just twisted round, sometimes placed elsewhere in the grave; in three cases the jawbone is placed separately.[38] Some more elaborate variants include: the skull and left femur on the chest, the right tibia and fibula repositioned, a stone replacing the left femur; the jawbone between the tops of the femurs; the skull on the left knee, the left foot missing; the cranium (without the jawbone) on the right humerus next to the clavicle, the legs tied.[39] Holding the corpse down with iron tools—a sickle across the body, or a large ploughshare on the left shoulder—occurs in four late cases, all post-1200.[40]

Even in the absence of visible staking or heart-piercing, there is a strong case for seeing these as post-burial mutilations of suspect corpses. As elsewhere, actions like rotating the head, removing the jawbone, or repositioning limbs—without leaving chop-marks—are hard to perform unless the corpse is semi-decomposed. An eighth- to ninth-century grave at Varbyane has a large slashing cut across the neck and chest; the cranium and jawbone are in the side of the grave; and ribs and vertebrae have been placed where the skull should be.[41] This looks like just the kind of hasty, violent action, performed (perhaps at night) by frightened grave-openers on a semi-decayed corpse, which is documented elsewhere in this book. It is notable that this behaviour persisted without radical change through the conversion of the Bulgars to Christianity from the 860s. Even so, around a third of the burials date from the century or so following that event, which may tell the familiar story of heightened fears in the face of spiritual destabilization.

Did corpse-killing have anything to do with the duallist Christian sects—Paulician and Bogomil—that would become established in regions around the Black Sea? The duallist belief that demonic powers ruled the physical world could have led, without too much difficulty, to the conception of demons controlling corpses. An isolated reference occurs in 1141, when two Anatolian bishops were accused of 'Bogomil practices', including digging up the bodies of Christians buried in churches because 'they died in sin and demons inhabited their corpses'.[42] This looks promising, but unfortunately we know too little about Bogomil practice to take it further.

Another point emerges from Parvanov's distribution maps: mutilated burials before about 950 are confined to the eastern half of Bulgaria (closest to the Black Sea), and only thereafter spread westwards.[43] This glimpse of change over time could—just possibly—reveal early stages of the dynamic that eventually brought the dangerous dead westwards to the Adriatic coast and northwards into Romania. And can it be a coincidence that Debelt/Deultum, with its late Roman nailed burials (p. 172), is on the Black Sea coast of Bulgaria? Despite the takeover by Slavs and Bulgars, the Romanised Thracians left a considerable cultural legacy.[44] More than two centuries separate the 'killed' burials at Deultum from the first Bulgarian ones, and the procedure is different. Still, there seems to be a case for suggesting continuity from late Roman to medieval and eventually post-medieval practices.

Did the north-westward drift continue? Burials in the tenth- to twelfth-century range at Vukovar-Lijeva Bara (Croatia), Hodoni (Transylvania), and Trjane (Serbia) had long bones repositioned in a crossed formation.[45] This looks like a persuasive corpse-killing action, though apparently a rare one. The landmark piece of evidence is Serbian, a clause in Tsar Stefan Dušan's law-code issued in 1349: 'if any person be taken out of his grave for magic and be burned: any village that does this shall pay a fine; and if any priest shall come to it, let his priesthood be taken from him.'[46] It is interesting to note that this law-code followed the first onslaught of the Black Death, which had devastated the region and displaced populations.[47] Of various possible scenarios, a westward-spreading wave of anxieties about the dead during the fourteenth century, fanned up by bubonic plague, is worth keeping in view.

To move from Serbia to Byzantium is to encounter a far better-documented medieval society. Given the later intensity of dangerous-dead beliefs in Greece, we should expect early sources to mention them if they had existed: this is one context where the absence of evidence has some weight as negative evidence.

In fact, the early Byzantine texts that are sometimes claimed to mention the walking dead do not withstand close examination.[48] Likewise, canonists of the ninth to twelfth centuries (who would have been concerned with such matters) make no reference either to walking corpses or to the strange doctrine—so prominent later—that posthumous incorruption could actually be *imposed* by excommunication:[49] that first appears in a patriarchal mandate from 1370.[50] The Emperor Michael VIII Palaiologos died excommunicate in 1282, but it is a commentator in the 1390s who first mentions (with derision) the belief that his body therefore remained incorrupt.[51]

For an explicit reference to the exhumation of sinister incorrupt bodies we must wait for the canonist Ioasaph of Ephesos (died 1437), who responded to the question 'If a so-called *katachthonian* [earth-dweller] is found among us, what should be done about it?': 'When people, lacking complete faith, dig up the grave to find the body, the devil takes over the body, which has blood, flesh, nails and hair. So they take it out and burn it, and thereby they perish in the eternal fire, because the cremated remains will rise at the Resurrection, and the people who did it will be judged and condemned if they do not repent.'[52]

The silence of earlier written sources in the case of Greece strengthens what would otherwise be mere conjecture in the case of Serbia: that corpse-killing reached both regions around the mid-fourteenth century, perhaps emanating from Bulgaria. The references to Serbs and Greeks burning suspect corpses, rather than mutilating them in the Bulgarian style, raise the possibility that this practice eventually spread to Bulgaria, explaining the cessation of visibly mutilated corpses in Bulgaria around 1350.

All this suggests a working hypothesis: that late Roman anxieties about the noxious power of corpses survived over many centuries in their Bulgarian reservoir, gradually trickling into other parts of the Balkan peninsula, and then flowing more strongly in the wake of the existential terror brought by plague during 1347–9.[53]

After 1400, the balance of the evidence changes. Written sources become richer, expanding to include theological commentary and eventually ethnographic reporting. Excavated burials remain useful, but there are fewer of them. The regions where 'vampires' are popularly located today emerge more clearly.

This chapter has shown, however, that these phenomena were not static, but took shape in fluid geographical and cultural contexts that had been mutating since Roman times. Little more would be heard of the dangerous dead in Britain, the Rhineland, the Alps, or the Mediterranean. By contrast, beliefs in northern Germany, Poland, and Bohemia would intensify and spread south-eastwards, eventually linking up with their counterparts in the Balkans.

PART V

Late Medieval and Early Modern Europe

AFTER 1400, *printing, widening horizons, and religious conflict accelerated the flow of ideas across Europe and beyond. To explore the impact of those developments, Part V will now start at a different point. Since leaving the Roman Empire, this book has concentrated on northern and central Europe, where the dead who refused to die were in a unique category. In chapters 24 and 25, we return to the Eurasian context introduced in Part II: a complex world of nature-spirits and other supernatural forces where unquiet corpses interacted with other beings. When revenants appear in the early modern eastern European zone, it is against this background of different and potentially older belief-systems.*

Returning then to western Europe, we will continue to find regional ebbs and flows. Beliefs faded in Britain and the Rhineland but intensified and extended eastwards. The revenants of Britain and Saxony can be placed in relatively clear-cut categories. But as we progress through Silesia and Bohemia to Moravia and the Carpathians, associations with magic and witchcraft will gradually intensify, and the boundary between the unquiet human dead and demonic beings will start to blur. Eventually, we will re-join the Balkan traditions and see how oral transmission and the expansion of popular print after 1600 encouraged a cross-fertilization between the dangerous dead of the west and the east.

24

The Eurasian Reservoir of Beliefs

NIGHT-BATTLERS, DAMNED HUNTSMEN, AND BLOODSUCKING CORPSES

This *obur* problem is worse than a widespread plague. It is especially common in the lands of Muscovy, the Cossacks, the Poles and the Czechs.

—EVLIYA ÇELEBI, 1666

THE FURTHER EAST we look, the more the dangerous dead recall the Asian motifs discussed in Chapters 8 and 9, and the more the 'vampire' motif broadens from the animated corpse to include were-animals and living magicians. The Lamia/Gello motif-complex lived on across the eastern Mediterranean and Near Eastern zone, where it could assimilate to conceptions of human/animal transitions and unruly spiritual forces. Whereas corpses in western and central Europe have no dedicated terminology because they are just people (once alive, now not-quite-dead), in the east they are described by a range of terms that originally meant shape-shifters, bloodsuckers, or flying demons.

In western Europe, some of that occasionally surfaces. The English revenants who shape-change, dance with animals, or wander with barking dogs recall later eastern European material to a surprising level of detail, as does the corpse in south-west Scotland uniquely described as a 'bloodsucker' (p. 254): these cases imply an otherwise invisible milieu of motif-exchange before the thirteenth century. The ashes of an Icelandic revenant generate a monstrous bull (p. 246). Another saga describes two terrifying women who appear in dreams: one whose son is a supernaturally-charged ox, the other who replaces the dreamer's entrails with brushwood.[1] Burchard of Worms had already condemned the second belief (p. 126), which recalls one version of the classical *strix*.[2] The eagle's and fox's feet in the Elsau burial suggest interaction with animal-spirits (p. 218). These are residual, half-buried traces of a supernatural world that, in later centuries, is more visible east of the Vistula and south of the Carpathians.

The Night-Flyers and the Wild Hunt

In 1691, in what is now Latvia, a routine trial for theft took a strange turn when a witness—one 'Old Thiess'—was casually described in court as a werewolf. The judge's perplexity increased when Thiess acknowledged cheerfully that he had indeed been a werewolf, but had given it up when a sorcerer had hit him on the nose. Where did that happen? In hell, while Thiess was rescuing grain-blossoms that his opponent had stolen from earth to cause a famine. So was he in league with the Devil? Of course not, Thiess responded indignantly: werewolves are God's hounds, and they combat the evil sorcerers who carry all the food off to hell and make people starve.[3]

The walking dead do not figure in this story. It matters here, however, because it describes ritualized warfare between two ambiguous kinds of being: people transformed into wolves, who are good (but in other contexts can be evil), and magicians who consume people's resources, and are alive (but in other contexts can be dead). Interchanges between people and animals, animals and magicians, and magicians and the dead, will recur in this chapter and the next. We need to enter Thiess's strange world if we are to understand how animated corpses could be viewed as members (usually rogue ones) of the same supernatural company.

Thiess's story contributed to Carlo Ginzburg's famous hypothesis of an ancient Eurasian tradition of agrarian rituals, which breaks surface at various different times and places scattered across Europe and beyond.[4] His starting-point was an association in the Friuli region known in the sixteenth century as the *benandanti* ('good walkers'). These people believed that they regularly went out at night in spirit to battle against witches and warlocks with fennel stalks, protecting crops and livestock that would otherwise have been devastated: they were on God's side. Being 'born with the caul' (that is, with part of the amniotic membrane draped over the baby's head like a veil) marked them from birth, and they often carried it like a relic. It conferred supernatural powers, variously identified as the ability to shape-shift into wolves or other animals, to operate outside the body, to foretell the future, and to communicate with the dead.[5]

If these were the good forces, what were the evil ones? Essentially, those were demons and sorcerers, but variants appear on the fringes. When a *benandante* goes wrong and his body is buried, says one source, 'the spirit goes wandering and is called a *malandante*'.[6] A werewolf in sixteenth-century Riga fought a witch in the form of a butterfly.[7] Recurrently woven into the 'night-battles' complex are distinct templates featuring supernatural huntsmen, diabolical processions of damned souls, assemblies to venerate a dominant female deity or spirit, and battles between demonic forces in the sky.[8] One such variant, from the world of powerful supernatural females, is the terrifying ride of valkyries in the Old English text quoted on p. 142.

One does not have to accept every detail of Ginsburg's courageous tour-de-force to acknowledge the broad reality of his 'system', its likely shamanic origins, and—for present purposes—its frequent interchanges between the worlds of the living and the dead. As he says, the adversaries in the 'night-battles' symbolize that great divide and the paths that cross it: 'On the one hand, [they were] the living assimilated to the dead through ecstasy; on the other, depending on the particular case, [they were] the dead, sorcerers, other members of the same initiatory group. . . . Metamorphoses, cavalcades, ecstasies, followed by the egress of the soul in the shape of an animal—these are different paths to a single goal. Between animals and souls, animals and the dead, animals and the beyond, there exists a profound connection.'[9]

This kaleidoscopic intersection of motif-sequences presents a set of immensely powerful images: people born with the caul; people changing into wolves; wolves battling sorcerers; good and evil forces battling in the sky; an army of ferocious women riding over a barrow; demons, lost souls, and barking dogs sweeping wildly across the countryside. When dead people appear in these contexts they are usually spirits, not corpses, but several of their attributes—the caul, shape-shifting, sorcery—are ascribed elsewhere to corpses that will not stay quiet. And one very bizarre but very important narrative describes predatory corpses taking part in night-battles.

Turkic Bloodsuckers Again: Evliya Çelebi in the Caucasus

High in the Caucasus near the present Russian/Georgian border, on the night of 24 April 1666, the Ottoman traveller Evliya Çelebi 'observed' a drama that cannot really have happened: a mighty battle in the sky between Circassian and Abkhazian *obur*s (a version of the Turkic word that would eventually produce 'vampire'). Riding dead horses, oxen, and camels, they fought for six hours amid thunder, lightning, and screams, leaving debris strewn over the hills. Just before dawn, seven Circassian *obur*s and seven Abkhazian witches put their heads under each other's necks, and fell to earth: '[two] Abkhazian *obur*s got to drink the blood of two Circassian *obur*s from their necks and died. Of the seven Abkhazian witches, five of them were alive and able to levitate and go away. In that place, Circassians burned the Abkhazian witches who drank the Circassian *obur*s' blood'.

Evliya goes on to relate that *obur*s kill people at night by drinking their blood: 'in this way, *obur*s can be cured [temporarily?] from being an *obur*. Despite this, the sign of being an *obur* can be seen in his/her eyes.' After an *obur*-related death, specialist *obur*-catchers—wise and respected elders of good birth—are called in (if the family can afford it) and paid to find the culprit's grave:

> They see that an *obur* indeed came out from the grave the other night, which they understand from the disturbed soil. Then, people come

and dig up the *obur* grave. They see that his/her eyes are filled with blood and his/her face is crimson red, which indicates that he/she has drunk human blood. They immediately remove the filthy carcass of the accursed *obur* from the grave and drive a hawthorn stake through the stomach, nailing him/her to the ground. This, with God's help, breaks the *obur*'s spell. . . . [But] some people burn the filthy carcass together with the stake in order to prevent another *obur* from entering the body of the dead *obur*. . . . Yet, it is a divine mystery that carcasses of these accursed *obur*s do not decompose.

'No one can recognize an *obur* when he/she is alive and walking', Evliya continues, but after attacking someone, the *obur* is sometimes imprisoned by *obur*-catchers:

On the third day of captivity, his/her *obur* features gradually become clearer. He/she says, 'I drank the blood of a certain person. Here is his/her blood behind my ear. I smeared it on myself so that when I am buried next to my *obur* ancestors, my body will not decay. I did it because I will resuscitate several times to battle in the sky.' Upon this, with everybody's permission, they drive a hawthorn stake into the *obur*'s stomach. When they smear *obur*'s blood on the face of the sick whose blood was sucked, he/she heals, and they burn the *obur*. These *obur* witches and sorcerers are a different species/lineage.[10]

Evliya's ethnographic reporting has been overshadowed by the wild fantasy preceding it, but it deserves more respect. He wrote well before the flood of German vampire commentary: no Western printed material could have provided these motifs. The framework is a version of the 'night-battles' theme, though without the struggle for agrarian fertility.[11] *Obur*s are a 'different species', but they still need to smear a victim's blood behind one ear to activate their posthumous incorruption and their flying and fighting strength. They can be either alive or dead. If alive, they can seem like ordinary people (beyond the look in their eyes), but must drain a victim's blood to be freed (temporarily?) from their lethal compulsion; they also give eloquent accounts of their exploits. If dead, they burrow through their grave-earth when they come out at night, and can be destroyed by staking or burning. Sometimes an *obur* is immaterial enough to occupy another *obur*'s corpse. Finally, neutralising them is the work of specialists.

Some very different ideas have been amalgamated here. The *oburs* combine traits of ecstatic 'night-battlers' with those of predatory magicians, demons, and dangerous corpses. Their 'different species' (possibly implying that they were born with the caul?), and their crossing of the life/death frontier, recall the Subarctic shape-shifters and the living 'vampires' of Kamchatka, just as the corpse-switching recalls the Mongolian *bong* (pp. 104, 107). All this seems decidedly shamanic. One fixed point, in conjunction with bloodsucking, is the term derived from Proto-Turkic **ōpyr* 'sucker': we can at least be confident that a bloodsucking demon with that name was an ancient inheritance from the Central Asian steppe. By contrast, exhumation, staking, and burning are familiar Western motifs, specific to unquiet corpses.

That comes to the heart of the matter: when was the animated corpse assimilated into the rest of Evliya's motif-complex? A date quite soon before 1666 cannot be excluded: comparable ideas were spreading around central Europe at the time. But he writes as though the corpse motif were already intense and deep-rooted; later appearances of the same fusion further west in the Black Sea zone, in western Turkey (where the harmful corpses were female) and southern Moldova, strengthen that impression.[12]

So many mobile peoples have occupied the shores of the Black Sea, and have left such complex and intersecting traditions, that it is futile to assert a clear or unique origin for these beliefs. One possibility—given the nailed burials at Deultum and the early medieval mutilations in Bulgaria (pp. 172, 283)—is that they were at least partly a Hellenistic and late Roman inheritance, from the world in which Philinnion had seduced Machates. A completely different source could be Viking influence, percolating down the Dnieper to the Black Sea from Kyivan Rus'. In either of these cases (or a combination of both, or some different one), the assimilation of Turkic speakers added the prototype of the word 'vampire', and the activity with which vampires are most associated today.

There is another problem: does Evliya's narrative describe the epicentre and heartland of this amalgamated belief-complex, or is it merely an unusually early and graphic description of something more widespread? In post-1800 folklore collections, its components do certainly occur across Eastern Europe. As we review them in the next chapter, the challenge will be to assess when, and how intensely, dangerous corpses penetrated the world of shape-shifters and flying demons.

25

Life-Forces, Shape-Shifters, and Dangerous Corpses

EASTERN EUROPE, 1400–1750

'If someone gathers a hundred cartloads of aspen wood to make a bonfire and cremates me in that fire, then he will have stopped me! Only they would have to be careful when cremating me, because vipers, maggots and other vermin will crawl out of my belly. Daws, magpies and crows will fly out. They will have to catch them and throw them into the fire. If even one small maggot escapes, it will all be to no avail! I will sneak away inside that maggot!'

—A RUSSIAN VAMPIRE IN A NINETEENTH-CENTURY FOLK STORY

THE SOURCES for central and western Europe are patchy, but at least they exist. In vaster expanses of territory—east of the Baltic, the Vistula, the Danube, and the Adriatic—there is even less to go on. The burial evidence is sparser, and (except in Greece) there are fewer pre-1750 written sources. In compensation, there are abundant collections of folklore and ethnography, from Russia, Belarus, Ukraine, Romania, and every country of the

Balkan peninsula, in which beings within the spectra from were-animals to magicians to dangerous corpses surface in various combinations.

The sheer volume of this folkloric material can mesmerize, but it has two big drawbacks. Most obviously, it is very late in date. A consequent but more insidious problem is that it can seem outside time, as though these recent reports described beliefs that 'always' existed. The dangerous dead were certainly feared across much of the zone by 1800, but they were not ubiquitous (they barely touched Hungary or Slovakia, for instance), nor self-evidently immemorial. In fact, there are good reasons for suspecting that they expanded from the southern Balkan core during the centuries after 1400.

In a time of hugely complex political, cultural, and religious change, this process is impossible to track in all details. (How did the motif of a woman who dies without anyone to watch her corpse, and therefore becomes a lethal shroud-swallower, find its way into an early sixteenth-century Jewish source from Egypt?[1] Its presence is certain, but its background is irrecoverably lost.) Still, if we revisit the material as historians rather than folklorists, some new perspectives on change through time and space may emerge.

Finland and the Baltic States

Finland is a good starting-point for this survey, since it stood at a crossroads between Scandinavian and Baltic cultures. The western and southern zone, with its 'weapon-killed' burials from the late Viking age (p. 273), was a Scandinavian island in a Balto-Finnic sea: northwards and eastwards, extending into Karelia, were populations of Western Uralic origin. In this conjunction, two distinct belief-systems interpenetrated.

Generally speaking, the Finnish dead did not return as corpses, though ensuring their proper transition to the next world was of great importance, and there are occasional folkloric references to leg-binding or even staking.[2] Ambiguous appearances of dead relatives, whose powers verged on the physical, have been common until recently (p. 37).

The widespread idea of the *etiäinen*, an external manifestation of a living human personality that sometimes travels ahead, reflects a quasi-shamanic background involving multiple life-forces and spirit entities.[3]

Another difficult term, *väki* 'power', had senses ranging from 'an essence or intentional nature of the entity in which it resides' (in Karelia), to the more personalized 'crowd of [supernatural] beings' (in western Finland).[4] The entity(ies) called *kirkonväki* ('churchyard-force/crowd') were said to 'appear in graveyards, on the road or even in farmhouses after someone has died or when death-related objects have been brought to the house. Belief legends also tell about their nightly church services. Some people describe churchyard-*väki* as decomposing bodies, while others tell it is an airy swarm of small, human-like figures which reek of death. Many accounts present it as an invisible agent which is brought along in the form of a small amount of graveyard soil to haunt a house'.[5] The motif of a congregation of the more-or-less physical dead (who in one story destroy a fur coat, mistaking it for a man) is prominent in the west and south-west, whereas further east the *kirkonväki* is conceived as an invisible or translucent crowd.[6]

The closer to Scandinavian influence, in other words, the more like dead humans the *väki*-entities seem, even though they are never explicitly defined as walking corpses. The fundamental contrast is between an animistic world where *väki* flows freely through all living things, and a Germanic/Scandinavian one where it is restricted by being confined to individuals.

In rural western Finland, near the Swedish border, residual beliefs had one unique outcome: a painted image of a European rampant corpse that apparently draws on genuine folk-belief. During 1774–9, Haukipudas church was brightly decorated, a last fling of the old pre-Reformation tradition. In its Last Judgement scene, the spectacular monstrosities who torment the damned include an unambiguous animated corpse, blood dripping from its teeth as it takes a bite from an unfortunate soul (Figure 56). The artist, Mikael Toppelius, is noted for incorporating vernacular material into the baroque repertoire that he learned as an apprentice: 'he would use ethnographic and local details that enhanced links with folk-culture'.[7] The Haukipudas schene was commissioned by a group of local farmers: did one of them suggest this last survivor of the Nordic dangerous dead?

Shape-shifting and werewolf motifs are prominent in Estonia, Latvia, and Lithuania, as the Thiess story illustrates. Dangerous corpses appear

FIGURE 56: Haukipudas church (Finland): a biting corpse in the Last Judgement scene painted by Michael Toppelius of Oulu in 1774. The overall scheme of the painting is conventional, but this detail seems to be unique, and presumably derives from local folklore.

in the folklore occasionally; there is an apparently widespread motif of a corpse bursting out of its coffin or shroud.[8] The dead could have a brooding presence, no less oppressive because they did not arise physically (p. 54). It looks as though these cultures were affected by Scandinavian ideas about the corporeal dead, but not very deeply.

Overall, the eastern Baltic zone illustrates how dangerous-dead ideas could infiltrate belief-cultures that had lacked them. They did not always infiltrate strongly, but they contributed to a mind-set in which corpse-killing epidemics might potentially erupt.

Russia and Belarus

Across this vast territory, extending into Siberia and the Shamanic north, there was a strong emphasis on wicked magicians and other evildoers, and on how their sins in life deprived them of peace in death. It is only west of the Urals, however, that ravenous and lethal corpses enter the picture, and they show distinct differences from their southern neighbours in Ukraine, Romania, and the Balkans.

There was a ubiquitous folk-belief in 'unclean force', which (like the Finnish *väki* but more negatively) could be either generalized or embodied in individuals.[9] As in regions further south, the human soul could take the form of an insect, butterfly, or small animal, not just a wolf.[10] A widespread belief was in *rusalki*: young women who—having drowned or died unbaptized—were yoked to these unclean forces and appeared as predatory water-nymphs.[11]

These were spirits, but the post-1850 folklore from south and west Russia includes lethally dangerous walking corpses. They were people who had either lived bad lives as magicians, witches, or evildoers, or had died bad deaths by suicide or drowning.[12] This strongly moralistic framework is emphasized by the application of yet another term that normally means something completely different: 'heretic'. As Felix Oinas explains, it 'has acquired a strongly negative connotation as "a person engaged in black magic, witch, sorcerer, wizard," and is used as a word of abuse. The same term with its different variants has also come to denote various types of vampires: *eretik*—the deceased who comes out of the grave and eats people; *erestun*—a living vampire, revived by a sorcerer who has penetrated a person's body at the moment of his death; and *eretica*—whose eye functions as a full-fledged vampire. The means for destroying heretic-vampires are burning and staking, and, in the case of the *erestun*, flogging'.[13] In the south, in Tambov province, *ereticy* were 'women who have sold their souls to the devil during their lifetimes and are now [after their deaths] roaming the earth, turning people away from their genuine faith. In daytime they walk around as ugly old women in rags, by the evening they gather in "heathen" ravines, but at night they enter sunken graves and sleep in the coffins of the impious dead'.[14] That these various sinister beings should be labelled 'heretics' reflects the popular demonization of actual doctrinal heretics, possibly with some influence from the Greek Orthodox idea that the flesh of the excommunicated did not decay.[15]

This strong identification of the troublesome in death with the wicked in life (great sinners, the violent, the godless, suicides, and above all evil sorcerers) distances these revenants from some other European ones. The stress on culpability, rather than failure of process between death and burial, explains why—again in contrast to the West (p. 55)—suicides were conspicuous among the Russian undead. What mattered was not incompletion, but the heinousness of sin and the consequent power of their evil, carried undiminished across the frontier of death.

It is plausible enough to trace these 'magicians' back to the circumpolar shamanic past (p. 104), and we know of at least one prominent werewolf. According to an early twelfth-century text, Prince Vseslav of Polotsk (now Belarus) was conceived in enchantment and born (in about 1029) with a caul, which was bound to him permanently to make him 'pitiless in bloodshed'; another source says that he could turn into a wolf or other wild beast.[16] The werewolf template was certainly very ancient in the region: Herodotos (c. 430 BC) had written that the Neuri (inhabitants of what are now Belarus and Ukraine) spent some days each year as wolves.[17]

Dangerous corpses are more elusive: supposed late eleventh-century references to the *upir'*, and to pre-emptive measures, do not bear scrutiny.[18] It was in Vseslav's reign that demons—described in one text as 'the dead'—killed people at Polotsk in 1092, but their nature remains vague.[19] In fact, the first solid reference to Russian corpse-fears comes only in 1274: a statement by the bishop of Vladimir that burials of 'drowned and hanged men' do *not* cause droughts, floods, and crop failures.[20] The idea that unholy corpses did precisely that surfaces regularly from the fifteenth century onwards. A recent analysis explains it as a fear that because the dead are thirsty and hungry, they drain life-giving fluids from the land and living things.[21] This looks like a fusion of the grave-bound unquiet corpse with the despoilers of fruitfulness in the 'night-battles' template, a hypothesis encouraged by Vseslav's werewolf identity.

Corpses that walk at night, and eat people, are only mentioned in very late sources. Dmitry Zelenin observed that the bloodsucking *upir'* motif extended northwards from the Balkans into Ukraine and southern Russia, and suggested that it assimilated readily to ideas of the unclean dead established there.[22] That is probably true, but leaves uncertain whether the Russian unclean dead had ever taken physical form outside their graves before that fusion took place. Alternatively, we should not forget the Viking origins of the Rus' state: Scandinavian influence is as plausible here as in northern Germany or Poland.

Ukraine, Moldova, and Romania

In the zone between the northern Slavic peoples and the Black Sea, the interpenetration of motifs was complex. The southern *obur/upir'* term fused with beliefs resembling Russian ones: among the Gagurz Turks in Moldova, for instance, it was especially suicides and sorcerers who became *oburs* in the grave.[23] But it could describe living people: near Kyiv in 1727, a man confessed that because he was born an *upir* he immediately knew everything that was going on in the world, and was recruited by the witches when he reached twelve.[24] Terminology is bewilderingly prolific, notably the several variants of *strigoi* from *strix*, *moroi* from *mara*, and *vukodlak* from the Slavic prototype 'wolf-hair' (see pp. 15–16).

These labels described a range of supernatural beings in a range of contexts, among whom unquiet corpses seem likely to be relative latecomers. The Romanian *strigoi* came to mean a dangerous corpse, but a shamanic shape-shifter born with the caul (like the Hungarian *táltos*, who had no corpse associations) looks like an older sense.[25] The *moroi* originates etymologically in the presser/squeezer of the night-mare paralysis.[26] The *vukodlac/vârcolac*—certainly a werewolf—had monstrous cosmic powers to eat the sun and moon, mentioned in Serbia in 1262 and later known across the southern Slavic zone.[27] In Romania, unlike the southern Balkans, this term usually still meant werewolf rather than unquiet corpse into modern times.[28]

Category-shifting has been regularly noted by modern ethnographers. When Pëtr Bogatyrëv conducted fieldwork in south-western Ukraine in the 1920s, he found a rich, fluid landscape of belief where undead corpses blended conceptually with other supernatural entities. Any of the dead could be threatening, but dead sorcerers were most threatening of all.[29] The *opyr* could be living or dead, could take human or animal form, and could be ambiguously identified as a night-spirit, nature-spirit, sorcerer, witch, or werewolf (*vovkun'*). The material does include the beheading and staking of unruly corpses, but as one motif-complex among several.[30]

In Romania, werewolves and witches were integrated into rituals that reinforced social stability and a sense of community, and were therefore not wholly bad, whereas 'vampires' were beyond the pale.[31] In practice, however, there was no hard boundary between living 'vampires' (*strigoi vi*) and dead ones (*strigoi mort*), whose misdeeds were often much the same,[32] and who both absorbed the power (*mana*) of people, animals, and insects.[33] For children born with the caul, this career-path was pre-ordained.[34] *Strigoi, moroi,* and *vârcolaci* met each other on the boundaries between village communities to formulate their wicked plans.[35] And it needs considerable perceptual flexibility to make sense of this Transylvanian story:

> A young woman found her father dead one day, and she herself died. A young man from the village found her dead in her bed. The young man left the house and when he came back later she was sitting up in the bed. The young man's mother forbade him to return to that house. The girl who was no longer dead married someone else from the village although she was in love with the first young man. The young man was in the fields one day when a wolf appeared in front of him, running back and forth like a dog with its master. The boy took a wooden stick and began to beat the wolf. The wolf fell to the ground and stayed there. The next day the young girl was found in bed; her ribs were cracked. The boy was afraid; he knew she was the wolf and might kill him.[36]

This is deeply ambiguous. We expect the girl to become a vampire, but in fact she becomes a werewolf. And is she really alive or dead?

The fictional 'Romanian vampire' of modern literature should not blind us, then, to the problems surrounding its origins and identity. This need for caution is confirmed by the long, thorough list of superstitions in Moldavia/Moldova (north-eastern Romania) compiled by Demetriu Cantemiru in 1714: it makes no reference to animated corpses. It does include three other beings: the *striga,* an evil baby-killing female; the *zburatorul,* a spectre in the form of a beautiful young man who attacks maidens at night; and the *tricolicz* (i.e., *vricolac*) or werewolf.[37] From these ingredients, the Romanian vampire motif would eventually crystallise. But Cantemiru's negative evidence is weighty: evidently that development had not yet happened by 1714, at least in Moldova.

Bulgaria and Serbia

Corpse-killing was practised by the fourteenth century in Greece and Serbia, and long before that in Bulgaria; in the nineteenth century it remained prominent in all three countries (pp. 284–285, 407). It is therefore a reasonable assumption that it became permanently endemic in the southern Balkan peninsula. In 1577, an Orthodox interpreter told a Lutheran delegation visiting Istanbul that 'in Bulgaria and Greece certain dead and buried people, who were excommunicated or otherwise infidels, did not decay. The Devil came to these at night, so that they left their graves and frightened people, and sometimes even infected and poisoned them. They were therefore dug up again and burned. Everyone would bring along one or two pieces of wood for the fire; the priests would stand by censing, and singing "Lord have mercy on us."'[38]

For Serbia and the adjoining Banat of Temesvár (now in Romania), we have reports spanning 1717–75 about corpses regularly called 'bloodsuckers', including a case in 1732 where a woman 'smeared herself with a vampire's blood to avoid being killed by one'.[39] Bulgarian corpses were also enthusiastic blood-drinkers, and were fought by professional vampire-killers (*vampirdžii, sâbotniki*) whose powers derived from their birth circumstances.[40] These recall Evliya Çelebi's 'respected, wellborn and wise looking old Circassians . . . who can recognize the *oburs*'.[41] They had counterparts in Greece (*alaphostratoi*), Serbia (*vampirovići*, 'the foul-smelling, boneless and toothless vampire children who alone can kill vampires'), and among Roma in Kosovo (*dhampir*, born to the widows of vampires); in Albania there were 'vampire families' who knew how to keep vampires down but were 'better avoided'.[42] In these adversaries of the noxious dead—born not made—we can perhaps recognize the virtuous werewolves of the 'night-battles' template, but in a context where the 'vampire complex' had almost completely absorbed that idea.[43]

Istria and Dalmatia

We noted slight hints that Roman corpse-killing could have survived at a low level in the Veneto/Friuli region (p. 281). An isolated if dramatic later case is a woman who died in Venice, apparently in the plague of 1629–31: a large piece of brick was forced between her jaws when the corpse was still articulated.[44]

On the Istrian and Dalmatian seaboard of the Adriatic (modern Slovenia, Croatia, and Bosnia-Herzegovina) the data are superficially richer, but again there are chronological uncertainties. The Paduan scholar G. F. Tomasini's description of Istria in the 1650s, like Cantemiru's account of Moldova, is eloquent in what it does *not* say. Tomasini observes that certain special individuals were *chresnichi* (good beings); that their adversaries were *vucodlachi* (evil beings), who 'go by night in spirit on the crossroads and also into houses to inspire fear or do damage'; and that these adversaries fought each other to produce abundance or scarcity of produce.[45] Clearly this is the 'night-battles' template, but (so far as Tomasini tells us) no corpse is in sight.

More forthcoming is the geographer and topographer Baron Valvasor, who published his great work on the region in 1689:

> The country and farming folk in Istria firmly believe that there are certain magicians and sorcerers who suck the blood out of children. They call such a bloodsucker *strigon*, or alternatively *vedarèz*. When a *strigon* dies, they think he goes around the village at midnight, knocking and banging on the houses, and when he knocks on a house, someone will die there within a day. When someone dies like that, the farmers say that the *strigon* has eaten him. What is more, these credulous farmers also believe that such returning *strigons* satisfy their wives at night . . .
>
> And they firmly believe that this ghost will not give them any peace until they drive a stake made of thorn-wood through his body. For that reason some of the bravest men do this, and always after midnight, because they believe that before midnight [the s*trigon*] is not in the grave but walks around. So they open the grave, and push

> or hit through his stomach a stake the thickness of a fist or small arm, horribly disfiguring him. Then blood flows out, and the corpse twists and bends as though it were alive and in pain. Then [the attacker] backfills the grave and goes away. This procedure is common among the Istrian farmers in the countryside, although the authorities always try to suppress it with harsh punishment, because it goes against the Faith.[46]

Distinctive ingredients here are bloodsucking, and corpses so unambiguously physical that they leave their graves empty when they walk. The *strigon* of course descends from the life-sucking *strix*; *vedarèz* is a version of *vedomec*, a widespread Slavic term for a living human with supernatural attributes including shape-shifting. Like *strigoi* and *moroi* in Romania and *vrykólakas* in Greece, these words—originally of different meanings—have been pressed into service to describe walking corpses. In later Slovene folklore, the *vedomec* is evil and predatory like Tomasini's *vucodlac*, while the *volkodlac* is a werewolf with similar unpleasant tendencies, including bloodsucking and continued activity after death.[47] A Dalmatian trial record of 1737 concerns walking corpses with several names (*kosac, pricosac, tenjac, vukodlac, lupi-manari*) that had sex with their widows, ate hearts and intestines, drank blood, and had to be staked; there was a similar episode ten years later.[48] In 1774, it was feared that a prospective vukodlak among the Dalmatian Morlachs would 'have a great thirst for children's blood' (p. 91).

All this recalls Evliya Çelebi's report, but there are difficulties. If blood-drinking corpses were already feared in the 1650s, why does Tomasini not mention them? And why does Valvasor equate the *vedarèz* with the walking corpse that he also calls *strigon*? The 1737 description is in line with Valvasor's, but uses a bewildering range of additional and apparently interchangeable terms.

The most famous example of an Istrian *strigon* deepens the puzzle. At Kringa in 1672, Valvasor tells us, one Giure Grando appeared after his burial: walking around, sitting behind a door, and paying some very unwelcome visits to his widow. He knocked on the doors of houses, whose inhabitants began to die. A posse of brave men, led by the sheriff, set out with lanterns and a crucifix to open his grave. Giure's face was red; he smiled at them and opened his mouth, at which the heroic corpse-killers fled. The sheriff—asking acidly how one dead man could turn nine living ones into frightened rabbits—tried to drive a hawthorn stake into his stomach, but it bounced off. The priest took a different approach: he held a crucifix in front of Giure's face, shouting 'Look, you *strigon*, here is Jesus Christ, who redeemed us from hell and died for us, and you, *strigon*, can have no rest.' Giure began to weep. Then one of the posse made a bungled attempt to behead him with a hoe. Another finished the job, at which the head screamed and the grave filled with blood.[49]

Valvasor claims to have interviewed eye-witnesses, and an almost identical story was reported near Ljubljana in 1883.[50] Yet Giure had not been a magician, and does not shape-shift or suck blood: he is more like the revenants of central Europe than Valvasor's *strigon/vedarèz*. Taken in conjunction with Tomasini's silence, Valvasor's category-confusions suggest that beliefs really were fluid and evolving. A plausible scenario is that Tomasini observed ancient beliefs of the 'night-battles' kind, which by Valvasor's time—three decades later—were being infiltrated both by bloodsucking corpses from Serbia and Bulgaria, and by narratives and motifs spread (through popular print?) from the north. Given that Istria adjoined both the maritime powerhouse of Venice and the violently contested Habsburg/Ottoman border, not to mention the Catholic/Orthodox frontier, such contrasting influences are hardly surprising.

Greece and the Aegean

Post-medieval Greece is rich in folklore, some of it perpetuating the supernatural beings of the ancient Greek world.[51] Conspicuous among them were the *gelloudes* (p. 126): still viciously attacking children, still ambiguously poised between demons, dead humans and living witches.[52] Popular belief often assimilated them to the *nereides*, close cognates of the Russian *rusalki*: beautiful young females who seduced men, attacked women during childbirth, and stole babies.[53] On Naxos, *gelloudes* were revealingly confused with *lamies* who appeared as young and beautiful women, and *stringles* who looked old and ugly.[54]

This survival of Gello, Lamia, and the *strix* shows a remarkable long-term coherence for the ancient demonic pantheon. Against that background, dangerous corpses—of both sexes—seem to be more recent arrivals in Greece, becoming visible (so far as the sources go) in the later fourteenth century (p. 285). Thereafter, references in canonical and other ecclesiastical texts are abundant. They describe lay practice through the strongly ideological lens of Orthodox theology, but Karen Hartnup's excellent analysis has now clarified many of the issues.[55]

The distinction between 'active' revenants who walk, and 'passive' ones who lie in their graves (but usually work harm from them), has appeared several times in this book. In Greece—uniquely—it took the form of a stark and officially prescribed moral contrast. The *vrykólakas* was the familiar kind of malevolent corpse that left its grave to wander at night, preying on people and injuring them. It was irredeemably evil, and in the pre-modern period was usually destroyed by burning. The Orthodox Church consistently opposed both the belief and the countermeasure: *vrykólakoi* were just diabolical phantoms, and burning such corpses was an abomination.[56] That did not prevent the enthusiastic participation of some clergy down to the nineteenth and even twentieth centuries.

The *tympaniaios*, by contrast, was defined in theology as an ordinary human sinner unlucky enough to die under excommunication. The natural process of dissolution was therefore halted, leaving the soul in a state of painful suspense, and the corpse intact though grotesquely swollen.[57] Such corpses did no harm to others, and were neither evil nor frightening: some boys used one as a trampoline, 'from which they bounced off as though from a drum'.[58] The state of being a *tympaniaios* arose through the rite of excommunication by a bishop or priest: the formula came to include a phrase explicitly condemning the victim to incorruption, elaborated in stages between the 1530s and 1620s.[59]

What was the source of this remarkably strange theology? As a 'half-way house' between heaven and hell, it fulfilled some of the functions of purgatory in the Catholic system.[60] But another strong factor must be that it bolstered Orthodoxy's moral authority in the face of encroaching Islam. Admittedly the first known case is from 1370 (p. 285), but the practice became much more prominent after the fall of Constantinople and the Byzantine state in 1453. In a set-piece story, the Ottoman sultan challenged Patriarch Maximos (1476–82) to prove the truth of Christianity. Maximos had the intact corpse of an excommunicate brought in, and pronounced absolution. The corpse disintegrated on the spot, and the sultan was duly impressed.[61]

Popular perceptions were another matter. For villagers, the *vrykólakas* was no illusion but an all-too-physical corpse. It might be created because of mishaps between death and burial, as du Boulay would later record (p. 49), or because the deceased was wicked or cursed; in any case it was in the Devil's power.[62] Later shepherds of the Epirus explained that the dead individuals were sinners whose souls had already been taken by the Devil, 'and since the body and soul, whatever the internal tension between them, form a unity, the body also falls into the power of the Devil, remains undissolved in the earth, and possessed by his spirit emerges from the grave to mock the sacred institutions of family life by attacking or terrifying those to whom it owed, in life, the greatest obligations'.[63]

The Greek laity internalized the theological conception of the *tympaniaios*, and later explained the distinction to researchers.[64] Even so, it is clear that both villagers and writers could easily, in practice, conflate the two beings.[65] A fearsome monster roaming at night must always have been a more compelling image than an inert corpse under ecclesiastical censure. It could well be that both mobile and grave-bound corpses were components of an inherited lay belief-system, before the Church outlawed one and re-moulded the other for its own ends.

Vocabulary gives pointers here. Three terms were in widespread use by the sixteenth century: *katachthonios*, *tympaniaios*, and *vrykólakas*.[66] The first ('under-earth') is attested before the others (p. 285); it is ambiguous, if more suggestive of a grave-bound corpse. The second term ('drum-like') is self-explanatory. *Vrykólakas* is different: not a Greek word, but a borrowing of *vukodlak* with the new sense of 'walking vampire'. The *vukodlak* as a werewolf had a deep Slavic background, but once the walking-corpse motif entered Greece, it swamped the werewolf motif there as it did elsewhere in the Balkans. (Faint memories of the original sense survived: *vrykólakas* has occasionally been used in Greece for living sleep-walkers who 'seized by a thirst for blood go forth at night from their shepherd's-huts and scour the country biting and tearing all that they meet both man and beast'.[67]) Orthodox theology would massage this fluid vocabulary into a more coherent scheme.

Corpse-killing episodes reported between the seventeenth and twentieth centuries concentrated heavily in the Aegean and its islands, and the Peloponnese, with far fewer cases from the west and north of Greece; penetration of the mountainous inland seems to have been much more limited than in coastal areas.[68] The intensity of the practice in the Aegean world amazed both educated Greeks and western European travellers during the seventeenth to nineteenth centuries, as many lurid narratives show.[69] The island of Santorini was believed (at least by Westerners) to be especially infested, so that 'sending vampires to Santorini' became a proverb like 'sending coals to Newcastle'.[70]

Muslim Reactions: The Ottoman Empire

What of the Islamic world, extending east from the Balkans towards Evliya's Caucasian *obur*s? In sixteenth-century Istanbul, the jurist Ebussuud Efendi issued three fatwas on the subject. In one, he rules that a corpse—of *tympanaiaos* type and probably in Greece—should simply be reburied 'if it is Muslim' (p. 240). In the other two, a *vrykólakas* among Greek Christians near Thessaloniki had visited houses at midnight saying 'Let's go to such-and-such a place together', with fatal consequences. Ebussuud proposed a familiar sequence—staking through the heart, beheading, then burning only as a last resort—but struggled to find Islamic authority for what was evidently an unfamiliar problem.[71]

From this it seems that in sixteenth-century Ottoman eyes, undead corpses were a Greek and primarily Christian phenomenon, even if Muslims (presumably living among Christians) could potentially end up in a *tympanaiaos*-like state. A late seventeenth-century religious commentator—who lived, perhaps significantly, on the north coast of the Black Sea—discussed the physical incorruption of Muslim corpses, rationalizing it as divine punishment in the grave.[72] A judicial process in 1701 addressed two dangerous grave-bound corpses in a Muslim community in Edirne, north-west of Istanbul.[73] A high-profile episode in

1833, involving former janissaries, took place in Bulgaria.[74] All this suggests that Balkan dangerous-dead beliefs did to some extent penetrate Ottoman consciousness, but only where they already existed among subject populations.

Common to this vast region were residues of ancient belief-systems, involving shamanic magicians, nature-spirits, shape-shifters, and 'night-battlers'. Into those systems, corpse-killing embedded itself like a virus. Perhaps Scandinavian versions percolated from the north through Finland and Russia, as they did through Germany and Poland. A different fusion took shape in Bulgaria, the Black Sea zone, and the Caucasus, where the origins of the dangerous-corpse motif could have been Roman, Hellenistic, or ultimately even Mesopotamian. The possibility that this fusion started in the first millennium BC—with Turkic bloodsuckers thrown into the mix later—is just a guess, but not an implausible one.

A strong case can at least be made that Bulgaria was the endemic early medieval nucleus, from which corpse-killing eventually spread to other parts of the Balkans and beyond. The virus found easier hosts in some regions than in others. Serbia and Greece were absorbing the Bulgarian practice around 1350 if not earlier, and retained it for centuries. Relatively unsuccessful among the Ottomans, corpse-killing eventually had a considerable impact in Romania, Ukraine, and further north, though perhaps at a later date than is normally assumed.

Did that happen in a series of tidal waves, generated by the geopolitical stresses of the early modern era? It is a tempting hypothesis, especially since sixteenth- to seventeenth-century Central Europe underwent a parallel expansion. Eventually, the two tidal waves collided in Serbia and the Banat in the 1720s. Elsewhere, by contrast, the tide was flowing out, most visibly in the British Isles.

26

The Dead Retreat Northward Again

ENGLAND AND SCOTLAND, 1200–1750

They hadna been a week from her,
  A week but barely three,
When word came to the carlin wife
  That her sons she'd never see.

'I wish the wind may never cease,
  nor fashes in the flood,
Till my three sons come hame to me,
  In earthly flesh and blood.'

It fell about the Martinmass,
  When nights are lang and mirk,
The carlin wife's three sons came hame,
  And their hats were o the birk.

—*THE WIFE OF USHER'S WELL*

IF THE WALKING dead were boringly common in William of Newburgh's England, they then beat a rapid retreat. All sources suggest that most of them moved north of the Humber after 1200, and north of the Scottish border after 1400 (see Map 5). In Britain as in the Rhineland, the contraction of beliefs stands in contrast to zones further east. Folkloric sources do suggest a shadowy afterlife, in secluded areas of western England as well as Scotland and Ireland, up to recent times. But the disappearance of dangerous corpses from mainstream popular culture and belief is remarkable, and underlines the epidemic character of what had gone before. In broad terms, this was a northward-retreating frontier, edging back towards the Nordic regions.

England from 1200 to the Black Death

A unique source is the clutch of 'ghost' stories from Byland Abbey on the edge of the North York Moors, apparently compiled around 1400. While hard to contextualize, it offers clues to how physical revenants now related to other supernatural entities. Most of the tales concern incorporeal spirits (usually dead sinners), but sometimes their nature is ambiguous. One story defeats all attempts to distinguish physical from ghostly: 'It is said that a woman took a ghost (*spiritus*) and carried it into a house on her back in the presence of men, one of whom recounted that he saw the woman's hands sinking deeply into the ghost's body, as though the ghost's flesh were rotten, and not solid but illusory (*fantastica*).'[1] A single report stands out as more explicit:

> Old men relate that one James Tankerlay, formerly rector of *Kereby* [Cold Kirby], was buried in front of the chapter-house at Byland. He had the habit of going out by night to *Kereby*, and one night he put out an eye of his concubine there. It is said that the abbot and convent had his body dug out of his grave with his coffin, and ordered Roger Wayneman to cart it to Gormire [an enclosed lake (Figure 57)]. As he was dumping the coffin in the water, the oxen almost sank through fear. May I not be in any danger for writing such things, for I have simply written what I heard from the old people. May the Almighty have mercy on him, if it is possible for him to be among the saved.[2]

FIGURE 57: Gormire (north Yorkshire), where James de Tankerlay's unquiet corpse was thrown in the fourteenth century. The name means 'dirt marsh'. This eerily still and enclosed lake (probably in fact fed by an underground spring) has no visible inflow or outflow, and was once thought to be bottomless. It illustrates the prison-like locations chosen as repositories for some of the noxious dead.

The compiler, who equivocated over the substance of ghostly flesh, clearly found this stark description disconcerting. Perhaps set in the early fourteenth century, it was a throwback to an era when the motifs would have been familiar: the priest who abuses his calling by a wicked life, the posthumous depredations, the consignment to a watery prison, the conundrum of whether such a soul might still be saved. The maddened oxen replicate the same motif in the Icelandic 'Eyrbyggja Saga', and the frightened reindeer in the Sámi case of Grigori Riisä (pp. 246, 105). This archaic template is anomalous within the Byland collection, where most of the returning dead are just ghosts.

Some thirty miles from Byland is Wharram Percy, with its bizarre deposit of shattered revenant remains (p. 259). Although the radiocarbon results locate most of them during the great dead-killing epidemic, two individuals died between 1250 and 1300.[3] Coming from what was presumably a normal village, this supports the impression that in northern England, the epidemic finally petered out around 1300. After generations of revenant-burning episodes, the accumulated remains were cleared up and buried in a pit, outside the churchyard but due west of the parish church. Like the dumping of James Tankerlay's coffin in Gormire, this was an act of closure: it marked the end of an era.

Late Medieval and Early Modern England: The Comforts of Purgatory and Providence

The bubonic plague, one of humanity's most traumatic misfortunes, hit Western Europe in 1348–9. We saw that in the Balkans and Aegean, it may have stimulated an epidemic of dangerous-dead beliefs (p. 285). In the Catholic West, including England, it did nothing of the kind. Instead, it encouraged an affective devotional culture that emphasized intercession for the purgatorial sufferings of the dead, and an artistic culture replete with images of decaying corpses and Death personified (Figure 58).[4]

Why did the dangerous dead fade away, and why did they not reappear in disrupted, plague-ridden England after 1349? One explanation may lie in the economy of salvation maintained by chantries and parish guilds, in which parishioners interceded for the souls of past friends and relatives. Perhaps this answered the same needs by creating a mutually supportive community of the living and the dead: when suffering souls were so palpably close, and so needy of prayers and masses, their physical return was superfluous.[5] There may be a sense, therefore, in which the rise of purgatory suppressed the dangerous dead (in contrast to Orthodox Greece, where the *tympaniaios* may have helped to fill a conceptual gap left by the absence of purgatory). Even so, there was no lack of appearances by unquiet or suffering ghosts.[6] Socio-economic and cultural explanations are possible, but a puzzle remains.

A sermon by the Augustinian preacher John Mirk (died c. 1414) provides one reference, but even that is equivocal. Mirk relates how the Devil occupied and re-animated a man's corpse, and used it to deceive the living, because the last rites had been neglected; the soul, we are told, was unharmed.[7] The threat of demonic hijacking—in this case as a warning against careless observance—is a standard clerical rationalization, though the fault has shifted from evil-living to failure to observe the new art of 'dying well'.[8] But did the people of Shropshire, where

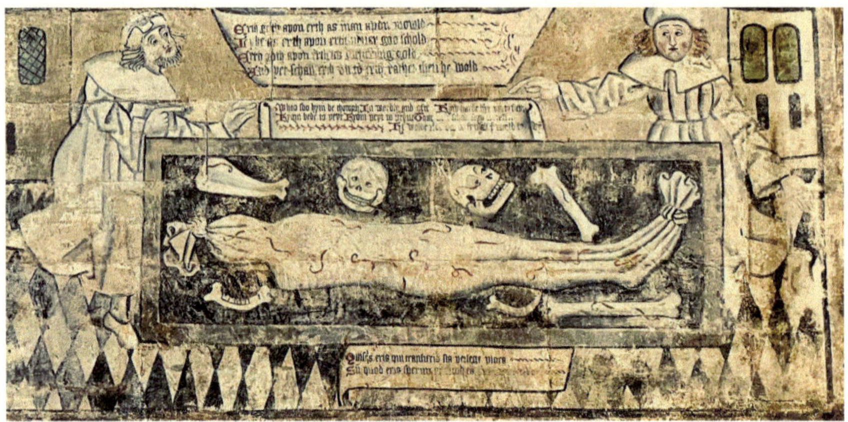

FIGURE 58: A death-obsessed society without dangerous corpses. This fifteenth-century wall-painting in the guild chapel at Stratford-upon-Avon (Warwickshire) shows a shrouded corpse amid scattered bones, framed by verses from the devotional poem *Erthe upon Erthe,* a reminder of human mortality. Such scenes were visible throughout late medieval England, despite the near-disappearance of beliefs in dangerous corpses.

Mirk worked, believe that corpses moved around? That is not impossible—we will find patches of residual belief in western England much later—but it may be relevant that Mirk's own background was northern and possibly Scandinavian.[9] Or maybe not: nearby in Herefordshire, in 1397, a Welsh chaplain made the extraordinary boast 'that he goes about at night with fantastic spirits'—an isolated but unmistakable reference to the 'night-battles' template.[10]

From the 1540s, reformed religion swept away purgatory and intercession, replacing them with providence and divine judgement beyond human reach. However traumatic this may have been,[11] the trauma did not re-activate the English dangerous dead: there is no hint of a corpse-killing epidemic like the one gripping parts of central Europe by 1600.[12]

The practice of staking suicides might look suggestive, but in fact it is a red herring. Rather than a survival—the pre-emptive 'killing' of potentially restless corpses—it was a late Tudor measure of social control, re-invented after a long gap.[13] That is not to say that the instinctive link between staking and prevention never suggested itself; indeed, in a play from 1636 the heroine asks that her lover who has killed himself should be buried 'as the custome of the Country is, and drive a stacke through him, so perhaps I that had no quietnes with him whil'st he liv'd, may sleepe in peace now he's dead'. For most people, though, it expressed straightforward abhorrence of suicide, like the newspaper correspondent of 1735 who thought that 'every one that commits so monstrous an Act' should be 'publickly expos'd naked, for so many Days, and then buried in the Highway, with a Stake drove throw them'.[14] Here as earlier, the restless dead and the self-slain were decisively different kinds of monster.

That said, the residual, muted anxieties implied by later folklore must occasionally have persisted through these centuries. There are rare deviant burials: a London man from the plague year 1666 with a big stone in his mouth (Figure 59: could he have belonged to a German immigrant community?), or another—trussed, prone, and with the head pulled off—next to a Norfolk church.[15] Apparently English beliefs in the dangerous dead never *quite* vanished. North of the border, they persisted more visibly.

Scotland: A Scandinavian Culture of Belief?

The chronicle of Lanercost Priory recounts events from 1295, set in the Clyde valley west of Glasgow.[16] A member of a religious community (Paisley Abbey?), who has died badly and under excommunication, returns from his grave to visit a knight's house. 'Having assumed a body—it is uncertain whether natural or aerial, but it was dank, gross and tangible'—he regularly comes at noonday dressed as a monk, and (like the Icelandic revenants Thórólf and Glám, pp. 246–247) settles on the roofs of houses or outbuildings. People try to shoot or stab him, but anything penetrating 'that damned substance' immediately burns up. He attacks people, and kills the knight's eldest son. This chronicler—like the Byland compiler, but unlike the more straightforward twelfth-century writers—worries about whether the revenant's substance is physical or spiritual. But behind the rhetoric, this apparition is clearly another late and northerly relative of William of Newburgh's revenants.

FIGURE 59: This man died in the great London plague of 1665, and was buried in the church of St Botolph, Billingsgate. Why was it thought necessary to put a stone in his mouth, in the corpse-killing tradition then current in central Europe but not in England?

Two fourteenth- to fifteenth-century burials from Scottish friaries (Perth and Linlithgow) are remarkable in recalling English cases from nearly a millennium earlier.[17] Both were young adult females, and both lay prone; the wildly splayed posture of one made the excavator fantasize that she was 'attempting press-up exercises in the grave'. Not much can be built on just two cases, but readers of this book will note the implications.

The most abundant and convincing evidence for walking-dead beliefs in Scottish popular culture comes from the rich body of oral ballads.[18] Most of them were collected after 1750, and they embody general folklore motifs that are hard to pin down. Still, it is clearly not a coincidence that the dead returning in physical form are so prominent in Scottish versions. The Wife of Usher's Well, quoted above, wants her dead sons to come home 'in earthly flesh and blood'. (When they do so she is delighted, not realizing that their flesh and blood does not make them living humans.) These revenants are pathetic rather than threatening: mourning their own bleak state, comforting those who have been dear to them, and warning against the damp and worms of the grave. This motif is Scandinavian, foreshadowed in an Eddic poem where the distraught Sigrun makes a bed for herself and her dead lover Helgi in his own barrow, and he warns her that he belongs to another world.[19]

We know one case of pre-emption by sharp iron, at Pencaitland on the Forth estuary. It concerns the sisters Isobel and Agnes Bennet, born in 1620 and 1626.[20] Isobel was in trouble with the Presbyterian authorities for sabbath-breaking in April 1651, and seems to have died soon afterwards. That October, Agnes was summoned to the kirk session (the parish disciplinary body) for 'putting a nail in a dead coope [i.e., corpse] after it was winne [i.e., shrouded]'. In November, Agnes confessed that 'she gat a kist naile [i.e., coffin-nail] from her sister, and put it betwixt the winding sheit and the corpe, q(ui)lk she said was to keip her spirit from coming again, and denyd that the naile was bro(ugh)t in purpose, but it was a kistnaile; and she confest she learned it at Bessie Craig in Saltoun'.[21]

This seems to mean that Agnes took a nail from her sister's (presumably Isobel's) coffin and put it inside the shroud. The authorities wanted to know whether she had brought the nail specially (which would have been worse), and who had given her the idea. This looks like a weak belief-survival maintained by wise-women, and Agnes—or at least the session clerk—defined the problem as Isobel's spirit not her corpse. But its origins are obvious, and the context suggestive: these were young unmarried women, and Isobel's death so soon after the moral crime of sabbath-breaking could have put her in the high-risk category.

Like Mirk, Scottish Calvinist theologians came to understand the reanimation of corpses as diabolic possession. But now the link with evil-living was broken: Satan could potentially hijack *any* corpse, however virtuous its former occupant. Writing in the 1590s, King James VI accepted that such entities could move around and open doors and windows. Then—wondering why God should allow the corpses of the faithful to be thus insulted—the scholar-king mused: 'What more is the reste troubled of a dead bodie, when the Devill carryes it out of the Grave to serve his turne for a space, nor when the Witches takes it up and joyntes it, or when as Swine wortes upp the graves? . . . And that the Devill may use aswell the ministrie of the bodies of the faithfull in these case, as of the un-faithfull, there is no inconvenient; for his haunting with their bodies after they are deade, can no-waies defyle them: In respect of the soules absence.'[22]

This version suited a Scottish Calvinist world where Satan, ever-present, could plague the elect but never harm their souls, and where witches were regularly thought to abuse corpses. But was it much more than a veneer? The returning corpses of the ballads—more plausible reflections of popular belief—are not demonic, but dead people with human feelings. The theological rationalization was needed in Scotland, in a way that it no longer was in England, because Scots retained a belief—endemic and enduring, but relatively low-key—that the dead could walk. In that respect, as in so many others, Scotland is best understood as part of the Scandinavian culture-zone.

This book has had little to say about the Gaelic world since the seventh century (p. 214), but some faint echoes can be picked up in the Isles. The celebrated Gaelic poet Màiri nighean Alasdair Ruaidh (Mary MacLeod) was buried face-down on Harris in c. 1707. The same was reputedly done to other Gaelic poetesses, apparently because they composed heroic verses reserved for men.[23] The need to constrain corpses of disconcertingly powerful females is a theme we recognize.

———

A century after James VI, a Scottish minister puzzled about a godless dead woman whose walking troubled her neighbours: 'But what could her *Apparition* be? It behoved, either to be her reall Body informed and acted by the Devil (for her soul could not be brought back) or only the Devil taking upon him her shape and form, acting and imitating her to the life, which is more probable.'[24]

Active corpses, even controlled by Satan, were hard for reflective Scottish clergy to accept by the 1680s. Their Continental counterparts—Catholic and Lutheran—had long been facing the same dilemma, as they struggled to make sense of similar beliefs among the people to whom they ministered.

27

Noxious Corpses and Noisy Shroud-Eaters

THE GERMAN-SPEAKING LANDS IN THE AGE OF REFORMATION

> A wonderfully strange thing sometimes happens in times of plague: people have experienced that those who have died of the plague, especially women, have [lip-]smacked in the grave like a sow when she eats, and that because of this smacking the plague increased greatly, especially in the same family.
>
> —MARTIN BÖHM, PASTOR OF LAUBAN [NOW, LUBAN, POLAND], 1601

EXCAVATED BURIALS show that the restless dead were feared widely—though not necessarily acutely—across the North European plain by 1050. One zone of belief was the Rhineland; another was the Viking-influenced regions between the Elbe and the Vistula (pp. 217, 273–279). Corpse-fears died down in the first of these, but continuing endemic concerns in the second probably underpinned the epidemics that would erupt in Saxony, Silesia, and Bohemia after 1540. Moving further eastward, sources become thinner, and it becomes difficult to distinguish evidence of absence from absence of evidence. Such references as do exist suggest a series of eastward-flowing waves, but was it simply that theologians in Saxony and Silesia raised consciousness among their counterparts in Moravia, Slovakia, and so onwards to Serbia?

That argument can only be pushed so far. The reports cluster in distinct areas, which do not correspond tidily with political boundaries or modes of documentation. It is true that the grave-bound and lip-smacking dead are mainly reported by Lutherans, the mobile dead mainly by Catholics. But the Reformation cannot have created such broad contrasts, which were entrenched by the later sixteenth century. What does seem possible is that preaching, and the circulation of ideas within distinct confessional groups, heightened and consolidated the distinctiveness of motifs already established at the grassroots level. And it is very likely indeed that migration, colonization, and the spiritual traumas of the Reformation played upon latent anxieties, especially during outbreaks of plague, whipping them up to epidemic levels.

Lutheran Lip-Smackers: Noisy Eating in the Grave, c. 1540–1600

Martin Luther liked a good lunch, and he liked holding forth while he ate it. On one such occasion, between 1531 and 1546, a less appetising kind of feasting was brought to his notice. A pastor in rural Saxony had written to his secretary for advice: a recently dead woman was eating herself in the grave, and in consequence nearly everyone in the village had died. What should he do? Luther replied:

> That's the Devil's deceit and malice. If they didn't believe it, it wouldn't hurt them. It's just a phantom of the Devil, and they only keep dying because they are so superstitious. And if they realized that, they wouldn't throw people into the grave so readily, but would say 'Eat, Devil! You're a fraud! You can't take us in!' . . . Write back to the pastor that they should certainly accept and believe that it was no ghost or soul, but the Devil himself. So they should all go to church and ask God to forgive their sins for Christ's sake, and to ward off the Devil.

For the rural pastor, it was a new problem. Whether Luther had heard of it before is unclear, but in any case his mind jumped automatically to the Devil's trickery. Perhaps he did not find it very interesting: he knew the Devil too well. But his off-the-cuff reaction would take on a life of its own from 1566, when his friends and pupils gathered such conversational remarks into a volume, *Table Talk*.[1] Thereafter, any Lutheran minister could consult it when confronted with this particularly weird pastoral concern, and it would inform responses until the early Enlightenment made the issue redundant.

This idea of a corpse 'eating itself' was meanwhile evolving into a distinctive template, linked almost exclusively to plague deaths, that would remain stable in Lutheran discourse until around 1600. The corpse is normally female, and seems to embody an impersonal energy: its activities after death spread the plague, but they do not imply wrongdoing in life. It eats its own shroud, followed by other available textiles and then (less frequently) its own body. In the process, it makes a lip-smacking noise sometimes compared to a sow eating: the 'smacking of the dead' (*Schmatzen der Toten*).

This belief could have developed from the shroud-swallowing idea (presumably corpses are not dainty eaters), and Paul Barber shows how decomposition can generate strange noises.[2] It is, however, specific to this time and place, and may have originated in a single episode. It had an important and panic-enhancing implication: dangerous corpses could be identified without digging. The remedy became standard too: open the grave, check for evidence of shroud-swallowing, and then cut off the head with an iron-edged spade.

These practices become visible in an intensive corpse-killing epidemic, which erupted during 1546–1553 in a series of small Saxon towns and then gradually wound down towards the 1590s (Maps 6 and 7).[3] The immediate catalysts were the recurrent outbreaks of bubonic plague, which gripped eastern and central Europe in a series of regular cycles.[4] After the isolated appearance of a lip-smacking corpse—a male shepherd—at Groß-Mochbern/Muchobór Wielki near Breslau/Wrocław (Poland) in 1516,[5] attacks on female lip-smackers are reported at Clausnitz in 1546, Dittersbach in 1551, Freiberg and Hermsdorf in 1552, and Lauban/Lubań (now Poland) in 1553.[6] There are then stories from Helsa near Kassel in 1558, Sangerhausen in 1565, and Brottrode near Schmalkalden in 1566.[7]

Thereafter it slackened, with lip-smacking episodes reported at Merseburg in 1581 and Jüterbog in 1584.[8] The other cases lay well outside Saxony: eastwards (Lossen/Łosiów near Wrocław, and Lemberg/Lviv in Ukraine, both in 1572); and northwards (Mühlhausen/Młynary in 1564, a village near Wismar in 1579, Schivelbein/Świdwin in 1584, and Niedstedten near Hamburg in 1603).[9] The dynamic is fairly clear: over time the panic weakened, but also diffused geographically. The many German-speaking Lutherans in Polish towns could have carried the template with them.[10] Stories must have spread into Silesia/Moravia and the Baltic zone, fanning the flames of endemic local tradition.

Why was it specifically in Saxony, among the regions preserving traces of the Viking-generated beliefs, that such panic broke out in the 1540s? Educated Lutherans viewed it as a strange new side-effect of plague. As in some other contexts, disease was a necessary condition for a corpse-killing epidemic but not a sufficient one: that required additional and more psychic stimuli. One such, surely, was the recent Lutheran Reformation, and the impenetrable barrier that it built between the living and the dead.[11] Fear and sorrow demand action, and an action available until recently had been to pray for the dead. Now, purgatory did not exist: all souls were in the hand of God, their fate sealed, and intercession through the saints was pointless. Those now dying in horrific numbers were denied all posthumous contact with their friends and relatives. The bereaved needed new answers.

In northern Europe, ancient fears of powerful women may never have been far below the surface. Female shroud-swallowing predated the Reformation, as shown by the *Hammer of Witches* story and an earlier Bohemian one (pp. 281, 334), but its explanatory basis was conveniently vague. Plague-struck Lutherans (unlike some Catholics) had to accept that the souls of the malicious dead could not inhabit their corpses. On the other hand, a narrative that depersonalized the corpse, while still making it a site of lethal energy, allowed them to fight back. Plague was spread mysteriously by the mechanism of female corpses swallowing their shrouds: the plague could be stopped, therefore, by making the corpses unable to swallow.

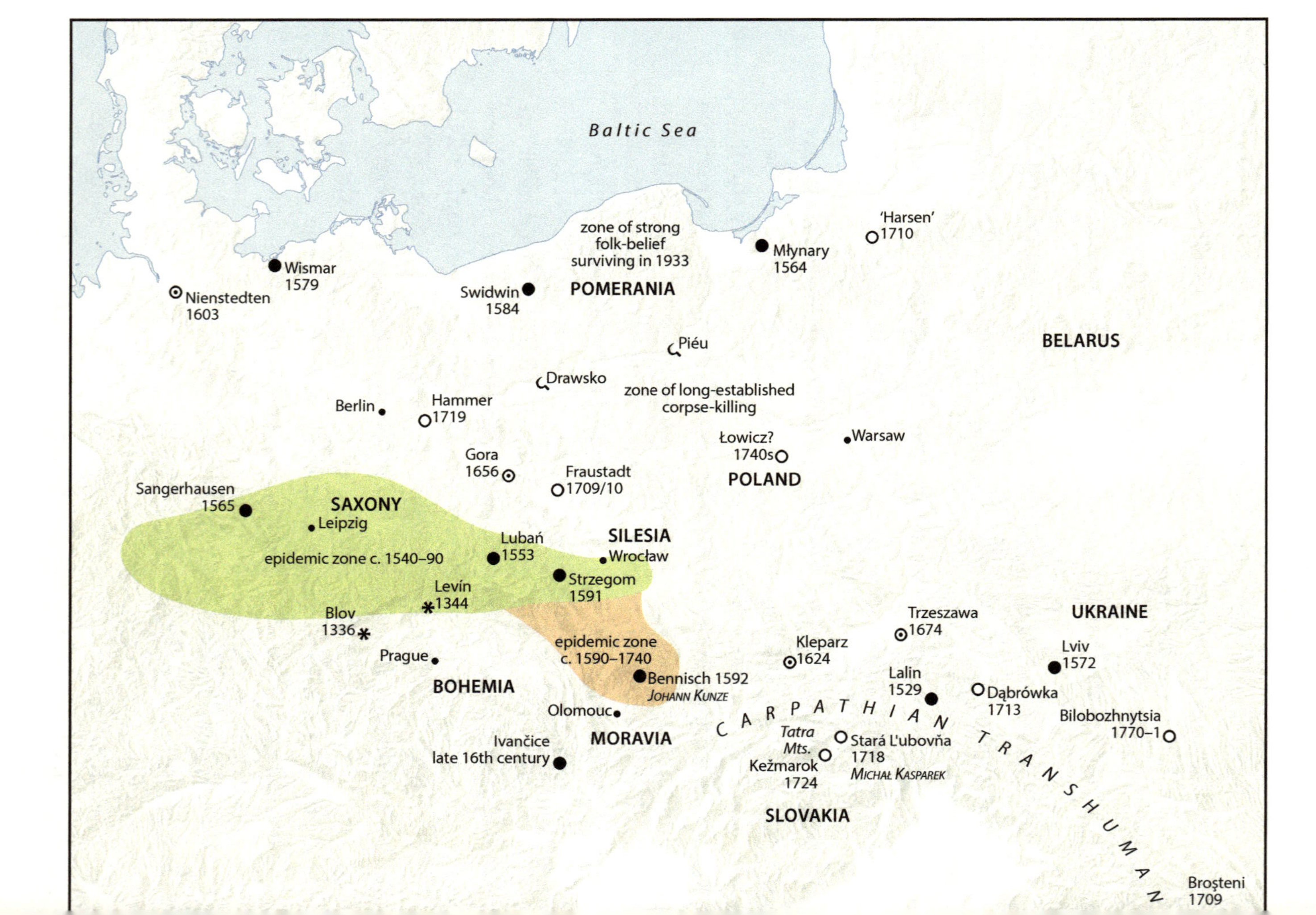
Baltic Sea
zone of strong folk-belief surviving in 1933
'Harsen' 1710
Wismar 1579
Nienstedten 1603
Swidwin 1584
POMERANIA
Młynary 1564
BELARUS
Piéu
Drawsko
zone of long-established corpse-killing
Berlin
Hammer 1719
Łowicz? 1740s
Warsaw
Gora 1656
Fraustadt 1709/10
POLAND
Sangerhausen 1565
SAXONY
Leipzig
Lubań 1553
SILESIA
Wrocław
epidemic zone c. 1540–90
Strzegom 1591
Levín 1344
Blov 1336
Trzeszawa 1674
UKRAINE
epidemic zone c. 1590–1740
Kleparz 1624
Lviv 1572
Prague
Bennisch 1592
Johann Kunze
Lalin 1529
Dąbrówka 1713
BOHEMIA
Olomouc
Bilobozhnytsia 1770–1
CARPATHIAN
TRANSHUMANZ
Tatra Mts.
Stará L'ubovňa 1718
Michał Kasparek
Ivančice late 16th century
MORAVIA
Kežmarok 1724
SLOVAKIA
Broşteni 1709

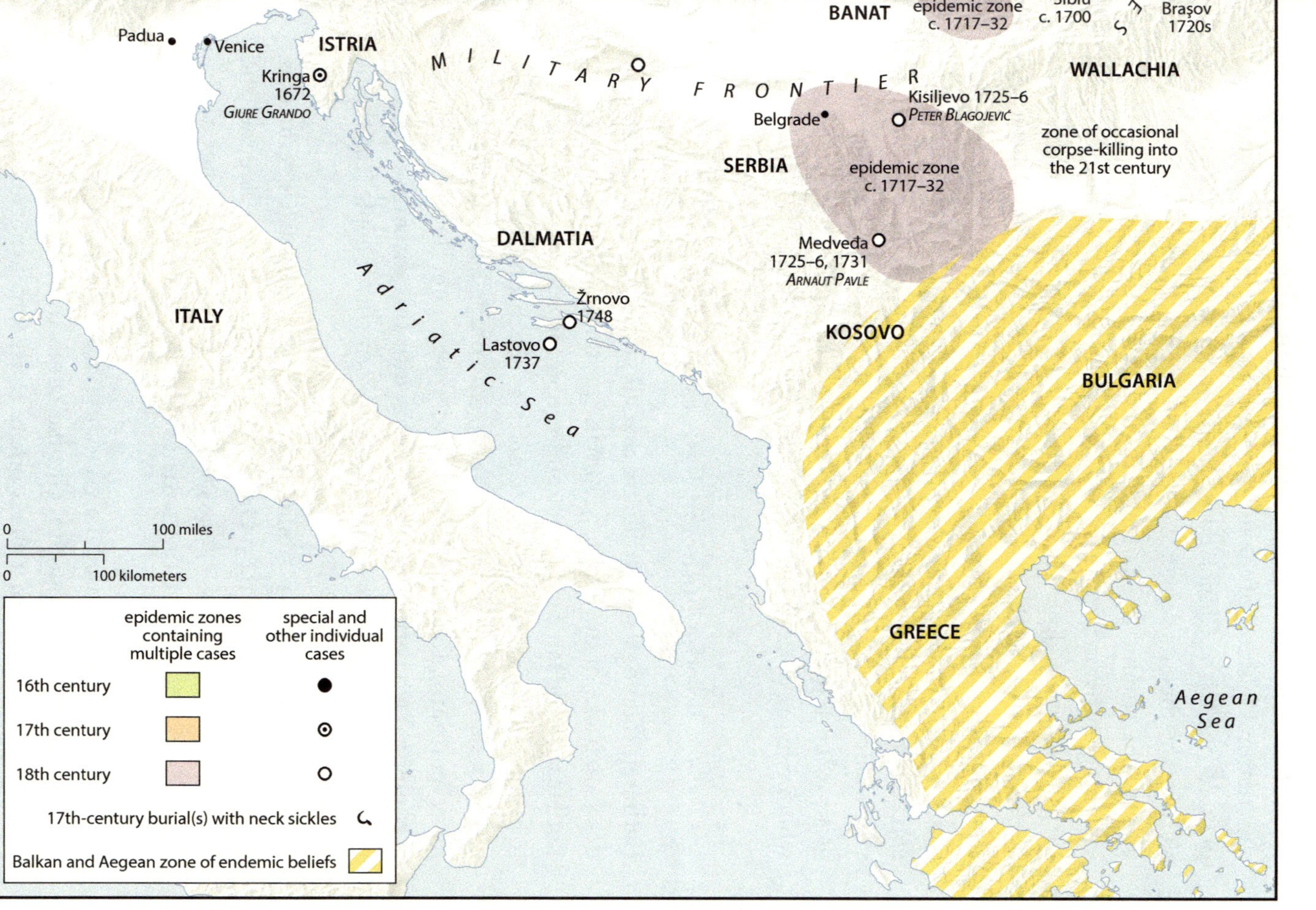

MAP 7: Patterns of corpse-killing in central to south-east Europe, 1500–1750: an overview.

There is an obvious parallel with witch-hunting—the other great supernatural hysteria of the mid-sixteenth century—but not a simple or direct one.[12] The Rhineland would become a centre of witch persecution, but by then its dangerous dead had largely faded from view. Conversely, the witch craze had little impact on the north German plain, including Lutheran Saxony with its chomping dead.[13] Witch-killing and corpse-killing usually affected different zones: perhaps they were *alternative* responses to the traumas of the age. A helpful analogy is the strange anxiety about 'greasing' in Europe further south, where the smearing of special ointments on buildings or animals was supposed to spread plague.[14] That was an activity of the living, so it led naturally to witchcraft accusations. Shroud-swallowing also caused plague, but it was by definition an activity of the dead. A culprit had to be found: whether living or dead was perhaps less fundamental.

The Lutheran Pastoral Response

Lutheran theology was emphatic that all ghostly appearances of the dead are tricks of the Devil.[15] Humane pastors, taking their cue from Luther, took the same view of shroud-eating corpses: to attack them was to become Satan's dupe. Yet they could also see that traumatized people, powerless in the face of sudden death, felt compelled to do *something,* however bizarre. Rational thinking had to be taught through reasoned argument. Two sermons offer insights into this discourse between popular and educated world-views: between what people feared, and how the Church responded.

Heinrich Roth was a pastor in the small Saxon town of Sangerhausen, where plague raged in 1565. One of its victims was the esteemed and respectable wife of a local judge, and Roth preached at her funeral. But disturbing rumours surfaced, and he felt obliged to preach again:[16]

> As deaths have increased daily and risen to a peak, this worthy Christian matron now in our thoughts has come, through fruitless gossip, under a suspicion: that she is one of those female persons who lip-smack in the grave and eat themselves, as is supposed to have been

> observed in other places; and that as long as the lip-smacking continues, the mortality will grow worse and worse. And if we were to follow what has happened elsewhere, these people would have to be dug up, the veils and shrouds that they have eaten (I can't think how) torn out, and their necks cut with a grave-spade, as has happened in places that I don't want to name.

Many people, Roth continues, have honestly believed that attacking the lip-smacking dead in order to save lives must accord with God's will. But we have plenty of experience that the Devil plays monkey-tricks with the dead. If a corpse could injure people by lip-smacking, that would undermine divine providence. But God holds life and death in his hands, and now he has given us relief from the plague. Satan tried to lure us into a sinful path by encouraging us to behead the corpse of this Christian lady, but she has been God's instrument to bring us to understanding and repentance.

Another compassionate Lutheran theologian (and prolific hymn-writer) was Martin Böhm, from Lauban, where he became senior pastor in 1586. In a collection of sermons on the scourges of war, famine, and pestilence, he turns his mind to the lip-smacking problem.[17] Like Roth, he considers corpse-killing an ungodly act. The smacking cannot come from the corpse in the grave: where there is no soul in the body there is no life or movement, so there can be no chewing, smacking, or biting. Death separates body and soul, and there is no way back. It can only be a diabolic illusion.

But why should the Devil play such tricks? Here Böhm goes further than Luther or Roth in suggesting motives. First—in a striking attack on misogyny—he explains that because the Devil has hated Eve's descendants since the Fall, he does everything possible to slander, demean, and diminish the female sex. Then the Devil wants to make people think that they are at the mercy of lip-smacking corpses, so that God cannot help them. He wants to distract people from repenting their sins, to blacken the reputations of the dead, and to make people slander others. He wants to cause enmity between people, 'for it embitters and corrodes an honest friendship to dig up someone's relative and cut off their head. Could anyone with a Christian and honour-loving streak in their body be at peace with that?' And he does it to spread plague by encouraging the opening of victims' graves, so that the contagion will escape and kill people. Anyone who colludes in these deceits becomes the Devil's servant and mocks God.

Böhm anticipates the counter-objections: that people can see with their own eyes that the corpses have eaten their shrouds; that the whole family often dies after the smacking starts; and that the plague stops once the corpse is beheaded. His responses are to invoke the Devil's trickery in the first case, and rationality in the others: whole families die of plague anyway, and there are counter-examples where the plague gets worse. So 'if the Devil assails you, don't cause such tragedies: he is sure to stop. At Sangerhausen and Merseburg and other places they let the dead rest, let the corpse be at peace, let the Devil make smacking sounds for a time; and then his nonsense stopped.'

A Stone in the Mouth

A gentler compromise—presumably less shocking to clergy—was also available: the placing of coins or stones in the mouths of suspect corpses (Figure 59). In about 1600, this was said to have been widespread in Saxony.[18] At Lauban in 1567 a man and his wife, accused of being *Pielweisen* (a fluid term with a range between 'nature-spirits' and 'sorcerers'[19]), swore their innocence and called God to blind one and maim the other if they lied—which duly happened. Then 'the woman died, and as she was carried out, a black goat walked behind the corpse and bleated, and then the corpse [lip-]smacked in the coffin. The gravedigger took the coffin out of the grave, put a penny and a stone in her mouth, closed the coffin, and reburied it. The mayor was very unhappy when he heard about it, but the gravedigger said, "It's nothing new to me, that will stop her mouth now"'.[20] If the mayor favoured beheading, the gravedigger was sure enough about his well-tried alternative: with her mouth wedged open literally, she would have to keep it shut metaphorically.

This episode explicitly links the lip-smacking epidemic to practices that had long left a mark on the burial record, and now re-emerged. A contemporary case from the Baltic zone is an infant—one of the first tuberculosis victims in the region—buried around 1600 at Rendsburg-Eckernförde near Kiel: coffined, in a privileged location, but with an amuletic button, a probable coin in the mouth, and a large stone wedged between the jaws.[21] As a less visible alternative, a stone or tile placed *under* the chin would block contact between the mouth and the shroud.[22] By such means—maybe with discreet clerical guidance—a respectable family might evade the scandal of lip-smacking followed by beheading.

Modern readers, doubtless agreeing with Luther, Roth, and Böhm that the chewing and smacking were illusions, will tend to prefer Paul Barber's forensic explanations over their diabolic ones. Why so many people were so convinced that they could hear and see corpses munching away at their shrouds defies modern explanation, but there can be no question that the belief was deep-held and widespread. Perhaps it was reinforced by the sensational stories now spreading in cheap print, or even by the sermons preached against it.

28

Movers and Shakers

ACTIVE CORPSES IN BOHEMIA AND SILESIA, 1330–1600

> Peter Weigel, a miller, died in the little mill [on 1 February 1575] and was buried. After his death a spectre appeared, whereupon he was suspected of being a magician. Accordingly, with the judicious advice and consent of the Governor . . . , he was dug up on 14 March, and he lay on the ground flexible and red. On 2 April following, his head was cut off and he was reburied. But because the spectre was not laid by these means, the said corpse, with further advice and consent of the Lord Governor, was again dug up on 29 April, and was burned to ashes. . . . God forbid any further misfortune!
>
> —TOWN RECORDS OF BOLKENHAIN (NOW, BOLKÓW, POLAND), 1575

THE TROUBLESOME CORPSES of Bohemia and Silesia (now in the Czech Republic and Poland respectively) differ from those of Saxony, even if the Saxon plague contributed to their new visibility. Offshoots of the 'lumpen' prototype, they are mobile and often male. They are sometimes associated with plague, but not always. They are given to

FIGURE 60: The posthumous killing of the bishop of Kamianets-Podilskyi (formerly Poland, now Ukraine) in 1757, from a sensational popular pamphlet. The corpse was initially beheaded, but then it walked around holding its head; it was therefore dug up again and burned. That episode is dubious, but the woodcut is unique as a contemporary depiction of the ritual for disposing of unquiet corpses in central to eastern Europe. It is the kind of illustration that might have embellished the lost pamphlet about Johann Kunze.

violence, especially night-mare attacks. They sometimes talk, and the things that they say can be strange. And they are not merely beheaded, but end up on the pyre (Figure 60). One of them, Johann Kunze, is in a class of his own for the scale of his depredations, though we will find that his story is not quite what it seems.

From now on, we will be in regions where ethnic co-existence (or lack of it) must always have been a major factor, but its impact is not straightforward to read. Communities in Slavic zones with substantial German populations (notably urban ones) dominate this chapter and the next two. But to identify the revenants as straightforward German imports would be too simple: they are just too different from their Saxon counterparts. What seems more likely is that tensions—especially between insecure settlers and aggrieved locals—generated an atmosphere of brittle unease in which endemic fears were luridly magnified.

Late Medieval Bohemia

Two passages in the chronicle of Jàn Neplach (c. 1360)[1] show that rural communities in Bohemia already believed in active corpses before the Black Death. Both episodes took place near what is now the north-west border of the Czech Republic. The first, dated to 1336, is set in the village of Blov near Kadaň:

> A shepherd called Myslata died. Rising up every night, he went around all the surrounding villages to terrify and kill people, and he talked. When a stake was driven through him, he said 'They hurt me badly, but they gave me a club to defend myself from dogs'. When he was dug up to be burned, he swelled up like an ox and became frightfully red. When he was put on the fire, someone grabbed a stake and drove it into him, and immediately blood burst out as though from a pitcher. Further, after he had been dug out and put on the cart, he pulled his feet together as though alive. Once he had been burned, all the evil ceased; previously, anyone whom he had called by name in the night had died within eight days.

The second story is dated to 1344:

> A woman in Levín [near Leitmeritz/Litoměřice, north of Prague] died and was buried, but after her burial she rose up and killed many, and leapt around after every one. When she was transfixed, blood flowed as though from a living animal. She swallowed more than half of her own shroud, and when it was pulled out it was covered with blood. When they tried to burn her it was impossible to light the wood, except with shingles from the church as advised by some old women. After she had been transfixed she rose up again, but once she had been burned, all the evil ceased.

Alongside the familiar shroud-swallowing, there are more distinctive motifs here that would reappear in the region two centuries later: the walking, talking predatory dead; red and swollen corpses; blood spurting from wounds; an attempted solution by staking (or in other cases beheading), followed by burning as a last resort.

The vignette of old women who knew how to get the fire going suggests that at least some of this was well embedded in folklore, and indeed the Göda cemetery, with its mutilated eleventh-century corpses, was not far away (Map 6). This looks like an endemic rather than epidemic level of anxiety, and Neplach's failure to mention any eruption of corpse-killing from 1348–9 implies that here—as in England—the Black Death did not fan the flames. Rather, the beliefs must have continued at a muted level before they erupted in the late 1560s.

A Regiment of Violent Corpses, c. 1570–1610

When similar stories do reappear (Maps 6 and 7), it is in the wake of the lip-smacking epidemic in Saxony.[2] Maybe eastwards-flowing ripples stimulated endemic fears into more conspicuous eruptions, or maybe the Lutheran publications made Catholic intellectuals more aware of the phenomenon. Both could be true. There is an overlap in time, region and to some extent motifs between the lip-smackers and the mobile dead, but the latter tend to concentrate further east and be slightly later, peaking at the end of the sixteenth century when the lip-smacking phenomenon was subsiding. They are mostly in places with a strong German presence, though we cannot know how much of that is an effect of differential reporting and publication.

Indicative cases are recorded in 1567 at Trautenau/Trutnov, involving a wealthy merchant who had died in honour but whose corpse ('occupied by Satan') went around strangling people;[3] and in 1575 at Bolkenhain/Bolków, involving a dead miller who visited women at night.[4] The remedy (or should we say punishment?) for both was exhumation and public burning, documented at Bolkenhain by an official process like that from a criminal trial.

More complex is the 1591 episode in the Silesian town of Striegau/Strzegom, involving a shoemaker who (very exceptionally) committed suicide.[5] This fact was suppressed, and he was buried honourably. But then a fearsome revenant in the shoemaker's form roamed by night and day, hitting and squeezing the living, lying on them as though to suffocate, and terrifying the sleeping with ghastly dreams. Finally, the body was exhumed after eight months in the ground. It was sound and undecayed, though 'swollen and inflated like a drum', with joints flexible, the wound in the throat gaping, and (in a detail drawn straight from witch-trials) a magical mark like a rose on the right big toe. They buried him under the gallows, but when the disturbances increased, even his widow accepted drastic measures. The corpse—which had meanwhile grown even fleshier—was dismembered, the heart was cut out from behind, everything was burnt, and the troubles ceased.

An apparent pendant to this story (though its context is confused) describes a maid of the shoemaker who died after him.[6] Eight days later she lay on a fellow-servant, making her eyes swell, and attacked a baby. The next night she appeared in the form of a hen, and when one of the maids chased her she grew huge and squeezed the maid's throat. In the course of a month she hit people, pulled the beds from under them, and appeared in the shapes of a woman, dog, cat and goat. She too ended up on the pyre.

Another case, perhaps of c. 1580–1610, takes us southwards into Moravia, which would become famous for its restless corpses a century later. An 'honest citizen' of Eibenschütz/Ivančice was buried in the churchyard, but he took to getting up at night and killing people. He always left his shroud by the grave, and one night the church guards spotted and removed it. When he came back to the grave he missed his shroud, and threatened to strangle the guards unless they returned it. Wisely, they complied, but in daylight the authorities opened the grave. The hangman pulled from the corpse's mouth a long veil, which he had eaten off the head of his wife who was buried next to him. As they lifted him from the grave, he observed sardonically that they were doing the right thing, since otherwise he and his wife would have killed half the town. The hangman chopped him up and the evil stopped.[7]

We have these stories because they attracted the interest of scholars. But they transmit a genuine and distinct regional tradition, which ranged across what are now the northern and eastern Czech Republic and south-west Poland. Remarkable corroboration comes from parish registers, which—perhaps uniquely in such a case—substantiate the Striegau story.[8] The suicidal shoemaker is identified as Hans Opitz, whose burial entry was struck out after his exhumation. Two years later, on 17 October 1594, a certain 'old Anna' was buried, then moved to another location, and finally, on 25 November, exhumed and burnt. She is called a witch (*veneficia*), and is said to have lived with Hans Opitz the *Pülweissen* (see p. 330): this is surely the maid in the subsidiary story.

Unnaturally flexible corpses associated with frightening apparitions were also reported at Braunseifen/Ryžoviště in 1597, 1600, and 1611, and at Friedland/Břidličná in 1610 and 1617.[9] At Wittgendorf/Witków Śląski in 1595, a man and woman emerged from their graves at night and troubled people and animals. The corpses were exhumed, coins and stones were placed in their mouths, their heads were bound, and they were laid face-down in their coffins, which were suspended to prevent contact with the earth, and kept under armed guard. Later the hearts were removed, the corpses quartered and burnt, and the ashes thrown in the river. All earth that had been in contact with the bodies was scraped out and thrown in the river, and the graves were bricked up.[10] That certainly left nothing to chance.

Archival references then tail off, resuming in earnest after 1650. This substantiates the impression, conveyed by the printed narratives, that there really was an anxiety-peak in the region in the decades around 1600. Indeed, they offer a powerful rebuttal to any idea that the narratives are simply lurid fiction. But that is not to say that fiction played no part: one substantial narrative remains to be discussed.

Johann Kunze on the Rampage

The best-known of these stories concerns one Johann Kunze, a rich citizen of the Moravian mining town of Bennisch/Horní Benešov near the Czech/Polish border, who died there in 1592. It survives embedded in a long preface in elegant Latin (also containing the Striegau story) by the natural philosopher Martin Weinrich, introducing an earlier work on demons and published in 1612.[11] Weinrich says that he has translated it from the German of an anonymous author, a 'pious and learned man' who was himself a victim of the revenant, and that he has omitted many stories to avoid repetition.[12] Given that the Latin text runs to over 6,000 words, the original must have been on a different scale from anything else like it. Its details are supposedly based on direct experience—which, as we will see, is almost certainly untrue. In fact, it is very interesting in a different way: the first modern vampire novel aimed at a popular audience.

The framework is familiar, but the details are abundant and often strange. Kunze is kicked in the testicles by his horse, and dies in great pain despite the lack of any visible injury. On his deathbed he dismisses all hope of salvation, protesting that his sins are huge and past all forgiveness (at which point some people remember that he was rumoured to have sold one of his sons and to have made a pact with a demon). As he dies, a black cat opens the window, rushes in, and scratches his face. Even before his burial, there are rumours of a spirit in his shape trying to rape a woman. The undertakers arranging his corpse are disconcerted when one hand keeps moving to his genitals. Nonetheless, he is buried in the church, next to the altar; a violent storm during the funeral ends as the grave is closed.

That is just the beginning. Kunze now embarks on a rampage of vampiric mayhem that leaves Count Dracula standing, and he omits scarcely any possible misdemeanor of revenant, ghost, or poltergeist. Things are thrown around, gates open by themselves, animals go mad, dogs howl, and horses kick and bite. He returns to ask a friend to deal with some unfinished business, stamping so heavily around the upper rooms that the roof shakes. He hits walls to make the house tremble, and in the morning there are footprints of strange creatures in the snow. He gallops around the courtyard of his house, riding through the streets and out into the countryside, the ground flashing beneath him. He drinks milk from bowls, replaces it with blood, and throws filth. He pulls up big posts. He threatens sleepers and tries to strangle them. He regularly squeezes and presses people at night, especially women, whom he tries to rape. He comes into the minister's house and makes a noise 'like a hog eating grain, smacking and grunting sonorously'. He makes a horrible smell in the supposed narrator's house. He defiles the font and altar-cloth. His gravestone is twisted over, with small holes below it going down to the coffin.

Eventually, a town meeting is held. The minister speaks against exhumation, using familiar Lutheran arguments: 'I don't know what sort of idolater thinks that you can kill a demon by exhuming or burning a corpse. If demons are completely non-physical, which is certain, they can't be harmed through physical elements, nor tortured or expelled in this way or any other.' But sterner views prevail: Kunze is exhumed, together with several other corpses as a control. All those are decayed, but Kunze himself is intact after more than five months in the grave. His skin is fresh, the joints flexible, and when a staff is put in his hand he grasps it firmly. His eyes open and shut, and when a vein is opened the blood spurts out. The corpse has, however, become puffy and inflated, with a swollen mouth, 'looking like a very fat butchered pig'. The inevitable burning follows.

Deconstructing Kunze: The Invention of the Sensational Vampire Novel

Going far beyond the 'normal' walking dead, the Kunze story includes ghost-story motifs (the request to a friend to complete a task), poltergeist phenomena (objects thrown around and smashed), the 'wild hunt' (his horse-shoes striking sparks[13]), and witchcraft ingredients (the diabolic pact, the black cat). Lip-smacking like a pig is elsewhere specific to the grave-bound dead. In fact, the story is a remarkably thorough compendium of activities that unwelcome supernatural visitors get up to. The debate, the minister's objection, and the description of the corpse likewise pile up the detail, as though an amalgam of several stories.

For a piece of serious first-hand reportage, all this seems strange. So does the unusually strong emphasis on Kunze's sexual predations. So again the style and incidental content (even as mediated through Weinrich's humanistic Latin), which put an inordinate emphasis on lurid or salacious details. For instance:

> He also appeared to a woman who was lying in bed, and asked to enjoy her body, but she said, 'You don't want that, Kunze, just look at my wrinkles and the ravages of age', and he left with raucous laughter. When another woman got up at dawn to start work, she saw the demon sitting at the bottom of the stairs, spreading his arms to embrace her. Frightened, she said 'Get out, Satan, you don't rule me'; the family came running, and he vanished. One night Kunze attacked a sleeping man, grabbed his penis, and pulled it out so far that he seemed to be tearing it off.[14]

What really gives the game away is the narrative of Kunze's exhumation and cremation. To appreciate that, we must revert to the Icelandic 'Eyrbyggja Saga' with its story of Thórólf (p. 246):

> Then he had a hole broken through the wall behind Thórólf, and had him pulled outside through this opening. Then oxen were hitched to a sled; Thórólf was laid on it, and they drove it up through Thórsárdalur, but not without a struggle. . . . [He is buried, then exhumed:] By then the oxen were exhausted and had to be replaced by another pair to drag him farther along the ridge. [He is exhumed again:] When they tried to move him they could not shift him. Thórodd then had a lever pushed underneath him . . . [and] they rolled him down to the foreshore and built a great pyre there; they set fire to it and bundled Thórólf onto it and burnt everything to ashes. Even so, it was a long time before the fire took hold on Thórólf.[15]

Compare the eventual disposal of Kunze's body:

> Two masons were brought, who made a hole through the walls next to the altar and prepared for the removal of the corpse. . . . The corpse was pulled out of the church through the hole with ropes, but it was so heavy that a rope broke, and the body could scarcely be shifted. Outside a cart was prepared. . . . But the corpse was so difficult to draw, because of its weight, that the massively-built horse pulled it painfully. . . . The corpse was placed on the pyre . . . , where it lay for a long time, for not all of it would burn. . . . [So the executioner

> chopped it up and threw the pieces on, but] during the following night it could scarcely be reduced to ashes.[16]

How the narrator obtained this motif-sequence raises intriguing questions, but what is beyond doubt is that he shamelessly passes it off as an eye-witness account. Since he does that once, he surely does it elsewhere: a systematic comparison would probably reveal other borrowings. For instance, the earth was scraped out of Kunze's grave, which was blocked with stones: exactly what happened at Wittgendorf in 1595.

Weinrich's 'pious and learned man' was evidently educated, and knowledgeable about folklore, but what he wrote was sensational fiction. The nature of the lost German text is easy to guess: it was surely a cheap printed pamphlet. Huge numbers of these—often with gruesome woodcuts—were being produced by the 1590s, especially to report lurid crimes and executions. Joy Wiltenburg's account emphasises the ubiquity of this material, and explains why a scholar such as Weinrich might have taken it seriously:

> Broadsides and pamphlets were by far the cheapest of printed materials. . . . Those with money were certainly the printers' target audience, but these works were sold in the streets and largely designed for oral performance or visual 'reading' rather than for silent consumption by a lone individual. . . . The potential audience for such literature was quite broad and could extend to people of relatively humble status. . . . But being broad, the audience was anything but uniform. It would be a mistake to assume, on the basis of relatively low cost and low literacy requirements, that consumers were concentrated at the lower end of the social spectrum. . . . Although elites sometimes expressed scorn for lying and scurrilous pamphlets—and authorities sought to censor them—they also made use of these forms.[17]

Lutheran clergy, all too familiar with Satan's intrusions into human affairs, could be involved in writing these pamphlets.[18] The Kunze source-text must have been similar in style to those describing witchcraft cases, which aimed to point a moral, to convince, but also—for mass sales—to entertain and titillate.[19] Its resourceful author probably used a genuine story about Johann Kunze of Bennisch on which hang his elaborate compilation, drawing on wide experience of revenants and other spectral happenings in Silesian towns.

———

The Kunze story is the first modern vampire novel, but it has further implications for us. A century later, and 200 kilometres to the north, a pastor would rage against sensational lies in cheap print that were making his townsfolk panic about vampires (p. 363). Kunze shows that the same could have happened as early as 1600. Pamphlets informed and moulded mass opinion: imaginative readers could easily have interpreted events in their own towns and villages in the light of Kunze. Once again, the feedback loops preclude any clear line between written and oral, or between educated and popular.

29

The Dangerous Dead between Witchcraft and the Enlightenment

EAST-CENTRAL EUROPE, 1550–1700

> After death has separated the soul from the body, the Devil's power has not yet been put to sleep entirely. He can do several things to the soul: he can do several things to the body. . . . As for the bodies of the dead, he sometimes clothes himself and appears in them. . . . But someone is going to press the point, 'Are you therefore claiming that the spirits of human beings also enter corpses (something evil spirits certainly do)?' As far as the souls of the damned are concerned, I see no reason why they should not do this.
>
> —MARTÍN DEL RÍO, 1598

IN A CONFESSIONALLY divided Europe, approaching the Scientific Revolution and the Enlightenment, the dangerous dead still flourished (Map 7). Printing meant that stories and motifs could travel more readily, crossing kingdoms and religious boundaries, as Johann Kunze illustrates.

At the same time, new motifs from the western Balkan peninsula began to penetrate northwards, apparently fusing with the central European belief-complex as it drifted south-eastwards.

The witch-hunting craze infected both Catholic and Protestant regions, but only Catholic thinkers assimilated unquiet corpses to witches and damned souls. Especially after 1670, Lutherans and rationalistic Catholics—increasingly sceptical about the whole business—diverged from those local Catholic leaders who responded to lay fears by ascribing personal guilt and malevolence to corpses.

Witches in the Grave: Catholic Perspectives, 1550–1610

The last two chapters examined motifs and interpretations in different confessional contexts. Lutheran pastors in Saxony preached against disturbing the dead; their lay flocks, even if inclined to behead shroud-eating female corpses with spades, ascribed their activity to impersonal forces rather than wickedness while alive. The Bohemian and Silesian stories, by contrast, picture men and women who are evil (even 'witches') in life, and whose posthumous antics cause mayhem. Although actually less deadly—they inflict bumps and bruises, not death by plague—they are mutilated and burnt in gruesome rituals of execution.

While the broad regional contrasts must surely have predated the Reformation, it is significant that the Bohemian, Silesian, and Moravian narratives mainly come to us through Catholic writers, even though the populations were now confessionally mixed. Modes of explanation were diverging. Catholic intellectuals were more inclined to identify malevolent corpses as the posthumous versions of malevolent women, an idea rooted in the scholarly conceptions of demonic evil that grew ever more intense and complex during c. 1540–1600. Even if witch-burning and corpse-burning were alternative outlets for the anxieties of unlearned layfolk, Catholic intellectuals were ready to bring them within the same moral framework of crime and retribution.

The Bohemian scholar and politician Václav Hájek—a Catholic convert—published his *Czech Chronicle* in 1541. This huge, influential but unreliable work contains various tall stories, among them a highly elaborated re-working of the Levín narrative (p. 334):

> In Bohemia, in a little town known as Levín, lived a potter called Ducháč. He had a wife called Brodka who was a real diabolical sorceress. The priest exhorted her to refrain from such wicked deeds, but although she complied in public she did them secretly. While summoning her spirits, she suddenly died: nobody could say whether strangled by them, or by divine dispensation. She was therefore excluded from burial among faithful Christians, and buried at a crossroads.
>
> Soon, people believed that she was walking around, often appearing to the shepherds in the fields and changing her shape into various animals. The shepherds were frightened and the cattle strayed, causing great misery. Sometimes she showed herself as she had been in life. After that, she often came by night into the little town and surrounding villages in people's houses, appearing in various forms. She talked to the people and frightened them, and even grabbed them by the throat and throttled them.
>
> Making common cause, the people of the little town and the peasants from surrounding villages chose a competent man to open the grave. When this had been done, everyone could see that she had half-eaten the veil that had been wrapped around her head, and when it was pulled from her mouth, it was found covered with blood. An oak stake was driven into her between the breasts; there was a great noise, and blood immediately spurted out of her body as though from a cow, so that everyone marvelled. She was buried again.
>
> After a short time, she appeared again much more than previously, terrified and killed people, and trampled her victims under her feet. The same man therefore uncovered her again, and found that she was holding in her hands the stake that had been driven into her body. After that, she was pulled out and burned together with the stake, and the ashes were thrown into the grave with the earth and thus buried. From that time on, the evil ceased. On many days a whirlwind was seen in the place where she was burned, but it did people no harm.[1]

The additions are dramatic. The anonymous woman of Neplach's story is given a name, a family, and—most strikingly—a career as a demonic witch. Was this a genuine tradition that Neplach had summarized incompletely, or Hájek's invention? Hájek's crude prejudices elsewhere (including antisemitic slanders that contributed to the expulsion of Jews from Bohemia) do not inspire confidence. Be that as it may, he clearly implies that Brodka's wickedness after death stemmed from her wickedness in life.

Fifty years later, the physician and medical teacher Ercole Sassonia ('Hercules of Saxony'), a native and graduate of Padua who spent time at the imperial court in Vienna, picked up the theme. In a monograph of 1600, he speculates on the potential causes of plague. One possibility, he believes, is supported by bizarre but incontrovertible evidence:

> What is to say that plague cannot also be caused by witchcraft? In fact, I worked out a compelling argument for this, but one that seemed so past all believing that I did not dare to present it: that in Poland and Germany, it is not uncommon for plague to be started by certain maleficent little women after they have died and been buried; and that is does not stop until a corpse is found with its own wrappings—or others from nearby—held bitten in the mouth, like a starving person desperate for food.

Three informants gave Ercole the courage to publish this idea. One was a medical scholar, Dr Jan Ursinus of Lemberg/Lviv, who reported a case there in 1572 (p. 352). The other two were grandees: Giovanni I Cornaro (Venetian nobleman and future Doge) and Prince-Cardinal Jerzy Radziwiłł. Both testified that this capacity to cause plague, and this mode of doing it, had existed for a long time in Germany.[2]

In 1612 another Catholic—our friend Martin Weinrich—prefaced the Striegau and Bennisch stories with a similar reflection:

> In recent years, so much has become known about these demons . . . through writing and word of mouth, that there is no corner of Germany and neighbouring realms to which at least some news of this astonishing thing has not penetrated. It is in the public interest for uneducated people to be warned against the amazing snares of our common enemy, and for those who wield power to learn by what means, and in what circumstances, these almost unheard-of mobs of turbulent demons have been dealt with, and must be dealt with in similar cases.[3]

Meanwhile, the Jesuit Martín Del Río had given voice to the intensified angst about demons, witches, magic, and heresy that afflicted educated Catholics in the 1590s.[4] In his huge book on demonology, he argues that the Devil's power over humans does not entirely end at death: he and other evil spirits can occupy corpses, and there is no reason why damned souls (though not blessed ones) should be unable to do the same.[5] That line of argument allows for a wicked person's soul and personality to function in a wicked corpse. However questionable theologically, Del Río's formulation could be seized upon by clergy and secular authorities in affected regions as a justification for corpse-killing.

Del Río, Ercole, and Weinrich (all born around 1550) worked in an intellectual tradition that embodied 'a highly intricate mixture of reasoned curiosity and unreasoned credulity which produced a surge in many kinds of occult study'.[6] Ercole describes the kind of passive, shroud-chewing corpse that the Lutheran laity feared in times of plague, but his framework is different: Poland and Germany are full of female witches, he thinks, and some pursue their malevolence in the grave. Weinrich's model is not gender-specific, and like the Lutheran pastors he envisages 'snares of the common enemy'. But he too would have assumed a different framework—witches and the satanic pact—and like Del Río he speculates on the possibility of souls occupying corpses.[7]

The Silesian and Bohemian cases substantiate Weinrich's appeal to secular magistrates: the denouement in nearly every case was a solemn and well-attended dismemberment and burning by the public executioner, ritualized like executions of living miscreants. But they also had a supernatural aspect, which could verge into sympathetic magic. Weinrich observes of the 1591 Striegau case that the ashes were carefully poured into the river 'so that they should not be collected by some busybody, or kept for any evil use, as has sometimes happened in such cases'.[8] The boundary between witchcraft and Paracelsian medicine is not entirely clear here.

Poland Looking Northward: Sickles at the Throat

After the 1610s, intellectual interest faltered for some decades and reported cases declined to a trickle. A dramatic exception is a man in a plague cemetery from 1638 at Anklam (Western Pomerania), buried with a wooden bowl over his head and nails through his wrists and right hip.[9] Overall, however, the Thirty Years' War (1618–48) did *not* generate revenant cases, despite the appalling combination of brutality with plague as the Swedish army moved through German lands in the early 1630s.[10] That may say something about the psychological roots of corpse-fears: stemming from human violence, war needs no such explanations. The most plausible reason for the drying-up of academic comment is that the later sixteenth century had genuinely been an epidemic phase, and that the epidemic had now subsided.

The war was, however, followed by a striking episode in northern Poland, towards Pomerania and the Baltic coast, where earlier cases had been reported in 1564 and 1584 (p. 325). Here the evidence is archaeological, displaying popular fears unmediated through texts.[11] Of the nearly 300 burials from c. 1650–1700 excavated at Drawsko, north-west of Poznań, about a third—preponderantly female—contained copper coins. Five graves—an adult male, three adult females, and an adolescent female—contained iron sickles: one of these lay over the pelvic area (of a corpse that also had a stone on its throat and a coin in its wide-open mouth), but the other four were hooked across the throat just under the chin (Figure 61). A female burial on a different site, at Pień near Toruń, had a sickle placed upright across her throat and a padlock on the big toe of her left foot. South of Gdańsk, as late as 1933, a respondent to the German Folklore Survey said that a sickle should be placed around the neck of an unquiet corpse.[12]

The Drawsko cemetery shows variable levels of concern: a coin used as a mild restraint for a large minority, tougher measures applied to a small minority. In both cases, the suspect corpses were mainly but not exclusively female. Scientific analysis shows that the high-risk individuals were local people. Sickles as grave-goods have variable meanings (p. 47), but these examples hooked under the chins—and in one case a stone laid on the throat—were surely to pre-empt biting or shroud-chewing.

Psychological trauma here is unsurprising, given that the region was contested in politics and religion and devastated by cholera outbreaks.[13] The strong female bias implies a concern to prevent witches from reviving in the grave and spreading disease. These burials corroborate reports

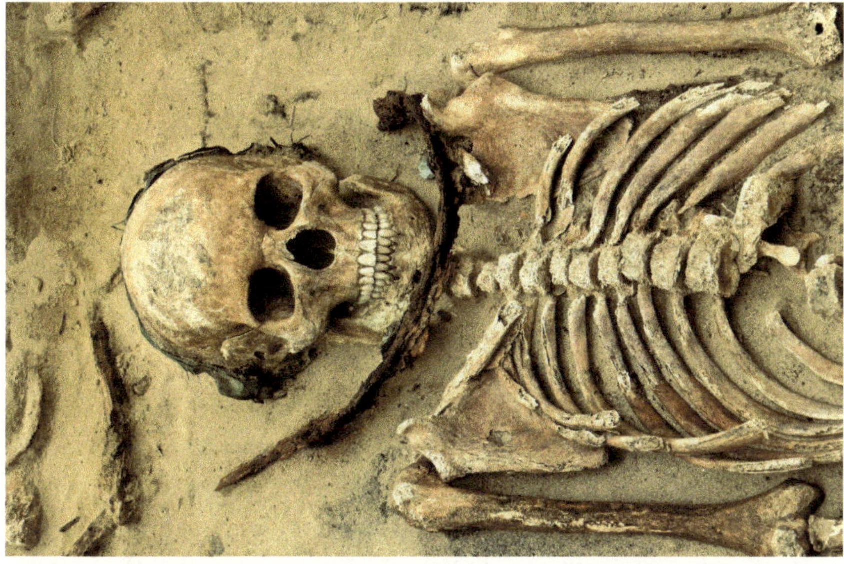

FIGURE 61: Drawsko (Poland), grave 6/2012: a teenage girl buried with a copper headband, a copper-alloy coin by her left jaw (presumably fallen from her mouth), and a sickle across her throat, c.1650–70.

suggesting that unquiet corpses (of both sexes) became more prominent again in Poland from the 1660s onwards.[14]

The Front Moves Eastward: Southern Silesia, Moravia, and the Bishopric of Olomouc

More significant than the Thirty Years' War was the Counter-Reformation, which swept across central Europe—and especially the Habsburg lands—during the seventeenth century. The outcome was a fragmented confessional landscape: officially Catholic, but with many pockets of resistance, and bearing the scars of violent re-conversion.[15] Also, as European revenants moved eastward, they started to make contact with their counterparts in the Orthodox world. If the Lutheran Reformation had stirred up the active dead, the anxious Counter-Reformation environment of religious conflict and instability could have done the same a century later. And new influences brought new fantasies.

The most prominent focus of this emerging fear-complex was northern Moravia, where we have already noted episodes during the 1590s.[16] The nucleus—in the mountainous Czech/Polish borderland at the north end of the Carpathians—lay mostly within the northernmost part of Olomouc diocese, and partly on the estates of its bishops. Both the corpse-killings and the broader religious culture are well documented, in sources that offer an unusually fine-grained understanding of how spiritual trauma exacerbated fears of the dead.

Olomouc so dominates these chapters that we need to ask why it assumed such exceptional importance in the annals of corpse-killing between the 1650s and 1750s.[17] The episodes erupted on a Slav/German cultural border, mostly though not exclusively among frontier Germans, and where protagonists are named in case records those names are mainly German. We are familiar with corpse-killing in ethnically tense contexts; what evidently made Olomouc different was that the bottom-up fears and pressures were fostered by top-down encouragement. It seems that there must have been some old-fashioned demonologists in the Olomouc consistory, who extended their enthusiasm for persecuting witches to persecuting corpses, and had free rein in that activity during long periods of negligent episcopal rule. This helps to explain the apparently unique convergence at Olomouc of witch-killing with corpse-killing, and the resemblance here between witches and corpses as objects of fear and aggression.

In the city, religious tensions between Lutheran townsfolk and the powerful, staunchly Catholic bishopric had grown through the sixteenth century. Measures against non-Catholics (facilitated by the new Jesuit university) intensified from the 1570s. After 1620, in line with aggressive imperial policy, the mainly Lutheran and Utraquist rural population were forcibly converted, sometimes with great brutality: purgatory was back whether people wanted it or not.[18] By 1636, the bishop of Olomouc could boast that 110,000 out of 150,000 non-Catholic Moravians had already been converted.[19]

In the wake of these upheavals, the first northern Moravian witch-hunt erupted during 1636–48. It is surely no coincidence that the endemic but hitherto sporadic practice of corpse-killing intensified close on its heels, with a distinct peak during 1651–70 (see Figure 64 in Chapter 30), nor that the legal and ritualized procedures for condemning and executing witches were enthusiastically extended to corpses. In an extraordinary documentary survival, expenses from 1635 detail the burning of a dead widow at Sternberg/Šternberk for 'running around, pressing and scaring people at night, and repeatedly making noises in houses'. Payments are listed for the imperial magistrate's consent, for 'fumigation against the foul smell', for masons opening and closing a hole in the churchyard wall to extract the corpse, for ropes, digging tools, and other equipment, and for the executioner's fee.[20]

During his long reign as bishop of Olomouc (1664–95), Charles of Liechtenstein-Castelkorn fostered baroque culture and an intense, theatrical Catholic devotion.[21] Pastoral care of his rural flock interested him much less, especially in the mountainous north: by 1700 the parishioners in one village had received no preaching for thirty years, did not know how to make the sign of the cross, and could not say how many gods there were.[22] A still darker aspect of Charles's reign was his support for Heinrich Franz Boblig's notorious witch persecutions—again in the north—during 1678–95.[23] A more poisonous mix of fear, ignorance, and spiritual insecurity would be hard to imagine.

Corpse-killing duly took a lurid and highly-coloured turn. At Lichtewerden/Světlá Hora in 1674, a disreputable man who scared and plagued people at night was exhumed, found guilty, burned on a boundary between villages with the coffin and all tools, and the grave blocked up.[24] At Friedland/Břidličná in 1685, a dead woman who roamed around 'like the living devil', crying, drumming, dancing and torturing people day and night, received the same treatment.[25] Those are the highlights: in the mountainous borderland of northern Moravia with Silesia, Ádám Mézes and Karen Lambrecht have documented a minimum of twenty-four further exhumations of this kind up to 1700, most of them after 1650 (Figure 64).[26] Trauma in the countryside, with an overlay of theatrical Catholicism in the view from Olomouc, moulded a distinctively legalistic approach to corpse-killing.

The Front Moves Southward: The Bloodsucking Strigon

By this time a new culture-zone of revenant fears, around the northern Carpathian arc, had emerged in succession to the one subsiding in Bohemia. The first known case is from the great Polish plague of 1572, when the corpse of a peasant-woman was brought into Lemberg/Lviv for burial. The plague intensified around that church, and she was exhumed on suspicion of being a witch. 'When they found her naked, with the remains of her eaten shroud in her mouth, they cut off her head with a sharp iron-edged spade, as is the custom, and dark-red corrupt bloody matter gushed out'; the plague duly stopped.[27] Female shroud-eaters were reported in 1624 at Kleparz near Krakow ('red from head to foot'), and in 1625 during the Warsaw plague.[28]

The first signs of new contacts with the south-east now start to appear. We saw that the Istrian *strigon* Giure Grando seemed surprisingly Western in his activities and personality (p. 307). If that reflects the percolation of motifs from the German- and Polish-speaking worlds, the influences also seem to have operated in the reverse direction. For the first time in central Europe, a Polish case of 1674 calls a bloated corpse a *stryga* and explicitly mentions bloodsucking:

> At Trzeszawa a man died, and harmed his relatives by strangling, beating and sucking blood: they say it is a *strxyga*. The tomb was opened, and they found him like a sack filled with blood. They turned him face-down, but the same night he went to his son and struck him, so that yesterday it was said that he had died. The parishioners want to behead him with a spade. They are not sure whether the Church is allowed to act so brutally, so the question is: Can the head of a corpse that commits crimes (*maleficia*) after burial be severed in the grave so that the crimes stop? [Answer:] Therefore it is permitted to kill the *stryga*.[29]

Trzeszawa lies well to the east of the earlier Polish cases. The word *stryga* is a significant import from Balkan terminology; so is the 'sack filled with blood', an image also found in Bulgaria.[30] Cross-fertilization was evidently an important background to the phenomena that would erupt so spectacularly on the Habsburg military frontier half a century later (Chapter 31).

Towards the Enlightenment: The Restless Dead in Later Seventeenth-Century Scholarship

Occasional authors, both Catholic and Protestant, recycled restless-dead stories in derivative compilations of marvels;[31] the contemporary episodes in the Aegean, as reported by travellers like Father Richard (p. 76), further sustained curiosity. In 1659, the Cambridge philosopher Henry More pre-empted the later Spiritualist idea of ectoplasm on the strength of Weinrich's narratives: they 'doe prove not onely the *appearing* of Souls after they have left this life, but also that some thickning Matter, such as may be got either from Bodies alive, or lately dead, or as fresh as those that are but newly dead . . . , or lastly from thick vaporous Air, may facilitate much their appearing'.[32] This original if eccentric contribution had no impact on Continental debates.

Lutheran philosophers, theologians, and medics re-engaged with the topic from the 1670s. Although coinciding with a rise in new reports, these works were retrospective, and not adventurous intellectually. The first were by Leipzig academics: Christian Friedrich Garmann's *On the Miracles of the Dead* (1670), and Philip Rohr's resoundingly titled *Historico-Philosophical Dissertation on the Mastication of the Dead* (1679; Figure 62). Building on a Leipzig and Wittenberg tradition of scholarly debate on werewolves,[33] they rejected any idea that corpses can act of their own volition, while accepting the orthodox Lutheran position that the Devil (or a demon) uses them to deceive mankind. They cite the usual examples, with a sceptical emphasis on lip-smacking (which actually had not been featured in new cases since around 1600). In the same genre, though more highly-coloured, is Erasmus Francisci (Finx)'s massive *The Infernal Proteus* (1690), which devotes 48 pages to *der schmätzende Todte* (Figure 63).[34]

Soon, these authors would seem old-fashioned. By the 1680s, Lutheran theologians were abandoning the interpretation of spectral phenomena

I. N. J.
DISSERTATIO
HISTORICO-PHILOSOPHICA
De
MASTICATIONE
MORTUORUM,
Quam
Dei & Superiorum indultu,
in illuſtri Academ. Lipſ.
ſiſtent
PRÆSES
M. PHILIPPUS Rohr/ Marckran-
ſtadio-Miſnic.
&
RESPONDENS
BENJAMIN FRIZSCHIUS, Muſilaviâ-Miſnicus,
Alumni Electorales.
ad diem XVI. Auguſti Ann. M. DC. LXXIX.
H. L. Q. C.

LIPSIÆ,
Typis MICHAELIS VOGTII.

FIGURE 62: Despite its unforgettable title, Philip Rohr's Leipzig dissertation on the 'mastication of the dead' was rather out-of-date in 1679: chewing corpses had not been newly reported for several decades.

FIGURE 63: The frontispiece of Erasmus Finx's demonological work from 1690, which includes one of the longest accounts of the unquiet dead before Calmet. It illustrates the kind of sensationalist packaging that was already responding to a popular market.

as deceits of Satan: increasingly, spirits were to be dismissed as misunderstandings or frauds.[35] Even so, these books were widely read, recycling a wide range of motifs into milieux where they could influence the new fears emerging around the Carpathians and the Balkans.

The Catholic position was more fragmented.[36] The likes of Del Río and Weinrich had validated the idea that to mutilate or burn an occupied corpse was to attack diabolic power. That was not the up-to-date view in Rome, far from the zones of dangerous-dead beliefs. In 1696 the Jesuit Revisors-General, charged with assessing the impact of science on doctrine, prescribed medicine, exorcism, and intercessions but deplored fighting magic with magic: beheading corpses was mere savagery towards the dead.[37] A provincial priest or bishop, already believing in witches and now confronted by laity plagued by night-mare attacks, might see matters differently, as the Trzeszawa verdict illustrates. In 1716, the Polish Jesuit Jerzi Gengell acknowledged the weight of opinion against beheading, but still preferred not to take chances: in a nutshell, 'a corpse is better off without a head and without a demon than with a head and with a demon'.[38]

In fact, the next great epidemic of corpse-killing was endorsed by a Catholic intellectual. The Observant Franciscan Amandus Hermann, whose work on philosophy and metaphysics 'shows no gleam of modernity',[39] is uncompromising about the moral culpability of corpses: 'What should be done with people buried in a cemetery who are suspected of magic and infest people?', he asks in 1698. He tells how he had passed through Moravia when corpses of both sexes were plaguing the countryside, throwing people out of bed and biting their fingers and toes. Hermann advised that this was a matter for the bishop or his consistory. Leaping at this helpful advice (which validated their existing practice), the Olomouc consistory ruled that guilty corpses should be beheaded and burned.[40]

Interpreting the Counter-Reformation in a local spirit, the Catholic establishment in Olomouc assimilated restless corpses to witches, and used witch-hunting principles to foment what would become the greatest corpse-killing epidemic in recorded history. This was one of the world's few cases of an institutionalized regime for trying, condemning, and executing the dead, persisting intermittently into the 1750s. By thus setting up a tangible target for Enlightenment scorn and outrage, it helped to frame the abnormal circumstances in which the vampires of central and eastern Europe were eventually introduced to western European audiences.

30

From Moravia to Transylvania

THE CARPATHIAN ARC, 1700–25

> I conjure up Maevia the *strix*: the posthumous witch, whose wickedness lived on after her burial, who did not rest in peace but, wandering restlessly, disturbed men and flocks; a demon, a shade who glided around her tomb. What you will read here cannot easily be read elsewhere.
>
> —KARL VON SCHERTZ, 1703

AFTER 1700, the dangerous dead were marching on again—first eastwards and then southwards—along a route conforming very closely to the great mountainous arc of the Carpathians (Map 7). This strange geographical pattern cannot be accidental, and it demands some attempt at explanation. Meanwhile, however, the dramatic events in Olomouc diocese remained centre-stage.

The Moravian Epidemic, 1690–1740

Between 1695 and 1738, the bishops of Olomouc were absentees: day-to-day governance devolved by default on the episcopal consistory, a body of senior clergy headed by the dean.[1] Its members do not seem to have questioned the essential reality of predatory corpses, and they systematized the procedure for dealing with them, as described by Amandus Hermann. The rural dean held an enquiry, the gravedigger exhumed the corpse, and the secular executioner burned it on the boundary of two districts. The coffin, the gravedigger's tools, and anything with the corpse were burned too, and the ashes thrown in a river.[2] Some suspects were not buried at all, but kept for six or seven weeks and then handed over to the executioner for burning if they showed no signs of decay. 'And it is certain that even the discarded clothes of those people have moved on their own', Hermann remarks in an unexpected aside.[3]

What happened after 1700—now clarified by the research of Ádám Mézes—was spectacular (Figure 64).[4] The established pattern of burning between one and three suspect corpses was now punctuated by mass exhumations and burnings. One account describes about fifty child corpses being put on a pyre.[5] At the town of Liebau/Libavá, a sequence of episodes climaxed in 1708 with the exhumation and burning of about forty corpses, and then—in the biggest known corpse-killing panic of all time—a further eighty in surrounding villages in 1727–8. Mézes was able to count at least 253 such 'executions' in the region during 1701–40. It is clear that these accusations against the dead were generated locally, not imposed from above.

Although certainly incomplete, these data are firmer than for any earlier period in any part of the world: this was a true epidemic. What had changed? To develop a well-known argument by Gabor Klaniczay, the best option seems to be a sense of unfinished business after the terror of Boblig's persecutions.[6] When the threat (or psychological release) of witch-burning ended, people sought an alternative release in intensified corpse-burning. Perhaps it gave a sense of agency to villagers who—only too used to accusations of supernatural malevolence from above—could now conduct their own autonomous witch-hunts among the dead. For their part, enthusiastic persecutors in the Olomouc consistory were happy to respond.

Karl von Schertz (whom we will meet soon) illustrates the new-style Moravian revenants with 'Maevia': a dead woman who appeared sometimes in human form and sometimes as a cat, pressing down on people and squeezing their hearts and throats. Cows collapsed, dogs barked,

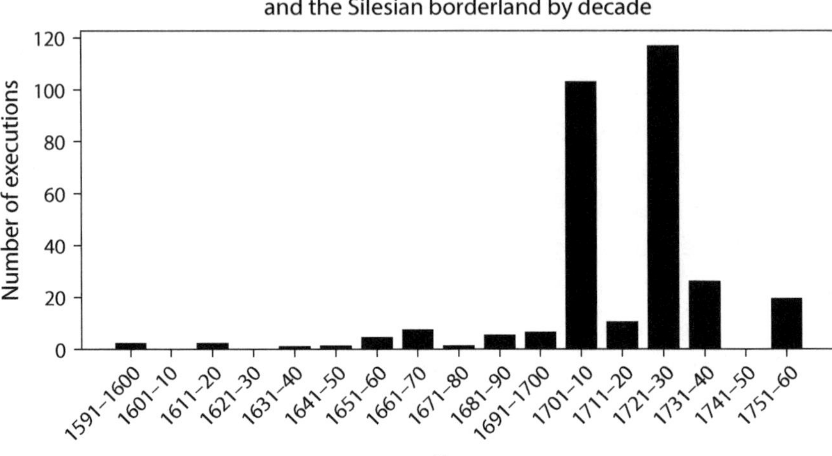

FIGURE 64: The incidence of recorded corpse executions in northern Moravia / southern Silesia. It is important to remember that many cases must have gone unrecorded (for instance, the gap in the 1740s probably reflects non-reporting during the reign of a vampire-sceptic bishop), but the overall picture may be accurate.

and horses sweated and trembled. One man reported that she urinated into his mouth so that he vomited.[7] A slightly later account claims that in Hotzenplotz/Osoblaha (another German settlement),

> people frequently returned after death to their families, to eat and drink with them, and even to have sexual relations with the wives whom they had left behind. And when travellers passed through the village at the hour of night when they left their graves, they ran after them and sat on their backs. In these various ghastly ways they are said to afflict both people and animals. Because of this, it is not uncommon for all the dogs to flee the village together at midnight and rush to the district boundaries, eventually returning after the first hour when the vampires are thought to return to their graves.[8]

Such extreme imaginings, including what sound like exceptionally nasty night-mare effects, might well reflect a community traumatised by persecutory violence but also habituated to it.

Another stimulus, however, was that a different and terrifying fear had entered the repertoire of motifs. If a predatory corpse were not burned, says Schertz in 1703, 'a greater evil would unfold: for everyone subsequently dying after her, and buried in the same cemetery, would likewise become "spectres" (*spectra*), and debilitating upheavals would increase, as witnesses from several places show: *The common man believes that the first ghost* (Gespenst) *blows upon* (anzublasen) *the other dead bodies buried nearby* (I use the actual terms); and that because of this blowing (*afflatus*) they must all wander around afterwards'.[9]

This fear of corpse-to-corpse contagion is possibly foreshadowed by the care with which grave-earth had been scraped out, and graves blocked with stones, in cases from the 1590s (pp. 337, 341). It is different from fearing that the *living* victims of vampires become vampires, another new idea that we will meet shortly. It is neither an ancient motif nor a common one, though it was re-worked a century later in New England with the idea of a lethal vine-like plant creeping from coffin to coffin (p. 392). It may derive from medical theory cycled into folk-belief (though contagion by breathing was not a mainstream early modern explanation for the spread of plague), or from a demonological concept of the Devil penetrating the human body in the form of breath.[10] At all events it is another factor behind the extreme and unusual character of the Moravian mass corpse-burnings.

Catholic Jurisprudence: Schertz and 'Posthumous Magic'

The Olomouc consistory sought advice from the authorities in Rome, who ignored what they presumably considered a ludicrous question.[11] But the director of the bishop's estates, Karl Ferdinand von Schertz, took the initiative in an elegant little book, *Posthumous Magic*, written in 1703 and published in 1706 (Figure 65).[12] The work of a practical lawyer, it is in stylish Latin replete with references to Roman literature and canon law, witnessing 'to the intensity of classical influence on Czech Baroque culture'.[13] Why deploy such resources on such a theme?

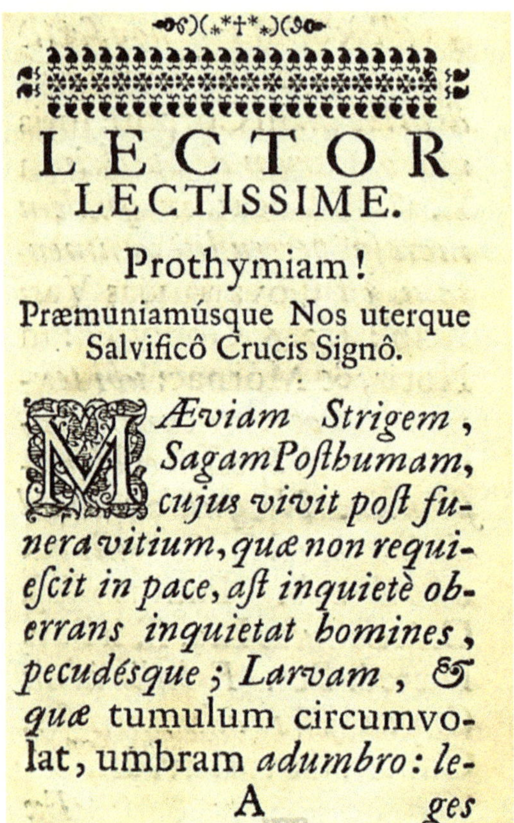

LECTOR
LECTISSIME.

Prothymiam!
Præmuniamúsque Nos uterque
Salvificô Crucis Signô.

MÆviam Strigem, SagamPoſthumam, cujus vivit poſt funera vitium, quæ non requieſcit in pace, aſt inquietè oberrans inquietat homines, pecudéſque; Larvam, & quæ tumulum circumvolat, umbram *adumbro: le-*

A *ges*

FIGURE 65: *Magia Posthuma*: Karl von Schertz's stylishly composed and printed treatise on the Moravian epidemic. The main text, with his account of 'Maevia the *strix*, the posthumous witch', starts on this page.

Schertz's book is framed as a legal 'for-and-against' disputation, so even-handedly that his personal views are slightly elusive.[14] He acknowledges ample testimony that corpses really can do harm, and that destruction is a necessary last resort in clear cases. Indeed, he comically scolds the English philosopher Thomas Hobbes for not believing in ghosts: 'If Hobbes were still alive, I'd invite him to our region . . . and spirits of a different kind would teach him and his combative spirit'.[15] But he also gives much space to sceptical common-sense: corpses can remain flexible for natural reasons; incorruption need not imply wickedness; ill-health or imagination produce night-mare experiences; and it is ludicrous to burn the corpses of children who have had no time to become wicked magicians.[16] Masses and exorcisms are a better approach: Schertz tells how he persuaded an old man to have masses and public prayers said for his restless dead wife instead of digging her up, which solved the problem.[17] Turning to clergy who condone superstition, he scolds curates who—pandering to rustic fears unsupported by medical knowledge—encourage poor peasants to pay for an executioner to burn corpses.[18]

Printed in Olomouc to a high standard, this book was an exclusive item for the educated and discriminating: only four copies are now known.[19] In giving approval, the episcopal court hoped 'that by its influence this magic may be buried in murky shadows'.[20] It all looks like an attempt by the more level-headed elements in the Olomouc establishment to influence the clergy and nobility of the diocese: not to suppress corpse-killing completely, but to control it through rigorous procedures and standards of proof. In practice, as we will see, the consistory would prove less resistant when rural communities and clergy demanded direct action.

Lutheran Scepticism: The Fraustadt Panic and Sensational Journalism, 1710

A plague epidemic during 1709–10 at Fraustadt/Wschowa weighed heavily on its devoted and scholarly Lutheran pastor, Samuel Friedrich Lauterbach, who loved Poland and his home town. That people started fearing corpses was an unwelcome distraction; that unscrupulous journalists then whipped that fear up into a panic drove Lauterbach to righteous fury. His diatribe is of great interest here, since it describes what may in fact have been a widespread dynamic that elsewhere can only be inferred.

The trouble started with a tragically commonplace scenario: a woman died, followed by her husband, three children, and grandmother. Soon, people were calling her 'a witch and sorceress who would after-feed on her family'. Speculations came to be taken for truth:

> the gossip grew here, and was written from many places, whether such-and-such signs would be found on the corpse if it were dug up.

> Furthermore, vagrants had already made songs, and sang them now and again in market-places. You should not be surprised at a bunch of people like that, since roaming around lying and cheating is their profession. But equally, there are ignorant printers who—just for a small profit—publish these false newspapers, thereby harming their neighbours, insulting honest families, and putting people under public pressure.
>
> I confess that I was shocked to the bottom of my heart to read that kind of thing. So many gross lies and slanders all at once have scarcely been heard, especially about the violent gestures in death, the fire-red figure in the coffin, the huge raven at the burial, and the bloody sight during the digging. It is all set out in detail as though the shameless poet had seen it with his own eyes, but not a word is true. It is also stated that a spirit was summoned, who declared that if the corpse were to be left undisturbed for another fourteen days, the plague would fall on the entire country. This blasphemer seems to be one of those people who are angry with the good Fraustadt, which has done no harm.[21]

We have seen that a lost sensational pamphlet lies behind the story of Johann Kunze (and might the same be true of Giure Grando?). The Fraustadt pamphlet is lost too, but Lauterbach shows that it was not only distributed and read in all its lurid detail, but also turned into a public performance by street-singers. That may explain a good deal about the expanding geographical spread of dangerous-dead beliefs from the 1690s, and also about the wider range of motifs now manifesting at a popular level.

Poland and Prussia: Continuity and Fragmentation

As the epidemic focus moved on, beliefs lingered in their earlier heartlands. But they diversified, partly because they became less intense, partly because of ramifying influences. The Fraustadt case encourages speculation that German-language printed material from the West was melding with oral material from the Carpathians. Meanwhile, scholarly interest remained lively, but was taking a more scientific and sceptical turn.

The *Collection for Natural and Medical History*, a progressive scientific journal for Prussian, Silesian, and Bohemian research, carried several restless-dead stories during the 1720s.[22] In 1722, one of these described after-eating corpses being beheaded in Podolia (west Ukraine) to stop plague, with an unpleasant but intriguing comment: 'It is no wonder that such a superstition is found in Poland and Podolia, where the people have much to do with Jews and unbelievers, but it is surprising that even in our Prussia, among the Protestants, you can still find people who indulge in such fantasies'.[23] This author evidently saw corpse-killing as a mobile rather than rooted belief, encouraged by Jewish and Turkish elements in Polish society. Irrespective of those specific links, the perception is interesting.

In Poland, Silesia, and Prussia, practices became more muted and less coherent. Corpses were manipulated rather than beheaded or burned, and there is less sense of common, locally rooted understandings of causes and remedies. Instead, people panicked because they picked up circulating ideas, sometimes garbled ones. Two isolated episodes are enlightening here for their novel and rather random character.

During a plague in 1710, villagers near Angerburg/Węgorzewo in east Prussia were determined to find a guilty self-eating corpse. So 'they had some corpses dug up by the gravediggers, but could not find one that was eating itself. They urged them to dig up more, and find the culprit. When the gravediggers gave up in frustration, they agreed to take a random corpse, chop it by the hands and armpits and tear it apart, and then call it a self-eating corpse. Then the execution was carried out: a few death-songs were sung, the corpse was solemnly beheaded with a grave-spade, and then it was thrown back into the grave with a live dog'.[24]

The other case, again in time of plague, concerns two adjoining Polish villages. In 1719, a beggar died in one and was taken to the other for burial. The next day, seventy people from the first village came to the cemetery and exhumed the corpse, because—as they told the pastor—the body had been taken out of their village 'in a bad way', that is, upside-down: if it were not retrieved and then returned to its grave the right way up, they said, the whole village would die.[25]

These episodes are notable for their confusion. In the first, the villagers evidently thought that the solution lay not in stopping the eating action but in dismembering *any* corpse. The second seems to depend on a muddled inversion of the idea that laying a corpse in a prone position would *stop* it from doing harm. These are incoherent outgrowths from earlier belief-systems: surely classic products of the rumour-mill.

Stories along the Carpathian Corridor?

So far, this chapter has remained in the long-established Moravian, Silesian, and Polish zones of dangerous-dead beliefs. But the decades after 1700 brought a broader if thinner scatter of cases running south-eastwards. Manifestations in what is now northern Slovakia, and then in Transylvania, were a prelude to the more dramatic eruption further south, in Serbia on the Habsburg-Ottoman frontier.

All these regions were within the early eighteenth-century Habsburg monarchy. This facilitated the flow of ideas, both among intellectuals and between the widely separated urban and mercantile communities. But the ideas must also have travelled at a vernacular and non-literate level: the eastern and south-eastern zones of Europe were multi-lingual in a way that western Europe was not.[26] The interpenetration of groups speaking German, Hungarian, and the various Slavic languages, and following the Orthodox, Catholic, Lutheran, and Muslim faiths, involved cross-cultural spoken communication on a large scale. Frontier Germans are a persistent presence in the stories, even though the dominance of German-speaking intellectual elites in writing and publication probably heightens that effect.

All the scattered instances of corpse-killing between Moravia and Serbia lie on or near the Carpathians (Map 7). This is in sharp contrast to the intervening Habsburg territories of Austria and Hungary, where cases are virtually unknown.[27] The distribution, Ádám Mézes observes, 'coincides with the migration route of Wallachian shepherding groups along the ridges of the Carpathian Mountains, from Wallachia . . .

through Transylvania and the Tatra Mountains to Moravia during the later middle ages'.[28] Transhumant herding communities tend to have a distinctive folk-culture that is receptive to elements from the cultures they encounter, and can transmit them over long distances. Mézes is surely right to suggest this as one possible conduit for conceptions about the dangerous dead, operating in both directions.

Of course, there would have been social, political, and commercial conduits of other kinds, and a long-standing capacity to spread stories. As early as 1529, a local priest at Lalin, in the outer western Carpathians, allowed parishioners 'who practiced witchcraft' to exhume, behead, and stake a male corpse.[29] Whether this was an isolated episode is unclear. At all events a growing influence of literate culture on vernacular culture seems likely after 1650, through a combination of cheap print with contacts and movements generated by the Habsburg-Ottoman wars.

Northern Slovakia: Michał Kasparek and Others

Tracking eastwards from Moravia, corpse-killing emerges in the Tatra Mountains region of what is now northern Slovakia. A Lutheran synod, held there at Rózsahegy/Ružomberok in 1707, discussed—with evident puzzlement—the belief that 'souls' of the dead come out of their coffins and go home. After the usual sentiments about Satan's tricks and the need for prayer, the synod condemned exhumation and decapitation 'as has been happening in some places'. They added that pastors should make sure that people are really dead before burying them: a pointer to how some members were rationalizing this new problem.[30]

A decade passed before the first specific report from the region, but it is a spectacular one. For sheer drama, events in the German- and Polish-settled town of Lubló/Stará L'ubovňa in 1718 compare with the rampages of Johann Kunze. The difference is the first-hand character of the documentation: no irresponsible, lurid-minded pamphleteer stoked up this hysteria.

Michał Kasparek, citizen and wine-merchant of Lubló, died on 28 February 1718 and was buried honourably. But he immediately began attacking people in bed by night and in the countryside by day. He rode around on a white horse: banging on doors, breaking into houses and inns, eating and drinking, and interrupting wedding-parties (Figure 66). He made his widow and four maids pregnant. At a town meeting on 26 March, his victims all told the same story: 'On going to bed they felt something cold on their bodies, which hit, bit and strangled them. All of them had visible wounds on their hands and necks.' Two Uniate priests performed a fruitless exorcism. On 15 April, witnesses reported that Kasparek was roaming around dressed in red, and had knocked a man down and torn his beard.

The grave was opened: Kasparek lay as though alive, but bloated, with torn hair in his hands and blood on his clothes. The citizens wrote to the bishop in Kraków for authority to proceed, and this letter survives. Exiles from (Polish) civilization, they profess their inability to cope with such terrors on their own. 'The horror of the phantasm, recovering from this respite and resuming its strength, forces the whole city to turn the nights meant for rest into days. . . . Such effects are usually resolved by exhumation of the main cause, as our reverend priest has taught many times by example here and in nearby places', but he lacks the authority to do it on his own. From this it seems that exhumations had become common in the region, that clergy led them, and also that an episcopal licensing system operated.

The permission arrived on 24 April. Two days later the corpse was carried out to the boundary, where many onlookers saw with amazement that it was fresh, plump, and beautiful. The heart was cut out and placed in a wooden box under a dunghill, but eventually given to Kasparek's brothers. Then the corpse was beheaded and burnt on a pyre, where it raised and lowered its right and then left foot, making frog-like croaking noises.

That did not stop Kasparek. He still appeared on horseback, wearing stylish, bright-coloured clothes and attacking neighbouring villages. When a nobleman accosted him, he replied 'Get lost if you don't want me to hurt you'. There was a brief respite in May when he went off to collect debts in Warsaw, but within three weeks he was back. 'You burn me, I'll burn you better!', he threatened, and kept his word: thirty houses were destroyed in a series of fires. The townsfolk went crazy: barely

FIGURE 66: Michał Kasparek on the rampage, riding through Lubló on his white horse and gate-crashing parties. He must count as the most flamboyantly dressed of all vampires.

working, keeping vigil day and night, carrying their belongings to the town square and sleeping in the open.

Kasparek's widow and brothers were interrogated, but swore that they had never known him to use magic. On 20 June the city council sent for monastic exorcists, who did their best with incense and holy water. But Kasparek raged on: 'Lubló will burn again on 8 July, and this time the town hall and church will go up in flames'. With much of the town now in ruins, people remembered the boxed-up heart. It was brought to the town hall, burned at a nearby church, and the troubles finally ended.[31]

The sources, including a report written as the fires still burned, have an almost unique immediacy. Whatever bizarre collective self-deception was at work here, the citizens really believed that they were suffering these gross predations. A spate of night-mare attacks, coincidentally followed by a series of fires in the hot summer of 1718, seems likely. The case shows that a highly-wrought narrative, replete with lurid detail, could be generated spontaneously. But that could scarcely have happened without cultural influence, perhaps from printed material that more impressionable townsfolk had absorbed beforehand.

The other case known from the region was in the forest village near Késmárk/Kežmarok, only twenty-five kilometres from Lubló. An innkeeper's wife, who had wasted away and died of tuberculosis, made strangling attacks at night. Her corpse remained flexible, so the villagers kept it unburied. After a week it (unsurprisingly) looked horrible, and the panic intensified. So the village authorities made her husband take the corpse to a boundary in the high forest and burn it on the road, in front of a big crowd. But for some weeks afterwards, people still complained of attacks.[32]

It may not be coincidence that three motifs here—keeping a suspect corpse unburied, burning it on a boundary, and subsequent continuing problems—echo the reports of Hermann and Schertz from Moravia; the last two are also in the Kasparek story. An innovation, however, is that the starting-point was not plague but tuberculosis: this medical updating points the way to New England a century later. So does the motif of placing potentially dangerous organs in a box, which would reappear in Massachusetts in 1788 (p. 393).

Into Transylvania

Meanwhile, what is now the Transylvanian region of Romania had received its first reports from Sámuel Köléseri, a rationalistic physician (from a Calvinist background) working there during a plague in 1709. He mentions bloated and shroud-chewing corpses at Kiskerék/Broşteni (one man, two women, and a girl exhumed after thirty-four deaths); at Pókafalva/Păuca (an old Vlach woman and her granddaughter exhumed after eleven deaths); and at ?Ogra (a cow-herd exhumed after deaths in his own family). He then notes two earlier Transylvanian cases *not* during plague: near Hermannstadt/Sibiu (a soldier who appeared at night and strangled flocks and people); and at Bábolna/Rapoltu Mare (a Vlach wise-woman). The remedies were inversion, mouth-stones, and staking.[33] Further Transylvanian cases at Braşov and Devá were reported in the 1720s.[34]

All these episodes were in the Sibiu and Braşov region, at the heart of the Saxon-settled *Siebenbürgen*, but also on the Carpathian transhumance route. They could derive from Saxony, but the night-strangling and staking recall Bohemian and Croatian cases, not the grave-bound Saxon ones. They immediately followed the Moravian epidemic, which reinforces the sense of a mobile focus of intensity drifting southeastward. Once again, we find that a milieu of German colonization was a catalyst but not necessarily the source.

The Moravian epidemic permits—for the first time in this book—some tentative quantification. But even these data must surely be compromised by serious under-counting. We might set aside as atypical the mass corpse-burnings, but individual cases were regular in the villages of the affected regions, and we can only know a fraction of them. Earlier epidemics lack numbers completely, but are there any grounds for thinking that any fewer corpses were 'killed' in (for instance) Reformation Saxony?

This raises the larger question of how corpse-killing has compared numerically across time with witch-killing. The witch-killings are far better recorded. Boblig's witch persecution in northern Moravia up to the mid-1690s claimed about a hundred living victims, and is famous.[35] Far more corpses were 'killed' in the region over the next three decades, but who remembers that? In terms of human misery, of course, the witch-burnings were incomparably worse, but that is precisely the point. Everyone knows about witch persecution, but this far less tragic alternative has been erased from popular consciousness, and from all but a fringe of academic consciousness.

Whatever was happening on the ground, Köléseri's report shows that the educated gaze on corpse-killing had been moving along the Carpathians. It now turned southwards to its spectacular climax in a traumatised war-zone, as the intellectual inquisitiveness of German scholarship converged with the bureaucratic inquisitiveness of Habsburg governance.

31

Vampires in the News, 1725–57

> We have observed with displeasure . . . what recently happened in our margravate of Moravia: . . . various corpses were exhumed from a cemetery by clergy under pretext that they were afflicted with the so-called 'posthumous magic', and one of them was burned, even though investigation of the case revealed nothing unnatural. Since this often involves superstition and fraud, and we will in no way allow such sinful abuses in our territories, they will henceforth be subject to the most severe penalties.
>
> —THE EMPRESS MARIA THERESIA, DECREE OF 1 MARCH 1755

IT WAS ON the grim Balkan frontier between the Habsburg and Ottoman empires—unstable, heavily militarized, and crowded with displaced people—that the most famous vampire-killing episodes occurred in 1725 and 1731–2. They have been described more times, and received more commentary, than all other European appearances of the dangerous dead put together. Indeed, their importance has been grossly inflated, to the extent that some recent authors have placed the 'invention of the vampire' in this context (which is indeed when that specific word enters European printed discourse).

This book treats the epidemic like any other, highlighting significant new motifs and how they impacted on popular and learned perceptions: readers seeking more detail have abundant resources.[1] These episodes are still significant: for their motifs, their fame, and the impact that they had on perceptions in Europe and beyond.

Trauma on the Habsburg Military Frontier, 1725–32

The Ottoman Empire, which within living memory had threatened Austria and indeed Christendom, was in violent, spasmodic retreat. Its frontier zone now crossed the Habsburg territories of Bosnia-Herzegovina, Serbia, and the Banat of Temeswar. Most of Serbia and northern Bosnia were in Habsburg hands between treaties in 1718 and 1739, and in Turkish hands earlier and later. The zone was traversed by a militarized frontier under Habsburg rule. A poor terrain even in normal times, the combination of military rule, famine, and epidemic disease had brutalised it. The many rootless Serbs displaced from Ottoman zones included *hajduks*, free-wheeling bands of Serbian warriors and semi-bandits. These people hated the Ottomans, and the Austrians formed some of them into a militia.

Again it is thanks to Ádám Mézes's research that we can glimpse the scale of the epidemic in these south Habsburg borderlands (Figure 67).[2] To judge from the (certainly incomplete) evidence, it was shorter than the Moravian one, though perhaps sustained at a consistently higher level if we exclude the Moravian mass-burnings. Starting in the 1710s, it shows peaks in the 1720s to the 1740s and a climax in the 1750s, with an average of around fifteen known 'killings' per decade. Compared with other epidemics, this scale need not have been exceptional.

During 1725–6, two unquiet corpses in Serbia, Peter Blagojević in Kisilova/Kisiljevo and a *hajduk* called Arnaut Pavle ('Albanian Paul') in Medvedia/Medveđa, caused nine and four deaths respectively, and were exhumed and burned. The Habsburg authorities investigated the first case, but did not pursue it. Another outbreak at Medvedia in 1731, claiming thirteen victims, had started with Arnaut Pavle but intensified as further suspects emerged. The imperial administration in Belgrade sent

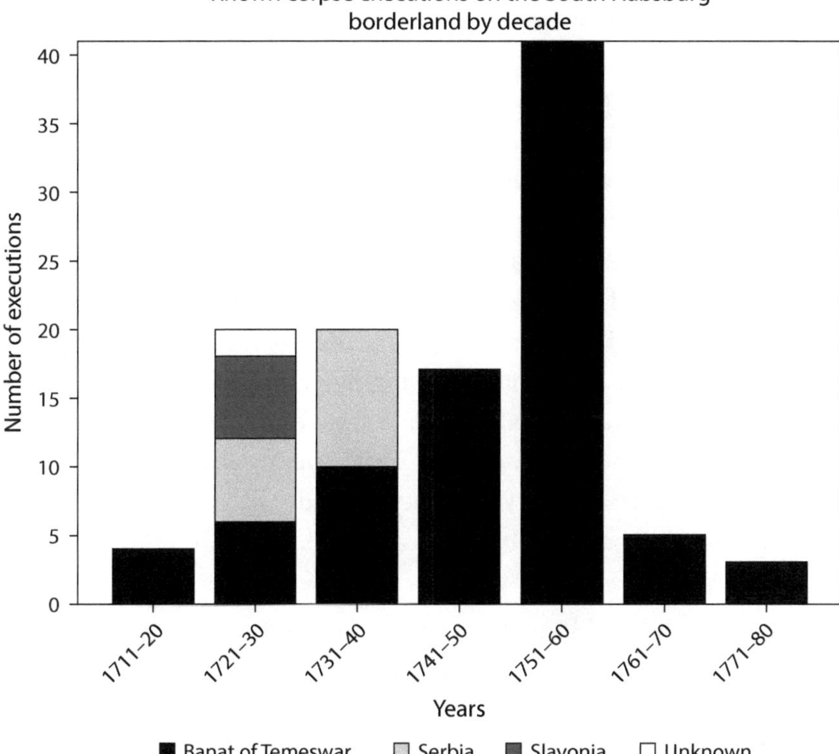

FIGURE 67: The incidence of recorded corpse executions in the region of the Habsburg military frontier. It is important to remember that many cases must have gone unrecorded, but the overall picture may be accurate.

another team of investigators, who reluctantly agreed to twelve exhumations and burnings.

These events interest us here for three different reasons. First, the military zone was a melting-pot of central European and Balkan cultures, and also of the catholic, Protestant, Orthodox, and Islamic faiths. Its psychological traumas, combined with the mobility of its inhabitants, made it exceptionally fertile soil in which fears of the dangerous dead could mutate. For instance, Arnaut Pavle had come from Turkish-controlled Serbia and had encountered a vampire there.

Secondly, this was when central European revenants converged with Balkan ones. Blagojević was a conventional night-strangler, but he came home to collect his shoes, and—like the Trzeszawa revenant of 1674 (p. 352)—he killed his own son. He also had in his mouth 'some fresh blood which, as all agreed, he had sucked from those he had murdered'.[3] Arnaut Pavle had been plagued by a vampire in Kosovo, but cured himself by eating soil from the vampire's grave, and (like Evliya Çelebi's *obur* victims, p. 293) by smearing himself with its blood. Even so, he became a vampire after breaking his neck in a fall. In turn, one of the women who started the 1731 epidemic died from eating the meat of sheep that Pavle and his victims had killed, while the other confessed on her deathbed to smearing herself with corpse-blood to protect herself from vampires.

This is a unique combination of highly-coloured motifs, formed in the context of acute trauma. A strange vagary of chance was to make it the staple of later vampire literature. That happened because of the third outcome: the extraordinary intensity of academic interest in the topic during 1732–3, unequalled before or since.

Hitting the Headlines: The Intellectual Response and Popular Media

This dynamic started with the Habsburg bureaucracy, which responded to the strange rumours by dispatching a series of investigators. District Provisor Frombald's report on the Blagojević case was then picked up by the Leipzig scholar Michael Ranft in a monograph of 1725, which quoted it as 'the most recent and memorable case' in what is otherwise a derivative reprisal of Garmann and Rohr.[4] In an enlarged edition three years later, he developed the thoroughly rationalistic line that Blagojević's wife had murdered him and that his 'victims' died of contagion or terror.[5]

The reports from 1731–2, by Imperial Physician Glaser and Regimental Surgeon Flückinger, had a more dramatic impact. The first pebble in the avalanche was a letter written on 3 February 1732 by Glaser's father, Dr Johann Friedrich Glaser, and published in a Nuremberg scholarly journal.[6] In his phrase *Omnibus igitur his* Vampyris *(sic scilicet in iiis oris vocantur)*... ('So from all these *vampires*—for thus they are called in those parts...'), the word 'vampire' entered western European vocabulary, where it would quickly swamp all the various alternatives. The response was electrifying: the popular press quickly picked up the story, which reached even London papers in March. For academics—notably in Leipzig, where Garmann and Rohr had written their gently sceptical accounts—it became a nine-month wonder. No fewer than twelve books on the subject, in Latin and German, were published before the end of 1732.[7]

These works are of some interest in the intellectual and scientific history of the Enlightenment. Several of them, and the medical reports on which they were based, were digested by Michael Ranft into a third and much larger version of his treatise (in German rather than Latin, to tap a market that had expanded beyond academic circles).[8] Like the events, this material has been very thoroughly discussed: suffice it to say here that the pervading tone was sceptical.[9] Whatever ideas may have lingered in certain Catholic circles, it was becoming untenable for scholars to take seriously any idea of dead people occupying their own corpses, or even of demons doing so.

Olomouc's Last Fling: Debate and Suppression, 1733–55

Meanwhile, back in Moravia, corpse-killing had subsided from the epidemic level of the 1720s, but was still regularly reported up to 1738 (Figure 64). Thereafter, no condemnations by the Olomouc consistory are recorded until 1755. It is hardly coincidence that a new and more engaged bishop, Jacob Ernst of Liechenstein-Kastelkorn, arrived there in 1738. Committed to better religious education and pastoral care, he may temporarily have suppressed this aspect of the consistory's work: perhaps vampire-plagued villagers and clergy did not make official reports, knowing that they would fall on deaf ears.[10]

Jacob Ernst typified a new and more sceptical generation of Church leaders. The bishop of Poznań condemned corpse-killing in 1739, only two decades after the bishop of Kraków had allowed Kasparek to be burned.[11] The Venetian authorities were now taking a rationalistic approach to corpse-killing outbreaks on the Dalmatian coast.[12] And in 1741, the archbishop of Trani wrote an analysis of the problem with entirely sceptical conclusions, ascribing vampire phenomena to the collective imagination.[13] Habsburg administrators in the Transylvanian zone shifted in the early 1750s from authorizing burnings (in the interests of calming people down) to banning and punishing them.[14] In Olomouc, another change of bishop in 1745 brought Ferdinand Julius Troyer, a reformer and devoted supporter of Habsburg rule who 'made first attempts to limit pomp and eccentricity of some devotions'.[15]

In that context, the last spectacular episode comes as a surprise. In 1754–5, the Olomouc consistory and a local estate court responded to an outbreak of vampire infestation in the village of Frei Hermersdorf/ Svobodné Heřmanice. After investigations and witness depositions, nineteen exhumed corpses were condemned in a highly ritualized and theatrical spectacle. On 30 January 1755 the judges assembled outside the cemetery, the verdict was read out, and the corpses were dragged through a hole in the cemetery wall. At dawn the next day they were loaded onto a cart and burned by the executioner, together with the shrouds, coffins, and grave-crosses.[16]

That was too much for the outraged sensibilities of Empress Maria Theresia. She dispatched investigators, who reported back to her trusted court physician Gerard van Swieten (Figure 68). He in turn conducted the most meticulous enquiry, including witness interrogations, and wrote a thorough report. Van Swieten and the Empress were of one mind: all the strange effects could be explained medically, there was no such thing as an unquiet corpse, and much blame should be laid on the superstitious and fraudulent ways of many Catholic clergy.[17]

Maria Theresia's decree of 1 March, condemning superstition and fraud and bringing such matters under imperial control, 'attests to an intense clash between local and central levels of authority and expertise'.[18] (Bishop Troyer's role here is an enigma: perhaps he had simply left such matters to the consistory, though the Empress held him responsible and scolded him soundly.[19]) Pope Benedict XIV (1740–58), a confirmed vampire-sceptic, eagerly supported the Empress, and now proposed banning all trials of corpses.[20] That was not quite the end of high-profile cases: in 1757—supposedly—Bishop Mikołaj Dembowski of Kamianets-Podilskyi (now western Ukraine) was posthumously beheaded and then burned by his own cathedral clergy because his corpse

FIGURE 68: The man who tried to kill corpse-killing: bust of Gerard van Swieten by F. X. Messerschmidt, 1769. For the educated world, van Swieten's meticulous investigation provided the final proof that undead corpses are imaginary.

became aggressive (Figure 60).[21] But we only have this story from a polemicist with a grudge, and increasingly such episodes seemed anomalous and bizarre.

It was thus in the mid-1750s that the academic debate shifted decisively: from gently sceptical respect for different opinions to Enlightened scorn of clerical obscurantism, superstition, and greed.[22] Of future consequence was the gulf that this opened between educated Catholics and Protestants on the one hand, who increasingly ridiculed the whole idea of vampires, and Orthodox clergy on the other, for whom they were built into theology and pastoral care. Defining the Habsburg monarchy as the home of Enlightened reason meant defining the Orthodox east as the home of barbarous stupidity: as van Swieten put it, 'all these occurrences are only to be found in areas where ignorance still prevails. It is also likely that the schismatic Greeks are the principal source'.[23] Orthodox clergy had both a confessional and a financial interest in the importance of clean white bones, and in the power of excommunication over those unfortunates who resisted decay.[24] The western boundary of Orthodox belief would increasingly become a frontier of corpse-killing.

Calmet and Voltaire

Augustin Calmet (1672–1757), Benedictine abbot of Senones near the French border with Lorraine, dominates the history of vampire studies (Figure 9). He was an omnivorous scholar—in the traditional monastic mode—and an amiable man: sociable, tolerant, and unpretentious. He became interested in vampires when an official of the Duke of Lorraine (the bishop of Olomouc's brother) sent him information about the Moravian cases.[25] The treatise that he wrote on the subject was a minor item in a huge literary output that included an influential Bible commentary. He drew the ridicule—but also the satirical affection—of a far greater figure, today almost synonymous with the French Enlightenment.

Calmet's *Dissertations on . . . Revenants and Vampires of Hungary, Bohemia, Moravia and Silesia,* first published in 1746, broke with the cut-and-paste style of earlier works, to which Ranfft and others had merely grafted the new medical reports. He chose examples widely but selectively: from the classical and Jewish worlds, modern Greece, William of Newburgh's England, and of course the sensational recent cases. He writes as a historian, philosopher, and theologian, for unprejudiced people who want to assess the evidence fairly, while making clear that he thinks that the case for vampires is weak.[26]

Calmet had no illusions about his reception: 'I risk being criticized however I go about it. Those who think [vampires] are real will accuse me of temerity and presumption for casting doubt on them, or even denying their actual existence. Others will blame me for having spent my time on this matter, which seems trivial and fruitless from the viewpoint of sensible people.'[27] The book proved a best-seller, though it did attract the predicted grumbles. Calmet engaged and corresponded with his critics, and produced enlarged and revised editions in 1749 and 1751.[28] German and English translations followed, reflecting abiding popular interest.[29]

Calmet's problem was that he was applying the Enlightenment virtue of rigorous, impartial enquiry to a subject which—in the eyes of Enlightenment thinkers—represented the worst kind of obscurantism and superstition. His aims were admirable, but his determination to reconcile scientific observation with scriptural infallibility drew him into logical contortions.[30]

That was the background to his engagement with Voltaire, who had earlier used Calmet's monumental commentary as a tool for demonstrating that scripture cannot be infallible.[31] Curiously enough, Voltaire stayed at Senones with Calmet for three weeks in 1754, using his host's library and taking full advantage of his good-nature.[32] When Calmet died in 1757—just two years after the Empress banned vampire-killing—Voltaire sent warm condolences to Senones, with a verse praising his learning, faith, and 'simplicity' (possibly in both senses of the word).[33] But seven years later he wrote, ungratefully and unfairly: 'What? This is our eighteenth century, and there are vampires? It is after the reign of Locke, Shaftesbury, Trenchard, Collins; it is during the reign of d'Alembert, Diderot, Saint-Lambert, Duclos: and we believe in vampires! The Reverend Father Dom Augustin Calmet . . . , abbot of Senones, an abbey with rents of 100,000 livres, printed and reprinted the history of vampires. . . . The real vampires are the monks, who eat at the expense of kings and peoples.'[34] This ambiguous relationship marks a symbolic watershed in our story: between the old world where belief in animated corpses was at least arguable, and the modern world where it just seems crazy.

Voltaire did not get the last word: corpse-killing still had more than a century's life ahead of it in pockets across the empire and German lands. The 1750s did, however, see a perceptual shift from the arena of serious debate to that of amused detachment: local survivals became objects of official annoyance, ethnographic curiosity, or literary inventiveness, rather than of theological or scientific concern. The Empress, Van Swieten, Calmet, and Voltaire all contributed to transforming dangerous corpses from a present fear into a fictional construct.

PART VI

The Modern World

TOWARDS FOLKLORE AND FICTION

AFTER 1750, few Europeans with educational or intellectual pretensions would admit to believing in vampires. Corpse-killing practices retreated into increasingly confined pockets in Europe and its colonial diaspora, but in some of those pockets they proved resilient.

Like some religious ideas from the Old World, the restless dead had a vigorous future life beyond the Atlantic. The belief in grave-bound but noxious corpses had helped sixteenth-century German Lutherans to fight disempowerment in the face of plague. Now it would do the same service for their colonial descendants, battered by the equally terrifying and inexplicable scourge of tuberculosis.

But increasingly, genuine folk survivals melded with motifs recycled from the published accounts, and then with Romantic fiction. These final chapters take the story on from eighteenth-century believers and sceptics to modern devotees of Count Dracula.

32

Vampires for a Scientific Age

PENNSYLVANIA AND NEW ENGLAND

Bodies to be Exhumed. The subscriber being the only survivor of a large family of brothers and sisters, all of whom have died of that dread disease, consumption, and whose children are following them by the same disease, has consented that the bodies of some of the first who died may be exhumed to satisfy the belief entertained that it will arrest the further progress of the disease. . . . The exhumation will take place on Saturday, April 29th, at 10 o'clock A.M. . . . This notice is given that all interested may be present.

—ADVERTISEMENT IN A PENNSYLVANIA NEWSPAPER, 1871

AS THE ONLY significant epidemic of corpse-killing in a modern Western society, the events in post-Revolutionary New England are not quite like anything else. It is thanks to the pioneering work of Michael E. Bell that the evidence is accessible, and this chapter could not have been written without him.[1] The unusually plentiful sources document interactions between medicine and folk-belief, and between written and oral circulation of ideas, that escape us in most other contexts.

Consumption's Vampire Grasp

During the nineteenth century, pulmonary tuberculosis ('consumption') killed up to a quarter of the population in the north-eastern United States. The heart-rending decline of victims, coughing up blood and already corpse-like before their almost certain deaths, readily suggested the image used in an elegy of 1838: 'consumption's vampire grasp'.[2] Some people took that literally. Between 1784 and 1892, consumption-wracked families blamed the disease on the still-active internal organs of dead relatives, and took appropriate action. About seventy exhumations are recorded in New England (at least nineteen of them in Rhode Island), thirteen in New York State, three (probably a serious under-estimate) in Pennsylvania, and one in Canada.

Why New England in particular? Very reasonably, Bell invokes the convergence of 'several different cultural groups, and in several variations', including diverse northern European settlers.[3] Even so, other eighteenth- and nineteenth-century communities were ravaged by tuberculosis, and influenced by quack-doctors, without developing a belief in vampires. Likewise, Americans could read lurid vampire stories disseminated by the European press, but so could a worldwide reading public that absorbed such entertainment without taking it seriously.

There must have been an exceptional convergence of factors, brought together and energized by medical tragedy. Bell's more recent work emphasizes a distinctive ingredient: the New England tradition of Paracelsian remedies, using body-parts and human blood, from the time of the poet Edward Taylor (c. 1642–1729).[4] One might add the stresses of a colonial society that had recently won a war of independence: Haiti comes to mind in that respect, extremely different though it is in others (p. 428). More elusively, it seems possible to glimpse anxieties about young adult females that resonate with New England's earlier witch-hunting tragedy, as well as with themes familiar from this book.

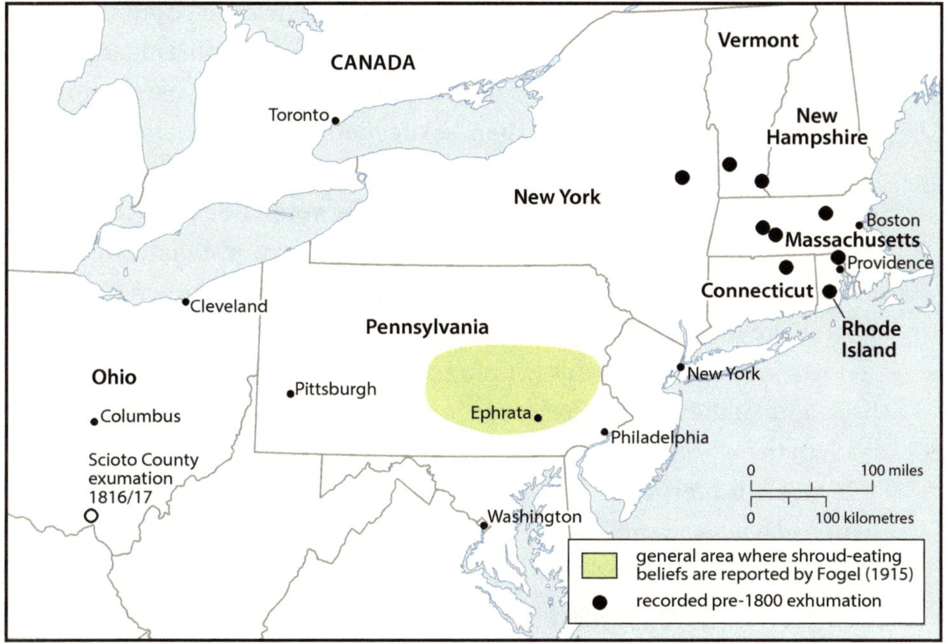

MAP 8: Corpse-killing in the United States up to 1800.

The Shroud-Chewer Emigrates to Pennsylvania

Tens of thousands of German speakers, mainly from the Rhenish Palatinate, settled in eastern Pennsylvania between the 1680s and 1760s. There they retained their language—a Palatinate dialect of German—and a distinct identity.[5] A collection of their oral folk-culture, published in 1915, contains this revealing item: 'If there are many deaths in a family in rapid succession, the grave of the first of those to die should be opened, to see whether the corpse has not drawn a part of its shroud into its mouth.'[6]

It will be recalled that the Rhineland was outside the European zone where the most alarming beliefs and practices flourished after 1500, and that its older culture of corpse-killing had faded. Accordingly, some motifs were *not* exported, notably the lip-smacking idea and the practice of beheading. It was more muted approaches to shroud-chewing that the colonists took with them, to be preserved in this enclosed community. A Pennsylvania newspaper in 1857 ran the story of Sophia Bauman, daughter of Peter Bauman of Ephrata, who had died of consumption some nine years earlier. Since then, every member of this large family had died, except one brother who feared the same fate: 'The belief was seriously entertained and acted upon, that by some hocus pocus the winding sheet of the corpse had got into her mouth, and that by continual suction, (the *modus operandi* of which was only known to the spirits) she had actually drawn the other five members of the family after her; and that unless this winding sheet was speedily removed from the mouth of the corpse, she would in like manner cause the premature death of the whole connection.'[7]

In this mild response, it seems likely that the shroud-chewer paradigm had been softened by the assimilation of different folklore motifs about shrouds and grave-clothes, where it is the wrappings rather than the corpse itself that cause problems. The idea (also recorded in Pensylvania in 1915)[8] that if a corpse is buried in clothes belonging to a living person, the owner will wither and die, figures in what must be the latest of all the American 'vampire' exhumations, performed in 1949 (Figure 69).

New England and Central European Influences in the Eighteenth Century

In one way or another, the New England vampires must go back to Central European traditions. It is hard to think of any other source, and it is indicative that, like the shroud-chewers of Saxony, they lay inert in their graves. The new environment was associated with other modifications: whereas the *first* to die was normally targeted as the culprit in German cases, it was the *last* to die in most New England cases. German sectarians from Pennsylvania, some with links to occultists, are known to have influenced Connecticut and Rhode Island's rich mix of magico-religious beliefs during the eighteenth century,[9] but New England also contained many direct immigrants from the Rhineland and neighbouring regions.

PRINCIPALS IN WITCHCRAFT CASE

REUBEN ROCK
"The thing crawled."

MRS. ROSELLA ROCK
"She was wasting away."

Dead GI's Body Exhumed To Break "Spell" on Widow

"Reuben's body is now at peace with the Lord."

With these words the family of Arthur Dively explained to Altoona Mirror representatives last evening a strange graveside ritual over the body of a dead veteran whose "restless spirit" had disturbed their household and brought his 22-year-old widow to the verge of a nervous breakdown.

The ritual, performed the morning of George Washington's birthday, consisted of exhuming the body of Pvt. Reuben C. Rock in Upper Claar cemetery. The United States army uniform in which Pvt. Rock was buried was stripped from the body and burned at the grave. Then the body was sprinkled with salt and enclosed in a sheet and blanket before being committed once again to the grave.

Thus was exorcised the evil influence which had upset the Dively house since their son-in-law was buried on Jan. 16. And now, according to the family, Rosella, his widow, has been freed from the spell which had held her in its grip since her veteran husband died.

Tied in with the weird tale of Reuben Rock is a series of charges and counter-charges of witchcraft which has upset the entire Bulls

(Continued on page 2, column 6)

FIGURE 69: The shroud-chewer's last descendant. After Private Reuben Rock died at Altoona, Pennsylvania, in 1949, his widow Rosella seemed to be wasting away. Remembering that the uniform in which they had buried him was technically Rosella's property, the family exhumed him and burnt it. This seems to be the last known corpse-killing in a non-Balkan and non-Aegean Western society. *Altoona Mirror*, 4 March 1949.

After the 1760s, increasing numbers of healers, surgeons, and medicine-sellers, alongside other would-be experts and practitioners from England, Germany, and France, were also active there. These itinerant and often suspect entrepreneurs, who operated through taverns, coffee-houses, and newspaper advertisements, targeted precisely those backwoods and marginal communities in Connecticut and Rhode Island where vampire-exhuming would flourish over the next century.[10] These 'other' New Englanders, writes Bell, 'participated in various hybrid religions that were unofficial combinations of Christian beliefs and folk practices', and 'experimented with a worldview that tapped into alchemy, astrology, divination, seeing stones, dowsing, and other practices that Puritans viewed as diabolical'.[11] Ideas about dangerous corpses—whether from Pennsylvania or direct from Germany—landed on this fertile ground and took root.

To complicate matters further, this was also an age of mass print media. German practitioners, if literate, could have read some of the central European exhumation reports, or Calmet. And on top of established Paracelsian ideas, sensational stories in the popular press could have enriched the mix. On 21 January 1765, the *Connecticut Courant* ran a front-page article titled 'The surprising account of those spectres called vampyres', re-cycling one of the standard narratives of Balkan vampire-killing.[12] The *Boston Evening Post* replicated it on (significantly) 1 April 1765. An outraged correspondent protested on 15 April that such nonsense was 'calculated to frighten old women and children, to amuse the ignorant and superstitious, and to promote deism and infidelity in the world'. If the April Fool was too subtle for this reader, less literate consumers could have taken it seriously. Did this light-hearted page-filler help to convince 'ignorant and superstitious' New Englanders, devastated by consumption, that vampires were real? At any rate some of them held that view by the mid-1780s.

Eighteenth-Century Cases in New England

During 1784–99, ten exhumations are recorded in New England (Map 9).[13] Circumstances were diverse. In 1784, one Moses Holmes of Hartford, Connecticut, complained that 'of late years there has been advanced

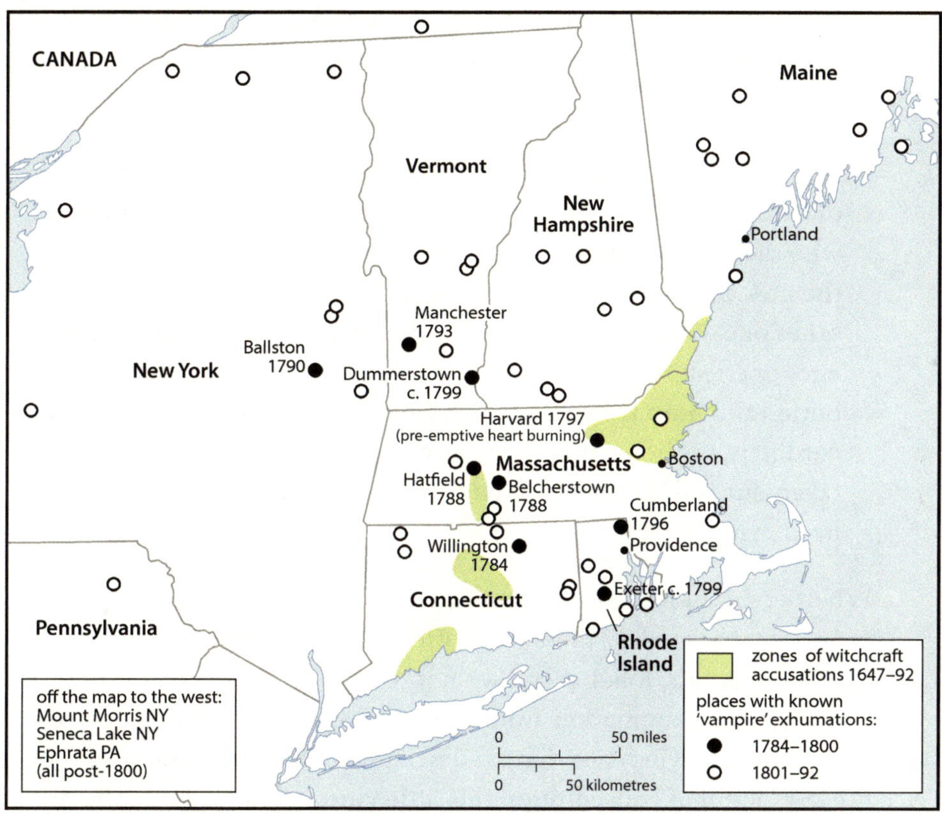

MAP 9: Corpse-killing in New England and adjoining states, 1784–1892.

for a certainty, by a certain Quack Doctor, a foreigner, that a certain cure may be had for consumption, where any of the same family has before that time died of the same disease: directing to have the bodies of such as had died to be dug up, and further said that out of the breast or vitals might be found a sprout or vine fresh and growing, which, together with the remains of the vitals, being consumed in the fire, would be an effectual cure to the same family'. He adds that two bodies (children of Isaac Johnson) had recently been dug up at Willington; and that although the remains looked normal, 'under the coffin was sundry small sprouts about one inch in length, then fresh, but most likely was the produce of sorrel seeds which fell under the coffin when put in the earth.'[14]

This procedure resurfaces in the late 1790s, when several members of a family at Dummerston, Vermont, had died of consumption and another daughter was failing:

> Among the superstitions of those days, we find it was said that a vine or root of some kind grew from coffin to coffin, of those of one family, who died of consumption, and were buried side by side; and when the growing vine had reached the coffin of the last one buried, another one of the family would die; the only way to destroy the influence or effect, was to break the vine; take up the body of the last one buried and burn the vitals, which would be an effectual remedy. Accordingly, the body of the last one buried was taken up and the vitals taken out and burned, and the daughter, it is affirmed, got well and lived many years.[15]

Whether this motif of a grave-generated creeping plant was a folk-belief or an eccentric medical theory, it is otherwise unknown in vampire folklore. At all events, folk-belief is what it soon became. The narrative of a New England exhumation around 1840 observes that 'there is a tradition among the Germans that if a descendant pluck from the corpse of the last victim of consumption this little vine, it will eradicate the disease from the family.'[16]

Other cases look different again. In 1786, there is a frustratingly laconic reference at Charleston, New Hampshire, to the body of an Irish traveller being exhumed and boiled—a procedure unique in this book.[17] In 1788, at Belchertown (Massachusetts), an educated and open-minded minister named Justus Forward, with three children dead of consumption and two more in imminent danger, 'consulted many about opening the graves of some of the deceased, to see whether there were any signs of the *dead preying on the living*'. Having first exposed and rejected a fully decayed corpse, they exhumed his daughter who had died nearly six years earlier:

> On opening the body, the lungs were not dissolved, but had blood in them, though not fresh, but clotted. The lungs did not appear as we would suppose they would in a body just dead, but far nearer a state

> of soundness than could be expected. The liver, I am told, was as sound as the lungs. We put the lungs and liver in a separate box, and buried it in the same grave, ten inches or a foot, above the coffin.[18]

In contrast to this restrained treatment, in 1790 Josiah Hewitt (a Connecticut man who moved to Ballston, New York) exhumed his dead daughter, when two other children were sick with consumption, and burned her whole body (Figure 10).[19] At Cumberland, Rhode Island, in 1796, Stephen Staples was enigmatically permitted to exhume his daughter Abigail 'in order to Try an Experiment' on Livinia, Abigail's living sister, and then rebury her.[20] That leaves three cases involving young female subjects—to which we will return—in which the organs were extracted and burned.

While the European origins of the dangerous-dead beliefs are obvious, other influences were probably also at work. Most intriguing is the longstanding New England tradition of Paracelsian medicine, which could have laid the ground for beliefs in the power and danger of specific organs. That helps to explain why such a strong emphasis was now placed on the internal organs as the seat of a lethal vitality, and a consequent need to destroy them.

Even so, the web of beliefs retained older strands: these backwoods communities were as receptive to traditional magic as to modern medicine. If we dig deeper, we might find some more organic traditions and instincts at work.

Dangerous Girls?

The known exhumations show a marked imbalance in both age and gender: most of the subjects were in the age-group fourteen to thirty—especially fourteen to twenty-four—and of those nearly two-thirds were female.[21] Objectively, there is a straightforward explanation. In New England during 1850–80, young women were heavily over-represented among victims of tuberculosis, which caused nearly half of all female deaths between the ages of fifteen and twenty-nine.[22] It is possible, though, that this medical fact has cognitive implications. We have repeatedly noted the spiritually-charged quality of this demographic group, which was now so eerily targeted by the dreaded consumption.

One earlier episode might offer some context. Notoriously, the Puritan communities of New England saw enthusiastic witchcraft prosecutions through the second half of the seventeenth century.[23] Activity fluctuated between peaks and lulls during c. 1647–70, and then died off until the last and worst outburst, in Essex County (including Salem, Andover, and Danvers) in 1692. Reactions of horror and guilt to the Salem disaster fed an already emergent scepticism about witchcraft, and encouraged its eventual decriminalization. This tragic episode sprang from a combination of internal social stress, failures of leadership, and paranoia as the brittle, inflexible regime of the Puritan 'saints' felt increasingly threatened.

Were witch-hunting and vampire-hunting divergent responses—one severely orthodox, the other off-beat and eclectic—to the same deep layer in the New England psyche? The point of comparison is not with the accused in the witch-trials, but with one group among their accusers: the people who were supposedly bewitched. Their age and gender profile were similar: of forty-three people diagnosed as 'afflicted' in seventeenth-century Massachusetts Bay, more than three-quarters were females, and nearly half were females aged between sixteen and twenty-two.[24] And here we are back in a familiar world: of young women engaging in extreme and transgressive behaviour, claiming to have acquired second-sight and access to the occult through their supernatural afflictions.[25] Later, one of the bewitched had a vision of her brother's death at the moment when it happened, forty miles away.[26] Such a woman fitted into society uneasily: she was a victim, but the experience had given her an uncanny new identity.

The vampire epidemic began nearly a century after Salem, and—as Map 9 illustrates—its heartlands in Rhode Island and Connecticut largely avoided the old centres of witchcraft persecution. There is one tenuous link: the Isaac Johnson who exhumed his children in 1784—the first known case in New England—was apparently related to Elizabeth Johnson, a young woman convicted of witchcraft in 1692.[27] Did family stories of her supernatural power weigh on him? A more important question is whether the dead women who would later be exhumed and mutilated in New England were likened—possibly at some level of collective consciousness preserved in oral tradition—to the earlier 'afflicted'. They were victims too, strangled in 'consumption's vampire grasp', but they also spread an insidious, lethal poison from their undead internal organs.

The rather clinical accounts of exhumations rarely offer individualized perceptions of the dead. The few subjects who do emerge as active agents, however, were all young females. Two of them were resolute enough to pre-empt their posthumous fate. In 1797 a dying girl in the town of Harvard, Massachusetts (probably Anna Bowles) 'extracted from friends a solemn promise that her heart should be consumed for the benefit of her sisters'.[28] Another in about 1847, at Chesterfield, Massachusetts, 'determined that her own "vitals" should never become ghoulish creatures feeding upon the life blood of nearest kindred', so ordered them to be cut out and burned before her burial.[29] Apparently less altruistic was Rachel Burton (née Harris), 'a fine, healthy, beautiful girl' who died at Manchester, Vermont, in 1790 after a year's marriage (Figure 70). Her husband quickly remarried, but the new wife sickened with consumption. In 1793, therefore, Rachel was exhumed and her organs burned, as a 'sacrifice to the Demon Vampire who it was believed was still sucking the blood of the then living wife'.[30]

Another familiar stratum of terror breaks surface with Sarah Tillinghast of Exeter, Rhode Island. After she died in 1799, five of her sisters died in succession and her brother and mother sickened, Sarah having visited all the sickbeds in night-mare form (p. 29). When her body was exhumed it 'was found to be in a very remarkable condition. The eyes were open and fixed. The hair and nails had grown and the heart and the arteries were filled with fresh red blood'.[31] Unfortunately this narrative only occurs in a source from 1888, which could have been influenced by the vampire literature then current. Still, this exhumation really happened, and an authentic sleep-paralysis case (unique among documented American vampires if so) may underlie the embellished story.

In their different ways, these young women are ascribed emotional power and agency while conforming to recognizable vampire templates.

FIGURE 70: The headstone of Rachel Burtun (born Harris), 1790, in Factory Point cemetery, Manchester, Vermont. 'Amiable Consort' though she may have been, her husband re-married quickly. Suspected of 'sucking the blood of the then living wife', Rachel was exhumed in 1793, and her heart, liver, and lungs burnt in the blacksmith's forge.

There is a strange convergence here between embedded folk-belief and fictional Romantic overtones. An observer at the exhumation of a sixteen-year-old girl at Plymouth, Massachusetts, in 1807 would report to the newspapers in 1822:

> Displacing the flat lid, they lifted the covering from her face and discovered what they had indeed anticipated, but dreaded to

> declare—Yes, I saw the visage of one who had been long the tenant of a silent grave, lit up with the brilliancy of youthful health. The cheek was full to dimpling, and a rich profusion of hair shaded her cold forehead, while some of its richest curls floated upon her unconscious breast. The large blue eye had scarcely lost its brilliancy, and the livid fullness of her lips seemed almost to say, 'loose me and let me go'.[32]

This eye-witness sounds thoroughly convinced by what he saw, and even reworked his experience as an eerie little poem (p. 432). But there must surely be some influence here from the beautiful, seductive female vampires evoked by Goethe and his literary successors. Did belief that mirrored fiction converge with fiction that mirrored belief?

Nineteenth-Century New England: Folk-Belief, Paracelsian Theory, and Modern Medicine

After 1800, the practice of exhumation diffused into the more northerly regions of New England and New York State, while remaining strong in Rhode Island and Connecticut (Map 9).[33] It acquired a more stable form that Bell calls the 'consumption ritual', moving through the stages of (1) exhumation; (2) diagnosis, by finding fresh blood in the heart or other organs; (3) neutralization, by extracting and burning the organs, turning the corpse face-down, or occasionally burning it completely; and (4) restoration of the afflicted, who might ingest the ashes of the offending organs or inhale smoke from their burning.[34]

While metropolitan newspapers and later commentators deplored the ignorance and superstition, some exhumations were carried out in the presence of doctors and religious leaders who expressed no disapproval.[35] What did people think was really going on? A fear of 'the dead preying on the living' seems implicit, if rarely stated directly, in some of the earlier cases. But were these conscious predators, or vehicles for some impersonal lethal force?

In 1837, a doctor recalled the case of a consumptive patient in Essex County, Massachusetts, around 1812:

> She was a young woman, and of a family predisposed to this disease, of which several had already died—at this juncture a strolling Indian doctor came into the neighborhood, and hearing of her sickness called at the house. With great solemnity he told her father that the course of her disease, and the continual wasting of her flesh were occasioned by a brother who had last died of the disease, three years before, and whose heart he affirmed was still fresh and plump, and drew in some mysterious manner its support from her blood. The remedy proposed, he said was infallible; which was to take up the dead body of her brother, separate the heart from its attachment, burn it to ashes; and let the sick woman drink it in a decoction which he would prepare from 'roots and herbs.'[36]

The culprit here is not the brother but his heart, and if its operations are 'mysterious' the remedy is essentially medical. There are other statements of this idea, including this report of a case in the 1840s: 'The story said that, when one member of a family died with consumption, his or her "vitals", meaning by that term the lungs, heart, and liver, became animated after burial and came back to earth in invisible form to prey upon the "vitals" of others in the family.'[37]

This reads like an inversion of Paracelsian medical theory, the link with universal spirit matter becoming lethal rather than beneficial. There are obvious reasons why bereaved relatives might prefer it to the idea that their dead children and siblings were attacking them. In that sense, it is a new and more scientific re-invention of the noxious but impersonal energy released by shroud-chewing corpses in Lutheran Germany.

Through the mid- to late nineteenth century, this kind of explanation co-existed with a traditional 'fear of the dead' but gradually gained ground. It resonated with the ideas of Joseph von Görres, who thought that vampiric corpses spread 'consumption' from the grave (p. 401) and whose book could have reached German-speaking Catholics in the United States. From 1869—when handbooks of popular science were widespread—one account envisages 'a sort of vital current existing between the living and dead', another that 'there exists between blood relations a sympathetic link which death does not entirely sever, and which, unless interrupted, oftentimes works injury'.[38] To dismiss such ideas as delusional is anachronistic: they belonged to the same experimental and speculative surge that has created modern physics, electronics, and medicine. Vampires were re-invented for a scientific age.

There would probably have been no vampires in New England without the groups of German-speaking immigrants, who transported stories of grave-bound dangerous corpses to ready listeners. Equally, the shroud-chewer would not have transmuted into a host for death-dealing bodily organs without the tradition of Paracelsian medicine, practised in New England from the later seventeenth century. And, operating though it did in a 'modern' society, the belief stirred up a more deeply-rooted fear: of young females cut off at the height of their uncanny power.

These ideas would not, however, have had traction in popular practice without the deadly scourge of tuberculosis. For parents and siblings, paralyzed and helpless in the face of multiple deaths, a procedure that was ritualized, comprehensible, and (within its own terms) scientific offered an escape-route. The New England vampire-killing episode counts as an epidemic, but it also illustrates once again how epidemics erupt out of endemic beliefs. In some ways the strangest of them all, it still followed the rules.

33

'The Horrible Scenes of Old Time'

EUROPE AFTER 1750

The horrible scenes of old time, when the suspected body was dragged from its grave and dismembered by a panic-stricken and desperate mob, when the heart, as sometimes happened, was torn out and boiled to shreds in vinegar, or when the ghastly remains were burnt on a public bonfire, have certainly become rarer. . . . None the less the superstition itself still holds a firm place among the traditional beliefs of modern Greece.

—J. C. LAWSON, 1910

CORPSE-KILLING continued in Romania, Greece, Bulgaria, Serbia, Poland, and Prussia beyond 1900, and lower-level concerns have been noted by folklorists much more widely across Europe east of the Rhine. The big eighteenth-century change was not that these beliefs became extinct, but that they became largely extinct among the educated and urban. The Habsburg military frontier makes the point: a trickle of corpse-killings continued into at least the 1770s (Figure 67), but by then they were covert, and punished when brought to official notice.

Even so, exceptions can be found. Reportedly, King George II of England (died 1760) 'had no doubt of the existence of vampires and their banquets of the dead'.[1] He had lived for thirty years in Hannover, on the edge of the shroud-chewer belt, and the vampire craze of 1732 must have impinged on him. If this stolid, unintellectual ruler with rudimentary theology continued to take vampires seriously, other secular aristocrats may have done the same.

Among intellectuals, one throwback was the Catholic Romantic polemicist Joseph von Görres, a professor at Munich. In his *Christian Mysticism* (1840) he argued that vampiric corpses retained a 'vegetal' life, preserving them intact and full of blood. Such corpses spread contagion to the living, who wasted away with 'consumption', died, and then resumed a life-like appearance as they became vampires themselves. Burning, Görres thought, was the only remedy for this malady, which would otherwise spread on an epidemic scale.[2] This would have seemed cranky to most educated Germans, but Görres was a popular author—especially in Catholic circles—and his ideas resonated with what was currently happening in America.[3]

The faintly sinister figure of Montague Summers (1880–1948) brings educated belief in vampires to its eccentric finale. A brilliant scholar of Restoration drama, he posed as a Roman Catholic priest and immersed himself (to an unclear extent) in occultism. His *The Vampire: His Kith and Kin* (1928) and *The Vampire in Europe* (1929) were the most substantial works on the subject since Calmet; they combine encyclopaedic knowledge with startling lapses in critical judgement. Perhaps it should not matter that Summers believed in the real existence of his subjects, but it is surprising—to put it mildly—in a modern academic work. 'To burn the body of the Vampire is generally acknowledged to be by far the supremely efficacious method of ridding a district of this demoniacal pest, and it is the common practice all over the world', he tells us with a straight face.[4]

By then, in more mainstream circles, vampires had long been objects of ethnographic interest rather than belief. An early illustration is the work of the Italian priest Alberto Fortis, whose book on Dalmatia and its Morlach inhabitants was published in 1774. His account of how the Morlachs forestalled vampirization (see p. 91) is embedded in a long description of their customs, song, and dance, pointing the way to Romantic interest in folklore and eventually to anthropology.[5]

Folklore, Fiction, and the Construction of Stories

If the likes of Görres and Summers could be taken seriously, survivals at the level of popular culture are hardly surprising. From 1850 onwards, folklore collections preserve stories and beliefs about the dangerous dead in abundant profusion. For historical purposes, it is hard to know what to make of them. While there is some stability in broad regional patterns, the material has been churned through the mill of greatly increased circulation—especially in print—and multiple re-workings.

In general, the late folklore collections ring the changes on older motifs described in this book, often worked up into elaborately extended narratives.[6] In the age of Romanticism and the Brothers Grimm, the line between 'genuine' folklore and scholars' creative re-working of it becomes hopelessly confused. Even items transcribed orally from storytellers can seem more like novellas than reports of what people really believed, as this Greek example illustrates:

> A soldier killed in a war became a vampire. His sergeant, who buried him, sent a letter to his wife about her husband's death. The vampirized soldier succeeded in avoiding being eaten by dogs (if a vampire can avoid dogs, it regains human form).
>
> So the soldier went back to his wife. They lived together except on Thursday and Saturday nights, which he spent outside his house. He returned at dawn holding pieces of liver. His wife fried them, but she did not eat them, for the liver smelled of soil (this shows that he took the liver from the dead). Each Sunday her husband went to church, but some people observed that he left at the point when the priest was preparing to take the sacred objects out of the sanctuary. He had two children whom he fed with livers.

> Such behaviour alerted and upset the villagers, who started suspecting him. Their suspicion turned to certainty when the sergeant who had buried him happened to come to the village. He went to the vampire's wife and told her to press the skin of her husband to see whether he had bones or not. Indeed she did as the sergeant told her and she discovered that her husband was just skin, swollen and boneless.
>
> Next Sunday all the villagers agreed to lock the doors and the windows in the church at the point when the vampire decided to leave. In fact, when the sacred objects were brought out they shut the doors and windows. The vampire and his children ran to leave the church, but they found the doors closed. At this moment, the priest came out of the sanctuary with the holy objects and a loud crack was heard. The vampire and his children exploded and they scattered like smoke, without leaving a trace.[7]

This speaks to the informed: 'becoming a vampire' is taken for granted, and the *tympaniaios* motif implied by the swollen skin does not need explaining. But did anyone really believe the narrative? Would some people believe it today in a tabloid newspaper? 'Believing' can mean different things. This kind of material does intersect with actual corpse-fearing and corpse-killing, but it also merges into fantasy fiction.

Favourable Climates for Corpse-Killing

Since the Enlightenment, the mutilation of corpses has offended the laws and sensibilities of much of Europe: the pockets where it survived require specific explanations. Three factors look especially important, though they mattered more in some regions than others.

One was continued Ottoman dominance—often chaotic and exploitative—over Christian populations in the Aegean, the Balkans, and Wallachia. Greece freed itself from the Turks in 1829, which was also when Wallachia and Romanian Moldova switched from Turkish to Russian control, finally gaining independence in 1859. Bulgaria became free, after a brutal independence war, in 1878. Until then, these regions were remote from the scientific and Enlightenment approaches that had been infiltrating western and central Europe for two centuries. For the rural laity, an oppressive colonial master with a different religion was conducive to the kind of brittle, adversarial resentment that breeds vampires.

The second factor was the Orthodox Church (Figure 71). In regions where it was under the Ottoman yoke, it was insulated from Catholic or Protestant criticism but existed on sufferance: it needed every supernatural weapon that it could muster, including the power to make corpses incorrupt (p. 309). It was everywhere more resistant to Enlightenment influence than its Western counterparts, less interested in educating the rural laity, and keener on quasi-magical ritual. Western observers were contemptuous: one commented in 1762 that Bulgarian village clergy 'do not know anything of their religion except for the fasts and holidays, the sign of the cross, the cult of some image'; for another in 1785, Moldovan clergy were 'beggarly and hypocritical riff-raff'.[8]

Eventually, Orthodox theologians did understand that belief in vampires, and the claim to control corpses, made them a laughing-stock for their Western counterparts: by 1800 they were rejecting them.[9] That did not necessarily have much impact on rural priests. An observer of Romanians in the Banat of Temeswar in 1774 noted that priests 'visit people's houses, spreading false stories about miracles that had happened, or walk around with spells to banish the devil or *strigoi*'.[10] Long afterwards, priests in Greece and Romania would do little to discourage beliefs in sinister forces residing in human remains, and indeed would sometimes affirm them.

The third factor was differences in family structure, which meant that inter-generational conflict varied between regions in its nature and intensity. The long-accepted idea of contrasting western and eastern European marriage patterns is too simple: there was actually quite a complex mosaic, many of the details of which remain to be worked out.[11] Suffice it to say that until recently, the regions where dangerous-dead fears survived late have tended to be marked either by extended, multi-generation family structures, or by nuclear families in which elders exercised fierce control over the marriage choices of the young.

These were the contexts of the dead Wallachian mothers who pursued their sons to Sweden; of the cross-grained mothers-in-law in Am-

FIGURE 71: An Orthodox funeral: the priest is putting a passport to the next world into the dead man's hand. This engraving of 1723 illustrates the continuing importance of 'ritual magic' for the safe passage of the dead.

béli; and of 'Saint Friday' as a ferocious grandmother (pp. 39, 43, 129). The iron grip of the Russian *babushka* on her sometimes chaotic household is legendary; in Karelia and other Finno-Ugric regions, the mother-in-law could be a fearsome, sometimes hated figure for a young bride (Figure 5).[12] In this institutionalized power-struggle, the harshly subjected bride would eventually supplant the mother-in-law as mistress of the house, as for instance in Greece.[13] But might the offended matriarch fight back after death?

One scholar ascribes corpse-fears in the Greek folkloric material to 'indifference shown by the deceased to his or her parents, or lack of respect on the part of the daughter-in-law towards her mother-in-law. Both of these causes stem from failure to observe basic components of cultural capital that, when correctly observed, contribute to the perpetuation of the traditional kinship structure'.[14] In one story, a dead mother returns to mix flour with blood and tip over the cauldron in her disobedient daughter's house, but cleans the fireplace in her obedient daughter's.[15] Georges Drettas argued that Greek vampire predation and vampire-slaying sprang from social systems where younger generations were pitted against older ones: 'we have here a very powerful quasi-oedipal model, which operates in a context of violence extending to all relatives, and which necessitates the murderous dexterity of certain living people in response to the gluttonous hostility of the dead.'[16]

Unpleasant though all this sounds, the vampires in such adversarial relations were at least dead. But some folklore collections make a more sinister allegation: that prematurely buried people who woke up in their coffins, and successfully attracted attention, were assumed to be vampires and killed. It could have happened (these societies certainly had their brutal sides), but caution is needed. As a rhetorical demonstration that corpse-killers are idiots, the story looks slightly too good to be true. One version—ghastly in its detail—is from a prejudiced British officer determined to denigrate Bulgarian culture.[17] Two out of three collected in Greece in 1963 (in the form 'I heard my grandmother say . . .') resemble each other so closely as to suggest an established story-format.[18] Others from Russia are also reported second-hand.[19] This question remains open.

The Eastern European Zones of Survival

In western Russia, Belarus, and Ukraine, corpse-killings continued up to at least the 1880s, and fears of the wicked dead for some decades more.[20] Likely factors are obvious: a very traditional rural society, rigid family structures, serfdom, Orthodox clergy unconcerned to disenchant the world, and ethnically diverse populations. In 1910, a classic corpse-killing prompted by epidemic disease occurred in a Muslim Tatar community in the Urals.[21] In an episode near the Polish border with Belarus in 1914, 'a priest told his people to exhume the body and found the revenant lying prone in his coffin, with his fingers all bitten as if he had been "eating himself". While the priest uttered his prayer, the head of the revenant was cut off with a spade.'[22] Thereafter, war, revolution, and collectivization devastated folk-culture. During fieldwork near the Russian border with Belarus and Latvia in 1995, Elizabeth Warner found that 'none of our informants . . . expressed either fear of the dead or any strong belief that they might come to life in any circumstances'.[23]

Bulgaria—it is argued above—was the cradle of dangerous-dead ideas in the Balkans. The abundant folkloric collections, ably analyzed by Bruce McClelland, show that a rich texture of belief—including corpse-killing—remained alive and well in the late nineteenth century.[24] McClelland writes: 'One informant in the Rhodope Mountains, a certain Tsvetana Dimitrova, at the time ninety years old, told of the time when it was permitted to go to the graveyard to exhume vampires. She went to the graveyard, saw a hole in a grave (a certain sign that the body beneath is a vampire), and dug up the corpse. The dead woman was pure red. Tsvetana took red-hot skewers and punctured the corpse, and it disappeared'.[25]

This book has often mentioned Western travellers' fascination with Greek vampires. That interest continued well into the twentieth century, when Lawson and the Blums documented the practices abundantly.[26] Although Juliet du Boulay did not encounter actual exhumation in her Ambéli case-study, it survived through most of the twentieth century in some parts of Greece. In a narrative from the 1960s, '[the priest] advised [my sister] to exhume and burn my aunt, as she had become a vampire. They went to the grave. The priest read some chants. The daughter-in-law took my aunt out of the grave and burnt her bones. The priest advised her not to leave even a trace. After burning the body, the daughter-in-law scattered the ashes. My aunt did not visit her again'.[27]

In Serbia, staking and beheading continued as a regular and public practice into the 1830s, despite energetic attempts by the reformist Prince Miloš Obrenović and his bishops to suppress it.[28] Roma communities on the Orthodox/Ottoman interface in Serbia and Kosovo still retained many of the complex Balkan beliefs about vampires into the 1950s, including apparently the practice of staking.[29]

Earlier chapters have discussed several episodes of corpse-killing, from the sixteenth century onwards, within what are now the boundaries of Poland. The survival of belief in the restless dead across much of this huge area is clear from sources recently assembled by Łukasz Kozak.[30] They show, in abundant detail, a culture of corpse-killing that was fully accepted in rural communities through the eighteenth and nineteenth

FIGURE 72: Nineteenth-century Romanian peasants killing a vampire by moonlight. The man on the right has just driven a stake into the heart of the corpse; the others are finishing the job with guns.

centuries, despite the fierce disapproval of ecclesiastical and lay authorities. From the 1870s it subsided, with the last known cases in 1906, 1913, and 1933, but many must have gone unrecorded. A Polish dictionary printed in 1919 still included the word *upiorobójstwo* ('vampiricide').[31]

Poland was Catholic, and outside Turkish dominance. It has conventionally been located in the 'eastern' zone of family structure; recent work shows that its marriage and household patterns were actually quite diverse, but household matriarchs have traditionally been strong.[32] In this case, it is perhaps more likely that Poland's political and social traumas fostered the survival of corpse-killing. Dysfunctional government, an impoverished and often servile rural society under exploitative landlordship, and the successive partitions between 1772 and 1918, were amply productive of trauma and misery.

The one part of Europe where counter-measures still involve physical mutilation today is south-western Romania: the region of Wallachia west of Bucharest. Folkloric material shows beliefs concentrated in this region,[33] but the explanation for their exceptional modern resilience is unclear. Bor-

FIGURE 73: Vâlcea, south-western Romania: the hole in the grave and its ghastly message, in a video by Stirile Pro-TV. The idea that vampires make holes through their grave-earth as they come and go is often mentioned, but this may be the only photographic record of the phenomenon. This corpse was exhumed and staked in 2019.

dered by Bulgaria, Serbia, and the south Carpathians, this zone has perhaps had a particularly intensive exposure to surrounding corpse-killing traditions. The Wallachians just inside Serbia, with their 'Timok family type' and vampiric grandmothers, are probably a factor (p. 39). Another may be the continued failure of Orthodox clergy—in defiance of Church discipline—to discourage these practices. In the latest corpse-killing reported before this book went to press, at Vâlcea in 2019, a parish priest was prosecuted, and temporarily suspended by his archbishop, for alleged complicity in the exhumation and staking of a woman (Figure 73).[34]

The West Prussian and Pomeranian Zone of Survival

West Prussia/Pomerania (now the Pomeranian Voivodeship, Poland), on the Baltic coast west of Gdansk, is unique in the later stages of European corpse-killing (Map 10). It was within the broad zone of late medieval to

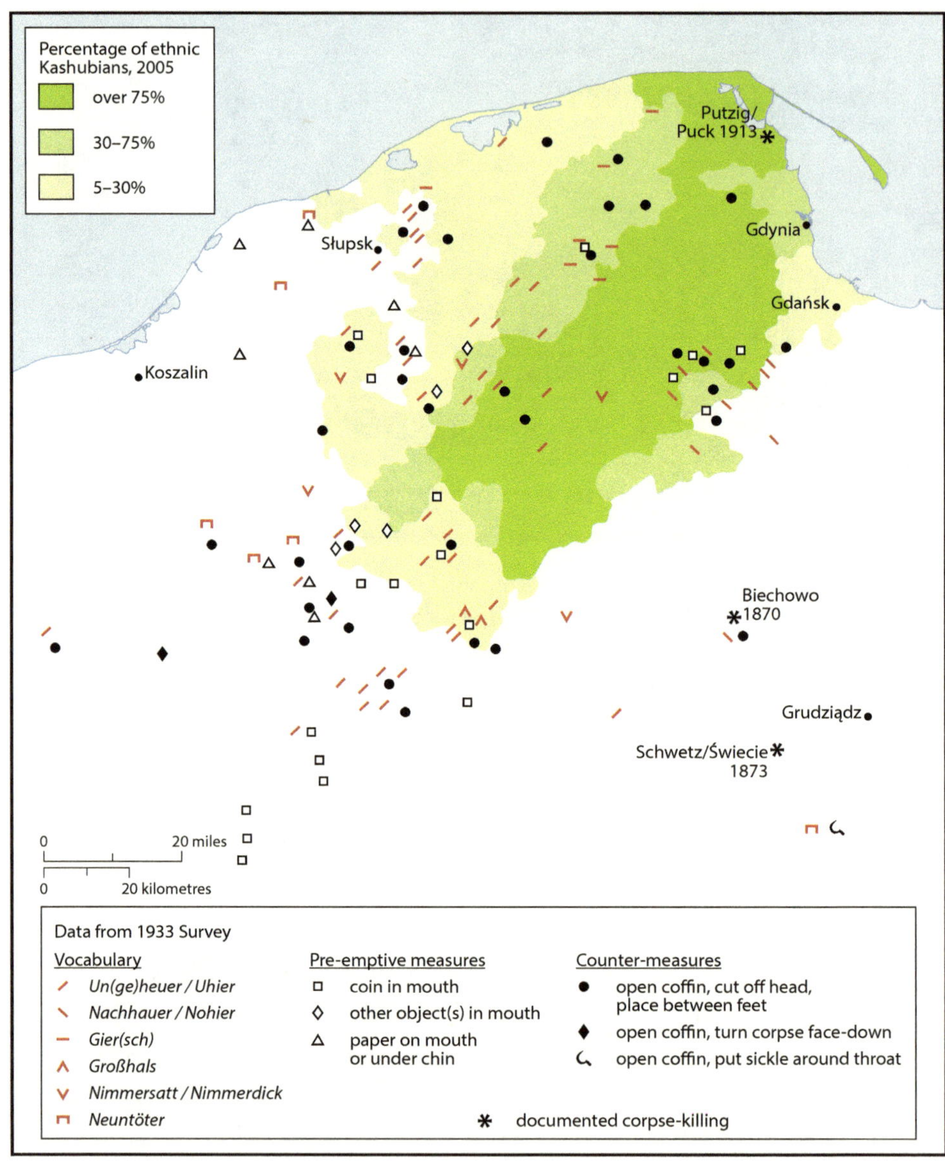

MAP 10: Dangerous-dead beliefs in West Prussia and Pomerania, according to the 1933 folklore survey, shown in relation to the proportion of ethnic Kashubians in 2005.

early modern outbreaks: to its west and east were Mühlhausen and Schivelbein, where cases had been reported in 1564 and 1584 (p. 325). But it conspicuously lacks medieval deviant burials, and does not emerge as any kind of special focus in the well-documented sixteenth to seventeenth centuries. It seems, therefore, that the complex beliefs recorded in the nineteenth to twentieth centuries intensified at quite a late stage.

It was here that corpses were exhumed and beheaded with spades in 1870–3, and again (by a workman who attacked his mother's corpse to suppress a tuberculosis outbreak) in 1913.[35] In 1933, the Survey of German Folklore found beliefs—much stronger and more complex than anywhere else in German-speaking Europe—concentrated in this confined region.[36] Uniquely, respondents still mentioned beheading the corpse or turning it over, though as past rather than current practices.[37] Again, it was only here that coins were still regularly placed in a corpse's mouth, or the feet bound.[38] Werewolves were mentioned, and being born with the caul, teeth, or other peculiarities were thought to presage the undead condition.[39]

At least one distinctive motif was deep-rooted in the general region. In the 1564 Mühlhausen case, the pastor reported that local farmers asked him to bury a plague victim 'behind the door'. When he refused, they said that 'the first person to die of plague in the village would sit up and eat the shroud, and so long as there was still some of it to eat, people would not stop dying in that place; and that this also happened at [*place*], but when they dug up the first one, they found [*name*] sitting and eating, and they cut the neck with a spade, and then it stopped'.[40] Compare this with a later folkloric story from Trzebiatkowa, in which some brave men go to a churchyard and open a grave, 'and there the *unhîr* sat in the coffin and gnawed at his chest and hands. The people now tried to turn the corpse over, so that the *unhîr* would eat into the earth and not come back to people again, but the dead man fought against this with all his might. Then a strong man called Witt took a sharp peat spade and knocked off his head with one stroke'.[41]

This motif of a sitting corpse was rooted in a local tradition where *all* the dead sit. The 1933 Survey picked up this account of normal funeral practices in East Prussia:

> When the mourners return from the churchyard on the day of the funeral, an empty chair is placed in the door of the room. Above the chair, a nail is driven into the wall. The long 'corpse-bands' with which the coffin was lowered into the grave are hung on this nail. The dead man, sitting on the chair, hides in these bands: his spirit has not yet left the house. He remains on the chair until midnight, and it is arranged for dinner to be eaten after that. When everything is set up, the bearers go out first with the other guests following, and everyone accompanies the spirit of the dead person to the grave . . . [or] to the field boundary.[42]

There was also an exceptionally varied vocabulary for the undead: *Neuntöter* ('nine-killer'[43]), *Un(ge)heuer/Uhier* ('uncanny'/'horrible'), *Nachheuer/Nohier* ('after-[eating] monster'), *Nimmersatt/Nimmerdick* ('insatiable'/'never-fat'), *Großhals* ('big-throat'), *Gier(sch)* ('greedy').[44] This luxuriant abundance of synonyms leaves no doubt about the extraordinary continuing importance of dangerous corpses for the population of this region. In 1933, it resembled a time-capsule for the beliefs discussed in earlier chapters.

Why was this region so different? What most obviously set it apart was the indigenous population of Slavic Kashubians, who retained a vigorous identity despite centuries of German colonization and acculturation. They were noted for their exceptionally restrictive and endogamous marriage practices. Kashubians resisted intermarriage with other ethnic groups (though of course it sometimes happened); even marriage outside one's own village was strongly discouraged. Marriages were arranged by parents and brokers, who prioritised economic and dynastic considerations over emotional ones: animosity between parents and children was therefore common.[45] If oppressive family structures create vampires, this looks like a prime candidate.

But it is not so simple. This was historically a mixed society of Catholic Kashubians, Catholic Germans, and Lutheran Germans, around a central zone of strong Kashubian ethnicity. As Map 10 shows, the dangerous-dead beliefs reported in 1933 cluster *around* this Kashubian core more than inside it. That must reflect incomplete reporting: Kashubian speakers probably ignored the German-language questionnaire. In fact, their vampire beliefs were strong enough to travel with emigrants to Ontario and flourish there.[46] Even so, the beliefs clearly spread well beyond Kashubians, and there are both German and Slavic names among the corpse-killers brought to trial.

There surely must be *some* link between the exceptional family structures and the exceptional survival of corpse-killing. Explanations can only be tentative, but a plausible one might go like this: A distinctive local motif-complex about the dangerous dead, drawing on both German and Slavic traditions, had coalesced much earlier. But the coexistence of brittle, defensive in-groups, with multiple fissures running along ethnic, confessional, and generational lines, increasingly made for stress and insecurity as the outside world changed. Hence the corpse-killing culture intensified and perpetuated itself in an exceptional way, because a traumatically contested environment demanded avenues for psychological release. Perhaps animosity towards neighbours and parents was sublimated into animosity towards the dead.

After-Tastes: Central Europe

Further west, corpse-killings now appear as rare exceptions. In the late nineteenth century, the troublesome corpse of an old man in the Schleswig-Flensburg district was turned face-down so that afterwards he 'could only go down into the earth'.[47] Some recently nailed and stoned corpses were found near Dresden in 1877 (though they were apparently the work of a lone enthusiast, and puzzled the locals).[48] But in general, the fear and the countermeasures both tended to soften over time. Bohemian and Moravian folklore, for instance, was rich in stories of the unquiet and evil dead—including *upíři* and *vampýři*—down to c. 1900, but by then they were conceived more as spirits than as corpses.[49]

The 1933 survey of German folklore provides a uniquely fine-grained source for beliefs and customs in the German-speaking lands, revealing much that usually escapes us.[50] Suspicion of newly-dead corpses with red cheeks, red lips, or smiling expressions, and concern to separate the mouth from anything that might be chewed, survived in the expected and familiar regions: the Rhineland, Mecklenburg/Brandenburg, Saxony, Silesia, and Moravia.[51]

More surprisingly, mild concerns about incorrect funeral rituals, and corpses with open eyes, were found over the whole of western and southern Germany and Austria, as were minority beliefs in 'fetching', 'sucking', or 'greedy' corpses that sap energy or life. In pockets north of Regensburg, Passau, and Vienna, corpse-fears of some kind were acknowledged by more than 30 percent of respondents.[52] That is harder to decode, but intriguing. Does the 1933 survey pick up an ancient and widespread sub-stratum of latent anxiety? Or did the zone of belief shift south-westwards after 1750, but in a social milieu where mutilating corpses was so completely off-limits that sources failed to register it? In either case, it is a salutary reminder of how much escapes record before the age of folklore collection.

During the twentieth century, counter-measures became gentler but sometimes idiosyncratic, almost verging on parody. In 1970s Euboea, vampire-hunters would peer down the hole that the vampire had made through the grave-earth and see its gleaming eyes. A mixture of boiling oil and vinegar was then poured into the hole as the priest read an exorcism, thus annihilating the vampire.[53] In the 1950s, Serbians and Albanians thought that 'a vampire's left sock must be taken, filled with earth from the grave (dug from the spot under which its head rests), and cast anywhere beyond the village boundaries into another village. It is believed that the vampire will then go after its sock to the latter place, and that in its flight it may drown itself'.[54] In Bulgaria, men stripped naked, rubbed strong-smelling herbs on their bodies, and ran around the houses and yards with knives, axes, and icons, before throwing soil from the vampire's grave into the river—which sounds more like having fun than slaying a monster.[55]

Such 'rituals' suggest lip-service to tradition when real belief and anxiety had weakened. The ultimate reduction to absurdity was a Polish game in which a child lay face-down, pretending to be in a coffin, while others circled around calling 'first hour, *strigon* is sleeping, second hour, *strigon* is sleeping'. When they reached twelve, the make-believe *strigon* jumped up and chased them, as they ran away calling '*strigon*, get up, give us some dumplings!'.[56]

But the rhetoric lives on. Apparently a stake was driven into the corpse (or at least the grave-earth) of the Serbian leader Slobodan Milošević, who died in 2006.[57] And in July 2023, the last resident of a bombed Ukranian village began each day by cursing Vladimir Putin, wanting 'to see him spinning in his coffin, tormented, unshriven and damned for all eternity'.[58]

After-Tastes: Ireland and England

Occasional stories and practices persisted in the Gaelic-speaking world, though it is hard to know how seriously they were taken and how they were understood. The Irish folk-tale of the womaniser Teig O'Kane, who has to carry a sentient, moaning corpse on his back until he finds a graveyard to receive it, seems essentially comic.[59] More mainstream is the idea, reported both in Galway and among the expatriate Irish of Connecticut in the 1880s, that a corpse in unsuitable grave-clothes (with stolen thread, or simply with ties and fastenings) will not lie quiet, so that it must be exhumed and the offending items removed.[60]

Did the dead still walk in Victorian England? Only rarely, but there are occasional faint hints and traces up to c. 1900. An explicit case of exhumation and inversion in response to haunting comes from Longtown on the Welsh border: 'I helped myself to turn a man in his grave, up at Capel-y-fin; he come back, and we thought to stop him, but after we turned him he come back seven times worse'.[61] Devon remained another foothold. Four years after the publication of *Dracula*, this conversation took place there between a squire and a farmer:

FARMER: S'pose you've a-yeard th' old 'umman [*name*] is dead to last.

SQUIRE: No, I had not heard of it. Where did she die? Not in this parish, I hope. She was here living not very long ago.

FARMER: Oh, no; her wid'n bide here. Her zaid how they was trying to pwoison her, so her made 'em take her home, and they drawed her home in a carriage. Her was that wicked, her died awful. Her died cussin' and dam'in [*name*] wi' the words in her mouth.

SQUIRE: Poor thing! I suppose she was mad. When did she die?
FARMER: Her died last Monday, and her's going to be buried t'arternoon to Culmstock.
SQUIRE: It's a good thing for us she is not going to be buried here, for she's sure to be troublesome wherever she lies.
FARMER: Oh, no, her 'ont, sir. You knows Joe, don't 'ee, sir? Well, I seed Joe this morning, and he's gwain to help car' her; so I sez to Joe, say I, 'For God's sake, Joe, be sure and put her in up'm down'.
SQUIRE: Do you mean that the coffin is to be turned upside down?
FARMER: Ay, sure, and no mistake! Her 'ont be troublesome then, 'cause if her do begin to diggy, her can on'y diggy downwards.[62]

In England as in the German-speaking world, the First World War seems to mark the final end of physical corpse-killing. It is ironic that the first serious study of English medieval vampires was by a German scholar, and published in 1914.[63] A year later, the war provided a theatre for the very last act: the Glám-like image of a 'huge, scowling' German soldier fighting a slim English youth. An officer observed: 'the German it was who died, and I remember his face afterwards. He might have been asleep dreaming of some wickedness. Later, I found our men burying him most carefully—face downwards. You know why. If he began digging his way out he would only go deeper'.[64] Even in twentieth-century England, grief, hatred, and paranoia could still summon up the malevolent dead. Meanwhile, the long-term effects of European colonization and exploitation had summoned them up in some very different parts of the globe.

34

Vampires of Colonialism and Slavery

> In every community where [slavery] exists, it presses like a night-mare on the body politic. Or, like the vampire, it slowly and imperceptibly sucks away the life-blood of society, leaving it faint and disheartened to stagger along the road to improvement.
>
> —ELIJAH LOVEJOY, ANTI-SLAVERY EDITORIAL IN THE ST. LOUIS *OBSERVER*, 1835

TWO REGIONS, outside the heartlands of belief that are the main subjects of this book, nonetheless have some stories of the restless dead: Australia and West Africa (pp. 17, 60). Understanding them is peculiarly difficult because—in default of relevant archaeology—we have to study the beliefs of these very ancient cultures through the eyes of recent and often colonial observers. Such sources are problematic: even when not actually hostile or patronizing, they can fundamentally misinterpret observed phenomena.[1]

Accordingly, the arguments of this chapter are hypotheses only, made in full acknowledgement that sources from which we might draw firm conclusions do not exist. They are still worth making, since curious aspects of both regions point tentatively to the same conclusion: that although conceptions of a permeable frontier with the spirit world are probably age-old, they only hardened into fears of the physical dead under the traumas of colonialism and slavery.

Australia

The indigenous hunter-gatherers of Australia, who preserved their cultures and ways of life for millennia, might seem a perfect testing-ground for psychological arguments that belief in unquiet corpses is hard-wired. Such beliefs are indeed recorded there in colonial contexts, but the story is not so simple. First, northern Australia was exposed to influences from Indonesia and New Guinea.[2] An underlying stratum of beliefs related to South-east Asian ones—at the extreme end of the 'vampire belt' (Map 1)—is therefore possible (though in that case one might have expected female flying demons to influence the tradition). Secondly, the lack of any reference in oral histories and modern anthropological work raises questions about the strange isolation of the nineteenth-century colonial references that do exist. A case can be made that these scraps of evidence reflect a limited, externally-induced epidemic.

Australians have traditionally practised elaborate and extended funeral rites, including secondary burial, reflecting beliefs in multiple spirits whom the living must help on their journey to the spirit world or back into the landscape. Spirits can be vengeful and aggressive, they can hang around while flesh remains on the body, and their return is feared. Thus the Yolngu of the north coast believe in two souls, *mokuy* and *birrimbirr*. Whereas the *birrimbirr* returns to the land to be reincorporated into the reservoir of ancestral power associated with that place, the *mokuy* continues as a ghost, which may cause trouble for anyone against whom the deceased had held a grudge; this is especially likely if the individual died an 'unnatural' death or was not adequately cared for.[3] As we saw, corporeal-revenant beliefs can sometimes emerge from this kind of ghost-belief complex, but are not the same thing. Those categories must be kept clearly distinct—all the more so since all the evidence comes from colonial observers, who may report accurately what they saw but misunderstand what it meant.

The ethnographer A. W. Howitt began work in the 1870s, and his *The Native Tribes of South-East Australia* was published in 1904. Naturally he writes as a colonial observer, though his approach is more sympathetic than many. His statements about the dangerous dead are based on his own recent fieldwork and that of two informants, so they offer more than a single perspective.[4] Howitt reports that the Gunaikurnai of the south-east coast identified the human spirit as a *yambo*, which could leave the body during sleep and followed a path to the sky after death. In the guise of a *mrart*, the *yambo* could become more interventionist. *Mrarts* were more than purely immaterial, for they could be heard jumping down from trees to the ground, and could even carry people off in bags. Male and female *mrarts* were believed to wander about the country that they inhabited during life, and at worst they could be daunting enemies.[5]

Thus far we are dealing essentially with ghosts, although verging on the corporeal, but the Diyari of the Blanchewater area, north of Adelaide, also took measures at funerals to restrain the corpse: 'They tie the toes together, and thumbs behind the back, sweep a clear space round the grave at dusk each evening, and inspect it to look for tracks early each morning for a month after death. Should tracks be found, the body is removed and reburied, as they think that the deceased is not satisfied with his first grave.'[6] The Dhudhuroa of north-east Victoria, not so far away, believed that the dead sometimes left their graves, which were therefore dug like cylindrical pits, with side chambers in which the corpses were blocked in with pieces of wood.[7]

In the Cape York area of north-east Australia, the funeral practices of people near the Herbert River seem still more explicit. The body was put in the grave and violently beaten, after which incisions were made on the stomach, shoulders, and lungs, which were filled with stones. Grave-goods, food, and water were provided, and

> the legs are generally broken to prevent the ghost from wandering at night. The beating is given in order to so frighten the spirit that it would be unlikely to haunt the camp, and the stones are put in the

> body to prevent it from going too far afield. . . . These burial customs . . . show that the deceased might follow his kindred corporeally and injure others. Hence it is that the body is tied up tightly in its cerements and placed in a grave, blocked in some cases with wood before being filled with earth. . . . The breaking of the bones by the Herbert River tribes is a very clear example of the precautions taken to prevent the ghost from wandering, although it is an exceptionally severe means of doing so.[8]

Also at Cape York, the police commissioner Frederic Urquhart observed in the 1880s that the Kutjal people decapitated their dead before burying the body, roasted the head on a fire, and broke it up among the hot coals. 'The theory is that the spirit rising from the grave misses its head, and goes groping about to find it', gets burnt, and is frightened back into its grave.[9] This again seems 'exceptionally severe'. Howitt and Urquhart use the words 'ghost' and 'spirit', but it is unclear how accurately concepts are translated: these dead people behave very physically.

These are first-hand reports and must be taken seriously, but the lack of external verification that the practices were mainstream raises the possibility of recent and specific causes. If trauma and insecurity can be catalysts for the walking-dead syndrome, we scarcely need to look further than the impact of colonization on Indigenous Australians. (Urquhart, one of the very witnesses just cited, committed horrible crimes against them.) There is also a more specific factor that seems compelling. Because the dead were thought to be white, the first Europeans seen in Australia were often identified as dead ancestors.[10] At Cape York, not far from the Herbert River peoples and the Kutjal, intermittent encounters with white people—sometimes brutal—had happened since the first Dutch landing in 1606, and white men were automatically assigned (like ghosts) to the Corpse Clan.[11] Once aggressive, lethal, and obviously corporeal 'ancestors' had appeared on the scene, it is hardly surprising if corpses came to be feared: it seems significant that the most extreme practices are recorded relatively near the sites of the first Dutch landings.

Although the recorded episodes were widely dispersed, and included some groups whose intensive contacts with Europeans were only from the 1850s onwards, that still leaves scope for rapid change to have taken place before contact with the first ethnographers. Europeans had mapped the whole coastline by the late eighteenth century. The Herbert River peoples were coastal; in the south, ideas could have been transmitted inland from the Gunaikurnai to the Diyari and Dhudhuora. Australia is large, but its people were very mobile, with a consistency of social practice that helped ideas to travel: stories of the malevolent white dead could have spread quickly.

Accordingly, it is arguable that the (relatively few) walking corpses reported from Australia in the 1890s represent a specific and potentially quite recent epidemic phenomenon. Traditional ideas of helping the dead on their journey back into the landscape, and fears of ghosts that had failed to complete it, were intensified by colonial disruption and by perceptions of white settlers as violent and dangerous dead people.

An important wider implication would follow from that. None of the western European colonizers retained any significant memory of restless corpses by the point of contact, which tends (South-east Asian influences aside) to suggest that the idea emerged autonomously. It illustrates humanity's latent capacity—given a suitable combination of traditions, influences, and stresses—to believe in the dangerous dead, even if only a minority of the world's population has ever believed in them at any one time.

West Africa

Africa lies completely outside the 'vampire belt', but expatriate West African communities since 1800 have produced some distinctive and well-known manifestations of the dangerous dead. These had a longer and more complicated back-story than can ever be reconstructed. The sub-Saharan west coast has been highly cosmopolitan since the Middle Ages, linked by regular coastal and cross-desert trade and traffic to Asia and Europe.[12] Tragically, it was also the scene of both internal and external slave-raiding and slave-trading through the same centuries. The belief-systems known from recent ethnography and biography are multi-layered, with ramifying complexities in the expatriate, slave-descended communities of the Caribbean. Our inevitably limited exploration here—confined to the African homeland, Jamaica, and Haiti—picks up two linked strands: the permeable boundary between life and death, and the impact of trauma and abuse inflicted by slavery on the inherited belief-system. That background helps to explain one famously bizarre outcome: *zombis*, the walking 'dead' who are not really dead.

The frontier of life and death, hazily defined in many pre-industrial societies, seems especially flexible in West Africa. Rather than a recognition of death as a moment in time, a funeral is a protracted and multi-stage negotiation transferring an individual from this world to the next. Malidoma Patrice Somé, of the Dagara people (Burkina Faso and Ghana), describes how his grandfather died yet was not dead: he responded to stimuli, opened his eyes, sat up, then stood up and walked out of the room:

> He moved strangely—too straight, too rigid, unnatural, yet very conscious of any obstacle. . . . The four-mile walk took an equal number of hours. Dead people don't walk very fast. They are not in a hurry. We must have reached home around noontime . . .
>
> Different cultures have different relationships with their dead, and I know very well that in a culture of skyscrapers and high technology, dead people don't walk. Instead, they are placed in nice expensive caskets and driven to the cemetery in elegant black cars. They are put quickly out of sight so that life can go on.
>
> Why do the dead walk where I come from? They walk because they are still as important to the living as they were before. They are even more meaningful, as the breadth and depth of our funeral ritual shows. . . . True, every dead person is not asked to walk. My grandfather died on the mission hill, thus in a foreign land. He was an elder and a leader of great power, and should have died at home. The only way to correct a death of such an important person when it occurs in the wrong place is to walk the dead home. . . . Grandfather's eyes were peering at something beyond them, his face and body expressionless.[13]

How are outsiders to conceive life and death in a society where such experiences are reality? At least Malidoma's insight illustrates how other representatives of the walking not-quite-dead—zombis, for instance—

may have seemed as natural to contemporaries as they are strange to modern Western people.

Traditional African belief-systems, spread out over a huge continent, are naturally both complex and varied: the reductionist umbrella label 'witchcraft' does less than justice. It is also implausible that beliefs were immemorially unchanging, especially in the west where international contacts were so long established. For instance, the term *zumbi* in late seventeenth-century Angola simply meant a dead person or spirit, notwithstanding its lurid later connotations.[14] It is probably a fair assumption that beliefs in the malevolent ghosts of unpleasant, marginal, and outcast individuals, as recorded in the nineteenth century, were deep-rooted.[15] The same *may* be true for more physical conceptions of the dead, but we should hesitate to assume that without good evidence. They are rarities among the African beliefs recorded by anthropologists, even in societies that have been very thoroughly studied.[16]

In West Africa, a tradition of noxious corpses that lie immobile but work harm appears in 1687, in a work on Angola which describes how undecayed corpses were beheaded to harvest curative blood and to stop them from harassing the living (p. 72). Later, corpses of women who died pregnant or in childbirth were especially feared.[17] In nineteenth-century Kongo, the corpse of a man whose relatives were often ill after his death was exhumed and burnt, to destroy the spirit of the witch (*ndoki*) occupying it.[18] On the Gold Coast in the 1840s, a Western observer noted a belief that

> compels the exhumation of the bodies of those people who have been suspected of being too intimately concerned with the supernatural influences during their lifetime. Natives who have been prematurely cut off, either from the inroads of some occasional epidemic, or the ordinary maladies of the season, are frequently supposed to become endowed with the potent prerogative of generating disease and destroying life; hence it is not an uncommon occurrence, when two or three members of the same family die in succession, to attribute their departure to the agency of the first sufferer or sufferers, the corpses of which, after satisfactory evidence has been adduced, are

> summarily removed from their houses within the sanctuary of which they have been interred, are ignominiously burned on the outskirts of the town, and their ashes scattered to the winds, amid the mingled groans and execrations of the populace. It matters not how innocent the unfortunate persons might have been, nor yet how long they may have slept in the calm tranquility of the grave. The voice of public opinion is unanimous; they are branded with the stigma of posthumous murderers.[19]

This was clearly different from those situations in which corpses walked. And some details (death from epidemic causing high risk, the absence of culpability in life, the 'domino-effect' where one person dies and relatives follow), look—for whatever reason—remarkably similar to the beliefs in Lutheran Germany described in Chapter 27.

Also widely attested, on the other hand, are belief-systems of a completely non-European kind, in which the active dead or seeming dead are controlled or enslaved by living specialists. One version is recorded in seventeenth-century Kongo: if an ancestor's ghost returned to do harm, the corpse was dug up and handed to a *nganga atombola* ('priest of the resurrected'), who made it appear to walk, speak, and explain why the funeral rites had gone wrong.[20] In 1665, King Antonio I of Kongo claimed to be 'lord of the *matambulas*, who are interpreted as dead and resurrected men',[21] which looks like the same conception of a revived corpse manipulated by a specialist in control of its spirit (*etombola*).

Hans-W. Ackermann and Jeanine Gauthier have shown that the two main ingredients of the *zombi* concept—the captured soul without a body and the enslaved body without a rational soul—can be found widely across west and central Africa.[22] Whether they are right to conclude that 'the *zombi* concept is very old and possibly predates the historical Bantu migration'[23] is perhaps not quite so self-evident, since it has been capable of self-generation in at least one recent case: the impact of economic development and globalization on Cameroon during the later twentieth century produced a new magical system, *ekong*, in which witches turned their victims into *zombi*-like slaves (rather than, as previously, eating them).[24]

Along similar lines are the stories, recounted among the Dahomey of Benin in 1931, of 'dead' people being seen in neighbouring regions: 'They were soulless beings, whose deaths were not real but resulted from the machinations of sorcerers who made them appear as dead, and then, when buried, removed them from their graves and sold them into servitude in some far-away land.'[25] None of this seems far removed from Luise White's argument that accusations of *living* vampirism in twentieth-century Africa reflect socio-economic stresses of colonialism.[26] The common factor seems to be oppression. Is it possible that the origins—or at least crystallization—of the belief lie in the African slave-trade?

The African Diaspora

Ideas of multiple souls and the not-quite-dead survived—in distinct but still recognizable forms—among the Afro-Caribbean people of the Antilles, descendants of the enslaved.[27] In Jamaica, for which we have the 1930s fieldwork of the anthropologist Zora Neale Hurston, the 'duppy' (a central African word and idea) is the life-force soul, unconstrained by morality or intellect. The duppy of a good-living person could be expected to stay with the corpse, but the more wicked the deceased, the more likely their duppies would be to leave their graves: throwing things around, making people sick, acting in a generally crude and disorderly fashion.

Hence the importance of funeral rituals to keep the duppy in the coffin, or—when those failed—of binding the grave with a strong chain (preferably made in Manchester).[28] The 'Nine Night', also an African import, was an elaborate wake ritual to keep the duppy in its body and coffin. An old man told Hurston:

> 'One day you see a man walking the road, the next day you come to his yard and find him dead. Him don't walk, him don't talk again. He is still and silent and does none of the things that he used to do. But you look upon him and see that he has all the parts that the living have. Why is it that he cannot do the thing that the living do? It is because the thing that gave power to those parts is no longer there. That is the duppy, and that is the most powerful part of any man.

Everybody has evil in them, and when a man is alive, the heart and the brain controls him and he will not abandon himself to many evil things. But when the duppy leaves the body, it no longer has anything to restrain it and it will do more terrible things than any man ever dreamed of. It is not good for a duppy to stay among living folk. The duppy is much too powerful and is apt to hurt people all the time. So we make Nine Night to force the duppy to stay in his grave.'[29]

The duppy displays some classic vampire characteristics (like obsessive-compulsive counting of seeds),[30] and can be sealed down in a very physical fashion (p. 90). Fundamentally, though, it is a 'spirit *zombi*': an incorporeal being capable of action (and also capable of being imprisoned), not a walking corpse.

What happens when the physical body and the animal life-force stay together, but the soul embodying intellect and morality departs? The bodily *zombis* of Haiti illustrate that variant in an especially lurid guise.[31] In common belief there, young people are targeted by magical specialists (*bokors*) who induce a death-like trance, steal them from their graves after their funerals, revive them to a semi-conscious state, and set them working in slave-gangs (Figure 74). Today, the Haiti penal code (article 246) solemnly states: 'The use made against a person of substances which, without giving death, will cause a more-or-less prolonged state of lethargy . . . is considered an attempt on life by poisoning. If the person was buried as a consequence of this state of lethargy, the attempt will be considered a murder.' Scientific research—while still a matter of debate[32]—leaves open the possibility that at least some of this has really happened, and recently living Haitians claimed to be able to show their own graves and death certificates (Figure 75).

For present purposes, the reality of zombification matters less than some of its perceived aspects. The belief-system distinguishes the *corps cadavre* (physical body), with its *gwo-bon anj* (life-force) that still animates the revived zombi, from the *ti-bon anj* (agency, awareness, memory), stored elsewhere by the *bokor*.[33] Most victims are unpopular or antisocial people who have transgressed social norms, and 'die' before

FIGURE 74: Slave *zombis* in Haiti being returned to a tomb by their *bokor* master: painting by Hector Hyppolite, 1946.

their time: *bokors* are seen (or see themselves) as executing a kind of justice.[34] Pre-emptive measures can be taken before the funeral: 'the body may be killed again, with a knife through the heart or by decapitation. . . . [S]eeds may be placed in the coffin so that whoever appears to take the body will be obliged to count them, a task that will take him perilously into the dawn.'[35]

Zombification is a strange offshoot from 'normal' walking-dead beliefs. Plural souls, high-risk individuals, lives unfulfilled, beheading and heart-piercing, seed-counting, and revenancy as a judicial penalty: we have met them all in this book. But through structures of control and

FIGURE 75: A *zombi* returned: Clairvius Narcisse (1922–94) sits beside his own tomb. In 1982, the anthropologist Wade Davis achieved the perhaps unique feat of photographing a self-declared member of the undead tribe. However dubious Narcisse's claim, his story illustrates the intensity of the belief in modern Haiti.

subservience, *zombis* have become something even more horribly different.

This is a nightmare of the disempowered: whatever deep roots may go down into traditional African cultures, the surface beliefs were surely intensified during the historical tragedy of the slave-trade, the slave colony in Haiti, and then its transition to a fragile republic. Haiti illustrates starkly the mirror-like quality of revenant beliefs: for those who know the trauma of slavery and displacement, the walking dead are slaves on secret plantations.[36]

Conclusion

THE DANGEROUS DEAD AS MIRRORS OF REALITY

> 'I long to go through the crowded streets of your mighty London, to be in the midst of the whirl and rush of humanity, to share its life, its change, its death, and all that makes it what it is.'
>
> —COUNT DRACULA

THIS BOOK BEGAN with the Serbian sensation of 1731–2, and its appearance in Western newspapers as an exotic horror story. That episode also makes a suitable ending, since most modern ideas of the vampire go back to it. Accidentally, the spotlight on the obscure Serbian *hajduk* Arnaut Pavle, and on the unusual combination of motifs surrounding his case, generated an enduring template that established itself almost immediately in the medical, philosophical, creative, and political discourse of Germany, France, and England.

That was not because Westerners believed in vampires literally. Rather, the vampire was useful: as a superstition against which the bright light of modern science could contrast itself; as a compelling character-type in Romantic and sensational fiction; and as a metaphor—which it had always been—for the outrageous, inexplicable, life-sapping forces that disrupt human happiness.

None of this should make us forget those other parts of Europe, and of the world, where the neutralizing of dangerous corpses remained and still remains an urgent and very physical task: a job that has to be done, undertaken by the resolute for the sake of their families and neighbours.

Science

Symbolically, Maria Theresia issued her Enlightened ban on corpse-killing between the first edition of Calmet's treatise of 1746 and its English translation in 1759. The work of the Leipzig academics, and van Swieten's meticulous documentation of the supposed Moravian vampires, had demonstrated in abundant detail how biological processes could be mistaken for unholy continuing life. Revenants were being nudged from the world of reality.

It was also becoming understood that some of the 'dead' might occasionally still be alive in a normal medical sense. In December 1732, a Scottish coal-miner called James Blair was overcome by poisonous fumes, hauled out as a corpse, but then revived by a local doctor—one William Tossach—with the world's first successful use of mouth-to-mouth resuscitation (Figure 76).[1] During the preceding nine months—since news of the Serbian events had broken—there had been a flow of publications on the subject in Latin and German: it is tempting to infer that Tossach had been reading these latest thoughts about the frontier between life and death.

In 1742 the Danish anatomist Jakob Winsløw published his path-breaking study of ambiguity in the signs of death; four years later, its English translation added an account of the Blair episode.[2] One outcome of these medical advances was heightened fear of premature burial, which lasted into the twentieth century. Another was the emergent scientific interest in the electro-chemical basis of life, prompting attempted 'revivals' of corpses by magnetism and electric charges.[3] The traditionally supernatural undead took a back seat.

FIGURE 76: The living dead demystified: William Tossach resuscitates James Blair, 3 December 1732.

Literature

Thus it was increasingly as a fictional and Romantic genre that French and German writers developed the templates learned from Calmet: vampires were ethnographically interesting, and rich sources for creative writing, but they did not actually exist. A French popular survey of 1820 concluded: 'all the narratives of ghosts, revenants, spectres, demons, *stryges, broucolaques,* and vampires deserve more attention than the amazing adventures of the Thousand and One Nights and the Tales of Mother Goose; but a sane mind will put no more faith in those narratives than in those tales'.[4]

The tapping of older sources of another kind, with different emotional resonances from Arnaut Pavle and his kin, began in 1798, when Johann Wolfgang Goethe published his poem 'The Bride of Corinth'. This was a re-working of the Philinnion story,[5] which it introduced to English authors at the point when, as Nick Groom puts it, 'vampires flashed through Romanticism like lightning, driven on by the obsessively necrophiliac imagination of the period' (Figure 77).[6]

In New England, where the vampire-killing epidemic was reaching its peak, the topic was still deadly reality rather than entertainment. Even so, some startling verses about the exhumation of a sixteen-year-old girl in Plymouth, Massachusetts, in 1807 (perhaps the only vampire poem ever written by a believing eye-witness) suggest that popular fears had acquired the same Romantic colouring:

I saw her, the grave sheet was round her,
  Months had passed since they laid her in clay;
Yet the damps of the tomb could not wound her,
  The worms had not seized on their prey.

O, fair was her cheek, as I knew it
  When the rose all its colours there brought;
And that eye—did a tear then bedew it?
  It gleam'd like the herald of thought.

She bloom'd, though the shroud was around her
  Her locks o'er her cold bosom wave,
As if the stern monarch had crown'd her,
  The fair speechless queen of the grave.

But what lends the grave such a lustre?
  O'er her cheek what such beauty had shed?
His life-blood, who bent there, had nurst her,
  The living was food for the dead![7]

FIGURE 77: A typical Romantic-era visualisation of vampires, in an engraving of 1820.

Two distinct models were thus available for authors of fiction: on the one hand, Calmet's stolid male subjects with their earthy, forensic solidity; on the other, the beautiful but deadly *lamia*-type females like Goethe's 'bride' or the Massachusetts girl, tragically torn between involuntary predation and normal human love.[8] And these, of course, were the two templates—'lumpen male' and 'dangerous female'—that this book has traced through millennia of human history.

The most notable progeny of the male template was Lord Byron's Giaour, quickly followed by Polidori's Lord Ruthven (based on Byron!).[9] It is no coincidence that both these authors belonged to the Shelley circle, and that the Creature in Mary Shelley's *Frankenstein,* made of body-parts recovered from 'vaults and charnel-houses', reflects the contemporary interest in re-vivifying corpses by scientific rather than supernatural means.[10] Thus the lurid stories of Slavic vampires converged with modern science. The female template, on the other hand, was explored through the seductive characters of Geraldine (Coleridge), Thalaba (Southey), Lamia (Keats), and La Belle Dame Sans Merci (also Keats).[11]

The literary potentials of both gender templates were finally realized in the later nineteenth century. Sheridan Le Fanu's *Carmilla* (1872) sensitively reinvents the Philinnion type, at once tragic heroine and deadly monster (Figure 22). But there is, of course, no question about the ultimate exemplar of the male prototype. If we were to name one year in which the indigenous English walking dead were irrevocably sealed in their graves it would be 1897, when Bram Stoker's *Dracula* was published to immediate popular acclaim (Figure 1). However flawed and misleading, *Dracula* is the most powerful story of the walking dead that has ever been written, and much of its power comes from the juxtaposition of exotic with familiar: the vampiric Transylvanian noblemen lurking in the terraced houses of Victorian London.

Count Dracula, unlike Carmilla, is pure invention: wily and resourceful, he bears no resemblance to the 'lumpen male' template. Stoker had read Calmet and East European folklore, and drew on them heavily, but he still chose to create an entirely original anti-hero. Yet this fictional image would prove overwhelmingly more powerful than anything inherited from real beliefs.[12] Despite the lingering memories in southwestern England, *Dracula* quickly smothered such traces with its spectacular success and its progeny of adaptations and films. Few modern readers or viewers have any inkling that their ancestors shared the terrors of Jonathan Harker and Abraham van Helsing.

Metaphor

Echoes of the Serbian vampires sound today whenever the French national anthem, the revolutionary 'Marseillaise', is sung: 'These bloodthirsty despots . . . who mercilessly tear their mother's breast . . . Let impure blood water our furrows'. Reformists and radicals found vampires an irresistible metaphor for exploitative institutions and energy-sapping parasites (Figure 78).[13] 'Capital is dead labour, which, vampire-like, lives only by sucking living labour, and lives the more, the more labour it sucks', wrote Karl Marx.[14]

Yet the essence of a vampiric corpse—what distinguishes it from a ghost, angel, or demon—is that it is physical. It is a tangible proxy for the inexplicable, indefinable anxieties, terrors, and tragedies of life: a scapegoat that can be beheaded, impaled, or burned. Since it is in fact insentient, it is the best and most harmless of scapegoats, infinitely preferable to all conscious victims of human paranoia. Nor (contrary to Freud) does attacking corpses imply hatred of the dead. By a remarkable and apparently intuitive sleight-of-hand, it occupies a different mental silo from feelings about remembered individuals, as in the parallel understandings of the soul in rural Greece (p. 101).

But the vampire is indeed a metaphor, and an infinitely malleable one: a dark mirror for the countless unacceptable facets of human behaviour. It breaks all rules, knows no limits, and indulges in monstrous excess: it represents the wild disorder against which political, social, and familial conventions stand as bulwarks.[15] Vampires have been flying demons, brutal thugs, antisocial relatives and neighbours, domineering grandmothers, cunning wise-women, heretics, deadly seducers, rebellious teenagers, and witches. They have reified the unaccountable horrors of bubonic plague and tuberculosis. They have been safety-valves

FIGURE 78: The vampire as satirical metaphor: *Punch* caricatures the Irish nationalist leader Charles Stewart Parnell in the run-up to the general election of late 1885.

when religious and socio-cultural change has up-ended all sense of security. This easy sliding between corpse and metaphor makes deeply satisfying emotional sense, even when it defies all logic. It was intuited in 1569 by the German gravedigger who thought that the best way to keep a chomping corpse's mouth shut was to wedge it open (p. 330).

But the dangerous dead are also products of their own times: if they are to mirror psychological realities, they must be given shape by historical, cultural, and religious ones. The bias towards females—especially young adults—may say a lot about male insecurities, but it also reflects contexts in which women were genuinely powerful. By contrast, lumpen, brutish male corpses have tended to inhabit male-dominated worlds. Folklore, story-telling, preaching, literate fiction, and the sensational press have all added layers, importing motifs from distant regions and different cultures. If compatible with the mental ecosystem, these have taken root and flourished; if not, they have faded.

Getting the Job Done

If this book has a central message, it is that corpse-killing is mainstream and not marginal, therapeutic and not pathological. Like other extreme rituals, it is distressing at the time but leaves people feeling good afterwards.[16] When I started this project, I would not have believed that I would find the dangerous dead in such a variety of contexts. Nor would I have believed that they would so often be hiding in plain sight, unnoticed (or tacitly ignored) by regional or period specialists.

A striking instance is early modern central Europe, where witchcraft persecution has attracted such widespread interest and such intensive research. Were fewer corpses 'executed' there than witches? There is no compelling reason to think so. Of course, the procedures against witches are far better documented, but poor documentation does not usually deter historians. Rather—without consciously articulating it like this—they have shied away from a topic that has seemed too marginal, too weird, or too disgusting (as if burning living people as witches were any less disgusting).

In sanitized Western societies, engagement with decaying human flesh is mainly off-limits. It is accepted that some people have to do it because their work is necessary and urgent: paramedics, rescue workers, police, forensic scientists, and undertakers. But the people who impaled and beheaded corpses were just as convinced about the urgency of their own tasks: to disable monsters, or to stop plague from spreading. Many world cultures—notably those practising secondary burial—do not see the decomposition process as repellent, but instead a natural moving-on that becomes sinister only if it is supernaturally halted. When Greek villagers remember the dead with love, their best hope for them is to see their clean white bones and know that they have reached 'joy and gladness' (p. 50).

In the Romanian village of Marotinu de Sus, a farmer named Petre Toma died and was buried. Remarkable events followed, and we are lucky to have them described by the main protagonist in the countermeasures, a shepherd called Mircea Mitrica:

> 'His heart was still beating when we took it out. . . . This is how we knew he was a *moroi*. If we hadn't done that, she would have died in two days. . . .
>
> 'There was this guy, he died a while ago. He was telling me, "Son, if you want to start doing this, go ahead. You need courage and a strong heart. Don't be afraid when you enter there. You can find the dead lying on their side, the same way you lie in bed".
>
> 'A horse killed him, he wasn't sick or anything. He was drunk driving his wagon, and fell under the horse. . . . [Soon afterwards his niece] was sick in bed. Her husband and father-in-law came to me, and they invited me to their house to drink plum brandy. When I got there the girl was sick in bed. The *moroi* withered her. All she could say was, 'Look, he's on top of me, he's killing me!' . . . The dead man's sister realized that Petre had become a monster. How could we save her? . . .
>
> 'We went at midnight to the cemetery and dug him up. His face was red and his beard had started to grow. He had fresh blood on the

> left corner of his mouth. When we cut him open there was a pool of blood. You cut him open with a scythe from the neck to the chest. You open the ribcage to take the heart out. I took his heart out and went to a crossroads. We started a fire and singed the heart on a pitchfork. We went home and made another fire. We burnt the heart to ashes and mashed it. We made it into a tea and gave it to the girl to drink. The next morning the girl came to my place by herself and said 'Let's eat and let's drink!' . . .
>
> 'The wife of the dead man turned us in to the authorities. The relatives approved of what we did, we saved a human being. . . . All the villagers said that this has been going on since the olden times. It's better to take the heart out than let the corpse kill children. The elders are wise and know things.'[17]

Readers of this book will feel on familiar ground here. They may be more surprised to learn that this passage is translated from Mitrica's spoken words in front of a video camera, and that the episode happened in 2004. When the police arrived at the cemetery they were followed by a journalist, and for the first (and perhaps last) time ever, the aftermath of a vampire-killing was captured on film. So we can all watch the lurid scene: the cemetery with police-car lights flashing, the violated tomb, and Mitrica brandishing his pitchfork at the camera. It also emerged that Mitrica had drunk half a litre of plum brandy before his enterprise: a detail that may have been more central to corpse-killing rituals in the past than we can ever know.

More important than sensationalism is the obvious sincerity and compassion with which those words were spoken. Many of Mitrica's fellow-villagers agreed. One of them, whose reactions are also recorded on video, can be allowed to speak for all conscientious killers of the dead in past ages:

> The dead have to be dead—not undead or half-dead. So they brought him something good, not something bad. It's about the universe, the cosmic harmony of the dead with the dead, the living with the living. For the community it's very good, for the dead it's very good, so where is the harm for them?

NOTES

Introduction

Epigraph: Dundes 1998a, p. viii.

1. Auerbach 1995 and Groom 2018 are good guides.

2. I am especially grateful to Bane 2010 and Melton 2011 for providing starting-points. Among countless other modern general works, readers may find these especially useful: Barber 1988; Bohn 2019; Cacciola 2016; Dundes 1998a; Groom 2018; Lecouteux 1999; Livermore 2021; Sugg 2019.

3. Littlewood 2009, p. 249.

Chapter 1: Who Were the Dangerous Dead?

Epigraph: English translation in Calmet 1759, p. vi.

1. Stoker 1897, p. 289.

2. *Gentleman's Magazine*, 2 (1732): 681; cf. Calmet 1759, p. 202, and Barber 1988, pp. 16–17, 57. These go back to the same small group of Serbian sources as the bloodsucking emphasis.

3. McGill 2022, p. 265.

4. Cf. Barber 1988, p. 14.

5. See pp. 67, 376. K. M. Wilson (1985) misleadingly dates one English-language occurrence of the word *vampire* to 1688, whereas it is actually in an annotation to a letter dated 17 January 1733: Charles Forman, *Some Queries and Observations upon the Revolution in 1688, and its Consequences*, 2nd ed. (London, 1741), p. 11n.

6. Lawson 1910, pp. 381–383, and below, p. 412.

7. Stachowski and Stachowski 2017, with Stachowski 2020 as an addendum, and Stachowski 2024; all contain useful bibliographies. Another helpful account is Mézes 2019, pp. 134–138.

8. Murgoci 1998, pp. 13–14.

9. Stachowski 2022 (especially pp. 386–387 for his conclusions).

10. Stachowski 2022, pp. 373, 375, 383–384; cf. Burkhardt 1966.

11. The sources for Map 1, where not otherwise found in this book, derive from Bane 2010, Melton 2011, and other standard works of reference.

12. Forth and Kukharenko 2012; below, p. 58. To the cases that they list should be added the Philippines: Demetrio 1970, 2.286–287.

13. Graeber and Wengrow 2021, pp. 103–104.

14. Hutton 2017, pp. 11, 285. Thanks to Ronald Hutton for a discussion on this point.

15. See Hutton 2017, pp. 23–35, for such direct action in witch cases.

16. Goodare 2002, pp. 20 (not universal), 23, 53 (social benefit), 187n32 (mothers), 21, 137 (endemic or epidemic), 25–29 (gender variability), and 211–212 (literary stimulus).

17. Hutton 2017, p. 14.

18. Holzem 2023, p. 715.

Chapter 2: Fearing Dead Friends, Killing Dead Enemies

Epigraph: L. Tolstoy, *War and Peace*, trans. R. Pevear and L. Volokhonsky (London: Vintage Books, 2007), p. 718.

1. Pettitt 2018.
2. Freud 1918, pp. 98–99.
3. Kleinpaul 1898, pp. 119–129.
4. Jones 1931, pp. 98–130.
5. Jones 1931, pp. 103, 106, 120.
6. See Melton 2011, pp. 554–562, for a useful digest of psychological approaches (Jung and this quotation are on p. 556).
7. Dundes 1998b, pp. 161, 163–170.
8. Especially Littlewood 2009; see also, for instance, Geschiere 1998.
9. Bahna 2015 (quotations on pp. 286, 291).
10. See Xygalatas 2022, especially pp. 210–213, for extreme ritual and 'effort justification'.
11. Hufford 1982; Adler 2011. Thanks also to Alan Lenzi for his very helpful advice.
12. Hufford 1982, especially pp. x–xviii, 245–250.
13. Hufford 1982, p. 221.
14. Cf. Jones 1931, pp. 116–118, for Romanian vampires making sexual attacks on victims of the opposite gender; and the several cases of night-mare, pressing and strangling mentioned by Barber 1988, pp. 6, 7, 12, 16, 184, 186–187.
15. Weinrich 1612, especially pp. 7–9; Adler 2011, p. 87, for the psychological context.
16. Bell 2011, p. 66.
17. Adler 2011, p. 2.
18. Adler 2011, pp. 97–98.
19. Adler 2011, p. 115.
20. Adler 2011, p. 111.
21. Adler 2011, pp. 124–133 (on 'Brugada syndrome').
22. Cf. Adler 2011, pp. 126–128.
23. Barber 1988.
24. Barber 1988, pp. 195–196.
25. D. E. Brown 2004 (quotation on p. 47).
26. D. E. Brown 2004, pp. 49–50.
27. D. E. Brown 2004, p. 53.

Chapter 3: The Dangerous Dead in Society

Epigraph: English translation in Calmet 1759, p. 208.

1. See Vitebsky 1993 for this section.
2. Vitebsky 1993, pp. 82, 139, 205.
3. Vitebsky 1993, pp. 3–4.
4. Vitebsky 1993, pp. 102, 128–129.
5. Vitebsky 1993, p. 97.
6. She was my wife's grandmother, and I was present on this occasion.
7. Information from Kanerva Blair-Heikkinen.
8. Frazer 1913–1924, 1933–1936.
9. Frazer 1933–1936, 2.63–94.
10. Swancutt 2008.
11. Schierup 1986, pp. 189–190.

12. Schierup 1986, p. 173.
13. Schierup 1986, p. 184.
14. Schierup 1986, p. 189.
15. Du Boulay 1982. The contextual arguments are developed at greater length in Du Boulay 2009.
16. Du Boulay 1982, p. 231.
17. Du Boulay 1982, pp. 224, 233.
18. Du Boulay 1982, pp. 234–235.
19. Du Boulay 1982, p. 236.
20. Du Boulay 1982, pp. 231–232.
21. Du Boulay 2009, pp. 164–165.
22. Lewis Everett Peck, farmer of Rhode Island, interviewed in 1981: quotation in Bell 2011, p. 10.

Chapter 4: Rest in Peace (and Don't Come Back)

1. Van Gennep 1960, pp. 146–165, at 146.
2. The classics are Hertz 1960 and Metcalf and Huntingdon 1991, building on Van Gennep 1960. McClelland 1999, pp. 108–140, discusses the importance of these rites to prevent vampirism in Bulgaria.
3. See Storå 1971, pp. 224–225, for Skolt Sámi; below, p. 415, for grave clothes in Ireland; Barber 1988, p. 49, for revenants untying knots.
4. Storå 1971, pp. 219–220. Cf. Kanerva 2013, pp. 209–210, for Iceland.
5. Janowski and Kurasiński 2010, figure 7 and p. 93.
6. Du Boulay 1982, pp. 224–225.
7. Storå 1971, p. 230. Cf. Pettersson 1957, pp. 76–77.
8. Du Boulay 1982, pp. 224–229; du Boulay 2009, pp. 223–301.
9. Du Boulay 1982, p. 225.
10. Barber 1988, p. 58. The Sámi are a good example: Pettersson 1957, pp. 79–81, and Storå 1971, p. 241. This idea applies to walking corpses where those are believed in, but much more widely to ghosts.
11. Pettersson 1957, pp. 79–81.
12. Danforth 1982, pp. 48–50. See also du Boulay 2009, pp. 74–77, 285–299, for the earth as a 'devourer and cleanser' and the need for physical dissolution.
13. Richardson 1993 (quotation on p. 92).
14. 'Vita S. Cuthberti Anon.' c.13, ed. B. Colgrave, in *Two Lives of Saint Cuthbert* (Cambridge, 1940), p. 130.
15. Fonseca 1995, p. 249.
16. Herskovits 1937, p. 206.
17. Pentikäinen 1968.
18. Pentikäinen 1968, pp. 152–153.
19. Gardeła and Duma 2013.
20. Angélopoulou 1999, pp. 79–82.
21. Pentikäinen 1968, p. 233.
22. Cf. Barber 1988, pp. 21, 29–30.
23. A. H. Tammsaare, *Vargamäe* (first published 1926; trans. I. Feldbach and A. P. Trei [Glasgow: Vagabond Voices, 2018]), p. 314.
24. At first sight, early modern Greece looks like an exception, but suicides there were posthumously excommunicated, and the unquietness of the corpse was integral to the penalties of

excommunication (p. 308). Another big exception is Russia, apparently because different criteria applied (p. 300). Suicides were resentful and dangerous among the Sora (p. 35), but their malevolence was not exercised in corporeal form.

25. *Nicomachean Ethics*, book V, cited in Murray 2023, pp. 73–74.

26. Murray 1998–2000, 1.110–113, 2.469.

27. Murray 1998–2000, 2.471–481, and Murray 2023, p. 82, noting that this seems to have changed somewhat in the early modern period (which is the context for the Striegau episode).

28. I owe this suggestion to Kanerva Blair-Heikkinen. Thanks also to Alexander Murray for discussions.

Chapter 5: Understanding Stories (1)

1. Thompson 1955–1958, 2.404–517 (section E).

2. Brown 2004, p. 47.

3. Forth and Kukharenko 2012, p. 160.

4. Forth and Kukharenko 2012, p. 169.

5. Disconcertingly, Forth and Kukharenko (p. 156) are 'confident' that they would find cases in Africa and native North America if they searched further, which makes one wonder how seriously they have considered alternatives.

6. Witzel 2012.

7. Notably Lincoln 2015, which seems rather unfair to me.

8. See the map in Witzel 2012, p. 235, showing the hypothetical spread of the Laurasian system.

9. Kelly and Metcalf 2021 is a collection of studies on the ancient world that embrace both positions, with thoughtful reflections by the editors on pp. 1–15. Thanks to Christopher Metcalf and Selena Wisnom for their advice.

10. Ginzburg and Lincoln 2020.

11. Ginzburg and Lincoln 2020, p. 176.

12. Currie 2021, pp. 138–140.

13. See Blair 2005, pp. 166–181, and Watkins 2007, pp. 1–22, for rejections of the 'two cultures' model.

14. Hansen 1980, p. 74 (and pp. 74–76 for other Irish variants on the same theme).

15. Martin 1979.

16. Richard 1657, p. 212. Cf. Hartnup 2004, pp. 193–194.

17. Thompson 1955–1958, 3.454–456 (motifs H970–H987). Cf. McClelland 1999, p. 85, for Bulgaria. Trzaska 2023, pp. 342–345, discusses the wider occurrence of this motif in Greece.

18. James 1922, p. 422.

19. Danforth 1982, p. 22.

20. Black 2016, p. 88.

Chapter 6: Understanding Stories (2)

Epigraph: *Gentleman's Magazine* 2 (March 1732): 681.

1. [Anonymous] 1820.

2. For this paragraph: Gordon-Grube 1993; Sugg 2011, especially pp. 181–188; Bell 2024. I am very grateful to Michael Bell for introducing me to this aspect of Paracelsian medicine.

3. Sugg 2011, p. 118.

4. Gordon-Grube 1993.

5. Cavazzi 1687, p. 222: 'Quando siano di fresco soterrati, ed intieri, egli stesso tronca loro dal busto la testa, da cui diconi uscire il sangue (e può essere che ciò succeda mediante qualche illusione, ò prestigio), indi raccoltolo, ne forma empiastri per l'infermo, ò glie lo distempra nelle vivande, promettendogli infallibile la sanità; e che in avvenire il defonto, perdute le forze, non potrà più molestarlo.' Grateful thanks to John Thornton for helping me to understand the context of this text.

6. Mallet 2019.

7. Pierre des Noyers to Ismael Bouillaud, 13 December 1639, in *Lettres de Pierre des Noyers* (Berlin: Behr, 1859), p. 561, letter CCXXXV.

8. *Mercure Galant*, May 1693, pp. 62–70 (prompted by a reference in the March issue to shroud-eating corpses in Poland and their decapitation). For the context and aftermath of this episode, see Vermeir 2012, and Bohn 2019, pp. 59–61.

9. 'Quand on les trouve de cette sorte [i.e., undecayed], ayant la figure de ceux qui ont apparu en songe, on leur coupe la teste, et on leur ouvre le cœur, et il en sort quantité de sang. On le ramasse, et on le mêle avec de la farine pour la pêtrir, et en faire ce pain, qui est un remede seur pour se garantir d'une vexation si terrible. Aprés qu'on leur a coupé la teste, ceux que l'Esprit tourmentoit la nuit, n'en sont plus troublez, et se portent bien en suite.'

10. Perkowski wrote vaguely that this 'also occur[s]', but his source was probably Calmet's paraphrase of des Noyers: Perkowski 1989, p. 124 (though it does not in fact occur in any of the stories that he analyses there).

11. *Mercure Galant*, February 1694, pp. 13–119.

12. Calmet 1746, pp. 297–298 (= Calmet 1759, pp. 212–213).

13. Bohn 2019, pp. 60–61.

14. Kozak 2021, pp. 171–172.

15. Calmet 1751a, pp. 72–73. I have been unable to verify the context, but this story was among news gathered since 1749 that Calmet added to the 1751 edition.

16. This, however, is from a late source: Tettau and Temme 1837, pp. 275–276.

17. Kozak 2021, pp. 177–178.

18. Kozak 2021, pp. 84, 171.

19. Kozak 2021, p. 85.

20. Bohn 2019, pp. 140–145; Barber 1988, p. 64, for Pomerania; Kozak 2021, pp. 172–181, for Poland and Kashubians.

21. Murgoci 1998, pp. 16–18; below, p. 439, for the 2004 case.

22. Richard 1657, pp. 215–216; Pitton de Tournefort 1717, p. 134. Cf. Barber 1988, p. 23, and Bohn 2019, pp. 69–73.

23. Ginzburg 1980, p. 117.

24. The sources that I have used here are Groot 1892–1910, 5.723–761; Louie and Edwards 1996; and Yi and Branscum 2021.

25. Groot 1892–1910, 5.749–750; Louie and Edwards 1996, pp. 90–91.

26. Groot 1892–1910, 5.745n.

27. Rawski and Rawson 2005, pp. 35–37.

28. J. M. Synge, *The Playboy of the Western World* (Dublin: Maunsel & Co., 1907), act 3.

Chapter 7: Understanding Corpses

1. I am very grateful to Anna Kjellström for her helpful comments on this chapter.

2. Principally (but not exclusively): Murphy 2008; Reynolds 2009; Klevnäs 2013; Devlin and Graham 2015; Gardeła and Kajkowski 2015; Cangle 2015; Aspöck et al. 2020; Betsinger et al. 2020; Klevnäs et al. 2021; Pergola et al. 2023.

3. For instance, Blaziot 2022, pp. 26–31.

4. Knüsel and Schotsmans 2022.

5. Noterman 2021, p. 22; Aspöck et al. 2022, pp. 290–291.

6. Barber 1988, pp. 102–119.

7. Alfsdotter et al. 2022.

8. Barber 1988, pp. 90, 103.

9. Hori 1962; Jeremiah 2010.

10. Reginald of Durham, 'Libellus', c.2 (ed. J. Raine [Surtees Society, 1835], pp. 3–4).

11. Levin 2003, p. 97.

12. Du Boulay 2009, pp. 302–303.

13. Levin 2003, pp. 85–87.

14. Barber 1988, pp. 164, 167–169.

15. Peterson 1976.

16. Du Boulay 2009, pp. 297–298.

17. This paragraph draws on Baines and Lacovara 2002, and on Richard Parkinson's helpful advice, for which I am most grateful. There was possibly a phase of more physical corpse-fear in pre-dynastic Egypt: see Marei 2016.

18. Barber 1988, p. 167.

19. Arcini 2009, figure 2.

20. Arcini 2009, p. 196.

21. Dierkens 1996. The motive ascribed in 1137—that it was to expiate his father's sins—has no contemporary support.

22. Toplak 2018; Alterauge et al. 2020, pp. 17–22.

23. Also Barber 1988, p. 49.

24. Cf. Arcini 2009, p. 187.

25. Alterauge et al. 2020, pp. 23–25.

26. *Hamlet*, act 5, scene 1.

27. Barber 1988, p. 79.

28. Barber 1988, pp. 73, 157.

29. Anna Kjellström (pers. comm.) writes : 'Diagnostic traces of posthumous decapitation in bone depend on the freshness of the bone, and thus the plastic response of the bone to trauma. . . . Absence of sharp force trauma, in a skeleton where the cranium is clearly separated from the rest of the body, suggest manipulation but not primarily beheading.'

30. Alfsdotter et al. 2022, p. 199 (the atlanto-occipital joint).

31. Alfsdotter et al. 2022, p. 199 ('mandible gravitating toward base of coffin' after 52 days).

32. Barber 1988, pp. 54–55.

33. Ginzburg 1991, p. 230, suggests a different mythological context for mutilation of the feet and ankles.

34. Barber 1988, pp. 53–74, 71–72, 157–158.

35. Hurston 1981, p. 58.

36. Fortis 1774, p. 64.

37. Barber 1988, p. 52.

38. Barber 1988, pp. 50–51; Wittkopp 2009; Janowski and Kurasiński 2010; Polcyn and Gajda 2015, pp. 1380–1382.

39. Barber 1988, p. 47.

40. Du Boulay 2009, pp. 72, 254, interprets placing a piece of clay tile on the mouth of the corpse as emphasising an 'understanding of man as clay'. But could this be a rationalisation of what was originally a countermeasure?

41. Also Barber 1988, pp. 21–22, 25, 63, 73–74.

42. Hennius et al. 2016 (Rissne on p. 156). I owe this reference to Anna Kjellström.

43. Murgoci 1998, p. 17.

44. Kurasiński et al. 2018.

45. E. O'Brien, *Post-Roman Britain to Anglo-Saxon England: Burial Practices Reviewed* (BAR British Ser. 289, 1999), p. 55; R. Shoesmith, *Hereford City Excavations; I: Excavations at Castle Green* (London: Council for British Archaeology, 1980), pp. 27–29.

46. Klevnäs 2013; Noterman 2021; Aspöck et al. 2022.

Chapter 8: The Circumpolar World and Northern Asia

Epigraph: Humphrey 1996, pp. 221–222.

1. See Poo 2022, pp. 177–181, for a good overview.

2. Herskovits 1938, 2.233–236. Cf. Pulkkinen 2014, pp. 143–147, for Finland, and Barber 1988, pp. 180, 186, 190–191, for other cultures.

3. Shirokogoroff 1935, pp. 52–53, 134–136.

4. Pettersson 1957, pp. 41–55, 72–75. Cf. Storå 1971, pp. 186–198.

5. Du Boulay 1982, pp. 226–227.

6. Lester 2023. See also Kastrup, Crabtree, and Kelly 2018 for further implications about universal consciousness.

7. For this paragraph: Humphrey 1996; Hunt 2003; Hutton 2017, pp. 74–95; Price 2019, pp. 230–271.

8. See Ogden 2021b, especially pp. 60–80, for these associations of werewolves in the ancient world and beyond.

9. Hunt 2003, p. 53.

10. King 1999, p. 59.

11. Swancutt 2008.

12. MacDonald 1983, p. 29.

13. Storå 1971, pp. 262–263.

14. Humphrey 1996, pp. 328–333.

15. Shirokogoroff 1935, pp. 136–137.

16. Shirokogoroff 1935, p. 213. For the same reason, Cantonese Taoist female shamans cared for the spirits of unmarried girls excluded from their birth-family altars: Reed 1987, p. 171.

17. Humphrey 1996, pp. 195, 221–222.

18. Groot 1892–1910, 5.520, 743–748.

19. A Yuan Mei story: Groot 1892–1910, 5.743–744.

20. Ahern 1973, pp. 172–173. Cf. Groot 1892–1910, 5.744–745, for the same Chinese belief.

21. Bane 2010, pp. 44–45, 75; Melton 2011, p. 127.

22. Yiwu 2009, pp. 29–30.

23. Stachowski and Stachowski 2017, pp. 652–653, 683–684. Many thanks to Kamil Stachowski for discussions.

24. Kozak 2021, pp. 107–108, for animals' milk; Angélopoulou 1999, pp. 79–82, for vampiric babies, deprived of their mothers' milk, who suck to death young mothers and milk-giving ewes.

25. Sarpkaya and Yaltırık 2022, pp. 40–50, 59–62, 66–71.

Chapter 9: India and China

Epigraph: Quoted by Ji Yun in *The Shadow Book*: Yu and Branscum 2021, p. 133.

1. Huang 2009.

2. D. G. White 2006, pp. 201–207; I. Ramos 2020, pp. 47–50.

3. D. G. White 2006, 2020; I. Ramos 2020, pp. 54–60.

4. D. G. White 2006, pp. 27–29; D. G. White 2020, pp. 64–65.

5. Translation from D. G. White 2006, pp. 193–194.

6. D. G. White 2020, p. 73.

7. Yu and Branscum 2021, pp. 6–9.

8. Groot 1892–1910, 4.406–407, 5.724, 744, 752–754; Strickmann 2002, pp. 74–79; Poo 2022, pp. 38–39; Yu and Branscum 2021, pp. 5–6.

9. Yu and Branscum 2021, pp. 4–5.

10. Groot 1892–1910, 5.734–738.

11. Campany 1996, pp. 253–255; Strickmann 2002, pp. 258–265; Poo 2022, pp. 94–95, 109–111; Yu and Branscum 2021, pp. 114, 228.

12. See the Ji Yun story in Yu and Branscum 2021, pp. 241–242.

13. Poo 2022, pp. 11–12.

14. Poo 2022, p. 37, citing the *Zuo Zhuan*.

15. For this paragraph: Jamison 1991, pp. 68–81; D. G. White 2020, pp. 73–74.

16. D. G. White 2020, p. 74.

17. Strickmann 2002, p. 259; see Xinjiang 2004 for the chronology of Buddhism, and Dalrymple 2024, pp. 94–108, for a new overview. Cf. Humphrey 1996, pp. 328–333, for fox-spirits among the Daur Mongols.

18. Strickmann 2002, pp. 261–265; D. G. White 2020, p. 70.

Chapter 10: Flying Demons and Dangerous Women

Epigraph: Naveh and Shaked 1998, p. 201.

1. Matos Moctezuma and Solís Olguín 2002, pp. 205–206, 222–223, 435.

2. Briggs 1920, p. 129; cf. Bane 2010, pp. 46–47, and Melton 2011, p. 372.

3. Maxwell 1881, p. 28.

4. García Arévalo 1998, pp. 112–114, 120–122; Poviones-Bishop 2001.

5. D. G. White 2020, pp. 70–73.

6. D. G. White 2020, p. 71.

7. Bane 2010, entries for *aswang/mannananggal, balbal, (hantu-)langsuir, mandurugo, mati-anak, penangglan, pontianak, tanggal*; Demetrio 1970, 2.232–252; M. Ramos 1969.

8. Bane 2010, entries for *khmoch-long, krappa, ma cá rông, phii krasue, yasha*. In Sri Lanka the *bodrimár* is 'a sort of Banshee, the ghost of a pregnant Sinhalese woman who died, and was buried with her undelivered child still alive. From time to time her weary spirit wails round houses' (note in *The Taprobanian*, 1 [1887], p. 38). Thanks to Shamara Wettimuny for this reference.

9. Bane 2010, entries for *camazotz, cihuacoatl, cihuateteo, ciuapipiltin, coatlicue, itzapapalotl, tlaciques*.

10. Scobie 1978, pp. 83–100, emphasizing the Hispanic context. As he says (p. 99), 'the question as to whether an imported Spanish folkbelief about strigiform witches merely reinforced an analogous pre-existing indigenous belief, or led to the grafting of a fresh belief onto already existing local traditions about the ability of *nahuales* to transform themselves into other animals, cannot at present be answered with certainty'.

11. Matos Moctezuma and Solís Olguín 2002, pp. 302–303, 463.

12. Bane 2010, entries for *bhuta, churel, gayal*.

13. Bane 2010, entries for *asema, loogaroo, obayifo, soucayant*.

14. Bane 2010, entries for *boginki, latawiec, mahr, mwère, navi, veshtitza*. The Portugese *bruja/bruxa* is also sometimes identified as a diabolical, bloodsucking night bird (Jones 1931, p. 107; Bane 2010, p. 40; Campagne 2008); in early modern sources, she is a witch transported to

'Diana's hunt', as with the Basque belief that 'illas maleficas et sortilegas mulierulas . . . que vulgariter broxe nuncupantur posse transferri de loco in locum per realem mutationem': Martin of Arles, *Tractatus de Superstitionibus* (Rome: Vincentio Luchino, 1559), p. 8. See Scobie 1978 for further discussion of these beliefs in Iberia.

15. For what follows: Patai 1990, pp. 221–222; Wiggermann 2000; Scurlock 2016; Ogden 2021a, pp. 50–51; Finkel 2021, pp. 61–64; Crear 2022, pp. 120–127; Clegg 2023, pp. 28–43. Many thanks to Selena Wisnom and Martin Worthington for their guidance.

16. Wiggermann 2000, p. 249; Selena Wisnom, pers. comm.

17. The two seals in Figure 20, and another apparently showing the same squatting female, are discussed by Briggs Buchanan, *Early Near Eastern Seals in the Yale Babylonian Collection* (New Haven, CT: Yale University Press, 1981), pp. 200–201. His rejection of the demonic interpretation seems unconvincing.

18. Burkert 1992, pp. 82–87; cf. Ogden 2021a, pp. 50–51.

19. Johnston 1999, pp. 169–170; cf. pp. 22, 72–73, 161–167.

20. Ogden 2021a; Hutton 2017, pp. 69–72; D. G. White 2020, pp. 60–63.

21. Ogden 2021a, pp. 21–23, 61; M. Ramos 1969, pp. 239–242.

22. For what follows: Sorlin 1991; Viscuso 2000; Hartnup 2004.

23. Campagne 2008, and note 14 above.

24. Ignatios the Deacon, 'The Life of Patriarch Tarasios', c.5, ed. S. Efthymiadis (Aldershot: Ashgate Variorum, 1998), pp. 172–173. For context: Sorlin 1991, pp. 413–415; Hartnup 2004, pp. 88–89, 92–95; Clegg 2023, pp. 65–69.

25. Hartnup 2004, pp. 85–157.

26. *'Decreta'*, book 19.5 (Burchard 1853, col. 973). See D. G. White 2020, pp. 59–63, for this substitution motif.

27. Naveh and Shaked 1998, pp. 113–133, 159–163, 173, 199–214; Patai 1990, pp. 221–254; Crerar 2022, pp. 120–127; Clegg 2023, pp. 89–114. In some of these sources Gello is assimilated to Lamia.

28. García Arévalo 1998, p. 112; Poviones-Bishop 2001.

29. Crerar 2022, pp. 123–127.

30. Hufford 1982, pp. 236–237, commenting that 'the Old Hag and the *aswang* often keep company'.

31. Du Boulay 2009, pp. 325–326.

Chapter 11: The 'Carmilla Template' in China and the Eastern Roman Empire

Epigraph: Hansen 1996, pp. 26–27.

1. Le Fanu 1993, p. 263. Cf. Groom 2018, pp. 143–146.

2. Campany 1996, pp. 253–255. Greater clarity on when this motif first appears would be helpful.

3. Poo 2022, pp. 109–111. Gan Bao also gives this story, but omitting the discovery of the fox-spirit: Diming and Wangdao 2004, pp. 930–931, No. 398.

4. Diming and Wangdao 2004, pp. 932–933, No. 399.

5. Groot 1892–1910, 4.424–425, citing *'Kwang I Ki'* and *'Kwei tung* chapter 2'. The first of these is evidently the *Taiping Huanyu Ji* of Yue Shi (930–1007).

6. Groot 1892–1910, 5.518–520, 723–761; Louie and Edwards 1996; Yu and Branscum 2021.

7. Louie and Edwards 1996, pp. 100–103.

8. Louie and Edwards 1996, pp. 128–129.

9. Philostratus, 'Life of Apollonios of Tyana', iv.25, in *Apollonius of Tyana*, 2 vols., ed. Christopher P. Jones, Loeb Classical Library (Cambridge MA: Harvard University Press, 2005), 1:372–377; Ogden 2009, pp. 65–66.

10. Johnston 1999, pp. 28, 181–182; Clegg 2023, pp. 46–49.

11. Phlegon of Tralles, 'Book of Marvels', c.1, in Hansen 1996, pp. 25–28, 68–85, 200. The author is unknown; the text survives (incomplete) in a collection of marvels compiled c. AD 120–130, and there is a later but independent summary. The story is set around 340 BC. See Doroszewska 2015 for further commentary.

12. Cf. Ogden 2009, p. 161.

13. Most obviously, the story of Orpheus and Eurydice. Hansen 1996, pp. 79–81, notes resemblances with a modern Irish folktale.

14. Diming and Wangdao 2004, Nos. 146, 177, 359, 360, 363, 368, 370–373, 381, 383, 395–398, 433.

15. Benjamin 2018 makes a sustained argument for the maximalist 'First Silk Roads' hypothesis (though on pp. 3–6 he acknowledges the sceptics). Dalrymple 2024, pp. 17–19, re-states the sceptical position with an emphasis on India.

16. Hiebert and Cambon 2011, pp. 141–142; Benjamin 2018, pp. 200–202.

17. Benjamin 2018, p. 234; Xiong and Fu 2022, pp. 165–166, 185.

18. Patai 1990, pp. 233–234, citing the 'Book of Zohar', a late thirteenth-century compilation by Moses of León.

19. Dickie 2001, pp. 178–181, 245–249, 302–303.

20. Yu 1987, p. 429 (though the anthropology he cites does not support this statement).

21. Poo 2022, pp. 94–96 (though he is essentially sceptical of Yu's argument).

22. Enthoven 1924, p. 240.

23. Jordan 1972, pp. 140–155 (quotation at p. 144).

24. Reed 1987, p. 170.

25. Poo 2022, pp. 95–96.

26. Pomeroy 1995, pp. 120–148 (pp. 131–136 for philosophers).

Chapter 12: Wonder-Working Women

Epigraph: Hall 2007a, pp. 1–3 (Alaric Hall's translation).

1. Nissinen 2017, pp. 297–325; see also Nissinen 2020 for the overlapping roles of shamans and prophets.

2. See Keller 2002 for a sustained critique of this view through the lens of feminist theory.

3. See Nissinen 2019, especially pp. 102–104.

4. See Nissinen 2017, pp. 310–314, for some good examples.

5. Van Buylaere 2019.

6. Quast 2011, especially essays by Enright, Istvánovits and Kulcsár, Simek, and Ljungkvist. Simek 2015 reviews the written sources, but with conclusions that are strangely (and surely unreasonably) negative.

7. Robinson 1993.

8. See Simek 2015 for an extreme statement that women did not have a formal role in cults.

9. Vitebsky 1993, pp. 18–20, 60–61 (quotation on pp. 19–20).

10. Girshick Ben-Amos 1994 (quotation pp. 130–131). Compare the remarkably similar status and roles of Taoist female shamans in China: Reed 1987, pp. 169–172.

11. Hall 2007b. Cf. Adler 2011, pp. 44–47.

12. Inference from Hufford 1982, pp. 33–34, 40–41, 73, 82, 88, 112, 221, 237; there is one counter-example on p. 102. This was also the tradition in ancient Mesopotamia: Scurlock 2016, p. 79.

13. O'Sullivan 2021, p. 173.

14. O'Sullivan 2021, pp. 223–224.

15. O'Sullivan 2021, pp. 225–226.
16. O'Sullivan 2021, pp. 257, 261. It is interesting to compare and contrast this with the theoretical feminist perspective on similar phenomena in Keller 2002.
17. Holmes 1993, p. 60n.
18. Holmes 1993, p. 65.
19. Roll and Persinger 2001, pp. 143–145.
20. See Figuer [c. 1880], pp. 477–512, for this and other cases of *les filles électriques*.
21. Roll 1977, pp. 405–408.
22. Roll 1977, pp. 386–387, 409.
23. Schürmann 1990, p. 59.
24. Mézes 2019, pp. 479–495.
25. Kreuter 2007, pp. 231–234; Bohn 2019, pp. 83–84, 103–104.
26. Kreuter 2007, p. 237.

Chapter 13: Mesopotamia, Greece, and Rome before Christ

Epigraph: Translation after Johnston 1999, p. 173.
1. See Wisnom 2025 for an introduction and guide.
2. Finkel 2021, p. 55. See also Scurlock 2016.
3. MacDougal 2014.
4. The Old Babylonian Dream Compendium (BM 96951), 79–81. I am very grateful to Elyse Zomer for supplying this still-unpublished text via Selena Wisnom.
5. Brereton 2018, pp. 100–117.
6. The texts of the *Descent of Ištar*, *Gilgameš*, and *Nergal and Ereškigal*, and the relationships between them are discussed by Wisnom 2024; see also Scurlock 2016, p. 80, and Finkel 2021, pp. 139–150. There was a Middle Assyrian version of the *Descent*, but this part is not preserved; otherwise, there are no manuscripts certainly predating the early Neo-Assyrian period. However, if one accepts Wisnom's argument that *Gilgameš* cites this passage, it must have been composed by c. 1200 BC. My handling of these sources, and of the other Assyrian material in this chapter, would have been impossible without the help of Selena Wisnom; grateful thanks also to Frances Reynolds for her comments.
7. Al-Rawi 2008, pp. 119–124; Finkel 2021, pp. 37–38.
8. Freedman 1998, pp. 308–309. The first seventeen clauses use the logogram $UŠ_2$ 'dead [person]', but clause 18 switches to $LU_2.UŠ_2$ 'corpse', at a point when the opening formulation also changes.
9. Finkel 2021, p. 32, argues that these are references to premature burial. But that involves assuming that the 'dead person' is not *really* dead, which seems forced and unconvincing. A contemporary letter describes a dream in which a boy comes out of his tomb to deliver a message (Frahm 2010): it may say something about the culture that this image was embedded in the dreamer's psyche.
10. See *Chicago Assyrian Dictionary*, s.v. *karāku*, 'to obstruct, to dam, to intertwine' etc., giving an example in a charm against impotence ('who has dammed you up?'), and another in the context 'he gagged (*ú-kar-rik*) his tongue with wool combings, he bound his hands and feet'. This is an incantation, edited by T. Abusch and D. Schwemer, *Corpus of Mesopotamian Anti-Witchcraft Rituals*, vol. 2 (Leiden: Brill, 2016), p. 59, where it is translated: 'The witch formed a figurine to bind the companion. She obstructed his tongue with (a ball of) combed-out hair, she tied his limbs, she seized his mouth so that he was not able to open it'.
11. Kreppner 2014; see Matney et al. 2002, pp. 55–56 and figure 8 (where the burials are misidentified as kilns); see Matney et al. 2011, p. 71 for a less formal pit containing partly-burnt

bodies. It must be emphasized that this idea is my own, not the excavators', and as a non-specialist I offer it with all due humility. But Mesopotamian archaeology has barely engaged with the possibility that these are 'deviant' burials, and it needs to be suggested.

12. *The Magical Ceremony Maqlû*, ed. T. Abusch (Leiden: Brill, 2016), pp. 297 (quotation), 301, 304.

13. *Gilgameš* XII, lines 305–306; translation from S. Helle, *Gilgamesh* (New Haven, CT: Yale University Press, 2021), p. 119. These lines are preserved only in a Sumerian poem: see Gadotti 2014, pp. 116–117, 160, 301, for context. Gadotti thinks that the implications of burning to death did not apply to cremation, but gives no explicit evidence.

14. Urned cremations do occasionally occur in Neo-Assyrian contexts, but they are rare and clearly in some way exceptional: Ferreri 2015, pp. 23–24, 36; Ökse and Eroglu 2013, pp. 173–174. Thanks to Frances Reynolds for her help.

15. Hauser 2012, pp. 253–254, suggests that they could be witches, Assyrians in some special category, or foreigners. Ferreri 2015 ascribes the cremation rite to immigrant groups, but that seems unconvincing given that the grave-goods are normal Assyrian ones, and she takes no account of the gender bias.

16. Kreppner 2014, p. 180 (my calculations). Compare the Palestinian cemetery at Tell 'Atlīt (Johns 1936–1937): out of twenty-three cremations, fifteen are identifiable, comprising three women, two unsexed adults, one adolescent, and nine children (my calculations).

17. See Burkert 1992 for a sustained argument.

18. Johnston 1999, pp. 8, 10–27, 31 (quotation), 87–94.

19. Johnston 1999, pp. 39–43.

20. Johnston 1999, pp. 127–137; Ogden 2009, p. 146.

21. Johnston 1999, pp. 47–54, 96–98, 129–130.

22. Johnston 1999, pp. 71, 85–86.

23. Johnston 1999, pp. 145–147.

24. Johnston 1999, pp. 156–159; Ogden 2009, p. 162.

25. Johnston 1999, pp. 28, 67–69, 133–137, 161–199.

26. Johnston 1999, pp. ix, 184–199 (quotation p. 196).

27. Vergil, *Aeneid*, VI, lines 305–332; Horace, *Odes*, I.28. Cf. Ogden 2009, p. 148.

28. Johnston 1999, pp. 130–135.

29. Dolansky 2019.

Chapter 14: The Later Roman World and Christianity

1. I owe this point to Claudia Rapp.

2. Hansen 1996, pp. 27–28.

3. Luke 24: 2–12.

4. D. A. Smith 2010, pp. 23, 47–61.

5. Chariton, 'Chaereas and Callirhoe', 3.3.1–3.3.7: D. A. Smith 2010, pp. 47–49 (and p. 198, note 4 for dating).

6. 2 Kings 4:18–37; John 11:1–44; Mark 5:35–43; Acts 20:7–12. Grateful thanks to Diarmaid MacCulloch for his guidance.

7. Tertullian, 'De Anima', cc.56–57, in Ogden 2009, pp. 149–151.

8. Hansen 1996, pp. 28–37, 92.

9. Apuleius, 'Metamorphoses', 9.29–9.31, in Ogden 2009, pp. 152–154.

10. Ogden 2004.

11. Pseudo-Quintilian, 'Declamationes maiores', 10, in Ogden 2009, pp. 164–166. This text was circulating in the Roman world by the later fourth century.

12. This rather general word could mean 'sword-blades', but also any instrument with a sharp point.

13. E.g., Strasbourg, Kastel, Scarponna, Veroli (Wernet 1970, pp. 5–11, 15–16; Alfayé 2009, pp. 201–206).

14. Dadea 2023.

15. L. de Tillemont, *Memoires pour server a l'histoire ecclesiastique*, vol. 4 (Venice: F. Pitteri, 1732), p. 497; Jullian and Gaidoz 1902.

16. Mariotti et al. 2023, pp. 31–34 (graves 109 and 76).

17. Suellacabras, Aguilar de Anguita, Luzaga, El Pedregal near Molina de Aragón, and Montuenga; Italica and Carmona: Andrès de la Pastora 1883; Olóriz 1897, pp. 261–269; Taracena 1933, p. 66; Obermaier 1933, pp. 169–170; Zeiss 1934, pp. 90–91.

18. Daniels 1966, pp. 24–25.

19. Balbanov 2011, pp. 111–113. The only firm chronology seems to be that they post-date an earlier Roman sequence and pre-date a tumulus built c. AD 400.

20. Mladenović 2009, pp. 104–108, which also interprets mouth-coins as intended to suppress posthumous activity rather than to pay Charon. I owe this reference to Andrew Wilson.

21. Faraone 1991.

22. Alfayé 2009, pp. 187–188; Alfayé Villa 2010.

23. Soren and Soren 1995. The mouth-stone burial was found later: see '"Vampire Burial" Reveals Efforts to Prevent Child's Return from Grave', Archaeology Wiki, October 15, 2018, https://www.archaeology.wiki/blog/2018/10/15/vampire-burial-reveals-efforts-to-prevent-childs-return-from-grave/.

24. Augustine, 'De cura pro mortuis gerenda', cc. 12–16, in *Corpus Scriptorum Ecclesiasticorum Latinorum*, vol. 41, ed. J. Zycha (Prague, 1900), pp. 619–660, at pp. 639–649). Foxhall Forbes 2013, pp. 267–271, 313–314, discusses the views of Augustine and Gregory on these issues.

25. Gregory the Great, 'Dialogorum Libri Quatuor', iv.40, 55, in *Patrologiae Cursus Completus: Series Prima*, vol. 77, ed. J.-P. Migne (Paris, 1849), cols. 396–397, 416–421.

26. Paulinus of Milan, 'Vita Beati Ambrosii', c.32, translated in *The Western Fathers*, trans. F. R. Hoare (London: Sheed and Ward, 1954), pp. 173–174.

27. Thacker 2002, pp. 48–52.

Chapter 15: The British Isles and Northern Francia, 200–600

1. Aldhouse Green 2001.

2. Giles 2012, pp. 1–3, 214–215, 241–244.

3. Trow et al. 2024, p. 24.

4. Allen and Rylatt 2002, p. 30; A. Smith et al. 2018, p. 228. For the calibrated radiocarbon date of 180 BC–AD 30, see Heritage Gateway, North Lincolnshire HER, https://www.heritagegateway.org.uk/Gateway/Results_Single.aspx?uid=MLS20030&resourceID=1034.

5. O'Brien 2020, p. 137.

6. For a recent full discussion, see A. Smith et al. 2018, pp. 226–230, 329–330, where references to other work can be found. Among those, Taylor 2008 remains useful.

7. Klevnäs 2015, p. 199 (Baldock, Herts.); Taylor 2008, p. 101 (Cambridge); note in *Oxoniensia*, 15 (1950) p. 105, and pl. VIIIc (Cassington, Oxon.).

8. Allason-Jones 1989, pp. 157–163.

9. Calkin 1947.

10. Barber and Bowsher 2000, pp. 230, 317 (Burial 733).

11. Apart from as single late medieval Breton story (p. 62).

12. A. Smith et al. 2018, maps on p. 227.
13. O'Brien 2020, pp. 140–150.
14. O'Brien 2020, pp. 159–164.
15. O'Brien 2020, p. 139.
16. O'Brien 2020, pp. 153–155.
17. Parker Pearson et al. 2018, pp. 21–41. However, the radiocarbon date given there has been drastically revised: see Noble and Evans 2022, p. 207, which I follow here.
18. See p. 445, note 2, for a general bibliography; particularly relevant here are Klevnäs 2013, 2015; Klevnäs et al. 2021; Aspöck et al. 2022; and the essays in Aspöck et al. 2020. It is especially Alison Kelvnäs's work that gives due weight to corpse-killing and aligns most closely with my own thinking.
19. See also Simmer 1982.
20. Klevnäs 2015, p. 199.
21. Chenal and Barrand Emam 2014.
22. Van Haperen 2017, pp. 114–115.
23. Van Haperen 2017, pp. 121–123.
24. Dickinson 2005; Blair 2011; Semple 2011.
25. With what follows, read the much longer discussion by Reynolds 2009, pp. 61–95.
26. Meaney 1964, pp. 18, 134, 190, 241, 285; Noble and Evans 2022, p. 208, for another case in Fife.
27. King et al. 1996, pp. 28–29; Leeds and Harden 1936, pp. 31, 36, 40–41.
28. P.D.C. Brown 1967.
29. Meaney 1964, pp. 16–17.
30. Dickinson 1993.
31. Felder 2014.
32. Felder 2014, pp. 317–341.
33. Felder 2014, pp. 338–339. Cf. Stoodley 2000, pp. 465–466.
34. Fell 1984, pp. 29–32.
35. For this section, see also Reynolds 2009.
36. Felder 2014, pp. 163, 172.
37. Grave 80: Mortimer et al. 2017, pp. 311–312; Felder 2014, p. 224; Sayer 2020, pp. 121, 156–158.
38. Sayer 2020, pp. 4–6.
39. Haughton and Powlesland 1999, pp. 185–188, 234–237, 264–269; Felder 2014, pp. 190–198.
40. Haughton and Powlesland 1999, pp. 25, 144–145, 189–190, 223–226, 291.
41. Hirst 1985, pp. 40–43 (and p. 95 for date).
42. Sherlock and Welch 1992, pp. 26–27.
43. Frankopan 2023, pp. 214–227.

Chapter 16: The Christian English, 600–700 (1)

Epigraph: Bede, 'Historia Ecclesiastica', iv.19, in Colgrave and Mynors 1969, pp. 394–395.
1. Blair 2011; Blair 2016, pp. 4–9.
2. Blair 2005, pp. 169–181; Blair 2016, pp. 6–14.
3. Hines and Bayliss 2013; Hamerow 2016.
4. Yorke 2003a; Blair 2005, pp. 166–168.
5. Bede, 'Historia Ecclesiastica', iii.8, in Colgrave and Mynors 1969, pp. 236–237.

6. Bede, 'Vita Sancti Cuthberti', c.3, in *Two Lives of Saint Cuthbert*, ed. and trans. B. Colgrave (Cambridge: Cambridge University Press, 1940), pp. 162–164.

7. Blair 2018, pp. 103–176; see Naismith 2023, chapter 8, for a radical reappraisal from a numismatic perspective.

8. Maddicott 1997.

9. Blair 2005, pp. 79–91; Yorke 2003b.

10. Rudolf of Fulda, 'Life of Saint Leoba', in Talbot 1954, p. 212.

11. Rudolf of Fulda, 'Life of Saint Leoba', pp. 208–209.

12. Barber 1988, p. 69 (citing a 'Serbian schoolbook').

13. See. for instance, the biography by A. Thacker in *Oxford Dictionary of National Biography* 1.429–432. The main source is Bede, 'Historia Ecclesiastica', iv.19–20, in Colgrave and Mynors 1969, pp. 390–401.

14. Stephen, 'Vita Wilfridi', cc.24, 39, in *The Life of Bishop Wilfrid by Eddius Stephanus*, ed. and trans. B. Colgrave (Cambridge: Cambridge University Press, 1927), pp. 48, 78.

Chapter 17: The Christian English, 600–700 (2)

Epigraph: See p. 432.

1. See p. 198, and Gibson 2022.

2. Lucy et al. 2009, p. 112.

3. Evison 1987, p 18.

4. Hancock and Zeepvat 2018, pp. 25, 119.

5. Boyle et al. 1998, pp. 85–86, 167.

6. Evison 1987, pp. 234–235, figures 37 and 73, pl. 3d.

7. This remains uncertain—the extreme flexing of the right leg could have happened when the corpse was turned over—but a decapitated male in the cemetery at Winnall (Hants.) was in the same peculiar attitude: Meaney and Hawkes 1970, pp. 14–15, 22.

8. Lucy et al. 2009.

9. I take burial 9 to be female (beads) and 3 and 4 to be male (knives).

10. Blair 2005, pp. 232–233.

11. Lucy et al. 2009, pp. 91–94, 112. I am very grateful to Professor Chris O'Callaghan for his help with the anatomical aspects of this complex burial.

12. Lucy et al. 2009, p. 126.

13. See Klevnäs 2015, pp. 179–193, for further details. Good examples are: Little Carlton (Lincolnshire), mature female, tightly bound, legs dislocated and rotated at the hips and knees, head slightly detached (Willmott et al. 2021, pp. 194–195, SK96); Tubney Wood (Berkshire), female, radiocarbon date AD 535–640, cranium on upper legs, legs cut off just below knees, one tibia by left shoulder (Simmonds et al. 2011, pp. 137–138); Buckland Dinham (Somerset), female with wire rings and beads, cranium on chest (Meaney 1964, p. 218); Edix Hill (Cambridgeshire), female, poorly dated, mandible carefully lifted out and placed between the legs, rest of skeleton undisturbed (Malim and Hines 1998, pp. 64, 143, grave 49); Worthy Park (Hants), male, savagely twisted and partly missing, cranium upside-down on chest, mandible near pelvis (Hawkes and Granger 2003, pp. 47–49, grave 41); Melbourn (Cambridgeshire), 'an old male', cranium relocated to his pelvis leaving the mandible in situ (D. M. Wilson 1956, p. 31).

14. Hancock and Zeepvat 2018, pp. 118–119 and burials 2197 and 2387. Note that, despite the description, burial 2168 was *not* prone.

15. Simmer 1988, pp. 138–153 (gender calculation based on the grave catalogue).

16. O'Brien 2020, p. 137.

17. O'Brien 2020, pp. 138–139.

18. *Beowulf*, line 112; Blair 2018, p. 78.

19. The point is very effectively made by Lapidge 1993.

Chapter 18: Francia, England, and Scandinavia, 700–1000

Epigraph: Larrington 1996, p. 243 (Larrington's translation).

1. MacLeod and Mees 2006, p. 75.

2. MacLeod and Mees 2006, p. 232; Toplak 2023, p. 153 (with image).

3. Yin Liu 2021, p. 145: 'exquirere strigas et fictos lupos credere'. Two centuries later, Rhineland beliefs in werewolves and night-battles were described explicitly by Burchard of Worms, *'Decreta'* (1853), 19.5, cols. 963–964, 971, 973–974).

4. 'Capitulatio de Partibus Saxoniae' cc.6–7, in *Leges Saxonum und Lex Thuringorum*, ed. C. von Schwerin (Hannover: MGH, 1918), p. 38.

5. Krapp 2006, p. 68.

6. Schaub 2009, section 3.3.1, photograph at https://stadt.bad-windsheim.de/fileadmin/Dokumente/Broschueren/arch-fenster-englisch.pdf, accessed April 2024.

7. Mariotti et al. 2023, pp. 37–38.

8. Brundke 2013.

9. Wild 2006.

10. Hey 2004, pp. 161–163, 257, 321–323.

11. E. West et al. 2025, pp. 151–152; Hardy, Charles, and Williams 2007, pp. 140–145, 206–207. It is proposed that the Higham Ferrers woman was executed, hung upside-down, and then buried when semi-decayed and after having been bitten by carnivores. That is possible, but the mutilations of semi-decayed bodies discussed above suggest an alternative scenario that is at least as plausible.

12. Perhaps a sixth-century case of the same practice is an adult woman, twisted into a chaotic parcel in the fill of an Iron Age ditch at Edix Hill (Cambridgeshire): Malim and Hines 1998, pp. 58–59, 141.

13. O'Brien 2020, pp. 164–167.

14. Semple 1998; Blair 2018, pp. 82–83.

15. 'Vita et miracula S. Kenelmi', c.16, in *Three Eleventh-Century Anglo-Latin Saints' Lives*, ed. and trans. R. Love (Oxford: Oxford University Press, 1996), pp. 70–73.

16. Blair 2023b.

17. Rahtz and Hirst 1974; Murphy et al. 2016.

18. Price 2019; Gardeła 2016; Gardeła et al. 2023.

19. Price 2019, pp. 84–119; Gardeła 2013, p. 118.

20. Gardeła 2013a, pp. 112–114; Gardeła 2013b, pp. 119–123.

21. Gardeła 2013a, p. 114; Gardeła 2013b, pp. 123–124.

22. Gardeła 2013b, p. 124.

23. Gardeła 2013a, p. 114.

24. Gardeła 2013b for a catalogue and analysis; Toplak 2023, pp. 149–153.

25. Blindheim and Heyerdahl-Larsen 1995, pp. 44–45, 117, 120; Nordberg 2002.

26. Artelius 2005.

27. Saxo Grammaticus, 'Gesta Danorum', v.7.1–4, in Friis-Jensen and Fisher 2015, 1.334–339. The same story is in the fourteenth-century 'Egils Saga ok Ásmundar'.

28. See Chadwick 1946 for an exhaustive survey of this material. Cf. Gardeła 2017, pp. 225–227.

29. Bill and Daly 2012; Gardeła 2017, pp. 223–227; Klevnäs 2023.
30. Saxo Grammaticus, 'Gesta Danorum', i.7.2, pp. 54–55.

Chapter 19: Motifs Taking Shape

Epigraph: Bartlett 2002, pp. 196–197.

1. Burchard of Worms, *'Decreta'* 19.5, ed. 1853, cols. 974–975. See Maraschi 2019, pp. 30–32, 45, for context.

2. But see Ginzburg 1991, pp. 264–265, for the idea that face-cloths represented the birth-caul.

3. See p. 458, note 11.

4. Thompson 1955–1958, 2.426 (motifs E261.2 and E261.2.1).

5. Bartlett 2002, pp. 194–199.

6. Anglo-Saxon Chronicle 'E' (Whitelock 1961, p. 194); Thompson 1955–1958, 2.463–472 (motif E501). See also Watkins 2007, pp. 215–217, and Cacciola 2016, pp. 157–205.

7. Sariyannis 2013, pp. 194–195; Kırgı 2017, pp. 29–32.

8. Havekost 1914, p. 47. Note that he only cites (p. 39) a single piece of supposed primary medieval evidence, the Czech gloss *vilkodlac* for entries in a dictionary manuscript of c. 1250. These, however, are modern forgeries: see *České Glossy V "Mater Verborum"*, ed. A. Patera (Prague: J. Otto, 1877), pp. 29–31, 52.

9. Havekost 1914, pp. 39–49.

Chapter 20: An Icelandic Epidemic?

Epigraph: Magnús Magnússon 1999, p. 363.

1. A good deal has been written about them and need not be repeated here. Boberg 1966, pp. 95–99, classifies the motifs. Among a very large secondary literature, helpful contributions include Davidson 1981; Sayers 1996; Martin 2005; Ármann Jakobsson 2011; Kanerva 2011, 2013, 2017; Merkelbach 2012, 2019; Hay 2018.

2. Byock 1984 makes a strong argument for the authenticity of the oral element.

3. See Wickham 1992, pp. 238–241, for introduction and further reading.

4. Wickham 1992, pp. 239–240.

5. Merkelbach 2012, pp. 7–10.

6. The arguments of Merkelbach 2012, pp. 29–34, support this.

7. Kanerva 2013, p. 211; Gardeła 2017, pp. 193–194.

8. Ármann Jakobsson 2011, pp. 289–293; Scudder 2005, pp. 38–40.

9. Magnús Magnússon 1999, pp. 600–601.

10. Today often called *draugar*, though that is not the usual term in contemporary sources: Ármann Jakobsson 2011, pp. 283–285; Merkelbach 2019, p. 46n4.

11. Sayers 1996, p. 258. Cf. Merkelbach 2012, pp. 11–19.

12. Merkelbach 2012, pp. 11–12.

13. This motif of the 'sentinel burial' is Irish: Magnús Magnússon and Hermann Pálsson 1969, p. 37; O'Brien 2020, pp. 167–169.

14. Magnús Magnússon and Hermann Pálsson 1969, pp. 61–62, 77–80, 100–103.

15. Magnús Magnússon 1999, pp. 285, 323–329. Cf. Kanerva 2013, pp. 214–219.

16. Magnús Magnússon 1999, pp. 329–330.

17. Glám and the Lanercost revenant also climb on roofs (pp. 247, 317), as do living magicians in 'Laxdaela Saga' (Magnús Magnússon and Hermann Pálsson 1969, pp. 134–135).

18. Magnús Magnússon 1999, pp. 330–332.

19. Magnús Magnússon 1999, pp. 376–378.

20. Scudder 2005, pp. 76–86.

21. Magnús Magnússon and Hermann Pálsson 1969, p. 235.

22. Magnús Magnússon 1999, pp. 357–359. Cf. Merkelbach 2012, pp. 25–26, identifying her with the witch-like Thórgunna in 'Eiríks Saga'.

23. Magnús Magnússon 1999, pp. 359–360.

24. Magnús Magnússon 1999, pp. 360–363.

25. By Herodotos in the 420s BC: Periander's dead wife Melissa 'appeared and said that . . . she was cold and naked. The clothes that had been buried with her were of no use because they had not been burned' (Ogden 2009, pp. 188–189).

26. The same motif of drowned dead men occurs in 'Laxdæla Saga': Magnús Magnússon and Hermann Pálsson 1969, p. 234. Cf. Ármann Jakobsson 2011, p. 287, and Hay 2018.

27. Magnús Magnússon 1999, pp. 340, 363–364.

28. Magnús Magnússon 1999, pp. 365–366.

29. See J. D. Martin 2005, pp. 79–81, for the socio-legal context; also Kanerva 2011, though I am sceptical about the sexual undertones.

30. Chadwick 1946, p. 51; Lapidge 1993.

31. Ármann Jakobssen 2011, p. 297; cf. Barber 1988, pp. 41, 84, and Lapidge 1993 for Glám and Grendel.

32. Scudder 2005, p. 85.

33. Magnús Magnússon and Hermann Pálsson 1969, p. 39.

Chapter 21: The English Walking Dead, 1000–1200 (1)

Epigraph: William of Newburgh, 'Historia rerum Anglicanum', v.23 (Howlett 1885, p. 477).

1. Blair 2018, pp. 311–380; Naismith 2023, chapter 9.

2. Watkins 2007 provides an excellent introduction to these writings and their intellectual world. See also Simpson 2003.

3. William of Newburgh, 'Historia rerum Anglicanum', v.23. See Gordon 2015 for a particular view of William's stories.

4. In the following notes I cite the best editions of the original texts, followed by references to recent commentary. William of Newburgh might well call some of the latter 'nimis operosum et onerosum', and I have been selective.

5. Herman the Archdeacon, 'Miracula Sancti Edmundi', c.4, and Goscelin of Saint-Bertin, 'Miracula Sancti Edmundi', c.3 (Licence 2014, pp. 12–15, 142–145).

6. William of Malmesbury, 'Gesta pontificum Anglorum', v.259 (Winterbottom 2007, pp. 614–615). There may be a confusion between two Brihtwolds: S. E. Kelly (ed.), *Charters of Malmesbury Abbey* (London: British Academy, 2005), pp. 111–113.

7. Geoffrey of Burton, 'Vita Sancte Moduenne Virginis', c.47 (Bartlett 2002, pp. 190–199). Cf. Blair 2009, pp. 539–540, 556–559.

8. Walter Map, 'De nugis curialium', ii.27 (James et al. 1983, pp. 203–205). During the episcopate of Gilbert Foliot. Cf. Gordon 2020, pp. 102–129, for Walter's stories.

9. Walter Map, 'De nugis curialium', ii.28 (James et al. 1983, pp. 204–205). During the episcopate of Roger.

10. Walter Map, 'De nugis curialium', ii.30 (James et al. 1983, pp. 206–207).

11. William of Newburgh, 'Historia rerum Anglicarum', v.24 (Howlett 1885, pp. 479–482). William heard it from an elderly priest. I am grateful to Fiona Edmonds for discussions indicat-

ing that the location of this story, 'castellum quod Anantis dicitur', is more likely to be Annan than Alnwick.

12. William of Newburgh, 'Historia rerum Anglicarum', v.24 (Howlett 1885, pp. 478–479). Told to William 'a few years ago' by Melrose monks.

13. William of Newburgh, 'Historia rerum Anglicarum', v.23 (Howlett 1885, pp. 476–477).

14. William of Newburgh, 'Historia rerum Anglicarum', v.22 (Howlett 1885, pp. 474–475). Told to William by Stephen, archdeacon of Buckinghamshire from c. 1194.

15. William of Newburgh, 'Historia rerum Anglicarum', v.22.

16. Anglo-Saxon Chronicle C, D, under 1040 (Whitelock 1961, p. 105); William of Malmesbury, 'Gesta regum Anglorum', ii.188.2 (Mynors et al. 1998, pp. 336–370); E. A. Freeman, *The History of the Norman Conquest of England, Its Causes and Results* (Oxford: Clarendon Press, 1867), 1.570–572. Tom Licence points out to me the potentially comparable treatment by Harold II of the corpse of his brother Tostig: Guy of Amiens, 'Carmen de Hastingae proelio', line 138, ed. F. Barlow, *The 'Carmen de Hastingae Proelio' of Guy Bishop of Amiens* (Oxford: Oxford University Press, 1999), p. 10.

17. William of Malmesbury, 'Gesta regum Anglorum', ii.24 (Mynors et al. 1998, pp. 196–197).

18. Cf., for a slightly different emphasis, Watkins 2007, pp. 5–12. I wholeheartedly agree with his rejection of a 'two cultures' model, though personally I think he understates the role of embedded popular belief. See also Simpson 2003. I am unpersuaded by the view of Black 2016, p. 73, that 'the rise and subsequent disappearance of medieval revenants are indicative of anxieties held by scholastic authors'.

19. See detailed analysis in Blair 2009, pp. 556–559.

20. West and Palmer 2014, pp. 136, 344–345.

21. Mays et al. 2017.

22. Thanks to Ian Meadows and Claire Finn for information about this burial, which is currently being studied for a forthcoming excavation report.

23. Channing [2005], p. 49, figure 3.29 and pl. 11 (burial c995). Thanks to John Channing and Elizabeth O'Brien for discussions of this surprising burial and its date.

Chapter 22: The English Walking Dead, 1000–1200 (2)

Epigraph: Howlett 1885, pp. 479–480.

1. Moore 1987.

2. Foxhall Forbes 2013, pp. 320–323.

3. See above, this page, note 17. I am very grateful to Carl Watkins and Tom Licence for debating the problems in this section; they have no responsibility for my conclusions.

4. I Corinthians 5:5. J. Barton and J. Muddiman (eds.), *The Oxford Bible Commentary* (Oxford: Oxford University Press, 2001), p. 1116, discuss the passage but are unable to explain it.

5. Watkins 2007, pp. 183–185.

6. *Homilies of Ælfric*, vol. 2, ed. J. C. Pope (London: Oxford University Press for the Early English Text Society, 1968), p. 796.

7. 'Gesta regum Anglorum', i.204 (Mynors et al. 1998, 1.377–379). Cf. Livermore 2021, pp. 44–45. Gordon 2020, pp. 30–43, suggests that the story has Continental origins and proposes (rather implausibly) a political subtext. I do not see why it should not be an authentic English story re-worked by William in the light of parallels. The idea of malefactors hauled demonically from their coffins is a folklore motif: Thompson 1955–1958, 2.442 (motif E411.9); Ginzburg and Lincoln 2020, p. 12.

8. Foxhall Forbes 2013, pp. 202–219; Watkins 2007, pp. 185–193.

9. This section rehearses the argument of Blair 2009, pp. 549–555, which gives further detail.

10. Reynolds 2009; Foxhall Forbes 2013, pp. 271–278.

11. Thompson 2004, pp. 49–50, 95–96, 124; Lockett 2011, pp. 23, 287–298.

12. See Blair 2009, pp. 552–553, for references.

13. Foxhall Forbes 2013, pp. 294–300, argues cogently that shameful burial was not envisaged by the learned as *causing* damnation. But to the uneducated laity, it must surely have seemed at least to affirm it.

14. Semple 2003, pp. 240, 243; cf. Semple 1998.

15. Cambridge, Corpus Christi College, MS 41, p. 433; Foxhall Forbes 2013, pp. 294–295.

16. See Blair 2009, pp. 553–554, for references.

17. 'Northumbrian Priests' Law', 61-3.3, in *Councils and Synods I, 879–1204*, ed. D. Whitelock, M. Brett, and C.N.L. Brooke (Oxford: Oxford University Press, 1981), 1.465–466; I Æthelred 4.1, in F. Liebermann, *Gesetze, der Angelsachsen*, 3 vols. (Halle: M. Niemeyer, 1903–16), 1.220–221.

18. Thompson 2004, pp. 171–172.

19. Cf. Watkins 2007. Gordon 2015 and Gordon 2020, pp. 102–129, argue that Walter Map and William of Newburgh use the walking dead as a satirical subtext for criticizing late twelfth-century politics.

20. Moore 1987.

21. Moore 1987, pp. 58–59.

22. Moore 1987, pp. 63, 111. See Biller 1999 for the context of William of Newburgh's knowledge of heretics. For the preoccupation with contagion, cf. Gordon 2015, pp. 454–456; Livermore 2021, pp. 49–50; Gordon 2022.

23. Biller 1999, p. 16.

24. Barbezat 2018 is now the standard work on heretic burning.

25. See p. 458, note 6.

Chapter 23: Central and Southern Europe, 1000–1400

Epigraph: See p. 461, note 24.

1. Wickholm [Wessman] 2006, 2010. The implements used are often Merovingian-era weapons recovered from cremation burials. I am unconvinced by the author's argument that these practices aim to link and bond with ancestors rather than to keep the dead down.

2. Moilanen 2018.

3. Pollex 2010, pp. 252–255 (and pp. 183–184 for the significantly similar incidence of iron fragments in graves).

4. For stoned, prone, beheaded, and other deviant burials in the north/ central European zone, see Alterauge et al. 2020; Brather 2007; Franz and Nösler 2016; Gardeła 2020; Gardeła and Kajkowski 2013; Grenz 1967; Jankowiak 2021, pp. 167–168; Schaub 2009, section 3.5.1; Schürmann 1990, pp. 36–42; Stülzebach 1998. For prone, decapitated, and stoned burials in Poland, see Gardeła 2017, pp. 91–204.

5. Wüstemann 1981; Kasbohm 1953.

6. Gehrke 1989, pp. 156–158; Gardeła 2020, pp. 256–257.

7. Gardeła 2017, pp. 220–221.

8. Gehrke 1989, pp. 155–156; Grenz 1967, pp. 258–260.

9. Gardeła and Kajkowski 2013, pp. 783, 789–790; Gardeła 2017, pp. 82–83; Gardeła 2020, pp. 256, 258; Schaub 2009, section 3.7.1.

10. Herbach 1925, p. 109; [Anonymous], 'Die Alte Schanze von Göda', https://www.1000lusatia.de/site/assets/files/5072/broschuere_-_die_alte_schanze_von_goeda.pdf, accessed April 2024.

11. Wachowski and Domański 1992, pp. 90–91; Gardeła 2017, pp. 96–100, 104 (with reconstruction showing stakes only).

12. Matchak et al. 2021.

13. Kaszewscy and Kaszewscy 1971, pp. 405, 525; Gardeła 2017, pp. 71–73, 78–79.

14. Buko 2015, pp. 130–131, 134, 307–311, 322, 377–379, 873.

15. Jungklaus 2008, pp. 380, 383.

16. Alterauge et al. 2020, p. 21.

17. Nösler 2014.

18. Broderus Boissen, 'Chronicon Slesvicense', in J. B. Mencke (ed.), *Scriptorum rerum Germanicarum, praecipue Saxonicarum* (Leipzig: J. C. Martin, 1730), cols. 564–630, at col. 597. Cf. Lecouteux 2011, pp. 80–81.

19. Baug et al. 2024.

20. Jankowiak 2021.

21. Urbańczyk 2016; Buko 2015, pp. 22–38.

22. Biermann 2016.

23. M. Müller-Wille in Buko 2015, pp. 479–510.

24. Caesarius of Heisterbach, 'Dialogus miraculorum', xi.56, xii.15, xii.20, in J. Strange (ed.), *Caesarii Heisterbacensis Monachi Ordinis Cisterciensis Dialogus Miraculorum*, 2 vols. in 1 (Cologne: H. Lempertz, 1851), 2.309, 327, 330. Other—more equivocal—references to animated corpses are in xi.40, xi.63–64, and xii.11 (pp. 300–301, 313–314, 324). Cf. Cacciola 2016, pp. 219–220; Livermore 2021, pp. 50–52.

25. Cf. Lecouteux 2011, pp. 56–59 (and pp. 256–257 for a late Irish version).

26. Caesarius of Heisterbach, 'Libri VIII miraculorum' [fragments], ii.50, in *Die Fragmente der Libri VIII Miraculorum des Cesarius von Heisterbach*, ed. A. Meister (Rome, 1901), pp. 122–123; Cacciola 2016, pp. 154–156.

27. I exclude Thietmar of Merseburg's stories (Cacciola 2016, pp. 109–152; Livermore 2021, pp. 41–43) because it is not clear to me that they refer to animated corpses.

28. See the analysis of his thought in Cacciola 2016, pp. 185–197.

29. Balther, 'Vita Fridolini Confessoris', c.29 addendum, in *Monumenta Germaniae Historica: Scriptores Rerum Merovingicarum*, vol. 3, ed. B. Krusch (Hannover: MGH, 1896), pp. 351–369, at pp. 367–368, footnote.

30. Berszin 1994, pp. 127–134, at pp. 133–134 (with photo).

31. *The Hammer of Witches: A Complete Translation of the Malleus Maleficarum*, trans. C. MacKay (Cambridge: Cambridge University Press, 2009), p. 237; cf. p. 38 for the inquisitor Henry Institoris, much of whose work was in the neighbourhood of Ravensburg.

32. See Pergola et al. 2023 for sporadic Italian cases of prone and decapitated burials, cited in several of the papers there. But most of these cannot compellingly be ascribed to corpse-killing.

33. Franz and Nösler 2016, p. 89; report in *Kleine Zeitung Kaernten*, 8 September 2013.

34. Grilletto 1989, pp. 346–347. I owe this reference to Gisella Cantino Wataghin.

35. Taracena 1933; Obermaier 1933. The cemeteries other than Deza—all poorly reported—appear to be Sigüenza, Valdenebro, and Luzaga.

36. Obermaier 1933, p. 171.

37. Parvanov 2016. The main respect in which I depart from Parvanov is that he sees many of these burials as judicial executions or mutilations.

38. Parvanov 2016, pp. 61–62.

39. Pliska Outer City East feature 77; Devnya-2 feature 74; Krasen feature 11; Madara feature 2: Parvanov 2016, catalogue numbers 48, 59, 61, 115.

40. See Parvanov 2016, pp. 93–95, and catalogue numbers 73, 80, 89, 95. Two of these, at Sozopol and Perperikon, attracted media interest, so that multiple images can be found on the internet.

41. Parvanov 2016, p. 97 and catalogue number 39 (though he interprets it as judicial mutilation).

42. *Les Regestes des Actes du Patriarchat de Constanople: I: Les Actes des Patriarches*, Fasc. II and III, ed. V. Grumel (Paris: Institut Français d'Études Byzantines, 1989), pp. 472–473, No. 1012.

43. Parvanov 2016, pp. 43, 49, 57, 66.

44. For instance, Whittow 2007.

45. Parvanov 2023, pp. 305–308.

46. Burr 1949, p. 202 (Article 20).

47. Fine 1994, pp. 314–321.

48. Notably the supposed seventh-century reference to revenants by Anastasios of Sinai that persuaded J. C. Lawson (Lawson 1910, pp. 403–404). In fact this is the work of a continuator, first known from a manuscript of 1062 (Florence, Biblioteca Laurenziana, MS Plut.4.6 fos.78–79r); cf. *Corpus Christianorum SG* 59 (2006), p. lviii. In any case it is part of a debate on necromancy that developed from a statement by Isidore ('Etymologiae', VIII.ix.11), and has no apparent relevance to contemporary Greek beliefs. Likewise, the idea of Judas as a bloated walking corpse (Hartnup 2004, pp. 231–232) seems to be a late development.

49. Hartnup 2004, pp. 178, 215–216.

50. F. Miklosich and J. Müller (eds.), *Acta et Diplomata Graeca Medii Aevi*, vol. 1 (Vienna: C. Gerold, 1860), pp. 524–525 (document 269).

51. Nicol 1971, pp. 137–138 and footnote, referring to Manuel Kalekas, 'Adversus Graecos', Book IV.

52. Mouzakēs 1989, pp. 64–66, citing 'Responses to George Drazinos', question 42; cf. Viscuso 2000.

53. Burkhardt 1966, pp. 250–252, argues along similar lines, though expressed rather differently.

Chapter 24: The Eurasian Reservoir of Beliefs

Epigraph: Yaşar 2014, p. 83.

1. Laxdæla Saga: Magnús Magnússon and Hermann Pálsson 1969, pp. 116–117, 171, 176.

2. Ogden 2021, pp. 21–23; cf. Ginzburg 1991, p. 90.

3. Ginzburg and Lincoln 2020, pp. 13–32. See also Ogden 2021b, pp. 109–136, for werewolves and soul projection.

4. Ginzburg 1983, 1991.

5. Jacobson and Szeftel 1966, pp. 341–353; Ginzburg 1983, pp. 6–7, 12, 14, 16, 37, 66.

6. Ginzburg 1983, p. 59.

7. Ginzburg 1983, p. 31.

8. Ginzburg 1983, pp. 33–68; Ginzburg 1991, pp. 89–103, 153–156; Lecouteux 2011.

9. Ginzburg 1991, pp. 262–263.

10. The source is discussed by Sariyannis 2013, pp. 197–200; Yaşar 2014, pp. 80–83; Kırgi 2017, pp. 40–47; Sarpkaya and Yaltırık 2022, pp. 94–106; Kafardar 2022. I owe these translations to Yaşar 2014, with small changes in the light of Kafadar 2022.

11. Cf. Ginzburg 1991, pp. 163–164.

12. Sarpkaya and Yaltırık 2022, pp. 48–49 (Gagauz Turks, southern Moldova), 55–59 (Sarıgöl, western Turkey).

Chapter 25: Life-Forces, Shape-Shifters, and Dangerous Corpses

Epigraph: Perkowski 1989, p. 20.

1. Epstein and Robinson 2012.

2. Hukantaival 2016, p. 138; Honko 1973, pp. 351–352.

3. Pulkkinen 2014, pp. 146–147.

4. Koski 2008, pp. 48–49.

5. Koski 2008, p. 46.

6. Koski 2008, pp. 49–50, 52, 62n2.

7. C. J. Gardberg, 'Toppelius, Mikael (1734–1821)', in *Suomen Kansallisbiografia*, vol. 9 (Helsinki: Suomalaisen Kirjallisuuden Seura, 2007), pp. 878–879. Thanks to Kanerva Blair-Heikkinen for help with this, and to Katri Heikkinen for introducing me to Haukipudas.

8. Thompson 1955–1958, 2.15, 424–425, 426 (motifs D113.1, E251, E261.2).

9. Ivanits 1989, p. 38.

10. Burkhardt 1966, p. 218.

11. Ivanits 1989, pp. 47–48, 75–77; Zelenin 1994, pp. 141–293; Warner 2011, pp. 162–164.

12. Jaworskii 1898, p. 331; Ivanits 1989, pp. 119–122; Zelenin 1994, pp. 45–50, 57–66, 88–93; Ryan 1999, pp. 72–74; Warner 2000, pp. 75–78.

13. Oinas 1978, pp. 433–436 (quotation p. 436). See Kovács 1973, p. 77, for *eretik* as (living) magician.

14. Oinas 1978, p. 434 (quoting A. Zvonkov); Ivanits 1989, p. 122.

15. Oinas 1978, p. 437.

16. Jacobson and Szeftel 1966; Ryan 1999, p. 13.

17. Herodotos, 'Histories', iv.105, in A. D. Godley, ed. and trans., *Herodotus*, vol. 2, rev. ed. (Cambridge, MA: William Heinemann, 1938), pp. 306–307. Cf. Ogden 2021b, pp. 24–26.

18. The word *upir'* was known in Russia by the 1040s, but apparently had a rather vague meaning (something like 'supernatural wretch'): see McClelland 1999, pp. 253, 256–259, for the two occurrences. The marginal note *upir' likhyi* in a manuscript of 1047 (known from a facsimile of 1499) is apparently a scribal humility formula meaning something like 'miserable wretch'; it seems unlikely that even the most humble scribe called himself 'miserable vampire'. The various instances of *upir'* in personal names (Oinas 1978, p. 436) do not get us much further. A supposed reference in the Russian Primary Chronicle to putting a coin in the mouth of a condemned magician in 1071 (Jacobson and Szeftel 1966, p. 350) seems in fact to mean that the man was gagged.

19. Jacobson and Szeftel 1966, p. 350; see Lecouteux 2011, pp. 29–31, for the textual problems.

20. Warner 2011, p. 166.

21. Warner 2000, p. 74; Warner 2011, pp. 156–158, 164–169. Cf. Kozak 2021, pp. 231–232.

22. Zelenin 1927, pp. 393–394 (and cf. Burkhardt 1966, p. 243, and Warner 2011, p. 168). Oinas disagreed (1978, p. 436), but his argument seems to rely on preconception more than evidence.

23. Sarpkaya and Yaltırık 2022, p. 49.

24. Kovács 1973, pp. 82–83; Kozak 2021, pp. 85–88.

25. Ginzburg 1991, pp. 161–162, 166; Murgoci 1998, pp. 33–34.

26. Burkhardt 1966, pp. 232–234.

27. Burkhardt 1966, p. 239; Perkowski 1989, pp. 37–53; Murgoci 1998, pp. 24–25.

28. Murgoci 1998, pp. 24–25.

29. Bogatyrëv 1998, p. 111.

30. Bogatyrëv 1998, pp. 119–121, 132–139.

31. Senn 1982, pp. 10–24.

32. Senn 1982, pp. 114–119.

33. Murgoci 1998, p. 21.

34. Murgoci 1998, pp. 19–20.

35. Murgoci 1998, pp. 20–21.

36. Senn 1982, p. 108, from Marginea (Bihor).

37. Cantemiru 1872, pp. 141–143. I owe knowledge of this important text to Alexandra Nachescu.

38. Stephan Gerlich, *Tage-Buch* (Frankfurt: J. and D. Zunners, 1674), p. 375.

39. Mézes 2019, pp. 480–487.

40. McClelland 1999, pp. 82–83, 331–338, 345–353.

41. Yaşar 2014, p. 82.

42. Burkhardt 1966, p. 224; Vukanović 1959, pp. 44–49; Drettas 1985, pp. 210–211.

43. Cf. Burkhardt 1966, pp. 215, 239, 251–252.

44. Nuzzolese and Borrini 2010.

45. Ginzburg 1991, pp. 160–161. Cf. Burkhardt 1966, pp. 225–226.

46. Valvasor 1689, vol. 2, book 6, p. 335.

47. Kropej 2012, pp. 193–200. Cf. Burkhardt 1966, p. 215.

48. See Benyovsky 1996 for eighteenth-century Dalmatia; Perkowski 1989, pp. 85–100, for the Lastovo case; and Čoralić et al. 2013 for the Žrnovo case.

49. Valvasor 1689, vol. 3, book 11, pp. 318–319; transcribed in Equiamicus 2023, pp. 340–343; translated in Lecouteux 1999, pp. 114–116. See also Evans 1979, pp. 178–179, for Valvasor.

50. Kropej 2012, pp. 193–194.

51. Lawson 1910 is a superb survey that has weathered more than a century. But now we have Nina Anna Trzaska's comprehensive thesis on Greek vampire beliefs (Trzaska 2023), which appeared when this book was almost finished. I am very grateful to her for giving me access; it should now be the first port of call.

52. Hartnup 2004, pp. 85–172.

53. Hartnup 2004, pp. 140–146, 157.

54. Hartnup 2004, p. 157.

55. Hartnup 2004. See also Mousakēs 1989, pp. 70–93, for the canonical sources.

56. Hartnup 2004, pp. 180–185.

57. Hartnup 2004, pp. 199–205.

58. Allatius 1645, p. 148.

59. Hartnup 2004, p. 224; Ricaut 1679, pp. 271–276.

60. Hartnup 2004, pp. 205–212.

61. Hartnup 2004, p. 219. The contribution of this belief to Orthodox authority is explored by Zelepos 2014, pp. 268–274.

62. Hartnup 2004, pp. 185–198.

63. Campbell 1964, p. 337.

64. Lawson 1910, pp. 376–384; Du Boulay 1982, p. 222.

65. Hartnup 2004, pp. 175–177, 226–233.

66. See p. 16; Hartnup 2004, pp. 174–176. See also Lawson 1910, pp. 381–383, for other terms used in specific Greek islands.

67. Lawson 1910, pp. 379–380.

68. See especially the map in Trzaska 2023, p. 331. Many of the cases are reported in Lawson 1910 and Mouzakēs 1989.

69. Allatius 1645, pp. 142–158; Richard 1657, pp. 208–226; Ricaut 1679, pp. 276–283; Pitton de Tournefort 1717, pp. 131–134; Lawson 2010, pp. 361–412; Mousakēs 1989.

70. Lawson 1910, pp. 363–364. However, Trzaska 2023, pp. 328–330, concludes that the notoriety of Santorini was to some extent a western construct.

71. Kırgi 2017, pp. 29–36; Sarpkaya and Yaltırık 2022, pp. 85–92. As Kırgi observes, the precedents that Ebussuud cites do not in fact refer to unquiet corpses.

72. Kırgi 2017, pp. 48–55.

73. Köhbach 1979; Sariyannis 2013, pp. 195–197; Kırgi 2017, pp. 37–39; Sarpkaya and Yaltırık 2022, pp. 115–121.

74. Kırgi 2017, pp. 62–66; Sarpkaya and Yaltırık 2022, pp. 122–127.

Chapter 26: The Dead Retreat Northward Again

Epigraph: Child 1883–1898, 2.238–239.

1. James 1922, pp. 418–419. This is an extreme illustration of the main point made by McGill 2022. Simpson 2003, pp. 399–400, plausibly suggests that the Byland stories are so hard to pin down because they embody a fusion of very different belief-systems.

2. James 1922, p. 418. The identification is problematic. The only known James de Taunkerleye was parson of Walesby (Lincolnshire) in the 1290s and 1300s (*Calendar of Patent Rolls 1292–1301*, p. 123; eyre roll, 1308–1310: National Archives, JUST1/1347 m.377d), and Cold Kirby was a chapelry of Easingwold until the 1740s.

3. See p. 259; Mays et al. 2017, p. 450.

4. See Binski 1996 and Townsend 2009 for the art.

5. Watkins 2013, pp. 1–24, is an evocative introduction to the issues. The classic defence and celebration of the late medieval 'economy of salvation' is Duffy 1992.

6. See Schmitt 1998, and the many clearly or ambiguously incorporeal ghosts discussed by Gordon 2020 and Livermore 2021. This ambiguity is (over?)-emphasized by McGill 2022.

7. John Mirk, 'Festial', Addition 2, in Susan Powell (ed.), *John Mirk's Festial*, vol. 2 (Oxford: Oxford University Press, 2011), pp. 257–258. Cf. Gordon 2020, pp. 144–146; Livermore 2021, p. 60. I believe that Mirk's other discussion of the 'walking dead' (cf. Gordon 2020, pp. 137–144) refers to ghosts, not corpses.

8. See Binski 1996 for the 'good death'.

9. S. Powell, 'John Mirk', in *Oxford Dictionary of National Biography*, vol. 38 (Oxford: Oxford University Press, 2004), pp. 368–369.

10. I. Forrest and C. Whittick (eds.), *The Visitation of Hereford Diocese in 1397* (Woodbridge: Boydell Press, 2021), pp. 34–35: 'fecit pompam suam quod de vadit tempore nocturno cum spiritibus fantasticis'.

11. Watkins 2013, pp. 41–55; Duffy 1992.

12. Examples are often proposed, but usually they turn out to be references to ghosts, or just misunderstandings. Of the cases in Gordon 2020, pp. 221–223, it seems to me that the Meg Shelton and George Hodgson episodes are inadequately supported, while those of Sir Walter Long and the 'sin-eaters' are misunderstandings. Likewise, the cases discussed by Keyworth 2006, pp. 245–246, are essentially just ghosts. The so-called *Suffolk Miracle* ballad, in which the corpse of a young man pursues his love-affair with a farmer's daughter, is merely a late version of a ubiquitous European tale: Child 1883–1998, 5.58–66; cf. Livermore 2021, p. 109.

13. Harte 2011; Cusack 2021, pp. 59–70.

14. Quotations from Cusack 2021, pp. 62, 72.

15. Schofield 2019, p. 87; Rogerson et al. 1987, p. 74.

16. J. Stevenson (ed.), *Chronicon de Lanercost* (Edinburgh: Bannatyne Club, 1839), pp. 163–164. It is located four miles from Paisley, in the house of a knight called Sir Duncan de Insula. For commentary, see Cacciola 2016, pp. 220–221; Gordon 2020, pp. 1–2; Livermore 2021, pp. 54–55.

17. D. Brodie et al., 'Four Excavations in Perth, 1979–1984', *Proceedings of the Society of Antiquaries of Scotland* 125 (1995): 917–999, at p. 944; J. A. Stones et al. (eds.), *Three Scottish Carmelite Friaries* (Edinburgh: Society of Antiquaries of Scotland, 1989), Fiche 1: C.12–13 and Fiche 6: A.11–12.

18. See Wimberly 1928, pp. 229–239, locating some of the Scottish motifs in a Scandinavian context.

19. Chadwick 1946, p. 57; Larrington 1996, pp. 140–141. Compare the Scottish ballad 'The Unquiet Grave'.

20. It is an inference that these daughters of John Bennet and Marion Powe, baptized at Haddington, are the women who later appear in nearby Pencaitland.

21. National Records of Scotland, CH2/296/1: Pencaitland kirk session, fol. 37 (Issobell Binnet to do public penance for drying corn on the Sabbath), fols. 37–37v (summons and confession of Agnes Binnet). The case is listed among other apotropaic rituals by Joyce Miller in Goodare 2002, p. 104.

22. [King James VI], *Daemonologie* (Edinburgh: Robert Waldegrave, 1597), p. 59; cf. Livermore 2021, p. 103.

23. Matheson 1951–1952, pp. 15–16.

24. George Sinclair, *Satan's Invisible World Discovered* (Edinburgh, 1685) p. 153; Livermore 2021, pp. 92–93. Cf. McGill 2022 for this ambiguity in early modern discourse.

Chapter 27: Noxious Corpses and Noisy Shroud-Eaters

Epigraph: Böhm 1601, fol. 141, transcribed in Schürmann 1990, p. 143.

1. [J. Mathesius et al. (eds.)], *Tischreden oder colloquia Doct. Mart: Luthers* (Eisleben: Urban Gaubisch, 1566), fol. 298; edited *D. Martin Luthers Werke: Kritische Gesamtausgabe: Tischreden*, vol. 6 (Weimar: Hermann Böhlaus Nachfolger, 1921), p. 214.

2. Barber 1988, pp. 126–130.

3. Schürmann 1990; Schürmann 2009, pp. 238, 242–243, table and map.

4. Eckert 1996, p. 1.

5. Nicolaus Pol, *Zeitbucher der Schlesier*, vol. 3, ed. J. G. Büsching (Breslau: Graß und Barth, 1819) pp. 1–2; Schürmann 1990, pp. 44–45. Since the sources are all much later in the century, it cannot be assumed that the lip-smacking described in this story was necessarily alleged in 1516.

6. Andreas Möller, *Theatri Freibergensis Chronici Pars Posterior* (Freiberg: Georg Beuther, 1653), pp. 254–255; Christian Gotthold Wilisch, *Kirchen-Historie der Stadt Freyberg* (Leipzig: Friedrich Lanckisch, 1737); p. 378. See also Böhm 1601, fol. 141; Schürmann 1990, pp. 46–47, 144.

7. Schürmann 1990, pp. 48–49, 141–144.

8. Böhm 1601, fol. 141; Schürmann 1990, p. 51.

9. Schürmann 1990, pp. 48–52, 144, 147. See p. 352 for the Lviv case.

10. MacCulloch 2003, pp. 340–341.

11. See Koslofsky 2000, pp. 19–77, and MacCulloch 2003, pp. 115–137, for Luther and Saxony.

12. For recent overviews, see MacCulloch 2003, pp. 563–575; Holzem 2023, pp. 687–730.

13. See Holzem 2023, pp. 700–703, for regional contrasts.

14. MacCulloch 2003, pp. 568–569.

15. Rieger 2011, pp. 9–16.

16. Roth 1587, sigs. Kk3, Ll3v–Mm2.

17. Böhm 1601, fols. 141–143v; reprinted in Schürmann 1990, pp. 143–147, and Equiamicus 2023, pp. 352–358.

18. Kornmann 1610, chapter 64, citing Gabriel Rollenhagen (but the reference he gives makes no sense).

19. Wojtucki 2020a, p. 279n36.

20. H. B. Schindler, *Der Aberglaube des Mittelalters* (Breslau: W. G. Korn, 1858), p. 144 (citing Lauban Chronicle).

21. Wehner and Grüneberg-Wehner 2014.

22. See Gardeła 2017, pp. 175–176, for excavated Polish examples; this volume, Map 10, for later German folklore.

Chapter 28: Movers and Shakers

Epigraph: Steige 1795, pp. 136–137.

1. 'Summula chronicae tam Romanae quam Bohemicae', in J. Emler (ed.), *Fontes Rerum Bohemicarum*, vol. 3 (Prague: Nadání F. Palakého, 1882), pp. 480–481.

2. Schürmann 2009, table and map, pp. 238, 242–243.

3. Andreas Hondorff, *Theatrum Historicum* (Frankfurt: Sigismund Feierabend, 1590), p. 169, transcribed in Schürmann 1990, pp. 142–143.

4. Contemporary official documents printed by Steige 1795, pp. 135–139.

5. Weinrich 1612, pp. 1–13; English translation in More 1655, pp. 209–213. See Barber 1988, pp. 10–14, for the forensic aspects. This story is often misattributed to Breslau/Wrocław.

6. Weinrich 1612, pp. 46–48. Weinrich in fact attaches it to the Johann Kunze story; for reasons unknown, More 1655, pp. 213–214, transposes it to follow the Striegau story. The evidence of the parish register (see note 8 below) suggests that More must have been right, and I accept his correction here. See Lecouteux 1999, pp. 161–162, for a translation.

7. François de Rosset, *Theatrum Tragicum, Das Ist, Newe Wahr-Hafftige, Traurig, Fläglich und Wunderliche Geschichten*, trans. with commentary by Martin Zeiller, 3rd ed. (Tübingen: Philibert Brunn, 1628), pp. 24–25. Zeiller, a keen topographer, visited the town in 1617–1618, was told the story by 'reliable citizens', and shown the grave site, which probably puts it no more than two or three decades earlier.

8. Wojtucki 2018, pp. 86–87; Wojtucki 2020a, p. 279.

9. Wojtucki 2020a, pp. 280–281.

10. Wojtucki 2018, pp. 85–86; Wojtucki 2020a, p. 277.

11. Weinrich 1612, pp. 13–46. The bibliography is huge, but for context and some references, see Bohn 2019, pp. 39–44. More 1655, pp. 213–226, and Lecouteux 1999, pp. 150–161, print summaries in English.

12. Weinrich 1612, p. 38. Stieff 1737, p. 381, comments that 'es ist Schade, daß man itzund dieses *Original* in keiner Bibliotheck mehr findet'. I cannot trace the attribution to Johann Vogt mentioned by Bohn 2019, p. 40.

13. Cf. Lecouteux 2011, p. 49.

14. Weinrich 1612, pp. 32–33: 'et arreptum eius penem adeo protraxit ut avulsurus eum videretur'.

15. Magnús Magnússon 1999, pp. 330–331, 377.

16. Weinrich 1612, pp. 44–45.

17. Wiltenburg 2012, pp. 9–11

18. Wiltenburg 2012, pp. 91, 96–98.

19. Warfield 2020.

Chapter 29: The Dangerous Dead between Witchcraft and the Enlightenment

Epigraph: Maxwell-Stuart and García Valverde 2023, pp. 496–497, 520–521.

1. Václav Hájek z Libočan, *Kronyka Czeská* [Prague, 1541], fols. 313v–313r. German translation: Wenceslaus Hagecius, *Böhmische Chronica* (Prague, 1596), fols. 419v–420r. Grateful thanks

to Robert Evans, both for correcting my translation from the German back to the Czech original and for identifying Levìn, which was, indeed, celebrated for its pottery.

2. Sassonia 1600, pp. 50–53. Cf. Kozak 2021, pp. 162–165.

3. Weinrich 1612, p. 1.

4. Maxwell-Stuart and García Valverde 2023, pp. 10, 17. Cf. Evans 1979, p. 384.

5. Maxwell-Stuart and García Valverde 2023, pp. 496–497, 520–521.

6. Evans 1979, p. 33.

7. Weinrich 1612, pp. 48–60.

8. Weinrich 1612, p. 12.

9. Fries 1996.

10. Eckert 1996, pp. 128–140; Schürmann 1990, pp. 55–56.

11. For Drawsko, see Betsinger and Scott 2014, 2020; Gregoricka et al. 2014; Polcyn and Gajda 2015. The Pień burial, found in 2022, was widely reported in the media but is still unpublished.

12. Grober-Glück 1981, p. 440.

13. Betsinger and Scott 2014, p. 468; Polcyn and Gajda 2015, p. 1382.

14. Kozak 2021, pp. 131–132, 304–306.

15. For context, see Louthan 2009; Evans 1979; MacCulloch 2003, pp. 442–464.

16. Wojtucki 2018 gives further details of the pre-1670 cases; see also Schürmann 2009, table and map, pp. 238, 242–243.

17. For the ecclesiastical institutions, personnel, and culture of Olomouc, see Zuber 1987 and 2003, and the essays in Kalous 2015.

18. See Louthan 2009, especially chapter 6; Kalous 2015, pp. 72–94, 108–115.

19. Kalous 2015, pp. 114–115.

20. Mézes 2019, p. 211.

21. Kalous 2015, pp. 124–139.

22. Kalous 2015, p. 143.

23. Evans 1979, pp. 404, 409–410; Zuber 2003, pp. 313–322; Kreuz 2006.

24. A. Schmidt, 'Ein Dokument zur Geschichte der schles. Hexenprozesse', *Zeitschrift für Geschichte und Kulturgeschichte Österreichisch-Schlesiens* 2 (1906/7): 193–194; see also Mézes 2019, pp. 213–215.

25. Mézes 2019, p. 489.

26. Mézes 2019, pp. 206–217, 488–490, to which I have added (as also in Figure 64) the cases, mostly now on the Polish side of the border, listed by Lambrecht 1994, pp. 57–65.

27. Sassonia 1600, pp. 51–52.

28. Rzaczynski 1721, pp. 364–368; Schürmann 1990, pp. 148–150; Kozak 2021, p. 298.

29. Schürmann 1990, pp. 147–148.

30. McClelland 1999, p. 351.

31. Notably Kornmann 1610, chapters 23, 35, 63–64; Gaspar Schott, *Physica Curiosa* (Würzburg: Job Hertz, 1662), pp. 29–30, 313–314, 319–321; Praetorius 1666, pp. 317–359. For the intellectual context, see Evans 1979, pp. 340–344, and p. 385 for Pretorius.

32. More 1659, p. 293; cf. McGill 2022, p. 277.

33. Ginzburg 1991, pp. 158–159, 176.

34. Garmann 1670, pp. 24–41; Rohr 1679; Francisci [Finx] 1690, pp. 253–300 (reprinted in Equiamicus 2023, pp. 358–385). Cf. Schürmann 1990, pp. 7–8, 75–79, for these writers.

35. Rieger 2011, summarized on pp. 279–282.

36. Cf. Evans 1979, p. 345: 'the Catholic Church was different precisely because it built on the miraculous and the sacramental, and laid such weight on the supernatural'. The more violent Catholic attacks on corpses may have some link with the greater violence of Catholic populations in their urge to eliminate the pollution of Protestantism (MacCulloch 2003, pp. 308–309).

37. Gengell 1716, p. 123.

38. Gengell 1716, p. 123. Another Jesuit who remained faithful to supernatural explanations was Rzaczynski 1721, pp. 364–368.

39. Evans 1979, p. 320.

40. Hermann 1698, pp. 368–369. He merely locates the episode 'in Confiniis Silesiae at Moraviae', but he and Schertz are clearly describing the same events.

Chapter 30: From Moravia to Transylvania

Epigraph: Schertz 1706, sig. A.

1. Kalous 2015, pp. 142–143, 153–154.

2. Schertz 1706, sigs. A7–A8.

3. Hermann 1698, pp. 368–369.

4. See Mézes 2019, pp. 218–245, 488–495, for the cases listed here; also Zuber 2003, pp. 322–328; Kalous 2015, pp. 143–144; Wojtucki 2020a, pp. 281–284; and Wojtucki 2020b.

5. Scherz 1706, sig. B12.

6. See Klaniczay 1990, pp. 178–188, for the first formulation of this argument, and Mézes 2019, pp. 93–95, for further discussion and critique.

7. Schertz 1706, sigs. A3, B4v–5; the urine episode is also mentioned by Hermann 1698, p. 368.

8. Report by Professor Geelhausen, *Commercium Litterarium* 2 (1732): 138–139.

9. Schertz 1706, sigs. B11v–12; the phrase italicized here is in German, the rest Latin. Cf. Mézes 2019, pp. 222–226.

10. Mézes 2019, pp. 223–224.

11. Calmet 1746, pp. 270–271.

12. Schertz 1706. Petersen 2021, p. 42, points out that although the imprimatur was issued in 1704, publication is dated to 1706 by the chronogram on the title-page.

13. Kysučan 2020, pp. 108–109.

14. See Mézes 2019, pp. 221–228.

15. Schertz 1706, sig. C1v.

16. Schertz 1706, sigs. A10, B5–6, B12.

17. Schertz 1706, sigs. B2v–3.

18. Schertz 1706, sigs. A10v–11v.

19. Petersen 2021, p. 42.

20. Schertz 1706, sig. E5.

21. Lauterbach 1710, pp. 23–25. Cf. Kozak 2021, pp. 166–168.

22. *Sammlung von Natur- und Medicin- (Wie auch hierzu gehörigen Kunst- und Literatur)-Geschichten* (quarterly, Leipzig and Bautzen: David Richter); hereafter *Sammlung N&M*.

23. [Anonymous], 'Von dem Polnischen *Upiertz* oder sich selbst fressenden Todten', *Sammlung N&M*, Winter Quarter 1722 (1723): 82–88, at pp. 82–83.

24. [Anonymous], 'Von dem Polnischen *Upiertz*', p. 83; Schürmann 1990, p. 109. This was in the village of *Harsen*, not identified.

25. Schurmann 1990, pp. 111–112.

26. Hetzer and Hoerder 1987, especially pp. 31–39.

27. See Dömötör 1982 for the absence of dangerous corpses in Hungarian folklore. However, for one potential medieval case, see Vargha 2017.

28. Mézes 2019, pp. 201–202. As he acknowledges, 'far-reaching conclusions cannot be drawn from this scattered data'. Robert Evans suggests to me (pers. comm.) that the transhumant Vlachs in Moravia were spread thinly while true Aromanians from the Balkans mixed little with

other ethnicities, which would have limited transmission possibilities. This question clearly needs more work, but meanwhile, the distribution of cases does strongly suggest a Carpathian transmission of *some* kind.

29. Kozak 2021, pp. 245, 295–296.

30. M. Zsilinsky, *Forradalmi Zsinat Története (1707–1715)* (Budapest: Viktor Akad. Könyvkereskedése, 1889), pp. 57–58, 71. Grateful thanks to Graeme Murdock for finding this publication, and for his advice.

31. My version conflates the two contemporary accounts, in Bertalan Matirkó, 'Egy Szepességi Népmondáról', *Ethnographia: a Magyarországi Néprajzi Társaság Értesitöje* 1 (June 1890): 261–272 (extracts from narrative and statements in the city archive, including the letter to the bishop); *Der Europäische Niemand* 11 (1719): 972–975 (report from Liptó county, July 1718). Matirkó also gives (pp. 262–264) a much-expanded folkloric version. An independent narrative from the physician Georg Buchholz, written down by his son in 1754, adds further details: summary in Bohn 2019, p. 113. Matthias Bel, *Hungariae Antiquae et Novae Prodromus* (Nuremberg, 1723), pp. 108–109, merely summarises.

32. Georg Buchholz, 'Von einem nach dem Tode verbrannten Weibe', *Sammlung N&M*, Spring Quarter 1724 (1725): 635.

33. Köléseri 1709, pp. 112–114.

34. Klaniczay 1990, pp. 179, 237n20 (but I have been unable to check his sources).

35. Kreuz 2006.

Chapter 31: Vampires in the News, 1725–57

Epigraph: J. Linden, *Abhandlungen über Cameral- und fiscalämtliche Gegenstände* (Vienna: Carl Gerold, 1834), p. 192.

1. A complete bibliography is impossible here, but the rich details of the phenomena and their literary reception can be traced through: Hamberger 1992 and Equiamicus 2023 (for the texts); essays in Augustynowicz and Reber 2011; Mézes 2019 (now the most thorough account); Barber 1988, pp. 5–9, 15–20 (medical aspects); Lecouteux 1999, pp. 140–145; Bräunlein 2012; Pickering 2013, 2020; Bohn 2019, pp. 78–94; de Ceglia 2023.

2. Mézes 2019, pp. 111–195, 479–487.

3. Bräunlein 2012, p. 7.

4. Ranft 1725, pp. 6–7.

5. Ranft 1728, pp. 93–94. Cf. Ceglia 2011, pp. 497–499, for the intellectual context.

6. *Commercium Litterarium* 2 (1732): 82–84. It immediately prompted a string of pieces from other contributors in the same issue.

7. Bohn 2019, pp. 92–99.

8. Ranft 1734.

9. Notably Bräunlein 2012; Vermeir 2012; Mézes 2019; Bohn 2019, pp. 94–99. Many of the primary texts are printed by Hamberger 1992 and Equiamicus 2023.

10. Mézes 2019, pp. 399–401; Kalous 2015, pp. 155–159.

11. Kozak 2021, p. 254.

12. See p. 306.

13. Ceglia 2011. The work circulated in manuscript but was not published until 1774.

14. Mézes 2019, pp. 483–487.

15. Kalous 2015, pp. 159–160.

16. Zuber 2003, pp. 328–335; Mézes 2019, pp. 402–417, 495.

17. Mézes 2019, pp. 417–440.

18. Mézes 2019, pp. 440–442.

19. Mézes 2019, p. 443.
20. Vidal 2009, pp. 170–171.
21. Emden 1758; Kozak 2021, pp. 72–77.
22. Bräunlein 2012, pp. 12–13; Mézes 2019, pp. 445–451.
23. See Wolff 1994 for the emergence of conceptions of 'Eastern Europe' as a primitive 'other'.
24. Bräunlein 2012, p. 13; Mézes 2019, pp. 130–134.
25. Calmet 1746, p. 270; Mézes 2019, p. 221.
26. Calmet 1746, pp. iv, vii–viii.
27. Calmet 1746, p. 253.
28. Calmet 1749, 1751a. For the criticism and responses, see Fangé 1762, pp. 377–388.
29. Calmet 1751b, 1759.
30. For Calmet's method, see Vidal 2009; Morris 2015; Craig 2021. Cf. Kozak 2021, pp. 252–264, for Enlightenment approaches.
31. Pearson 2005, pp. 129–130.
32. Fangé 1762, pp. 142–146; Pearson 2005, p. 239. Morris 2015, pp. 191–196, provides some explanation for Voltaire's unattractive behaviour.
33. I am grateful to Roger Pearson for discussions on this point and for his view that the verse is double-edged, implying that Calmet was a well-meaning simpleton.
34. *Œuvres complètes de Voltaire*, vol. 43 (Gotha: Charles-Guillaume Ettinger, 1784), pp. 386–392.

Chapter 32: Vampires for a Scientific Age

Epigraph: *Montrose Democrat*, 26 April 1871, signed 'W.M.B. Tourje'.
1. Bell 2006, 2011, 2021, 2024; Bell and Bellantoni 2023. I am deeply grateful to Michael Bell for his generously given knowledge and expertise, and for answering so many questions. It is thanks to him that I found most of the source-material used in this chapter.
2. Quoted in Bell 2011, pp. xxix–xxx.
3. Bell 2011, p. xxxiii.
4. See p. 72; Bell 2024, pp. 13, 34–35, 173–177.
5. Fogel 1915, pp. 1–2.
6. Fogel 1915, p. 129.
7. *Lancaster Examiner and Herald*, 3 June 1857.
8. Fogel 1915, pp. 133–134. There was also a Danish belief that 'a corpse is not allowed to be buried in the clothes of a living person, lest as the clothes rot in the grave, that person to whom they belonged should waste away and perish': T. F. Thiselton-Dyer, *Domestic Folk-Lore* (London: Cassell, [1881]), pp. 83–84.
9. Brooke 1995, pp. 122–124.
10. Benes 1992, pp. 97–99, 106–107; Benes 1995, pp. 131–137; Brooke 1995.
11. Bell 2006, p. 107. Cf. Benes 1995, pp. 137–139.
12. The source is a short tract called *The Travels of Three English Gentlemen from Venice to Hamburgh* (1745). I owe these references to J. L. Bell's blog *Boston 1775* at https://boston1775.blogspot.com/2020/01/vampire-reports-in-colonial-american.html.
13. See the list in Bell 2024, pp. iii–vi.
14. *Connecticut Courant and Weekly Intelligencer*, 22 June 1784, quoted in Bell 2011, pp. xxx–xxxi; Bell 2024, pp. 51–54.
15. D. L. Mansfield, *The History of the Town of Dummerston* (Ludlow, VT: A. M. Hemenway, 1884), p. 27; Bell 2011, pp. 219–220; Bell 2024, pp. 151–156.

16. *Chicago Daily Tribune*, 24 October 1885; Bell 2024, pp. 37–38. See Bell 2011, pp. 254–255 for another case.

17. Higgins 2003: petition of 8 August 1787 by seven freeholders of Charleston, requesting a meeting to 'prosecute the persons who dug up and boiled the body of James O'Neill'.

18. 'A curious old letter' printed in *Greenfield Gazette and Courier*, 10 September 1877, 1 (italics in original); cited from Bell 2024, pp. 25–27.

19. *Albany Gazette*, 26 April 1790; Bell 2024, pp. 69–71.

20. Bell 2011, p. 301; Bell 2024, p. 53.

21. Data compiled by Michael Bell: Bell 2024, pp. 55–56.

22. N. L. Smith 2008, based on four Connecticut case-studies. She shows that this female bias disappeared after 1880.

23. Weisman 1984; Baker 2006; Moyer 2020.

24. Calculated from data in Weisman 1984, pp. 222–223.

25. Moyer 2020, pp. 143–144, 162–170; Weisman 1984, pp. 45–47.

26. Moyer 2020, p. 169.

27. Information from Richard Hite: Bell 2024, p. 54.

28. H. S. Nourse, *History of the Town of Harvard Massachusetts, 1731–1893* (Harvard, MA: printed for Warren Hapgood, 1894), pp. 104–105; Bell 2024, pp. 163–167.

29. A. M. Tirrell, 'Vampire Vitals', *Springfield [MA] Republican*, 25 August 1929, cited here from Bell 2024, pp. 233–236.

30. J. S. Pettibone, 'Early History of Manchester', *Proceedings of the Vermont Historical Society*, n.s., 1 (1930):147–166, at p. 158; cf. Bell 2011, pp. 215–217, and Bell 2024, pp. 149–151. This is an edition of a narrative from the 1860s, which says that it was 'furnished me by an eye witness of the transaction'.

31. Bell 2011, pp. 65–67; Bell 2024, pp. 247–250.

32. *The Alexandria Gazette and Daily Advertiser*, 16 March 1822 (among other papers); Joseph R. Chandler, 'Superstitions of New England, No. 1', *The Lady's Book* 6 (January 1833): 31–32; cf. Bell 2011, pp. 270–272, and Bell 2024, pp. 238–242. Notwithstanding some ambiguity, it seems likely that Chandler quoted the eye-witness report and poem rather than being their author.

33. The cases are listed and discussed by Bell 2011, and in Bell 2024, pp. iii–vi. For one excavated case—a burial in which the bones have been rearranged—see Sledzik and Bellantoni 1994; Bell and Bellantoni 2023.

34. Bell 2024, pp. 9–13.

35. Bell 2011, pp. 204–206, 253–255, 301.

36. [S. P. Hildreth], 'Extracts from the Diary of an Old Physician', *Western Journal of the Medical and Physical Sciences*, 10.iv (1837): 500–504, at p. 501; Bell 2024, pp. 49–50.

37. Tirrell, 'Vampire Vitals', quoted in Bell 2024, p. 233.

38. *Springfield Republican*, 3 September 1869; *Cincinnati Daily Gazette*, 29 September 1869; both cited in Bell 2024, pp. 93, 97.

Chapter 33: 'The Horrible Scenes of Old Time'

Epigraph: Lawson 1910, pp. 371–372.

1. Horace Walpole to the Countess of Ossory, 1785, in P. Cunningham (ed.), *The Letters of Horace Walpole* (London: H. G. Bohn, 1861), pp. 537–538.

2. Görres 1840, pp. 283–288; Steiner 1959, pp. 26–33.

3. There was a sequel of a kind. In 1861 a German naturalist, Maximilian Perty, published a brief account that does not endorse the literal truth of vampires (though it needs to be read quite carefully to grasp that), but nonetheless uses the language of 'epidemic disease' for the

mental suffering of those who thought themselves afflicted. See Perty 1861, pp. 336–339; Steiner 1959, pp. 33–35.

4. Summers 1929, p. 206.

5. Fortis 1774; Wolff 1994, pp. 315–331.

6. Abundant quantities of such material can be found in, or located through, Perkowski 1989; Schürmann 1990; Dundes 1998a; Bohn 2019; Sugg 2019; Kozak 2021; Trzaska 2023. See also note 20 below.

7. Avdikos 2013, p. 312.

8. Both quoted in Wolff 1994, pp. 175, 293.

9. Zelepos 2014, pp. 374–381.

10. J. J. Ehrler, *Banatul de la Origini pină Acum (1774)* (Timisoara, Romania: Editura Facla, 1982), p. 37. Compare Fortis's comment that Morlach priests sell people 'superstitious scrolls': Wolff 1994, p. 322.

11. See Szołtysek 2012 for a useful overview, along with a strong critique of the classifications associated with John Hajnal.

12. This is very clear from verses in Honko et al. 1993, for instance 'Mother, forgive and bless: you gave me hell' (p. 360).

13. Du Boulay 2009, pp. 164–165.

14. Avdikos 2013, p. 316.

15. Avdikos 2013, pp. 317–318.

16. Drettas 1985, p. 209, 211.

17. S.G.B. St. Clair and C. A. Brophy, *Twelve Years' Study of the Eastern Question in Bulgaria* (London: Chapman and Hall, 1877), pp. 52–53; Sugg 2019, pp. 8–9. Sugg takes the story (set in Enekli village) seriously, but St. Clair's career suggests that he was an erratic and unpleasant individual with a deep hatred of Bulgarians.

18. Blum and Blum 1970, pp. 71–72.

19. Sugg 2019, pp. 11–12 (oral account after a fifty-year lapse), 224–225 (set in Volhynia, Russia, 1888, source not stated), 226–227 (in several English provincial newspapers, from a journalist in St Petersburg, 1890).

20. For a few cases, and much folklore, see Jaworskii 1898; Oinas 1978; Ivanits 1989; Perkowski 1989, 1998; Warner 2000, 2011; Bohn 2019, pp. 148–156; Kozak 2021, pp. 63–67, 130.

21. Kozak 2021, pp. 102–103.

22. Gardeła 2020, p. 262. This was at Mierzwice Stare.

23. Warner 2000, p. 71.

24. McClelland 1999, pp. 66–98; see also Bohn 2019, pp. 186–190.

25. McClelland 1999, pp. 94–95.

26. Lawson 2010; Blum and Blum 1970. The new standard reference, with copious documentation of this material, is Trzaska 2023.

27. Avdikos 2013, p. 314.

28. Fine 1998; Bohn 2019, pp. 174–178.

29. Vukanović 1958 (including pp. 117–118 for staking); Vukanović 1959.

30. Kozak 2021, especially pp. 56, 62, 88–97, 308–355.

31. Kozak 2021, p. 200.

32. Guzowski 2021.

33. Perkowski 1998, p. 41, map.

34. The priest denied his complicity; he and others involved were acquitted on appeal in February 2024. There are various reports in Romanian online media, for instance https://www.antena3.ro/actualitate/locale/preot-vanator-de-strigoi-valcea-usurat-decizia-instantei-familia-strigoaicei-inchisoare-acord-700923.html, or https://adevarul.ro/stiri-locale/ramnicu-valcea/au-dezgropat-mortul-si-i-au-infipt-un-cutit-in-2339627.html. I owe knowledge of this case to Alexandra Nachescu.

35. Steiner 1959, pp. 36–42; Franz and Nösler 2016, pp. 175–178; Schürmann 1990, p. 73.
36. Grober-Glück 1981; Schürmann 1990, pp. 98–108; Kozak 2021, p. 173.
37. Grober-Glück 1981, pp. 440–441.
38. Grober-Glück 1981, pp. 442–443, 445–446, and map NF 75.
39. Grober-Glück 1981, p. 450.
40. Schürmann 1990, pp. 48, 141. Cf. Schürmann 2009, pp. 244–245.
41. Schürmann 1990, p. 104.
42. Wiegelmann 1966, p. 173.
43. This word also means the red-backed shrike, *lannius coluro*, which is apparently a metaphor: Schürmann 1990, pp. 98–99.
44. Grober-Glück 1981, pp. 450–451, and map NF 76. Compare the multiple synonyms on the Dalmatian coast (p. 306).
45. Kwaśniewska 2019.
46. Perkowski 1972.
47. Nösler 2014, p. 16.
48. Schürmann 1990, pp. 95–96.
49. Navrátilová 2005.
50. Wiegelmann 1966; Gröber-Gluck 1981; Schürmann 1990, pp. 79–124.
51. Grober-Glück 1981, pp. 428–435, 442–445, 449–453, and map NF 73.
52. Grober-Glück 1981, maps NF 74–75.
53. Du Boulay 1982, p. 226.
54. Vukanović 1958, pp. 116–117.
55. A. Stojnev (ed.), *Bălgarska mitologija. Enciklopedičen rečnik* (Sofia: Izdatelstvo Zaharij Stojanov, 2006), pp. 45–47.
56. Kozak 2021, p. 203.
57. Widely reported in the Western press, for instance in the *Herald*, 10 March 2007, https://www.heraldscotland.com/default_content/12768421.vampire-slayer-impales-milosevic-stop-return/.
58. Simon Tisdall, 'Putin Has Become a Global Bogeyman. Russians Must Exorcise This Ghoul', *The Guardian*, 23 July 2023, https://www.theguardian.com/commentisfree/2023/jul/23/putin-has-become-a-global-bogeyman-russians-must-exorcise-this-ghoul.
59. Livermore 2021, pp. 123–124.
60. Lady Wilde, *Ancient Cures, Charms, and Usages of Ireland* (London: Ward and Downey, 1890), p. 67; *Syracuse Herald*, 21 February 1886. I owe these references to Michael Bell. See p. 388 for comparable practices among German immigrants in Pennsylvania.
61. E. M. Leather, *The Folk-Lore of Herefordshire* (London: Sidgwick and Jackson, 1912), 35.
62. F. T. Elsworthy, 'How to Bury a Witch', *Transactions of the Devonshire Association* 34 (1902): 83–84; cf. R. Tongue, 'Odds and Ends of Somerset Folklore', *Folklore* 69 (1958): 43–45. Note also a nineteenth-century Somerset view that a conventionally buried corpse could be turned over in the grave by the Devil: F. T. Elsworthy, *An Outline of the Grammar of the Dialect of West Somerset* (London: Trubner & Co., 1877), 99.
63. Havekost 1914.
64. *The Times*, 29 July 1915, p. 5; repr. in *Folklore* 27 (1916): 224–225.

Chapter 34: Vampires of Colonialism and Slavery

Epigraph: Quoted in Bell 2011, p. xxviii.
1. I am very grateful to Meleisa Ono-George for her effective criticisms of this chapter, and especially for advice on handling colonial sources.
2. Witzel 2012, pp. 291–300.

3. Morphy 1984, p. 40. Philip Jones, Howard Morphy and Veronica Strang gave me much-needed and much-appreciated advice while I was writing this section, though I take full responsibility for the somewhat heterodox views expressed here.

4. The relevant informants were Frank James and John Gaggin, both working in the 1890s.

5. Howitt 1904, pp. 436–439.

6. Howitt 1904, p. 449 (information from James).

7. Howitt 1904, pp. 460–461.

8. Howitt 1904, pp. 474–475 (information from Gaggin).

9. Urquhart 1885, p. 88.

10. Howitt 1904, pp. 444–445. I am very grateful to Philip Jones for this explanation (pers. comm.): 'The basis of this likeness was apparently linked to the practice in Ngarrindjeri country (Lower Murray River, Lakes and Coorong) of smoking a deceased individual's body on a platform, with mourners beneath. Apparently the black skin peeled off in this process, exposing a white layer beneath. The language term for this was *grinkar'* and this was the term applied to white people. It is still used today, but without any direct reference to the funeral ritual. Particular facial features of white men were considered to belong to those deceased ancestors—that was enough for the *grinkari* appellation to be applied.'

11. Sharp 1952, pp. 17–18, 22.

12. As beautifully illustrated by Berzock 2019.

13. Somé 1994, pp. 46–48.

14. Cavazzi 1687, pp. 221–222. I am very grateful to John Thornton for his guidance on West African sources.

15. Parker 2021, pp. 210–227.

16. For instance, they do not feature among the LoDagaa of Ghana: Goody 1962, pp. 365, 371. In North Kenya the *loip* (shadow or spiritual manifestation) can—in cases of early or bad death—appear as a fire or mist, throw stones, or occasionally manifest as a night-mare, but it is not identified with the corpse: Straight 2007, pp. 161–162, 167–170, 173–174.

17. Herskovitz 1938, 1.399; Parker 2021, pp. 212–218. Compare this characteristic of female demons discussed in Chapter 10.

18. Weeks 1909, p. 55.

19. Daniell 1856, p. 19.

20. Hilton 1985, pp. 10–11.

21. 'Senhor dos . . . Matambulas, que se interpretam homens mortos, e resucitados': [Antonio de Sousa de Macedo], *Mercurio Portuguez* (Lisbon, July 1666), sig. B2[v]; reprinted in Visconde de Paiva Manso, *Historia do Congo* (Lisbon: Typographia da Academia, 1877), p. 244. John Thornton (pers. comm.) suggests that this is a Portuguese forgery, 'intended to undermine Antonio's commitment to Christianity and to belittle the customs of Kongo', but in any case it shows that the concept existed in 1666. See Topa 2019 for later literary uses of *matumbola*.

22. Ackermann and Gauthier 1991.

23. Ackermann and Gauthier 1991, p. 489.

24. Geschiere 1998, pp. 820–824. Ardener 1970, pp. 147–149, describes the same process among the Bakweri of west Cameroon.

25. Herskovits 1938, 2.243–244.

26. White 1993, 2000. There are critical reviews by James L. Giblin (*African Studies Review* 44 [2001]: 83–87) and Peter Geschiere (*Journal of African History* 43 (2002): 499–501).

27. See Paton 2015 for a modern study of the cultural and religious context.

28. Hurston 1981, pp. 58–61. Cf. Paton 2015, pp. 222–224, for rituals against duppies and other supernatural beings.

29. Hurston 1981, p. 59.

30. Hurston 1981, pp. 61–62.

31. For the socio-religious background, see Deren 1953; Davis 1985, 1988.

32. Davis 1985 and Davis 1988 are strong positive statements. Littlewood and Douyon 1997 are more measured, and emphasise psychological explanations; they tentatively entertain the theory of poisoning by tetrodotoxin, but not the idea of secret farms cultivated by enslaved *zombis*. Littlewood 2009 has moved in a more sceptical direction.

33. Littlewood and Douyon 1997, p. 1094; Davis 1985, pp. 181–182.

34. Davis 1985, pp. 186–188, 212–213, 237–238, 253.

35. Davis 1985, p. 185.

36. Cf. Littlewood 2009, p. 249: 'The Haitian fear of zombification graphically represents the possibility of the loss of self-determination for the Haitian peasant.'

Conclusion

Epigraph: Stoker 1897, p. 21.

1. Tossach 1744; Blair 2023a, pp. 151–154, 162–164.

2. Winsløw 1742, 1746.

3. Ruston 2021, pp. 61–120.

4. [Anonymous] 1820, p. 247.

5. Hansen 1996, pp. 70–71, 201–207; Groom 2018, p. 100. See also this volume, p. 136.

6. Groom 2018, p. 97. Cf. Ruston 2021, 19–40, and Hock 1900 for the German background, and Kozak 2021, pp. 265–281, for vampires in the Polish Romantic movement.

7. In various newspapers, cited here from *The Alexandria Gazette and Daily Advertiser*, 16 March 1822. Cf. Bell 2011, pp. 269–272, and pp. 396–397 in this volume.

8. Cf. Hock 1900, pp. 108–115.

9. Groom 2018, pp. 104–112; Ruston 2021, pp. 30–32.

10. Ruston 2021.

11. Groom 2018, pp. 100–101, 123–125.

12. Auerbach 1995, 38–69.

13. Klaniczay 1990, pp. 180–188; Groom 2018, pp. 33–40. See p. 381 in this volume for Voltaire.

14. For this and other uses by Marx of the vampire metaphor, see Neocleous 2003.

15. Cf. Drettas 1985, pp. 206–208.

16. Xygalatas 2022.

17. The context is described by Panea and Preda 2019, who accept the sincerity of Mitrica and his companions, and emphasise the tension between traditional belief and the concern of the mayor and other authorities to avoid reputational damage. Clips of the cemetery scene, and of the filmed interviews translated here, are widely available online, for instance, at https://www.youtube.com/watch?v=5O28Vz-YS2I&t=101s, accessed 11 February 2025.

BIBLIOGRAPHY

Ackermann, H.-W. and J. Gauthier 1991. 'The Ways and Nature of the Zombi'. *Journal of American Folklore* 104: 466–494.

Adler, S. R. 2011. *Sleep Paralysis: Night-Mares, Nocebos and the Mind-Body Connection*. New Brunswick, NJ: Rutgers University Press.

Ahern, E. M. 1973. *The Cult of the Dead in a Chinese Village*. Stanford, CA: Stanford University Press.

Aldhouse Green, M. 2001. *Dying for the Gods*. Stroud: Tempus.

Alfayé, S. 2009. '*Sit Tibi Terra Gravis*: Magical-Religious Practices against the Restless Dead in the Ancient World'. In F. Marco Simón, F. P. Polo, and J. R. Rodríguez (eds.), *Formae Mortis: El Tránsito de la Vida a la Muerte en las Sociedades Antiguas*. Barcelona: Universitat de Barcelona, pp. 181–216.

Alfayé Villa, S. 2010. 'Nails for the Dead: A Polysemic Account of an Ancient Funerary Practice'. In R. L. Gordon and F. Marco Simón (eds.), *Magical Practice in the Latin West*. Leiden: Brill, pp. 427–456.

Alfsdotter, C. et al. 2022. 'An Actualistic Taphonomic Study of Human Decomposition in Coffins'. *Bioarchaeology International* 6: 190–215.

Allason-Jones, L. 1989. *Women in Roman Britain*. London: British Museum Publications.

Allatius, L. 1645. *De templis Graecorum recentioribus*. Cologne: J. Kalckhoven.

Allen, M. and J. Rylatt 2002. 'Phase 5, The Bridles, St Barnabas Road, Barnetby le Wold, North Lincolnshire'. Unpublished excavation report. Lincolnshire: Pre-Construct Archaeology.

Al-Rawi, F.N.H. 2008. 'Inscriptions from the Tombs of the Queens of Assyria'. In J. E. Curtis et al. (eds.), *New Light on Nimrud—Proceedings of the Nimrud Conference 2002*. London: British Institute for the Study of Iraq, pp. 119–138.

Alterauge, A. et al. 2020. 'Between Belief and Fear: Reinterpreting Prone Burials during the Middle Ages and Early Modern Period in German-Speaking Europe'. *PLoS ONE* 15(8). https://doi.org/10.1371/journal.pone.0238439.

Andrés de la Pastora, R. 1883. 'Antigüedades prehistóricas del partido de Molina de Aragón'. *Boletín de la Real Academia de la Historia Madrid* 3: 154–159.

Angélopoulou, A. 1999. 'Vampires d'Orient: L'écriture d'un mythe'. *Cahiers de Littérature Orale* 45: 63–86.

[Anonymous.] 1820. *Histoire des vampires et des spectres malfaisans*. Paris: Masson.

Arcini, C. 2009. 'Losing Face: The Worldwide Phenomenon of Ancient Prone Burial'. In Postdoctoral Archaeology Group, *Döda Personers Sällskap*. Stockholm: Stockholm University, pp. 187–202.

Ardener, E. 1970. 'Witchcraft, Economics and the Continuity of Belief'. In M. Douglas (ed.), *Witchcraft Confessions and Accusations*. London: Routledge, pp. 141–160.

Ármann Jakobsson 2011. 'Vampires and Watchmen: Categorizing the Mediaeval Icelandic Undead'. *Journal of English and Germanic Philology* 110: 281–300.

Artelius, T. 2005. 'The Revenant by the Lake: Spear Symbolism in Scandinavian Late Viking Age Burial Ritual'. In T. Artelius and F. Svanberg (eds.), *Dealing with the Dead*. Sweden: National Heritage Board, pp. 261–276.

Aspöck, E., K. Gerdau-Radonić, and A. Noterman 2022. 'Reopening Graves for the Removal of Objects and Bones'. In Knüsel and Schotsmans 2022, pp. 277–310.

Aspöck, E., A. Klevnäs, and N. Müller-Scheeßel (eds.). 2020. *Grave Disturbances: The Archaeology of Post-Depositional Interactions with the Dead*. Oxford: Oxbow.

Auerbach, N. 1995. *Our Vampires, Ourselves*. Chicago: University of Chicago Press.

Augustynowicz, C. and U. Reber (eds.). 2011. *Vampirglaube und Magia Posthuma im Diskurs der Habsburgermonarchie*. Münster: LIT Verlag.

Avdikos, E. 2013. 'Vampire Stories in Greece and the Reinforcement of Socio-Cultural Norms'. *Folklore* 124: 307–326.

Bahna, V. 2015. 'Explaining Vampirism: Two Divergent Attractors of Dead Human Concepts'. *Journal of Cognition and Culture* 15: 285–298.

Baines, J. and P. Lacovara 2002. 'Burial and the Dead in Ancient Egyptian Society'. *Journal of Social Archaeology* 2: 5–36.

Baker, E. W. 2006. *A Storm of Witchcraft: The Salem Trials and the American Experience*. New York: Oxford University Press.

Balbanov, P. 2011. 'Mortuary Archaeology in Roman Thrace: The "Helikon" Funerary Complex'. In I. P. Haynes (ed.), *Early Roman Thrace: New Evidence from Bulgaria*. Portsmouth, RI: Journal of Roman Archaeology, pp. 107–114.

Bane, T. 2010. *Encyclopaedia of Vampire Mythology*. Jefferson, NC: McFarland and Company.

Barber, B. and D. Bowsher 2000. *The Eastern Cemetery of Roman London: Excavations 1983–1990*. London: MOLA.

Barber, P. 1988. *Vampires, Burial, and Death: Folklore and Reality*. New Haven, CT: Yale University Press.

Barbezat, M. D. 2018. *Burning Bodies: Communities, Eschatology and the Punishment of Heresy in the Middle Ages*. Ithaca, NY: Cornell University Press.

Bartlett, R. (ed.). 2002. *Geoffrey of Burton, Life and Miracles of Saint Modwenna*. Oxford: Oxford University Press.

Baug, I. et al. 2024. 'Norse Whetstones in Slavic Areas—Indicators of Long-Distance Networks during the Viking Age and the Middle Ages'. *Medieval Archaeology* 68: 48–71.

Bell, M. E. 2006. 'Vampires and Death in New England, 1784 to 1892'. *Anthropology and Humanism* 31: 124–140.

Bell, M. E. 2011. *Food for the Dead: On the Trail of New England's Vampires*. 2nd ed. Middletown, CT: Wesleyan University Press.

Bell, M. E. 2021. 'New England Vampires as Local Variants of a Belief Tradition'. *Journal of Vampire Studies* 1: 165–191.

Bell, M. E. 2024. *Vampire's Grasp: The Hidden History of Consumption in New England*. Queensbury, NY: Warren History Press.

Bell, M. E. and N. F. Bellantoni 2023. 'Fear of the Undead: An Archaeological and Folkloristic Interpretation of the New England Vampire Tradition'. *Bulletin of the Archaeological Society of Connecticut* 85: 29–47.

Benes, P. 1992. 'Itinerant Physicians, Healers, and Surgeon-Dentists in New England and New York, 1720–1825'. In P. Benes (ed.), *Medicine and Healing*. Annual Proceedings of the Dublin Seminar for New England Folklife. Boston: Boston University, pp. 95–112.

Benes, P. 1995. 'Fortunetellers, Wise-Men, and Magical Healers in New England, 1644–1850'. In P. Benes (ed.), *Wonders of the Invisible World: 1600–1900*. Annual Proceedings of the Dublin Seminar for New England Folklife. Boston: Boston University, pp. 127–148.

Benjamin, C. 2018. *Empires of Ancient Eurasia: The First Silk Roads Era 100 BCE–250 CE*. Cambridge: Cambridge University Press.

Benyovsky, I. 1996. 'Vampiri u dubrovačim selima 18 stoljeća'. *Otium* 4: 118–130.

Berszin, C. 1994. 'Der Spitalfriedhof Heiliggeist-Hospital in Konstanz'. In S. Brather et al. (eds.), *Archäologie als Sozialgeschichte*. Rahden: Verlag Marie Leidorf GmbH, pp. 127–134.

Berzock, K. B. (ed.). 2019. *Caravans of Gold, Fragments in Time*. Evanston, IL: Block Museum of Art, Northwestern University.

Betsinger, T. K. and A. B. Scott 2014. 'Governing from the Grave: Vampire Burials and Social Order in Post-Medieval Poland'. *Cambridge Archaeological Journal* 23: 467–476.

Betsinger, T. K. and A. B. Scott 2020. 'Does Health Define Deviancy? Non-Normative Burials in Post-Medieval Poland'. In Betsinger, Scott, and Tsaliki 2020, pp. 276–291.

Betsinger, T. K., A. B. Scott, and A. Tsaliki (eds.). 2020. *The Odd, the Unusual and the Strange: Bioarchaeological Explorations of Atypical Burials*. Gainesville: University of Florida Press.

Biermann, F. 2016. 'North-Western Slavic Strongholds of the 8th–10th Centuries AD'. In N. Christie and H. Herold (eds.), *Fortified Settlements in Early Medieval Europe*. Oxford: Oxbow, pp. 85–94.

Bill, J. and A. Daly 2012. 'The Plundering of the Ship Graves from Oseberg and Gokstad: An Example of Power Politics?' *Antiquity* 86: 808–824.

Biller, P. 1999. 'William of Newburgh and the Cathar Mission to England'. In D. Wood (ed.), *Life and Thought in the Northern Church, c.1100–c.1700*. Woodbridge: Boydell, pp. 11–30.

Binski, P. 1996. *Medieval Death: Ritual and Representation*. London: British Museum Press.

Black, W. 2016. 'Animated Corpses and Bodies with Power in the Scholastic Age'. In J. Rollo Koster (ed.), *Death in Medieval Europe*. New York: Routledge, pp. 71–92.

Blair, J. 2005. *The Church in Anglo-Saxon Society*. Oxford: Oxford University Press.

Blair, J. 2009. 'The Dangerous Dead in Early Medieval England'. In S. Baxter et al. (eds.), *Early Medieval Studies in Memory of Patrick Wormald*. Farnham: Ashgate, 539–559.

Blair, J. 2011. 'Overview: The Archaeology of Religion'. In H. Hamerow et al. (eds.), *The Oxford Handbook of Anglo-Saxon Archaeology*. Oxford: Oxford University Press, 727–741.

Blair J. 2016. *Bede and the Culture of the Laity: The Jarrow Lecture 2010*. Jarrow: The Parish Church Council.

Blair, J. 2018. *Building Anglo-Saxon England*. Princeton, NJ: Princeton University Press.

Blair, J. 2023a. 'Life, Death and Near-Death in the Sauchie Colliery, c.1670–1820: the Case of the Blair Family'. *Forth Naturalist and Historian* 46: 120–167.

Blair, J. 2023b. 'Restraining the Unquiet Dead: The Burials containing Iron Nails'. In Randall and Poulton 2023, pp. 63–66.

Blaizot, F. 2022. 'Methodological Guidelines for Archaeothanatological Practice'. In Knüsel and Schotsmans 2022, pp. 23–41.

Blindheim, C. and B. Heyerdahl-Larsen 1995. *Kaupang-Funnene*. Vol. 2. Oslo: Institutt for Arkeologi.

Blum, R. and E. Blum. 1970. *The Dangerous Hour: The Lore of Crisis and Mystery in Rural Greece*. London: Chatto and Windus.

Boberg, I. M. 1966. *Motif-Index of Early Icelandic Literature*. Copenhagen: Munksgaard.

Bogatyrëv, P. 1998. *Vampires in the Carpathians: Magical Acts, Rites and Beliefs in Subcarpathian Rus'*. New York: Columbia University Press. [Translation of *Actes magiques, rites et croyances en Russie subcarpathique*, Paris, 1929.]

Böhm, M. 1601. *Die Drey Grossen Landtplagen*. Wittenberg: Lorenz Säuberlich.

Bohn, T. M. 2019. *The Vampire: Origins of a European Myth*. New York: Berghahn. [English translation of *Der Vampir. Ein europäischer Mythos*, 2016.]

Boyle, A. et al. 1998. *The Anglo-Saxon Cemetery at Butler's Field, Lechlade*. Vol. 1. Oxford: Oxford Archaeological Unit.

Brather, S. 2007. 'Wiedergänger und Vampire? Bauch- und Seitenlage bei westslawischen Bestattungen des 9. bis 12. Jh'. In G. H. Jeute, J. Schneesweß, and C. Theune (eds.), *Aedificatio Terrae: Festschrift für Eike Gringmuth-Dallmer*. Rahden: Marie Leidorf, pp. 109–117.

Bräunlein, P. J. 2012. 'The Frightening Borderlands of Enlightenment: The Vampire Problem'. *Studies in History and Philosophy of Biological and Biomedical Sciences* 43: 710–719.

Brereton, G. (ed.). 2018. *I Am Ashurbanipal*. Catalogue of British Museum exhibition. London: Thames and Hudson and British Museum.

Briggs, G. W. 1920. *The Chamārs*. Calcutta: Association Press.

Brooke, J. L. 1995. "'The True Spiritual Seed": Sectarian Religion and the Persistence of the Occult in Eighteenth-Century New England'. In P. Benes (ed.), *Wonders of the Invisible World: 1600–1900*. Annual Proceedings of the Dublin Seminar for New England Folklife. Boston: Boston University.

Brown, D. E. 2004. 'Human Universals, Human Nature and Human Culture'. *Daedalus* 133: 47–54.

Brown, P.D.C. 1967. 'The Anglo-Saxon Cemetery at Harwell, Grave 7'. *Oxoniensia* 32: 73–74.

Brundke, N. 2013. 'Das Gräberfeld von Mockersdorf—Frühmittelalterliche Sonderbestattungen im slawisch-fränkischen Kontaktbereich'. *Beiträge zur Archäozoologie und Prähistorischen Anthropologie* 9: 141–150.

Buko, A. 2015. *Bodzia: A Late Viking-Age Elite Cemetery in Central Poland*. Leiden: Brill.

Burchard. 1853. 'Burchard of Worms'. In *'Decreta'*, book 19, edited by J.-P. Migne. Patrologiae Cursus Completus, Series Secunda, 140. Paris, 1853, cols. 943–1014.

Burkert, W. 1992. *The Orientalizing Revolution: Near Eastern Influence on Greek Culture in the Early Archaic Age*. Cambridge, MA: Harvard University Press.

Burkhardt, D. 1966. 'Vampirglaube und Vampirsage auf dem Balkan'. In *Beiträge zur Südosteuropa-Forschung*. München: Dr Dr R. Trofenik, pp. 211–252.

Burr, M. 1949. 'The Code of Stephan Dušan, Tsar and Autocrat of the Serbs and Greeks'. *The Slavonic and East European Review* 28: 198–217.

Byock, J. L. 1984. 'Saga Form, Oral Prehistory, and the Icelandic Social Context'. *New Literary History* 16: 153–173.

Cacciola, N. M. 2016. *Afterlives: The Return of the Dead in the Middle Ages*. Ithaca, NY: Cornell University Press.

Calkin, J. B. 1947. 'Two Romano-British Burials at Kimmeridge'. *Proceedings of the Dorset Natural History and Archaeological Society* 69: 33–41.

Calmet, A. 1746. *Dissertations sur les apparitions des anges, des démons et des esprits, et sur les revenans et vampires de Hongrie, de Boheme, de Moravie et de Silesie*. Paris: De Bure l'aîné.

Calmet, A. 1749. *Dissertations sur les apparitions des anges, des démons et des esprits, et sur les revenans et vampires de Hongrie, de Boheme, de Moravie et de Silesie*. Rev. ed. 2 vols. Einsiedeln: Jean Everhard Kalin.

Calmet, A. 1751a. *Traité sur les apparitions des esprits, et sur les vampires ou les revenans de Hongrie, de Moravie, etc.* 2 vols. Paris: De Bure l'aîné.

Calmet, A. 1751b. *Gelehrte Verhandlung der Materi, Von Erscheinungen der Geisteren, und denen Vampiren in Ungarn, Mahren etc.* 2 vols. Augsburg: Rieger. [German translation of Calmet 1751a.]

Calmet, A. 1759. *Dissertations upon the Apparitions of Angels, Dæmons and Ghosts, and Concerning the Vampires of Hungary, Bohemia, Moravia and Silesia*. London: M. Cooper. [English translation of Calmet 1746.]

Campagne, F. A. 2008. 'Witch or Demon? Faries, Vampires and Nightmares in Early Modern Spain'. *Acta Ethnographica Hungarica* 53: 381–410.

Campany, R. F. 1996. *Strange Writing: Anomaly Accounts in Early Medieval China*. Albany: State University of New York Press.

Campbell, J. K. 1964. *Honour, Family and Patronage: A Study of Institutions and Moral Values in a Greek Mountain Community*. Oxford: Clarendon Press.

Cangle, J. N. 2015. 'A Study of Post-Depositional Funerary Practices in Medieval England'. Unpublished Ph.D. thesis, University of Sheffield.

Cantemiru, D. 1872. *Operele Principelui: I: Descriptio Moldaviae*. Bucuresti: Lucratorii Associati.

Cavazzi da Montecuccolo, G. A. 1687. *Istorica descrizione de' tre regni, Congo, Matamba et Angola*. Bologna: Giacomo Monti.

Ceglia, F. P. de. 2011. 'The Archbishop's Vampires: Guiseppe Davanzati's *Dissertation* and the Reaction of "Scientific" Italian Catholicism to the "Moravian Events"'. *Archives Internationales d'Histoire des Sciences* 61: 487–510.

Ceglia, F. P. de. 2023. *Vampyr: Storia naturale della resurrezione*. Turin: Einaudi.

Chadwick, N. K. 1946. 'Norse Ghosts (a Study in the *Draugr* and the *Haugbúi*)'. *Folklore* 57: 50–65, 106–127.

Channing, J. [2005]. 'N6 Kilbeggan to Kinnegad Dual Carriageway: Archaeological Resolution. Final Report 1: Ballykilmore 6. Unpublished report. Valerie J. Keeley, Castlecomer, Co. Kilkenny.

Chenal, F. and H. Barrand Emam 2014. 'Nouvelles données concernant le pillage des sepultures mérovingiennes en Alsace'. *Revue archéologique de l'Est* 63: 489–500.

Child, F. J. 1883–1898. *The English and Scottish Popular Ballads*. 10 vols. Boston: Houghton, Mifflin & Co.

Clegg, S. 2023. *Woman's Lore: 4000 Years of Sirens, Serpents and Succubi*. London: Head of Zeus.

Colgrave, B. and R.A.B. Mynors (eds.). 1969. *Bede, Historia Ecclesiastica Gentis Anglorum*. Oxford: Oxford University Press.

Čoralić, L., Ž. Dugac and S. Sardelić 2013. 'Vampires in Dalmatia: The Example of the Village of Žrnovo on the Island of Korčula in the Eighteenth Century'. *Review of Croatian History* 9: 61–76.

Craig, C. 2021. 'Augustin Calmet and the Construction of the Eighteenth-Century Vampire'. *Central Europe Yearbook* 3: 54–70.

Crerar, B. 2022. *Feminine Power: The Divine to the Demonic*. London: British Museum.

Currie, B. 2021. 'Etana in Greece'. In Kelly and Metcalf 2021, pp. 126–144.

Cusack, A. R. 2021. 'The Marginal Dead of London, c.1600–1800'. Unpublished Ph.D. thesis, Birkbeck, University of London.

Dadea, M. 2023. 'Corpi santi e sepulture anomale in Sardegna attraverso i dati d'archivio'. In Pergola et al. 2023, pp. 187–201.

Dalrymple, W. 2024. *The Golden Road*. London: Bloomsbury.

Danforth, L. M. 1982. *The Death Rituals of Rural Greece*. Princeton, NJ: Princeton University Press.

Daniell, W. F. 1856. 'On the Ethnography of Akkrah and Adampe, Gold Coast, Western Africa'. *Journal of the Ethnological Society of London* 4: 1–32.

Daniels, C. M. 1966. 'Excavation on the Site of the Roman Villa at Southwell, 1959'. *Transactions of the Thoroton Society* 70: 13–54.

Davidson, H.R.E. 1981. 'The Restless Dead'. In H.R.E. Davidson and W.M.S. Russell (eds.), *The Folklore of Ghosts*. Woodbridge: D. S. Brewer, pp. 155–175.

Davis, W. 1985. *The Serpent and the Rainbow*. New York: Simon and Schuster.

Davis, W. 1988. *Passage of Darkness: The Ethnobiology of the Haitian Zombie*. Chapel Hill: University of North Carolina Press.

Demetrio, F. R. 1970. *Dictionary of Philippine Folk Beliefs and Customs*. 4 vols. Cagayan de Oro City, Philippines: Xavier University.

Deren, M. 1953. *Divine Horsemen: The Living Gods of Haiti*. London: Thames and Hudson.

Devlin, Z. L. and E.-J. Graham (eds.). 2015. *Death Embodied: Archaeological Approaches to the Treatment of the Corpse*. Oxford: Oxbow.

Dickie M. W. 2001. *Magic and Magicians in the Greco-Roman World*. London: Routledge.
Dickinson, T. M. 1993. 'An Anglo-Saxon 'Cunning Woman' from Bidford-on-Avon'. In M. Carver (ed.), *In Search of Cult*. Woodbridge: Boydell, pp. 45–54.
Dickinson, T. M. 2005. 'Symbols of Protection: The Significance of Animal-Ornamented Shields in Early Anglo-Saxon England'. *Medieval Archaeology* 49: 109–163.
Dierkens, A. 1996. 'La mort, les funérailles et la tombe du roi Pépin le Bref (768)'. *Médiévales* 31: 37–51.
Diming, Huang and Ding Wangdao (eds. and trans.). 2004. *Gan Bao, Anecdotes about Spirits and Immortals*. Beijing: Foreign Languages Press.
Dolansky, F. 2019. 'Nocturnal Rites to Appease the Untimely Dead: The *Lemuria* in Its Socio-Historical Context'. *Mouseion*, ser. 3, vol. 16, suppl. 1: 37–64.
Dömötör, T. 1982. *Hungarian Folk Beliefs*. Budapest: Corvina.
Doroszewska, J. 2015. 'When the Dead Love the Living: A Case Study in Phlegon of Tralles's *Mirabilia*'. *Scripta Classica* 12: 137–149.
Drettas, G. 1985. 'Questions de vampirisme'. *Études rurales* 97/98: 201–218.
Du Boulay, J. 1982. 'The Greek Vampire. A Study of Cyclic Symbolism in Marriage and Death'. *Man* 17: 219–238. [Reprinted in Dundes 1998a, pp. 85–108.]
Du Boulay, J. 2009. *Cosmos, Life and Liturgy in a Greek Orthodox Village*. Evia, Greece: Denise Harvey.
Duffy, E. 1992. *The Stripping of the Altars: Traditional Religion in England c.1400–c.1580*. New Haven, CT: Yale University Press.
Dundes, A. (ed.). 1998a. *The Vampire: A Casebook*. Madison: University of Wisconsin Press.
Dundes, A. 1998b. 'The Vampire as Bloodthirsty Revenant: A Psychoanalytic Post-Mortem'. In Dundes 1998a, pp. 159–171.
Eckert, E. A. 1996. *The Structure of Plagues and Pestilences in Early Modern Europe: Central Europe 1560–1640*. Basel: S. Karger AG.
Emden, J. 1758[–62?]. *Sefer Shimmush*. 'Amsterdam' [In fact published clandestinely in Altona near Hamburg].
Enthoven, R. E. 1924. *The Folklore of Bombay*. Oxford: Clarendon Press.
Epstein, S. and S. L. Robinson. 2012. 'The Soul, Evil Spirits and the Undead: Vampires, Death and Burial in Jewish Folklore and Law'. *Preternature* 1: 232–251.
Equiamicus, N. 2023. *Historia Vampyrorum: Eine Geschichte der Wiedergänger, Nachzehrer und Blutsauger*. Norderstedt: BoD.
Evans, R.J.W. 1979. *The Making of the Habsburg Monarchy 1550–1700*. Oxford: Oxford University Press.
Evison, V. I. 1987. *Dover: Buckland Anglo-Saxon Cemetery*. London: Historic Buildings and Monuments Commission.
Fangé, A. 1762. *La vie du trés-réverend père D. Augustin Calmet*. Senones: Joseph Pariset.
Faraone, C. A. 1991. 'Binding and Burying the Forces of Evil: The Defensive Use of "Voodoo Dolls" in Ancient Greece'. *Classical Antiquity* 10: 165–220.
Felder, K. 2014. 'Girdle-Hangers in 5th- and 6th-Century England. A Key to Early Anglo-Saxon Identities'. Unpublished D.Phil. thesis, University of Cambridge.
Fell, C. 1984. *Women in Anglo-Saxon England*. London: British Museum Publications.
Ferreri, S. 2015. 'Cremation Burials in North Mesopotamia in the First Millennium BC'. Unpublished M.Phil thesis, University of Cambridge.
Figuier, L. [c. 1880]. *Les mystères de la science*. Vol. 2. Paris: La Libraire Illustrée.
Fine, J.V.A. 1994. *The Late Medieval Balkans*. Ann Arbor: University of Michigan Press.
Fine, J.V.A. 1998. 'In Defense of Vampires'. In Dundes 1998a, pp. 57–66. Reprinted from *East European Quarterly* 21 (1987): 15–23.
Finkel, I. 2021. *The First Ghosts*. London: Hodder and Stoughton.

Fogel, E. M. 1915. *Beliefs and Superstitions of the Pennsylvania Germans*. Philadelphia: American Germanica Press.

Fonseca, I. 1999. *Bury Me Standing: The Gypsies and Their Journey*. London: Chatto & Windus.

Forth, G. and S. Kukharenko 2012. 'Animals Crossing: Analytical Observations on a Cross-Culturally Ubiquitous Mortuary Belief'. *Folklore* 123: 152–178.

Fortis, A. 1774. *Viaggio in Dalmazia*. Vol. 1. Venice: Alvise Milocco.

Foxhall Forbes, H. 2013. *Heaven and Earth in Anglo-Saxon England*. Farnham: Ashgate.

Frahm, E. 2010. 'Hochverrat in Assur'. In S. M. Maul and N. P. Heeßel (eds.), *Assur-Forschungen*. Wiesbaden: Harrassowitz Verlag, pp. 89–139.

Francisci [Finx], E. 1690. *Der höllische Proteus*. Nürnberg: Wolfgang Moritz.

Frankopan, P. 2023. *The Earth Transformed*. London: Bloomsbury.

Franz, A. and D. Nösler 2016. *Geköpft und Gepfählt: Archäologen auf der Jagd nach den Untoten*. Darmstadt: Theiss.

Frazer, J. G. 1913–1924. *The Belief in Immortality and the Worship of the Dead*. 3 vols. London: Macmillan.

Frazer, J. G. 1933–1936. *The Fear of the Dead in Primitive Religion*. 3 vols. London: Macmillan.

Freedman, S. M. 1998. *If a City Is Set on a Height*. Vol. 1. Philadelphia: University of Pennsylvania Museum.

Freud, S. 1918. *Totem and Taboo*. New York: Moffat, Yard & Co.

Fries, H. 1996. 'Eine ungewöhnliche Bestattung auf dem Anklamer Pferdemarkt aus der Zeit des Dreißigjähren Krieges'. *Archäologische Berichte aus Mecklenburg-Vorpommern* 3: 80–83.

Friis-Jensen, K. and P. Fisher (eds.). 2015. *Saxo Grammaticus, Gesta Danorum*. 2 vols. Oxford: Oxford University Press.

Gadotti, A. 2014. *'Gilgamesh, Enkidu and the Netherworld' and the Sumerian Gilgamesh Cycle: Untersuchungen zur Assyriologie und Vorderasiatischen Archäologie*. Vol. 10. Boston: de Gruyter.

García Arévalo, M. A. 1998. 'The Bat and the Owl: Nocturnal Images of Death'. In F. Bercht et al. (eds.), *Taíno: Pre-Columbian Art and Culture from the Caribbean*. New York: El Museo del Barrio, pp. 112–123.

Gardeła, L. 2013a. 'The Dangerous Dead? Rethinking Viking-Age Deviant Burials'. In L. Słupecki and R. Simek (eds.), *Conversions: Looking for Ideological Change in the Early Middle Ages*. Vienna: Fassbaender, pp. 99–136.

Gardeła, L. 2013b. 'The Headless Norseman: Decapitation in Viking Age Scandinavia'. In L. Gardeła and K. Kajowski (eds.), *The Head Motif in Past Societies in a Comparative Perspective*. Bytów: West-Cassubian Museum, pp. 88–155.

Gardeła, L. 2016. *(Magic) Staffs in the Viking Age*. Vienna: Fassbaender.

Gardeła, L. 2017. *Bad Death in the Early Middle Ages: Collectio Archaeologica Ressoviensis*. Vol. 36. Rzesów: Wydawca.

Gardeła, L. 2020. 'Atypical Burials in Early Medieval Poland'. In Betsinger et al. 2020, pp. 246–275.

Gardeła, L., S. Bonding, and P. Pentz (eds.). 2023. *The Norse Sorceress*. Oxford: Oxbow.

Gardeła, L. and P. Duma 2013. 'Untimely Death: Atypical Burials of Children in Early and Late Medieval Poland'. *World Archaeology* 45: 314–332.

Gardeła, L. and K. Kajkowski 2013. 'Vampires, Criminals or Slaves: Reinterpreting "Deviant Burials" in Early Medieval Poland'. *World Archaeology* 45: 780–796.

Gardeła, L. and K. Kajkowski (eds.). 2015. *Limbs, Bones and Reopened Graves in Past Societies*. Bytów: Muzeum Zachodniokaszubskie.

Garmann, C. F. 1670. *De miraculis mortuorum*. Leipzig: Christian Kirchner.

Gehrke, W. 1989. 'Das slawische Gräberfeld am Spandauer Burgwall'. In A. von Müller and K. von Müller-Muči (eds.), *Ausgrabungen, Funde und naturwissenschaftliche Untersuchungen auf dem Burgwall in Berlin-Spandau*. Berlin: Volker Spiess, pp. 143–197.

Gengell, G. 1716. *Eversio atheismi, seu pro Deo contra atheos libri duo*. Braunsberg: Jesuit College.

Geschiere, P. 1998. 'Globalization and the Power of Indeterminate Meaning: Witchcraft and Spirit Cults in Africa and East Asia'. *Development and Change* 29(4): 811–837.

Gibson, A. 2022. *Early Anglo-Saxon Christian Reliquaries*. Oxford: Archaeopress.

Giles, M. 2012. *A Forged Glamour*. Oxford: Windgather Press.

Ginzburg, C. 1980. *The Cheese and the Worms*. Baltimore: Johns Hopkins University Press. [Translation of *Il formaggio e i vermi* (1976).]

Ginzburg, C. 1983. *The Night Battles: Witchcraft and Agrarian Cults in the Sixteenth and Seventeenth Centuries*. Baltimore; Johns Hopkins University Press. [Translation of *I Benandanti* (1966).]

Ginzburg, C. 1991. *Ecstasies: Deciphering the Witches' Sabbath*. New York: Pantheon Books. [Translation of *Storia notturna* (1989).]

Ginzburg, C. and B. Lincoln 2020. *Old Thiess, a Livonian Werewolf*. Chicago: University of Chicago Press.

Girshick Ben-Amos, P. 1994. 'The Promise of Greatness: Women and Power in an Edo Spirit Possession Cult'. In T. D. Blakely, W.A.E. van Beek, and D. L. Thomson (eds.), *Religion in Africa: Experience and Expression*. London: James Currey, pp. 118–134.

Goodare, J. (ed.). 2002. *The Scottish Witch-Hunt in Context*. Manchester: Manchester University Press.

Goody, J. 1962. *Death, Property and the Ancestors: A Study of the Mortuary Customs of the Lodagaa of West Africa*. London: Tavistock.

Gordon, S. 2015. 'Social Monsters and the Walking Dead in William of Newburgh's *Historia rerum Anglicarum*'. *Journal of Medieval History* 41: 446–465.

Gordon, S. 2020. *Supernatural Encounters: Demons and the Restless Dead in Medieval England, c.1050–1450*. London: Routledge.

Gordon, S. 2022. "'Agite, agite et uenite!" Corrupted Breath, Corrupted Speech and Encounters with the Restless Dead in Geoffrey of Burton's *Vita sancte Moduenne virginis*'. *Journal of Medieval History* 48: 183–198.

Gordon-Grube, K. 1993. 'Evidence of Medicinal Cannibalism in Puritan New England'. *Early American Literature* 28: 185–221.

Görres, J. von 1840. *Die christliche Mystik*. Vol. 3. Regensburg: G. Joseph Manz.

Graeber, D. and D. Wengrow 2021. *The Dawn of Everything*. London: Allen Lane.

Gregoricka, L. A. et al. 2014. 'Apotropaic Practices and the Undead: A Biogeochemical Assessment of Deviant Burials in Post-Medieval Poland'. *PLOS ONE* 9(11): e113564.

Grenz, R. 1967. 'Archäologische Vampirbefunde aus dem westslawischen Siedlungsgebiet'. *Zeitschrift für Ostforschung* 16: 254–265.

Grilletto, R. 1989. 'Le sepolture e il cimitero della chiesa abbaziale della Novalesa'. *Archeologia medievale* 16: 329–355.

Grober-Glück, G. 1981. 'XXI: Der Verstorbene als Nachzehrer'. In M. Zender (ed.), *Atlas der Deutschen Volkskunde: Neue Folge: Erläuterungen zu den Karten 43–48*. Marburg: N. G. Elwert, pp. 427–456.

Groom, N. 2018. *The Vampire: A New History*. New Haven, CT: Yale University Press.

Groot, J.J.M. de. 1892–1910. *The Religious System of China*. 6 vols. Leiden: E. J. Brill.

Guzowski, P. 2021. 'The Peasant Family'. In P. Guzowski and C. Kuklo (eds.), *Framing the Polish Family in the Past*. London: Routledge, pp. 24–42.

Hall, A. 2007a. *Elves in Anglo-Saxon England*. Woodbridge: Boydell Press.

Hall, A. 2007b. 'The Evidence for *Maran*, the Anglo-Saxon "Nightmares"'. *Neophilologus* 91: 299–317.

Hamberger, K. 1992. *Mortuus non mordet: Kommentierte Dokumente zum Vampirismus 1689–1791*. Vienna: Turia und Kant.

Hamerow, H. 2016. 'Furnished Female Burial in Seventh-Century England: Gender and Sacral Authority in the Conversion Period'. *Early Medieval Europe* 24: 423–447.

Hancock, A. J. and R. J. Zeepvat. 2018. *Wulfhere's People: A Conversion-Period Anglo-Saxon Cemetery at Wolverton, Milton Keynes*. Aylesbury: Buckinghamshire Archaeological Society.

Hansen, W. F. 1980. 'An Ancient Greek Ghost Story'. In N. Burlakoff and C. Lindahl (eds.), *Folklore on Two Continents*. Bloomington, IN: Trickster Press, pp. 71–77.

Hansen, W. F. 1996. *Phlegon of Tralles' Book of Marvels*. Exeter: Exeter University Press.

Hardy, A., B. M. Charles, and R. J. Williams 2007. *Death and Taxes: The Archaeology of a Middle Saxon Estate Centre at Higham Ferrers, Northamptonshire*. Oxford: Oxford Archaeology.

Harte, J. 2011. 'Maimed Rites: Suicide Burials in the English Landscape'. *Time and Mind* 3: 263–82.

Hartnup, K. 2004. *'On the Beliefs of the Greeks': Leo Allatios and Popular Orthodoxy*. Leiden: Brill.

Haughton, C. and D. Powlesland. 1999. *West Heslerton: The Anglian Cemetery*. Vol. 2. Yedingham: Landscape Research Centre.

Hauser, S. R. 2012. *Status, Tod und Ritual. Stadt und Sozialstruktur Assurs in neuassyrischerzeit*. Wiesbaden: Harrassowitz.

Havekost, E. 1914. *Die Vampirsage in England*. Halle: Buchdruckerei Hohmann.

Hawkes, S. C. and G. Granger 2003. *The Anglo-Saxon Cemetery at Worthy Park, Kingsworthy*. Oxford: Oxford University School of Archaeology.

Hay, A. 2018. '"From Beneath the Waves": Sea-*Draugr* and the Popular Conscience'. In J. Hackett and S. Harrington (eds.), *Beasts of the Deep: Sea Creatures and Popular Culture*. East Barnet: John Libbey, pp. 11–25.

Hennius, A., E. Sjöling, and S. Prata. 2016. *Människor kring Gnistahögen: Begravningar från vendeltid, vikingatid och tidig medeltid. Upplandsmuseets Rapporter*. 2016:02. Uppsala: Upplandsmuseet.

Herbach, K. 1925. 'Skelettfunde in der Schanze bei Göda'. *Bautzner Geschichtshefte* 3: 100–109.

Hermann, A. 1698. *Ethica sacra: Pars secunda*. Würzburg: Job Hertz.

Herskovits, M. J. 1937. *Life in a Haitian Valley*. New York: Alfred A. Knopf.

Herskovits, M. J. 1938. *Dahomey: An Ancient West African Kingdom*. 2 vols. New York: J. J. Augustin.

Hertz, R. 1960. *Death and the Right Hand*. Aberdeen: Cohen and West.

Hetzer, A. and D. Hoerder. 1987. 'Linguistic Fragmentation or Multilingualism among Labor Migrants in North America: The Socio-Historical Background to Eastern and Southeastern Europe: A Research Note'. In D. Hoerder (ed.), *The Immigrant Labor Press in North America, 1840s–1870s: An Annotated Bibliography*. Westport, CT: Greenwood Press, pp. 9–52.

Hey, G. 2004. *Yarnton: Saxon and Medieval Settlement and Landscape*. Oxford: Oxford University School of Archaeology.

Hiebert, F. and P. Cambon (eds.). 2011. *Afghanistan: Crossroads of the Ancient World*. London: British Museum Press.

Higgins, J. 2003. 'The Unsolved Mystery of James O'Neill'. *Soo Nipi Magazine*. [Consulted from a transcript provided by Michael Bell.]

Hilton, A. 1985. *The Kingdom of Kongo*. Oxford: Clarendon Press.

Hines, J. and A. Bayliss (eds.). 2013. *Anglo-Saxon Graves and Grave Goods of the 6th and 7th Centuries AD: A Chronological Framework*. London: Society for Medieval Archaeology.

Hirst, S. M. 1985. *An Anglo-Saxon Inhumation Cemetery at Sewerby, East Yorkshire*. York: York University.

Hock, S. 1900. *Die Vampyrsagen und ihre Verwertung in der deutschen Litteratur*. Berlin: Alexander Duncker.

Holmes, C. 1993. 'Women: Witnesses and Witches'. *Past and Present* 140: 45–78.

Holzem, A. 2023. *Christianity in Germany 1550–1850*. Paderborn: Brill und Schöningh.

Honko, L. 1973. 'Finnische Mythologie'. In H. W. Haussig (ed.), *Götter und Mythen im alten Europa*. Stuttgart: Ernst Klett Verlag, pp. 263–371.

Honko, L. et al. 1993. *The Great Bear*. Helsinki: Finnish Literature Society.

Hori, Ichiro 1962. 'Self-Mummified Buddhas in Japan'. *History of Religions* 1: 222–242.

Howitt, A. W. 1904. *The Native Tribes of South-East Australia*. London: Macmillan.

Howlett, R. (ed.). 1885. *Chronicles of the Reigns of Stephen, Henry II and Richard I*. Vol. 2. London: H. M. Treasury.

Huang, Po-chi 2009. 'The Cult of Vetāla and Tantric Fantasy'. In M. Poo (ed.), *Rethinking Ghosts in World Religions*. Leiden: Brill, pp. 211–235.

Hufford, D. J. 1982. *The Terror That Comes in the Night: An Experience-Centred Study of Supernatural Assault Traditions*. Philadelphia: University of Pennsylvania Press.

Hukantaival, S. 2016. *'For a Witch Cannot Cross Such a Threshold!' Building Concealment Traditions in Finland c.1200–1950*. Archaeologia Medii Aevi Finlandiae 23. Turku: Suomen Keskiajan Arkeologian Seura.

Humphrey, C. 1996. *Shamans and Elders*. Oxford: Oxford University Press.

Hunt, N. B. 2003. *Shamanism in North America*. New York: Firefly Books.

Hurston, Z. N. 1981. *Tell My Horse*. Reprint. Berkeley, CA: Turtle Island.

Hutton, R. 2017. *The Witch*. New Haven, CT: Yale University Press.

Ivanits, L. J. 1989. *Russian Folk Belief*. Armonk, NY: M. E. Sharpe.

Jacobson, R. and M. Szeftel. 1966. 'The Vseslav Epos'. In *Roman Jacobson: Selected Writings*, vol. 4: *Slavic Epic Studies*. The Hague: Mouton, pp. 301–368.

James, M. R. 1922. 'Twelve Medieval Ghost-Stories'. *English Historical Review* 37: 413–422.

James, M. R. et al. (eds.). 1983. *De Nugis Curialium* by Walter Map, rev. C.N.L. Brooke and R.A.B. Mynors. Oxford: Oxford University Press.

Jamison, S. W. 1991. *The Ravenous Hyenas and the Wounded Sun*. Ithaca, NY: Cornell University Press.

Jankowiak, M. 2021. 'Tracing the Saqaliba: Slave Trade and the Archaeology of the Slavic Lands in the Tenth Century'. In F. Biermann and M. Jankowiak (eds.), *The Archaeology of Slavery in Early Medieval Northern Europe*. Cham: Springer, pp. 161–181.

Janowski, A. and T. Kurasiński 2010. 'Rolnik, wojownik czy "odmieniec"? Próba interpretacji obecności sierpów w grobach wczesnośredniowiecznych na terenie ziem polskich'. *Acta Archaeologica Lodziensia* 56: 79–95.

Jaworskij, J. 1898. 'Südrussische Vampyre'. *Zeitschrift des Vereins für Volkskunde* 8: 331–336.

Jeremiah, K. 2010. *Living Buddhas: The Self-Mummified Monks of Yamagata*. Jefferson, NC: McFarland.

Johns, C. N. 1936–1937. 'Excavations at Pilgrim's Castle, 'Atlīt (1933): Cremated Burials of Phoenician Origin'. *Quarterly of the Department of Antiquities in Palestine* 6: 121–52.

Johnston, S. I. 1999. *Restless Dead: Encounters between the Living and the Dead in Ancient Greece*. Berkeley: University of California Press.

Jones, E. 1931. *On the Nightmare*. London: Hogarth Press.

Jordan, D. K. 1972. *Gods, Ghosts and Ancestors: The Folk Religion of a Taiwanese Village*. Berkeley: University of California Press.

Jullian, C. and H. Gaidoz 1902. ' Cadavres Percés des Clous'. *Revue des Études Anciennes: Annales de la Faculté des Lettres de Bordeaux* 4: 300–301.

Jungklaus, B. 2008. 'Sit tibi terra levis—"Die Erde möge dir leicht sein". Sonderbestattungen auf dem Friedhof des mittelalterlichen Diepensee, Lkr. Dahme-Spreewald'. In F. Biermann et al. (eds.), *"Die Dinge beobachten . . .": Archäologische und historische Forschungen zur frühen Geschichte Mittel- und Nordeuropas*. Rahden: Verlag Marie Leidorf GmbH, pp. 379–387.

Kafadar, C. 2022. '"Vampire Trouble Is More Serious than a Mighty Plague": The Emergence and Later Adventures of a New Species of Evildoers'. In A. Payne (ed.), *The Land between Two Seas*. Leiden: Brill, pp. 126–151.

Kalous, A. (ed.). 2015. *The Transformation of Confessional Cultures in a Central European City: Olomouc, 1400–1750*. Rome: Viella.

Kanerva, K. 2011. 'The Role of the Dead in Medieval Iceland: A Case Study of *Eyrbyggja Saga*'. *Collegium Medievale* 24: 23–49.

Kanerva, K. 2013. 'Rituals for the Restless Dead: The Authority of the Deceased in Medieval Iceland'. In S. Kangas et al. (eds.), *Authorities in the Middle Ages: Influence, Legitimacy and Power in Medieval Society*. Berlin: de Gruyter.

Kanerva, K. 2017. 'From Powerful Agents to Subordinate Objects? The Restless Dead in Thirteenth- and Fourteenth-Century Iceland'. In J. Rollo Koster (ed.), *Death in Medieval Europe*. New York: Routledge, pp. 40–70.

Kasbohm, W. 1953. 'Das slawische Körpergräberfeld von Damm, Kreis Rostock'. *Bodendenkmalpflege in Mecklenburg: Jahrbuch 1953*: 108–125.

Kastrup, B., A. Crabtree, and E. F. Kelly 2018. 'Could Multiple Personality Disorder Explain Life, the Universe and Everything?'. *Scientific American*, 18 June. https://blogs.scientificamerican.com/observations/could-multiple-personality-disorder-explain-life-the-universe-and-everything/.

Kaszewscy, E. and Z. Kaszewscy. 1971. 'Wczesnośredniowieczne cmentarzysko w Brześciu Kujawskim, pow. Włocławek'. *Materiały Starożytne Wczesnośredniowieczne* 1: 365–434.

Keller, M. 2002: *The Hammer and the Flute: Women, Power and Spirit Possession*. Baltimore: Johns Hopkins University Press.

Kelly, A. and C. Metcalf (eds.). 2021. *Gods and Mortals in Early Greek and Near Eastern Mythology*. Cambridge: Cambridge University Press.

Keyworth, G. D. 2006. 'Was the Vampire of the Eighteenth Century a Unique Type of Undead Corpse?'. *Folklore* 117: 241–260.

King, A. D. 1999. 'Soul Suckers: Vampiric Shamans in Northern Kamchatka, Russia'. *Anthropology of Consciousness* 10: 57–68.

King, R., A. Barber, and J. Timby 1996. 'Excavations at West Lane, Kemble'. *Transactions of the Bristol and Gloucestershire Archaeological Society* 11: 15–54.

Kırgi, S. F. 2017. 'An Early Modern Horror Story: The Folk Beliefs in Vampire-like Supernatural Beings in the Ottoman Empire and Consequent Responses in the Sixteenth and Seventeenth Centuries'. Unpublished M.A. thesis, Central European University, Budapest. [Published in Turkish as *Osmanlı Vampirleri: Söylenceler, Etkiler, Tepkiler*. Istanbul: Iletişim Yayınları, 2018.]

Klaniczay, G. 1990. *The Uses of Supernatural Power*. Princeton, NJ: Princeton University Press.

Kleinpaul, R. 1898. *Die Lebendigen und die Toten in Volksglauben, Religion und Sage*. Leipzig: G. J. Göschen'sche Verlagshandlung.

Klevnäs, A. M. 2013. *Whodunnit? Grave-Robbery in Anglo-Saxon England and the Merovingian Kingdoms*. Oxford: BAR.

Klevnäs, A. M. 2015. 'Overkill: Reopening graves to Maim the Dead in Anglo-Saxon England'. In Gardeła and Kajkowski 2015, pp. 177–211.

Klevnäs, A. M. 2023. 'Surely Every Live Man Fades among the Dead: Fear and Desire in the Afterlife of Viking Age Graves'. In Gardeła et al. 2023, pp. 171–184.

Klevnäs, A. M. et al. 2021. 'Reopening Graves in the Early Middle Ages: from Local Practice to European Phenomenon'. *Antiquity* 95: 1005–1026.

Knüsel, C. and E.M.J. Schotsmans (eds.). 2022. *The Routledge Handbook of Archaeothanatology: Bioarchaeology of Mortuary Behaviour*. Abingdon: Routledge.

Köhbach, M. 1979. 'Ein Fall von Vampirismus bei den Osmanen'. *Balkan Studies* 20: 83–90.

Köléseri, S. 1709. *Pestis Daciae anni 1709 scrutinium et cura*. Sibiu: Michael Heltzdörfer.

Kornmann, H. 1610. *De miraculis mortuorum*. [Frankfurt am Main]: Johann Wolff.

Koski, K. 2008. 'Conceptual Analysis and Variation in Belief Tradition: A Case of Death-Related Beings'. *Folklore: Electronic Journal of Folklore* 38: 45–66.

Koslofsky, C. M. 2000. *The Reformation of the Dead: Death and Ritual in Early Modern Germany, 1450–1700*. Basingstoke: Macmillan.

Kovács, Z. 1973. 'Die Hexen in Rußland'. *Acta Ethnographica Academiae Scientiarum Hungaricae* 22: 51–87.

Kozak, Ł. 2021. *Upiór: Historia naturalna*. Warsaw: Evviva L'arte.

Krapp, K. 2006. 'Ein Dorf verschwindet'. *Archäologie in Deutschland*, January–February: 64–69.

Kreppner, F. J. 2014.'The New Primary Cremation Custom of Iron Age Tell Sheikh Hamad/ Dūr-Katlimmu (North-Eastern Syria)'. In P. Pfälzner et al. (eds.), *Contextualising Grave Inventories in the Ancient Near East*. Wiesbaden: Harrassowitz, pp. 171–185.

Kreuter, P. M. 2007. 'The Role of Women in Southeast European Vampire Belief'. In A. Buturovič and Í. C. Schick (eds.), *Women in the Ottoman Balkans*. London: I. B. Tauris, pp. 231–241.

Kreuz, P. 2006. 'Moravia'. In R. M. Golden (ed.), *Encyclopedia of Witchcraft: The Western Tradition*. Vol. 3: *K–P*. Santa Barbara, CA: ABC-CLIO.

Kropej, M. 2012. *Supernatural Beings from Slovenian Myth and Folktales*. Ljubljana: Slovenian Academy of Sciences and Arts.

Kurasiński, T., K. Skóra, and V. Gayduchlik. 2018. 'A Grain against a Vampire? Some Remarks on So-Called Anti-Vampire Practices in the Light of Archaeological and Folkloristic-Ethnographic Data'. *Sprawozdania Archeologiczne* 70: 173–202.

Kwaśniewska, A. 2019. 'Endogamia i zwyczaje małżeńskie na Kaszubach a kwestia tzw. genu kaszubskiego'. *Studia Etnologiczne i Antropologiczne* 19: 138–157.

Kysučan, L. 2020. 'Classical Tradition in Czech Renaissance and Baroque Literature'. In G. Siedina (ed.), *Essays on the Spread of Humanistic and Renaissance Literary Civilization in the Slavic World*. Florence: Firenze University Press, pp. 98–116.

Lambrecht, K. 1994. 'Wiedergänger und Vampire in Ostmitteleuropa—posthume Verbrennung statt Hexenverfolgung?' *Jahrbuch für Deutsche und Osteuropäische Volkskunde* 37: 49–77.

Lapidge, M. 1993. 'Beowulf and the Psychology of Terror'. in H. Damico and J. Leyerle (eds.), *Heroic Poetry in the Anglo-Saxon Period*. Kalamazoo: Medieval Institute Publications, pp. 373–402.

Larrington, C. (trans.). 1996. *The Poetic Edda*. Oxford: Oxford University Press.

Lauterbach, S. F. 1710. *Kleine Fraustädtische Pest-Chronica*. Leipzig: J. F. Gledisch & Son.

Lawson, J. C. 1910. *Modern Greek Folklore and Ancient Greek Religion: A Study in Survivals*. Cambridge: Cambridge University Press.

Lecouteux, C. 1999. *The Secret History of Vampires*. Rochester, VT: Inner Traditions.

Lecouteux, C. 2011. *Phantom Armies of the Night*. Rochester, VT: Inner Traditions. Translation of *Chasses fantastiques et cohorts de la nuit au moyen age* (1999).

Leeds, E. T. and D. B. Harden 1936. *The Anglo-Saxon Cemetery at Abingdon, Berkshire*. Oxford: Ashmolean Museum.

Le Fanu, S. 1993. *In a Glass Darkly*. Edited by R. Tracy. Oxford: Oxford University Press.

Lester, R. J. 2023. 'The Community of Ella'. *Scientific American* 328(6).

Levin, E. 2003. 'From Corpse to Cult in Early Modern Russia'. In V. A. Kivelson and R. H. Greene (eds.), *Orthodox Russia: Belief and Practice under the Tsars*. University Park: Pennsylvania State University Press, pp. 81–103.

Licence. T. (ed.). 2014. *Herman the Archdeacon and Goscelin of Saint-Bertin: Miracles of St Edmund*. Oxford: Oxford University Press.

Lincoln, B. 2015. Review of Witzel 2012. *Asian Ethnology* 74: 443–449.
Littlewood, R. 2009. 'Functionalists and Zombis: Sorcery as Spandrel and Social Rescue'. *Anthropology and Medicine* 16: 241–252.
Littlewood, R. and C. Douyon 1997. 'Clinical Findings in Three Cases of Zombification'. *The Lancet* 350: 1094–1096.
Livermore, C. 2021. *When the Dead Rise: Narratives of the Revenant from the Middle Ages to the Present Day*. Cambridge: D. S. Brewer.
Lockett, L. 2011. *Anglo-Saxon Psychologies in the Vernacular and Latin Traditions*. Toronto: University of Toronto Press.
Louie, K. and L. Edwards (eds. and trans.). 1996. *Censored by Confucius: Ghost Stories by Yuan Mei*. Armonk, NY: M. E. Sharpe.
Louthan, H. 2009. *Converting Bohemia: Force and Persuasion in the Catholic Reformation*. Cambridge: Cambridge University Press.
Lucy, S. et al. 2009. 'The Burial of a Princess? The Later Seventh-Century Cemetery at Westfield Farm, Ely'. *Antiquaries Journal* 89: 81–141.
MacCulloch, D. 2003. *Reformation: Europe's House Divided*. London: Allen Lane.
MacDonald, G. F. 1983. *Haida Monumental Art*. Vancouver: University of British Columbia Press.
MacDougal, R. 2014. 'Remembrance and the Dead in Second Millennium BC Mesopotamia'. Unpublished Ph.D. thesis, University of Leicester.
MacLeod, M. and B. Mees 2006. *Runic Amulets and Magic Objects*. Woodbridge: Boydell Press.
Maddicott, J. R. 1997. 'Plague in Seventh-Century England'. *Past and Present* 156: 7–54.
Magnús Magnússon (trans.). 1999. *The Icelandic Sagas*. London: Folio Society.
Magnús Magnússon and Hermann Pálsson (trans.). 1969. *Laxdæla Saga*. Harmondsworth: Penguin.
Malim, T. and J. Hines 1998. *The Anglo-Saxon Cemetery at Edix Hill (Barrington A), Cambridgeshire*. York: Council for British Archaeology.
Mallet, D. 2019. 'Pierre des Noyers, a Scholar and a Courtier'. *Kwartalnik Historii Nauki i Techniki* 64: 139–146.
Maraschi, A. 2019. 'There Is More than Meets the Eye: Undead, Ghosts and Spirits in the *Decretum* of Burchard of Worms'. *Thanatos* 8: 29–60.
Marei, S. 2016. 'Displaced Human Remains in Predynastic Period'. Unpublished master's thesis, American University in Cairo.
Mariotti, V., M. Milella, and M. G. Belcastro 2023. 'Duri a morire: comportamenti persistenti intorno al defuncto'. In Pergola et al. 2023, pp. 29–44.
Martin, H. 1979. 'À la recherche de la culture populaire bretonne à travers les manuscrits du bas Moyen Age'. *Annales de Bretagne et des pays de l'Ouest* 86: 631–633.
Martin, J. D. 2005. 'Law and the (Un)dead: Medieval Models for Understanding the Hauntings in *Eyrbyggja Saga*'. *Saga-Book* 29: 67–82.
Matchak, M. et al. 2021. 'A Multidisciplinary Study of Anti-Vampire Burials from Early Medieval Culmen, Poland: Were the Diseased and Disabled Regarded as Vampires?' *Archaeologia Historica Polona* 29: 219–252.
Matheson, W. 1951–1952. 'Notes on Mary MacLeod'. *Transactions of the Gaelic Society of Inverness* 41: 11–25.
Matney, T. et al. 2002. 'Archaeological Excavations at Ziyaret Tepe, 2000 and 2001'. *Anatolica* 28: 47–89.
Matney, T. et al. 2011. 'Excavations at Ziyaret Tepe, Diyarbakir Province, Turkey, 2009–2010 Seasons'. *Anatolica* 37: 67–114.
Matos Moctezuma, E. and F. Solís Olguín 2002. *Aztecs*. London: Royal Academy of Arts.

Maxwell, W. E. 1881. 'The Folklore of the Malays'. *Journal of the Straits Branch of the Royal Asiatic Society* 7: 11–29.

Maxwell-Stuart, P. and J. M. García Valverde 2023. *Investigations into Magic: An Edition and Translation of Martín del Río's 'Disquisitionum magicarum libri sex'*. Vol. 2. Leiden: Brill.

Mays, S. et al. 2017. 'A Multidisciplinary Study of a Burnt and Mutilated Assemblage of Human Remains from a Deserted Medieval Village in England'. *Journal of Archaeological Science: Reports* 16: 441–455.

McClelland, B. A. 1999. 'Sacrifice, Scapegoat, Vampire: The Social and Religious Origins of the Bulgarian Folkloric Vampire'. Unpublished Ph.D. thesis, University of Virginia.

McGill, M. 2022. 'Bodies of Earth and Air: Corporeality and Spirituality in Pre-Modern British Narratives of the Undead'. *Journal of Medieval History* 48: 265–281.

Meaney, A. L. 1964. *A Gazetteer of Early Anglo-Saxon Burial Sites*. London: George Allen and Unwin.

Meaney, A. L. and S. C. Hawkes 1970. *Two Anglo-Saxon Cemeteries at Winnall*. London: Society for Medieval Archaeology.

Melton, J. D. 2011. *The Vampire Book*. 3rd ed. Canton, MI: Visible Ink Press.

Merkelbach, R. 2012. 'Hann lá eigi kyrr'—Revenants and a Haunted Past in the Sagas of the Icelanders'. Unpublished master's thesis, University of Cambridge.

Merkelbach, R. 2019. *Monsters in Society: Alterity, Transgression and the Use of the Past in Medieval Iceland*. Berlin: de Gruyter.

Metcalf, P. and R. Huntingdon 1991. *Celebrations of Death*. 2nd ed. Cambridge: Cambridge University Press.

Mézes, A. 2019. 'Doubt and Diagnosis: Medical Experts and the Returning Dead of the Southern Habsburg Borderland, 1718–1766'. Unpublished Ph.D. thesis, Central European University, Budapest.

Mladenović, D. 2009. 'Roman Moesia Superior: The Creation of a New Provincial Entity and Processes of Multicultural Adjustment'. 3 vols. Unpublished D.Phil. thesis, University of Oxford.

Moilanen, U. 2018. 'Facing the Earth for Eternity? Prone Burials in Early Medieval and Medieval Finland (c.AD 900–1300)'. In L. Damman and S. Leggett (eds.), *The Others—Deviants, Outcasts and Outsiders in Archaeology: Archaeological Review from Cambridge* 33(2): 19–36.

Moore, R. I. 1987. *The Formation of a Persecuting Society*. Oxford: Basil Blackwell.

More, H. 1655. *An Antidote against Atheism*. London: J. Flesher.

More, H. 1659. *The Immortality of the Soul*. London: J. Flesher.

Morphy, H. 1984. *Journey to the Crocodile's Nest*. Canberra: Australian Institute of Aboriginal Studies.

Morris, K. 2015. 'Superstition, Testimony, and the Eighteenth-Century Vampire Debates'. *Preternature* 4: 181–202.

Mortimer, R., D. Sayer, and R. Wiseman 2017. 'Anglo-Saxon Oakington: A Central Place on the Edge of the Cambridgeshire Fen'. In S. Semple et al. (eds.), *Life on the Edge: Social and Religious Frontiers in Early Medieval Europe*. Brunswick: Braunschweiges Landesmuseum, pp. 305–316.

Mouzakēs, S. A. 1989. *Hoi vrikolakes: Doxasies, prolēpseis kai paradoseis*. Athens: Vivliopoleio tōn Vivliophilōn.

Moyer, P. B. 2020. *Detestable and Wicked Arts: New England and Witchcraft in the Early Modern Atlantic World*. Ithaca, NY: Cornell University Press.

Murgoci, A. 1998. 'The Vampire in Roumania'. In Dundes 1998a, pp. 12–34. Reprinted from *Folklore* 37 (1926): 320–349.

Murphy, E. M. (ed.). 2008. *Deviant Burial in the Archaeological Record*. Oxford: Oxbow.

Murphy, K. et al. 2016. 'Excavation at St Patrick's Chapel 2016'. Unpublished interim report. Llandeilo: Dyfed Archaeological Trust.

Murray, A. 1998–2000. *Suicide in the Middle Ages*. 2 vols. Oxford: Oxford University Press.

Murray, A. 2023. 'Medieval Suicide'. In H. Skoda (ed.), *A Companion to Crime and Deviance in the Middle Ages*. Leeds: ARC Humanities Press, pp. 66–83.

Mynors, R.A.B., R. M. Thomson, and M. Winterbottom (eds.). *William of Malmesbury, Gesta Regum Anglorum*. Oxford: Oxford University Press.

Naismith, R. 2023. *Making Money in the Early Middle Ages*. Princeton, NJ: Princeton University Press.

Naveh, J. and S. Shaked 1998. *Amulets and Magic Bowls: Aramaic Incantations of Late Antiquity*. 3rd ed. Jerusalem: Magnes Press.

Navrátilová, A. 2005. 'Revenantství v české lidové tradici jako obraz cizího, nepřátelského světa'. *Studia Mythologica Slavica* 8: 115–136.

Neocleous, M. 2003. 'The Political Economy of the Dead: Marx's Vampires'. *History of Political Thought* 24: 668–684.

Nicol, D. M. 1971. 'The Byzantine Reaction to the Second Council of Lyons, 1274'. *Studies in Church History* 7: 113–146.

Nissinen, M. 2017. *Ancient Prophecy: Near Eastern, Biblical and Greek Perspectives*. Oxford: Oxford University Press.

Nissinen, M. 2019. 'The Ritual Aspect of Prophecy'. In L.-S. Tiemeyer (ed.), *Prophecy and Its Cultic Dimensions*. Göttingen: Vanderhoeck & Ruprecht, pp. 101–114.

Nissinen, M. 2020. 'Why Prophets Are (Not) Shamans?' *Vetus Testamentum*, 70: 124–139.

Noble, G. and N. Evans 2022. *Picts: Scourge of Rome, Rulers of the North*. Edinburgh: Birlinn.

Nordberg, A. 2002. 'Vertikalt placerade vapen in vikingatida gravar'. *Fornvännen* 97: 15–24.

Nösler, D. 2014. 'Untote und Bann. Zwei mittelalterliche Wiedergängerbestattungen aus dem Kreuzgang des Benediktinerklosters Harsefeld'. In D. Alsdorf (ed.), *Geschichte und Gegenwart 2014*. Harsefeld: Verein für Kloster- u. Heimatgeschichte, pp. 11–20.

Noterman, A. A. 2021. *Approche archéologique des réouvertures de sepultures mérovingiennes dans le nord de la France (Vie–VIIIe siècle)*. Oxford: BAR.

Nuzzolese, E. and M. Borrini 2010. 'Forensic Approach to an Archaeological Casework of "Vampire" Skeletal Remains in Venice: Odontological and Anthropological Prospectus'. *Journal of Forensic Sciences* 55: 1634–1637.

Obermaier, H. 1933. 'Leichennagelung im spanischen Mittelalter'. *Forschungen und Fortschritte* 9: 169–171.

O'Brien, E. 2020. *Mapping Death: Burial in Late Iron Age and Early Medieval Ireland*. Dublin: Four Courts Press.

Ogden, D. 2004: 'Eucrates and Demainete: Lucian, *Philopseudes* 27–8'. *Classical Quarterly* 54: 484–493.

Ogden, D. 2009. *Magic, Witchcraft and Ghosts in the Greek and Roman Worlds*. Oxford: Oxford University Press.

Ogden, D. 2021a. *The Strix-Witch*. Cambridge: Cambridge University Press.

Ogden, D. 2021b. *The Werewolf in the Ancient World*. Oxford: Oxford University Press.

Oinas, F. 1978. 'Heretics as Vampires and Demons in Russia'. *The Slavic and East European Journal* 22: 433–441.

Olóriz, F. 1897. 'Estudio de una calavera antigua, perforada por un clavo, encontrada en Itálica'. *Boletín de la Real Academia de la Historia* 31: 257–308.

Ökse, T. and S. Eroglu, 2013. 'The Tradition of Burning the Corpse in the Iron Age: A Case Study on Zeviya Tivilki in the Upper Tigris Region'. *Akkadica* 134: 159–185.

O'Sullivan, S. 2021. *The Sleeping Beauties, and Other Stories of Mystery Illness*. London: Picador.

Panea, N. and V. Preda 2019. 'Fear, Ghouls and Politics: Obscure Power Games in an Equally Obscure Village in the Danube Plains'. In C. Ghita and R. Beshara (eds.), *Fear and Anxiety in the 21st Century: The European Context and Beyond*. Leiden: Brill, pp. 107–115.

Parker, J. 2021. *In My Time of Dying: A History of Death and the Dead in West Africa*. Princeton, NJ: Princeton University Press.

Parker Pearson, M. et al. 2018. *Cille Pheadair: A Norse Farmstead and Pictish Burial Cairn in South Uist*. Oxford: Oxbow.

Parvanov, P. 2016. 'Medieval Deviant Burials from Bulgaria (7th–14th Centuries)'. Unpublished M.A. thesis, Central European University, Budapest.

Parvanov, P. 2023. 'Making a Deviant: Intentional Skeletal Dislocations in Reopened Graves from the Medieval Balkans'. In Pergola et al. 2023, pp. 303–313.

Patai, R. 1990. *The Hebrew Goddess*. 3rd ed. Detroit: Wayne State University Press.

Paton, D. 2015. *The Cultural Politics of Obeah*. Cambridge: Cambridge University Press.

Pearson, R. 2005. *Voltaire Almighty*. New York: Bloomsbury.

Pentikäinen, J. 1968. *The Norse Dead-Child Tradition*. Helsinki: Suomalainen Tiedeakatemia.

Pergola, P., S. Roascio, and E. Dellù (eds.). 2023. *Sit tibi terra gravis: Sepolture anomale tra età medievale e moderna*. Oxford: Archaeopress.

Perkowski, J. L. 1972. *Vampires, Dwarves and Witches among the Ontario Kashubs*. Ottawa: National Museums of Canada.

Perkowski, J. L. 1989. *The Darkling: A Treatise on Slavic Vampirism*. Columbus, OH: Slavica Publishers.

Perkowski, J. L. 1998. 'The Romanian Folkloric Vampire'. in Dundes 1998a, pp. 35–46. Reprinted from *East European Quarterly* 16 (1982): 311–322.

Perty, M. 1861. *Die mystischen Erscheinungen der menschlichen Natur*. Leipzig: C. J. Winter'sche Verlagshandlung.

Petersen, N. K. 2021. 'Magia Posthuma: Karl Ferdinand von Schertz, Calmet and Revenant Beliefs'. *Bulletin of the Transylvanian University of Braşov*, ser. 4, 14(63): 41–50.

Peterson, N. 1976. 'Mortuary Customs of Northeast Arnhem Land: An Account Compiled from Donald Thomson's Fieldnotes'. *Memoirs of Museum Victoria* 37: 97–108.

Pettersson, O. 1957. *Jabmek and Jabmeaimo: A Comparative Study of the Dead and the Realm of the Dead in Lappish Religion*. Lund: University of Lund.

Pettitt, P. 2018. 'Hominin Evolutionary Thanatology from the Mortuary to Funerary Realm'. *Philosophical Transactions of the Royal Society B: Biological Sciences* 373(1754): 20180212.

Pickering, M. [G.] 2013. '"Sie Mußten ins Feuer": Changing Policies within the Habsburg Monarchy on the Destruction of Vampire Bodies'. In K. Sarma and B. Livings (eds.), *Evil and the State: Interdisciplinary Perspectives*. Oxford: Inter-Disciplinary Press, pp. 11–29.

Pickering, M. G. 2020. 'Vampires, Ottomans and the Specter of Contagion: The Intersectionality of Fear on the Periphery of the Habsburg Monarchy'. In T. J. Kehoe and M. G. Pickering (eds.), *Fear in the German-Speaking World, 1600–2000*. London: Bloomsbury Academic.

Pitton de Tournefort, [J.] 1717. *Relation d'un voyage du Levant*. Vol. 1. Paris: Imprimerie Royale.

Polcyn, M. and Gajda, E. 2015. 'Buried with Sickles: Early Modern Interments from Drawsko, Poland'. *Antiquity* 89: 1373–1387.

Pollex, A. 2010. *Glaubensvorstellungen im Wandel. Eine archäologische Analyse der Körpergräber des 10. bis 13. Jahrhunderts im nordwestslawischen Raum*. Rahden: Verlag Marie Leidorf GmbH.

Pomeroy, S. B. 1995. *Goddesses, Whores, Wives, and Slaves*. 2nd ed. New York: Schocken Books.

Poo, Mu-chou 2022. *Ghosts and Religious Life in Early China*. Cambridge: Cambridge University Press.

Poviones-Bishop, M. 2001. 'The Bat and the Guava: Life and Death in the Taino Worldview'. https://www.yumpu.com/en/document/read/65135990/the-bat-and-the-guava-life-and-death-in-the-taino-worldview-by-maria-poviones-bishop, 30 July.

Praetorius [Schultze], J. 1666. *Anthropodemus Plutonicus*. Magdeburg: Johann Lüderwald.
Price, N. 2019. *The Viking Way: Magic and Mind in Late Iron Age Scandinavia*. 2nd ed. Oxford: Oxbow.
Pulkkinen, R. 2014. *Suomalainen kansanusko*. Helsinki: Gaudeamus.
Quast, D. (ed.). 2011. *Weibliche Eliten in der Frühgeschichte*. Mainz: Verlag des Römisch-Germanischen Zentralmuseums.
Rahtz, P. and S. Hirst 1974. *Beckery Chapel, Glastonbury, 1967–8*. Glastonbury: Glastonbury Antiquarian Society.
Ramos, I. 2020. *Tantra: Enlightenment to Revolution*. London: Thames and Hudson/British Museum.
Ramos, M. 1969. 'The Aswang Syncrasy in Philippine Folklore'. *Western Folklore* 28: 238–248.
Randall, N. and R. Poulton 2023. *A Later Saxon and Norman Cemetery at Priory Orchard, Station Road, Godalming, Surrey*. Woking: Surrey County Archaeological Unit.
Ranft, M. [1725]. *Dissertatio Prior Historico-Critica de Masticatione Mortuorum in Tumulis*. Leipzig: Breitkopf.
Ranft, M. 1728. *De Masticatione Mortuorum in Tumulis*. Leipzig: August Martin.
Ranft, M. 1734. *Tractat von dem Kauen und Schmatzen der Todten*. Leipzig: Teubner.
Rawski, E. S. and J. Rawson 2005. *China: The Three Emperors 1662–1795*. London: Royal Academy of Arts.
Reed, B. 1987. 'Taoism'. In A. Sharma (ed.), *Women in World Religions*. Albany: State University of New York Press, pp. 161–181.
Reynolds, A. 2009. *Anglo-Saxon Deviant Burial Customs*. Oxford: Oxford University Press.
Ricaut, P. 1679. *The Present State of the Greek and Armenian Churches*. London: John Starkey.
Richard, F. 1657. *Relation de ce qui s'est passé de plus remarquable a Saint-Erini*. Paris: Sebastien Cramoisy.
Richardson, R. 1993. 'Death's Door: Thresholds and Boundaries in British Funeral Customs'. In H. E. Davidson (ed.), *Boundaries and Thresholds*. Stroud: Thimble, 1993, pp. 91–101.
Rieger, M. 2011. *Der Teufel im Pfarrhaus: Gespenster, Geisterglaube und Besessenheit im Luthertum der frühen Neuzeit*. Stuttgart: Franz Steiner Verlag.
Robinson, F. C. 1993. 'The Prescient Woman in Old English Literature'. In *The Tomb of Beowulf and Other Essays*. Oxford: Blackwel, pp. 155–163.
Rogerson, A. et al. 1987. *Three Norman Churches in Norfolk*. Gressinghall: Norfolk Archaeological Unit.
Rohr, P. 1679. *Dissertatio historico-philosophica de masticatione mortuorum*. Leipzig: Michael Vogt.
Roll, W. G. 1977. 'Poltergeists'. In B. B. Wolman (ed.), *Handbook of Parapsychology*. New York: Van Nostrand Reinhold, pp. 382–413.
Roll, W. G. and M. A. Persinger 2001. 'Investigations of Poltergeists and Haunts: A Review and Interpretation'. In J. Houran and R. Lange (eds.), *Hauntings and Poltergeists: Multidisciplinary Perspectives*. Jefferson, NC: McFarland, pp. 123–163.
Roth, H. 1587. *Leichpredigten*. Eiszleben: Gaubisch.
Ruston, S. 2021. *The Science of Life and Death in Frankenstein*. Oxford: Bodleian Library.
Ryan, W. F. 1999. *The Bathhouse at Midnight*. University Park: Pennsylvania State University Press.
Rzaczynski, G. 1721. *Historia naturalis curiosa regni Poloniae*. Sandomierz: Jesuit College.
Sariyannis, M. 2013. 'Of Ottoman Ghosts, Vampires and Sorcerers: An Old Discussion Disinterred'. *Archivum Ottomanicum* 30: 191–216.
Sarpkaya, S. and M. B. Yaltırık. 2022. *Türk Kültüründe Vampirler*. Ankara: Karakum.
Sassonia, Ercole. 1600. *De plica quam Poloni gwoździec, Roxolani kołtunum vocant*. Padua: Officina Laurentii Pasquati.

Sayer, D. 2020. *Early Anglo-Saxon Cemeteries: Kinship, Community and Identity*. Manchester: Manchester University Press.

Sayers, W. 1996. 'The Alien and the Alienated as Unquiet Dead'. In J. J. Cohen (ed.), *Monster Theory: Reading Culture*. Minneapolis: University of Minnesota Press, pp. 242–263.

Schaub, H. 2009. 'Knochen und Bestattungsriten: Die Bedeutung archäologischer Funde zum Wiedergänger- bzw. Vampirglauben'. *Kakanien Revisited*. https://www.kakanien-revisited.at/beitr/vamp/HSchaub1.pdf.

Schertz, K. F. von. 1706. *Magia Posthuma*. Olomouc: Ignatius Rosenburg.

Schierup, C.-U. 1986. 'Why Are Vampires Still Alive? Wallachian Immigrants in Scandinavia'. *Ethnos* 51: 173–198.

Schmitt, J.-C. 1998. *Ghosts in the Middle Ages: Living and the Dead in Medieval Society*. Chicago: University of Chicago Press.

Schofield, J. 2019. 'London's Waterfront 1100–1666'. *Antiquaries Journal* 99: 63–94.

Schürmann, T. 1990. *Nachzehrerglauben in Mitteleuropa*. Marburg: N. G. Elwert.

Schürmann, T. 2009. 'Schmatzende Tode und ihre Bekämpfung in der frühen Neuzeit'. *Ethnographisch-Archäologische Zeitschrift* 50: 235–247.

Scobie, A. 1978. 'Strigiform Witches in Roman and Other Cultures'. *Fabula* 19: 74–101.

Scudder, B. (trans.). 2005. *The Saga of Grettir the Strong*. London: Penguin.

Scurlock, J-A. 2016. 'Mortal and Immortal Souls, Ghosts and the (Restless) Dead in Ancient Mesopotamia'. *Religion Compass* 10: 77–82.

Semple, S. 1998. 'A Fear of the Past: The Place of the Prehistoric Burial Mound in the Ideology of Middle and Later Anglo-Saxon England'. *World Archaeology* 30: 109–126.

Semple, S. 2003. 'Illustrations of Damnation in Late Anglo-Saxon Manuscripts'. *Anglo-Saxon England* 32: 231–245.

Semple, S. 2011. 'Sacred Spaces and Places in Pre-Christian and Conversion Period Anglo-Saxon England'. In H. Hamerow et al. (eds.), *The Oxford Handbook of Anglo-Saxon Archaeology*. Oxford: Oxford University Press, pp. 742–763.

Senn, H. A. 1982. *Were-Wolf and Vampire in Romania*. New York: Colombia University Press.

Sharp, L. 1952. 'Steel Axes for Stone-Age Australians'. *Human Organization* 11: 17–22.

Sherlock, S. J. and M. G. Welch. 1992. *An Anglo-Saxon Cemetery at Norton, Cleveland*. London: Council for British Archaeology.

Shirokogoroff, S. M. 1935. *Psychomental Complex of the Tungus*. London: Kegan Paul.

Simek, R. 2015. 'Females as Cult Functionaries and Ritual Specialists in the Germanic Iron Age?' In Frog and K. Lukin (eds.), *Between Text and Practice: Mythology, Ritual and Research: Retrospective Methods Network Newsletter*. Helsinki: University of Helsinki, pp. 71–78.

Simmer, A. 1982. 'Le prélèvement des crânes dans l'est de la France à l'époque mérovingienne'. *Archéologie médiévale* 12: 35–49.

Simmer, A. 1988. *Le cimetière Mérovingien d'Audun-le-Tiche (Moselle)*. Paris: Editions Errance.

Simmonds, A. et al. 2011. 'Excavations at Tubney Wood Quarry, 2001–9'. *Oxoniensia* 76: 105–172.

Simpson, J. 2003. 'Repentant Soul or Walking Corpse? Debatable Apparitions in Medieval England'. *Folklore* 114: 389–402.

Sledzik, P. S. and N. Bellantoni 1994. 'Brief Communication: Bioarcheological and Biocultural Evidence for the New England Vampire Folk Belief'. *American Journal of Physical Anthropology* 94: 269–274.

Smith, A. et al. 2018. *Life and Death in the Countryside of Roman Britain*. London: Society for the Promotion of Roman Studies.

Smith, D. A. 2010. *Revisiting the Empty Tomb: The Early History of Easter*. Minneapolis: Fortress Press.

Smith, N. L. 2008. 'The Problem of Excess Female Mortality: Tuberculosis in Western Massachusetts'. Unpublished master's thesis, University of Massachusetts–Amherst.

Somé, M. P. 1994. *Of Water and the Spirit: Ritual, Magic and Initiation in the Life of an African Shaman*. New York: Penguin Compass.

Soren, D. and N. Soren. 1995. 'Who Killed the Babies of Lugnano?' *Archaeology* 48: 43–48.

Sorlin, I. 1991. 'Striges et géloudes. Histoire d'une croyance et d'une tradition'. *Travaux et Mémoires* 11: 411–436.

Stachowski, K. 2020. 'Etymologies of *Vampire* with *pirЪ* "a feast"'. *Journal of Vampire Studies* 1: 5–18.

Stachowski, K. 2022. 'Etymologising the Slavic Werewolf'. *Die Welt der Slaven* 67: 369–392.

Stachowski, K. 2024. 'Etymologies of Vampire'. In S. Bacon (ed.), *The Palgrave Handbook of the Vampire*. Cham, Switzerland: Palgrave Macmillan/Springer Nature Switzerland, pp. 55–72.

Stachowski, K. and O. Stachowski. 2017. 'Possibly Oriental Elements in Slavonic Folklore. *Upiór ~ Wampir*'. In M. Németh et al. (eds.), *Essays in the History of Languages and Linguistics Dedicated to Marek Stachowski*. Kraków: Księgarnia Akademika, pp. 643–693.

Steige, B. G. 1795. *Bolkenhainische Denkwürdigkeiten*. Hirschberg: Krahnschen Schriften.

Steiner, O. 1959. *Vampirleichen: Vampirprozesse in Preussen*. Hamburg: Kriminalistik.

Stieff, C. 1737. *Schlesisches Historisches Labyrinth*. Breslau: Michael Hubert.

Stoker, B. 1897. *Dracula*. Westminster: Archibald Constable.

Stoodley, N. 2000. 'From the Cradle to the Grave: Age Organization and the Early Anglo-Saxon Burial Rite'. *World Archaeology* 31: 456–472.

Storå, N. 1971. *Burial Customs of the Skolt Lapps*. Helsinki: Suomalainen Tiedeakatemia.

Straight, B. 2007. *Miracles and Extraordinary Experience in Northern Kenya*. Philadelphia: University of Pennsylvania Press.

Strickmann, M. 2002. *Chinese Magical Medicine*. Stanford, CA: Stanford University Press.

Stülzebach, A. 1998. 'Vampir und Wiedergängererscheinungen aus volkskundlicher und archäologischer Sicht'. *Concilium medii aevi* 1: 97–121.

Sugg, R. 2011. *Mummies, Cannibals and Vampires: The History of Corpse Medicine from the Renaissance to the Victorians*. Abingdon: Routledge.

Sugg, R. 2019. *The Real Vampires: Death, Terror and the Supernatural*. Stroud: Amberley.

Summers, M. 1928. *The Vampire: His Kith and Kin*. London: Kegan Paul.

Summers, M. 1929. *The Vampire in Europe*. London: Kegan Paul.

Swancutt, K. 2008. 'The Undead Genealogy: Omnipresence, Spirit Perspectives and a Case of Mongolian Vampirism'. *Journal of the Royal Anthropological Institute*, n.s., 14: 843–864.

Szołtysek, M. 2012. 'Spatial Construction of European Family and Household Systems: A Promising Path or a Blind Alley?'. *Continuity and Change* 27: 11–52.

Talbot, C. H. (trans.). 1954. *The Anglo-Saxon Missionaries in Germany*. New York: Sheed and Ward.

Taracena, B. 1933. 'Cadáveres atravesados por clavos en el cementerio judío de Deza (Soria)'. *Investigacion y Progreso* 7: 65–71.

Taylor, A. 2008. 'Aspects of Deviant Burial in Roman Britain'. In Murphy 2008, pp. 91–114.

Tettau, W.J.A. von and J.D.H. Temme. 1837. *Die Volkslagen Ostpreußens, Litthauens und Westpreußens*. Berlin: Nicolaischen Buchhandlung.

Thacker, A. 2002. 'The Making of a Local Saint'. In A. Thacker and R. Sharpe (eds.), *Local Saints and Local Churches in the Early Medieval West*. Oxford: Oxford University Press, pp. 45–73.

Thompson, S. 1955–1958. *Motif-Index of Folk-Literature*. Rev. ed. 6 vols. Copenhagen: Rosenkilde and Bagger.

Thompson, V. 2004. *Dying and Death in Later Anglo-Saxon England*. Woodbridge: Boydell and Brewer.

Topa, F. 2019. 'An Ancient Angolan Zombie: *Juca, a Matumbola* by Ernesto Marecos'. *Diadorim* 21: 175–183.

Toplak, M. 2018. 'Deconstructing the Deviant Burials'. *META Historiskarkeologisk Tidskrift* 2018: 79–109.

Toplak, M. 2023. 'Ritualised Executions and Human Sacrifices in the Viking World'. In Gardeła et al. 2023, pp. 145–160.

Tossach, W. 1744: 'A Man Dead in Appearance, Recovered by Distending the Lungs with Air'. In *Medical Essays and Observations Revised and Published by a Society in Edinburgh*, vol. 5, pt. 2. Edinburgh, pp. 605–608.

Townsend, E. 2009. *Death and Art: Europe 1200–1530*. London: V&A Publishing.

Trow, R. et al. 2024. 'Buried at Bodicote'. *Current Archaeology* 416: 18–24.

Trzaska, N. A. 2023. 'Grecki wampiryzm w ujęciu diachronicznym na podstawie źródeł literackich i piśmiennictwa nieliterackiego'. Unpublished D.Phil. thesis, Adam Mickiewicz University.

Urbańczyk, P. 2016. 'Early Medieval Strongholds in Polish Lands'. In N. Christie and H. Herold (eds.) *Fortified Settlements in Early Medieval Europe*. Oxford: Oxbow, pp. 95–106.

Urquhart, F. C. 1885. 'Legends of the Australian Aborigines'. *Journal of the Anthropological Institute* 14: 87–88.

Valvasor, J. W. von 1689. *Die Ehre deß Herzogthums Crain*. 15 books in 4 volumes. Laybach: Endter.

Van Buylaere, G. 2019. 'The Decline of Female Professionals—and the Rise of the Witch—in the Second and Early First Millennium BCE'. *Magic, Ritual and Witchcraft* 14: 37–61.

Van Gennep, A. 1960. *Rites of Passage*. London: Routledge and Kegan Paul.

Van Haperen, M. 2017. *In Touch with the Dead*. Leiden: Leiden University.

Vargha, M. 2017. 'Deviant Burials in Rural Environment in the High Middle Ages—Ritual, the Lack of Ritual, or Just Another Kind of It?' In C. Bis-Worch and C. Theune (eds.), *Religion, Cults and Rituals in the Medieval Rural Environment*. Leiden: Sidestone Press, pp. 271–280.

Vermeir, K. 2012. 'Vampires as Creatures of the Imagination: Theories of Body, Soul, and Imagination in Early Modern Vampire Tracts (1659–1755)'. In Y. Haskell (ed.), *Diseases of the Imagination and Imaginary Disease in the Early Modern Period*. Turnhout: Brepols, pp. 341–373.

Vidal, F. 2009. 'Ghosts of the European Enlightenment'. In Mu-chou Poo (ed.), *Rethinking Ghosts in World Religions*. Leiden: Brill, pp. 163–182.

Viscuso, P. 2000. 'Vampires, Not Mothers: The Living Dead in the Canonical Responses of Ioasaph of Ephesos'. *St Vladimir's Theological Quarterly* 44: 169–179.

Vitebsky, P. 1993. *Dialogues with the Dead: The Discussion of Mortality among the Sora of Eastern India*. Cambridge: Cambridge University Press.

Vukanović, T. P. 1958. 'The Vampire' [Parts II and III]. *Journal of the Gypsy Lore Society*, 3rd ser., 37: 21–31, 111–118.

Vukanović, T .P. 1959. 'The Vampire' [Part IV]. *Journal of the Gypsy Lore Society*, 3rd ser., 38: 44–55.

Wachowski, K. and G. Domański 1992. *Wczesnopolskie cmentarzysko w Starym Zamku*. Wrocław: Wrocław University.

Warfield, A. 2020. 'Witchcraft and the Early Modern Media'. In J. Dillinger (ed.), *The Routledge History of Witchcraft*. Abingdon: Routledge, pp. 208–218.

Warner, E. A. 2000. 'Russian Peasant Beliefs and Practices concerning Death and the Supernatural Collected in Novosokol'niki Region, Pskov Province, Russia, 1995: I: The Restless Dead, Wizards and Spirit Beings'. *Folklore* 111: 67–90.

Warner, E. A. 2011. 'Russian Peasant Beliefs concerning the Unclean Dead and Drought, within the Context of the Agricultural Year'. *Folklore* 122: 155–175.

Watkins, C. S. 2007. *History and the Supernatural in Medieval England*. Cambridge: Cambridge University Press.

Watkins, C. [S.] 2013. *The Undiscovered Country: Journeys among the Dead*. London: Bodley Head.

Weeks, J. H. 1909. 'Notes on Some Customs of the Lower Congo People (Continued)'. *Folklore* 20: 32–63.

Wehner, D. and K. Grüneberg-Wehner 2014. 'Mit Stein im Mund. Ein Fall von Nachzehrerabwehr in der St. Catharinenkirche am Jellenbek, Kr. Rendsburg-Eckernförde?' *Arkæologi i Slesvig* 15: 55–68.

Weinrich, M. 1612. *Iohanni Francisci Pici Mirandulae . . . , Strix sive de ludificatione daemonum dialogi tres. Nunc primum in Germania eruti*. Strasbourg: Paul Ledertz.

Weisman, R. 1984. *Witchcraft, Magic and Religion in Seventeenth-Century Massachusetts*. N.p.: University of Massachusetts Press.

Wernet, P. 1970. 'Les cranes cloués de la Butte Saint-Michel à Strasbourg'. *Cahiers Alsaciens d'Archéologie et d'Histoire* 14: 5–26.

West, E. et al. 2025. *Time Travellers' Tales. Essays from the A14 Cambridge to Huntingdon Archaeological Excavations*. London: MOLA Headland Infrastructure.

West, J. J. and N. Palmer 2014. *Haughmond Abbey: Excavation of a 12th-Century Cloister in its Historical and Landscape Context*. Swindon: English Heritage.

White, D. G. 2006. *Kiss of the Yogini: "Tantric Sex" in Its South Asian Contexts*. Chicago: University of Chicago Press.

White, D. G. 2020. 'Were-Creatures of the Eurasian Ecumene: Variations on a Theme'. *Journal Asiatique* 308: 57–77.

White, L. 1993. 'Vampire Priests of Central Africa: African Debates about Labor and Religion in Colonial Northern Zambia'. *Comparative Studies in Society and History* 35: 746–772.

White, L. 2000. *Speaking with Vampires: Rumor and History in Colonial Africa*. Berkeley: University of California Press.

Whitelock, D. (trans.). 1961. *The Anglo-Saxon Chronicle*. New Brunswick, NJ: Rutgers University Press.

Whittow, M. 2007. 'Nicopolis ad Istrium: Backward and Balkan?' In A. Poulter (ed.), *The Transition to Late Antiquity, on the Danube and Beyond*. Oxford: Oxford University Press, pp. 375–389.

Wickham, C. 1992. 'Problems of Comparing Rural Societies in Early Medieval Western Europe'. *Transactions of the Royal Historical Society*, 6th ser., 2: 229–246.

Wickholm [Wessman], A. 2006. '"Stay Where You Have Been Put!" The Use of Spears as Coffin Nails in Iron Age Finland'. In H. Valk (ed.), *Ethnicity and Culture: Studies in Honour of Silvia Laul: Muinasaja Teadus*, vol. 18. Tartu: Tallinn-Tartu School of Archaeology, 2006, pp. 193–207.

[Wickholm] Wessman, A. 2010. *Death, Destruction and Commemoration: Tracing Ritual Activities in Finnish Late Iron Age Cemeteries (AD 550–1150)*. Helsinki: Finnish Antiquarian Society, 2010.

Wiegelmann, G. 1966. 'Der "lebende Leichnam" im Volksbrauch'. *Volkskunde* 62 (1966): 161–183.

Wiggermann, F.A.M. 2000. 'Lamaštu, Daughter of Anu: A Profile'. In M. Stoll (ed.), *Birth in Babylonia and the Bible: Its Mediterranean Setting*. Groningen: Styx, pp. 217–252.

Wild, W. 2006. 'Unter Adler und Fuchs begraben: Ein aufsehenerregendes Frauengrab des 9. Jahrhunderts in Elsau, Kanton Zürich'. *Mittelalter: Zeitschrift des Schweizerischen Burgenvereins* 11: 20–60.

Willmott, H. et al. 2021. 'Rethinking Early Medieval "Productive Sites": Wealth, Trade and Tradition at Little Carlton, East Lindsey'. *Antiquaries Journal* 101: 181–212.

Wilson, D. M. 1956. 'The Initial Excavation of an Anglo-Saxon Cemetery at Melbourn, Cambridgeshire'. *Proceedings of the Cambridgeshire Antiquarian Society* 49: 29–41.

Wilson, K. M. 1985. 'The History of the Word "Vampire"'. *Journal of the History of Ideas* 46: 577–583. Reprinted in Dundes 1998a, pp. 3–11.

Wiltenburg, J. 2012. *Crime and Culture in Early Modern Germany*. Charlottesville: University of Virginia Press.

Wimberly, L. C. 1928. *Folklore in the English and Scottish Ballads*. Chicago: University of Chicago Press.

Winsløw, J. B. 1742. *Dissertation sur l'incertitude des signes de la mort*. Paris: Cl.-Fr. Simon, fils.

Winsløw, J. B. 1746. *The Uncertainty of the Signs of Death*. London: M. Cooper.

Winterbottom, M. (ed.). 2007. *William of Malmesbury, Gesta Pontificum Anglorum*. Oxford: Oxford University Press.

Wisnom, S. 2024. 'Journey towards Death: The Cedar Forest in the SB *Gilgamesh* Epic from an Intertextual Perspective'. In D. Shehata and K. Sonik (eds.), *Contemporary Approaches to Mesopotamian Literature*. Leiden: Brill, pp. 158–182.

Wisnom, S. 2025. *The Library of Ancient Wisdom*. London: Allen Lane.

Wittkopp, B. 2009. 'Der Dominikanerfriedhof in Strausberg. Sonderbestattungen, Sicheln und ihre Interpretation'. *Ethnographisch-Archäologische Zeitschrift* 50: 3–12.

Witzel, E.J.M. 2012. *The Origins of the World's Mythologies*. Oxford: Oxford University Press.

Wojtucki, D. 2018. 'Procesy i egzekucje "żywych trupów" przed sadami miejskimi i wiejskimi w XIV–XVIII wieku'. *Opolskie Studia Administracyjno-Prawne* 16/4(1): 77–92.

Wojtucki, D. 2020a. 'The "Living Dead" in Modern Era Parish Records in Silesia and Moravia'. *Krakowskie Studia z Historii Państwa i Prawa* 13(3): 273–287.

Wojtucki, D. 2020b. '"Wampiryczne dzieci"—ofiary wierzeń w *magia posthuma* na Morawach w XVIII w'. *Klio: Czasopismo Poświęcone Dziejom Polski i Powszechnym* 53(2): 211–246.

Wolff, L. 1994. *Inventing Eastern Europe: The Map of Civilization on the Mind of the Enlightenment*. Stanford, CA: Stanford University Press.

Wüstemann, H. 1981. 'Slawische Bestattungen vom Fährberg in Rostock-Gehlsdorf'. *Bodendenkmalpflege in Mecklenberg: Jahrbuch 1981*: 239–244.

Xinjiang, Rong 2004. *Land Route or Sea Route?* Philadelphia: University of Pennsylvania.

Xiong, Z. and X. Fu 2022. *Hepu Han Tombs*. Singapore: Springer.

Xygalatas, D. 2022. *Ritual: How Seemingly Senseless Acts Make Life Worth Living*. London: Profile Books.

Yaşar, M. 2014. 'Evliya Çelebi in the Circassian Lands: Vampires, Tree Worshippers, and Pseudo-Muslims'. *Acta Orientalia Academiae Scientiarum Hungaricae* 67: 75–96.

Yin Liu 2021. 'Baptismal Renunciation and Moral Reform in Charlemagne's Christian Empire'. *Traditio* 76: 117–155.

Yiwu, Liao 2009. *The Corpse Walker*. New ed. New York: Anchor Books.

Yorke, B. 2003a. 'The Adaptation of the Anglo-Saxon Royal Courts to Christianity'. In M. Carver (ed.), *The Cross Goes North*. York: York Medieval Press, 243–257.

Yorke, B. 2003b. *Nunneries and the Anglo-Saxon Royal Houses*. London: Continuum.

Yu, A. C. 1987. '"Rest, Rest, Perturbed Spirit!": Ghosts in Traditional Chinese Prose Fiction'. *Harvard Journal of Asiatic Studies* 47: 397–434.

Yu, Yi Izzy and J. Y. Branscum 2021. *The Shadow Book of Ji Yun*. N.p.: Empress Wu Books.

Zeiss, H. 1934. *Die Grabfunde aus dem spanischen Westgotenreich*. Berlin: de Gruyter.

Zelenin, D. K. 1927. *Russische (Ostslavische) Volkskunde*. Berlin: de Gruyter.

Zelenin, D. K. 1994. *Isbrannye Trudy*. Moscow: Indrik.

Zelepos, I. 2014. 'Vampirglaube und orthodoxe Kirche im osmanischen Südosteuropa. Ein Fallbeispiel für die Ambivalenzen vorsäkularer Rationalisierungsprozesse'. In A. Helmedach et al. (eds.), *Das osmanische Europa*. Leipzig: Eudora-Verlag, pp. 365–381.

Zuber, R. 1987. *Osudy moravské církve v. 18 století*. Vol. 2. Olomouc: Matrice cyrilometodějská.

Zuber, R. 2003. *Osudy moravské církve v. 18 století*. Vol. 4. Prague: Česká katoliká Charata.

ILLUSTRATION SOURCES AND CREDITS

Figure 1: Illustration on the dust-jacket of the tenth edition of *Dracula* (London, 1913). Photo John Blair, with thanks to the Bodleian Library.

Figure 3: Stachowski 2024, figure 1: reproduced by kind permission of Kamil Stachowski.

Figure 4: *Contes de Charles Nodier* (Paris: J. Hetzel, 1846), plate opposite p. 31, illustrating Nodier's story 'Smarra'. Photo John Blair, with thanks to the Bodleian Library.

Figure 5: Photograph by I. K. Inha of a scene at Kiestinki/Kestenga. Reproduced by kind permission of the Finnish Literature Society (SKS).

Figure 6: Honko et al. 1993, plate after p. 576. Photo by the late Lauri Honko, with acknowledgement to his estate.

Figure 7: A. H. Gjelstad, *Big Heart, Strong Hands* (Stockport: Dewi Lewis Publishing, 2020), p. 121. Reproduced by kind permission of Anne Helene Gjelstad.

Figure 8: After F. R. Demetrio, *Dictionary of Philippine Folk Beliefs and Customs*, vol. 2 (Cagayan de Oro City, Philippines: Xavier University, 1970), p. 375.

Figure 9: Frontispiece of Fangé 1762. Photo John Blair, with thanks to the Bodleian Library.

Figure 10: [T. M. Harris], *The Triumphs of Superstition: An Elegy* (Boston: Isaiah Thomas and Ebenezer T. Andrews, 1790), pp. 9–10. Photos John Blair, with thanks to the Bodleian Library.

Figure 11: Reproduced by kind permission of Mirosław Kuźma.

Figure 12: Vienna: Kunsthistorisches Museum, inv. GG 991. Photo John Blair.

Figure 13: After Taracena 1933.

Figure 14: Reconstructed for display, Gotlands Museum, Visby. Photo John Blair.

Figure 15: Burial at Ust'-Uda. After A. P. Okladnikov, *Neolit i Bronzovy vek Pribakalia: Istoriko-Ar* (Leningrad: Nauka, 1950), p. 352.

Figure 16: Swancutt 2008, figure 2. Reproduced by kind permission of Katherine Swancutt.

Figure 17: Victoria and Albert Museum, IS.9-1969. Photo John Blair.

Figure 18: After Groot 1892–1910, vol. 5, plate opposite p. 736, illustrating a story by Pu Songling.

Figure 19: British Museum, Am1990, 10.1. Image Wikimedia Commons, United States public domain.

Figure 20: After J.-E. Gautier and G. Lampre, *Fouilles de Moussian* (Chartres, 1905), p. 136; L. Delaporte, *Catalogue des Cylindres*, vol. 1 (Paris, 1920), plate 4 (T.88); A. Parrot, *Glyptique Mésopotamienne* (Paris, 1954), No. 259. Re-drawn by John Blair.

Figure 21: After Wiggermann 2000, figure 3; Crerar 2022, figure 79. Re-drawn by John Blair.

Figure 22: From *The Dark Blue* 3 (March 1872). Photo John Blair, with thanks to the Bodleian Library.

Figure 23: Jordan 1972, p. 145. Photo by David K. Jordan, reproduced by his kind permission.

Figure 24: Museum of Archaeology and Anthropology, Cambridge, N.21390.LIN. Reproduced by their kind permission.

Figure 25: From data in E. Wamers, *Franconofurd*, vol. 2 (Regensburg: Schnell and Steiner, 2015), and J.-P. Urlacher et al., *La nécropole mérovingienne de la Grande Oye à Doubs* (Saint-Germain-en-Laye, 1998). Re-drawn by John Blair.

Figure 26: Girshick Ben-Amos 1994, plate 7.1. Photo by Paula Girshick, reproduced by her kind permission.

Figure 27: Figuer [c. 1880], opposite p. 480. Creative Commons, with thanks to the Wellcome Trust.

Figure 28: Al-Rawi 2008, figure 15-b. Reproduced by kind permission of Farouk Al-Rawi and the British Institute for the Study of Iraq.

Figure 29: After R. Wünsch, 'Eine antike Rachepuppe', *Philologus* 61 (1902): 26–31, at p. 27.

Figure 30: After Calkin 1947, figures 2–3; Barber and Bowsher 2000, p. 230. Re-drawn by John Blair.

Figure 31: After Parker Pearson et al. 2018. Re-drawn by John Blair and with hypothetical outlines added.

Figure 32: After P.D.C. Brown 1967, figures 14–15. Re-drawn by John Blair with anatomical detail added.

Figure 33: Photos reproduced by kind permission of Steve Sherlock and Tees Archaeology.

Figure 34: Reproduced by kind permission of Anthony Gibson.

Figure 35: After data in Hancock and Zeepvat 2018. Re-drawn by John Blair and with hypothetical outlines added.

Figure 36: After data in Boyle et al. 1998. Re-drawn by John Blair and with hypothetical outlines added.

Figure 37: After data in Evison 1987. Re-drawn by John Blair and with hypothetical outlines added.

Figure 38: After data in Lucy et al. 2009. Drawn by John Blair.

Figure 39: Copyright Cambridge Archaeological Unit. Reproduced by its kind permission, and with thanks to Sam Lucy.

Figure 40: After data in Lucy et al. 2009. Re-drawn by John Blair and with hypothetical body outlines added.

Figure 41: After illustrations in Wild 2006. Re-drawn by John Blair.

Figure 42: After Hey 2004, figure 7.20. Re-drawn by John Blair.

Figure 43: After *Oxford Archaeological Unit Newsletter*, March 1991. Reproduced by kind permission of Oxford Archaeology.

Figure 44: Photo MOLA Headland Infrastructure, working on behalf of National Highways. Reproduced by their kind permission, and with thanks to Emma West.

Figure 45: From data in Randall and Poulton 2023, and from primary site records kindly provided by Rob Poulton. Nails and spike are shown as on X-rays. Re-drawn by John Blair.

Figure 46: Reproduced by kind permission of Mirosław Kuźma.

Figure 47: Reproduced by kind permission of Mirosław Kuźma.

Figure 49: Photo Nicholas Palmer, reproduced by his kind permission.

Figure 50: Mays et al. 2017, figure 5. Reproduced by kind permission of Simon Mays.

Figure 51: Photograph John Channing. Reproduced by his kind permission.

Figure 52: British Library, Harley MS 603, fols. 67r and 72r. Reproduced by permission of the British Library and Bridgeman Images.

Figure 53: After Cambridge, Corpus Christi College, MS 41, p. 433. Re-drawn by John Blair.

Figure 54: For sources, see p. 460, note 11, and p. 461, notes 13 and 14. Re-drawn by John Blair.

Figure 55: Memorial stained-glass window, Swiss, 1547. Landesmuseum Zürich. Photo John Blair.

Figure 56: Photo John Blair.

Figure 57: View from Sutton Bank on an early twentieth-century postcard.

Figure 58: Photo John Blair.

Figure 59: After Schofield 2019, figure 19. Reproduced by kind permission of MOLA, by arrangement with John Schofield.

Figure 60: After Emden 1758[–62?]. Re-drawn by John Blair.

Figure 61: Polcyn and Gajda 2015, figure 8. Photo Marek Polcyn, reproduced by his kind permission.

Figure 62: Photo John Blair, with thanks to the Bodleian Library.

Figure 63: Frontispiece of Francisci 1690. Bayerische Staatsbibliothek München, Phys.m 66, urn:nbn:de:bvb:12-bsb10132606.2. Reproduced by kind permission of the Münchener DigitalisierungsZentrum.

Figure 64: Data from Mézes 2019, pp. 488–495, and Lambrecht 1994. Graph drawn by Kanerva Blair-Heikkinen.

Figure 65: National Library of the Czech Republic, 65 F 1382. Reproduced by kind permission.

Figure 66: Frontispiece of *Der Europäische Niemand* 11 (1719).

Figure 67: data from Mézes 2019, pp. 479–487. Graph drawn by Kanerva Blair-Heikkinen.

Figure 68: Vienna, Belvedere Palace. Photo John Blair.

Figure 69: Reproduced with the kind permission and help of Neil Rudel, editor of the *Altoona Mirror*, and Brenda Carberry.

Figure 70: Photo Cyril Place, reproduced by his kind permission.

Figure 71: B. Picard, *Ceremonies and Religious Customs* (English ed., London, 1736), vol. 5, opp. p. 307. Photo John Blair.

Figure 72: *Journal des Voyages et des Aventures de Terre*, 9 April 1893. Photo John Blair.

Figure 73: Still from Stirile Pro-TV news report of February 2024, accessible at https://stirileprotv.ro/divers/strigoiul-din-valcea-dezgropata-si-injunghiata-in-inima-de-fratele-ei-o-viseaza-ca-vine-la-el-ce-a-patit-preotul.html.

Figure 74: 'Vol de Zombis'/ 'An avan, an avan!' Reproduced by kind permission of the Musée d'Art Haïtien, Port-au-Prince.

Figure 75: Davis 1988, p. 81. Photo Wade Davis, reproduced by his kind permission.

Figure 76: Engraving by James Hulett in Winsløw 1746, opposite p. 81. Photo John Blair, with thanks to the Bodleian Library.

Figure 77: [Anonymous] 1820, frontispiece: engraving by Berthe. Photo John Blair, with thanks to the Bodleian Library.

Figure 78: *Punch*, 24 October 1885. Photo John Blair.

Map 10: Data from Grober-Glück 1981 (folklore) and Jan Mordawski, *Statystyka ludności kaszubskiej. Kaszubi u progu XXI wieku* (Gdańsk 2005) (for ethnicity data).

Part- and Chapter-Opening Vignettes

Coffin transfixed by a stake: Detail from a wood-engraving in [J. M. Rymer and T. P. Prest], *Varney the Vampire: A Feast of Blood* (London: E. Lloyd, 1845–7).

Female flying demon: A Malaysian *mannananggal*, drawing by John Blair.

Rock-cut tomb with stone rolled away: Galilee, near the Jezreel Valley, drawing from photographs by John Blair.

Skull transfixed by a spike: After K. Moszyński, *Kultura ludowa Słowian* (Kraków: Polska Akademja, 1934), p. 663, redrawn by John Blair.

Man detaching a head with a spade: Detail from the present Figure 60.

Angel's head and wings: Detail from the present Figure 70.

INDEX

A NOTE ON THE TYPE

This book has been composed in Arno, an Old-style serif typeface in the classic Venetian tradition, designed by Robert Slimbach at Adobe.